THE (MGMT) SOLUTION

Print

MGMT delivers all the key terms and all the content for the **Principles of Management** course through a visually engaging and easy-to-review print experience.

Digital   MindTap®

MindTap enables you to stay organized and study efficiently by providing a single location for all your course materials and study aids. Built-in apps leverage social media and the latest learning technology to help you succeed.

1 Open the Access Card included with this text.

2 Follow the steps on the card.

3 Study.

Student Resources

- Interactive eBook
- Practice Quizzes
- Flashcards
- Chapter Review Cards
- Online Glossary
- Chapter Visual Summaries
- You Make the Decision Activities
- Chapter Case Studies
- Management Decision Exercises

Students: **nelson.com/student**

Instructor Resources

- Access to All Student Resources
- Engagement Tracker and Gradebook
- Instructor Companion site
- Instructor's Manual
- PowerPoint Slides
- Updated Test Bank
- Additional Assignments and Activities
- Management Decisions Exercises and Cases

Instructors: **nelson.com/instructor**

NELSON

MGMT, Third Canadian Edition
by Chuck Williams, Terri Champion, and Ike Hall

VP, Product and Partnership Solutions:
Anne Williams

Publisher, Digital and Print Content:
Anne-Marie Taylor

Marketing Manager:
Christina Koop

Content Development Manager:
Lisa Peterson

Photo and Permissions Researcher:
Natalie Barrington

Production Project Manager:
Jaime Smith

Production Service:
MPS Limited

Copy Editor:
Top Copy Communications

Proofreader:
MPS Limited

Indexer:
MPS Limited

Design Director:
Ken Phipps

Managing Designer:
Pamela Johnston

Interior Design:
Dave Murphy Design

Cover Design:
Trinh Truong

Cover Image:
BlackJack 3D/iStock
by Getty Images

Compositor:
MPS Limited

Library and Archives Canada Cataloguing in Publication Data

Williams, Chuck, 1959-, author
    MGMT : principles of management / Williams, Champion, Hall. — Third Canadian edition.

Title from cover. Written by Chuck Williams, Terri Champion and Ike Hall. Includes bibliographical references and index.
ISBN 978-0-17-670348-6 (paperback)

    1. Management—Textbooks.
I. Champion, Terri, 1965-, author
II. Hall, Ike, author III. Title.

HD31.W51675 2017   658
C2016-904391-6

ISBN-13: 978-0-17-670348-6
ISBN-10: 0-17-670348-9

MGMT

Brief Contents

BlackJack 3D/iStock by Getty Images

Contents

Part 3
Organizing

Churchill/iStock

1 Management

Global Stock / istockphoto.com

LEARNING OUTCOMES

After studying this chapter, you will be able to...

1-1 Describe what management is.

1-2 Explain the four functions of management.

1-3 Describe different kinds of managers.

1-4 Explain the major roles and subroles that managers perform in their jobs.

1-5 Explain what companies look for in managers.

1-6 Discuss the top mistakes that managers make in their jobs.

1-7 Describe the transition that employees go through when they are promoted to management.

After you finish this chapter, go to **PAGE 20** for **STUDY TOOLS**

Build Your Brand

Taking a proactive approach has served Shaun Lichtenberger and Chris Sinclair well. Sean, a marketing graduate of Fanshawe College and Chris, an alumni from the Business Administration Marketing Program at Niagara College in Ontario, are co-owners and managing partners in Brand Blvd, a promotional products and corporate apparel firm. The pair met while working for a company that was struggling with serious operational and management challenges. Shaun and Chris decided to join forces and right the wrongs they had observed as employees. They started Brand Blvd in 2007, with limited management experience but with a vision to take a fresh and energetic approach to building a team that could succeed in the highly competitive promotional products industry. They pride themselves both on their ability to help clients "build their brand" and on having built a team of enthusiastic, customer-driven professionals to work with them. As the company began to succeed and grow in size, Shaun and Chris realized they needed to further define their management roles. Shaun is now the president, running the internal operations with the management team reporting to him, while Chris oversees the sales team and represents the company in a community and public relations capacity in his role as vice president. Brand Blvd has more than 20 employees. Although the company's organizational structure now defines specific management roles that complement their own individual strengths and weaknesses, the two partners share the same management philosophy—one that is based on getting to know your team.

Photos by Brent Porter, Form&Affect

1. How do you define success as a manager?

For us, management success translates into an engaged team with a clear purpose. Knowing that we have a productive, happy, challenged team in place means we are doing something right. Success as a manager is built on the success of the whole team.

2. What trait or skill has served you the best in your career as a manager?

Shaun: Listening skills. As a manager you find yourself dealing with lots of different people—not just your own employees. And what you sometimes notice is that many people aren't really listening during communication—they are simply waiting for their turn to speak. Listening has served me well over the years and allowed me to gain insight into not only my own team but also my clients, suppliers, and people in general.

Chris: Having a strong work ethic. I grew up on a farm and learned that from my father and grandfather. In the early years at Brand Blvd the workload was incredible; it was all about put your head down and get it done—and as a manager this sets a good example. I lead by example and I think that when your team sees that, they emulate it.

3. What have you learned about management that surprised you the most?

How much people care and will do for you if they believe in your vision. It also surprised us how much pride we have in our team's success.

4. Which management function (planning, leading, organizing, controlling) do you think is the most important function that you perform as a manager?

As co-owners and senior managers in the company, we believe that "steering the ship" through planning and leadership is the most important function we perform.

5. Which do you think is more important to achieve as a manager—efficiency or effectiveness?

Both are important, but if we had to choose, it would be effectiveness. If you are really efficient but not effective, then what's the point? Effectiveness means you are hitting your metrics—you can always backtrack and come up with ways to improve your efficiency.

6. When hiring a manager, which skills do you think are most important for a candidate to possess—technical skills, human relations skills, or conceptual skills?

No doubt about it—human skills. Management is all about people. You have to be able to get your people on board, working for you, wanting to work for you—and that is best achieved using human skills. You can teach someone about an industry or improve their technical skills, but if someone already has a natural ability when it comes to dealing with people, this is much more valuable as a potential manager.

7. What advice would you give someone about to step into a management position?

Shaun: Get rid of your ego—congratulations, you are a manager, now it's time to get to work. Be patient—get to know the lay of the land and what your people do. Be very transparent—be clear and let the team know what you expect of them, and at the same time let them know what management is doing.

Chris: Be realistic about your strengths and weaknesses. For me, my weakness has been assuming the disciplinary role with my team. I don't want to be the "bad guy" but I know that sometimes I need to be firm, so I've had to try and go outside my comfort zone to try and assume that role when I need to.

8. What is the most important thing you learned in business school that you use to this day?

Presentation skills.

For the full interview go online to nelson.com/student

Interview courtesy of Shaun Lichtenberger and Chris Sinclair.

MANAGEMENT IS . . .

Management issues are fundamental to any organization, regardless of size. How do we plan to get things done, organize the company to be efficient and effective, lead and motivate employees, and put controls in place to make sure our plans are followed and our goals are met? Good management is basic to starting a business, growing a business, and maintaining a business once it has achieved some measure of success.

To understand how important *good* management is, think about the following situation. Managers at Dunkin' Donuts Canada were accused of making critical management errors that severely affected the chain's Quebec operation. Their accusers were a group of franchisees who sued the company for what they saw as poor management. The franchisees blamed Dunkin' Donuts' management for making poor marketing decisions that failed to protect and enhance the brand in the face of rising competition, and for persuading franchisees to buy into a new business strategy that ultimately failed. The company saw the number of Dunkin' Donuts locations in Quebec decline rapidly, from 250 in 1995, to 115 in 2003, and down to 4 as of 2015. The Quebec Superior Court agreed with the franchisees and awarded them over $16 million in damages.[1]

Many of today's managers got their start working on the factory floor, clearing dishes off tables, helping customers buy a new pair of shoes, or wiping up a spill in a grocery store aisle. Similarly, you will likely start at the bottom and work your way up. There's no better way to get to know your competition, your customers, and your business. But whether you begin your career at the entry level or as a supervisor, your job is not to do the work but to help others do theirs. **Management** is getting work done through others. Canadian businessman and television personality Jim Treliving is co-owner and co-chairman of the Boston Pizza chain and the T&M Group of Companies, with an impressive portfolio of businesses that generate over $1 billion in sales annually. Jim started out as an RCMP officer but later traded in his uniform to become a Boston Pizza franchisee in Penticton, British Columbia. Working hands-on in the business, Jim learned how to manage and run a successful franchise, balancing two important management concepts—efficiency and effectiveness. He and his partner George Melville eventually purchased the entire Boston Pizza chain in 1983 and began expanding the brand across Canada; in the process, they began growing their own group of companies. According to Jim, "Behind every great company is a great team." Jim's entrepreneurial spirit coupled with his skills in strategic planning and marketing have served him well; however, when asked to explain his success, he says, "I think it's managing people. I think I get along with people well. I can understand people. I can read people fairly decently." As a testament to Jim and George's belief in the value of good management, their company has been recognized with numerous prestigious awards over the years, including Canada's 50 Best Managed Companies Platinum Club, Canada's 10 Most Admired Corporate Cultures, and the Canadian Franchise Association's Lifetime Achievement Award.[2]

Jim Treliving's experience with Boston Pizza suggests that managers have to be concerned with efficiency and effectiveness. **Efficiency** is getting work done with minimal effort, expense, or waste. How does the Shouldice Hospital in Toronto perform more than 7,500 hernia surgeries a year on patients from all over the world even though it employs only 10 full-time surgeons? The Shouldice Hernia Centre, founded in 1945, is a testament to the principles of efficiency and productivity. The hospital has five operating theatres, 89 hospital beds, and a staff of over 160, all focused on providing an extremely specialized high-quality and high-volume service. A well-organized admissions screening and scheduling system allows for efficient management of demand and capacity, and the delivery system allows for maximum patient involvement to ensure efficiency and low cost. The facility encourages exercise and rapid recovery—there are no TVs or telephones in patient rooms, but there *are* over 20 acres of gardens for patients to stroll in. The centre's results are impressive—at Shouldice, the chances of complications are 0.5 percent, and the chances of recurrence after hernia repair average less than 1 percent. Compare this to the average in North America for recurrence after hernia repair, which is 10 percent. In addition, recovery times and costs are lower compared to other hospitals and clinics.[3]

Overall, efficiency is an important focus for individual organizations and for Canada as a whole, given that labour productivity is tied to a country's economic success and standard of living. You'll learn more about labour productivity in Chapter 17 on managing service and manufacturing operations.

Management getting work done through others.

Efficiency getting work done with a minimum of effort, expense, or waste.

Efficiency alone is not enough to ensure success. Managers must also strive for **effectiveness**, which means accomplishing tasks that help fulfill organizational objectives such as customer service and satisfaction. In the world of ecommerce, shipping and delivery are key components of the online shopping experience and can make or break an online retailer's reputation. When a surge in online holiday shopping a few years ago overwhelmed UPS and led to tens of thousands of late deliveries, online retail giant Amazon.com began exploring new delivery options to improve customer service and satisfaction. Amazon began experimenting with its own fleet of delivery vehicles in a limited number of cities, as well as more "out of the box" options like using a crowdsourced network of drivers to make deliveries on their way to their destinations as well as arrangements with some retailers to store packages. For a company that ships over 5 billion items a year, having greater control over the "last mile" or final leg of a package's journey to the customer is critical to improving the company's overall effectiveness.[4]

<table>
<tr><td>1-2</td><td></td></tr>
</table>

1-2 MANAGEMENT FUNCTIONS

Henri Fayol, the managing director (chief executive officer, or CEO) of a large steel company in the early 1900s, was one of the founders of the field of management. You'll learn more about Fayol and management's other key figures when you read about the history of management in Chapter 18 (online at www.nelson.com/student). Based on his 20 years as a CEO, Fayol argued that "the success of an enterprise generally depends much more on the administrative ability of its leaders than on their technical ability."[5]

An exhaustive study undertaken at Google involving data-mining of quantitative data as well as qualitative information sought to shed light on what makes a successful manager. The results of the two-year study included a ranking of the most important managerial behaviours that produced some surprising results—even for Google executives. "In the Google context, we'd always believed that to be a manager, particularly on the engineering side, you need to be as deep or deeper a technical expert than the people who work for you," Google's vice president for people operations explains. "It turns out that that's absolutely the least important thing. It's important, but pales in comparison. Much more important is just making that connection and being accessible." As a case in point,

Exhibit 1.1
The Four Functions of Management

Planning | Organizing

Leading | Controlling

the top three behaviours identified were: (1) be a good coach; (2) empower; don't micromanage; and (3) be interested in direct reports' success and well-being.[6]

Managers need to perform five managerial functions in order to succeed, according to Fayol: planning, organizing, coordinating, commanding, and controlling.[7] Most management textbooks today have updated this list by dropping the coordinating function and referring to Fayol's commanding function as "leading." Thus, Fayol's management functions are known today in this updated form: planning, organizing, leading, and controlling. Studies indicate that managers who perform these management functions well are more successful, gaining promotions for themselves and profits for their companies. One study has found that the more time CEOs spend planning, the more profitable their companies are.[8] A 25-year study at AT&T found that employees with better planning and decision-making skills were more likely to be promoted into management jobs, to succeed as managers, and to be promoted into upper levels of management.[9] The evidence is clear. Managers at all levels of an organization and in small, medium, and large enterprises serve their companies well when they plan, organize, lead, and control. (That's why this book is organized around the functions of management outlined in Exhibit 1.1.)

Now let's take a closer look at each of the management functions: **1-2a planning, 1-2b organizing, 1-2c leading, and 1-2d controlling.**

Effectiveness accomplishing tasks that help fulfill organizational objectives.

1-2a Planning

Planning involves determining organizational goals as well as means for achieving them. As you'll learn in Chapter 4, planning is one of the best ways to improve performance. It encourages people to work harder, to work hard for extended periods, to engage in behaviours directly related to accomplishing goals, and to think of better ways to do their jobs. But most important, companies that plan have larger profits and faster growth than companies that don't plan.

For example, the question "What business are we in?" is at the heart of strategic planning, which you'll learn about in Chapter 5. If you can answer the question "What business are we in?" in no more than two sentences, chances are you have a very clear plan for your business. Although some would describe Instagram as a photo-sharing website, the founders of Instagram believe that their unique business model contributed to a new entertainment platform—one that allowed people to tell stories as well as discover the world around them. According to co-founder Kevin Systrom, "By no means do we think of Instagram as just a photo-sharing service. It's something that a lot of people lump us into, but we'd like to think of ourselves as a storytelling service. It's the way you go out in the world and tell a story about your life, and it's a new entertainment platform."[10]

You'll learn more about planning in Chapter 4 on planning and decision making, Chapter 5 on organizational strategy, Chapter 6 on innovation and change, and Chapter 7 on global management.

1-2b Organizing

Organizing is deciding where decisions will be made, who will do what jobs and tasks, and who will work for whom in the company. The organizational structure of a company can have a major impact on its ability to handle decisions and execute effectively, which is why managers will often examine the organization and, when necessary, make changes or suggest a reorganization of the company's structure. When upper management at Rogers Communications Inc. decided changes were needed to revitalize the company and improve the customer experience, they introduced a new strategy dubbed Rogers 3.0 that included a new organizational structure focused on consumer and business customers. To execute the strategy, new positions in marketing and customer relations were added while management positions in other areas were cut. In the new organizational structure, all elements of customer service were combined into a single unit (over 10,000+ employees) reporting directly to the CEO. One of the pillars of the new strategy was a commitment to empower employees with more training, better systems, and tools to be able to resolve customer complaints and provide higher levels of customer service. Rogers CEO Guy Laurence explained, "This structure will help streamline the organization, clarify accountabilities and make us more agile. We will focus on fewer, more impactful initiatives and execute with more precision." The plan has met with success; one year after launching Rogers 3.0, the company reported a reduction in the annual customer complaints by more than 30 percent from the previous year and successfully launched Rogers NHL Game Centre Live, a partnership with the NHL that allows customers to live stream hockey games and gain access to exclusive features.[11]

You'll learn more about organizing in Chapter 8 on designing adaptive organizations, Chapter 9 on leading teams, Chapter 10 on managing human resource systems, and Chapter 11 on managing individuals and a diverse workforce.

1-2c Leading

Our third management function, **leading**, involves inspiring and motivating employees to work hard to achieve organizational goals. John Stanton, founder and president of the Edmonton-based The Running Room chain of retail stores, which cater to running and fitness enthusiasts alike, knows how important leadership is to building a successful company. Since opening his first store in 1984, Stanton has grown his company into North America's largest specialty retailer of sporting goods, apparel, and footwear, with stores from coast to coast. Stanton's original vision for the company hasn't changed much over the years—locate stores near parks, trails, and post-run meeting places like cafés; provide specialized knowledge and technical expertise on shoe selection as well as health and nutrition; offer running clinics and weekly runs for everyone from beginners to avid runners and marathoners; and promote a lifestyle of wellness and community. Much of The Running Room's success in achieving this vision can be attributed to Stanton himself, who spends about 300 days a year on the road, visiting Running Room stores and participating in numerous

Planning (management functions) determining organizational goals and a means for achieving them.

Organizing deciding where decisions will be made, who will do what jobs and tasks, and who will work for whom.

Leading inspiring and motivating workers to work hard to achieve organizational goals.

Courtesy of John Stanton, Running Room Inc.

charity runs and marathons across North America. All of this allows him to stay up to date on the needs of his consumers and staff. Examples of his approachable and accessible leadership style are found throughout the company: his email address is posted on the company website; he acts as the voice of the company's voice mail receptionist; and he utilizes a company-wide computer network that allows store employees to stay connected with one another and with head office. The results speak for themselves: The Running Room boasts an employee turnover rate that is half the industry average. Although Stanton's two sons are now actively involved in the management of this family-owned business, the leadership style set by their father is still very much a part of the corporate culture, as are what he believes to be the three key elements to the company's success—earning customer loyalty and respect, becoming a part of customers' lives, and supporting the community. And, speaking of success, Stanton is also famous for saying, "True success is never knowing if you are working or playing."[12]

You'll learn more about leading in Chapter 12 on motivation, Chapter 13 on leadership, and Chapter 14 on managing communication.

1-2d Controlling

The last function of management, **controlling**, involves monitoring progress toward goal achievement and taking corrective action when progress isn't being made. The basic control process involves setting standards to achieve goals, comparing actual performance to those standards, and then making changes to return performance to those standards.

Vancouver-based retailer Mountain Equipment Co-op (MEC) is a haven for Canadian outdoors enthusiasts. Operating in a highly competitive industry that sees small independent stores going head to head with large-scale chains; management at MEC is well aware that monitoring the organization's progress and making changes when needed is an important part of the strategic planning process for the future. In crafting a new corporate strategy, MEC was able to harness the power of its own data to help set the company's future course—analyzing the vast amounts of customer data at management's disposal. MEC customers become lifetime members of the co-op for a one-time fee of $5.00, and with more than 4 million members, MEC has a healthy database to tap into. During a recent rebranding initiative, MEC was able to access such information as what products are being purchased, from which stores, and how often; where members live; and member demographics. By analyzing this information and comparing store results to projections, MEC management is able to make better decisions as to what strategic changes should be made and when.[13]

You'll learn more about the control function in Chapter 15 on control, Chapter 16 on managing information in a global world, and Chapter 17 on managing service and manufacturing operations.

1-3 KINDS OF MANAGERS

Not all managerial jobs are the same. The demands and requirements placed on the CEO of Apple are significantly different from those placed on the manager of your local Subway restaurant. However, managers at all levels have a role to play in terms of the core management functions of planning, organizing, leading, and controlling.

*As shown in Exhibit 1.2, there are four kinds of managers, each with different jobs and responsibilities: **1-3a top managers**, **1-3b middle managers**, **1-3c first-line managers**, and **1-3d team leaders**.*

1-3a Top Managers

Top managers hold positions like chief executive officer (CEO), chief operating officer (COO), chief financial officer (CFO), and chief information officer

Controlling monitoring progress toward goal achievement and taking corrective action when needed.

Top managers executives responsible for the overall direction of the organization.

Exhibit 1.2
What the Four Kinds of Managers Do

Jobs		Responsibilities
Top Managers		
chief executive officer	(CEO)	change
chief information officer	(CIO)	commitment
chief operating officer	(COO)	culture
chief financial officer	(CFO)	environment
vice president		
corporate heads		
Middle Managers		
general manager		resources
plant manager		objectives
regional manager		coordination
divisional manager		subunit performance
		strategy implementation
First-Line Managers		
office manager		nonmanagerial worker supervision
shift supervisor		teaching and training
department manager		scheduling
		facilitation
Team Leaders		
team leader		facilitation
team contact		external relationships
group facilitator		internal relationships

EDHAR/Shutterstock.com

YanLev/Shutterstock.com

Blend Images—ColorBlind Images/Getty Images

Marcin Balcerzak/Shutterstock

(CIO), and are responsible for the overall direction of the organization. Top managers have many responsibilities.[14]

First, they are responsible for creating a context for change. In many large corporations, it is not uncommon for a CEO to be fired because he or she failed to move fast enough to effect significant change. Andrew Mason, founder and CEO of Groupon, was fired because he did not bring about significant changes needed to reverse a 77 percent decline in the stock price and an $81 million loss in the last quarter of his tenure. In a surprising online memo to his employees, Mason wrote, "I was fired today. If you're wondering why . . . you haven't been paying attention. The events of the last year and a half speak for themselves. As CEO, I am accountable."[15]

Although Mason lasted four and a half years as CEO of Groupon, many believe that the most critical time for a CEO is the first 100 days. The concept of the first 100 days (also known as the *honeymoon period*) is widely used in the world of politics as well as business, indicating that organizations today expect to see results quickly and that the first few months of a top manager's tenure can be the "make or break" time period that will determine whether that person will succeed.[16] Creating a context for change includes forming a long-range vision or mission for the company.

Once that vision or mission is set, the second responsibility of top managers is to develop employees' commitment to and ownership of the company's performance. That is, top managers are responsible for creating employee buy-in.

Third, top managers must create a positive organizational culture through language and action. Top managers impart company values, strategies, and lessons through what they do and say to others both inside and outside the company. Above all, no matter what they communicate, it's critical for CEOs to send and reinforce clear, consistent messages.[17] A former *Fortune* 500 CEO said, "I tried to [use] exactly the same words every time so that I didn't produce a lot of, 'Last time you said this, this time you said that.' You've got to say the same thing over and over and over."[18]

Finally, top managers are responsible for monitoring their business environments. This means that they must closely monitor customers' needs, competitors' moves, and long-term business, economic, and social trends. You'll read more about business environments in Chapter 2.

1-3b Middle Managers

Middle managers hold positions like plant manager, regional manager, or divisional manager. They are responsible for setting objectives consistent with top management's goals and for planning and implementing subunit strategies for achieving those objectives.[19] One specific middle management responsibility is to plan and allocate resources to meet objectives.

A second major responsibility is to coordinate and link groups, departments, and divisions within a company. The use of just-in-time inventory practices to keep inventory costs at the lowest level possible is an important business practice that has become a mainstay of the North American automotive industry. For this practice to succeed, parts and supplies must be shipped in a timely manner to allow plant managers to reach production objectives and targets. However, since September 11, 2001, border wait times have increased, which has left plant managers dealing with frustrating delays, rescheduling of production runs, and increased costs. It is estimated that delays at the Canada–United States border have increased production costs for new vehicles by $800 per unit.[20]

A third responsibility of middle management is to monitor and manage the performance of subunits and of individual managers. Capitalizing on advances in customer relationship management (CRM) technology, Canada's upscale menswear retail chain, Harry Rosen Inc., continues to invest in software systems to help manage store operations and allow sales associates to better manage customer relationships. The company's over 700 employees can access the computer system via the Web and mobile devices to view sales and inventory reports and customer preferences and purchase history, as well as to share information between stores. The system provides valuable information for managers to allow them to evaluate inventory decisions and marketing strategies, as well as store and individual sales associate results. As a result, management is able to assess how stores and associates are performing in terms of key performance indicators, thereby ensuring that the Harry Rosen quality and brand image is maintained.[21]

Finally, middle managers are responsible for implementing the changes or strategies generated by top managers. Walmart's strategy reflects its mission, "Saving people money so they can live better." When Walmart began selling groceries in its supercentres, it made purchasing manager Brian Wilson responsible for buying perishable goods more cheaply than Walmart's competitors. When small produce suppliers had trouble meeting Walmart's needs, Wilson worked closely with them and connected them to RetailLink, Walmart's computer network, "which allows our suppliers immediate access to all information needed to help run the business." Over time, these steps helped the produce suppliers reduce costs and deliver the enormous quantities of fresh fruits and vegetables that Walmart's supercentres need.[22]

1-3c First-Line Managers

First-line managers hold positions like office manager, shift supervisor, or store or department manager, and are usually the only managers that do not supervise other managers. The primary responsibility of first-line managers is to manage the performance of the entry-level employees who are directly responsible for producing a company's goods and services. As such, first-line managers are expected to train, monitor, encourage, and reward the performance of frontline workers to ensure organizational objectives are achieved and quality is maintained.

In the restaurant industry, first-line managers work closely with wait staff to increase sales and server

Middle managers managers responsible for setting objectives consistent with top management's goals and for planning and implementing subunit strategies for achieving these objectives.

First-line managers managers who train and supervise the performance of non-managerial employees who are directly responsible for producing the company's products or services.

Why Middle Managers May Be the Most Important People in Your Company

A study conducted by Wharton School of Business professor Ethan Mollick may change the way the business community views middle managers. Mollick chose the video game industry for the basis of his research, and concluded that middle managers have more impact on revenue than senior managers or designers. According to Mollick, middle managers are often overlooked because they aren't directly producing anything or involved in higher level strategic planning, even though they play a large role in a firm's performance, particularly in industries that are innovative and knowledge-intensive, such as computer games, software, and biotech. Middle managers in these industries often have key roles related to project management and responsibilities that include resource allocation, meeting deadlines, nurturing and facilitating employee creativity, and fostering an innovative environment. In fact, in the computer game industry, "Success . . . relies not just on managers in charge of innovation, but also on project managers capable of organizing dozens of programmers and coordinating budgets that often reach into the tens of millions of dollars." In addition, although top management plays a major role in setting the overall vision and direction of a company, "They don't have a big part in deciding which individual projects are selected and how

© Gregg Segal/Corbis

they are run. At least for the computer game industry—and no doubt lots of knowledge-based industries—it is all about the middle managers."

Sources: T. Barkley, "Don't Count Out the Middle Manager," *Forbes*, November 25, 2013, accessed August 22, 2015, http://www.forbes.com/sites/xerox/2013/11/25/dont-count-out-the-middle-manager/; E. Mollick, "People and Process, Suits and Innovators: The Role of Individuals in Firm Performance," March 1, 2011; available at SSRN: http://ssrn.com/abstract=1630546 or http://dx.doi.org/10.2139/ssrn.1630546; E. Mollick, "Why Middle Managers May Be the Most Important People in Your Company" May 25, 2011, in *Knowledge@Wharton* at http://knowledge.wharton.upenn.edu/article.cfm?articleid=2783, accessed November 30, 2012.

productivity to ensure that operations run smoothly and financial goals are achieved. Technology like Avero's Slingshot program helps restaurant managers to accomplish these tasks by analyzing sales data for each member of a restaurant's wait staff. Using this specialized software program, restaurant sales figures are examined with a *Moneyball* mentality, identifying the specific strengths and weaknesses of each server and bartender—much the same way a baseball general manager would analyze the on-base and hitting percentages of players. For example, using a Slingshot report, a manager can compare individual server sales of beverages or appetizers as well as the per cheque dollar average to other servers and the overall restaurant's goals. This kind of data can be used by first-line managers to help improve individual employee performance and determine where

additional training might be required.[23] First-line managers also make detailed schedules and operating plans based on middle management's intermediate-range plans. By contrast to the long-term plans of top managers (three to five years out) and the intermediate plans of middle managers (6 to 18 months out), first-line managers engage in planning and actions that typically produce results within two weeks.[24]

For some organizations, the value of first-line managers is critical in terms of facilitating worker performance, however, sometimes their value is diluted. Studies show that on average across industries, first-line managers spend 30–60 percent of their time on administrative work and meetings and only about 10–40 percent actually managing frontline employees by coaching them directly.[25]

1-3d Team Leaders

The fourth kind of manager is the team leader. This form of management developed as companies shifted to self-managed teams, which by definition have no formal supervisor. In traditional management hierarchies, supervisors or first-line managers are usually involved with overseeing the quality of employee performance, resolving conflicts within the workplace, completing administrative tasks, and in some cases, hiring and firing employees. In the team leader structure, team members perform nearly all the functions traditionally performed by first-line managers under the direction of a team leader.

Team leaders are primarily responsible for facilitating team activities toward accomplishing a goal. However, this doesn't mean that team leaders are responsible for team performance—the team is. Team leaders help their team members by developing timelines, delegating work to members of the team, providing project information to supervisors, and giving updates on the team's progress and the project's status. If problems or conflicts arise, the team leader is expected to help team members address the issue quickly and effectively. Team leaders usually do the same level of work as the members of their team and the position may not come with extra pay, as the benefit is the prestige of being selected for the position, although some organizations will offer bonuses or stipends to team leaders to compensate them for the additional work.[26]

Relationships among team members and between different teams are crucial to good team performance and must be well managed by team leaders. Communication and interpersonal relationships are much more important in team structures because team members can't get work done without the help of their teammates. Take the healthcare industry for example. Healthcare can be described as a team sport; teams take care of patients. The quality and effectiveness of team communication, team monitoring, and team coordination are important—not just for safety, but also in terms of efficiency.

Studies have shown that it's not the surgeon but the interactions between the surgeon and all operating room team members that determine surgical outcomes. When team members like nurses, technicians, and other doctors find it difficult to speak up or voice a concern in the operating room, serious mistakes can occur no matter how talented the surgeon. Consequently, many surgeons now are using "safety pauses" to better involve members of their surgical teams. The surgeon will pause, ask if anyone has concerns, and address them if need be at that time. Studies show that safety pauses reduce errors, such as operating on the wrong leg or beginning surgery with key surgical instruments missing.[27]

You will learn more about teams in Chapter 9.

1-4 MANAGERIAL ROLES

Although all four types of managers engage in planning, organizing, leading, and controlling, if you were to follow them around during a typical day on the job, you would probably not use these terms to describe what they actually do. Rather, what you'd see is the various *roles* managers play. Canadian professor Henry Mintzberg is well known for his study of management roles and behaviours. Mintzberg followed five CEOs, shadowing each for a week, analyzing their mail, their conversations, and their actions. He concluded that managers fulfill three major roles while performing their jobs:[28]

▸ interpersonal roles

▸ informational roles

▸ decisional roles

In other words, managers talk to people, gather and give information, and make decisions. Furthermore, as shown in Exhibit 1.3, these three major roles can be subdivided into 10 subroles.

*Let's examine each major role—**1-4a interpersonal, 1-4b informational**, and **1-4c decisional roles**—and the 10 subroles.*

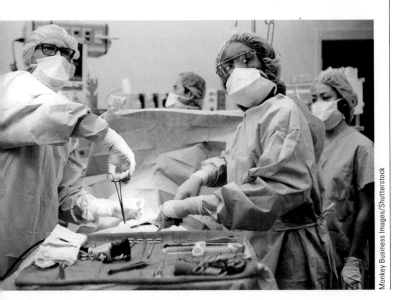

Monkey Business Images/Shutterstock

Team leaders managers responsible for facilitating team activities toward accomplishing a goal.

Exhibit 1.3
Mintzberg's Managerial Roles

Category	Role	Activity	Examples
Informational			
	Monitor	Seek and acquire work-related information	Scan/read trade press, periodicals, reports; attend seminars and training; maintain personal contacts
	Disseminator	Communicate/disseminate information to others within the organization	Send memos and reports; inform staffers and subordinates of decisions
	Spokesperson	Communicate/transmit information to outsiders	Pass on memos, reports, and informational materials; participate in conferences/meetings and report progress
Interpersonal			
	Figurehead	Perform social and legal duties, act as symbolic leader	Greet visitors, sign legal documents, attend ribbon cutting ceremonies, host receptions, etc.
	Leader	Direct and motivate subordinates, select and train employees	Interact with subordinates
	Liaison	Establish and maintain contacts within and outside the organization	Write business correspondence, participate in meetings with representatives of other divisions or organizations.
Decisional			
	Entrepreneur	Identify new ideas and initiate improvement projects	Implement innovations; plan for the future
	Disturbance Handler	Deal with disputes or problems and take corrective action	Strategic alternatives; overcome crisis situations
	Resource Allocator	Decide where to apply resources	Settle conflicts between subordinates; choose Draft and approve of plans, schedules, budgets; set priorities
	Negotiator	Defend business interests	Participate in and direct negotiations within team, department, and organization

R.Gino Santa Maria/Shutterstock.com

EDHAR/Shutterstock.com

Tuomas Kujansuu/iStockphoto.com

Source: Reprinted by permission of *Harvard Business Review* (an exhibit) from "The Manager's Job: Folklore and Fact," by H. Mintzberg, *Harvard Business Review,* July–August 1975. Copyright © 1975 by the Harvard Business School Publishing Corporation; all rights reserved.

1-4a **Interpersonal Roles**

More than anything else, management jobs are people-intensive. Estimates vary with the level of management, but most managers spend between two-thirds and four-fifths of their time in face-to-face communication with others.[29] If you're a loner, or if you consider dealing with people a pain, then you may not be cut out for management work. In fulfilling the interpersonal role of management, managers perform three subroles: figurehead, leader, and liaison.

In the **figurehead role**, managers perform ceremonial duties like greeting company visitors, speaking at the opening of a new facility, or representing the company at a community luncheon to support local charities. In the **leader role**, managers motivate and encourage workers to accomplish organizational objectives. Individuals assuming the leader role can be found in business, in government, and in nonprofit organizations. Peter Frates may not be well known as a business leader, however, his efforts on behalf of the Amyotrophic Lateral Sclerosis (ALS) Association led to the most viral fundraising campaign in history, the

Figurehead role the interpersonal role managers play when they perform ceremonial duties.

Leader role the interpersonal role managers play when they motivate and encourage workers to accomplish organizational objectives.

Ice Bucket Challenge. The same day Frates was diagnosed with ALS in 2012, the former Boston College baseball player decided to make it his mission to raise awareness and funds for this little-known debilitating neuro-degenerative disease that has no cure and no treatment and a life expectancy of two to five years after diagnosis. His goal was to bring the disease to the attention of philanthropists like Bill Gates, and his video did just that, sparking a viral social media phenomenon that had people dumping buckets of ice over their heads and then challenging others to do the same on YouTube, Facebook, and Twitter. In just six weeks, the Ice Bucket Challenge raised over $100 million in donations—compared to $2.8 million for the comparable period the year before. Frates did what inspiring leaders do—he articulated a bold vision and then inspired others to help rally around the vision.[30]

In the **liaison role**, managers deal with people outside their units. Studies consistently indicate that managers spend as much time with outsiders as they do with their own subordinates and their own bosses.[31] For example, it is not uncommon for a CEO to sit on another company's board of directors. Sarah Raiss, executive vice president of corporate services for TransCanada Corp.

in Calgary, sits on two different corporate boards, travelling to Toronto for meetings with Shoppers Drug Mart Corp. and to Montreal for the Business Development Bank of Canada's board meetings. "I get to use my experience and there is a tremendous intellectual challenge. In the process, I'm learning a lot about how to become a better manager," said Ms. Raiss. As a board member, a CEO can gain valuable perspective—not only about the company and its industry but also about other operational methods, different management styles, and business strategies—as well as build up his or her business network.

1-4b Informational Roles

Mintzberg found that the managers in his study spent 40 percent of their time exchanging information with others. In this regard, management can be viewed as processing information: gathering information by scanning the business environment and listening to others in face-to-face conversations, processing that information, and then sharing it with people inside and outside the company. Mintzberg described three informational subroles: monitor, disseminator, and spokesperson.

In the **monitor role**, managers scan their environment, actively communicate with others, and, because of their personal contacts, receive a great deal of unsolicited information. Besides receiving firsthand information, managers monitor their environment by reading local and national news publications like the *Globe and Mail* and the Business News Network to keep track of business news, customer trends, competitor news, and technological developments that may affect their businesses. In addition to traditional news sources, managers can also take advantage of electronic monitoring and distribution services that track the news wires for stories related to their businesses. These services deliver customized electronic newspapers that include only stories on topics the managers specify. For example, Canadian News Wire (CNW) (www.newswire.ca) connects organizations to relevant news and information, including social media releases that allow multimedia content. Business News Network (www.bnn.ca) is Canada's only all business and financial news channel. Globe Investor (www.theglobeandmail.com/globe-investor)

Marcos Mesa Sam Wordley/Shutterstock

Liaison role the interpersonal role managers play when they deal with people outside their units.

Monitor role the informational role managers play when they scan their environment for information.

offers up-to-date financial news and articles on stock trends. Canadian Press (www.thecanadianpress.com), in addition to being a multimedia real-time news agency, provides subscribers with news alerts to developing stories related to a specific company and/or industry.

Because of their numerous personal contacts and their access to subordinates, managers are often hubs for the distribution of critical information. In the **disseminator role**, managers share the information they have collected with their subordinates and others in the company. Yet technology is changing how information is shared and collected. Although the primary methods of communication in large companies are email and voice mail, managers are also using company intranets, online video, blogs, podcasts, and wikis to communicate internally with employees. Managers are also beginning to realize the value of social networking technologies like Facebook and Twitter to disseminate information internally. Tobias Lütke, CEO of Ottawa-based Shopify, an ecommerce company that provides a platform for small business owners to start selling online, wanted a way to quickly share information with employees and allow them to do the same. Taking a page from social media platforms like Facebook and Twitter, the company developed a custom-built social media platform named Unicorn to do just that. Lütke is now able to use the Unicorn system to share news of projects he is working on and also hear about interesting things his employees are doing. A major benefit of the system is that ideas and accomplishments can be shared with everyone in the company, widening the lines of communication between employees and managers.

In contrast to the disseminator role, in which managers distribute information to employees inside the company, in the **spokesperson role**, managers share information with people outside their departments and companies. One of the most common ways CEOs serve as spokespeople for their companies is at annual meetings with company shareholders or the board of directors. CEOs also speak to the media when their companies are involved in major news stories. Amazon founder and CEO Jeff Bezos attracted worldwide attention when he

announced that Amazon was actively working on a new transportation format—using drones to deliver packages directly to customers. The project dubbed "Prime Air" would use electrically powered drones to deliver packages up to five pounds in weight, which makes up 86 percent of the objects Amazon delivers. At the time of the announcement Bezos said, "I know this looks like science fiction; it's not," adding that the project would take several years before it would be ready to launch. Since the announcement, Amazon was able to gain approval from federal regulators to test the aircraft, a major step in helping to make this project a reality, and Bezos and his management team continue to lobby the Federal Aviation Administration to change drone-related regulations that would allow the use of drones for commercial activity. Time will tell whether Prime Air will "get off the ground."[32]

1-4c Decisional Roles

Mintzberg found that obtaining and sharing information is not an end in itself. Obtaining and sharing information with people inside and outside the company is useful to managers because it helps them make good decisions. According to Mintzberg, managers engage in four decisional subroles: entrepreneur, disturbance handler, resource allocator, and negotiator.

In the **entrepreneur role**, managers adapt themselves, their subordinates, and their units to change. For Manjit Minhas, management means staying close to her entrepreneurial roots. Manjit and her brother Ravinder learned about how to manage a business from watching their parents; their family started one of the first privatized liquor stores in Alberta, operating on the high volume, low price strategy. Although both brother and sister had planned a career in the oil industry, the Minhas siblings saw a greater opportunity in Calgary, and began selling deep-discount beer and spirits to bars and restaurants and then eventually to liquor stores. The pair began to slowly expand their product line and geographic coverage and now have two breweries and a distillery producing

Disseminator role the informational role managers play when they share information with others in their departments or companies.

Spokesperson role the informational role managers play when they share information with people outside their departments or companies.

Entrepreneur role the decisional role managers play when they adapt themselves, their subordinates, and their units to change.

Courtesy of Manjit Minhas

WANG ZHAO/AFP/Getty Images

160 varieties of beer and 90 spirits. Although her business has grown tremendously, Minhas continues to stick to her initial formula, capitalizing on new opportunities, offering low-cost options, and ruthlessly controlling expenses.

In the **disturbance handler role**, managers respond to pressures and problems so severe that they demand immediate attention and action. Managers often play the role of disturbance handler when the board of a failing company hires a new CEO to turn the company around. When Alan Mulally took over at Ford Motor Company in 2006, the company was in rough shape. Although the company had a huge portfolio of brands (97 in total), sales and market share were down 25 percent, high labour costs were contributing to low profit margins, and the company was lagging behind competitors in terms of new vehicle development. Mulally developed a plan (named One Ford) to restore the company's leadership position that included creating a new vision for Ford as a "mobility company" and not just a car company, reducing the number of vehicles produced, accelerating the development of new products and new technology, reducing the cost structure and the size of the workforce, and securing the financing necessary to fund the new plan. Mulally retired in 2014, however, his tenure at Ford will be remembered as one of the great turnarounds in automotive history.[33]

In the **resource allocator role**, managers decide who will get what resources and how much of each resource they will get. As part of the turnaround plan for Ford, management at Ford Motor Company committed to a multibillion-dollar investment into a major redesign of the Ford F-150, America's best-selling vehicle and Ford's best-selling truck in Canada for 48 years. There were many in the automotive industry who believed this was a huge risk. The redesign included the use of a lot more aluminum in the truck's construction, replacing traditional steel and thereby reducing the weight by 700 pounds. Although some worried that this decision would not sit well with die-hard truck customers who might question the truck's ability to perform, the change allowed Ford engineers to replace the truck's V8 engine with a turbocharged V6 engine, improve overall gas mileage by 16 percent, and still allow a towing capacity of 8,000 pounds—all of which was extremely well received by customers.[34]

In the **negotiator role**, managers may negotiate schedules, projects, goals, outcomes, resources, and employee raises. When Disney and Marvel Studios were planning the production and release of *Iron Man 3*, they entered into negotiations with DMG, a global entertainment and media company based in Beijing, to bring the film to China's 10,000+ theatres. However, DMG faced a major hurdle: only 31 foreign films are imported to China each year, and studios are limited to just 25 percent of the revenues. However, management at DMG were able to negotiate a creative solution— they proposed that *Iron Man 3* become a United

Disturbance handler role the decisional role managers play when they respond to severe problems that demand immediate action.

Resource allocator role the decisional role managers play when they decide who gets what resources.

Negotiator role the decisional role managers play when they negotiate schedules, projects, goals, outcomes, resources, and employee raises.

States–China coproduction by incorporating Chinese elements into the script and shooting part of the movie in China. Doing so increased the studio box office receipts in China from 25 to 38 percent. The film was a major hit, achieving global sales of over $1.2 billion and breaking opening-day records in China.[35]

1-5 WHAT COMPANIES LOOK FOR IN MANAGERS

I didn't have the slightest idea what my job was. I walked in giggling and laughing because I had been promoted and had no idea what principles or style to be guided by. After the first day, I felt like I had run into a brick wall.

—(*Sales Representative #1*)

Suddenly, I found myself saying, boy, I can't be responsible for getting all that revenue. I don't have the time. Suddenly you've got to go from [taking care of] yourself and say, "Now I'm the manager, and what does a manager do?" It takes a while thinking about it for it to really hit you . . . A manager gets things done through other people. That's a very, very hard transition to make.

—(*Sales Representative #2*)[36]

The above statements come from two star sales representatives, who, on the basis of their superior performance, were promoted to the position of sales manager. As their comments indicate, at first they did not feel confident about their ability to do their jobs as managers. Like most new managers, these sales managers suddenly realized that the knowledge, skills, and abilities that led to success early in their careers (and were probably responsible for their promotion into management) would not necessarily help them succeed as managers. As sales representatives, they were responsible for managing only their own performance. But as sales managers, they were now directly responsible for supervising all of the sales representatives in their sales territories. Furthermore, they were now directly accountable for whether those sales representatives achieved their sales goals.

If performance in nonmanagerial jobs doesn't necessarily prepare you for a managerial job, then what does it take to be a manager? When companies look for employees who would be good managers, they look for individuals who have technical skills, human skills, and conceptual skills.[37] Exhibit 1.4 shows the relative importance of these four skills to the jobs of team leaders, first-line managers, middle managers, and top managers.

Technical skills are the specialized procedures, techniques, and knowledge required to get the job done. For the sales managers like the ones quoted earlier, technical skills include the ability to find new sales prospects, develop accurate sales pitches based on customer needs, and close the sale. For a nurse supervisor, technical skills would include being able to insert an intravenous line or operate a crash cart if a patient goes into cardiac arrest. Technical skills are most important for team leaders and lower level managers because they supervise the workers who produce products or serve customers. Team leaders and first-line managers need technical knowledge and skills to train new employees and help employees solve problems, and to troubleshoot problems that employees can't handle. Technical skills become less important as managers rise through the managerial ranks, but they are still important.

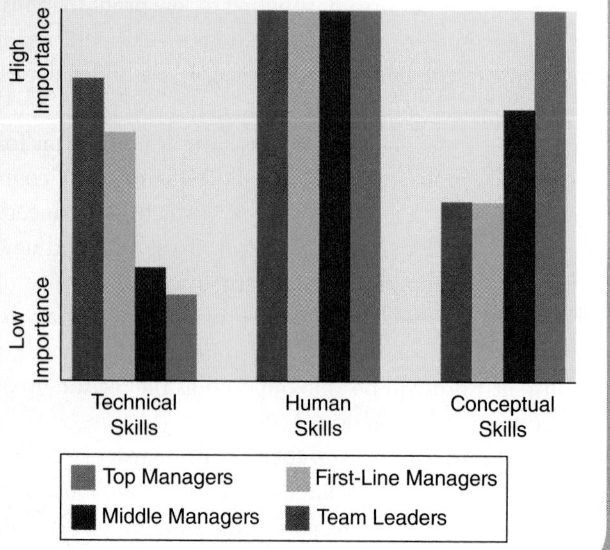

Technical skills the specialized procedures, techniques, and knowledge required to get the job done.

Exhibit 1.4
Management Skills

Legend:
- Top Managers
- Middle Managers
- First-Line Managers
- Team Leaders

(Vertical axis: Low Importance to High Importance)
(Horizontal axis: Technical Skills, Human Skills, Conceptual Skills)

Human skills can be summarized as the ability to work well with others. Managers with people skills work effectively within groups, encourage others to express their thoughts and feelings, are sensitive to others' needs and viewpoints, and are good listeners and communicators. Human skills are equally important at all levels of management, from first-line supervisors to CEOs. However, because lower-level managers spend much of their time solving technical problems, upper-level managers may actually spend more time dealing directly with people. On average, first-line managers spend 57 percent of their time with people, but that percentage increases to 63 percent for middle managers and 78 percent for top managers.[38]

Conceptual skills include the ability to see the organization as a whole, to understand how the different parts of the company affect one another, and to recognize how the company fits into or is affected by elements of its external environment such as the local community, social and economic forces, customers, and the competition. Good managers must be able to recognize, understand, and reconcile multiple complex problems and perspectives. In other words, managers have to be smart! In fact, intelligence makes so much difference to managerial performance that managers with above-average intelligence typically outperform managers of average intelligence by approximately 48 percent.[39] Clearly, companies need to be careful to promote smart workers into management. Conceptual skills increase in importance as managers rise through the management hierarchy.

Ryan McVay/Photodisc/Thinkstock

1-6 MISTAKES MANAGERS MAKE

It is generally accepted that good management will enhance organizational performance, and that some managers are better than others. However, reaching a consensus on what makes a good manager is more challenging than determining what makes for a *bad* manager. For that reason, one way to understand what it takes to be a good manager is to look at the common mistakes managers make. In other words, we can learn just as much from manager failures as we can from manager successes.

Management failure has typically been associated with managers who experience career "derailment" (related to the metaphor of a train coming off the track)—being demoted or fired, or finding themselves involuntarily stuck on a management plateau and performing below their level of expected achievement. Leadership derailment occurs in a situation when leaders who progress upward by capitalizing on their key strengths suddenly fail to develop more widely and are unable to deliver results when confronted by challenges that require a broader range of capabilities. It is obviously beneficial to study leadership from both sides—leadership successes and leadership failures (the dark side)—to gain better and more complete knowledge of leadership. As such, understanding the key characteristics of leaders who derail can be useful for managers who wish to avoid this potentially damaging career development.

Let's take a closer look at **1-6a key characteristics of leaders who derail**, *and* **1-6b strategies to prevent leadership derailment.**

Human skills the ability to work well with others.

Conceptual skills the ability to see the organization as a whole, understand how the different parts affect one another, and recognize how the company fits into or is affected by its environment.

© Mikael Damkier/Dreamstime.com

1-6a Key Characteristics of Leaders Who Derail

Leaders who derail often demonstrate some identifiable characteristics:

1. Difficulty in changing or adapting—they are resistant to change, and have trouble learning from mistakes and developing.

2. Problems with interpersonal relationship—they find it hard to develop good working relations with others.

3. Failure to build and lead a team—they experience difficulties in selecting and building a team.

4. Failure to meet business objectives—they are challenged in following up on promises and completing jobs.

5. Too narrow a functional orientation—they lack depth to manage outside of their current function.

Since leadership derailment impacts greatly on the followers, the leaders, and the different facets of organizational life and activities, it makes sense to address strategic options that can be utilized to prevent the consequences of the dark side of leadership.

1-6b Strategies to Prevent Leadership Derailment

Here are some strategies that can improve the quality of leadership:

1. Executive coaching: Equipping managers with the tools, knowledge, and opportunities they need to develop themselves and become more effective will help them better cope with the challenges that are likely to confront them in their higher job positions. Coaching provides opportunity for employees with high potential to learn valuable lessons that will help them deliver long-term results in the organization. Effective executive coaching that critically considers a leader's strengths and weaknesses can contribute to specific development plans for the leader and this can help prevent derailment.

2. Leadership training: This helps foster the development of needed skills and behaviour that help the leader perform and prevent derailment. Providing varied leadership challenges and developmental assignments can give managers learning opportunities for skill improvement.

3. Self-awareness: This is the first component of the needed changes that can help prevent a leader from derailing. Self-awareness helps a leader understand aspects of his or her personality which could lead to derailment, and to then proactively manage these as an important way of ensuring stable high performance and career progression.

4. Creating effective management processes and feedback: Organizations must develop effective management tools to identify early signals of derailment and address these during recruitment and selection processes. Strong management processes should be applied to promote only competent managers to higher job responsibility, and not to promote people beyond their levels of competence. Providing feedback for

iofoto/Shutterstock

leaders on their performance is very necessary, as good leaders seek out trusted, honest observers throughout their career to monitor how they are performing. Having intensive, honest, and systematic assessment of performance can prevent leadership derailment. This is a vital key to any leadership development effort.

1-7 THE TRANSITION TO MANAGEMENT: THE FIRST YEAR

Studies show that most derailment occurs following a management transition to a position with greater responsibility and greater scrutiny. In a well known study, Harvard Business School professor Linda Hill followed the development of 19 people in their first year as managers. Her study found that becoming a manager produced a profound psychological transition that changed the way these managers viewed themselves and others. As shown in Exhibit 1.5, the evolution of the managers' thoughts, expectations, and realities over the course of their first year in management reveals the magnitude of the changes they experienced.

Initially, the managers in Hill's study believed that their job was to exercise formal authority and to manage tasks—basically "to be the boss," telling others what to do, making decisions, and getting things done. In fact, most of the new managers were attracted to management

positions because they wanted to be in charge. Surprisingly, the new managers did not believe that their job was to manage people. The only aspects of people management mentioned by the new managers were hiring and firing.

After six months, most of the new managers had concluded that their initial expectations about managerial work were wrong. Management wasn't just about being the boss, making decisions, and telling others what to do. The first surprise was the fast pace and heavy workload involved. Said one manager: "This job is much harder than you think. It is 40 to 50 percent more work than being a producer! Who would have ever guessed?" The pace of managerial work was startling, too. Another manager said: "You have eight or nine people looking for your time . . . coming into and out of your office all day long." A somewhat frustrated manager declared that management was "a job that never ended . . . a job you couldn't get your hands around."

Informal descriptions like this are consistent with studies indicating that the average first-line manager spends no more than two minutes on a task before being interrupted by a request from a subordinate, a phone call, or an email. The pace is somewhat less hurried for top managers, who spend an average of nine minutes on a task before having to switch to another. In practice, this means that supervisors may perform 30 different tasks per hour, while top managers perform seven different tasks per hour, with each task typically different from the one that preceded it. A manager described this frenetic level of activity: "The only time you are in control is when you shut your door, and then I feel I am not doing the job I'm supposed to be doing, which is being with the people."

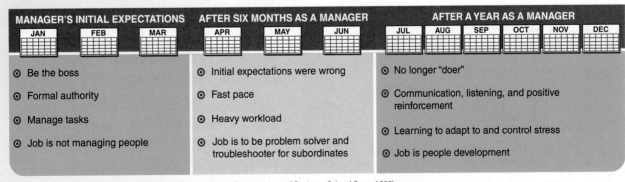

Exhibit 1.5
Stages in the Transition to Management

MANAGER'S INITIAL EXPECTATIONS			AFTER SIX MONTHS AS A MANAGER			AFTER A YEAR AS A MANAGER					
JAN	FEB	MAR	APR	MAY	JUN	JUL	AUG	SEP	OCT	NOV	DEC

MANAGER'S INITIAL EXPECTATIONS	AFTER SIX MONTHS AS A MANAGER	AFTER A YEAR AS A MANAGER
⊙ Be the boss	⊙ Initial expectations were wrong	⊙ No longer "doer"
⊙ Formal authority	⊙ Fast pace	⊙ Communication, listening, and positive reinforcement
⊙ Manage tasks	⊙ Heavy workload	⊙ Learning to adapt to and control stress
⊙ Job is not managing people	⊙ Job is to be problem solver and troubleshooter for subordinates	⊙ Job is people development

Source: L.A. Hill, *Becoming a Manager: Mastery of a New Identity* (Boston: Harvard Business School Press, 1992).

CHAPTER 1: Management 19

The other major surprise after six months on the job was that the managers' expectations about what they should do as managers were very different from their subordinates' expectations. Initially, the managers defined their jobs as helping their subordinates perform their jobs well. For the managers, who still defined themselves as doers rather than managers, assisting their subordinates meant going out on sales calls or handling customer complaints. But when the managers "assisted" in this way, their subordinates were resentful and viewed their help as interference. The subordinates wanted their managers to help them by solving problems they themselves couldn't solve. Once managers realized this distinction, they embraced their role as problem solvers and troubleshooters. They could then help without interfering with their subordinates' jobs.

After a year on the job, most of the managers thought of themselves as managers and no longer as doers. In making the transition, they finally realized that people management was the most important part of their job. One manager summarized the lesson that had taken him a year to learn: "As many demands as managers have on their time, I think their primary responsibility is people development. Not production, but people development." Another indication of how much their views had changed was that most of the managers now regretted the rather heavy-handed approach they had used in their early attempts to manage their subordinates. "I wasn't good at managing . . . so I was bossy like a first-grade teacher." "Now I see that I started out as a drill sergeant. I was inflexible,

Top managers spend an average of nine minutes on a given task before having to switch to another.

elnavegante/Shutterstock

just a lot of how-to's." By the end of the year, most of the managers had abandoned their authoritarian approach for one based on communication, listening, and positive reinforcement.

Finally, after beginning their year as managers in frustration, the managers came to feel comfortable with their subordinates, with the demands of their jobs, and with their emerging managerial styles. While being managers had made them acutely aware of their limitations and their need to develop as people, it also provided them with an unexpected reward of coaching and developing the people who worked for them. One manager said: "I realize now that when I accepted the position of branch manager that it is truly an exciting vocation. It is truly awesome, even at this level; it can be terribly challenging and terribly exciting."

Lane Oatey/Blue Jean Images/Getty Images

STUDY TOOLS 1

READY TO STUDY?

LOCATED IN TEXTBOOK:

☐ Rip out the Chapter Review Card at the back of the book to have a summary of the chapter and key terms handy.

LOCATED AT NELSON.COM/STUDENT:

☐ Access the eBook or use the ReadSpeaker feature to listen to the chapter on the go.

☐ Prepare for tests with practice quizzes.

☐ Review key terms with flashcards and the glossary feature.

☐ Work through key concepts with case studies and Management Decision Exercises.

☐ Explore practical examples with You Make the Decision Activities.

Learning like never before.

nelson.com/student

2 Organizational Environments and Cultures

Johnny Greig/iStockphoto

LEARNING OUTCOMES

After studying this chapter, you will be able to...

2-1 Discuss how changing environments affect organizations.

2-2 Describe the four components of the general environment.

2-3 Explain the five components of the specific environment.

2-4 Describe the process that companies use to make sense of their changing environments.

2-5 Explain how organizational cultures are created and how they can help companies succeed.

After you finish this chapter, go to **PAGE 41** for **STUDY TOOLS**

It's a Digital World

For Chelsea Macdonald, management is about continuous learning. Shortly after graduating from Algonquin College of Applied Arts and Technology in Ottawa, Chelsea was hired as a project manager for a digital strategy and implementation firm. Working closely with the firm's CEO, she was responsible for organizing the project documentation, resourcing, and budgets of client projects. More importantly, as project manager, her job was to ensure that the application was aligned with the client's expectations, timeline, and budget. As a manager, Chelsea recognized the need for business development both internally and externally in order to build her credibility with clients, who often looked to her to provide strategic guidance regarding their digital footprint.

Chelsea is quick to point out that she is constantly learning from those around her—and that is always the end goal, to be continuously learning. Even back when she attended Algonquin College, Chelsea didn't shy away from learning a little extra. Instead of leaving with just one diploma, first she took the two-year business marketing program (2007–09), earning a diploma in business marketing, and then she took a one-year extension program (2009–10), earning a diploma in business administration.

1. How important is it to monitor the organizational environments surrounding your business?

This is critical. Externally: running a business really means having your ear to the ground at all times, from understanding changes to regulations and industry best practices, to keeping up with economic news within your community. In a small business, every contract counts and competing means being aware of what's happening around you. Internally: A business is nothing without a good team of workers working toward a common goal. Being aware of employee skill, capabilities, and interests helps create a working culture that recognizes the strengths and weakness within your team.

2. In examining the external environment facing your company, which elements of the general environment have the greatest potential to influence your company?

The major external factors that affect the Web application development industry as a whole are technological, sociocultural, and regulatory. In our industry, new technology frameworks and new programming languages are regularly released and physical hardware is regularly improved. Knowing what kinds of processes to implement based on emerging technology in software and hardware can affect our business's efficiency, the ability to provide good service, and our bottom line. We are expected to advise our clients, and being aware of industry trends is critical to being able to provide good advice. Communities of online users dictate what makes for a good online experience, which in turn impacts the industry's adoption of new development standards. The standards become adopted by the online communities, and can then become actual legislation mandated by government.

3. What kind of customer monitoring do you do—is it reactive or proactive in nature?

We monitor our business development efforts by tracking interactions with existing and potential customers using a customer relationship management tool. Throughout our client engagements, we regularly incorporate client feedback to ensure that information is being delivered effectively and our processes are working. Once a project is delivered, we perform a post-mortem session with clients to look back at the project, identifying issues along the way and developing strategies to avoid the same issue in the next project.

4. How would you describe your company's organizational culture?

Our development shop has an open, flexible, and fun environment. Our management team is open to ideas, and we encourage open discussion among team members. We encourage creativity, trying new things, and professional development. Everyone has a voice on the projects we work on, and the technology we use. Everyone feels appreciated and that they provide value. That encourages loyalty and dedication from our team members.

5. How important do you think organizational culture is to the success of an organization?

Very important. An organization's culture makes employees love working somewhere, and makes potential employees want to work there. The more interesting and appealing the organizational culture is, the higher the volume of skilled applicants applying to open positions will be. The more skilled applicants you have to choose from, the better chance you have at staffing your organization with skilled employees.

6. What advice would you give someone about to step into a management position?

Make the effort to understand the individuals on your team as just that, individuals. Understand the way they communicate and make it easy for them to provide you with the information you need to perform your job.

7. What is the most important thing you learned in business school that you use to this day?

How to understand an audience.

For the full interview go online to nelson.com/student

Photo and interview courtesy of Chelsea Macdonald

CHAPTER 2: Organizational Environments and Cultures

2-1 CHANGING ENVIRONMENTS

MikeDotta/Shutterstock

This chapter examines the internal and external forces that affect business. First we'll examine the two types of external organizational environments: the general environment that affects all organizations, and the specific or task environment that is unique to each company. Then we'll learn how managers make sense of their changing general and specific environments. The chapter finishes with a discussion of internal organizational environments that focuses on organizational culture. But first, let's see how changes in external organizational environments affect the decisions and performance of a company.

External environments are the forces and events outside a company that have the potential to influence or affect it. In most cities, taxi fares (what is charged on the taxi meter) and taxi licences (for drivers and cars) are highly regulated. However, Uber, an Internet ride-hailing company that began in 2009, has shaken up the taxi industry by introducing customers to a new form of transportation. After signing up as an Uber customer, a person can use the Uber app on a smart phone to order a ride. Tap Uber. Enter a destination. Tap a button indicating your location. Then, the Uber app indicates the cost and how long until the car arrives. Uber connects users both to licensed drivers and, through the UberX service, to unlicensed drivers using their own cars for a cheaper fare. Afterward, it e-mails a receipt and automatically pays the driver. No cash changes hands. Customers love Uber because it's often faster than hailing a cab on the street. Taxi drivers and companies are not happy, however, arguing that Uber should be classified as a taxi service and be required to meet the same industry regulations, since the present format undercuts their ability to make a living. Uber has expanded globally, offering ride-hailing services in 300 cities in 58 countries and causing regulatory bodies and interest groups within the transportation industry to sit up and take notice. The local government body responsible for transport services in

London, England, has been lobbying the government to introduce specific policies that would help protect the rights of taxi companies and the famous London Black Cabs. Steve McNamara, a spokesperson for London's Licensed Taxi Driver Association, said, "We have nothing against competition. But Uber is being allowed to 'operate outside the law.'" In response to Uber, many cities have had to determine how to deal with companies that provide transportation services but don't technically own vehicles or employ drivers. While some cities have banned Uber and consider it illegal, other cities are working on proposals to introduce ride-sharing regulations. In Ontario, Kitchener–Waterloo became the first in Ontario to propose a ride-hailing bylaw that would require Uber drivers to have a global positioning system (GPS) and a closed-circuit television system installed in their vehicle, as well as a commercial auto insurance policy.[1] As such, monitoring the external environment is critical for many of the stakeholders identified above— for taxi companies that are in markets where Uber may be operating (or is expected to enter), for local municipalities who are unsure how legislation will impact the taxi industry, and for Uber itself, to ensure they remain up to date with respect to the specific laws and regulations governing the markets they expect to operate in.

*Let's examine the three basic characteristics of changing external environments: **2-1a environmental change, 2-1b environmental complexity, 2-1c resource scarcity,** and **2-1d the uncertainty that environmental change, complexity, and resource scarcity can create for organizational managers.***

2-1a Environmental Change

Environmental change refers to the rate at which a company's general and specific environments change. In a **stable environment**, the rate of environmental

---

External environments all events outside a company that have the potential to influence or affect it.

Environmental change the rate at which a company's general and specific environments change.

Stable environment an environment in which the rate of change is slow.

change is slow. Apart from occasional shortages due to drought or frost, the wholesale food distribution business—where dairy items, fresh produce, baked goods, poultry, fish, and meat are processed and delivered by trucks from warehouses to restaurants, grocery stores, and other retailers—changes little from year to year. Distributors take shipments from farmers, food manufacturers, and food importers, consolidate them in warehouses, and then distribute them to retailers. While recent adoption of GPS and radio frequency identification (RFID) devices might be seen as "change," wholesale food distributors began using them because, like the trucks they bought to replace horse-drawn carriages in the early 1900s, GPS and RFID improved the core part of their business—getting the freshest food ingredients to customers as quickly and inexpensively as possible—which has not changed in over a century.[2]

While wholesale food distribution companies have stable environments, smart phone manufacturers like Apple and Samsung compete in an extremely dynamic external environment. In a **dynamic environment**, the rate of environmental change is fast. The smart phone industry is heavily influenced by the actions of ferocious competitors, technological innovations, and changes in consumer demand. While Apple leads the industry in overall profitability, Samsung has been steadily gaining market share at the same time as Google's Android operating system continues to dominate the market. New product innovations are still widely anticipated by consumers and industry experts, signalling new opportunities for growth in this industry and inciting even more competitive reactions. Recently, mobile payments have given the major smart phone players an opportunity to shake things up again in this industry, offering customers the ability to make card-free and wallet-free payments from their smart phone simply by holding their phone up to a retailer's payment point of sale device. Shortly after Apple introduced Apple Pay, its mobile payment solution, Samsung responded with Samsung Pay, integrating magnetic secure transmission technology into its system and allowing retailers to utilize existing payment terminals to accept mobile payments instead of having to upgrade their card readers. With this latest technology, the smart phone war continues.[3]

You might expect a company's external environment to be *either* stable *or* dynamic. However, research suggests that companies often experience both. According to **punctuated equilibrium theory**, companies go through long periods of stability (equilibrium) during which incremental changes occur, followed by short periods of dynamic, fundamental change (revolutionary periods), which end with a return to stability (new equilibrium).[4]

One example of punctuated equilibrium is found in the Canadian airline industry. Twice in the past 30 years, that industry has experienced revolutionary periods. The first occurred in 1978 with the advent of airline deregulation, in response to US deregulation. Prior to deregulation, the industry was dominated by the "friendly duopoly" of CP Air and Air Canada, which shared over 95 percent of the market; however, the federal government controlled where airlines could fly, when they could fly, the prices they could charge, and the number of flights they could have on a particular route. Full deregulation was not seen in Canada until 1988, and when it was, airlines suddenly had more options. Many competitors—such as Wardair, which was primarily a charter airline, and Pacific Western Airlines, a regional carrier—expanded, and new air carriers were started. Competition among the airlines was fierce, with Pacific Western purchasing several smaller airlines, including Wardair and the much larger CP Air, to form Canadian Airlines. Although still smaller than Air Canada, Canadian Airlines' expansion allowed the company to compete with Air Canada on a more even basis, and once again, two companies dominated the skies and the industry settled into a period of relative stability. The dominance of these two carriers was not seriously challenged until 1996, when Calgary-based WestJet Airlines entered the scene. Competition once again increased, and eventually a faltering Canadian Airlines was purchased by Air Canada in 2000, leaving again only two national carriers, Air Canada and WestJet. Several smaller carriers (such as Porter Airlines, a regional flier that operates from Billy Bishop Airport on Toronto Island) have met with success by operating smaller aircraft and appealing to business travellers. Air Canada and WestJet still dominate the Canadian skies, however, change may be on the horizon for the airline industry. In 2015, WestJet faced two separate union drives: one involving pilots, and the other among flight attendants. By a narrow margin, WestJet pilots voted against unionization, preserving for now the non-union workplace

Dynamic environment an environment in which the rate of change is fast.

Punctuated equilibrium theory a theory according to which companies go through long, simple periods of stability (equilibrium), followed by short periods of dynamic, fundamental change (revolution), and ending with a return to stability (new equilibrium).

CHAPTER 2: Organizational Environments and Cultures

recognized to be one of WestJet's early competitive advantages against Air Canada. In addition, the airline that built its reputation on a low-cost structure has slowly become a more full-service carrier, introducing charges for checked baggage and premium seating, and expanding its fleet to include 767 aircraft that will allow the company to expand into trans-Atlantic flights to Europe. Time will tell whether these changes will impact the industry overall and whether increasing pressure on government to deregulate the industry further to allow more international competition will once again demonstrate the punctuated equilibrium theory.[5]

2-1b Environmental Complexity

Environmental complexity refers to the number and intensity of external factors in the environment that affect organizations. A **simple environment** has few environmental factors, whereas a **complex environment** has many environmental factors. The dairy industry is an excellent example of a relatively simple external environment. Even accounting for decades-old advances in processing and automatic milking machines, milk is produced the same way today as it was 100 years ago. And while food manufacturers introduce dozens of new dairy-based products each year, Canadian milk production has grown only 1.7 percent per year over the last decade. In short, producing milk is a simple but highly competitive business that has experienced few changes.[6]

At the other end of the spectrum, few industries today face a more complex environment than the newspaper industry. For a century, making money selling newspapers was relatively simple: sell subscriptions for daily home delivery, and then sell classified

ads and retail ads to reach those subscribers. In today's digital age, however, that business model doesn't work. First, revenues from classified ads—which had been extremely profitable for local newspapers—dropped 70 percent between 2000 and 2010 primarily because of popular sites like Craigslist.com, Kijiji.ca, and eBay-Classified.com, which allow free posting of classified ads.[7] Second, digital ads bring in substantially less revenue compared to print ads. Recent studies report that publishers only earn $1 in digital revenue for every $7 lost from print advertising, and these earnings don't generate enough revenue to cover the cost of "free" online versions of newspapers. Finally, because digital content is very inexpensive to distribute relative to print, most consumers expect Internet-based news to be free. As a result, many online newspapers—such as the *National Post*, the *New York Times*, and the *Wall Street Journal*—now charge for online access, but other newspapers may find it more difficult to do so. Says *Adweek* senior editor Mike Shields: "*The Wall Street Journal* is not free. They never wavered or changed that. That is as key to the success as the content they deliver. That precedent is enviable and hard for someone [else] to copy, particularly if you've been giving away your content for ten years."[8]

2-1c Resource Scarcity

The third characteristic of external environments is resource scarcity. **Resource scarcity** refers to the abundance or shortage of critical resources in the organization's external environment. Chenab Ltd., a garment manufacturer in Faisalabad, Pakistan, makes fashionable sportswear for global brands, ranging from Victoria's Secret to Tommy Hilfiger. Due to severe

Environmental complexity the number of external factors in the environment that affect organizations.

Simple environment an environment with few environmental factors.

Complex environment an environment with many environmental factors.

Resource scarcity the abundance or shortage of critical organizational resources in an organization's external environment.

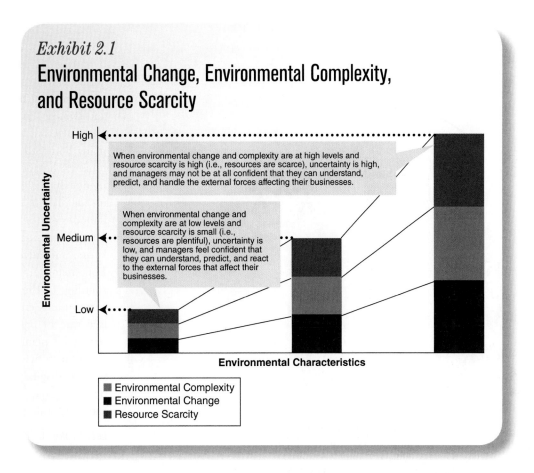

Exhibit 2.1

Environmental Change, Environmental Complexity, and Resource Scarcity

When environmental change and complexity are at high levels and resource scarcity is high (i.e., resources are scarce), uncertainty is high, and managers may not be at all confident that they can understand, predict, and handle the external forces affecting their businesses.

When environmental change and complexity are at low levels and resource scarcity is small (i.e., resources are plentiful), uncertainty is low, and managers feel confident that they can understand, predict, and react to the external forces that affect their businesses.

Environmental Uncertainty

High

Medium

Low

Environmental Characteristics

- ■ Environmental Complexity
- ■ Environmental Change
- ■ Resource Scarcity

electricity shortages in Pakistan, where demand for electricity exceeds supply by 50 percent, power outages often occur 12 to 18 hours a day. Chenab bought a $6 million generator to power the entire plant, but it goes unused because of gas shortages. Says Muhammad Latif, Chenab's owner, "I am asked to pay interest on my loans for 365 days a year, but I can only work my business for half that time." As a result, Chenab's clothing plant runs at only one-third of its capacity and is forced to turn down orders. Its 14,000-strong workforce, likewise, has shrunk to just 4,500 employees and its sales are down 75 percent.[9]

2-1d Uncertainty

As Exhibit 2.1 shows, environmental change, environmental complexity, and resource scarcity affect environmental **uncertainty**, which refers to how well managers can understand or predict the external changes and trends affecting their businesses. Starting at the left side of the figure, environmental uncertainty is lowest when environmental change and environmental complexity are low and resources are plentiful. In these environments, managers feel confident that they can understand, predict, and react to the external forces that affect their businesses. By contrast, the right side of the figure

shows that environmental uncertainty is highest when environmental change and complexity are high and resource scarcity is a problem. In these environments, managers may not be confident that they can understand, predict, and handle the external forces affecting their businesses.

2-2 GENERAL ENVIRONMENT

As Exhibit 2.2 shows, two kinds of external environments influence organizations: the general environment, and the specific or task environment. The **general environment** consists of the political/legal, economic, sociocultural, and technological trends that

Uncertainty extent to which managers can understand or predict which environmental changes and trends will affect their businesses.

General environment the economic, technological, sociocultural, and political trends that indirectly affect all organizations.

Exhibit 2.2
General and Specific Environments

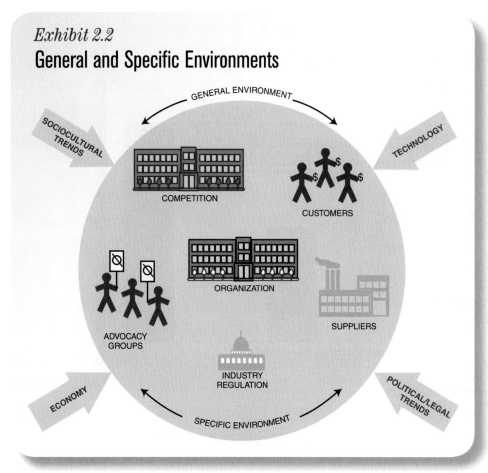

2014, Tim Horton's raised the price of an average coffee by 10 cents. Others in the coffee industry followed suit, including Starbucks Canada and Keurig, the makers of "K-cup" coffee pods used in many home coffee brew systems.[10] The specific environment, which will be discussed in detail in Section 2-3, includes customers, competitors, suppliers, industry regulators, and advocacy groups. For managers, an understanding of the environment surrounding an organization is a critical first step in the strategic planning process undertaken by managers, and will be discussed in greater detail in Chapter 5, "Organizational Strategy."

Let's take a closer look at the four components of the general environment: **2-2a economy, 2-2b technological component, 2-2c sociocultural component,** *and* **2-2d political/legal component,** *or trends that indirectly affect all organizations.*

indirectly affect all organizations. Changes in any part of the general environment eventually affect most organizations. For example, when the Bank of Canada lowers its prime lending rate, most businesses benefit because banks and credit card companies often reduce the interest rates they charge for loans. Consumers can then borrow money more cheaply to buy homes, cars, refrigerators, and computers. But each organization also has a **specific environment** that is unique to its industry and that directly affects how it conducts day-to-day business. For example, Tim Horton's carefully monitors coffee bean prices, as this important ingredient influences the chain's operational costs, as well as plays a major role in the company's business strategy. When coffee-growing regions like Brazil, the world's largest exporter of coffee beans, experienced record-breaking drought which impacted crop yields in

Specific environment the customers, competitors, suppliers, industry regulations, and advocacy groups that are unique to an industry and directly affect how a company does business.

2-2a Economy

The current state of a country's economy affects virtually every organization doing business there. In a growing economy, more people are working and wages are increasing, and as a result, consumers have more money to spend. More products are bought and sold in a growing economy than in a static or shrinking economy. Although an individual firm's sales will not necessarily increase, a growing economy does provide an environment favourable to business growth. In a shrinking economy, on the other hand, consumers have less money to spend and relatively fewer products are bought and sold. A shrinking economy thus makes growth for individual businesses more difficult. Because the economy influences basic business decisions—such as whether to hire more employees, expand production, or take out loans to purchase equipment—managers scan their economic environments for signs of significant change.

The Economic Ripple Effect

A sudden change in a country's economy can send a ripple effect through the entire country or even the world. Difficulties in the US housing market began in 2008 when a large number of Americans, many of whom had poor credit histories, took advantage of low interest rates and forgiving credit standards in the form of subprime mortgages. As home prices fell and interest rates began to rise, many borrowers found themselves unable to meet their mortgage payments; the result was a record number of loan defaults and foreclosures, which forced a number of financial institutions into bankruptcy. As a result, consumer confidence began to slide, stock prices fell, the credit market stalled, and retail spending on big-ticket items declined.

The economic challenges facing the United States, Canada's largest trading partner, led to a decrease in Canadian exports and resulting slowdowns in the manufacturing sector. Canadian exports to the United States (which represent about 78 percent of the total value of Canadian exports)

scyther5/Shutterstock

decreased by 31 percent from 2008 to 2009. The business and economic community kept a close eye on these economic developments and was relieved to see that by 2010, as global market conditions improved, so did Canada's trading results, with both exports and imports increasing.

Sources: P. Bergevin, "The Global Financial Crisis and Its Impact on Canada," Library of Parliament, December 2008; J. Lorio, "October Auto Sales Screech to a Halt," Automobile, November 7, 2008, http://www.automobilemag.com/news/october-2008-auto-sales-analysis; R. Ray, "Canada to Feel Impact From Slowing US Growth, Economists Say Good News Is the Worst Is Already Behind Us," Investment Executive, February 25, 2008; http://www.conferenceboard.ca/HCP/Details/Economy/forecast-2010.aspx.

Some managers try to predict future economic activity by tracking business confidence. **Business confidence indices** show how confident actual managers are about future business growth. The Conference Board of Canada surveys more than 1,500 business executives in Canada each quarter to compile the Index of Business Confidence (IBC), a measure of the business community's perceptions of the current economic situation and an indication of future plans relating to business growth. The same board surveys Canadian consumers to gauge consumer confidence by asking how they feel about the economy and their employment situation and whether they plan to purchase any big-ticket items. In addition, the Small Business Research Board surveys Canadian small business owners for their opinions on significant business issues and topics in order to gain valuable insights into the small business environment in Canada.[11] Managers often prefer business confidence indices to economic statistics because they know that other managers make business decisions that are in line with their expectations concerning the economy's future. So when business confidence indices are dropping, a manager may decide against hiring new employees, increasing production, or taking out additional loans to expand the business.

2-2b Technological Component

Technology is the knowledge, tools, and techniques used to transform inputs (raw materials, information, and so on) into outputs (products and services). For example, the inputs of authors, editors, and artists (knowledge and skills) and the use of equipment such as computers and printing presses (technology) transformed paper, ink, and glue (raw material) into this book (the finished product). In the case of a service company such as an airline, the technology consists of equipment, including airplanes, repair tools, and computers, as well as the knowledge of mechanics, ticketers, and flight crews. The output is the service of transporting people from one place to another.

Changes in technology can help companies provide better products or produce their products more

Business confidence indices indices that show managers' level of confidence about future business growth.

Technology the knowledge, tools, and techniques used to transform input into output.

efficiently. For example, advances in surgical techniques and imaging equipment have made open-heart surgery much faster and safer in recent years. While technological changes can benefit a business, they can also threaten it. Companies must embrace new technology and find effective ways to use it to improve their products and services or decrease costs. If they don't, they will lose out to those companies that do.

2-2c Sociocultural Component

The sociocultural component of the general environment refers to the demographic characteristics, general behaviour, attitudes, and beliefs of people in a particular society. Sociocultural changes and trends influence organizations in two important ways.

First, changes in demographic characteristics—such as the number of people with particular skills, the growth or decline in particular population segments, and evolving cultural norms (e.g., changes in gender roles)—affect how companies staff their businesses. Married women with children are much more likely to be working today than they were four decades ago. In 1976, only 31.4 percent of women with children under six years old and 39.1 percent of women with children under 16 living at home worked. By 2009, those percentages had risen to 66.5 percent and 72.9 percent, respectively.

Second, changes in behaviour, attitudes, and beliefs affect the demand for a business's products and services. With traffic congestion creating longer commutes and both parents working longer hours, employees today are much more likely to value products and services that allow them to recapture free time with their families. Balancing work with family is a major concern for many Canadians and is a factor in determining commitment to an employer. Edmonton-based VIP Concierge & Errand was launched to meet the needs of busy working Canadians who want to spend more time with family and leisure activities and less time running errands. The services it provides include these: shopping (personal and grocery), meal delivery, pet sitting and dog walking, travel planning, car cleaning, and a wait service for cable, phone, or other home services. A recent study found that employees with greater work–life support are more balanced and committed to their employers and are more likely to achieve greater work outcomes.[12]

Organizations pursuing international growth would be wise to do their research prior to entering a foreign market, for widely different social and cultural norms may exist there. Foreign investment carries a

monkeybusinessimages/iStock/Thinkstock

much higher risk for organizations that do not take this precaution.

2-2d Political/Legal Component

The political/legal component of the general environment includes the laws, regulations, and court decisions that govern and regulate business behaviour. New laws and regulations continue to impose additional responsibilities on companies. For example, in British Columbia, Bill 14 introduced amendments to the B.C. Workers' Compensation Act which allow employees who have been the target of bullying or harassment to have a potential worker's compensation claim for a mental disorder if that disorder was in reaction to a traumatic event in the work environment, or was caused by a work-related stressor. Passed in 2012, Bill 14 specifies that employers must create policies that define what constitutes bullying and harassment and also educate employees within the organization on how to deal with bullying in the workplace.[13] In 2015, the Ontario provincial government passed the Making Healthier Choices Act banning flavoured tobacco products, regulating the sale and advertising of electronic cigarettes and where they can be used, as well as requiring fast-food restaurant chains to include calorie counts on their menus. The legislation is aimed at reducing smoking rates as well as lowering obesity by helping families make informed and healthy food choices.[14] Even though the Canadian and American legal systems differ, there is sometimes a trickle-down effect whereby a law introduced in the United States may result in similar legislation being passed in Canada. The increasing number of climate change lawsuits levelled against US oil companies, automakers, and electrical utilities has signalled to many Canadian companies and legal advisers that it would be wise to prepare for similar developments in Canada.[15]

Helping Companies Enter New Markets

The Canadian government would like to see more Canadian companies follow in the footsteps of Valiant Machine and Tool Inc., a Canadian engineering design and manufacturing company headquartered in Windsor, Ontario, that invested in a high-tech manufacturing facility in Pune, India, and now employs 550 workers in Canada and India. To help other small and medium-sized enterprises navigate the challenging and often frustrating waters associated with foreign markets, the Canadian government promotes foreign investment, and has made protection agreements with countries like India. For many Canadian companies, the uncertainty and unfamiliarity of the sociocultural, political, and legal environment of foreign markets is a major stumbling block in terms of pursing international opportunities. However, the strength of Canadian economy, labour market, and quality of life increasingly depends on the ability of Canadian businesses to capitalize on opportunities in the wider global community. Initiatives

like foreign investment promotion and protection agreements help provide Canadian companies with a greater level of confidence in their global efforts. To date, Canada has agreements in force with 24 countries.

Sources: Foreign Affairs and International Trade Canada, "International Trade Minister Ed Fast Applauds Canadian Companies Expanding into High-Growth India," November 7, 2011, http://www.international.gc.ca/media_commerce/comm/news-communiques/2011/334.aspx?view=d; Export Development Canada, "Prospecting Growth in India and Other Markets Can Pay Long-Term," October 2, 2012, http://www.theglobeandmail.com/partners/advedc1111/prospecting-growth-in-india-and-other-markets -can-pay-long-term/article4582725/; Carol Stephenson, *Ivey Business Journal*, "Mitigating the Risk: Practical Steps for Expanding Your Business Abroad," March/April 2010, http://www.iveybusinessjournal.com/departments/from-the-dean/mitigating-the-risk-practical-steps-for-expanding-your-business-abroad#.UO4–GdTwfw.

Canadian companies looking to pursue international opportunities should carefully consider the political and legal practices in foreign markets, with a mind to navigating different political systems, government regulations, and laws about intellectual property, the labour force, and financial matters.

From a managerial perspective, the best mitigator against legal risk is prevention. As a manager, it is your responsibility to educate yourself about the laws and regulations that could affect your business. Failure to do so may put you and your company at risk of sizable penalties and fines.

2-3 SPECIFIC OR TASK ENVIRONMENT

As you just learned, changes in any sector of the general environment (economic, technological, sociocultural, political/legal) eventually affect most organizations. Each organization also has a specific or task environment that is unique to its industry and that directly affects the way it conducts day-to-day business. For instance, if your

customers decide to use another product, your main competitor cuts prices 10 percent, your best supplier can't deliver raw materials, federal regulators mandate reductions in pollutants in your industry, or environmental groups accuse your company of selling unsafe products, the impact from the specific environment on your business is immediate.

*Let's examine how the **2-3a customer**, **2-3b competitor**, **2-3c supplier**, **2-3d industry regulation**, and **2-3e advocacy group components** of the specific environment affect businesses.*

2-3a Customer Component

Customers purchase products and services. Companies cannot exist without customer support. Monitoring customers' changing wants and needs is therefore critical to business success. There are two basic strategies for monitoring customers: reactive and proactive.

Reactive customer monitoring involves identifying and addressing customer trends and problems after they occur. One reactive strategy is to listen closely to customer complaints and respond to customer concerns. Listen360 is a company that helps businesses monitor customer satisfaction and complaints by contacting their customers and asking two questions: "How likely are you to recommend this business?" and "Why?" Customer responses fall into three categories: *promoters*, who would recommend the business to others; *passives*, who are neither negative nor positive; and *detractors*, unhappy customers who would not recommend the business. When customers are unhappy, the business receives a report detailing what products and services the customer purchased, what it would cost the company if it lost that customer's business, and a "voice of the customer" report that scans the answers to the open-ended question ("Why?") for key words about specific likes, dislikes, and concerns. At the Italian restaurant chain Macaroni Grill, thanks to Listen360, servers now know whether returning customers are promoters, passives, or detractors, and can take specific actions to ensure great service and food.[16] Studies highlight that companies that respond quickly to customer complaint letters are viewed much more favourably than companies that are slow to respond or never respond.[17] In addition to traditional communication formats, communication channels like social media are now able to play a pivotal role in the monitoring of customers. How organizations choose to respond or react, however, is varied. When United Airlines passenger Dave Carroll's beloved guitar was broken after being tossed by baggage handlers, he spent over nine months attempting to communicate with the airline and asking for compensation to cover the cost of the repair. When his attempts failed he took to the Internet, posting a YouTube video ("United Breaks Guitars") that became a viral sensation, garnering nearly 16 million views to date. According to the *London Times*, within four days of the song going online, United Airlines' stock prices dropped by 10 percent. In a report that focused on the impact of the customer experience, 50 percent of consumers give brands only one week to respond to a question before they stop doing business with them, and 79 percent of consumers who shared complaints about poor customer service experiences online had their complaints ignored.[18]

Proactive monitoring of customers, on the other hand, means identifying and addressing customer needs, trends, and issues before they occur. Cable TV's *The Weather Channel* forecasts weather worldwide, relying on its 75 years of weather data to predict weather patterns. Recently, The Weather Co., the company that owns The Weather Channel, invested in data-crunching algorithms that analyze user behaviour patterns to help advertisers to identify consumer behaviour and shopping patterns in different geographic areas, relative to weather patterns. For example, Michaels, a North American arts and crafts retail chain, planned to advertise on The Weather Channel on rainy days, on the assumption that customers would be more likely to buy and then do arts and crafts projects during this type of weather. The Weather Co.'s data analytics unit examined daily sales for each Michaels store, which it then combined with corresponding weather data. It found that sales increased not on rainy days, but rather three days before rainy weather was to occur. In other words, people bought arts and crafts supplies at Michaels to have something to do before rainy weather arrived. This kind of proactive monitoring has proven so valuable that it now accounts for half of The Weather Co.'s advertising revenue.[19]

2-3b Competitor Component

Competitors are companies in the same industry that sell similar products or services to customers. For example, Ford, Toyota, Honda, Nissan, Hyundai, and Kia all compete for automobile customers. In Canada, Bell, Rogers Wireless, Fido, Wind Mobile, and Koodo (along with a number of regional carriers) compete for mobile customers' business. Often the difference between business success and failure comes down to whether your company is doing a better job of satisfying customer wants and needs than the competition. Consequently, companies need to keep close track of what their competitors are doing. To do this, managers perform **competitive analysis**, which involves deciding who your competitors are, anticipating their moves, and determining their strengths and weaknesses.

Managers often do a poor job of identifying potential competitors because they tend to focus on only two or three well-known competitors with similar goals and resources. For example, Hoover, Dirt Devil, and (more

Competitors companies in the same industry that sell similar products or services to customers.

Competitive analysis a process for monitoring the competition that involves identifying competition, anticipating their moves, and determining their strengths and weaknesses.

recently) Oreck were competing fiercely in the market for vacuum cleaners. Because these companies produced relatively similar vacuum cleaners, they paid attention to one another and competed mostly on price. When Dyson entered the market with its radically different vacuum cleaner, which developed and maintained significantly more suction power, the company garnered 20 percent market share within its first 12 months on the shelves. Only then did Hoover and Dirt Devil design their own bagless vacuums.[20]

Another mistake managers make is to underestimate potential competitors' capabilities. In the retail industry in particular, competition has intensified as retailers vie for many of the same consumers, and that means managers must keep a close eye on new competitors at all times. When US powerhouse retailer Target decided to enter the Canadian marketplace, many Canadian retailers took this into consideration when formulating future strategic plans. Walmart Canada invested $750 million in updates to existing stores and moved full speed ahead to increase grocery sections of its superstores, a defensive strategy that made sense in terms of competing with Target, which is known to be stronger in other areas, such as apparel and housewares. Sears Canada braced for Target's arrival by embarking on a strategy to reposition itself as a more "contemporary" retailer. Loblaw Companies and Canadian Tire sped up plans to update operations and focused on expanding their business through related acquisitions like Shoppers Drug Mart and Sport Chek. Although the decision to shutter Target's Canadian stores came within two years of their entry, the strategic decisions made by some retailers to gear up for Target's arrival had a positive impact on their current competitive position.[21]

2-3c Supplier Component

Suppliers are companies that provide material, human, financial, and informational resources to other companies. A key factor influencing the impact and quality of the relationship between companies and their suppliers is how interdependent they are. **Supplier dependence** refers to the degree to which a company relies on a given supplier because of the importance of its product to the company and the difficulty of finding other sources for that product. Even though Apple and Samsung are fierce competitors when it comes to smart phones and computer tablets, for over a decade Apple has been highly dependent on Samsung for computer chips, flash drives, and high resolution touch screens used in iPhones and iPads.[22]

Supplier dependence has historically been very strong in the diamond business, given that for many years De Beers Consolidated Mines enjoyed a monopoly in this industry, controlling the supply, distribution, and pricing of diamonds. Due to its control over supply, the company was able to stockpile inventory when markets were weak and then raise prices when demand was on the rise, relying on excess supply to maintain diamond prices at higher levels. The company's market share reached almost 90 percent in the late 1980s, however, as new world-class mines were discovered in Russia, Australia, and Canada, De Beers' control slowly decreased over time, and its current market share is about 35 percent. However, De Beers has partnered with Mountain Province Diamonds on a new large-scale diamond mine in Canada's Northwest Territories, which may elevate the company's presence in the diamond industry once again.[23]

Buyer dependence is the degree to which a supplier relies on a buyer because of the importance of that buyer to the supplier's sales and the difficulty of finding other buyers for its products. While Samsung is one of Apple's key suppliers (i.e., supplier dependence), Apple, in turn, is Samsung's key buyer of computer components. Apple's purchase of $10 billion of chips, flash memory drives, and touch screens in 2013 represented 17 percent of Samsung's $59.13 billion components business.

A high degree of buyer or seller dependence can lead to **opportunistic behaviour**, in which one

Pieter Beens/Shutterstock

Suppliers companies that provide material, human, financial, and informational resources to other companies.

Supplier dependence the degree to which a company relies on a supplier because of the importance of the supplier's product to the company and the difficulty of finding other sources for that product.

Buyer dependence the degree to which a supplier relies on a buyer because of the importance of that buyer to the supplier and the difficulty of finding other buyers for its products.

Opportunistic behaviour a transaction in which one party in the relationship benefits at the expense of the other.

party benefits at the expense of the other. Suppliers are beginning to hit back at automakers that expect them to supply parts at prices that are attractive for the automaker and crippling for the supplier, pushing many of the latter into bankruptcy or out of business. When Michael Lord, the CEO of Bluewater Plastics, refused to sell parts at a too-low price, the purchasing manager of a Detroit automaker told him, "Obviously, you don't want to be strategic with us." Lord, however, was confident that the purchasing manager would call back. "I know we aren't the only ones pushing back—the supplier world is changing."[24] Although opportunistic behaviour between buyers and suppliers will never be completely eliminated, many companies believe that both buyers and suppliers can benefit by improving the buyer–supplier relationship.[25]

In contrast to opportunistic behaviour, **relationship behaviour** focuses on establishing mutually beneficial, long-term relations between buyers and suppliers.[26] DreamWorks Studios, which makes films and TV shows, has a long-term strategic relationship with Hewlett-Packard (HP), a maker of computers and software. In fact, the DreamWorks animation data centre in Redwood City, California, is run completely on HP systems. DreamWorks, the buyer, advises HP, the supplier, on the advanced servers and data management it needs to produce animated films, or even traditional films, which today contain significant portions of computer generated images.[27] The average DreamWorks film is created using 300 graphics work stations, 60 million rendering hours (a rendering hour is an hour of computer time used to process an image), 17,000 computer core chips in simultaneous usage, and over 200 terabytes of storage.[28]

Relationship behaviour mutually beneficial, long-term exchanges between buyers and suppliers.

Industry regulation regulations and rules that govern the business practices and procedures of specific industries, businesses, and professions.

Advocacy groups groups of concerned citizens who band together to try to influence the business practices of specific industries, businesses, and professions.

Public communications an advocacy group tactic that relies on voluntary participation by the news media and the advertising industry to get the advocacy group's message out.

Media advocacy an advocacy group tactic that involves framing issues as public issues; exposing questionable, exploitative, or unethical practices; and forcing media coverage by buying media time or creating controversy that is likely to receive extensive news coverage.

2-3d Industry Regulation Component

The political/legal component of the general environment affects *all* businesses, whereas the **industry regulation** component consists of regulations and rules that govern the practices and procedures of *specific* industries, businesses, and professions. Regulatory agencies affect businesses by creating and enforcing rules and regulations to protect consumers, workers, and/or society as a whole. For example, the responsibility for toy safety is shared among governments, the toy industry, and safety associations as well as consumers. The Canadian Toy Association's mission is to work at a national and international level to protect and improve industry practices through various committees such as the Safety and Government Relations Committee, which helps develop toy safety standards. All toys sold in Canada must meet safety requirements defined in the Hazardous Products Act and the Hazardous Products (Toys) Regulations. The toy industry recognizes that liaison among the various stakeholders is needed especially in terms of packaging, labelling, advertising, and the environment.[29]

2-3e Advocacy Group Component

Advocacy groups are groups of concerned citizens who band together to influence the business practices of specific industries, businesses, and professions. The members of a group generally share the same point of view on a particular issue. For example, environmental advocacy groups might try to get manufacturers to reduce smokestack pollution emissions. Unlike the industry regulators, advocacy groups cannot force organizations to change their practices. They can, though, use a number of techniques to influence companies, including public communications, media advocacy, websites, and blogs, as well as product boycott campaigns.

The **public communications** approach relies on voluntary participation by the news media and the advertising industry to send out an advocacy group's message. Media advocacy is much more aggressive than the public communications approach. A **media advocacy** approach typically involves framing the group's concerns as public issues (affecting everyone); exposing questionable, exploitative, or unethical practices; and forcing media coverage by buying media time or creating controversy that is likely to receive extensive news coverage.

Bunny Butchers

PETA (People for the Ethical Treatment of Animals), which has offices in the United States, England, Italy, and Germany, uses controversial publicity stunts and advertisements to try to change the behaviour of large organizations, fashion designers, medical researchers, and anyone else it believes is hurting or mistreating animals. In one of its more recent protests, PETA released a series of attention-getting advertisements featuring nude celebrities who would "rather go naked than wear fur" and "rather bare skin than wear skin." A number of designers have pledged to go animal-free. PETA is active against those that have not, engaging in activities such as smearing the windows of Jean-Paul Gaultier's Paris boutique with red "blood."

s_bukley/Shutterstock

For example, the Liquor Control Board of Ontario's $1.6 million "Deflate the Elephant" media advocacy campaign was aimed at helping people start what is often an uncomfortable conversation (the elephant in the room) to prevent their friends and guests from drinking and driving. This campaign featured television commercials, online and print ads, and a special website; its purpose was to engage those people who are in a position to intervene when family or friends are at risk of getting behind the wheel when they have had too much to drink.[30]

In a **product boycott**, an advocacy group tries to persuade consumers not to purchase a company's products or services. Members of the Rainforest Action Network (RAN) have chained themselves to woodpiles at select Home Depot stores to get the company to stop selling old-growth lumber. RAN has also partnered with Greenpeace Canada as part of a Canadian/American coalition that promotes a boycott of products from Canada's boreal forest, one of the last intact forests in North America, which starts in Alaska and extends all the way to the Atlantic. In question are the logging practices used by the forest companies that supply many large US corporations with boreal wood. The coalition has sent correspondence to 500 major corporations, urging them to stop buying from logging companies that haven't shifted to sustainable logging and to decrease the number of flyers, catalogues, and magazines they produce.[31]

2-4 MAKING SENSE OF CHANGING ENVIRONMENTS

In Chapter 1, you learned that managers are responsible for making sense of their business environment. As our discussions of the general and specific environments have indicated, however, doing so is not an easy task. Because external environments can be dynamic, confusing, and complex, managers use a three-step process to make sense of changes in the external environment: 2-4a environmental scanning, 2-4b interpreting environmental factors, and 2-4c acting on threats and opportunities.

2-4a Environmental Scanning

Environmental scanning involves searching the environment for important events or issues that might affect an organization. Managers scan the environment to stay up to date on important factors in their industry and to reduce uncertainty. They want to know if demand will increase, or prices for key components will rise, and whether competitors' sales are rising or falling. This is why Google paid $500 million in 2014 to buy Skybox Imaging, a company that can capture high resolution satellite images from anywhere on Earth. Initial plans are to have six satellites in place to take complete images of the earth twice daily and, by 2018, to have 24 satellites taking images three times a

Product boycott an advocacy group tactic that involves protesting a company's actions by convincing consumers not to purchase its product or service.

Environmental scanning searching the environment for important events or issues that might affect an organization.

Andrey Armyagov/Shutterstock

day. The resolution will be sufficient to capture real-time video of vehicles travelling down a highway; count the number of cars in a shopping mall's parking lot to help estimate retail sales; or predict when the latest iPhone will be released by monitoring the number of trucks coming in and out of Foxconn factories in Taiwan, where the Apple iPhone is manufactured. Co-founder Dan Berkenstock says, "We think we are going to fundamentally change humanity's understanding of the economic landscape on a daily basis."[32]

Organizational strategies also affect environmental scanning. In other words, managers pay close attention to trends and events that are directly related to their company's ability to compete in the marketplace. Nearly 70 percent of China's water sources are polluted, making consumers understandably concerned about drinking tap water. China's water problem, however, represents a business opportunity for Nestlé's bottled water business, especially with sales being flat in North America and Europe. Chinese sales of bottled water, by contrast, are expected to grow significantly from $9 billion in 2012 to $16 billion in 2017. Therefore, Nestlé is rapidly expanding in China, selling water in five-gallon jugs, often through company-owned stores that provide free delivery to consumers' homes.[33]

Finally, environmental scanning contributes to organizational performance. Environmental scanning helps managers detect environmental changes and problems before they can become crises. Companies whose CEOs do more environmental scanning have higher profits.[34] CEOs in better performing firms scan their firm's environment more often and more thoroughly than do CEOs in more poorly performing firms.[35] Managers pay close attention to trends and events that are directly related to their company's ability to compete.

2-4b Interpreting Environmental Factors

After scanning, managers determine what environmental events and issues *mean* to the organization.

Typically, managers view environmental events and issues as either threats or opportunities. When managers interpret environmental events as threats, they take steps to protect the company from further harm. The growing popularity of food trucks now found on the streets of many Canadian cities has caused many restaurant owners to complain to municipal governments and to join forces to try and lobby for protection from these mobile competitors. In Toronto, city officials enacted a slew of restrictions on food truck operators, the most controversial being the 50-metre rule—food trucks cannot operate within 50 metres of a restaurant—and, in the downtown Toronto core, this has effectively banned food trucks from certain areas. Tony Elenis, president of the Ontario Restaurant Hotel and Motel Association, argues that the 50-metre rule is necessary to ensure a level playing field among food service competitors given that restaurant owners are paying either rent or property taxes for their bricks-and-mortar locations. The two sides will undoubtedly continue to square off in an effort to protect their interests, as the city continues to review the regulations and determine if any further changes are necessary.[36]

By contrast, when managers interpret environmental events as opportunities, they consider strategic alternatives for exploiting those events to improve company performance. Referring back to the restaurant industry, for those managers in the food service industry seeking growth opportunities, the baby boomers and seniors markets offer great strategic potential as these markets represent an increasing share of restaurant traffic. Older boomers (aged 55–64) and seniors (65 and up) eat out more often, and younger boomers (aged 45–54) will carry their frequent use of food service with them as they age. Restaurateurs would be wise to understand the buyer behaviour of these groups when deciding on a marketing strategy. Customers over the age of 45 are likely to frequent a

jewhyte/iStockphoto

restaurant based on habit and brand loyalty, often preferring smaller, independent operators that offer full service and that make them feel welcome as soon as they enter. In terms of menu offerings, boomers and seniors are more influenced by food quality, lighter meals, and menu options that offer reduced fat, sugar, and salt without compromising flavour.[37]

2-4c Acting on Threats and Opportunities

After scanning for information on environmental events and issues and interpreting them as threats or opportunities, managers have to decide how to respond to these environmental factors. Deciding what to do during times of uncertainty is always difficult. Managers can never be completely confident that they have all the information they need or that they correctly understand the information they have. Nonetheless, they must make decisions and take actions that minimize threats and take advantage of opportunities.

In the end, managers must complete all three steps—environmental scanning, interpreting environmental factors, and acting on threats and opportunities—to make sense of changing external environments. Environmental scanning helps managers more accurately interpret their environments and take actions that improve company performance. Through scanning, managers monitor what competitors are doing, identify market trends, and stay alert to current events that affect their company's operations. Armed with the environmental information they have gathered, managers can then minimize the impact of threats and turn opportunities into increased profits.

2-5 ORGANIZATIONAL CULTURES: CREATION, SUCCESS, AND CHANGE

We have been looking at trends and events outside of companies that have the potential to affect them. By contrast, the **internal environment** consists of the trends and events *within* an organization that affect the management, employees, and organizational culture. Internal environments are important because they affect what people think, feel, and do at work. The internal environment at SAS, the leading provider of statistical software, is unlike that of most software companies. Instead of expecting employees to work 12- to 14-hour days, SAS has a seven-hour workday and closes its offices at 6 p.m. every evening. Employees receive unlimited sick days each year. To encourage employees to spend time with their families, there's an on-site daycare facility, and the company cafeteria has plenty of high chairs and baby seats. Given SAS's internal environment, it shouldn't surprise you that almost no one quits. In a typical software company, 25 percent of the workforce quits each year to take another job. At SAS, only 4 percent leave.[38]

A key component in internal environments is **organizational culture**—that is, the key values, beliefs, and attitudes shared by members of the organization.

*Let's take a closer look at **2-5a how organizational cultures are created and maintained, 2-5b the characteristics of successful organizational cultures,** and **2-5c how companies can accomplish the difficult task of changing organizational cultures.***

2-5a Creating and Maintaining Organizational Cultures

A key source of organizational culture is the company founder. Founders like Bill Gates (Microsoft) create organizations in their own image and imprint them with their beliefs, attitudes, and values. Microsoft employees share founder Bill Gates's determination to stay ahead of software competitors. Says a Microsoft vice president: "No matter how good your product, you are only 18 months away from failure."[39] Although the founder is instrumental in the creation of the organization's culture, eventually that person retires, dies, or leaves the company. When the founder is gone, how are that person's values, attitudes, and beliefs sustained in the organization? It is through stories and heroes.

Internal environment the events and trends inside an organization that affect management, employees, and organizational culture.

Organizational culture the key values, beliefs, and attitudes shared by members of the organization.

Members tell **organizational stories** to make sense of events and changes in an organization and to emphasize culturally consistent assumptions, decisions, and actions.[40] At Walmart, stories abound about founder Sam Walton's thriftiness as he strove to make Walmart the low-cost retailer that it is today. Gary Reinboth, one of Walmart's first store managers, tells the following story:

In those days, we would go on buying trips with Sam, and we'd all stay, as much as we could, in one room or two. I remember one time in Chicago when we stayed eight of us to a room. And the room wasn't very big to begin with. You might say we were on a pretty restricted budget.[41]

Sam Walton's thriftiness permeates Walmart to this day. Everyone flies coach rather than business or first class—and that includes top executives and the CEO. When employees travel on business, it's still the norm for them to share rooms (although two to a room, not eight!) at relatively inexpensive motels. Likewise, Walmart will reimburse only up to $15 per meal on business travel, which is half to one-third the reimbursement rate at companies of similar size. (Remember, Walmart is one of the largest companies in the world.)

A second way in which organizational culture is sustained is by recognizing and celebrating heroes. **Organizational heroes** are admired for their qualities and achievements within the organization, at any level of the organization. Isadore Sharpe, founder of the luxury Four Seasons Hotels and Resorts, was well known for his long-standing commitment to the power of personal service and for passing that principle on to employees at all levels of the Four Seasons organization, as illustrated by this story:

An employee overheard a guest telling his wife how embarrassed he was to be the only one without a black tie at a formal function. The employee asked the man to take a seat in his office, and then quickly took off his own tuxedo and rushed it to laundry. Once the tux was clean, this employee called a seamstress to fit the guest. Not only does this story

teach the shared Four Seasons values, but the guest turned out to be the chairman and CEO of a leading consulting organization who subsequently directed all of his company's business (worth millions in food and lodging) to the Four Seasons. The man also took every opportunity to give a testimonial for Four Seasons.[42]

2-5b Successful Organizational Cultures

Preliminary research shows that organizational culture is related to business success. As shown in Exhibit 2.3, cultures based on adaptability, involvement, a clear vision, and consistency can help companies achieve higher profits, quality, sales growth, return on assets, and employee satisfaction.[43]

Adaptability is the ability to notice and respond to changes in the organization's environment. Cultures need to reinforce important values and behaviours; but at the same time, a culture becomes dysfunctional if it prevents change.

In cultures that promote higher levels of *employee involvement* in decision making, employees feel a greater sense of ownership and responsibility. Employee involvement has been part of the WestJet corporate culture since the Calgary-based airline was founded in 1996. Employees are empowered to rely on their own integrity and decision making to solve WestJet guest problems personally. They can issue flight credits to customers when situations arise such as overbookings or late plane arrivals; they can even order in refreshments for tired passengers who are stranded at the airport.

Organizational stories stories told by members to make sense of events and changes in an organization and to emphasize culturally consistent assumptions, decisions, and actions.

Organizational heroes people celebrated for their qualities and achievements within an organization.

Exhibit 2.3
Keys to Successful Organizational Culture

Adaptability

Employee involvement

Vision

Strong culture

matis/Shutterstock.com

In addition, the Employee Share Purchase Plan means that employees are also "owners" and are integral to the company's success.[44]

Company vision is the business's purpose or reason for existing. In organizational cultures with a clear company vision, the organization's strategic purpose and direction are apparent to everyone in the company. As discussed, at the Four Seasons luxury hotel chain, "treating all others as we would wish to be treated" is the company's Golden Rule that sums up its vision. Besides the Golden Rule, the company's goals, beliefs, and principles are formally communicated to help guide employees in their day-to-day activities and interactions with one another and with guests. As part of annual performance reviews, employees are evaluated on how well they embody the company's values as well as on their achievements in terms of development, mentorship, and interactions with people. President and COO Kathleen Taylor sums up the company's vision when she says: "Our founder had a theory that you couldn't have a guest focus in a luxury hotel business without an employee focus."[45]

Finally, in *consistent organizational cultures*, the company actively defines and teaches organizational values, beliefs, and attitudes. Consistent with its code of conduct to "Do no harm to people. Protect the environment, and comply with all laws and regulations," when

Royal Dutch Shell, the multinational energy company, buys smaller drilling companies, the first thing it does is shut down the drilling rigs for several weeks to retrain the workers in terms of safety and environmental procedures. J. R. Justus, Shell's general manager in Appalachia, says, "I don't think there's any question that the culture around safety has changed considerably since Shell came here. We've got a lot more technical resources to bring to bear than a smaller independent company would." In terms of Shell's improvements to environmental practices, Shell, unlike many smaller drilling companies, lines oil wells with steel pipe surrounded by cement, which fills the gaps between the pipe and surrounding earth, so that gas or fluids can't seep into rock layers or water sources. As a result, Shell receives environmental citations just 6.5 percent of the time, as compared to 14 percent for mid-sized drillers and 17 percent for small ones.[46]

2-5c Changing Organizational Cultures

As shown in Exhibit 2.4, organizational cultures exist on three levels.[47] On the first, or surface, level are the elements that can be seen and observed, such as symbolic artifacts (e.g., dress codes and office layouts) and workers' and managers' behaviours. Next, just below the surface, are the values and beliefs expressed by people in the company. You can't see these values and beliefs, but they become clear if you listen carefully to what people say and to how decisions are made or explained. Finally, there are unconsciously held assumptions and beliefs about the company, which are buried deep below the surface. These are the unwritten views and rules that are so strongly held and so widely shared that they are rarely discussed or even thought about unless someone attempts to change them or unknowingly violates them. Changing such assumptions and beliefs can be very difficult. Instead, managers should focus on the parts of the organizational culture they can control. These include observable surface-level items, such as workers' behaviours and symbolic artifacts, and expressed values and beliefs, which can be influenced through employee selection. Let's see how these can influence organizational cultures.

Yellow Media (famous for its telephone directories and formerly known as Yellow Pages Group) has

Company vision a business's purpose or reason for existing.

Exhibit 2.4
Three Levels of Organizational Culture

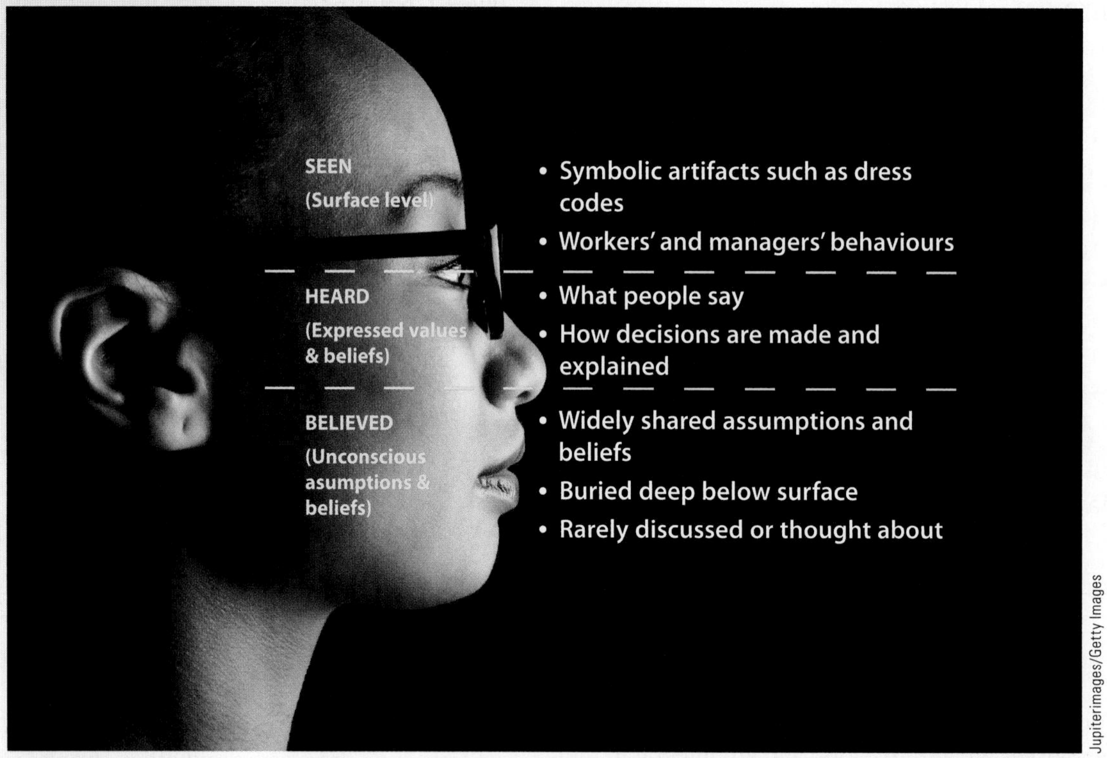

SEEN
(Surface level)
- Symbolic artifacts such as dress codes
- Workers' and managers' behaviours

HEARD
(Expressed values & beliefs)
- What people say
- How decisions are made and explained

BELIEVED
(Unconscious assumptions & beliefs)
- Widely shared assumptions and beliefs
- Buried deep below surface
- Rarely discussed or thought about

Jupiterimages/Getty Images

experienced a number of significant changes recently, including a major ownership change and reorganization in 2002, almost filing for bankruptcy protection in 2012, and installing a new CEO in 2014 to help reposition the company for the future. At the same time, Yellow Pages business customers and consumers turned away from bulky print directories in favour of online listings, causing the company's revenues to drop dramatically and its debt to spiral.

During the company's reorganization, management gave serious thought to the type of corporate culture they wanted to have and what values and behaviours were needed to achieve that vision. The desire for a customer-focused and performance-based culture emerged and, with that, six values were developed to help guide employee behaviour: customer focus, compete to win, teamwork, passion, respect, and open communication. To communicate the new values and ultimately achieve the desired corporate philosophy, management used traditional communication channels with a twist, printing the six values on employee security passes and running town-hall–style

meetings to spread the new vision. The company also refocused its selection process for new hires, looking for individuals with values and beliefs consistent with the company's desired culture. To facilitate the new organizational direction in a tangible way, the company brought its Montreal and Laval offices together in a new centralized head office complete with on-site fitness facility (with free memberships, organized walking groups, and instructor-led fitness classes); a healthy eating cafeteria; self-serve kitchen areas on every floor; outdoor eating areas to take advantage of the beautiful view of the St. Lawrence River; transit subsidies for employees; and a car pool sign-up system.

When new CEO Julien Bilot arrived in 2014, he spent time meeting with almost all the staff (over 2,000 people), having roundtable breakfasts and lunches with managers and members of the sales force, and physically visiting all of the company's locations across the country. Through these interactions he was able to gain valuable insight into the company's culture as well as its business operations, and subsequently introduced a new four-year strategic plan to restore profitability by increasing the focus on digital business services as well as rolling out mobile apps, in order to offset the declines in the traditional print business.[48]

The experience at Yellow Media demonstrates that, although it is a daunting task, changes to corporate culture can be accomplished. As Josée Dykun, VP of human resources, explains, "Strong corporate culture translates into alignment, performance, and then financial results."[49] According to Marty Parker, president and CEO of Waterstone Human Capital, organizations with successful corporate cultures place a high priority on creating great workplaces for their employees; however, they also enjoy financial returns. "Organizations want to deliver to their stakeholders and shareholders, and those with strong corporate cultures, quite simply, outperform their peers." All in all, a strong corporate culture is associated with more productive employees, greater customer satisfaction, better innovation, stronger confidence to develop new strategies, and improved hiring and employee retention; all of these have a positive impact on company performance. See Exhibit 2.5 for a list of the 10 most admired Canadian corporate cultures.

Exhibit 2.5
Canada's 10 Most Admired Corporate Cultures–Enterprise (2014)

AltaGas Ltd.—Calgary, AB
AltaLink—Calgary, AB
Ericsson Canada—Toronto, ON
Home Hardware Stores Ltd.—St. Jacobs, ON
Ivanhoe Cambridge—Montreal, QC
Ledcor Group of Companies—Vancouver, BC
Monsanto Canada Inc.—Winnipeg, MB
Munich Re—Toronto, ON
Starbucks Coffee of Canada—Toronto, ON
West Fraser Timber Co.—Quesnel, BC

Source: Waterstone Human Capital Ltd. Reprinted by permission.

STUDY TOOLS 2

READY TO STUDY?

LOCATED IN TEXTBOOK:

☐ Rip out the Chapter Review Card at the back of the book to have a summary of the chapter and key terms handy.

LOCATED AT NELSON.COM/STUDENT:

☐ Access the eBook or use the ReadSpeaker feature to listen to the chapter on the go.

☐ Prepare for tests with practice quizzes.

☐ Review key terms with flashcards and the glossary feature.

☐ Work through key concepts with case studies and Management Decision Exercises.

☐ Explore practical examples with You Make the Decision Activities.

3 Ethics and Social Responsibility

Jon Feingersh/Getty Images

LEARNING OUTCOMES

After studying this chapter, you will be able to...

3-1 Identify unethical workplace behaviours.

3-2 Describe ethics guidelines and legislation in North America.

3-3 Describe what influences ethical decision making.

3-4 Explain what practical steps managers can take to improve ethical decision making.

3-5 Explain to whom and for what organizations are socially responsible.

3-6 Explain how organizations can choose to respond to societal demands for social responsibility and how social responsibility impacts economic performance.

After you finish this chapter, go to **PAGE 64** for **STUDY TOOLS**

Leading in a Fast-Moving Industry

At a time when society applauds ethical decision making and social responsibility in the business world and demonizes companies that fail in these areas, Caroline Charter lives on the edge—she is an executive in high tech, where change is constant. Caroline set out on her corporate career path immediately after graduating in 2000 with a marketing diploma from the business administration program at Seneca College in Ontario. Her first professional career stop was in Dublin, where she worked at Gateway Computers. By mid-2015 she was the senior director of global partner enablement within Worldwide Operations at Microsoft Ltd., working out of Microsoft's corporate head office in Redmond, Washington (near Seattle). Recognition along the way has included being named to the 2013 list of Canada's Top 100 Most Powerful Women within the Corporate Executive Category, an award that the Women's Executive Network (WXN) created. In Caroline's new work role, she and her team are responsible for launching products and programs to Microsoft partners around the world. Previously at Microsoft, Caroline was general manager of the Latin America Operations Centre. Before that, she spent 12 years at Oracle Canada, where her final role was as a vice president.

1. Are there special challenges in terms of ethics and social responsibility within a fast-changing industry such as IT?

Huge challenges. Laws and regulations are changing all the time. The industry is evolving at such a rapid pace that it's often challenging for large companies to be nimble enough to evolve as quickly as is necessary. It's like trying to manoeuvre a huge tanker ship versus a little cruiser boat. It requires the right ability to build a solid, scalable, nimble framework and infrastructure to make sure things can move as quickly as they need to—while staying compliant with industry regulations and rules.

2. You've been called a trailblazer (in a *Financial Post* article on the 2013 WXN awards). Does that mean you feel any special degree of social responsibility?

Yes. I believe it's my responsibility to bring others along with me, and also help others learn from my lessons along the way. It's important to do that and give others a chance to demonstrate their full potential. I have done speaking engagements with the Federated Press in Toronto for women executives, regularly speak to MBA groups at various universities across the United States and Canada, and when at Oracle would guest speak in the Oracle Women's Leadership (OWL) program to help female employees at all levels of the organization get exposure and experience in networking events and the chance to be paired up with a suitable mentor. At Microsoft I am a participant in the Women in Operations group, where my social responsibilities are the same as they were in the OWL program and the objectives of the groups are very similar.

3. Does your work in partner enablement give you insights into ethics and social responsibility in the general business world?

Anybody who works at Microsoft feels this as part of their corporate responsibility. It's part of our DNA, and we are all encouraged to reach out and understand or explore these aspects within the general business world.

4. What do you love best about your job?

My team and the people and partners I work with every day. We have a large mandate, and it's wonderful to work with such talented and dedicated individuals. It's amazing to work with all types of partners—independent software vendors, systems integrators, original equipment manufacturers, resellers, cloud solution providers—and learn something about how they run their businesses, what their clients and customers are doing, and how the industry is ever changing and evolving. You learn something from each other every day, and it's great to see what we can all accomplish when we put our minds together.

5. What advice would you give someone about to do your kind of work?

Ask the right questions. Ask: What is right for the business? What *should* things be like? Where do we *really* want to be? Don't confine yourself to the restricted scope or box you may have been given. Think ahead, and, to quote Wayne Gretzky: Skate to where the puck is going.

6. What is the most important thing you learned as a student that you use today?

Common sense prevails. Far too often people get wrapped up in theory or structures that really can sometimes hinder progress. You are smarter than you think you are. Ask questions and use your common sense and don't be afraid to challenge. If something doesn't make sense, say so—you're probably not the only one in the room that thinks so. It's all about the growth mindset. Challenge yourself to grow and be bold about it.

For the full interview go online to nelson.com/student

Photo and interview courtesy of Caroline Charter

3-1 UNETHICAL WORKPLACE BEHAVIOURS

Today, it's not enough for companies to make a profit. We also expect managers to make a profit by doing the right things. Unfortunately, no matter what managers decide to do, someone or some group will be unhappy with the outcome. Managers don't have the luxury of choosing theoretically optimal, win–win solutions that are obviously desirable to everyone involved. In practice, solutions to ethical and social responsibility problems aren't optimal. Often, managers must be satisfied with a solution that just makes do or does the least harm. Rights and wrongs are rarely crystal clear to managers charged with doing the right thing; the business world is much messier than that.

Ethics is the set of moral principles or values that defines right and wrong for a person or group. In a work environment, individuals at every level of an organization make decisions on a daily basis with respect to how to behave and what course of action to take, often relying on their own personal ethical principles to guide them. A recent Ipsos poll on workplace ethics in Canada reported that 42 percent of Canadians have witnessed misconduct in the workplace including bribery, fraud, and misrepresentation of company results, and less than half have reported the misconduct. Sixty-two percent indicated they would feel obligated to report activities that they felt were seriously unethical. One-third of Canadians felt that delivering results was more important that doing the right thing and 22 percent felt they had to compromise their personal ethics to maintain their job.[1]

The Ethics and Compliance Initiative (ECI), a non-profit organization dedicated to supporting global ethics practices, identified two key influences reflected in today's business environment: the state of the economy, and the increased use of technology at work. During a period of economic difficulty, "the decisions and behaviours of their leaders are perceived by employees as a heightened commitment to ethics. As a result, employees adopt a higher standard of conduct for themselves."[2]

In addition, the increased use of the Internet in the workplace, including social networking, presents new challenges in terms of ethical behaviour. Active social networkers (defined as employees who spend at least 30 percent of their workday on social network sites) have a more tolerant attitude toward a number of workplace behaviours. Half of active social networkers believe it is acceptable to keep copies of confidential work documents for possible use in future jobs, compared to 15 percent of non-active social networkers. In addition, active social networkers are more likely to buy personal items with the company credit card, take home company software, and share less than flattering information about their workplace on personal social networking sites.[3]

A previous ECI survey explored the implications of online social networks and found that 74 percent of employees surveyed believed that it was possible to damage a company's reputation through social media; however, 53 percent believed that their social networking pages were none of their employers' business.[4]

Other studies contain more positive news, highlighting that ethics is a growing concern among employees. Ninety-four percent of respondents said it was either vital or important that the company they work for be ethical; and 82 percent of a group of employees surveyed said "they would work for less to be at a company that had ethical business practices, and more than a third left a job because they disagreed with the actions of fellow employees or managers."[5]

According to Sharon Allen, chairperson of Deloitte LLP, "Regardless of the economic environment, business leaders should be mindful of the significant impact that trust in the workplace and transparent communication can have on talent management and retention strategies. By establishing a values-based culture, organizations can cultivate the trust necessary to reduce turnover and mitigate unethical behavior."[6] In short, much needs to be done to make workplaces more ethical, but—and this is very important—most managers and employees want this to happen.

Ethical behaviour follows accepted principles of right and wrong. Depending on which study you look at, however, one-third to three-quarters of all employees admit that they have stolen from their employer, committed computer fraud, embezzled funds, vandalized company property, sabotaged company projects, faked injuries to receive workers' compensation benefits or insurance, or been "sick" from work when they weren't really sick. Experts estimate that unethical behaviours like these, which researchers call *workplace deviance*, may cost companies nearly $3.5 trillion a year, or roughly 5 percent of their revenues.[7]

Ethics   the set of moral principles or values that defines right and wrong for a person or group.

Ethical behaviour   behaviour that conforms to a society's accepted principles of right and wrong.

Exhibit 3.1
Types of Workplace Deviance

Organizational

Production Deviance	Property Deviance
• Leaving early • Taking excessive breaks • Intentionally working slowly • Wasting resources	• Sabotaging equipment • Accepting kickbacks • Lying about hours worked • Stealing from company

Minor ◄————————————————► **Serious**

Political Deviance	Personal Aggression
• Showing favouritism • Gossiping about coworkers • Blaming coworkers • Competing nonbeneficially	• Sexual harassment • Verbal abuse • Stealing from coworkers • Endangering coworkers

Interpersonal

Source: S.L. Robinson and R.J. Bennett, "A Typology of Deviant Workplace Behaviors," (Figure), *Academy Management Journal*, 1995, Vol 38.

Workplace deviance is unethical behaviour that violates organizational norms about right and wrong. As Exhibit 3.1 shows, workplace deviance can be categorized by how deviant the behaviour is, from minor to serious, and by the target of the deviant behaviour—whether it is the organization or particular people in the workplace.[8]

Company-related deviance can affect both tangible and intangible assets. One kind of workplace deviance, **production deviance**, hurts the quality and quantity of work produced. Examples include leaving early, taking excessively long work breaks, intentionally working more slowly, or wasting resources. Consider the common occurrence of employees participating in office sports pools or fantasy leagues. Some employees spend a lot of time talking about which teams did or didn't make advance, other workers are busy setting up and managing office pools for which participating employees will then spend time filling out their selections, while others may spend time at work researching teams and analyzing statistics. Based on US estimates, if about half of workers spent at least one hour on any of these activities, the cost to employers of that lost hour is $1.9 billion. And that doesn't even consider how much more time employees will spend not working as they watch the games at work online, or get updates via Twitter or special sports apps on their smartphones.[9]

Property deviance is unethical behaviour aimed at company property or products. Examples include sabotaging, stealing, damaging equipment or products, and overcharging for services and then pocketing the difference. Fifty-eight percent of office workers acknowledge taking company property for personal use, according to a survey conducted for Lawyers.com.[10] Property deviance also includes the sabotage of company property, such as using "software bombs" to destroy company programs and data.[11]

The theft of company merchandise by employees, called **employee shrinkage**, is another common form of property deviance. Retail shrinkage costs Canadian retailers on average over $10.8 million per shopping day, over $4 billion annually, and approximately 1.04 percent of sales.[12] Small and independent businesses feel the negative impact of shrinkage even more since they often have fewer resources and less effective theft controls in place. This means that losses experienced by smaller businesses have a greater impact than they would in larger organizations.[13]

Retail employees use a variety of methods to commit crimes against their employers: leaving the store with merchandise; stashing unloaded merchandise in dumpsters and then returning after their shift to retrieve it (referred to as "dumpster diving"); acting as "sweethearts" for friends and family by discounting purchases; not charging for items at the checkout counter; allowing refunds with no receipts; or passing on credit card numbers to process gift cards.[14]

Although production and property deviance harm companies, political deviance and personal aggression are unethical behaviours that hurt particular people within companies. **Political deviance** involves using

Workplace deviance unethical behaviour that violates organizational norms about right and wrong.

Production deviance unethical behaviour that hurts the quality and quantity of work produced.

Property deviance unethical behaviour aimed at the organization's property or products.

Employee shrinkage employee theft of company merchandise.

Political deviance using one's influence to harm others in the company.

one's influence to harm others in the company. Examples include making decisions based on favouritism rather than performance, spreading rumours about coworkers, or blaming others for mistakes they didn't make. **Personal aggression** is hostile or aggressive behaviour toward others. According to the Canadian Centre for Occupational Health and Safety, workplace violence is not just a physical act, but rather any act in which a person is abused, threatened, intimidated, or assaulted in his or her place of employment. Examples include threatening behaviour (e.g., shaking fists, destroying property, throwing objects), verbal or written threats (any expression of intent to inflict harm), harassment (behaviour that demeans, embarrasses, humiliates, or alarms a person and includes words, gestures, bullying, and inappropriate activities), verbal abuse (swearing, insults, or condescending language) or physical attacks (hitting, shoving, pushing, or kicking).[15] Almost one in five violent incidents in Canada occurs in the workplace of the victim, and 71 percent of all incidents of workplace violence are physical assaults.[16]

3-2 ETHICS GUIDELINES AND LEGISLATION IN NORTH AMERICA

Following a series of high-profile financial scandals in the early 2000s involving companies like Enron, WorldCom, and Tyco, the US government passed the Sarbanes-Oxley Act to address growing concern over the lack of accountability by public companies. This legislation was developed to improve corporate governance and protect shareholders and the general public from fraudulent practices and accounting errors by organizations. In addition to dealing with financial matters of a corporation, the Act also extends into other operational areas, specifying what type of business records a corporation should store and for how long. Organizations found to be in violation may face fines, imprisonment, or both.[17] Although the Sarbanes-Oxley Act did not translate to Canadian legislation, the Canadian Securities Administrators

(CSA) did introduce a series of policies that followed the Sarbanes-Oxley guidelines but reflected the unique nature of the Canadian financial market.[18] At present there is no national ethics legislation in Canada, however, there are a number of associations and regulatory bodies that have adopted their own code of ethics. For example, members of the Canadian Real Estate Association must adhere to the Realtor Code, which outlines responsibilities of its members to the public, clients, and fellow real estate agents. In 1997, an International Code of Ethics was released by a group of Canadian companies to provide a general guideline for acceptable standards of conduct when doing business at home and in other countries. This voluntary code covers issues relating to community participation, environmental protection, human rights, business conduct, and employee rights. The code is intended to establish Canadian businesses as respected members of the global business community and is supported by the Department of Foreign Affairs and International Trade.[19]

In the United States, the establishment of the US Sentencing Commission Guidelines for Organizations in 1991 signalled a change in the legal approach to handling unethical activities in business. Until that time, a company that was unaware of an employee's unethical activities could not be held responsible; however, since the new guidelines were established, companies can be prosecuted and punished *even if management doesn't know about the unethical behaviour*. Nearly all businesses are covered by the US Sentencing Commission's guidelines and this includes nonprofit organizations. Penalties can be substantial, with maximum fines approaching $300 million.[20] A 2004 amendment outlines much stricter ethics training requirements and emphasizes creating company cultures that value legal and ethical behaviour.[21]

3-3 INFLUENCES ON ETHICAL DECISION MAKING

Assume you are a human resources manager for a large public company preparing for your company's annual board of directors' meeting and you know that a review of hiring practices is on the agenda. With employee benefits costs rising, some organizations are now refusing to hire smokers and a few board members would like to discuss this option. Smokers are not hired at Union Pacific Railroad, Alaska Airlines, the Canadian Cancer

Personal aggression hostile or aggressive behaviour toward others.

Forget the Customers; Who's Watching Your Employees?

Employee theft can range from taking an extra plate of french fries without payment to being part of "a very sophisticated network of friends" facilitating theft and subsequent resale of items inside and outside of store operations. If you compare a dishonest retail employee to a typical shoplifter, the employee is far more harmful to the organization. Dishonest employees go to the same place every day, and the more they learn about the business, the more familiar they become with the tools that the loss prevention department employs. Ultimately they become more effective at stealing. Alcohol, apparel, and cosmetics are the most targeted categories and are highly resellable. Kaileen Millard-Ruff, director of retail at Toronto-based Match Marketing Group, said that technology now gives retail employees a greater opportunity than they would have had in the past to partner with external criminal networks, or resell goods anonymously online through sites such as eBay and Kijiji.

Source: H. Shaw, "Workers Steal 33% of All Goods That Go Missing at Retailers: Survey," *The Financial Post*, October 31, 2012, http://business.financialpost.com/2012/10/31/workers-steal-33-of-all-goods-that-go-missing-at-retailers-survey/.

Stockbyte/Getty Images

Society, or the Cleveland Clinic, where applicants are required to take a nicotine test. Supporters point to the long-term health benefits associated with trying to promote not smoking, while others focus on the fact that costs are a large part of what is driving the trend not to hire smokers. Studies show that a smoker costs about $4,200 more a year to employ—$3,800 in lost productivity due to unsanctioned smoking breaks (losing 39 minutes per day or over 1,800 hours annually) and another $400 in lost productivity due to absenteeism. In addition, employing smokers is linked to high costs relating to property damage, accident costs, and annual insurance premiums.

Ottawa-based Momentous Corp. made the decision to stop hiring smokers. As its president explains, "I'm not saying job applicants don't have a choice to smoke; I'm just saying they don't have the choice to work at Momentous if they do smoke." The company reports that health benefit costs have dramatically decreased and employee productivity has also increased because of the policy.

However, there are other considerations in this decision—namely whether or not denying employment to smokers will negatively impact individuals who are addicted to tobacco and disadvantage certain segments of society. You have been asked to respond directly to this issue. As you prepare for the meeting, what is the ethical thing to do?

Although some ethical issues are easily solved, many do not have clearly right or wrong answers. Although the answers are rarely obvious, managers do need to know *how* to arrive at an answer in order to manage this ethical ambiguity well.

*The ethical answers that managers choose depend on **3-3a the ethical intensity of the decision, 3-3b the moral development of the manager,** and **3-3c the ethical principles used to solve the problem.***

3-3a Ethical Intensity of the Decision

Managers don't treat all ethical decisions the same. The manager who has to decide whether to enforce a company-wide policy not to hire smokers is going to treat that decision much more seriously than the decision of how to deal with an assistant who has been taking computer paper home for personal use. These decisions differ in their **ethical intensity**, or the degree of concern people have about an ethical issue. When addressing an issue of

---

Ethical intensity the degree of concern people have about an ethical issue.

high ethical intensity, managers are more aware of the impact their decision will have on others. They are more likely to view the decision as an ethical or moral decision rather than as an economic decision. They are also more likely to worry about doing the right thing.

Six factors must be taken into account when determining the ethical intensity of an action, as shown in Exhibit 3.2. **Magnitude of consequences** is the total harm or benefit derived from an ethical decision. The more people who are harmed or the greater the harm to those people, the larger the consequences. **Social consensus** is agreement on whether behaviour is bad or good. **Probability of effect** is the chance that something will happen and then result in harm to others. If we combine these factors, we can see the effect they can have on ethical intensity. For example, if there is *clear agreement* (social consensus) that a managerial decision or action is *certain* (probability of effect) to have *large negative consequences* (magnitude of consequences) in some way, then people will be highly concerned about that managerial decision or action, and ethical intensity will be high. Policy decisions relating to hiring practices will potentially impact all future applicants, therefore, the magnitude of consequences and possibility of effect from this decision would be quite high. Although some ethical issues are easily solved, many do not have clearly right or wrong answers.

Exhibit 3.2
Six Factors That Contribute to Ethical Intensity

Magnitude of consequences
Social consensus
Probability of effect
Temporal immediacy
Proximity of effect
Concentration of effect

Source: T.M. Jones, "Ethical Decision Making by Individuals in Organizations: An Issue Contingent Model," *Academy of Management Review 16* (1991) 366–395.

Temporal immediacy is the time between an act and the consequences the act produces. Temporal immediacy is stronger if a manager has to lay off workers next week as opposed to three months from now. **Proximity of effect** is the social, psychological, cultural, or physical distance of a decision maker from those affected by his or her decisions. Thus, proximity of effect is greater for the human resources manager who is in direct communication with job applicants and is involved in making hiring decisions than it is for a manager who works in an area that does not have any communication with potential applicants. Finally, whereas the magnitude of consequences is the total effect across all people, **concentration of effect** is how much an act affects the average person. Temporarily laying off 100 employees for 10 months without pay is a greater concentration of effect than temporarily laying off 1,000 employees for one month.

Which of these six factors has the most impact on ethical intensity? Studies indicate that managers are much more likely to view decisions as ethical when the magnitude of consequences (total harm) is high and there is a social consensus (agreement) that a behaviour or action is bad.[22]

Andy Dean Photography/Shutterstock.com

Magnitude of consequences the total harm or benefit derived from an ethical decision.

Social consensus agreement on whether behaviour is bad or good.

Probability of effect the chance that something will happen and then harm others.

Temporal immediacy the time between an act and the consequences the act produces.

Proximity of effect the social, psychological, cultural, or physical distance between a decision maker and those affected by his or her decisions.

Concentration of effect the total harm or benefit that an act produces on the average person.

3-3b Moral Development

It's Friday. Another long week of classes and studying is over, and all you want to do is sit down and relax. "A movie sounds good," you think to yourself, but you don't want to spend $10 to trek down to the movie theatre and you are too tired to make the short trip down to the Redbox machine at your local Tim Hortons. Your room-mate says he's got the perfect solution and gives you the URL of a website that streams all the latest blockbuster movies and TV shows for free. The writers, actors, and producers won't earn a dime if you watch the pirated copy of the movie. Furthermore, it's illegal to download or watch streamed copies of pirated shows. But how will the movie studios ever find out? Are the police going to come through your door because you watched a pirated movie? Will you watch the movie? What are you going to do?

In part, according to psychologist Lawrence Kohlberg, your decision will be based on your level of moral development. Kohlberg identified three phases of moral development with two stages in each phase (see Exhibit 3.3).[23] At the **preconventional level of moral development**, people decide based on selfish reasons. For example, if you are in Stage 1, the *punishment and obedience stage*, your primary concern will be to avoid trouble for yourself. So you won't watch the pirated movie because you are afraid of being caught and punished. Yet in Stage 2, the *instrumental exchange stage*, you worry less about punishment and more about doing things that directly advance your wants and needs. So you watch the movie.

People at the **conventional level of moral development** make decisions that conform to societal expectations. In other words, they look to others for guidance on ethical issues. In Stage 3, the *good boy, nice girl stage*, you normally do what the other "good boys" and "nice girls" are doing. If everyone else is illegally watching pirated movies, you will, too. But if they aren't, you won't either. In the *law and order stage*, Stage 4, you again look for external guidance, but do whatever the *law* permits, so you won't watch the movie.

People at the **postconventional level of moral development** use internalized ethical principles to solve ethical dilemmas. In Stage 5, the *social contract stage*, you will refuse to copy the movie because, as a

whole, society is better off when the rights of others—in this case, the rights of actors, directors, producers, and writers—are not violated. In Stage 6, the *universal principle stage*, you might or might not watch the pirated movie, depending on your principles of right and wrong. Moreover, you will stick to your principles even if your decision conflicts with the law (Stage 4) or what others believe is best for society (Stage 5). For example, those with socialist or communist beliefs might choose to watch the pirated movie because they believe that goods and services should be owned by society rather than by individuals and corporations.

Kohlberg believed that people would progress sequentially from earlier to later stages as they became more educated and mature. But only 20 percent of adults ever reach the postconventional stage of moral development where internal principles guide their decisions. Most adults are in the conventional stage of moral development and look to others for guidance on ethical issues. This means that most people in the workplace look to and need leadership when it comes to ethical decision making.[24]

Exhibit 3.3
Kohlberg's Stages of Moral Development

Stage 1	Stage 2	Stage 3	Stage 4	Stage 5	Stage 6
Punishment and Obedience	Instrumental Exchange	Good Boy, Nice Girl	Law and Order	Social Contract	Universal Principle
Preconventional		Conventional		Postconventional	
Self-Interest		Societal Expectations		Internalized Principles	

Source: W. Davidson III and D. Worrell, "Influencing Managers to Change Unpopular Corporate Behavior Through Boycotts and Divestitures," *Business & Society* 34 (1995): 171–196.

Preconventional level of moral development the first level of moral development, in which people make decisions based on selfish reasons.

Conventional level of moral development the second level of moral development, in which people make decisions that conform to societal expectations.

Postconventional level of moral development the third level of moral development, in which people make decisions based on internalized principles.

3-3c Principles of Ethical Decision Making

Beyond an issue's ethical intensity and a manager's level of moral maturity, the particular ethical principles that managers use will also affect how they solve ethical dilemmas. Unfortunately, there is no one ideal principle to use when making ethical business decisions. According to Professor LaRue Hosmer, a number of different ethical principles can be used to make business decisions: long-term self-interest, personal virtue, religious injunctions, government requirements, utilitarian benefits, individual rights, and distributive justice.[25] All of these ethical principles encourage managers and employees to take others' interests into account when making ethical decisions. At the same time, however, these principles can lead to very different ethical actions, as we can see by referring back to the scenario involving whether or not to hire smokers.

According to the **principle of long-term self-interest**, you should never take any action that is not in your or your organization's long-term self-interest. Although this sounds as if the principle promotes selfishness, it doesn't. What we do to maximize our long-term interests (save more, spend less, exercise every day, watch what we eat) is often very different from what we do to maximize short-term interests (max out our credit cards, be couch potatoes, eat whatever we want). Because of the costs involved, it serves the company's long-term interest to do whatever it can to reduce operational costs and maintain a profitable financial position.

The **principle of personal virtue** holds that you should never do anything that is not honest, open, and truthful and that you would not be glad to see reported in the newspapers, on TV, or on the Internet. American investor Warren Buffett elaborates on what he refers to as the "Front Page of the Newspaper Test" when

Andres Rodriguez/Hemera/Thinkstock

he explains that, "Contemplating any business act, an employee should ask whether he or she would be willing to see it immediately described by an informed and critical reporter on the front page of the local paper, there to be read by his or her spouse, children and friends." Using the principle of personal virtue, the company may want to avoid enacting a hiring policy in order to avoid the potential for negative media coverage.

The **principle of religious injunctions** holds that you should never take an action that is unkind or that harms a sense of community, such as the positive feelings that come from working together to accomplish a commonly accepted goal. Using this principle, some would argue that the company should not introduce restrictive hiring practices that would limit the opportunity for otherwise qualified potential employees to pursue employment and earn a living.

According to the **principle of government requirements**, the law represents the minimal moral standards of society, so you should never take any action that violates the law. Using this principle, the company would want to consider provincial or federal laws relating to this issue. Currently, in Canada, the only provincial or federal laws that might apply are human rights codes that prohibit employers from discriminating against someone based on a disability. The question then arises as to whether or not smokers are considered to be disabled. There have been a few cases that have tested the waters of this issue, however, to date the Human Rights Tribunal of Ontario has not yet ruled on whether smoking is a disability.

Principle of long-term self-interest an ethical principle that holds that you should never take any action that is not in your or your organization's long-term self-interest.

Principle of personal virtue an ethical principle that holds that you should never do anything that is not honest, open, and truthful and that you would not be glad to see reported in the newspapers, on TV or on the Internet.

Principle of religious injunctions an ethical principle that holds that you should never take any action that is not kind and that does not build a sense of community.

Principle of government requirements an ethical principle that holds that you should never take any action that violates the law, for the law represents the minimal moral standard.

CEOs Who Fell From Grace

In a corporate structure, the board of directors has the ultimate say in most major business decisions, however, the position of chief executive officer (CEO) is one that carries a substantial amount of power, and can influence board members as well as set the tone for a company's ethical culture. This concentration of power can allow a CEO to do a lot to benefit the company or alternatively, that power can be used to support unethical decisions that can ruin a company. Below are some highlights of some of the most public corporate and CEO ethics violations that had a major impact on the view of business ethics in North America.

Enron Corporation—After it was discovered that company executives had manipulated accounting practices to hide massive business losses from shareholders and the public, allowing these executives to make huge personal profits while the company itself lost millions, an investigation by the US Securities and Exchange Commission (SEC) eventually led to the bankruptcy of this energy services giant and the conviction of CEO Kenneth Lay and other high ranking Enron executives. As a result of its association with Enron, the accounting firm Arthur Andersen was shut down. Between the two companies, close to 90,000 jobs were lost, employees lost more than $2 billion USD from pensions and savings plans, and shareholders lost another $70 billion USD. The hearings and corporate scandals that followed Enron led to the passage of the Sarbanes-Oxley Act in 2002.

WorldCom—When this telecommunications company began planning to merge with Sprint, the other major industry player at the time, the United States Department of Justice opposed the arrangement out of concern that it would lead to a monopoly; as a result, WorldCom's stock prices began to fall. CEO Bernard Ebbers margined the millions of dollars of stocks he held in World-Com to invest in other business ventures and, as stock prices fell after the failed merger, he was under pressure to cover more than $400 million in margin calls. To avoid having to sell his stocks, Ebbers convinced the board to lend him the money and then initiated a scheme to create fraudulent accounting entries. WorldCom's own internal audit department reported the accounting fraud to the audit committee and the resulting SEC investigation eventually led to the company filing for bankruptcy and to Ebbers receiving a 25-year sentence for fraud, conspiracy, and filing false documents.

Hollinger International—Canadian born Conrad Black's business empire, Hollinger Inc., was one of the largest media groups in the world, including publications like the *National Post, Chicago Sun-Times,* and London's *The Daily Telegraph.* In 2003, Hollinger's board of directors called in the SEC to investigate $200 million worth of payments made to Black as well as four other company directors. Black was eventually convicted of fraud, tax evasion, and racketeering and served five years in prison before being released in 2012. Black's actions may continue to impact future business dealings, as a recent decision handed down by the Ontario Securities Commission has permanently banned him from serving as a corporate director or officer of a public company in Ontario. At that hearing, Black told panelists he feels no guilt or shame over his criminal convictions.

Nortel—In its heyday, this Canadian multinational telecommunications company had a roster of more than 90,000 employees and a corporate value of over $300 billion. Following the technology crash of 2000–01, the company found itself in a fragile financial state and weakened by allegations that the company's CEO, CFO, and controller had doctored the books to present a stronger financial position to their shareholders and the public. The company filed for bankruptcy in 2009 with large debts and even larger legal issues to follow. In January 2013, after 10 years of litigation, one of the largest criminal trials in Canada's corporate history finally came to an end when three ex-Nortel senior executives, accused of manipulating accounting statements that shrouded the company's financial performance and led to the payout of more than $12 million in bonuses and share payments to themselves, were acquitted. Although comparisons were made to the Enron case, with many expecting a similarly harsh ruling for Nortel's executives, the judge in his final ruling concluded that although Nortel had a history of setting up inflated accounting reserves, "the burden [of proof] in my view was not met" in terms of the accounting decisions that formed the basis of the case.

MANDY GODBEHEAR/Shutterstock

Sources: "5 Most Publicized Ethics Violations by CEOs," Forbes.com, February 5, 2013, http://www.forbes.com/sites/investopedia/2013/02/05/5-most-publicized-ethics-violations-by-ceos/; Financial Post Staff, "Conrad Black Permanently Banned as Director or Officer of Any Ontario Public Company," Financial Post Online, February 27, 2015, http://business.financialpost.com/legal-post/conrad-black-banned-from-boards-of-ontario-public-firms-by-osc; G. Farrell and USA Today News, "Conrad Black Sentenced to 6 Years in Prison," ABC News.com, December 11, 2007, http://abcnews.go.com/Business/story?id=3981662&page=1; L. Nguyen, "Former Nortel Execs to Learn Fate Today," *Calgary Herald,* January 13, 2013, http://thechronicleherald.ca/business/425155-former-nortel-execs-to-learn-fate-today; J. McFarland and J. Blackwell, "Three Former Nortel Executives Found Not Guilty Of Fraud," *The Globe and Mail,* January 14, 2013, http://www.theglobeandmail.com/globe-investor/former-nortel-executives-claim-vindication-after-fraud-acquittal/article7319241/; L. Taylor, "Nortel Verdict: Pensioners Not Surprised By Verdict But Observers Consider It a Black Mark," *The Toronto Star,* January 14, 2013, http://www.thestar.com/business/companies/nortel/article/1314742--nortel-verdict-pensioners-not-surprised-now-await-outcome-of-mediation.

The **principle of utilitarian benefits** states that you should never take an action that does not result in greater good for society. In short, you should do whatever creates the greatest good for the greatest number. If the company is under pressure to reduce costs in order to stay profitable, a change in hiring practices may help the company to maintain its financial stability, thereby protecting workers' jobs and shareholders' investments. In this case, the principle does not lead to a clear choice.

The **principle of individual rights** holds that you should never take an action that infringes on others' agreed-upon rights. Using this principle, if you view smoking as an individual right, not hiring smokers is a form of discrimination. Some may argue that a company that doesn't want to hire someone they consider to have an unhealthy habit should also not hire people who don't exercise or have higher levels of cholesterol or tend to drink too much.

Finally, under the **principle of distributive justice**, you should never take any action that harms the least fortunate among us in some way. This principle is designed to protect the poor, the uneducated, and the unemployed. Following this principle, the company should not discriminate by not hiring smokers because of the economic impact it could have on certain members of society. Statistics show that smoking is unevenly distributed among the population—a larger percentage of people of lower socioeconomic status are smokers. In addition, according to US statistics, 45 percent of unemployed people smoke—which means that these hiring policies would risk hurting vulnerable groups that are already faced with higher unemployment rates, poor job prospects, and little job security. Using the

principle of distributive justice, the company should not change its hiring policies.

As mentioned at the beginning of this chapter, one of the practical aspects of ethical decisions is that no matter *what* you decide, someone or some group will be unhappy. This corollary is also true: No matter *how* you decide, someone or some group will be unhappy. Some will argue that you should have used a different principle or weighed concerns differently. Consequently, although all of these ethical principles encourage managers to balance others' needs against their own, they can also lead to very different ethical actions. The ethical spotlight is often cast on senior business executives, CEOs, and board members who in their role as business fiduciaries are legally authorized to manage the assets of others rather than for their own profit. **Self-dealing** refers to actions taken by a fiduciary that further his or her own best interest, rather than the benefit of the corporation. Examples may include appropriating funds for personal use, using corporate funds as a personal loan, or purchasing or selling stock based on inside information received through their own position.

(3-4) PRACTICAL STEPS TO ETHICAL DECISION MAKING

*Managers can encourage more ethical decision making in their organizations by **3-4a carefully selecting and hiring ethical employees**, **3-4b establishing a specific code of ethics**, **3-4c training employees to make ethical decisions**, and **3-4d creating an ethical climate**.*

3-4a Selecting and Hiring Ethical Employees

As an employer, how can you increase your chances of hiring honest employees, the kind who would return a wallet filled with money to its rightful owner? An **overt integrity test** estimates job applicants' honesty by asking them directly what they think or feel about theft or about punishment of unethical behaviours.[26] For example, an employer might ask an applicant, "Would you ever consider buying something from somebody if you knew the person had stolen the item?" or "Don't most people steal from their companies?" Surprisingly, unethical people will usually answer "yes"

Principle of utilitarian benefits an ethical principle that holds that you should never take any action that does not result in greater good for society.

Principle of individual rights an ethical principle that holds that you should never take any action that infringes on others' agreed-upon rights.

Principle of distributive justice an ethical principle that holds that you should never take any action that harms the least fortunate among us: the poor, the uneducated, the unemployed.

Self-dealing actions taken by a fiduciary that further his or her own best interest, rather than the benefit of the corporation.

Overt integrity test a written test that estimates job applicants' honesty by directly asking them what they think or feel about theft or about punishment of unethical behaviours.

to such questions, because they believe that the world is basically dishonest and that dishonest behaviour is normal.[27]

A **personality-based integrity test** indirectly estimates job applicants' honesty by measuring psychological traits such as dependability and conscientiousness. For example, prison inmates serving time for white-collar crimes (counterfeiting, embezzlement, and fraud) scored much lower than a comparison group of middle-level managers on scales measuring reliability, dependability, honesty, conscientiousness, and abiding by rules.[28] These results show that companies can selectively hire and promote people who will be more ethical.[29]

3-4b Establishing Codes of Ethics

Today, almost all large corporations have similar ethics codes in place. Still, two things must happen if those codes are to encourage ethical decision making and behaviour.[30] First, a company must communicate its code inside and outside the company. Johnson & Johnson's credo is an example of a well communicated code of ethics. Written in 1943 by Robert Johnson, a member of the founding Johnson family, the credo is widely available—featured prominently on the company website and throughout the company's worldwide corporate offices.

Second, besides having an ethics code with general guidelines like "Do unto others as you would have others do unto you," management must develop practical ethical standards and procedures specific to the company's line of business. Canadian Tire has established a set of ethical standards known as its Code of Business Conduct to help direct the actions of employees and individuals who act on behalf of the company. For example, a Canadian Tire employee who is unsure whether to accept an invitation to a business function can refer to the code and find that the expected procedure is to seek approval prior to accepting any invitation and to consider whether the event is relevant to his or her role in the company, whether the event is a networking opportunity, and whether acceptance would reduce his or her ability to be objective in making decisions regarding this business partner. The code is available on the company's website, so it is easily accessible to employees, suppliers, and customers alike. Complaints or concerns regarding potential violations of the code can be submitted to the company using the Business Conduct Hotline, or they can be reported through the company's website as part of the company's Business Conduct Compliance Program.[31]

3-4c Training in Ethics

In addition to establishing ethical standards, managers should also be involved in ethics and compliance training to develop employees' awareness of ethics.[32] This means helping employees to recognize which issues are ethical issues and then to avoid rationalizing unethical behaviour by thinking, "This isn't really illegal or immoral" or "No one will ever find out." To ensure that employees of the Royal Bank of Canada understand the company's code of conduct, at least once every two years, employees participate in a web-based ethics training program that incorporates role plays as well as a testing feature designed to evaluate awareness of company principles and how an employee would respond to an ethical dilemma.[33] Several companies have even created board games to improve awareness of ethical issues.[34] Defence contractor Lockheed Martin's ethics training program is aimed at creating "a culture of trust." Employees form small groups and engage in role playing and dialogue with one another about real-life scenarios such as managing relationships with coworkers, using company credit cards ethically while on business travel, and managing conflicts of interest. The groups then develop outcomes to the scenarios. Because it is collective, this program not only conveys information about ethical behaviour but also builds accountability and a sense of "We're all in this together."[35]

The second objective for ethics training programs is to achieve credibility with employees. Some companies have hurt the credibility of their ethics programs by having outside instructors and consultants conduct the classes.[36] Employees often complain that outside instructors and consultants are teaching theory that has nothing to do with their work and the practical dilemmas they actually face on a daily basis. Boeing has established a number of ways to educate employees about ethical issues and to help them manage those issues in-house. These include providing ethics advisers who serve as mentors, as well as disseminating a handbook that outlines how to make ethical decisions and that presents information in response to frequently asked questions. Answers to "What do I do if . . .?" questions are easily accessible in the handbook and through the company's Ethics Line, which is available to employees throughout the company as well as to concerned stakeholders.[37] Ethics training

Personality-based integrity test a written test that indirectly estimates job applicants' honesty by measuring psychological traits, such as dependability and conscientiousness.

Exhibit 3.4
A Basic Model of Ethical Decision Making

1. Identify the problem. What makes it an ethical problem? Think in terms of rights, obligations, fairness, relationships, and integrity. How would you define the problem if you stood on the other side of the fence?

2. Identify the constituents. Who has been hurt? Who could be hurt? Who could be helped? Are they willing players, or are they victims? Can you negotiate with them?

3. Diagnose the situation. How did it happen in the first place? What could have prevented it? Is it going to get worse or better? Can the damage now be undone?

4. Analyze your options. Imagine the range of possibilities. Limit yourself to the two or three most manageable. What are the likely outcomes of each? What are the likely costs? Look to the company mission statement or code of ethics for guidance.

5. Make your choice. What is your intention in making this decision? How does it compare with the probable results? Can you discuss the problem with the affected parties before you act? Could you disclose without qualm your decision to your boss, the CEO, the board of directors, your family, or society as a whole?

6. Act. Do what you have to do. Don't be afraid to admit errors. Be as bold in confronting a problem as you were in causing it.

Source: L.A. Berger, "Train All Employees to Solve Ethical Dilemmas," *Best's Review—Life Health Insurance Edition 95* (1995): 70–80. © A.M. Best Company. Used with permission.

becomes even more credible when top managers teach the initial ethics classes to their subordinates, who in turn teach their subordinates.[38]

The third objective of ethics training is to teach employees a practical model of ethical decision making. A basic model should help them think about the consequences their choices will have for others and consider how they will choose between different solutions. Exhibit 3.4 presents a basic model of ethical decision making.

Don't Be Evil

These three words form the basis for the Google Code of Conduct. The "Don't be evil" principle helps guide Googlers (Google employees) in how to approach and serve customers in order to provide customers with the best products and services possible, but also extends to how to treat fellow Googlers with respect. According to Google, the code recognizes that "Everything we do in connection with our work at Google will be, and should be, measured against the highest possible standards of ethical business conduct. Trust and mutual respect among employees and users are the foundation of our success, and they are something we need to earn every day." Google has a reputation for quirkiness and an unconventional work environment (rooftop miniature golf, relaxation rooms complete with aquariums and massage chairs, music, and DJ rooms); even so, the company is very serious about the ethics code. It covers topics such as serving users with integrity, treating one another with integrity and respect, addressing conflicts of interest, preserving confidentiality, and protecting Google assets. Googlers are expected to adhere to the code and to bring concerns forward if they feel that fellow Googlers are falling short on their interpretation of the code. For Googlers, failure to follow the code can result in disciplinary action, including termination of employment, but the code also extends to any outside individuals, contractors, or consultants that do business with the company. If you want to read more about the code, google it!

Andresr/Shutterstock.com

Source: Alphabet Code of Conduct from http://investor.google.com/corporate/code-of-conduct.html

3-4d Creating an Ethical Climate

Organizational culture is key to fostering ethical decision making. Management consultant Andrea Plotnick observes about an ethics code: "You want it to be about embedding the right behaviours and the right decision-making process within everybody in the organization, so that it becomes part of the culture. That is how you will have success."[39] As mentioned previously, economic conditions can also play a role in the ethical climate within organizations. During tough economic times, when a company's future is in jeopardy, management may emphasize the importance of high standards and project a heightened commitment to ethics. As a result, employees may be less inclined to participate in unethical behaviours, adopting a higher standard of conduct for themselves.[40]

The Ethics Research Center cautions that when the economic business environment improves, misconduct may rise unless a strong ethical culture is in place.[41] To achieve such a culture, management must set the tone. Studies have found that the two major drivers of ethics culture are senior executives and supervisors. When researchers ask, "What is the most important influence on your ethical behaviour at work?", the answer comes back, "My manager." The first step in establishing an ethical climate is for managers, especially top managers, to act ethically themselves.[42]

A second step in establishing an ethical climate is for top management to be active in and committed to the company ethics program.[43] Business writer Dayton Fandray says: "You can have ethics offices and officers and training programs and reporting systems, but if the CEO doesn't seem to care, it's all just a sham. It's not surprising to find that the companies that really do care about ethics make a point of including senior management in all of their ethics and compliance programs."[44]

A third step is to implement a reporting system that encourages managers and employees to report potential ethics violations. **Whistle blowing**, that is, reporting others' ethics violations, is a difficult step for most people to take. Potential whistle blowers often feel that their reporting won't make an impact and fear that they, and not the ethics violators, will be punished. In a recent study on ethics in the workplace, 69 percent of respondents said they did not report wrongdoing because they lacked faith that investigations would be conducted, 66 percent did not believe disciplinary measures would be consistently applied, and 23 percent claimed they did not report out of fear of retaliation for their actions.[45] Retaliation could include being excluded from decisions and work activities by supervisors or management, along with responses from coworkers and supervisors such as verbal abuse or being given the cold shoulder (see Exhibit 3.5). Retaliation may cause some

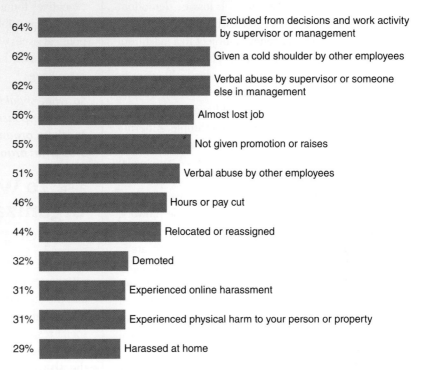

Exhibit 3.5

Types of Retaliation Experienced as a Result of Reported Misconduct (2011)

Percentage	Type of Retaliation
64%	Excluded from decisions and work activity by supervisor or management
62%	Given a cold shoulder by other employees
62%	Verbal abuse by supervisor or someone else in management
56%	Almost lost job
55%	Not given promotion or raises
51%	Verbal abuse by other employees
46%	Hours or pay cut
44%	Relocated or reassigned
32%	Demoted
31%	Experienced online harassment
31%	Experienced physical harm to your person or property
29%	Harassed at home

Source: 2011 National Business Ethics Survey. Workplace Ethics in Transition. Ethics Resource Center, available online at http://www.ethics.org/nbes/files/FinalNBES-web.pdf. Reprinted by permission of the Ethics Resource Center.

Whistle blowing reporting others' ethics violations to management or legal authorities.

employees to leave an organization, negatively impacting employee retention and workplace stability.

In 2004, an amendment to the Canadian Criminal Code offered whistle blower protection, making it a federal criminal offence for employers to make employment-related threats like job loss or demotion, or to retaliate against employees who report unlawful acts to law enforcement agencies, subject to a maximum penalty of five years' imprisonment. The Public Servants Disclosure Protection Act protects whistle blowers in the federal public sector and most recently, several provinces have also enacted whistle blower protection to protect public sector employees. For example, Alberta's Public Interest Disclosure Act, which came into effect in 2013, applies to the Alberta public service, provincial agencies, boards, and commissions, as well as academic institutions, school boards, and health organizations.

What does the most to discourage whistle blowers, however, is lack of company action on their complaints.[46] Thus, the final step in developing an ethical climate is for management to fairly and consistently punish those who violate the company's code of ethics. Amazingly, not all companies fire ethics violators. In fact, 8 percent of the companies surveyed admitted that they would promote top performers even if they had violated ethical standards.[47]

3-5 SOCIAL RESPONSIBILITY

Social responsibility is an individual's or a business's obligation to pursue policies, make decisions, and take actions that benefit society.[48] Over the years, the view of social responsibility has expanded somewhat, with the term **corporate social responsibility** being used to describe the voluntary activities undertaken by a company to operate in an economically, socially, and

Social responsibility an individual's or a business's obligation to pursue policies, make decisions, and take actions that benefit society.

Corporate social responsibility the voluntary activities undertaken by a company to operate in an economically, socially, and environmentally sustainable manner.

Shareholder model a view of social responsibility that holds that an organization's overriding goal should be to maximize profit for the benefit of shareholders.

environmentally sustainable manner. There are differing opinions over to whom and for what organizations are responsible, so it can be difficult for managers to know what socially responsible corporate behaviour is, or what will be perceived as such. A study of 1,144 top global executives found that 79 percent predicted that at least some responsibility for dealing with future social and political issues would fall on corporations; only 3 percent, however, said they were doing a good job of dealing with these issues.[49]

*So what should managers and corporations do to be socially responsible? This depends on determining **3-5a to whom organizations are socially responsible,** and **3-5b what organizations are socially responsible for.***

3-5a To Whom Are Organizations Socially Responsible?

There are two perspectives regarding to whom organizations are socially responsible: the shareholder model, and the stakeholder model. According to the late Nobel Prize-winning economist Milton Friedman, the only social responsibility that organizations have is to satisfy their owners, that is, company shareholders. This view—the **shareholder model**—holds that the only social responsibility businesses have is to maximize profits. By maximizing profits, the firm maximizes shareholder wealth and satisfaction. More specifically, as profits rise, the company shares owned by shareholders generally increase in value.

Friedman argued that it is socially irresponsible for companies to divert time, money, and attention away from maximizing profits toward social causes and charitable organizations. The first problem, he believed, is that organizations cannot act effectively as moral agents for all company shareholders. Although shareholders are likely to agree on investment issues concerning a company, it's highly unlikely they have common views on what social causes a company should or should not support. Instead of acting as moral agents, Friedman argued, companies should maximize profits for shareholders. Shareholders can then use their time and increased wealth to contribute to the charities, institutions, or social causes they want rather than to those that the company wants.

The second major problem, Friedman said, is that time, money, and attention diverted to social causes undermines market efficiency.[50] In competitive markets, companies compete for raw materials, talented workers, customers, and investment funds. A company that spends

The Most Hated Man in America

Martin Shkreli is not afraid to share his opinions on business and some of the controversial decisions that he has made over the years. Shkreli, known to some as "the most hated man in America," gained notoriety and media attention when his company, Turing Pharmaceuticals, after acquiring the rights to a pharmaceutical drug known as Daraprim, decided to raise the price by more than 5000 percent. Daraprim is the only approved drug for the treatment of toxoplasmosis, a rare parasitic disease that mainly strikes pregnant women, cancer patients, and AIDS patients. Public outrage and media attention erupted when it became known that the price of a Daraprim tablet had increased from $13.50 USD to $750 USD overnight. Following the controversy, Shkreli attended a Healthcare Summit and was asked by the media if, looking back at the controversy, he would have done anything differently. Shkreli responded, "I would have raised prices higher. That's my duty. My shareholders expect me to make the most profit. That's the ugly, dirty truth." He went on to say, "No one wants to say it, no one's proud of it, but this is a capitalist society, a capitalist system, and capitalist rules."

This is not the first time Shkreli has gained media attention. The 32-year-old former hedge fund manager and biotechnology firm owner was accused repeatedly of losing money for investors and lying to them about it, as well as illegally taking assets from one of his companies to pay off debtors in another. In December 2015, Shkreli was arrested on securities fraud and conspiracy charges.

Sources: D. Diamond, "Martin Shkreli Admits He Messed Up: He Should've Raised Prices Even Higher," Forbes.com, December 3, 2015, http://www.forbes.com/sites/dandiamond/2015/12/03/what-martin-shkreli-says-now-i-shouldve-raised-prices-higher/#37cfe1f71964; T. Hays, "Drug Industry's Villain' Martin Shkreli Arrested on Securities Fraud Charges," The Globe and Mail.com, December 17, 2015, http://www.theglobeandmail.com/report-on-business/international-business/us-business/turing-pharma-ceo-martin-shkreli-arrested-by-fbi-report/article27799692/; C. Smythe and K. Geiger, "Shkreli, Drug Price Gouger, Denies Fraud and Posts Bail," Bloomberg Business.com, December 17, 2015, http://www.bloomberg.com/features/2015-martin-shkreli-securities-fraud/.

money on social causes will have less money to purchase quality materials or to hire talented workers who can produce valuable products at good prices. If customers find the company's products less desirable, its sales and profits will fall. If profits fall, the company's stock price will decline, and the company will have difficulty attracting investment funds that will allow it to grow. In the end, Friedman argues, diverting the firm's money, time, and resources to social causes hurts customers, suppliers, employees, and shareholders. Russell Roberts, an economist at George Mason University, agrees: "Doesn't it make more sense to have companies do what they do best, make good products at fair prices, and then let consumers use the savings for the charity of their choice?"[51]

By contrast, under the **stakeholder model**, management's most important responsibility is the firm's long-term survival (not just maximixing profits), which is achieved by satisfying not just shareholders but also the interests of multiple corporate stakeholders.[52] **Stakeholders** are persons or groups that are interested in and affected by the organization's actions.[53] They are called stakeholders because they have a stake in what

those actions are. Consequently, stakeholder groups may try to influence the firm to act in their own interests.

Being responsible to multiple stakeholders raises two basic questions. First, how does a company identify its stakeholders? Second, how does a company balance the needs of different stakeholders? Distinguishing between primary and secondary stakeholders can help answer these questions.[54]

Some stakeholders are more important to the firm's survival than others. A **primary stakeholder** is any group on which the organization depends for its

Stakeholder model a theory of corporate responsibility that holds that management's most important responsibility, long-term survival, is achieved by satisfying the interests of multiple corporate stakeholders.

Stakeholders persons or groups with a "stake" or legitimate interest in a company's actions.

Primary stakeholder any group on which an organization relies for its long-term survival.

long-term survival. Primary stakeholders include shareholders, employees, customers, suppliers, governments, and local communities. When managers are struggling to balance the needs of different stakeholders, the stakeholder model suggests that the needs of primary stakeholders take precedence over the needs of secondary stakeholders. But among primary stakeholders, are some more important than others? In practice, yes, as CEOs typically give somewhat higher priority to shareholders, employees, and customers than to suppliers, governments, and local communities.[55] Addressing the concerns of primary stakeholders is important because if a stakeholder group becomes dissatisfied and terminates its relationship with the company, the company could be seriously harmed or go out of business.

A **secondary stakeholder**, such as the media or a special interest group, can influence or be influenced by the company. Unlike the primary stakeholders, however, they do not engage in regular transactions with the company and are not critical to its long-term survival. Nevertheless, secondary stakeholders are still important because they can affect public perceptions and opinions about socially responsible behaviour. The fight over Trans-Canada Corporation's proposed Keystone XL Pipeline lasted close to seven years before the US government eventually rejected the proposal shortly after the Liberal government won the federal election in Canada. The Keystone XL pipeline would have carried 800,000 barrels of crude oil per day from the tar sands in Alberta to oil refineries in Texas and Louisiana. Supporters pointed to the tens of thousands of jobs that would be created from this project, the benefit of having a reduced reliance on oil imports, and the minimal environmental impact as reasons why the project should be allowed to complete the last 3,800 miles of the pipeline network. However, environmental groups like the Natural Resources Defense Council, for example, argued that the pipeline would increase oil sands production, one of the most energy- and carbon-intensive methods of retrieving oil. Another environmental advocacy group, 350.org, which sponsors grassroots protests against projects that increase carbon production, held a 40,000-person rally in the nation's capital against the Keystone XL pipeline. It also supported the Do The Math Tour, which travelled to 20 cities, arguing that governments and energy companies should leave the oil sands in the ground.[56] In

John Rensten/Digital Vision/Getty Images

terms of the US government, support was divided—with the House of Representatives and the US Senate putting forward a bill in support of the project only to have it vetoed by President Obama.

So, to whom are organizations socially responsible? Many commentators, especially economists and financial analysts, continue to argue that organizations are responsible only to shareholders. Increasingly, however, top managers have come to believe that they and their companies must be socially responsible to their stakeholders. Surveys show that as many as 80 percent of top-level managers believe it is unethical to focus just on shareholders. Although there is not complete agreement, a majority of opinion makers would argue that companies must be socially responsible to their stakeholders.

3-5b For What Are Organizations Socially Responsible?

If organizations are to be socially responsible to stakeholders, what are they to be socially responsible *for*? Well, companies can best benefit their stakeholders by fulfilling their economic, legal, ethical, and discretionary responsibilities. Economic and legal responsibilities play a larger part in a company's social responsibility than do ethical and discretionary responsibilities. However, the relative importance of these various responsibilities depends on society's expectations of corporate social responsibility at a particular point in time.[57] A century ago, society expected businesses to meet their economic and legal responsibilities and little else. Today, when society judges whether businesses are socially responsible, ethical and discretionary responsibilities are considerably more important than they used to be.

Secondary stakeholder any group that can influence or be influenced by a company and can affect public perceptions about its socially responsible behaviour.

Historically, **economic responsibility**—making a profit by producing a product or service valued by society—has been a business's most basic social responsibility. Organizations that don't meet their financial and economic expectations come under tremendous pressure. For example, company boards are very, very quick these days to fire CEOs, who are three times more likely to be fired today than they were two decades ago. Typically, all it takes is two or three bad quarters in a row. William Rollnick, who became acting chairman of Mattel after the company fired its previous CEO, says: "There's zero forgiveness. You screw up and you're dead." Indeed, in both Europe and the United States, nearly one-third of CEOs are fired because of their inability to successfully change their companies.[58]

Legal responsibility is a company's social responsibility to obey society's laws and regulations as it tries to meet its economic responsibilities. For example, various municipalities across Ontario have adopted anti-drive-through ordinances in response to environmental concerns about emissions generated by vehicles using drive-throughs. These bans pose a challenge for businesses with drive-throughs. One of these is TDL, the parent company of Tim Hortons, which has responded by commissioning a study that concludes that drive-throughs actually generate lower vehicle emissions than

Renae McCann for Nelson Education

parking lots do. Tim Hortons cannot afford to walk away from this legal issue, considering that drive-throughs generate 50 percent of its revenue. TDL has succeeded in fighting restrictions in several Ontario cities. In Kingston, Ontario, however, the city planning committee has prohibited new drive-throughs in the city's historic downtown core.[59]

Ethical responsibility is a company's social responsibility not to violate accepted principles of right and wrong when conducting its business. For example, most people believe that KFC was wrong to run ads implying that its fried chicken was good for you and could help you lose weight. In one ad, one friend said to another, "Is that you? Man you look fantastic! What the heck you been doin'?" With his mouth full, the friend says, "Eatin' chicken." A voice-over then says, "So if you're watching carbs and going high protein, go KFC!" Two of KFC's fried chicken breasts, however, contain 780 calories and 38 grams of fat. Michael Jacobsen, executive director of the Center for Science in the Public Interest, says: "These ads take the truth, dip it in batter and deep-fry it. Colonel Sanders himself would have a hard time swallowing this ad campaign."[60] After running the ads for a brief period, KFC quietly pulled them.

A **discretionary responsibility** pertains to the social roles that businesses play in society beyond their economic, legal, and ethical responsibilities. Discretionary responsibilities are voluntary and can be undertaken by large, multinational corporations as well as by small businesses. The Royal Bank of Canada created the "RBC Generator" fund, a social finance initiative with a $10 million pool of capital for investment in new business models that address environmental and social change challenges. In addition, the company pledges $100 million to support children's programs in the arts, sports, and mental health and education.

After Hurricane Sandy, the largest Atlantic hurricane ever recorded, caused approximately $75 billion in damage in New York state and New Jersey, many

Economic responsibility the expectation that a company will make a profit by producing a valued product or service.

Legal responsibility a company's social responsibility to obey society's laws and regulations.

Ethical responsibility a company's social responsibility not to violate accepted principles of right and wrong when conducting its business.

Discretionary responsibility the expectation that a company will voluntarily serve a social role beyond its economic, legal, and ethical responsibilities.

Triple Bottom Line

The term *bottom line* has been used in business for quite some time, referring to the practice of using profitability as a measure of success. However, in recent years, the movement toward greater social responsibility and sustainability on the part of organizations both large and small has led to a new term being introduced. The phrase *triple bottom line* (TBL) refers to the belief that social and environmental factors should be considered along with financial indicators when it comes to assessing performance. According to John Elkington, cofounder of the consulting organization SustainAbility, companies should be preparing three distinct bottom lines that include an evaluation of how an organization is doing in terms of the three P's: profit, people, and planet.

▶ Profit: The traditional measure of profit—the bottom line of the profit-and-loss account—is a familiar and desired outcome for business, however, it should be considered to be only one part of a business plan. Profit represents total value for a company but also what benefits society at large.

▶ People: The second bottom line of a company's "people account" is a measure of how socially responsible a company has been throughout its operations in terms of its respect of employees, the community, and the region in which a corporation does business. This means taking actions that benefit all stakeholders—for example,

adopting fair trade practices to help sustain small producers in developing countries.

▶ Planet: The third bottom line is the company's "planet" account—a measure of how environmentally responsible it has been in terms of environmentally sustainable business practices.

The concept of TBL points to the fact that success of an organization should not be measured solely by economic performance, supporting somewhat the stakeholder model of social responsibility. By measuring other factors like the social and environmental performance of a company, the TBL encourages managers to pay attention to these issues and consider the full cost of doing business. At the same time, proponents of the shareholder model of social responsibility may also find support in the TBL concept if they view some of the people and planet initiatives as being a strategic competitive advantage, even though it may take some time to be able to measure those contributions to financial performance.

Sources: "Triple Bottom Line," *The Economist*, http://www.economist.com/node/14301663. © The Economist Newspaper Limited, London (November 17, 2009); R. Scott, "The Bottom Line of Corporate Good," *Fortune.com*, September 4, 2012, accessed November 1, 2015, http://www.forbes.com/sites/causeintegration/2012/09/14/the-bottom-line-of-corporate-good/; G. Davis, "The Triple Bottom Line Goal of Sustainable Businesses," Entrepreneur.com, April 24, 2013, https://www.entrepreneur.com/article/225948.

Used with the permission of the Bank of Canada.

Rawpixel.com/Shutterstock

leonello calvetti/Shutterstock.com

PROFIT   **PEOPLE**   **PLANET**

BOTTOM LINE

companies stepped in with donations, contributions, and other forms of valuable assistance. The J.P. Morgan Bank pledged $2 million to the Red Cross and allowed storm-affected customers to skip mortgage payments for 90 days and suspended all of its foreclosure activity in storm-damaged areas. Adidas, the sporting goods company, donated $600,000 worth of jackets, while

Terramar Sports, which makes outdoor clothing and gear, donated $500,000 worth of long underwear and thermal clothing to people displaced from their homes by the storm.[61]

At the opposite end of the spectrum, Bargains Group, a small, Toronto-based company that sources discounted clothing for resale to retailers, uses industry contacts and suppliers to donate sleeping bags and survival kits for street people, toys for the Salvation Army, and emergency supplies for victims of natural disasters.[62] Discretionary responsibilities such as these are voluntary. Companies are not considered unethical if they don't perform them. Today, however, corporate stakeholders expect companies to do much more than in the past to meet their discretionary responsibilities.

<table>
<tr><td>3-6</td><td></td></tr>
</table>

RESPONSES TO DEMANDS FOR SOCIAL RESPONSIBILITY AND IMPACT ON ECONOMIC PERFORMANCE

3-6a Responses to Demands for Social Responsibility

Social responsiveness refers to a company's strategy for responding to stakeholders' economic, legal, ethical, and discretionary expectations. A social responsibility problem exists whenever company actions do not meet stakeholder expectations. One model of social responsiveness identifies four strategies for responding to social responsibility problems: reactive, defensive, accommodative, and proactive. These strategies differ in the extent to which the company is willing to act to meet or exceed society's expectations.

A company using a **reactive strategy** will do less than society expects. It may deny responsibility for a problem or fight any suggestion that it should solve the problem. In 2014, General Motors (GM) publicly acknowledged that since 2001 it had knowingly produced 1.6 million GM cars with faulty ignition switches. The issue, which is linked to 12 auto-related deaths, could happen when turning the ignition key from "off" to "accessory" (used to power accessories, like radios, without the engine running) and then back "on."[63] The car would start, but the ignition switch, which was only partially engaged, could switch off, causing car engines to stop unexpectedly. Service technicians first documented the issue in 2001. Engineers knew in 2004. GM management found out in 2011.[64] Despite knowing about

the problem, GM did not issue a safety recall because engineering managers thought drivers could still maintain control of their cars even if their motors suddenly turned off. The defective switches were not redesigned until 2007 and the first vehicle recall did not occur until February 2013. Ironically, the problem is easily fixed with a $5 replacement part that takes minutes to install. GM is offering to either repair the switches or give customers a $500 allowance toward the purchase or lease of a new GM vehicle. It's estimated that GM will spend $1.3 billion just to fix affected vehicles.[65] The Center for Auto Safety, a nonprofit organization, has called for GM to waive legal immunity from lawsuits, which it obtained via its 2009 bankruptcy, and to set aside an additional $1 billion as a dedicated fund for victims.[66]

By contrast, a company using a **defensive strategy** will admit responsibility for a problem but do the least required to meet societal expectations. Foxconn, a Taiwanese electronics manufacturer, produces 40 percent of the world's consumer electronic products. Over the last four years, at the Foxconn factories that make iPhones and iPads, 18 employees attempted suicide, most by leaping to their deaths. After the eleventh suicide, the company placed suicide nets that reach 20 feet out around the perimeter of each building. An extensive *New York Times* investigation found that employees often worked seven days a week, were exposed to dangerous chemicals, and lived in crowded, company-supplied dorm rooms, some with as many as 20 people per three-bedroom apartment. However, Apple, which had been conducting audits of its suppliers' manufacturing facilities for many years, was slow to respond. A consultant with Business for Social Responsibility, a company Apple hired for advice on labour issues, said, "We've spent years telling Apple there are serious problems and recommending changes. They don't want to pre-empt problems; they just want to avoid embarrassments." A former Apple executive said, "If you see the same pattern of problems, year after year, that means the company's ignoring the issue rather than solving it. Noncompliance is tolerated, as long as the suppliers promise to try harder

Social responsiveness a company's strategy for responding to stakeholders' economic, legal, ethical, or discretionary expectations concerning social responsibility.

Reactive strategy a social responsiveness strategy in which a company does less than society expects.

Defensive strategy a social responsiveness strategy in which a company admits responsibility for a problem but does the least required to meet societal expectations.

next time. If we meant business, core violations would disappear." After the *New York Times* story, Apple began working with the Fair Labor Association, a nonprofit organization that promotes and monitors safe working conditions. Four years after the problems began, following the Fair Labor Association's report, Apple and Foxconn agreed to increase pay, limit workers to a maximum of 49 hours a week, build more dormitories, and hire thousands of additional workers.[67]

A company using an **accommodative strategy** will accept responsibility for a problem and take a progressive approach by doing all that can be expected to solve the problem. When a garment factory collapsed in Bangladesh in 2013, over 1,100 textile workers died in one of the most tragic industrial catastrophes in recent years. Garments for the Joe Fresh clothing line produced for Canadian food distributor Loblaw Co. Ltd. were manufactured at this factory. Reports showed the building was found to be in violation of building codes as a result of substandard construction, particularly in the upper floors of the building which had heavy generators installed there, causing the building to shake. The day before its collapse, the building was deemed to be unsafe by inspectors, however, the owners still allowed workers to report to work. Loblaw immediately came forward to acknowledge its relationship to the factory and propose a relief program that included providing financial assistance to injured workers and families, rehabilitating injured workers, and implementing a joint program with Save the Children Canada and Save the Children Bangladesh to "provide life skills and workplace support for garment industry workers and their families." Loblaw also joined a group of international retailers including Benetton and H&M, to commit to regularly inspecting individual factories where garments are produced and to make the reports public, with each retailer contributing $500,000 annually to the initiative.

Exhibit 3.6
Social Responsiveness

Source: A.B. Carrol, "A Three-Dimensional Conceptual Model of Corporate Performance," *Academy of Management Review*, 1979, Vol 4 497–505.

Finally, a company using a **proactive strategy** will anticipate responsibility for a problem before it occurs, do more than expected to address the problem, and lead the industry in its approach. In 2013, Unilever announced that it would no longer use microplastic beads in its soap products. The beads, about one-third of a millimetre in size, function like a gentle abrasive to remove dead skin. A single bottle of facial cleanser can contain as many as 360,000 microbeads. While it's not yet known with scientific certainty that microbeads are harmful, there is potential because they absorb chemicals and are easily ingested by sea animals because of their minuscule size. Rather than waiting for conclusive evidence, Unilever announced that it is completely eliminating microbeads from its products because, "We believe we can provide consumers with products that deliver a similar exfoliating performance without the need to use plastics. We are currently exploring which suitable alternatives can best match the sensory experience that the plastic scrub beads provide."[68] Exhibit 3.6 summarizes the discussion of social responsiveness.

3-6b Social Responsibility and Economic Performance

One question that managers often ask is, "Does it pay to be socially responsible?" Early research on this question showed no inherent relationship between social responsibility and economic performance.[69] Recent research, however, has led to different conclusions. There is a trad-eoff between being socially responsible and economic performance.[70] And there is a small, positive relationship between being socially responsible and economic

Accommodative strategy a social responsiveness strategy in which a company accepts responsibility for a problem and does all that society expects to solve that problem.

Proactive strategy a social responsiveness strategy in which a company anticipates responsibility for a problem before it occurs and does more than society expects to address the problem.

performance that strengthens with corporate reputation.[71] Let's explore what each of these results means.

First, managers don't need to choose between being socially responsible and maximizing economic performance.[72] Being socially responsible usually won't make a business less profitable. What this suggests is that the costs of being socially responsible—and those costs can be high, especially early on—can be offset by a better product or corporate reputation, which results in stronger sales or higher profit margins. The Patagonia Company sells expensive outdoor gear and clothing to customers who are willing to pay a higher price because of the company's environmental focus. Two decades ago, it switched to organic cotton, which costs three times as much as traditional cotton because it is grown without chemicals and irrigation. In 2011, Patagonia created the Common Threads Partnership, in which it pledged "to build useful things that last, to repair what breaks and recycle what comes to the end of its useful life," and in which customers are asked "to buy only what I need (and will last), repair what breaks, reuse (share) what I no longer need and recycle everything else."[73] Patagonia promoted the partnership with an advertising campaign proclaiming, "Don't Buy This Jacket." Environmental consumers demonstrated their willingness to pay more, as sales increased after the campaign, presumably taking market share from Patagonia's competitors.[74]

Second, it usually *does* pay to be socially responsible, and that relationship becomes stronger particularly when a company or its products have a strong reputation for social responsibility.[75]

Finally, even if there is generally a small positive relationship between social responsibility and economic performance that becomes stronger when a company has a positive reputation for social responsibility, and even if there is no tradeoff between being socially responsible and economic performance, social responsibility can have significant costs, and there is no guarantee that socially responsible companies will be profitable.

Socially responsible companies experience the same ups and downs in economic performance as traditional businesses. General Motors' Chevy Volt features a

DON'T BUY THIS JACKET

It's Black Friday, the day in the year retail turns from red to black and starts to make real money. But Black Friday, and the culture of consumption it reflects, puts the economy of natural systems that support all life firmly in the red. We're now using the resources of one-and-a-half planets on our one and only planet.

Because Patagonia wants to be in business for a good long time – and leave a world inhabitable for our kids – we want to do the opposite of every other business today. We ask you to buy less and to reflect before you spend a dime on this jacket or anything else.

Environmental bankruptcy, as with corporate bankruptcy, can happen very slowly, then all of a sudden. This is what we face unless we slow down, then reverse the damage. We're running short on fresh water, topsoil, fisheries, wetlands – all our planet's natural systems and resources that support business, and life, including our own.

The environmental cost of everything we make is astonishing. Consider the R2® Jacket shown, one

COMMON THREADS INITIATIVE

REDUCE
WE make useful gear that lasts a long time
YOU don't buy what you don't need

REPAIR
WE help you repair your Patagonia gear
YOU pledge to fix what's broken

REUSE
WE help find a home for Patagonia gear you no longer need
YOU sell or pass it on*

RECYCLE
WE will take back your Patagonia gear that is worn out
YOU pledge to keep your stuff out of the landfill and incinerator

REIMAGINE
TOGETHER we reimagine a world where we take only what nature can replace

of our best sellers. To make it required 135 liters of water, enough to meet the daily needs (three glasses a day) of 45 people. Its journey from its origin as 60% recycled polyester to our Reno warehouse generated nearly 20 pounds of carbon dioxide, 24 times the weight of the finished product. This jacket left behind, on its way to Reno, two-thirds its weight in waste.

And this is a 60% recycled polyester jacket, knit and sewn to a high standard; it is exceptionally durable, so you won't have to replace it as often. And when it comes to the end of its useful life we'll take it back to recycle into a product of equal value. But, as is true of all the things we can make and you can buy, this jacket comes with an environmental cost higher than its price.

There is much to be done and plenty for us all to do. Don't buy what you don't need. Think twice before you buy anything. Go to patagonia.com/CommonThreads or scan the QR code below. Take the Common Threads Initiative pledge, and join us in the fifth "R," to reimagine a world where we take only what nature can replace.

patagonia.com

TAKE THE PLEDGE

Courtesy of Patagonia

plug-in hybrid engine, producing outstanding fuel efficiency of 60 miles per gallon and the ability to drive 800 miles between fill-ups. The Volt is a tremendous technological and environmental product, but it's been a disaster for GM's bottom line. GM's investment in the Volt, so far, is estimated at $1.2 billion. But, because of the technology involved, the Volt is difficult and expensive to assemble, so much so that Reuters estimates that GM loses $50,000 per Volt! Sales have been incredibly disappointing. Priced at $39,995, GM has sold only 58,000 Volts in four years, far short of its goal of 60,000 per year. Sales picked up slightly only after GM offered a 25 percent discount on top of the Volt's already steep price discounts, which are three to four times higher than the rest of the auto industry. GM's attempt at building a highly fuel-efficient, environmentally friendly car may have been good for the planet, but it has been a drag on GM's profits and finances.[76]

Being socially responsible may be the right thing to do, and it is usually associated with increased profits, but it doesn't guarantee business success.

STUDY TOOLS ③

READY TO STUDY?

LOCATED IN TEXTBOOK:

☐ Rip out the Chapter Review Card at the back of the book to have a summary of the chapter and key terms handy.

LOCATED AT NELSON.COM/STUDENT:

☐ Access the eBook or use the ReadSpeaker feature to listen to the chapter on the go.

☐ Prepare for tests with practice quizzes.

☐ Review key terms with flashcards and the glossary feature.

☐ Work through key concepts with case studies and Management Decision Exercises.

☐ Explore practical examples with You Make the Decision Activities.

Learning like never before.

4LTR
PRESS

nelson.com/student

4 Planning and Decision Making

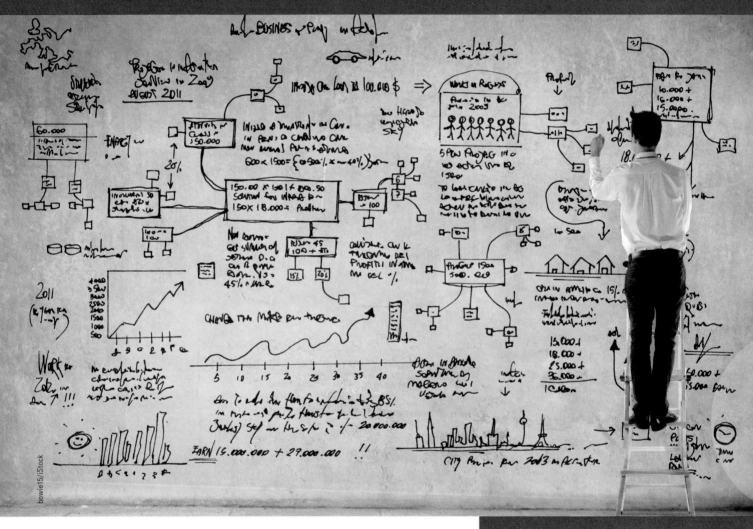

bowie15/iStock

LEARNING OUTCOMES

After studying this chapter, you will be able to...

4-1 Discuss the benefits and pitfalls of planning.

4-2 Describe how to make a plan that works.

4-3 Discuss how companies can use plans at all management levels, from top to bottom.

4-4 Explain the steps and limits to rational decision making.

4-5 Explain how group decisions and group decision-making techniques can improve decision making.

After you finish this chapter, go to **PAGE 85** for

STUDY TOOLS

Aiming for Success

Joining Yamaha Motor Canada was a decision with long-term—and high-flying—consequences for Peter Smallman-Tew. Over the years he has risen from sales rep to the top of the sales and marketing ladder and has travelled the world on business. Peter started work at Yamaha in 1986, the year he graduated from the Business Administration Marketing Program at St. Lawrence College in Kingston, Ontario. These days he is vice president of sales and marketing for Yamaha Motor Canada and also vice president of North American operations for the snowmobile division for Yamaha. His office is in Toronto, but he travels often to Yamaha's US offices, as well as to the parent company, Yamaha Motor Co., in Japan. Yamaha Canada has 180 employees and about 460 Canadian dealerships. It sells snowmobiles, motorcycles and scooters, all-terrain vehicles, outboard motors, personal watercraft, and accessories. The manufacturing is done outside Canada. The North American snowmobile industry alone is a multibillion-dollar one, and one in which Peter was part of a major planning and decision-making process a few years ago that resulted in Yamaha entering an unusual partnership with Arctic Cat, a US-based manufacturer of snowmobiles and ATVs. Under that partnership, Arctic Cat manufactures Yamaha snowmobiles in the United States using many Arctic Cat components and that company uses Yamaha engines in some of its products.

1. How important has planning been to you as a manager?

I believe planning is the key to the success of any action taken in business or your personal life. To be able to execute with excellence relies solely on how well you have planned and adhere to the process so you can truly control your objective or outcome.

2. Do you consciously use S.M.A.R.T. (specific, measurable, attainable, realistic, timely) guidelines for achieving goals?

Yes, I definitely use a similar process involving these steps. I have found that the amount of effort put into planning controls the outcome of your objective. When utilizing a planning tool like S.M.A.R.T., you can clearly focus on your objective and not overlook key components that are lost on poor or panic planning.

3. What's the most important factor in planning, in your experience?

Setting measurable, trackable goals. I often say to my executive team: "You cannot manage what you not measuring." Every plan needs KPI—key performance indicators.

4. What have you learned, in a nutshell, about decision making as a manager?

I would rather learn from making the wrong decision than lose an opportunity by not making a decision. Weaker managers will procrastinate to the point that the momentum of growth or positive change is lost in waiting for the perfect plan.

Decisions should always be taken seriously. I am a firm believer that in business you need to be committed to a decision. *Yes* and *no* are fairly straightforward decisions. There is nothing worse in my opinion than the word *maybe*—to me this is just a deferred *no*!

5. You played a major role in what is regarded as a daring decision for Yamaha to partner with Arctic Cat. How important is taking daring approaches like this?

It may be seen from outside that this was a daring approach, but it started from thinking outside the box, and looking at our current business practice with different eyes. This alliance was intriguing as it brought two different business processes together, a Japanese company with a North American company. Our processes and decision making were completely different, and rather than adapting to each other's processes we found the relationship flourished when we worked together to form a new business process taking the best from both companies. The benefit to Arctic Cat was learning a Japanese company's decision processes that give the same importance to every detail of a plan, where Yamaha learned from Arctic Cat that speed in the decision process can also yield excellence in the results.

6. Does creativity come into your work picture often?

Absolutely! I welcome it, as creativity reveals opportunity. In Japan, our engineers have "after-5 projects"—after 5 o'clock on their regular work day they are allowed to use the resources and systems to invent, dream, or be creative in pretty much anything they wish. I know for a fact that some of Yamaha Motors' most innovative products or product features come from allowing this creative freedom.

7. Have groups played much of a role in your decision-making experience?

Yes, a group or team approach, which I prefer to call it, allows everyone to have a voice but also understand why and how decisions are made. To make decisions is truly a skill. In business, sometimes the decision by a team may not be the right one for the company, and that's why it's important that the team understand the role and needs of the decision maker.

8. What is the best advice you've ever received?

Be accountable—don't live your life on "what if's."

For the full interview go online to nelson.com/student

Photo and interview courtesy of Peter Smallman-Tew

4-1 BENEFITS AND PITFALLS OF PLANNING

Even inexperienced managers know that planning and decision making are an important part of a manager's job. *Figure out what the problem is. Generate potential solutions or plans. Pick the best one. Make it work.* Experienced managers, however, know how hard it really is to make good plans and decisions. One seasoned manager says: "I think the biggest surprises are the problems. Maybe I had never seen it before. Maybe I was protected by my management when I was in sales. Maybe I had delusions of grandeur, I don't know. I just know how disillusioning and frustrating it is to be hit with problems and conflicts all day and not be able to solve them very cleanly."[1]

Planning is choosing a goal and developing a method or strategy to achieve that goal. Facing increased competition, changing consumer tastes, and a damaged reputation due to a deadly contaminated meat recall, Maple Leaf Foods, one of Canada's largest food producers, embarked on an ambitious five-year "value creation plan" to help restore the company's financial position. The plan included a major organizational restructuring, enhancements to the company's level of technology and infrastructure, and operational changes to significantly reduce costs and improve productivity. By the time the five-year plan wrapped up in 2015, the company had refocused its strategic direction (divesting itself of non-core businesses, consolidating, and closing unprofitable facilities), revamped its product line, and spent $1 billion in capital investment that included a new state of the art distribution facility. As soon as the company announced the successful end of its five-year plan, it launched its next initiative—a comprehensive sustainability strategy focused on advancing nutrition and health, community involvement, animal care, and environmental sustainability.[2]

Are you one of those naturally organized people who always make a daily to-do list and never miss a deadline? Or are you one of those flexible, creative, go-with-the-flow people who dislike planning because it restricts their freedom? Some people are natural planners. They love it and can see only its benefits. Others dislike planning and can see only its disadvantages. It turns out that *both* views have real value.

Planning choosing a goal and developing a strategy to achieve that goal.

*Planning has advantages and disadvantages. Let's learn about **4-1a the benefits of planning** and **4-1b the pitfalls of planning**.*

4-1a Benefits of Planning

Planning offers four important benefits: provides direction, intensifies effort, reduces uncertainty, and facilitates decision making.

First, having plans in place allows everyone in the organization to understand how their efforts can contribute to achieving an organization's goals. Planning through goal setting is particularly important when an organization is undergoing a major transition. According to Irving Wladowsky-Berger of the Institute for Data Driven Design, "A major way of rallying the organization to embrace the needed transformation is to have a compelling target to shoot for, a kind of promised land everyone can aim for instead of wandering in the desert without a clear path forward."[3]

Second, plans encourage managers and employees to direct greater efforts *toward* activities that help accomplish their goals and *away* from activities that don't.[4] Employees put forth greater effort when following a plan. Take two employees. Instruct one to "do your best" to increase production. Instruct the other to achieve a 2 percent increase in production each month. Research shows that the one with the specific plan will work harder.[5] There is no better way to improve the performance of the people who work in a company than to have them set goals and develop strategies for achieving those goals.

Third, planning reduces uncertainty. As part of the planning process, managers consider future changes and potential problems that might arise and then develop the appropriate strategies to respond. In doing so, planning can help minimize the negative impact that can occur as a result of future events and enhance a manager's ability to deal with change.

Fourth, planning facilitates decision making. When an organization has plans in place, managers and employees will be able to refer to those plans to help guide current decision making. In the absence of plans, individuals within an organization may not consider how actions may impact the organization as a whole and/or in the long run. On average, companies with plans have larger profits and grow much faster than companies that don't.[6] ***Despite the significant benefits associated with planning, planning is not a cure-all***.

4-1b Planning Pitfalls

Despite the significant benefits associated with planning, there are some criticisms of plans and, in fact, many management authors and consultants believe that planning can harm companies in several ways.[7]

The first pitfall of planning is that it can impede change and prevent or slow needed adaptation. Sometimes companies become so committed to achieving the goals set forth in their plans or following the strategies and tactics spelled out in them that they fail to notice when their plans aren't working or their goals need to change. When it comes to environmentally sound cars, General Motors initially dismissed the industry's increased interest in electric vehicles because of its "culture wedded to big cars and horsepower." In the mid-1990s, when Toyota formed its "green group"—which led to the development of the company's first electric hybrid, the Prius—GM decided to kill its electric car program to focus on profitable SUVs (sport utility vehicles). However, as oil prices began to rise drastically and interest in electric vehicles continued to surge, GM was forced to play "catch up" and restarted its work on hybrid vehicles. By 2010, GM launched the Chevy Volt, a battery-powered car that combines the use of off-peak electricity for overnight recharging of the batteries with daytime recharging by a small gas engine. However, the competitive arena for electric cars had changed quite a bit by then. The Volt now faces competition from a number of other manufacturers' models, including the Chevy Spark, Nissan Leaf, Toyota RAV4 EV, and Ford Focus, as well as new entries from Tesla Motors and BMW. Some still question GM's decision to abandon the electric car; a documentary titled *Who Killed the Electric Car?* speculated that other forces may have contributed to this costly decision, including pressure from large oil companies and other stakeholders in the automotive industry.[8]

The second pitfall is that planning can create a false sense of certainty. Planners sometimes feel that they know exactly what the future holds for their competitors, their suppliers, and their companies. However, all plans are based on assumptions. "The price of gasoline will increase by 4 percent per year." "Exports will continue to rise." For plans to work, the assumptions on which they are based must hold true. If the assumptions turn out to be false, then the plans based on them are likely to fail.

The third potential pitfall of planning is the detachment of planners. In theory, strategic planners and top-level managers are supposed to focus on the big picture and not concern themselves with the details of implementation (i.e., carrying out the plan). According to management professor Henry Mintzberg, detachment leads planners to plan for things they don't understand.[9]

4-2 HOW TO MAKE A PLAN THAT WORKS

Planning is a double-edged sword. If done right, it brings about tremendous increases in individual and organizational performance. If done wrong, it can have just the opposite effect and harm individual and organizational performance.

In this section, you will learn how to make a plan that works. As depicted in Exhibit 4.1, planning consists of 4-2a setting goals, 4-2b developing commitment to the goals, 4-2c developing effective action plans, 4-2d tracking progress toward goal achievement, and 4-2e maintaining flexibility.

4-2a Setting Goals

The first step in planning is to set goals. To direct behaviour and increase effort, goals need to be specific and challenging.[10] In 2011, the city of Vancouver announced details of an ambitious plan to become The Greenest City in the World by 2020. Spearheaded by Vancouver mayor Gregor Robertson, a team of local experts spent two years researching best practices from leading green cities around the world and then developed a plan to help Vancouver establish itself as the world's greenest city. The

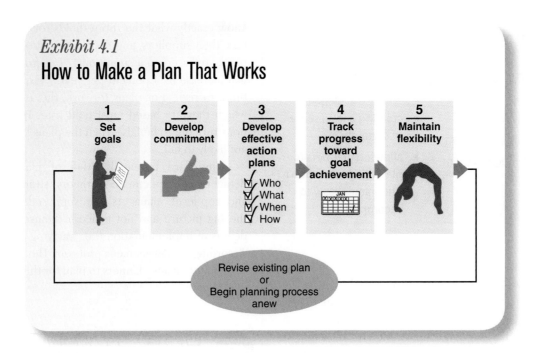

Exhibit 4.1

How to Make a Plan That Works

1	2	3	4	5
Set goals	**Develop commitment**	**Develop effective action plans**	**Track progress toward goal achievement**	**Maintain flexibility**

☑ Who
☑ What
☑ When
☑ How

Revise existing plan
or
Begin planning process
anew

result was the Green City Action Plan (GCAP), which outlined 10 goal areas and 15 measurable targets to serve as checkpoints to guide the execution of the plan.[11] See Exhibit 4.2 for the details of the GCAP goals.

One way of writing effective goals for yourself, your job, or your company is to use the S.M.A.R.T. guidelines. **S.M.A.R.T. goals** are **s**pecific, **m**easurable, **a**ttainable, **r**ealistic, and **t**imely.[12] Let's examine Vancouver's GCAP to see how it measures up to the S.M.A.R.T. guidelines for goals.

First, are the goals *specific*? Yes, because for each of the 10 overall goal areas, specific targets have been identified and serve as the benchmark for activities. For example, in the goal area relating to zero waste, the GCAP specifies that the target for 2020 is to reduce solid waste going to landfill and incinerator by 50 percent from 2008 levels or 480,000 tonnes.[13] Besides being specific, the goals are intended to be *measurable*, since for each goal area the GCAP has identified indicators as well as baseline measurements to serve as the comparison. For some of those goals, the measurement indicator is quite discrete, while other goals are more complex in terms of measurement capabilities. For example, in the access to nature area, the goal stipulated that 150,000 new trees be planted within the city and, as of 2014, city officials reported that 37,000 new trees had been planted. In the green transportation area, the goal was to make walking,

cycling, and public transit the preferred mode (over 50 percent) of transportation for Vancouver residents by 2020. Based on the measurement tools employed (trip diaries and panel surveys), Vancouver was able to achieve that goal by 2014, however, limited data availability and reliability of measurement tools for this initiative means these goals are not as easy to measure as other goal areas.[14] Whether the goal is *attainable* or not for the most part depends on the overall strategic plan Vancouver has in place to achieve this very ambitious goal, as well as the specific actions used to implement it. As of 2015, over 80 percent of the initial actions outlined in the GCAP were carried out and several goal areas have reported meeting their goals ahead of time, helping move the city closer to achieving the 2020 completion targets, thus the goals would appear to have been *realistic*.

Finally, the goals should be *timely*. As of 2015, Vancouver's overall plan has been well received, with some important highlights that include reducing Vancouver's greenhouse gas emissions by 7 percent and passing one of the greenest building codes in North America, as homes built in Vancouver now use 50 percent less energy than those built elsewhere. Moving forward, the city has identified over 50 new actions to be completed between 2015 and 2020 to help meet the overall targets. Time will tell whether Vancouver will be able to reach all the benchmarks set out in the GCAP and achieve the title, "Greenest City in the World," however, the city is optimistic and results are encouraging. Deputy city manager Sadhu Johnson explains, "You can't walk one block without seeing the impact the of the Greenest City Action Plan, whether it is a new composting container, a Car2Go vehicle you

S.M.A.R.T. goals goals that are specific, measurable, attainable, realistic, and timely.

Exhibit 4.2
Vancouver's Green City Action Plan

Goal 1: Green economy
- Double the number of green jobs over 2010 levels by 2020
- Double the number of companies that are actively engaged in greening their operations over 2011 levels, by 2020

Goal 2: Climate leadership
- Reduce community-based greenhouse gas emissions by 33% from 2007 levels

Goal 3: Green buildings
- Require all buildings constructed from 2020 onward to be carbon neutral in operations
- Reduce energy use and greenhouse gas emissions in existing buildings by 20% over 2007 levels

Goal 4: Green transportation
- Make the majority of trips (over 50%) by foot, bicycle, and public transit
- Reduce the average distance driven per resident by 20% from 2007 levels

Goal 5: Zero waste
- Reduce total solid waste going to the landfill or incinerator by 50% from 2008 levels

Goal 6: Access to nature
- Ensure that every person lives within a five-minute walk of a park, greenway, or other green space by 2020
- Plant 150,000 additional trees in the city between 2010 and 2020

Goal 7: Lighter footprint
- Reduce Vancouver's ecological footprint by 33% over 2006 levels

Goal 8: Clean water
- Meet or beat the most stringent of British Columbian, Canadian, and appropriate international drinking water quality standards and guidelines
- Reduce per capita water consumption by 33% from 2006 levels

Goal 9: Clean air
- Meet or beat the most stringent air quality guidelines from Metro Vancouver, British Columbia, Canada, and the World Health Organization

Goal 10: Local food
- Increase city-wide and neighbourhood food assets by a minimum of 50% over 2010 levels

Sources: VanCityBuzz, "Earth Day: 10 Goals to Vancouver's 2020 Greenest City Plan," April 22, 2015. Used with permission. Found at http://www.vancitybuzz.com/2015/04/vancouver-2020-greenest-city-plan/; City of Vancouver, http://vancouver.ca/green-vancouver/greenest-city-goals-targets.aspx.

Dan breckwold/Shutterstock

wouldn't have seen before this, an LED street light that shines above your head or a new community garden."[15]

4-2b Developing Commitment to the Goals

Just because a company sets a goal doesn't mean that people will try to accomplish it. If workers don't care about a goal, that goal won't encourage them to work harder or smarter. Thus, the second step in planning is to develop commitment to goals.[16]

Goal commitment is the determination to achieve a goal. Commitment to achieve a goal is not automatic; managers and workers must choose to commit themselves to it. Facing a company-wide slowdown in revenue, the management at 1-800-GOT-JUNK, North America's largest junk removal franchise network, came up with a business strategy for combating the recession, one that would allow the company to grow and become more sustainable in the future. The "100-Day Plan" was introduced with the clear expectation that the new strategy would be executed throughout the organization in 100 days. Brian Scudamore, founder and CEO

of the company, explains that "Having everyone moving with the same purpose in the same direction, we figured, would allow us to gain maximum momentum. With only 100 days to execute, we had to be driving hard every single day."[17] Put another way, goal commitment is about really wanting to achieve a goal.

So how can managers bring about goal commitment? The most popular approach is to set goals collectively, as a team. At 1-800-GOT-JUNK, each franchisee was asked to set a revenue goal for the 100-Day Plan and to sign a commitment to that goal. Goals are more likely to be realistic and attainable when individuals participate in setting them. Another technique for gaining commitment to a goal is to make that goal public, as was the case at 1-800-GOT-JUNK. It held a company-wide conference call and web presentation to introduce the plan, following that up with regular 100-Day Updates and a 100-Day Plan blog. Support from top management was also important; it included providing funds, speak-

Goal commitment the determination to achieve a goal.

The Canadian Press/Jeremy Hainsworth

Shutter_M/Shutterstock

ing publicly about the plan, and participating in the plan itself. At 1-800-GOT-JUNK, frequent communication from top management ensured that the plan was being adopted throughout the organization.[18]

4-2c Developing Effective Action Plans

The third step in planning is to develop effective action plans. An **action plan** lists the specific steps (how), people (who), resources (what), and time period (when) for accomplishing a goal. When Nissan Motor Co. introduced "Power 88," a six-year business plan developed to achieve the company's key corporate goals of renewing focus on the overall customer experience and increasing the brand's sales power, it included S.M.A.R.T. goals as well as an action plan to deliver on the plan. The name of the plan emphasizes its goals: by the end of 2016, the company aims to achieve a global market share of 8 percent as well as increase corporate operating profit to a sustainable 8 percent. In order to achieve the goals, Power 88 included plans to deliver, on average, an all-new vehicle every six weeks for six years; to introduce more than 90 new advanced technologies, averaging 15 per year; and to continue to emphasize sustainable mobility, including low and zero-emission vehicles as well as new vehicles to be developed for entry-level segments and emerging markets. Nissan incorporated specific time

frames in the Power 88 plan goals, providing a strong incentive for the company to achieve the strategic results set out in the plan. As of the end of 2015, the company announced gains in both market share and profit margin, reporting a 5.8 percent market share and an operating profit of 7 percent. However, the timeline for achieving the goal of 8 percent market share has been pushed back to allow Nissan time to include the full-year impact of a wave of new products introduced.[19] The company's new market share goal of 8 percent is to be achieved by the company's fiscal year-end of March 31, 2018—which means there still will be an "8" in the plan.[20]

4-2d Tracking Progress

The fourth step in planning is to track progress toward goal achievement. There are two accepted methods of tracking progress.

The first method is to set short-term and long-term goals. Short-term goals often define the preliminary levels of performance that need to be achieved in order to attain the long-term goal or ultimate level of performance. Short-term goals enable you to achieve a long-term goal one step at a time, making these goals less intimidating and often leading to higher levels of motivation directed toward goal attainment compared to relying on long-term goals that may seem very far off in the future, and as such, not as motivating or rewarding. As a result, using short-term as well as long-term goals often produces better performance than long-term goals alone.

The second method of tracking progress is to gather and provide performance feedback. Regular, frequent performance feedback allows workers and managers to track their progress toward goal achievement and make adjustments in effort, direction, and strategies. For many

Action plan the specific steps (how), people (who), resources (what), and time period (when) for accomplishing a goal.

organizations, this means setting annual goals in January, checking in if possible mid-year, and then doing a final performance evaluation at the end of the year. However, the time lag between goal setting and feedback can reduce the ability of employees to make necessary performance improvements. To combat this issue, IBM recently introduced a new app-based performance review system that allows managers and employees to set shorter-term goals and deliver more frequent feedback—managers assess performance every quarter instead of just once a year. The criteria employees are evaluated on also expanded to include business results, impact on client success, innovation, personal responsibility to others, and skills. Research indicates that the effectiveness of goal setting can be doubled by the addition of feedback.[21]

4-2e **Maintaining Flexibility**

Because action plans are sometimes poorly conceived and goals sometimes turn out not to be achievable, the last step in developing an effective plan is to maintain flexibility.

One method of maintaining flexibility while planning is to adopt an options-based approach.[22] The goal of **options-based planning** is to keep options open by making small, simultaneous investments in many alternative plans. Then, when one or a few of these plans emerge as likely winners, you invest even more in these plans while discontinuing or reducing investment in the others. In part, options-based planning is the opposite of traditional planning. Although the purpose of an action plan is to commit people and resources to a particular course of action, the purpose of options-based planning is to leave those commitments open by maintaining **slack resources**—that is, a cushion of resources such as extra time, people, money, or production capacity—that can be used to address and adapt to unanticipated changes, problems, or opportunities.[23] Holding options open gives you choices. And choices, combined with slack resources, give you flexibility.

4-3 PLANNING FROM TOP TO BOTTOM

Planning works best when the goals and action plans at the bottom and middle of the organization support the goals and action plans at the top of the organization. In other words, planning works best when everybody pulls in the same direction. Exhibit 4.3 illustrates this planning

> **Options-based planning** maintaining flexibility by making small, simultaneous investments in many alternative plans.
>
> **Slack resources** a cushion of extra resources that can be used with options-based planning to adapt to unanticipated change, problems, or opportunities.

Exhibit 4.3
Planning From Top to Bottom

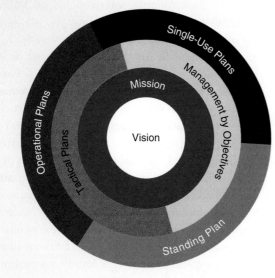

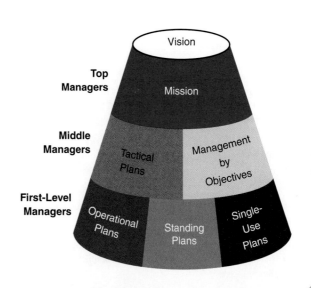

continuity, beginning at the top with a clear definition of the company vision and ending at the bottom with the execution of operational plans.

*Let's see how **4-3a top managers create the organizational vision and mission, 4-3b middle managers develop tactical plans and use management by objectives to motivate employee efforts toward the overall vision and mission, and 4-3c first-level managers use operational, single-use, and standing plans to implement the tactical plans.***

4-3a Starting at the Top

Top management is responsible for developing long-term **strategic plans** that make clear how the company will serve customers and position itself against competitors in the next two to five years. Strategic planning begins with the creation of an organizational vision or mission.

A **vision statement** is a statement of a company's purpose and the destination it hopes to reach. It serves as a guide to individuals in an organization. A vision statement should be brief—no more than two sentences—and should also be enduring, inspirational, clear, and consistent with widely shared company beliefs and values. An example: "To be the No. 1 executive recruiter in Alberta." Another, in this case Google's: "To organize the world's information and make it universally accessible and useful."[24]

An organization's mission, which should flow from its vision, is about how the organization plans to get there—in other words, how it plans to achieve its vision. To define the mission, a formal **mission statement** can be developed to provide a broad statement of an organization's purpose that distinguishes it from others of a similar type.[25] A mission statement can be an

effective way to inspire employees and create shared values. For example, here is the mission statement for Starbucks: "To inspire and nurture the human spirit—one person, one cup and one neighbourhood at a time." That statement guides everyone in the organization and provides a focal point for the delivery of the company's products to its customers around the world. Even though regional differences are integrated into the company's strategy around the globe, the vision is the same whether Starbucks is selling its Assam black tea latte in Tokyo, its lemon poppy muffin in Moscow, or its iced caffe latte in Edmonton. The Starbucks vision is clear, inspirational, and consistent with the company's values and principles, which are meant to guide the organization on a day-to-day basis.[26] Other examples of organizational visions include these: yoga-inspired athletic apparel company lululemon's "creating components for people to live a longer, healthier, more fun life," and the Royal Canadian Legion's "to serve veterans and their dependants, promote remembrance and act in the service of Canada and its communities."[27]

4-3b Bending in the Middle

Middle management is responsible for developing and carrying out tactical plans to accomplish the organization's mission. **Tactical plans** specify how a company will use resources, budgets, and people to accomplish specific goals within its mission. However, strategic plans and objectives are used to focus company efforts over the next two to five years, tactical plans and objectives are used to direct behaviour, efforts, and attention over the next six months to two years. When ecommerce giant Amazon set its sights on entering India, predicting the country would be its largest market after the United States within a decade, it was up to management in Amazon's international division to develop and execute the tactical plans necessary to increase the company's foothold in the country. Competing with two other established online retailers, Flipkart and Snapdeal, Amazon decided to pull out all the stops during the start of Diwali, the Hindu festival of lights and the busiest shopping week of the year for Indians. Amazon's full-scale marketing attack included blanketing roadsides and bus stations with billboards promoting huge sales on popular categories like furniture, clothing, and smart phones; publishing eight-page ads in local newspapers; and, taking an even more brash approach, running a lottery for customers with a prize of a gold brick. Amazon even went so far as

Strategic plans overall company plans that clarify how the company will serve customers and position itself against competitors over the next two to five years.

Vision statement a statement of a company's purpose and the ultimate destination it hopes to reach, acting as a guide to individuals in an organization.

Mission statement a broad statement of an organization's purpose that distinguishes the organization from others of a similar type.

Tactical plans plans created and implemented by middle managers that specify how the company will use resources, budgets, and people over the next six months to two years to accomplish specific goals within its mission.

to change the billboards within hours of its five-day sale ending to announce another three-day sale just a week later. For Amazon, the stakes are high: India has the world's fastest growing major economy and is estimated to represent trillions of dollars in sales.[28]

4-3c Finishing at the Bottom

Lower level managers are responsible for developing and carrying out **operational plans**, which are the day-to-day plans for producing or delivering the organization's products and services. Operational plans direct the behaviour, efforts, and priorities of operative employees for periods ranging from 30 days to six months. There are three kinds of operational plans: single-use plans, standing plans, and budgets.

ZUMA Press, Inc./Alamy

Operational plans day-to-day plans, developed and implemented by lower-level managers, for producing or delivering the organization's products and services over a 30-day to six-month period.

The Napkin Test

Mission statements are often a source of frustration for members of a committee charged with writing one. Employees often read a cliché mission statement such as "We continually revolutionize business data to allow us to quickly integrate unique solutions to stay competitive in tomorrow's world" with glazed eyes. Such documents are often uninspiring and get shoved in a drawer and make little impact on how people work. Mission statements may seem overused and unimportant, however a well-crafted mission can help to focus a business and provide employees with a context for the business and its purpose. In addition, a mission statement can help to provide a framework for evaluating opportunities and deciding whether or not to make changes to your core business model and strategy. Your mission statement must be a clear and concise declaration of your business strategy, and should answer these four essential questions:

1. What do we do?
2. How do we do it?
3. Whom do we do it for?
4. What value are we bringing?

According to communication coach Carmine Gallo, what makes a real difference in the work of an organization is not a bulky mission statement, but a concise and inspiring vision that can fit on the back of a napkin. It will stick. It will inspire members of the organization to be creative, and it'll motivate them to invest their energies into a shared dream. So, if you are asked to attend a meeting to help develop a mission statement, you might want to provide coffee at your meeting—as well as a stack of paper napkins!

RAGMA IMAGES/Shutterstock

Sources: P. Hull, "Answer 4 Questions to Get a Great Mission Statement," Forbes.com, January 20, 2013, http://www.forbes.com/sites/patrickhull/2013/01/10/answer-4-questions-to-get-a-great-mission-statement/#77e2965535e1; "Why You Need a Great Mission Statement," Time, January 24, 2013, http://business.time.com/2013/01/24/why-you-need-a-mission-statement/; C. Gallo, "The Napkin Test; Why It's Time to Replace Your Company's Bulky Mission Statement With a Vision Concise Enough to Fit on the Back of a Napkin." BusinessWeek Online, 10 December 2007, http://www.businessweek.com/smallbiz/content/dec2007/sb2007127_010305.htm?chan=search.

Single-use plans deal with unique, one-time-only events. For example, when its new owners took over Alberta-based Blue Falls Manufacturing (a maker of portable hot tubs and spas), they quickly found that there was no inventory control system to identify component parts needed to service older hot tub models that had been sold to customers and dealers. There were over 1,100 components that didn't have part numbers, and searching for parts became a frustrating exercise; it sometimes took hours to determine which part was needed for a particular model. So the company came up with a plan for an inventory system that would allow it to catalogue each piece of equipment for almost every model built since the company began in the late 1980s. Although time consuming, this plan allowed Blue Falls to continue servicing its network of existing customers and dealers; it also established a process by which subsequent hot tub models and components could be tracked.[29]

Unlike single-use plans, which are created, carried out, and then never used again, **standing plans** can be used repeatedly to handle frequently recurring events. If you encounter a problem that you've seen before, someone in your company has probably written a standing plan that explains how to address it. Using this plan rather than reinventing the wheel will save you time. There are three kinds of standing plans: policies, procedures, and rules and regulations.

A **policy** indicates the general course of action that company managers should take in response to a particular event or situation. A well written policy will also specify why the policy exists and what outcome the policy is intended to produce. Concerns surrounding the amount of time employees spend surfing the Internet while at work, as well as fears about computer virus attacks, have prompted many organizations to monitor web surfing

Rawpixel.com/Shutterstock

and develop policies for managing Internet use, including defining acceptable web browsing and blocking access to non-work-related sites.[30]

A **procedure** is more specific than a policy because it indicates the series of steps that should be taken in response to a particular event. A manufacturer's procedure for handling defective products might include the following steps.

▶ Step 1: Rejected material is locked in a secure area, with "reject" documentation attached.

▶ Step 2: Material Review Board (MRB) identifies the defect and how far outside the standard the rejected products are.

▶ Step 3: MRB determines the disposition of the defective product either as scrap or as rework.

▶ Step 4: Scrap is either discarded or recycled, and rework is sent back through the production line to be fixed.

▶ Step 5: If delays in delivery will result, MRB member notifies customer.[31]

Rules and regulations are even more specific than procedures because they specify what must or must not happen. They describe precisely how a particular action should be performed. For instance, many companies have rules and regulations forbidding managers from writing job reference letters for employees who have worked at their firms because a negative reference may prompt a former employee to sue for defamation of character.[32]

Single-use plans plans that cover unique, one-time-only events.

Standing plans plans used repeatedly to handle frequently recurring events.

Policy a standing plan that indicates the general course of action that should be taken in response to a particular event or situation.

Procedure a standing plan that indicates the specific steps that should be taken in response to a particular event.

Rules and regulations standing plans that describe how a particular action should be performed or what must happen or not happen in response to a particular event.

After single-use plans and standing plans, budgets are the third kind of operational plan. **Budgeting** is quantitative planning because it forces managers to decide how to allocate available money to best accomplish company goals. According to Jan King, author of *Business Plans to Game Plans,* "Money sends a clear message about your priorities. Budgets act as a language for communicating your goals to others."

4-4 STEPS AND LIMITS TO RATIONAL DECISION MAKING

Decision making is the process of choosing a solution from available alternatives.[33] **Rational decision making** is a systematic process in which managers define problems, evaluate alternatives, and choose optimal solutions that provide maximum benefits to their organizations.

Now, we will consider the eight steps in the rational decision-making process: 4-4a define the problem, 4-4b identify decision criteria, 4-4c weight the criteria, 4-4d generate alternative courses of action, 4-4e evaluate each alternative, 4-4f compute the optimal decision, 4-4g implement the decision, and 4-4h evaluate the decision. Then we'll look at 4-4i limits to rational decision making.

4-4a Define the Problem

The first step in decision making is to identify and define the problem. A **problem** exists when there is a gap between a desired state (what is wanted) and an existing state (the situation you are actually facing). For many companies, a discrepancy between forecasted and actual financial results is a red flag that a problem exists. During the last recession, international coffee giant Starbucks reported a decline in revenues and net income, likely related to the economic climate as well as to increased

competition from companies like McDonald's that were attempting to steal market share.[34]

The presence of a gap between an existing state and a desired state is no guarantee that managers will make decisions to solve problems. Several things must occur for this to happen. First, managers have to be aware of the gap. But that isn't enough: managers also have to be motivated to reduce the gap. In other words, managers have to know there is a problem and *want* to solve it. Finally, it's still not enough to be aware of a problem and be motivated to solve it: managers must also have the knowledge, skills, abilities, and resources to fix the problem. In the case of Starbucks, the company responded to its performance gap by closing nearly 1,000 stores and laying off employees in order to trim expenses by $100 million to help restore profits. But it wasn't until McDonald's rolled out a national advertising

NorGal/Shutterstock

campaign for its lower-priced McCafé mochas, lattes, and cappuccinos that Starbucks was finally motivated to cut product prices. CEO Howard Schultz said: "We know customers are looking for meaningful value, not just a lower price. In the coming days we're going to arm our consumers and partners with the facts about Starbucks coffee." Those facts included lowering the price of basic drinks. With profits down 77 percent and same-store sales down 8 percent, and with McDonald's now selling specialty coffee drinks, Starbucks was motivated to take steps to keep customers who might be tempted by McDonald's lower prices.[35]

4-4b Identify Decision Criteria

Decision criteria are the standards used to guide judgments and decisions. Typically, the more criteria a potential solution meets, the better that solution will be. The second step in decision making is to identify the decision criteria relevant to your situation.

Imagine that your regional sales manager asks for a recommendation on new laptops for the sales force, many of whom travel regularly. What general factors will be most important? Reliability, price, warranty, service, and compatibility with existing software and hardware will all be important, but you must also consider the technical details. With technology changing so quickly, you'll probably want to buy laptops with as much capability and flexibility as you can afford. But what will the sales force really need? How much memory and hard drive space will users need? Should you pay extra for durability, file encryption, larger screens, or extra-large batteries? Answering questions like these will help you identify the criteria that will guide the purchase of the new equipment.

4-4c Weight the Criteria

After identifying decision criteria, the next step is to decide which criteria are more or less important. Although there are numerous mathematical models for weighting decision criteria, all require the decision maker to provide an initial ranking of the criteria. Some use **absolute comparisons**, in which each criterion is compared to a standard or ranked on its own merits. For example, *Consumer Reports* uses nine criteria when it rates and recommends vehicles: predicted reliability, current owners' satisfaction, predicted depreciation (the price you could expect if you sold the vehicle), ability to avoid an accident, fuel economy, crash protection, acceleration, ride, and front seat comfort.

Different individuals will rank these criteria differently, depending on what they value or require in a vehicle. Exhibit 4.4 shows the absolute weights that someone buying a vehicle might use. Because these weights are absolute, each criterion is judged on its own importance, using a five-point scale, with "5" representing "critically important" and "1" representing "completely unimportant." In this instance, predicted reliability, fuel economy, and front seat comfort are rated most important, and acceleration and predicted depreciation are rated least important.

Decision criteria the standards used to guide judgments and decisions.

Absolute comparisons a process in which each criterion is compared to a standard or ranked on its own merits.

Exhibit 4.4

Absolute Weighting of Decision Criteria for a Car Purchase

5 critically important
4 important
3 somewhat important
2 not very important
1 completely unimportant

1. Predicted reliability	1	2	3	4	(5)
2. Owner satisfaction	1	(2)	3	4	5
3. Predicted depreciation	(1)	2	3	4	5
4. Avoiding accidents	1	2	3	(4)	5
5. Fuel economy	1	2	3	4	(5)
6. Crash protection	1	2	3	(4)	5
7. Acceleration	(1)	2	3	4	5
8. Ride	1	2	(3)	4	5
9. Front seat comfort	1	2	3	4	(5)

Exhibit 4.5

Relative Comparison of Home Characteristics

Home Characteristics	L	PS	IP	RR	QS	NBH
Daily commute (L)		+1	−1	−1	−1	0
Proximity to schools (PS)	−1		−1	−1	−1	−1
In-ground pool (IP)	+1	+1		0	0	+1
Recreation room (RR)	+1	+1	0		0	0
Quiet street (QS)	+1	+1	0	0		0
Newly built house (NBH)	0	+1	−1	0	0	
Total weight	+2	+5	−3	−2	−2	0

Another method uses **relative comparisons**, in which each criterion is compared directly to every other criterion. Exhibit 4.5 shows six criteria that someone may use when buying a house. Moving down the first column, we see that the time of the daily commute has been rated less important (−1) than proximity to schools; more important (+1) than having an in-ground pool, a recreation room, or a quiet street, and just as important as the house being brand new (0). Total weights, which are obtained by summing the scores in each column, indicate that the daily commute and proximity to schools are the most important factors for this home buyer, whereas an in-ground pool, a recreation room, and a quiet street are the least important.

4-4d Generate Alternative Courses of Action

After identifying and weighting the criteria that will guide the decision-making process, the next step is to identify possible courses of action that could solve the problem. The idea is to generate as many alternatives as possible. Let's assume that you're trying to select a city in Europe to be the location of a major office. After meeting with your staff, you generate a list of possible alternatives: Amsterdam, the Netherlands; Barcelona or Madrid, Spain; Berlin or Frankfurt, Germany; Brussels, Belgium; London, England; Milan, Italy; Paris, France; and Zurich, Switzerland.

4-4e Evaluate Each Alternative

The next step is to systematically evaluate each alternative against each criterion. Because of the amount of information that must be collected, this step can take much longer and be much more expensive than other steps in the decision-making process. When selecting a European city for your office, you could contact economic development offices in each city, systematically interview businesspeople or executives who operate there, retrieve and use published government data on each location, or rely on published studies such as Cushman & Wakefield's *European Cities Monitor*, which conducts an annual survey of more than 500 senior European executives who rate European cities on 12 business-related criteria.[36]

No matter how you gather the information, the key is to use it to systematically evaluate each alternative against each criterion once you have it. Exhibit 4.6 shows how each of the 10 cities on your staff's list fared on each of the 12 criteria (higher scores are better), from qualified staff to freedom from pollution. London has the most qualified staff and the best access to markets and telecommunications, and is the easiest city to travel to and from, but it is also one of the most polluted cities

> **Relative comparisons** a process in which each criterion is compared directly to every other.

Exhibit 4.6

Criteria Ratings Used to Determine the Best Locations for a New Office

Criteria Weights	Access to Markets 60%	Qualified Staff 53%	Telecommunications 52%	Travel to Other Cities 42%	Cost and Value of Office Space 33%	Cost of Staff 32%	Available Office Space 25%	Languages Spoken 21%	Travel Within City 20%	Business Climate 20%	Quality of Life 16%	Freedom from Pollution 16%	Weighted Average	Ranking
Amsterdam	0.42	0.40	0.39	0.68	0.30	0.19	0.30	0.96	0.34	0.47	0.44	0.63	1.7220	5
Barcelona	0.23	0.32	0.16	0.29	0.52	0.59	0.52	0.23	0.47	0.31	1.08	0.42	1.4473	8
Berlin	0.44	0.39	0.41	0.35	0.78	0.40	0.79	0.50	0.78	0.34	0.38	0.29	1.85	4
Brussels	0.46	0.43	0.37	0.48	0.44	0.17	0.42	0.98	0.29	0.37	0.41	0.27	1.6491	7
Frankfurt	0.68	0.57	0.70	1.17	0.38	0.11	0.44	0.57	0.35	0.38	0.17	0.18	2.1578	3
London	1.50	1.36	1.27	1.79	0.27	0.10	0.42	1.48	1.26	0.55	0.46	0.15	4.0295	1
Madrid	0.45	0.46	0.27	0.41	0.52	0.61	0.67	0.22	0.53	0.29	0.67	0.13	1.6989	6
Munich	0.34	0.47	0.48	0.37	0.18	0.03	0.18	0.30	0.47	0.22	0.62	0.57	1.3635	9
Paris	1.09	0.84	0.89	1.36	0.22	0.10	0.37	0.58	1.07	0.30	0.52	0.12	2.8285	2
Zurich	0.24	0.40	0.31	0.37	0.11	0.06	0.12	0.54	0.40	0.47	0.71	0.89	1.3015	10

Source: *European Cities Monitor 2011*, Cushman & Wakefield. Reprinted by permission.

on the list. Paris offers excellent access to markets and clients, but if your staff is multilingual, Amsterdam may be a better choice.

4-4f Compute the Optimal Decision

The next step in the decision-making process is to compute the optimal decision by determining the optimal value of each alternative. This is done by multiplying the rating for each criterion (Step 5) by the weight for that criterion (Step 3), and then summing those scores for each alternative course of action that you generated (Step 4). The 500 executives participating in Cushman & Wakefield's survey of the best European cities for business rated the 12 decision criteria in terms of importance, as shown in the first line of Exhibit 4.6.

Easy access to markets, availability of qualified staff, the quality of telecommunications, and transportation links with other cities were deemed most important. Freedom from pollution, on the other hand, while a concern, was not high on the list of priorities. To calculate the optimal value for London, its score in each category is multiplied by the weight for each category (0.60 × 1.5 in the access to markets category, for example). Then all of these scores are added together to produce the optimal value, as follows:

$$(0.60 \times 1.5) + (0.53 \times 1.36) + (0.52 \times 1.27) + (0.42 \times 1.79) + (0.33 \times 0.27) + (0.32 \times 0.10) + (0.25 \times 0.42) + (0.21 \times .48) + (0.20 \times 1.26) + (0.20 \times 0.55) + (0.16 \times 0.46) + (0.16 \times 0.15) = 4.029$$

Since London has a weighted average of 4.029 compared to 2.828 for Paris and 2.157 for Frankfurt, London clearly ranks as the best location for your company's new European office because of its large number of qualified staff; easy access to markets; outstanding ease of travel to, from, and within the city; excellent telecommunications; and top-notch business climate.

4-4g Implement the Decision

Once a decision has been made, the next step is to implement it. An important first step in the implementation process is for management to provide clear and concise communication of the decision to those who will be affected by the relocation to London. Management would be wise to foster group participation and involvement in the details of the move to facilitate a smooth execution of the decision and to minimize the resistance to change. Consideration should also be given to the allocation of resources and the timing of the execution to maximize efficiency and effectiveness.

Tischenko Irina/Shutterstock

And the winner is ... London. When all the weights are calculated and compared, London is the best city in Europe for business.

4-4h Evaluate the Decision

The final stage of the decision-making process is to evaluate the outcome of the decision and the success of the implementation. Analysis and feedback tools can provide management with a mechanism to determine the effectiveness of the decision. The use of periodic progress reports can help gauge how the implementation is going and also identify any potential problems before they occur.

4-4i Limits to Rational Decision Making

In general, managers who diligently complete all eight steps of the rational decision-making model will make better decisions than those who don't. So, when they can, managers should try to follow the steps in the rational decision-making model, especially for big decisions with long-range consequences.

To make completely rational decisions, managers would have to operate in a perfect world with no real-world constraints. Of course, it never actually works

like that in the real world. Managers face time and budget constraints. They often don't have time to make extensive lists of decision criteria. And they often don't have the resources to test all possible solutions against all possible criteria.

In theory, fully rational decision makers maximize by choosing the optimal solution. In practice, limited resources along with attention, memory, and expertise problems make it nearly impossible for managers to maximize decisions. Consequently, most managers don't maximize—they satisfice. **Maximizing** is choosing the best alternative; **satisficing** is choosing a "good enough" alternative. In reality, however, the manager's limited time, money, and expertise mean that only a few alternatives will be assessed against a few decision criteria. In practice, the manager may visit two or three online computer or ecommerce sites, read a few recent computer reviews, and get bids from computer companies like Apple, Dell, Lenovo, and Hewlett-Packard. The decision will be complete when the manager finds a good enough laptop computer that meets a few decision criteria.

 ## 4-5 USING GROUPS TO IMPROVE DECISION MAKING

According to Blanchard's annual survey on corporate issues, 84 percent of companies use teams to handle special projects (i.e., to make decisions).[37] Why so many? When done properly, group decision making can lead to much better decisions than those typically made by individuals. In fact, many studies have found that groups consistently outperform individuals on complex tasks.

| **Maximizing** | choosing the best alternative. |
| **Satisficing** | choosing a "good enough" alternative. |

Let's explore the **4-5a advantages and pitfalls of group decision making** and the following group decision-making methods: **4-5b structured conflict, 4-5c nominal group technique,** and **4-5d electronic brainstorming.**

4-5a Advantages and Pitfalls of Group Decision Making

Groups can do a much better job than individuals in two important steps of the decision-making process: defining the problem and generating alternative solutions. Group members usually possess different skills, experience, and knowledge, so groups are able to view problems from multiple perspectives and to gain access to more information. So groups find it easier to generate more alternative solutions. Studies have found that generating more solutions is critical to improving the quality of decisions. This can help groups perform better on complex tasks. It can also strengthen the commitment to making chosen solutions work.[38]

Still, group decision making has some pitfalls that can quickly erase these gains. One possible pitfall is groupthink. **Groupthink** occurs in highly cohesive groups when group members feel intense pressure to agree with one another so that the group can approve a proposed solution.[39] Because groupthink leads to consideration of a limited number of solutions and restricts discussion, it usually results in poor decisions. Groupthink is most likely to occur under the following conditions:

▶ The group is insulated from others with different perspectives.

▶ The group leader begins by expressing a strong preference for a particular decision.

▶ The group has no established procedure for systematically defining problems and exploring alternatives.

▶ Group members have similar backgrounds and experiences.[40]

Groupthink a barrier to good decision making caused by pressure within a group for members to agree with one another.

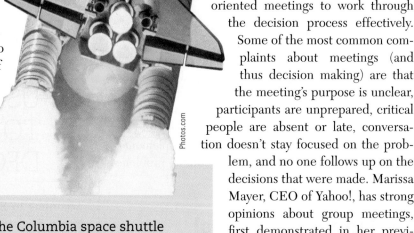

The Columbia space shuttle explosion is a tragic example of groupthink gone wrong.

Groupthink is thought to have contributed to the destruction of the US space shuttle *Columbia* in 2003. The foam used to insulate space shuttles often caused damage to the wing during launch. When *Columbia* reentered the atmosphere, wing damage allowed superhot gas to enter the wing, which caused the shuttle to explode. Previous shuttle missions had revealed this problem, and damage on this particular mission was suspected. However, NASA's culture did not allow individuals to be wrong, and its dependence on public and political support influenced decisions in favour of keeping missions on schedule even when delay would have allowed such problems to be investigated. Managers were reluctant to be the first to point out the problem, and requests for satellite images of the damage to *Columbia* during flight were ignored. The result? Loss of lives and a negative reputation for NASA— consequences worse than those that would have resulted from a delay to investigate the problems.[41]

A second potential problem with group decision making is that it takes considerable time. Reconciling schedules so that group members can meet takes time. Furthermore, it's a rare group that consistently holds productive task-oriented meetings to work through the decision process effectively. Some of the most common complaints about meetings (and thus decision making) are that the meeting's purpose is unclear, participants are unprepared, critical people are absent or late, conversation doesn't stay focused on the problem, and no one follows up on the decisions that were made. Marissa Mayer, CEO of Yahoo!, has strong opinions about group meetings, first demonstrated in her previous position as vice president of search products and user experience at Google. At Google she routinely held more than 70 meetings a week and was the last executive to hear a pitch before it was made to the cofounders. To keep meetings on track, Mayer set down six guidelines. Meetings must have (1) a firm agenda and (2) an assigned note taker. Meetings must occur (3) during established office hours, and (4) preferably as short, 10-minute micro-meetings. Those running the meeting should

Photos.com

(5) discourage office politics and rely on data, and above all, (6) stick to the clock. Mayer's guidelines at Google helped meetings stay focused and productive. As the head of Yahoo!, Mayer continued to demonstrate her belief that, when handled effectively, groups can improve the quality of decisions and business ideas. Her controversial decision to discontinue Yahoo!'s work-at-home policy for employees was based on her belief that in-person meetings provide greater insight and generate more business ideas.[42]

Strong-willed group members are a third possible pitfall to group decision making. Such an individual, whether the boss or a vocal group member, dominates group discussion and puts limits on how the problem is defined and what the solutions can be. Another potential problem is that the group members may not feel accountable for the decisions made and actions taken by the group unless they are personally responsible for some aspect of carrying out those decisions.

These pitfalls can lead to poor decision making, but this doesn't mean that managers should avoid using groups to make decisions. When facilitated well, group decision making can lead to much better

> When done properly, group decision making can lead to much better decisions.

decisions. The pitfalls of group decision making are not inevitable. Managers can overcome most of them by using the various techniques described next.

4-5b Structured Conflict

Most people view conflict negatively. Yet the right kind of conflict can lead to much better group decision making. **C-type conflict**, or "cognitive conflict," focuses on problem- and issue-related differences of opinion.[43] In c-type conflict, group members disagree because their different experiences and expertise lead them to view the problem and its potential solutions differently. C-type conflict is also characterized by a willingness to examine, compare, and reconcile those differences to produce the best possible solution.

By contrast, **a-type conflict**, meaning "affective conflict," refers to the emotional reactions that can occur

> **C-type conflict** (cognitive conflict) disagreement that focuses on problem-and issue-related differences of opinion.
>
> **A-type conflict** (affective conflict) disagreement that focuses on individual or personal issues.

A-type conflict: When disagreements become personal rather than professional.

CHAPTER 4: Planning and Decision Making   83

when disagreements become personal rather than professional. A-type conflict often results in hostility, anger, resentment, distrust, cynicism, and apathy. Unlike c-type conflict, a-type conflict undermines team effectiveness by preventing teams from engaging in the activities characteristic of c-type conflict that are critical to team effectiveness. Examples of a-type conflict statements are "your idea," "our idea," "my department," "you don't know what you are talking about," and "you don't understand our situation." Rather than focusing on issues and ideas, these statements focus on individuals.[44]

Experienced managers likely find it easier to accept the idea that conflict in teams is inevitable and, more importantly, is sometimes necessary for a team to succeed.

The **devil's advocacy** approach can be used to create c-type conflict by assigning an individual or a subgroup the role of critic. The following five steps establish a devil's advocacy program:

1. Generate a potential solution.

2. Assign a devil's advocate to criticize and question the solution.

3. Present the critique of the potential solution to key decision makers.

4. Gather additional relevant information.

5. Decide whether to use, change, or not use the originally proposed solution.[45]

When properly used, the devil's advocacy approach introduces c-type conflict into the decision-making process. Contrary to the common belief that conflict is bad, studies show that structured conflict leads to less a-type conflict, improved decision quality, and greater acceptance of decisions once they have been made.[46]

© alengo/iStockphoto.com

4-5c Nominal Group Technique

Nominal means "in name only." Accordingly, the **nominal group technique** received its name because it begins with a quiet time in which group members independently write down as many problem definitions and alternative solutions as possible. In other words, the nominal group technique begins by having group members act as individuals. After the quiet time, the group leader asks each group member to share one idea at a time with the group. As they are read aloud, ideas are posted on flipcharts or wallboards for all to see. This step continues until all ideas have been shared. In the next step, the group discusses the advantages and disadvantages of the ideas. The nominal group technique closes with a second quiet time in which group members independently rank the ideas presented. Group members then read their rankings aloud, and the idea with the highest average rank is selected.[47]

The nominal group technique improves group decision making by decreasing a-type conflict, but it also restricts c-type conflict. Consequently, the nominal group technique typically produces poorer decisions than does the devil's advocacy approach. Nonetheless, more than 80 studies have found that nominal groups produce better ideas than those produced by traditional groups.[48]

4-5d Electronic Brainstorming

Brainstorming, in which group members build on others' ideas, is a technique for generating a large number of alternative solutions. Brainstorming has four rules:

1. The more ideas, the better.

2. All ideas are acceptable, no matter how wild or crazy they might seem.

3. Other group members' ideas should be used to come up with even more ideas.

4. Criticism or evaluation of ideas is not allowed.

In terms of decision making, brainstorming can generate a large number of ideas and possible solutions, although there are some disadvantages associated with this process. Fortunately, technology has been able to address some of these challenges through **electronic brainstorming** (EBS), where team members share

Devil's advocacy a decision-making method in which an individual or a subgroup is assigned the role of a critic.

Nominal group technique a decision-making method that begins and ends by having group members quietly write down and evaluate ideas to be shared with the group.

Brainstorming a decision-making method in which group members build on one another's ideas to generate as many alternative solutions as possible.

Electronic brainstorming a decision-making method in which group members use computers to build on one another's ideas and generate many alternative solutions.

Brainwriting Techniques

Another take on traditional brainstorming is known as brainwriting, where group members sit together around a table; however, instead of expressing ideas through verbal communication, each participant writes down his or her ideas anonymously on sheets of paper or cards and then the ideas are distributed using a variety of formats to help spark more ideas. Some of the brainwriting approaches include the following:

▶ In the *6–3–5 technique*, 6 group members each write down 3 ideas and then hand in their paper. This is repeated 5 times so that in the end, 108 ideas can be collected in a short amount of time.

▶ *Brainpooling* has participants record their ideas on a sheet of paper, then place their paper in the middle of the table and pick up someone else's paper, adding or modifying the ideas on that paper and then handing that paper in. The process continues until no one has any other ideas left.

▶ *Idea card brainwriting* attempts to generate extreme creativity, as participants each write down an absurd,

off-the-wall idea or solution on an index card. The card is then passed to the person on the right, who then writes down the first thing that comes to mind after reading that card. The process continues for a few rounds and then the ideas are shared with the group.

Monashee Frantz/OJO Images/Getty Images

Sources: L. Thompson, "How to Neutralize a Meeting Tyrant," *CNN Money*, February 11, 2013, http://management.fortune.cnn.com/2013/02/11/meetings-conversation-dominator-work/; N. Michinov, "Is Electronic Brainstorming or Brainwriting the Best Way to Improve Creative Performance in Groups?" *Journal of Applied Social Psychology*, 2012, 42, S1, pp. E222–E243; "The Brainstorming Tweak: How to Boost Creativity in Groups," http://www.spring.org.uk/2013/02/the-brainstorming-tweak-how-to-boost-creativity-in-groups.php.

information online, using computers to communicate possible solutions. These systems have helped remove some of the drawbacks of traditional face-to-face brainstorming, which can inhibit effective group decision making.

In the typical layout for EBS, all participants sit in front of computers around a U-shaped table. This configuration allows them to see their computer screens, the other participants, a large main screen, and a meeting leader or facilitator. Step 1 in electronic brainstorming is to anonymously generate as many ideas as possible. Groups commonly generate 100 ideas in a half-hour period. Step 2 is to edit the generated ideas, categorize them, and eliminate redundancies. Step 3 involves ranking the categorized ideas in terms of quality. Step 4, the last step, has three parts: generate a series of action steps, decide the best order for accomplishing these steps, and identify who is responsible for each step. All four steps are accomplished with computers and EBS software.[49]

STUDY TOOLS 4

READY TO STUDY?

LOCATED IN TEXTBOOK:

☐ Rip out the Chapter Review Card at the back of the book to have a summary of the chapter and key terms handy.

LOCATED AT NELSON.COM/STUDENT:

☐ Access the eBook or use the ReadSpeaker feature to listen to the chapter on the go.

☐ Prepare for tests with practice quizzes.

☐ Review key terms with flashcards and the glossary feature.

☐ Work through key concepts with case studies and Management Decision Exercises.

☐ Explore practical examples with You Make the Decision Activities.

5 Organizational Strategy

Joshua Hodge Photography/iStockphoto

LEARNING OUTCOMES

After studying this chapter, you will be able to...

5-1 Specify the components of sustainable competitive advantage and explain why it is important.

5-2 Describe the steps involved in the strategy-making process.

5-3 Explain the different kinds of corporate-level strategies.

5-4 Describe the different kinds of industry-level strategies.

5-5 Explain the components and kinds of firm-level strategies.

After you finish this chapter, go to **PAGE 107** for **STUDY TOOLS**

Eyes on the World

For Tyra Bermudez, organizational strategy has wide-ranging significance—in her work, she deals only with situations in which two entities in two different countries are exchanging goods or services. She graduated from the BC Institute of Technology in 2014 and 2015, first from the international business and global supply chain management program and then from the bachelor in business administration program. She decided when she was 16 that she wanted to be involved in international business, and now she works for a large professional services firm where she provides trade and customs advice. Professional services companies usually include various business units (for legal, accounting, and trade and customs matters, for example) and, in Tyra's words, "They provide value through knowledge of everything." She says that when she tells people the story of how she got hired, she tells them she underwent a year-long interview, "and it's somewhat true!" She took part in a mentorship program at her university, and she and her mentor would meet monthly to discuss aspects of becoming a professional and achieving one's goals. When the mentorship was over, her mentor offered to stay in touch and said she would be a great fit for his team. "I joined his team a year later."

1. What principles of organizational strategy do you regularly use or draw upon in your position?

During my first week of training, I learned about my firm's strategy. I learned the legal and organizational structure as well as the global strategy. The methodology provided was not a nebulous and vague set of goals, but it clearly outlined how the company goals trickled down to my own goals, in both my personal and professional life.

Our strategy is everywhere around me. Our goals and objectives are set with the company strategy in mind. It was a pleasant surprise to see the logical progression of our strategy and how it aligns with my own personal goals.

2. How do you use what you have learned in terms of organizational strategy?

We use a VRIO analysis, to ensure our resources are **v**aluable, **r**are, not easy to **i**mitate and our **o**rganizational capabilities keep us at the top. Throughout the years, my firm has been through recessions—the most recent being the 2008 financial crisis and now the RMB monetary devaluation. Understanding the value added that we provide to our clients, our people, the economy, and our community is the reason why we [in my firm] are successful.

Individually, having a full understanding of the creation and execution of a strategy, I believe, has given me leverage to be hired at this cutting-edge organization. More importantly, it has allowed me to fully grasp where I fit into this strategy and how I can create value to an already world renowned firm.

3. Why is this kind of understanding important?

Having this understanding is critical—it is self-awareness and environmental awareness. One cannot build a path to success without understanding both the present and the past; in business school we call this a SWOT (strengths, **w**eaknesses, **o**pportunities, **t**hreats) or PESTEEL (**p**olitical, **e**conomic, **s**ocial, **t**echnological, **e**nvironmental, **e**xternal-employee, and **l**egal factors) analysis, or Porter's Five Industry Forces (i.e., environmental analysis). We use trends to forecast events that we outline in our SWOT and PEST analysis, to make educated decisions for both the firm and our personal actions.

The most fascinating thing is that these educated and informed methods of action-taking or understanding of the world around us are done across all disciplines; we simply call it different things, depending on the purpose of the exercise. Having a grasp of this fact is the first step toward understanding the interrelatedness of the individual, the firm, the community, the country, the world. In my new position, I deal with my firm's strategy, our clients' goals, different countries' laws and government agendas. I live intersectionality every day.

4. What is the most important thing you learned in your studies that you apply now?

Communication in every shape and form. I truly believe we will spend our entire lives trying to perfect the art of communication.

5. What advice would you give to someone about to do your kind of work?

I would give them the advice my boss gives me: "Don't sweat the small stuff, but sweat the details."

6. What are your plans for the future?

They involve working in the trade and customs advisory and legal field. It is my passion. My biggest goal is to actively be a part of improving our current worldwide socioeconomic situation. One of the reasons I truly cherish being a part of my firm is that it's part of our organizational culture to be inclusive on all levels. I have recently joined a not-for-profit foundation whose goal is to empower women and girls into leadership positions. My firm fully supports these endeavours and there are groups within the organization that are committed to helping both my firm and the communities around us to foster inclusivity.

For the full interview go online to nelson.com/student

Photo and interview courtesy of Tyra Bermudez

5-1 SUSTAINABLE COMPETITIVE ADVANTAGE

TonyV3112/Shutterstock.com

The iPod has been on top of the market for music players, but for how long?[1] The overall size of the MP3 music player market continues to contract amid cannibalization from smart phones like the iPhone. So wait, Apple is its own competition? Former chief executive Steve Jobs was famously quoted as saying, "If we don't cannibalize ourselves, someone else will," and with Apple selling upward of 70 million iPhones per quarter, it cuts into the iPod market tremendously.[2] Apple dominates the recording industry, yet it is a computer company; witness its release of the iPad 3 in 2013, and the iPad Pro and iPad Plus in 2015, and iPad Air 3 in 2016: all of these have shaken up the computer industry.[3]

Goodbye Google; hello Alphabet! What is Alphabet? Alphabet is mostly a collection of companies, the largest of which is, of course, Google (search, ads, maps, apps, YouTube and Android). Google's best known businesses continue to prosper, however Alphabet also includes newer business divisions such as Calico (life-extension biotech research); Nest (maker of the Nest Thermostat and other smart home products); Fiber (high-speed Internet service); Ventures and Capital (early and growth-stage investing); and, finally, X lab (Google[x] the "moonshot" research incubator that includes projects such as self-driving cars and delivery drones).[4] "Our company is operating well today, but we think we can make it cleaner and more accountable, so we are creating a new company, called Alphabet," wrote Google co-founder and current CEO Larry Page in a post to the official Google blog.[5] "Companies are doing the same strategic thing that they did 50 years ago, 20 years ago; that's not really what we need. This newer Google is a bit slimmed down, with the companies that are pretty far afield of our main Internet products contained in Alphabet instead."[6] The goal, it seems, is to run more nimbly in a portfolio of smaller companies rather than one behemoth of only loosely related things.[7] Exhibit 5.1 shows Alphabet's organizational chart.

Apple has also had a huge impact on the smart phone industry with its various new iPhone entries, but again, it is a computer company—or is it? Google is a computer company (of sorts!), yet it has entered the smart phone industry with its Android phone, with Microsoft and Motorola hard on its heels. Even so, Samsung (with its Galaxy line) and Nokia still dominate the smart phone market.[8] How does a company decide which industries to enter, in which markets, and with which products? Further, how can dominant companies like Apple, Microsoft, and Google maintain their competitive advantage once strong, well financed competitors enter the market? What can a company do to formulate better strategy? How does strategy relate to sustainable competitive advantage?

Resources are the assets, capabilities, processes, employees, information, and knowledge that an organization controls. Resources are vital to an organization's

> **Resources** the assets, capabilities, processes, information, and knowledge that an organization uses to improve its effectiveness and efficiency, create and sustain competitive advantage, and fulfill a need or solve a problem.

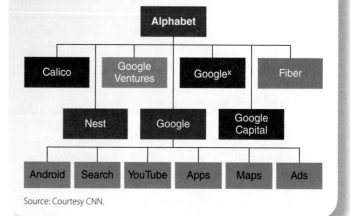

Exhibit 5.1
Alphabet Organizational Chart

Source: Courtesy CNN.

UPS and FedEx—Not Just Delivery

United Parcel Service (UPS) is a global leader in the package delivery market, moving packages each business day for 9 million customers in over 200 countries. UPS operates a ground fleet of more than 100,000 vehicles and an air fleet of more than 500. Another package delivery powerhouse, FedEx, moves 290 million packages per day and has more than 47,500 vehicles and more than 600 aircraft.

Online shopping using smart phones and tablets has fuelled the growing ecommerce industry, which has been driving up the need for package delivery services and benefited both FedEx and UPS. Many online retailers, such as Amazon and eBay, employ FedEx and UPS to deliver their products. UPS Supply Chain Solutions operates in order to deliver these products. Also FedEx has divisions (Caliber Logistics and Caliber Technology) that provide delivery services for manufacturers, wholesalers, and retailers. UPS's New Logistics division asked SaltWorks to test free shipping—and it paid off. Orders soared, topping the previous year by 1,600 more orders. The higher sales volume more than covered the cost.

Uber, the ride-sharing start-up that has shaken up the taxi industry, is now entering the package delivery market: what strategy will FedEx and UPS take in response? FedEx chief executive Fred Smith believes that Uber is unlikely ever to become a major competitor in package delivery. Smith says

FedEx came up with Uber-type services long before the tech start-up was around. While Uber's technology has revolutionized the taxi industry, UPS and FedEx are no slouches when it comes to tech and logistics. Their consistent innovation makes them comparatively less vulnerable to disruption than the taxi industry. In order to handle 290 million packages per day, FedEx employed strategic tactics which included increasing seasonal workers, using six-sided cameras to read package labels, investing in improving its network, and capping retailers' deliveries. For future strategic growth, FedEx purchased its Dutch rival TNT Express in an all-cash $6 billion deal. As part of its continued growth strategy, UPS will also continue its acquisitions of technology companies.

Sources: The Wall Street Journal, http://blogs.wsj.com/corporate-intelligence/2015/03/18/fedex-ceo-uber-is-terrific-but-no-threat/; Forbes, http://www.forbes.com/sites/greatspeculations/2015/06/18/can-uber-disrupt-fedex-and-ups/; http://www.proactiveinvestors.com/companies/news/60868/the-billion-dollar-merger-between-rivals-fedex-and-tnt-express-should-meet-little-opposition-60868.html; http://about.van.fedex.com/our-story/company-structure/express-fact-sheet/;http://investors.fedex.com/company-overview/Acquisition-History/default.aspx ; http://www.trefis.com/stock/fdx/articles/273734/three-key-strategies-driving-fedex-in-2015/2015-01-07; http://www.ups.com/content/us/en/bussol/browse/industries/retail.html?WT.svl=Footer.

strategy because they can help companies create and sustain an advantage over competitors.[9]

Organizations can achieve a **competitive advantage** by using their resources to provide greater value for customers than competitors can. For example, the newest iPod's competitive advantages continue to come from its simple, attractive design relative to its price. But Apple's most important advantage was being the first company to make it easy to legally purchase music online. Remember that prior to the iTunes store at iTunes.com; the only way to acquire digital music was by illegal file sharing. Apple negotiated agreements with nearly all of the major record labels to sell their music, and iTunes.com quickly became the

premier platform for music downloading. Apple was a computer company, not a music company. Even so, it was able to use its resources to create a competitive advantage with an easy-to-understand site that provided free downloadable software for customers to use when organizing and managing their digital music libraries.[10] What will Apple do now that Spotify is on the market, giving you unlimited songs for $10 per month?[11] Well, "Apple Music" might be a strategic answer, and Apple

> **Competitive advantage** providing greater value for customers than competitors can.

has sold more than a billion iOS devices and maybe those iOS users will purchase Apple Music (also at $10/month).[12] Even allowing for those Apple iOS devices no longer in use, and multiple devices owned by the same customers, that's a lot of customers. Additionally, thanks to extremely high adoption rates of new iOS versions, those customers will automatically be exposed to Apple Music.[13] Both companies are also trying to get strategic deals with automobile companies to have their systems installed as original equipment on new vehicles.[14]

The goal of most organizational strategies is to create and sustain a competitive advantage. A competitive advantage becomes a **sustainable competitive advantage** when other companies cannot match the value a firm is providing to customers. Sustainable competitive advantage is not the same as a *long-lasting* competitive advantage, although companies obviously want a competitive advantage to last a long time. Rather, a competitive advantage is *sustained* if competitors have tried and failed to duplicate the advantage and have, for the moment, stopped trying to do so. It's the corporate equivalent of your competitors saying, "We give up. You win. We can't do what you do, and we're not even going to try to do it anymore." Jay Barney introduced the VRIO framework, which stands for four questions asked about a resource (or capability) to determine its **v**alue, **r**arity, **i**mitability, and **o**rganization.

1. Is it *valuable*?

2. Is it *rare*?

3. Is it costly or difficult to *imitate*?

4. Is the firm *organized* to capture the value of the resources?

A resource or capability that meets all four requirements can bring sustained competitive advantage for the company.[15] Exhibit 5.2 shows a graphical depiction of the VRIO framework.

Valuable resources allow companies to improve their efficiency and effectiveness. Unfortunately, changes in customer demand and preferences, competitors' actions,

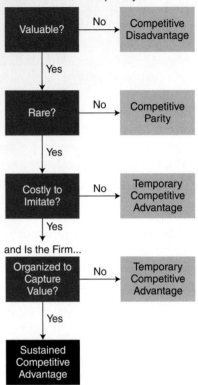

Exhibit 5.2
VRIO Model

Is the Resource or Capability...

Valuable? → No → Competitive Disadvantage
↓ Yes
Rare? → No → Competitive Parity
↓ Yes
Costly to Imitate? → No → Temporary Competitive Advantage
↓ Yes

and Is the Firm...

Organized to Capture Value? → No → Temporary Competitive Advantage
↓ Yes
Sustained Competitive Advantage

Source: Frank Rothaermel, *Strategic Management: Concepts and Cases*, 1st Edition. McGraw-Hill (2012) Copyright McGraw-Hill Education. Used with permission.

and technology can make once-valuable resources much less valuable. Also, for competitive advantage to be sustainable, the valuable resources must also be rare. Think about it: How can a company sustain a competitive advantage if all of its competitors have similar resources and capabilities? Consequently, **rare resources**—resources that are not controlled or possessed by many competing firms—are necessary in order to sustain a competitive advantage. When Apple introduced the iPod, it was unique. The technology that powered the iPod was readily available, however, so competitors were able to quickly imitate iPod's basic storage capacity. As competitors began introducing iPod look-alikes, Apple released new models for the iPod Touch, Nano, or Shuffle, the iPad Air 2, and the iPad Mini 3. With Wi-Fi and two cameras, these latest devices have the ability to play on-demand songs, surf, text, make phone calls, or open Skype as long as you have an Internet connection through Wi-Fi or a G4 chip.

Clearly, valuable and rare resources can create temporary competitive advantage. For sustained competitive advantage, however, other firms must be unable to imitate or find substitutes for those valuable, rare resources. **Imperfectly imitable resources** are impossible or extremely costly or difficult to duplicate. For example, despite many attempts by competitors to imitate it, iTunes is basically unique and has retained its competitive lock on the music download business. Because it capitalized on Apple's reputation for developing customer-friendly software, the library of music, movies, and podcasts on iTunes is still two to three times larger than those of other music download sites. Because the company has developed a closed system for iTunes and the iPod, iPod owners can only download music from Apple's iTunes store. But consumers don't seem to mind. Kelly Moore, a sales representative for a Texas software company, takes her iPod everywhere she goes and keeps it synchronized with her iPad and iPhone. She says, "Once I find something I like, I don't switch brands."[16] She's not alone: it is projected that, by 2017, people with iPads, iPods, iWatches and iPhones will be using iTunes to download more than 45 billion songs and 100 billion apps from Apple's App Store.[17] No other competitor will come close to those numbers. However, as noted earlier, Apple is "cannibalizing" its own iTunes with Apple Music. And right behind the Apple Music streaming service is plenty of competition in the form of SoundCloud, Spotify, Google Play, Pandora, iHeartRadio, and other music blogs (including YouTube and many podcasts).

Valuable, rare, imperfectly imitable resources can produce sustainable competitive advantage only if the firm is organized to capture the resources' value. The resources do not confer any advantage for a company if it's not organized to capture the value from them. A firm must organize its management systems, processes, policies, organizational structure and culture to be able to fully realize the potential of its valuable, rare, and costly to imitate resources and capabilities. Only then the companies can achieve sustained competitive advantage.[18]

In summary, Apple has reaped the rewards of first-mover advantage from its interdependent iPod and iTunes. Apple's customer-friendly software, the capabilities of its iPod, the simple sales model of iTunes, and the unmatched list of music and movies that Apple Music makes available for download or for streaming provide customers with a service that is valuable, rare, and relatively nonsubstitutable, and Apple has demonstrated that it has the organizational capability to continually deliver these services.

STRATEGY-MAKING PROCESS

*In order to produce sustainable competitive advantage, a company must have a strategy.[19] Exhibit 5.3 displays the three steps of the strategy-making process: **5-2a assess the need for strategic change, 5-2b conduct a situational analysis,** and then **5-2c choose strategic alternatives.** Let's examine each of these steps in more detail.*

5-2a Assess the Need for Strategic Change

The external business environment is much more turbulent than it used to be. With customers' needs constantly growing and changing, and with competitors working harder, faster, and smarter to meet those needs, the first step in creating a strategy is to determine the need for strategic change. In other words, the company should determine whether it needs to change its strategy to sustain a competitive advantage.[20]

Determining the need for strategic change might seem easy to do, but really it's not. There's a great deal of uncertainty in strategic business environments. Furthermore, top-level managers are often slow to recognize the need for strategic change, especially at successful companies that have created and sustained competitive advantages. Because they are acutely aware of the strategies that made their companies successful, they continue to rely on those strategies even as the competition changes. In other words, success often leads to **competitive inertia**—a reluctance to change strategies or competitive practices that have succeeded in the past.

Besides being aware of the dangers of competitive inertia, what can managers do to improve the speed and accuracy with which they determine the need for strategic change? One method is to actively look for signs of strategic dissonance. **Strategic dissonance** is a

Imperfectly imitable resources resources that are impossible or extremely costly or difficult for other firms to duplicate.

Competitive inertia a reluctance to change strategies or competitive practices that have been successful in the past.

Strategic dissonance a discrepancy between a company's intended strategy and the strategic actions managers take when implementing that strategy.

Exhibit 5.3
Three Steps of the Strategy-Making Process

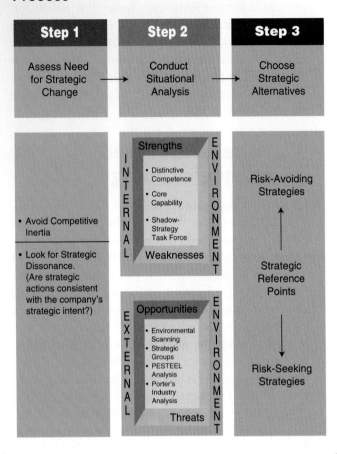

5-2b Conduct a Situational Analysis

A situational analysis can help managers determine the need for strategic change. A **situational analysis (SWOT analysis)** is an assessment of the **s**trengths and **w**eaknesses in an organization's internal environment and the **o**pportunities and **t**hreats in its external environment.[22] Ideally, as shown in Step 2 of Exhibit 5.3, a SWOT analysis helps a company determine how to increase internal strengths and minimize internal weaknesses while maximizing external opportunities and minimizing external threats. This is what Tyra was talking about in the opening vignette. It is important to note that external factors that are positive in nature are opportunities; negative external factors are called threats. The everyday English meaning of *opportunity* does not apply in strategy, however. A company never has an opportunity to *do* something; it is not action-oriented—it is a *factor*. An opportunity (similar to a threat) is an external factor that cannot be controlled by the firm (like interest rates, demographic changes, competition, and government action). In a macro sense, opportunities are factors from the PESTEEL (outlined later in this section), and in a micro sense, opportunities are factors from the Porter Industry Analysis (as outlined in Section 5-4a).

An analysis of strengths and weaknesses may be useful, but more vital to determining a strategic direction is an examination of the external forces acting on the company. Again, these external issues are called opportunities (if the forces are positive) or threats (if the forces might negatively affect the company).

However, let's start with an organization's internal environment—that is, its strengths and weaknesses. The internal assessment often begins with an assessment of its distinctive competencies and core capabilities. A **distinctive competence** is something that a company can make, do, or perform better than its competitors. For example, *Consumer Reports* magazine consistently ranks Toyota cars number one in quality and reliability.[23] Similarly, *PC Magazine* readers ranked Apple's desktop and laptop computers best in terms of service and reliability.[24]

Although distinctive competencies are tangible—for example, a product or service is faster, cheaper, or better—the core capabilities that produce distinctive competencies are not. **Core capabilities** are the less visible, internal decision-making routines, problem-solving processes, and organizational cultures that

discrepancy between a company's intended strategy and the strategic actions managers take when actually implementing that strategy.[21]

Strategic dissonance can indicate that managers are not doing what they should to carry out company strategy; but it can also mean that the intended strategy is out of date and needs to be changed.

Situational analysis (SWOT analysis) an assessment of the strengths and weaknesses in an organization's internal environment and the opportunities and threats in its external environment.

Distinctive competence what a company can make, do, or perform better than its competitors.

Core capabilities the internal decision-making routines, problem-solving processes, and organizational cultures that determine how efficiently inputs can be turned into outputs.

determine how efficiently inputs can be turned into outputs.[25] Distinctive competencies cannot be sustained for long without superior core capabilities. Offering Asian food products is a distinctive competency at T & T Supermarkets. At these stores, one can find every kind of Asian food imaginable. Most of the products T & T sells are exotic and unique. This company's goal is to enrich the lives of Asian families in Canada by offering them choice foods and household items in a comfortable shopping environment. It also hopes to introduce the colourful Asian food culture to Canada's multicultural society. "Freshness" is its most important operating value, one that it practises along with "customer satisfaction" to enhance its one-stop shopping convenience and personable service standards. This is an example of a focused differentiated approach. T & T Supermarkets is just one of Loblaw's acquisitions that were meant to enhance Weston's corporate strategy.[26]

The second part of a situational analysis, after examining internal strengths and weaknesses, is to assess the opportunities and threats in the external environment. In a situational analysis, managers use environmental scanning to identify specific opportunities and threats that can either improve or harm the company's ability to sustain its competitive advantage. They can do this by identifying strategic groups and forming shadow-strategy task forces.

The easiest way to examine factors in the external environment is to go through a **PESTEEL analysis** of **p**olitical, **e**conomic, **s**ocial, **t**echnological, **e**nvironmental, **e**xternal-**e**mployee, and **l**egal factors. Again, see Tyra's comments at the beginning of the chapter. *Political* forces include government trade agreements, taxation, government ownership,

Courtesy of T & T Supermarket, Inc.

and globalization issues. *Economic* forces include interest rates, exchange rates, gross domestic product (GDP) and other general economic indicators, unemployment, and other factors over which a company has no control. *Social* and demographic factors include age, ethnicity, housing, purchasing psychometrics, and other changes or trends that affect consumer behaviours. *Technological* factors include new processes, new methods, new discoveries,

> **PESTEEL analysis** analysis of the political, economic, social/demographic, technological, environmental, external-employee, and legal factors that affect a company and shape the company's strategy.

Shadow-Strategy Task Force

When looking for competitive issues, many managers look to competitors in the external environment. Others, however, prefer to examine the internal environment through a shadow-strategy task force. This strategy involves a company actively seeking out its own weaknesses and then thinking like its competitors, trying to determine how they can be exploited for competitive advantage. To make sure that the task force challenges conventional thinking, its members should be independent-minded, come from a variety of company functions and levels, and have the access and authority to question the company's current strategic actions and intent.

Sources: C. Sidle, "The Five Intelligences of Leadership," *Leader to Leader, (4)*43, 2007, 19–25; W.B. Werther, Jr., and J.L. Kerr, "The Shifting Sands of Competitive Advantage," *Business Horizons*, 1995, 11–17.

Strategic Innovation at Canadian Colleges and Universities

Ken Coates, Canada research chair in regional innovation at the University of Saskatchewan, states that people still have a false view that "If you are really smart, you go to university." He states that "It's an old-fashioned attitude . . . and it's not connected to the realities of today." Innovation and research are becoming a larger and larger part of the "college" system, with George Brown College, Centennial College, Humber College, Sheridan College, and Durham College having recently hammered out a deal with the Province of Ontario to indicate where their research and innovation would be channeled.

Another example of collaboration is Prometheus, which involves researchers from the University of British Columbia,

the University of Victoria, and the British Columbia Institute of Technology® collaborating to bridge the gaps between academia and industry so that British Columbia can become a global leader in engineering and materials science.

Sources: L. Brown, "Universities, Colleges Hammer Out Deal on What Programs They Can Expand," *The Toronto Star,* August 4, 2014; C. Abraham, "Why Colleges Are Increasingly Being Seen as the Smart Choice," *Maclean's,* November 30, 2015.

and new ways of communicating, again, none of which a company can control.[27] *Environmental* factors include effect on climate, waste, impact on nature, air/water/ground pollution, and energy usage. *External-employee* factors include concern for employees all the way down the chain (global suppliers), fair wages, providing healthy and safe work environments, providing workplaces free from harassment and discrimination, and employee assistance programs. Finally, *legal* factors would include laws and regulations that affect companies, compliance with provincial and federal laws (labour laws), international law, and legal obligations for things like pipelines and mining in Canada or other countries. A company's strategy must try to take advantage of external (positive) opportunities and leverage them in a beneficial manner, while trying to overcome or cope with external (negative) threats.[28]

5-2c Choose Strategic Alternatives

The entry of new and more aggressive retailers such as Walmart has caused Canadian Tire to sit up and take notice. In response to this, Canadian Tire revamped many of its stores, opened new stores in downtown locations, refurbished older stores, and overhauled many aspects of its strategy.[29] It is also now using new and highly innovative approaches to retail; one of these involves a business sustainability strategy that includes convenience kiosks, gas bar canopies, car washes, and other nontraditional "big box" offerings.[30] Many existing retailers already compete in housewares, including Sears, the Bay, Home Outfitters,

and Walmart, and even home improvement stores like Lowe's. How can Canadian Tire hope to win? "I think Canadian Tire can't just be tires or automotive. It has to be more than that," says Maureen Atkinson, a retail consultant at J.C. Williams Group. "They can't play everywhere so they are going to have to look for places they think they can play. I'm not sure housewares is the right place, but I think they do have to put a line in the sand and decide that this is going to be it."[31] Canadian Tire is certainly not going to be counted out in this round.

So even when (perhaps *especially* when) companies have achieved a sustainable competitive advantage, top managers must adjust or change strategic reference points in order to challenge themselves and their employees to develop new core competencies for the future.

5-3 CORPORATE-LEVEL STRATEGIES

To formulate effective strategies, companies must be able to answer these three basic questions:

1. What business are we in?

2. How should we compete in this industry?

3. Who are our competitors, and how should we respond to them?

These simple but powerful questions are at the heart of corporate-, industry-, and firm-level strategies.

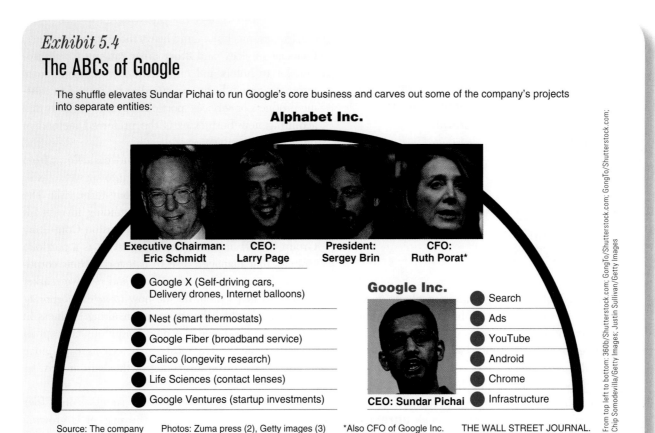

Exhibit 5.4
The ABCs of Google

The shuffle elevates Sundar Pichai to run Google's core business and carves out some of the company's projects into separate entities:

Alphabet Inc.

Executive Chairman: Eric Schmidt
CEO: Larry Page
President: Sergey Brin
CFO: Ruth Porat*

- Google X (Self-driving cars, Delivery drones, Internet balloons)
- Nest (smart thermostats)
- Google Fiber (broadband service)
- Calico (longevity research)
- Life Sciences (contact lenses)
- Google Ventures (startup investments)

Google Inc.

- Search
- Ads
- YouTube
- Android
- Chrome
- Infrastructure

CEO: Sundar Pichai

Source: The company   Photos: Zuma press (2), Getty images (3)   *Also CFO of Google Inc.   THE WALL STREET JOURNAL.

Corporate-level strategy is the overall organizational strategy that addresses the question "What business or businesses are we in or should we be in?" There are two main approaches to corporate-level strategy that companies use to decide which businesses they should be in: 5-3a portfolio strategy and 5-3b grand strategies.

5-3a Portfolio Strategy

A standard strategy for stock market investors is **diversification**, or owning stocks in a variety of companies in different industries. The purpose of this strategy is to reduce the risk in one's stock portfolio (collection of stocks). The basic idea is simple. If you invest in 10 companies in 10 different industries, you won't lose your entire investment if one company performs poorly. Furthermore, because they're in different industries, one company's losses are likely to be offset by another company's gains. Portfolio strategy is based on these same ideas. We'll start by taking a look at the theory and ideas behind portfolio strategy and then proceed with a critical review that suggests that some of the key ideas behind portfolio strategy are *not* supported.

Portfolio strategy is a corporate-level strategy that minimizes risk by diversifying investment among various businesses or product lines.[32] For example, portfolio strategy could be used to guide the strategy of a company like Alphabet, which we saw at the beginning of the chapter.

First, according to portfolio strategy, the more businesses in which a corporation competes, the smaller its overall chances of failing. Think of a corporation as a stool and its businesses as the legs of the stool. The more legs or businesses added to the stool, the less likely it is to tip over. Using this analogy, portfolio strategy reduces Alphabet's risk of failing because the corporation's survival depends on essentially seven different business sectors. Managers employing portfolio strategy can either develop new businesses internally or look for a potential new **acquisition**, that is, another company to buy.

Diversification a strategy for reducing risk by owning a variety of items (stocks or, in the case of a corporation, types of businesses) so that the failure of one stock or one business does not doom the entire portfolio.

Portfolio strategy a corporate-level strategy that minimizes risk by diversifying investment among various businesses or product lines.

Acquisition the purchase of a company by another company.

As shown in Exhibit 5.4, Google has jumped into dozens of new businesses in recent years, but it remains primarily an advertising company, generating most of its revenue and nearly all of its profit when people click ads in search results.

Second, beyond adding new businesses to the corporate portfolio, portfolio strategy predicts that companies can reduce risk even more through **unrelated diversification**—creating or acquiring companies in completely unrelated businesses (more on the accuracy of this prediction later). The leadership of Alphabet can take world-changing moonshots, and mature them to the level of Google and Android, now that the search engine and operating system are ready for other people to run. This also gives them the structure to add in another business line when they make additional acquisitions. According to portfolio strategy, when businesses are unrelated, losses in one business or industry should have a minimal impact on the performance of other companies in the corporate portfolio. Another example of unrelated diversification is the international company Samsung of Korea. Samsung has businesses in electronics, machinery and heavy industries, chemicals, financial services, and other areas ranging from automobiles to hotels and entertainment.[33] Because most internally grown businesses tend to be related to existing products or services, portfolio strategy suggests that acquiring new businesses is the preferred method of unrelated diversification.

Third, investing the profits and cash flows from mature, slow-growth businesses into newer, faster growing businesses can reduce long-term risk. The best-known portfolio strategy for guiding investment in a corporation's businesses is the Boston Consulting Group (BCG) matrix. The **BCG matrix** is a portfolio strategy that managers use to categorize their corporation's businesses by growth rate and relative market share; this helps them decide how to invest corporate funds. BCG, which began as a consulting business in 1963, also introduced the now-ubiquitous concept of the experience curve (costs go down as experience increases), followed by the growth share matrix, as shown in Exhibit 5.5.

The BCG matrix separates businesses into four categories based on how fast the market is growing (high-growth or low-growth) and the size of the business's share of that market (small or large). A **star** is a company that has a large share of a fast-growing market, much like Alphabet's Nest and Fibre. To take advantage of a star's fast-growing market and its strength in that market (large share), the corporation must invest substantially in it. The investment is usually worthwhile, however, because many stars produce sizable future profits. A **question mark** is a company that has a small share of a fast-growing market. If the corporation invests in these companies, they may eventually become stars, but their relative weakness in the market (small share) makes investing in question marks more risky than investing in stars; Google[x] is a great example of this. A **cash cow** is a company that has a large share of a slow-growing market, similar to YouTube, Google Search, Google Maps, and Android. Companies in this situation are often highly profitable. Finally, a **dog** is a company that has a small share of a slow-growing market. As the name suggests, having a small share of a slow-growth market is often not profitable. Alphabet does not have a dog yet, but some bets are on Calico.[34]

Since the idea is to redirect investment from slow-growing to fast-growing companies, the BCG matrix starts by recommending that the substantial cash flows from cash cows be reinvested in stars while the cash lasts (see arrow 1 in Exhibit 5.5), to help them grow even faster and obtain even more market share. Under

Unrelated diversification creating or acquiring companies in completely unrelated businesses.

BCG matrix a portfolio strategy, developed by the Boston Consulting Group, that categorizes a corporation's businesses by growth rate and relative market share and helps managers decide how to invest corporate funds.

Star a company with a large share of a fast-growing market.

Question mark a company with a small share of a fast-growing market.

Cash cow a company with a large share of a slow-growing market.

Dog a company with a small share of a slow-growing market.

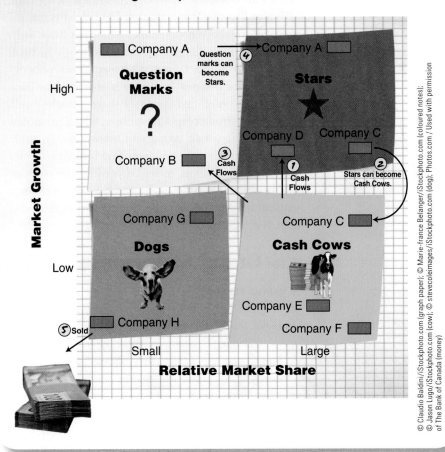

Exhibit 5.5
Boston Consulting Group Matrix

Question Marks — Company A, Question marks can become Stars. ④

Stars — Company A, Company D, Company C

Cash Flows ③ — Company B

① Cash Flows

② Stars can become Cash Cows.

Dogs — Company G, Company H

Cash Cows — Company C, Company E, Company F

⑤ Sold

High / Low — Market Growth

Small / Large — Relative Market Share

© Claudio Baldini/iStockphoto.com (graph paper); © Marie-france Belanger//iStockphoto.com (coloured notes); © Jason Lugo/iStockphoto.com (cow); © stevecoleimages/iStockphoto.com (dog); Photos.com / Used with permission of The Bank of Canada (money)

significant: contrary to the predictions of portfolio strategy, evidence suggests that acquiring unrelated businesses is *not* useful. As shown in Exhibit 5.6, there is a U-shaped relationship between diversification and risk. The left side of the curve shows that single businesses with no diversification are extremely risky (if the single business fails, the entire business fails). So, in part, the portfolio strategy of diversifying is correct—competing in a variety of different businesses can lower risk. However, portfolio strategy is partly wrong, too—the right side of the curve shows that conglomerates composed of completely unrelated businesses are even riskier than single, undiversified businesses.

A second set of problems with portfolio strategy has to do with the dysfunctional consequences that occur when companies are categorized as stars, cash cows, question marks, or dogs. The BCG matrix often yields incorrect judgments about a company's potential. This is because it relies on past performance (i.e., previous market share and previous market growth), which is a notoriously poor predictor of future company performance.

Furthermore, using the BCG matrix can weaken the strongest performer in the corporate portfolio, the cash cow. As funds are redirected from cash cows to stars, corporate managers essentially take away the resources needed to exploit the cash cow's new business opportunities. As a result, the cash cow becomes less aggressive in seeking new business and in defending its present business. Finally, labelling a top performer as a cash cow can harm employee morale. Cash cow employees realize that they have inferior status and that they are now working to fund the growth of stars and question marks instead of working for themselves.

So, what kind of portfolio strategy does the best job of helping managers decide which companies to buy or sell? The U-shaped curve in Exhibit 5.6 indicates that

this strategy, current profits help produce future profits. As market growth slows over time, some stars may turn into cash cows, potentially Google Ventures and Google Capital (see arrow 2).

Cash flows should also be directed to some question marks (see arrow 3). Although riskier than stars, question marks have great potential because of their fast-growing markets. Managers must decide which question marks are most likely to turn into stars (and therefore warrant further investment) and which ones are too risky and should be sold. It is hoped that, over time, some question marks will become stars as their small markets become large ones (see arrow 4). Finally, because dogs lose money, the corporation should "find them new owners" or "take them to the pound." In other words, dogs should either be sold to other companies or be closed down and liquidated for their assets (see arrow 5).

Although the BCG matrix and other forms of portfolio strategy are relatively popular among managers, portfolio strategy has some drawbacks. The most

Exhibit 5.6
U-Shaped Relationship Between Diversification and Risk

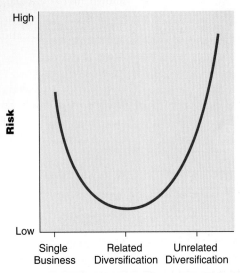

Sources: Reprinted with permission of Academy of Management, PO Box 3020, Briar Cliff Manor, NY, 10510-8020; M. Lubatkin & P.J. Lane, "Psst—The Merger Mavens Still Have It Wrong," *Academy of Management Executive 10* (1996) 21–39.

liked the name Alphabet because it means a collection of letters that represent language, one of humanity's most important innovations, and is the core of how we index with Google search!" Google founder Page said. "We also like that it means alphabet (*alpha* is investment return above benchmark), which we strive for!" They will still be calling the new phones Google Nexus 5 and Google Nexus 6, not *Alphabet Nexus* phones. The URL for the new company is abc.xyz; how cool is that? The new divisions still share Google's well established strong corporate culture, which promotes and encourages risk taking and innovation. In sum, in contrast to a single, undiversified business, or unrelated diversification, related diversification reduces risk because the different businesses can work as a team, relying on one another for needed experience, expertise, and support.

5-3b Grand Strategies

A **grand strategy** is a broad strategic plan to help an organization achieve its strategic goals.[35] Grand strategies guide the strategic alternatives that managers of individual businesses or subunits may use in deciding what businesses they should be in. There are three kinds of grand strategies: growth, stability, and retrenchment/recovery.[36]

The purpose of a **growth strategy** is to increase profits, revenues, market share, or the number of places (stores, offices, locations) in which the company does business. Companies can grow in several ways. For example, they can grow externally, by merging with or acquiring other companies in the same, or different, businesses.

Another way to grow is internally, directly expanding the company's existing business or creating and growing new businesses. In Canada, Staples sells office

the best approach is probably **related diversification**, in which the different business units have similar products, technologies, and approaches to manufacturing and marketing, as well as a similar culture. The key to related diversification is to acquire or create new companies with core capabilities that complement the core capabilities of businesses already in the corporate portfolio.

The Alphabet plan is to have more management scale (multidimensional measurements) by appointing strong CEOs for each business. They'll be run as various operations independently, as portfolios. According to one former Google executive, "It's easier to take the core business and run it like a *Fortune* 500 company," keeping the more speculative enterprises separate. "We

Related diversification creating or acquiring companies that share similar products, manufacturing, marketing, technology, or cultures.

Grand strategy a broad corporate-level strategic plan used to achieve strategic goals and guide the strategic alternatives that managers of individual businesses or subunits may use.

Growth strategy a strategy that concentrates on increasing profits, revenues, market share, or the number of places in which the company does business.

supplies in retail stores, online, and through catalogues to individuals as well as small and large businesses. The company wants to strengthen its ability to deliver supplies directly to consumers. In order to accomplish this, Staples is seeking to grow externally by acquiring other companies that specialize in delivery.[37]

With a **stability strategy**, the company keeps doing what it has been doing, just does it better. Companies following a stability strategy try to improve how they sell the same products or services to the same customers. For example, Subaru has been making four-wheel-drive station wagons for 30 years. Over the past decade, it has strengthened this concentration by manufacturing only all-wheel-drive vehicles, such as the Subaru Legacy and Outback; both are popular in snowy and mountainous regions.[38] Companies often choose a stability strategy when their external environment doesn't change much or after they have struggled with periods of explosive growth.

The purpose of a **retrenchment strategy** is to turn around very poor company performance by shrinking the size or scope of the business or, if a company is in multiple businesses, by shutting down different lines of the business. The initial steps in a retrenchment strategy often include making significant cost reductions; laying off employees; closing poorly performing stores, offices, or manufacturing plants; and/or closing or selling entire lines of products or services.[39] BlackBerry had to go through a retrenchment in 2014, after its sales and market share plummeted. Its stock lost more than two-thirds of its value in 2014 after its BlackBerry phones were overtaken by more powerful devices from Apple and from manufacturers running the Android operating software. The Waterloo, Ontario, device maker says it will refocus on its core enterprise market. It will also consider options for turning the company around that could include partnerships with rivals. We will see if the retrenchment strategy succeeds so that the company passes into the recovery stage.

After cutting costs and reducing a business's size or scope, the second step in a retrenchment strategy is recovery. **Recovery** involves taking strategic actions to return the company to a growth strategy. This two-step process of cutting and recovery is analogous to pruning roses. Before each growing season, roses should be cut back to two-thirds their normal size. Pruning doesn't damage the roses; it makes them stronger and more likely to produce beautiful, fragrant flowers. The retrenchment-and-recovery process is similar. Cost reductions, layoffs, and plant closings are sometimes necessary to restore companies to good health. Like pruning, those cuts are intended to allow companies

to eventually return to growth (i.e., recovery). When company performance drops significantly, a strategy of retrenchment and recovery may help the company return to a successful growth strategy. Daimler experienced just this after it split from Chrysler. The company's ability to focus on its strengths in the luxury car industry (Daimler makes Mercedes-Benz) took it from a loss of €12 million to a profit of €1.69 billion.[40]

 5-4 # INDUSTRY-LEVEL STRATEGIES

Industry-level strategy addresses the question, "How should we compete in this industry?"

*Let's find out more about industry-level strategies by discussing **5-4a five industry forces** that determine overall levels of competition in an industry and **5-4b positioning strategies** that companies can use to achieve sustained competitive advantage and above-average profits.*

5-4a **Five Industry Forces**

According to Harvard University professor Michael Porter, five industry forces determine an industry's overall attractiveness and potential for long-term profitability. These forces are as follows: the character of the rivalry, the threat of new entrants, the threat of substitute products or services, the bargaining power of suppliers, and the bargaining power of buyers (see Exhibit 5.7). The stronger these forces, the less attractive the industry becomes to corporate investors because it is more difficult for companies to make profits. Let's examine how these industry forces are bringing changes to several kinds of industries.

Stability strategy a strategy that concentrates on improving the way in which the company sells the same products or services to the same customers.

Retrenchment strategy a strategy that focuses on turning around very poor company performance by shrinking the size or scope of the business.

Recovery the strategic actions taken after retrenchment to return to a growth strategy.

Industry-level strategy a corporate strategy that addresses the question, "How should we compete in this industry?"

Exhibit 5.7
Porter's Five Industry Forces

Threat of New Entry
– Time and cost of entry
– Specialist knowledge
– Economies of scale
– Cost advantages
– Technology protection
– Barriers to entry

Threat of New Entry

Competitive Rivalry
– Number of competitors
– Quality differences
– Other differences
– Switching costs
– Customer loyalty

Supplier Power

Competitive Rivalry

Buyer Power

Supplier Power
– Number of suppliers
– Size of suppliers
– Uniqueness of service
– Your ability to substitute
– Cost of changing

Threat of Substitution
– Substitute performance
– Cost of change

Threat of Substitution

Buyer Power
– Number of customers
– Size of each order
– Differences between competitors
– Price sensitivity
– Ability to substitute
– Cost of changing

Competitive rivalry is a measure of the intensity or characteristics of competitive behaviour between companies in an industry. Is the competition among firms aggressive and cutthroat, or do competitors concentrate more on serving customers than on attacking one another? Industry attractiveness and profitability both decrease when rivalry is cutthroat. One does not have to look hard to notice the intensity of the rivalry between Molson Canadian and Labatt Blue.[41] The beverage industry is highly competitive in the soft drink sector as well, as illustrated by the intense rivalry between Coke and Pepsi. Does your school offer both, or has a deal been made that just offers the one product at your school? On the Internet, or in any Saturday paper across Canada, you will see pages and pages of car advertisements announcing "Year End Clearance," "Everything Must Go," and "New Models Now Available."[42]

Competitive rivalry a measure of the intensity of competitive behaviour between companies in an industry.

Threat of new entrants a measure of the degree to which barriers to entry make it easy or difficult for new companies to get started in an industry.

The current competition for selling automobiles is as hot and vicious as it always was. Competitive rivalry includes the number of competitors (the greater the number, generally the greater the rivalry); the quality differences (how much each firm tries to differentiate its products and product lines); switching costs (the cost to get a new supplier based on training, retooling, restocking, changing computer systems and contracts); customer loyalty (including brand awareness, usability, history, comfort, degree of dependence (i.e., for medical items/prescriptions)); other differences (such as location, amount of focus, size of company, how similar products might be, size of market). The stronger the forces, the less attractive the industry, and the more acute the chosen strategy must be.

The **threat of new entrants** is a measure of the degree to which barriers to entry make it easy or difficult for new companies to get started in an industry. If new companies can easily enter the industry, then competition will increase and prices and profits will fall. On the other hand, if there are sufficient barriers to entry, such as large capital requirements to buy expensive equipment or plant facilities or the need for specialized knowledge, then competition will be weaker and prices and profits will generally be higher. For instance, high costs and intense competition make it very difficult to enter the video game business. With today's average video game taking 12 to 36 months to create and millions of dollars to develop, and needing teams of highly paid creative workers to develop realistic graphics, captivating story lines, and innovative game capabilities, the barriers to entry for this business are obviously extremely high. The provinces of Quebec and British Columbia even compete with various tax incentives and tax breaks that help raise the entry barriers.[43] Threats of new entrants include:

▶ the time and cost of any entry (as in the video game example, above)

▶ specialist knowledge (it is easy to make a pizza, but not so easy to make an airplane)

▶ economies of scale (oil refineries, mines, and pulp and paper plants take billions of dollars to construct and require huge throughput)

▶ cost advantages, such as in shipping, resources (e.g., electricity), labour, inputs (e.g., coal, oil, and iron ore), technology protection (e.g., patents, copyright, or trademarks)

▶ other barriers to entry (political, legal, etc.)

The **threat of substitute products or services** is a measure of the ease with which customers can find substitutes for an industry's products or services. If customers can easily find substitute products or services, the competition will be greater and profits will be lower. If there are few or no substitutes, competition will be weaker and profits will be higher. Generic medicines are some of the best-known examples of substitute products. Under Canadian patent law, a company that develops a drug has exclusive rights to produce and market that drug for 17 years. Prices and profits are generally high during this period if the drug sells well. After 17 years, however, the patent will expire, and any pharmaceutical company can manufacture and sell the same drug. When this happens, individual drug prices drop substantially, and the company that developed that patented drug typically sees its revenues drop sharply. Threats of substitution include:

▸ substitute performance (margarine for butter, corn fructose for cane sugar)

▸ cost of change (switching costs that take into consideration training, familiarity, quantities, storage)

▸ availability (basketball game for football game, buns for bread, orange juice for apple juice, Coke for Pepsi).

Bargaining power of suppliers is a measure of the influence that suppliers of parts, materials, and services to firms in an industry have on the prices of these inputs. When companies can buy parts, materials, and services from numerous suppliers, the companies will be able to bargain with the suppliers to keep prices low or to ensure quality is high. Today, there are so many suppliers of inexpensive, standardized parts, computer chips, and video screens that dozens of new companies are beginning to manufacture flat-screen TVs. In other words, the weak bargaining power of suppliers has made it easier for new firms to enter the HDTV business. On the other hand, if there are few suppliers, or if a company is dependent on a supplier with specialized skills and knowledge, then the *suppliers* will have the bargaining power to dictate price levels. Bargaining power of suppliers includes:

▸ the number of suppliers (as noted with HDTVs)

▸ size of suppliers (larger firms can sometimes provide better terms, prices and product variety)

▸ uniqueness of service (which means delivery times, delivery volumes, payment schemes, JIT, special preparation)

▸ ability to substitute (which includes technical knowledge, quality, impact on finished product or service)

▸ cost of changing (again, switching costs involved in training, changing systems and processes, warehousing, retooling)

Bargaining power of buyers is a measure of the influence that customers have on the firm's prices. If a company sells a popular product or service to multiple buyers, then the company has more power to set prices. By contrast, if a company is dependent on just a few high-volume buyers, those buyers will typically have enough bargaining power to dictate prices. Remember that most buyers are other companies (business-to-business sales are far higher than direct retail sales for manufacturers in Canada). Walmart is the largest single buyer in the history of retailing in Canada. The company buys 30 percent of all toothpaste, shampoo, and paper towels made by toiletries manufacturers; 15–20 percent of all electronics, videos, and DVDs; 15 percent of all magazines; 14 percent of all groceries; and 20 percent of all toys. And, of course, Walmart uses its purchasing power as a *buyer* to push down prices.[44] All firms buy and sell, so everyone has a buyer and everyone has a supplier, but very few firms or individual consumers have Walmart's kind of buyer power. Buyer power includes:

▸ the number of customers (generally, with a lower number of buyers, the power balance favours the buyer)

▸ size of order (the larger the order, the larger the bargaining power)

▸ differences (similar to the supplier power, if the product or service is very differentiated—in quality, convenience, or service, for example—then the bargaining power shifts)

▸ price sensitivity (some buyers are very price sensitive—many manufacturers are, for example—and in that case the bargaining power would shift)

▸ ability to substitute (similar to the supplier power, if the buyer can substitute, then the buyer's bargaining power increases)

Threat of substitute products or services a measure of the ease with which customers can find substitutes for an industry's products or services.

Bargaining power of suppliers a measure of the influence that suppliers of parts, materials, and services to firms in an industry have on the prices of these inputs.

Bargaining power of buyers a measure of the influence that customers have on a firm.

▸ cost of changing (the old switching costs; if buyers can switch with no cost, then the buyer has relatively better bargaining power)

5-4b Positioning Strategies

After analyzing industry forces, the next step in industry-level strategy is to protect your company from the negative effects of industry-wide competition and to create a sustainable competitive advantage. According to Michael Porter, there are four positioning strategies: cost leadership, differentiation, cost focus, and differentiation focus (Exhibit 5.8). It is important to note that all firms want high quality, all firms want good customer service, and all firms want things like good prices, however, we have to clearly delineate that the benefits of cost and differentiation are comparable or relative to every other firm.[45]

A **cost leadership** strategy involves producing a product or service of comparable quality at consistently lower cost than competitors (because of production ability, sourcing ability, distribution ability, special processes, etc.) so that the firm can offer the product or service at the lowest price in the industry. The cost leadership strategy protects companies from industry forces by deterring new entrants, who will have to match low costs and prices. This strategy also forces down the prices of substitute products and services, attracts bargain-seeking buyers, and increases bargaining power with suppliers, who have to keep their prices low if they want to do business with the low cost producer.[46]

Differentiation means making your product or service sufficiently different from competitors' offerings that customers are willing to pay a premium price for the extra value or performance it provides. Differentiation protects companies from industry forces by reducing the threat of substitute products. It also protects companies by making it easier to retain customers and more difficult

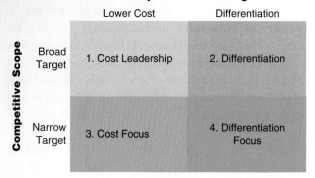

Exhibit 5.8
Four Generic Strategies

	Competitive Advantage	
	Lower Cost	Differentiation
Broad Target	1. Cost Leadership	2. Differentiation
Narrow Target	3. Cost Focus	4. Differentiation Focus

(Competitive Scope)

for new entrants trying to attract new customers. For example, why would anyone pay $2,300 for Whirlpool's Duet, a deluxe washer–dryer combination, when they could purchase a regular washer–dryer combination for $700 or less? The answer is that the Duet washer does huge loads, almost twice what normal washers hold, with less than half the water—just 60 litres compared to 160 litres for conventional washers. So it's incredibly efficient in terms of water and energy and saves consumers time because they can wash and dry twice as much at the same time.[47]

With a **focus strategy**, a company uses either a cost focus or a differentiation focus to produce a specialized product or service for a limited, specially targeted group of customers in a particular geographic region or market segment. Focus strategies typically work in market niches that competitors have overlooked or have

Differentiation is what makes Whirlpool's $2,300 washer–dryer combination a hot product.

Cost leadership the positioning strategy of producing a product or service of acceptable quality at consistently lower production costs than competitors can, so that the firm can offer the product or service at the lowest price in the industry.

Differentiation the positioning strategy of providing a product or service that is sufficiently different from competitors' offerings that customers are willing to pay a premium price for it.

Focus strategy the positioning strategy of using cost focus or differentiation focus to produce a specialized product or service for a limited, specially targeted group of customers in a particular geographic region or market segment.

Amazon's Fashion Strategy

Traditional retailers in Canada have continued to be troubled. Big names such as Target Canada, Future Shop, Eaton's, and Sony are just some of the traditional retailers that have closed their doors. Amazon is now trying to become something different from them, and has succeeded spectacularly, having now surpassed Walmart to become the largest retailer in the world.

Amazon.ca has expanded its clothing and shoe stores on its website, and these items will increase its inventory to more than 150 million items. An Amazon fashion marketing official recently told the Business of Fashion website that luxury brands are not part of the current picture despite reports to the contrary. In an article noting this, Business Insider said the Business of Fashion website had reported that Amazon already has partnered with such intermediate-level brands as Theory and Lacoste. But Busi-

ness of Fashion also stated that Amazon's business model doesn't really lend itself to high-fashion sales.

Back in 2012, though, Amazon CEO Jeff Bezos proclaimed that the ecommerce giant was investing significantly in luxury brands. The *New York Times* quoted him as saying, "It's Day 1 in the category" and "[Our job is to ensure] the designer brands are happy." Amazon will apparently never sell Louis Vuitton products, though. Yves Carcelle, the late Louis Vuitton CEO, told *Vogue UK* that his company had pioneered a model of direct control and would be the only company to sell Louis Vuitton goods. He suggested that this stance would ultimately be the one most luxury ecommerce would take.

It seems that Amazon is being pulled in several directions.

K Asif/India Today Group/Getty Images

Sources: M. Schlossberg, "Amazon Has Completely Changed Its Fashion Strategy," *Business Insider*, July 1, 2015, http://www.businessinsider.com/amazons-fashion-strategy-2015-7#ixzz3kWEEFu5q; A. Hathout, Amazon.ca Launches Clothing, Shoe Stores," *The Globe and Mail*, June 11, 2015, http://www.theglobeandmail.com/report-on-business/international-business/us-business/amazonca-launches-dedicated-clothing-and-shoe-stores/article24905958/; Bloomberg, "Amazon passes Wal-Mart as Largest Retailer," TheStar.com, July 24, 2015, https://www.thestar.com/business/2015/07/24/amazon-passes-wal-mart-as-largest-retailer.html; R. Mac, "Amazon's Purchase of Luxury Retailer Net-a-Porter Far From Certain, But Talks On-Going," Forbes, March 26, 2015, http://www.forbes.com/sites/ryanmac/2015/03/26/amazons-purchase-of-luxury-retailer-net-a-porter-far-from-certain-but-talks-on-going/#37dff0b0106c.

difficulty serving. Containerstore.com sells products in Canada to reorganize and rebuild your closets, sort out your kitchen drawers and cabinets, or add shelves, hooks, and storage anywhere in your home, office, or dorm room. But, unlike Walmart, IKEA, or Canadian Tire, that's all it does. You can never have just a "focus" strategy alone: it must be a differentiation focus or a cost focus (focus on whom, or where, is always useful to state; along with differentiate (how) or cost (how)).[48]

5-5 # FIRM-LEVEL STRATEGIES

Microsoft brings out its XboxOne video game console; Sony counters with its PlayStation 4. Telus drops prices and increases monthly cellphone minutes; Bell Mobility strikes back with better reception and even lower prices and more data streaming. Attack and

respond, respond and attack. **Firm-level strategy** addresses the question, "How should we compete against a particular firm?"

*Let's find out more about the firm-level strategies (i.e., direct competition between companies) by reading about **5-5a basics of direct competition,** and **5-5b strategic moves involved in direct competition between companies.***

5-5a Basics of Direct Competition

Although Porter's five industry forces indicate the overall level of competition in an industry, most companies do not compete directly with all the firms in their

Firm-level strategy a corporate strategy that addresses the question, "How should we compete against a particular firm?"

industry. For example, McDonald's and Boston Pizza are both in the restaurant business, but no one would characterize them as competitors. McDonald's offers low-cost, convenient fast food in a seat-yourself restaurant, while Boston Pizza offers mid-priced, sit-down pizza, pasta, and wings complete with servers and a bar.

Instead of competing with every other firm in an industry, most firms compete directly with just a few companies within the industry. **Direct competition** is the rivalry between two companies offering similar products and services that acknowledge each other as rivals and take offensive and defensive positions as they act and react to each other's strategic actions.[49] Two factors determine the extent to which firms will be in direct competition with each other: market commonality and resource similarity. **Market commonality** is the degree to which two companies have overlapping products, services, or customers in multiple markets. The more markets in which there is product, service, or customer overlap, the more intense the direct competition will be between the two companies. **Resource similarity** is the extent to which a competitor has similar amounts and kinds of resources—that is, similar assets, capabilities, processes, information, and knowledge for creating and sustaining an advantage over competitors. From a competitive standpoint, resource similarity means that your direct competitors can probably match the strategic actions that your company takes.

Exhibit 5.9 shows how market commonality and resource similarity interact to determine when and where companies are in direct competition.[50] The overlapping area in each quadrant (between the triangle and the rectangle, or between the different-coloured rectangles) depicts market commonality (overlapping products and services). The larger the overlap, the greater the market commonality. Shapes depict resource similarity (similar products and services), with rectangles representing one set of competitive resources and triangles representing another.

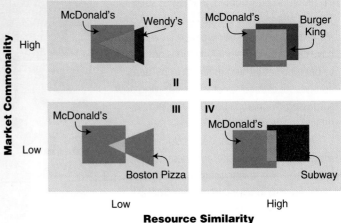

Exhibit 5.9
A Framework of Direct Competition

Sources: Reprinted with permission of Academy of Management via Copyright Clearance Centre, P O Box 3020, Briar Cliff Manor, NY, 10510-8020. M. Chen, "Competitor Analysis and InterFirm Rivalry: Toward a Theoretical Integration," *Academy of Management Review* 21 (1996): 100–134.) 21–39.

Quadrant I shows two companies in direct competition because they have similar resources at their disposal and a high degree of market commonality. These companies try to sell similar products and services to similar customers. McDonald's and Burger King would clearly fit here as direct competitors.

In Quadrant II, the overlapping parts of the triangle and rectangle show two companies going after similar customers with some similar products or services, but doing so with different competitive resources. McDonald's and Wendy's restaurants would fit here. Wendy's is after the same lunchtime and dinner crowds that McDonald's is. Nevertheless, with its more expensive hamburgers, fries, shakes, and salads, Wendy's is less of a direct competitor to McDonald's than Burger King is. For example, Wendy's Garden Sensation salads (using fancy lettuce varieties, grape tomatoes, and mandarin oranges) bring in customers who would have eaten at more expensive casual dining restaurants like Boston Pizza.[51] A representative from Wendy's says, "We believe you win customers by consistently offering a better product at a strong, everyday value."[52]

In Quadrant III, the very small overlap shows two companies with different competitive resources and little market commonality. McDonald's and Boston Pizza, with restaurants in most major Canadian cities, fit here. Although it sounds American, Boston Pizza was founded as a franchise by Jim Treliving, a

Direct competition the rivalry between two companies that offer similar products and services, acknowledge each other as rivals, and react to each other's strategic actions.

Market commonality the degree to which two companies have overlapping products, services, or customers in multiple markets.

Resource similarity the extent to which a competitor has similar amounts and kinds of resources.

Timmy's

Tim Hortons (affectionately known by customers as "Timmy's") is planning to open 500 new stores in Canada and 300 in the United States (where it already owns 800). In Canada, the iconic Tim Hortons has more than a 75 percent market share in coffee and baked goods, as well as an entry in the *Canadian Oxford Dictionary* for one of the chain's shorthand orders, a "double-double" (coffee with two creams and two sugars). Tim Hortons is now owned by 3G Capital (the financial holding company that also owns Heinz and Anheuser-Busch), as part of the newly formed Restaurant Brands International (RBI). Daniel Schwartz, the 36-year-old CEO of RBI, says that "It's all about growth, and bringing Tim Hortons around the world. We are going to be working really hard to accelerate the pace of the brand, finding great partners and exciting places." Schwartz goes on to state that "When we look at the Tim Hortons brand in Canada, we think there is no reason that the rest of the world shouldn't be able to experience what Canadians get to experience every day." As the biggest quick-serve restaurant chain in Canada, Timmy's is well positioned to grow. It has a leading market share of 27 percent in customer dollars and 42 percent in customer traffic, and its traffic

Jin Lee/Bloomberg via Getty Images

share is larger than the next 15 chains in Canada combined! Sixty percent of its customers are there for a single item, and 40 percent of that is the chain's core business—*coffee*. They hope to offset that by having more people ordering three-item combo meals. Additionally, part of Timmy's strategy is to have 80 percent of its restaurants renovated to its new café format with armchairs and flat screen TVs by 2018.

Sources: H. Shaw, "Tim Hortons Will Become Household Name Around the World, CEO Daniel Schwartz Says," *National Post*, February 17, 2015, http://business.financialpost.com/news/retail-marketing/tim-hortons-will-become-household-name-around-the-world-ceo-daniel-schwartz-says; H. Shaw, "Tim Hortons Inc. to Open 500 New Stores in Canada, 300 in U.S.," *National Post*, February 25, 2015, http://business.financialpost.com/news/retail-marketing/tim-hortons-inc-to-open-800-new-stores.

Royal Canadian Mounted Police officer from British Columbia, and now has more than 350 restaurants in Canada. Both McDonald's and Boston Pizza are in the fast food business, but there's almost no overlap in terms of products and customers. Furthermore, Boston Pizza's customers aren't likely to eat at McDonald's. In fact, Boston Pizza is not really competing with other fast food restaurants, but with eating at home. Boston Pizza sells pizza, pasta, wings and more.[53]

Finally, in Quadrant IV, the small overlap between the two rectangles shows that McDonald's and Subway compete with similar resources but with little market commonality. In terms of resources, McDonald's sales are much larger, but Subway, with more than 40,000 stores worldwide, has much faster growth (and a plan to add another 10,000 stores by 2017), compared to McDonald's total number of stores at 34,700.[54] Although Subway and McDonald's compete, they aren't direct competitors in terms of market commonality in the way that McDonald's and Burger King are, because Subway, unlike McDonald's, sells itself as a provider of healthy fast food. Thus, the overlap is much smaller in Quadrant IV than in Quadrant I. With the detailed nutritional information available in its stores, and its close relationship with various Heart Associations, Subway's goal "is to emphasize that the Subway brand represents all that is good about health and well-being."[55] Fast food customers eat at both restaurants, yet Subway's customers have been found to be twice as loyal as McDonald's customers, probably because of Subway's strategy of offering healthier foods.[56]

5-5b Strategic Moves of Direct Competition

Corporate-level strategies help managers decide what business to be in; industry-level strategies help them determine how to compete within an industry; firm-level strategies help managers determine when, where, and what strategic actions to take against a direct competitor. Firms in direct competition can make two basic strategic moves: attacks and responses. These moves are made all the time in virtually every industry, but they are most noticeable in industries where multiple large competitors are pursuing customers in the same market space.

An **attack** is a competitive move designed to reduce a rival's market share or profits. A **response** is a countermove, prompted by a rival's attack, that is designed to defend or improve a company's market share or profit. There are two kinds of responses.[57] The first is to match or mirror your competitor's move. For instance, GE sells 70 percent of the freight locomotive rail cars in the North American market, with the remaining 30 percent sold by Caterpillar. To become more competitive with GE, Caterpillar closed a unionized locomotive manufacturing plant in Ontario, replacing it with brand-new nonunionized plants in Muncie, Indiana, and Brazil. Bill Ainsworth, who leads Caterpillar's railroad business, says the new Muncie plant "will be the most efficient locomotive-manufacturing plant in the world."[58] In response to Caterpillar's cost-cutting moves, GE eliminated 950 jobs at its unionized plant in Pennsylvania, shifting production work to a new, nonunionized manufacturing plant in Texas. With GE's union wages running $25 to $36 an hour compared to the $14.50 an hour at Caterpillar's nonunionized Muncie plant, GE had to respond by finding a way to lower costs.[59]

Modfos/Shutterstock.com

Attack a competitive move designed to reduce a rival's market share or profits.

Response a competitive countermove, prompted by a rival's attack, to defend or improve a company's market share or profit.

Market commonality and resource similarity determine the likelihood of an attack or response—that is, whether a company is likely to attack a direct competitor or to strike back with a strong response when attacked. When market commonality is strong and companies have overlapping products, services, or customers in multiple markets, there is less motivation to attack and more motivation to respond to an attack. The reason for this is straightforward: when firms are direct competitors in a large number of markets, they have a great deal at stake. So when Caterpillar launched an aggressive price war with lower labour costs, GE had no choice but to respond by cutting its own costs of manufacturing.

Although market commonality affects the likelihood of an attack or a response to an attack, resource similarity largely affects response capability—that is,

Red Ocean, Blue Ocean

Using the ocean as a metaphor, Professors Renée Mauborgne and W. Chan Kim describe highly competitive markets as shark-infested waters. The water is red with blood from continual attacks and responses, and any gains made by one company are incremental at best and bound to be ceded in the next shark fight. The only hope for survival is to pursue innovations that take you out of the red ocean and into the deep blue ocean, where there are no competitors.

The war between GE and Caterpillar Locomotives is an example of a red ocean. Canadian Tire's new strategy of kiosks and new, smaller, more nimble stores could be seen as entering a blue ocean. Canada's own Cirque du Soleil is another clear example of a blue ocean,

Red Ocean Strategy	Blue Ocean Strategy
Compete in **existing** market space.	Create **uncontested** market space.
Beat the competition.	Make the competition **irrelevant**.
Exploit **existing** demand.	Create and capture **new** demand.
Make the value-cost trade-off.	**Break** the value-cost trade-off.
Align the whole system of a firm's activities with its **strategic choice of differentiation or low cost**.	Align the whole system of a firm's activities in **pursuit of differentiation or low cost**.

as Cirque du Soleil created a whole new category of entertainment. Perhaps Alphabet/Google will move into a blue ocean; time will tell.

Source: Renée Mauborgne, W. Chan Kem, *Blue Ocean Strategy, Expanded Edition: How to Create Uncontested Market Space and Make the Competition Irrelevant* (Harvard University Press, 2015). Used with permission.

Strategy at the Departmental Level

All strategies have to be executed by the various departments throughout the firm. We need to have strategic human resources policies and procedures, strategic manufacturing approaches, legal departments, and inbound and outbound logistics departments: all of these departments need to act in a strategic manner to successfully accomplish the firm's strategy. One example of this is the strategic marketing approach to pricing, one example of which is the *razor–razorblade model*. This pricing model approaches selling dependent goods for different prices—one good is sold at a low price, and the second, dependent good is sold at a much higher price. The razor–razorblade model is named after King Gillette (I've always wanted a name like that!), who invented the disposable razor. He sold his sturdy razor for a low cost and then made a fortune selling his patented high priced razor blades (which, coincidentally, were the only ones that worked with his razor). Think about the printer–print cartridge industry or the old camera–film industry. This can also apply to something as new as Software as a Service (SaaS) where the same advantages appear. People buy a low-priced application, and then get hooked on the service when the relationship, through monthly interaction, is built up.

The risk involved with this approach is that you can get your "razor blades" undercut (look at what the Dollar Shave Club has been doing). Customers can also feel tricked, or "nickeled and dimed," which could destroy customer loyalty if people don't understand what they've signed up for.

Sources: Picker, R.C. (2015) The Razors and Blades Myth(s). University of Chicago Law School. The Social Sciences Research Network. http://papers.ssrn.com/sol3/papers.cfm?abstract_id=1676444; Yu, E., (2013). Razor Blades: What They Can Teach You About Value Based Pricing. Price Intelligently.com. http://www.priceintelligently.com/blog/bid/179336/Razor-Blades-What-They-Can-Teach-You-About-Value-Based-Pricing; Savitz, E. (2014). *Razor-And-Blades Pricing Strategies In The Digital Age*. Forbes. http://www.forbes.com/sites/ciocentral/2012/12/19/razor-and-blades-pricing-strategies-in-the-digital-age/.

how quickly and forcefully a company can respond to an attack. When resource similarity is strong, the responding firm will generally be able to match the strategic moves of the attacking firm. Consequently, a firm is less likely to attack firms with similar levels of resources because it is unlikely to gain any sustained advantage when the responding firms strike back. On the other hand, if one firm is substantially stronger than another (i.e., there is low resource similarity), then a competitive attack is more likely to produce sustained competitive advantage.

In general, the more moves (i.e., attacks) a company initiates against direct competitors and the greater a company's tendency to respond when attacked, the better its performance. More specifically, attackers and early responders (companies that are quick to launch a retaliatory attack) tend to gain market share and profits at the expense of late responders. This is not to suggest that a full-attack strategy always works best. In fact, attacks can provoke harsh retaliatory responses. Consequently, when deciding when, where, and what strategic actions to take against a direct competitor, managers should always consider the possibility of retaliation. Implementing strategy goes beyond the scope of this textbook, but a Balanced Scorecard (discussed in Chapter 15) and the methods outlined in Chapter 4, along with load charts, Gantt charts, or Program Evaluation and Review Technique (PERT) diagrams, are useful in implementing strategy once it has been determined.

STUDY TOOLS 5

READY TO STUDY?

LOCATED IN TEXTBOOK:

☐ Rip out the Chapter Review Card at the back of the book to have a summary of the chapter and key terms handy.

LOCATED AT NELSON.COM/STUDENT:

☐ Access the eBook or use the ReadSpeaker feature to listen to the chapter on the go.

☐ Prepare for tests with practice quizzes.

☐ Review key terms with flashcards and the glossary feature.

☐ Work through key concepts with case studies and Management Decision Exercises.

☐ Explore practical examples with You Make the Decision Activities.

6 Innovation and Change

Stigur Karlsson/iStockphoto

LEARNING OUTCOMES

After studying this chapter, you will be able to...

6-1 Explain why innovation matters to companies.

6-2 Discuss the different methods that managers can use to effectively manage innovation in their organizations.

6-3 Discuss why not changing can lead to organizational decline.

6-4 Discuss the different methods that managers can use to better manage change as it occurs.

After you finish this chapter, go to **PAGE 129** for **STUDY TOOLS**

Managing in a Modern Setting—the Gastropub

When she was a business student in the 1990s, Melissa Reeves couldn't have begun to imagine where she would be working now, because her Nova Scotia village of Port Williams was a "dry" community with a prohibition on alcohol. But prohibition disappeared with a 2005 plebiscite, and since the spring of 2014, Melissa has been the general manager of a gastropub that opened in Port Williams once it became "wet." She graduated from the Nova Scotia Community College business program (then called accounting) in 1995, worked in a variety of companies, and then went back to school. In 2014, she graduated from St. Mary's University in Halifax with a master's degree in cooperative management and credit unions, and started work at the gastropub: The Port Pub and Bistro. Fondly known as "The Port," the 200-seat restaurant, an hour's drive from Halifax, has dozens of community shareholders and showcases local beer and wine. Melissa leads a team of up to 35 staff. The Port overlooks the Cornwallis River, which rises and falls with the highest tides in the world—those of the Bay of Fundy—and it draws tourists as well as locals. Gastropubs have been around only since the late 20th century, and The Port is part of the international Slow Food movement, which states on its website that it works to ensure everyone has access to good, clean, and fair food.

1. In a nutshell, how important are innovation and change in the gastropub business?

They're important in any type of business. *Innovation* and *change* can be very scary words to some people, but leaders know that in order to stay leaders in any industry, you have to be continually improving systems, processes, and yourself—through professional development—for better service or products to the clients. As humans we are hard-wired to be attracted to exciting new items or adventures, and businesses have to be hard-wired the same way, building a team culture of thinking outside the box and taking risks, guided by our values.

2. What role do innovation and change play in your day-to-day work?

Innovation is key to my day-to-day work and also to achieving strategic goals. It's vital to listen to the team, clients, and community; to incorporate the mission of the business; and to think outside the box, using a lens on all areas of the business to ask, "Why do we do it this way?" and "Is there a better way?" and "Does this meet our mission?"

3. Is creativity important in your job?

It's very important! The key is listening to the team members, and all stakeholders. Taking complaints or feedback and turning them into opportunities, and building on ideas to deliver success.

4. Change isn't always well received. Have you had to deal with that situation?

Yes, every leader has been in this situation. Change is very hard for some people, which is not a bad thing. You need diversity in the team, and sober second thought, which also requires more communication about the change to get the whole team going in one direction.

When developing a new team, you take the easy changes that the team usually come up with—changes they've wanted for a long time—and implement them. By doing this you are building a "trust bank" with the team, and it's a win–win situation. When it's time to make a difficult change, the team will be more supportive of the change given the trust that has been built.

5. How important is communication in the process?

Communication can make or break the team buy-in on the change. If the team doesn't support the change, disaster is ahead. Your communication style must be adjusted to the audience and the impact of the change. Some team members will be on board with just an email, while others will require a face-to-face, one-on-one information session. It's about knowing your teams personally—their individual strengths as well as weaknesses.

6. What is the most important thing you learned in your business studies that you apply to your current role?

Skills can be trained but personality is key to success. Success can't be defined by wealth—it grows out of building a satisfied, fun, hard-working team culture, and making a profit not at the expense of the people or the environment.

When you know how you define success, finding a job that fits that success will lead to a happy work life.

7. How much can you draw on your varied work background in your present job?

Because this is a privately owned restaurant, rather than a chain-run restaurant, the various processes, manuals, and systems that are needed to run the business have had to be specially designed. I draw on my finance experience to put these items in place, my sales and marketing experience to increase sales, and my experience in human resources to build the team to support the sales through the system changes.

OFF THE CUFF

8. What skills or traits have served you best?

Being flexible. And my listening skills—including listening to my gut, and then using an analysis of the numbers to support my gut.

9. What's your favourite app?

Facebook and YouTube . . . as research tools, not for selfies or cute-kitten videos. Facebook is great to see what's trending. YouTube is a great tool for learning about leadership. It's a key tool I used in developing a cooperative management training program.

For the full interview go online to nelson.com/student

6-1 WHY INNOVATION MATTERS

We are surrounded by Canadian innovations—including canola oil, alkaline batteries, and snowmobiles. Such innovations are at the heart of our economy. A patent provides its owner with the legal right to limit others' use or sale of an invention in Canada, and in exchange, the inventor must disclose the details of the invention to the public. Patents are a good measure of innovation at work, being a direct outcome of research and development. Computer and electronics manufacturing has accounted for a large and growing share of Canadian-led innovation over the past 20 years. Mining, quarrying, and oil and gas extraction have also seen a steady increase in innovation since 1990.[1] Canada's prosperity depends on succeeding in the global innovation economy, and this is not lost on the hundreds of thousands of Canadians who are clearly trying to get rich by commercializing ideas.[2] A recent report by the Global Entrepreneurship Monitor found that Canada ranked second to only the United States for its share of working-age population either engaged as an entrepreneur or working directly for one.[3] More than 140 publicly funded incubators are currently in operation in Canada today. Productivity in the innovation economy comes from generating new ideas that generate new revenue. *Intrapreneurship* is also a large part of innovation (where entrepreneurial ideas are created inside an existing company).[4]

Organizational innovation is the successful implementation of creative ideas in an organization.[5] **Creativity**, which is a form of organizational innovation, is the production of novel and useful ideas.[6] In the first part of this chapter, you will learn why innovation matters and how to manage innovation to create and sustain a competitive advantage. In the second part, you will learn about **organizational change**, which is a difference in the form, quality, or condition of an organization over time.[7] You will also learn about the risk of not changing. But first, let's deal with organizational innovations, like using body heat to warm buildings.[8]

*Let's begin our discussion of innovation by learning about **6-1a technology cycles** and **6-1b innovation streams**.*

6-1a Technology Cycles

In Chapter 2, you learned that *technology* consists of the knowledge, tools, and techniques used to transform inputs (raw materials, information, etc.) into outputs (products and services). Services in Canada make up more than 70 percent of our gross domestic product (GDP).[9] A **technology cycle** begins with the birth of a new technology; it ends when that technology reaches its limits and is replaced by a newer, substantially better technology.[10] Technology cycles occurred when air-conditioning supplanted fans, when Henry Ford's Model T replaced horse-drawn carriages, and when airplanes replaced trains as a means of crossing Canada.

From Gutenberg's invention of the printing press in the 1400s to the rapid advance of the Internet, studies of hundreds of technological innovations have shown that nearly all technology cycles follow an **S-curve pattern of innovation** (see Exhibit 6.1).[11] Early in a technology cycle, there is still much to learn, so progress is slow, as depicted by point A on the S-curve. The flat slope indicates that increased effort (i.e., money and research and development) brings only small improvements in

Organizational innovation the successful implementation of creative ideas in organizations.

Creativity the production of novel and useful ideas.

Organizational change a difference in the form, quality, or condition of an organization over time.

Technology cycle a cycle that begins with the birth of a new technology and ends when that technology reaches its limits and is replaced by a newer, substantially better technology.

S-curve pattern of innovation a pattern of technological innovation characterized by slow initial progress, then rapid progress, and then slow progress again as a technology matures and reaches its limits.

Exhibit 6.1
S-Curves and Technological Innovation

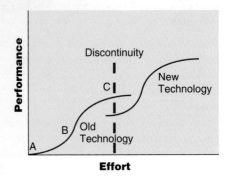

Source: R. N. Foster, *Innovation: The Attacker's Advantage* (New York: Summitt, 1986).

technological performance. Fortunately, as the new technology matures, researchers figure out how to get better performance from it. This is represented by point B of the S-curve in Exhibit 6.1. The steeper slope indicates that small amounts of effort will result in significant increases in performance. At point C, the flat slope again indicates that further efforts to develop this particular technology will result in only small increases in performance. More importantly, however, point C indicates that the performance limits of that particular technology are being reached. In other words, additional significant improvements in performance are highly unlikely because they are at the maturity stage of the product life cycle.

Intel's technology cycles have followed this pattern. Intel spends billions developing new computer chips, and has found that the technology cycle for its integrated circuits is about three years. In each three-year cycle, Intel improves the chip by making it a little bit faster, and, finally, replaces that chip at the end of the cycle with a brand-new chip that is substantially better. At first (point A), Intel produces only small improvements in performance. But, after six months to a year with a new chip design, Intel's engineering and production people typically figure out how to make the new chips much faster than they were initially (point B). Despite impressive gains in performance, Intel is unable to make a particular computer chip run any faster once the chip reaches its design limits.

After a technology has reached its limits at the top of the S-curve, significant improvements in performance usually come from radical new designs or new performance-enhancing materials (point C). In Exhibit 6.1, that new technology is represented by the second S-curve. The changeover or discontinuity between the old and new technologies is represented by the dotted line. At first, the old and new technologies will likely coexist; eventually, however, the new technology will replace the old. When that happens, the old technology cycle will be complete, and a new one will have started. The changeover between newer and older computer chip designs typically takes about one year and, over time, Intel has increased the speed of its computer processors by a factor of 300.[12]

Though the evolution of Intel's chips has been used to illustrate S-curves and technology cycles, it's important to note that technology cycles and technological innovation don't necessarily involve faster computer chips or cleaner-burning automobile engines. Remember that *technology* is simply the knowledge, tools, and techniques used to transform inputs into outputs. So a technology cycle occurs whenever there are major advances or changes in the *knowledge*, *tools*, and *techniques* of a field or discipline, whatever they may be.

Elena Elisseeva/Shutterstock

6-1b Innovation Streams

Twenty-five years ago, digital cameras replaced film-based technology. But with digital camera sales down 40 percent in four years (and still dropping), digital camera makers are losing their competitive advantage to smart phones with HD photo and video capabilities far better than basic digital cameras. Shigenobu Nagamori—CEO of Nidec, which makes electric motors used in consumer electronics—says that thanks to smart phones we should "assume that the inexpensive cameras are dead, just like PCs."[13] Tsugio Tsuchiya—a general manager at Tamron, which makes lenses for more advanced digital single-lens reflex cameras (DSLRs)—worries that "Smart phones pose a threat not just to compact cameras but to entry-level DSLRS," which start at $400 and use interchangeable lenses, such as telescoping zooms.[14] But even that advantage may soon be lost. HTC's Symon Whitehorn says, "I think we're looking at about 18 months to two years until that [zoom] lens barrier begins breaking down and it becomes much harder to justify buying a dedicated camera outside of specialist or nostalgia reasons."[15]

Companies that want to sustain a competitive advantage must understand and protect themselves from the strategic threats of innovation. In the long run, the best way for a company to do that is by creating a stream of its own innovative ideas and products year after year. Consequently, we define **innovation streams** as patterns of innovation over time that can create sustainable competitive advantage.[16] Exhibit 6.2 shows a typical innovation stream consisting of a series of three technology cycles.

Innovation streams patterns of innovation over time that can create sustainable competitive advantage.

Exhibit 6.2
Innovation Streams: Technology Cycles Over Time

Technological Substitution (3)

Technological Discontinuity (3)

| Incremental Change (3) | **Variation Selection** | Discontinuous Change (3) |

Dominant Design (3)

Technological Substitution (2)

Technological Discontinuity (2)

| Incremental Change (2) | **Variation Selection** | Discontinuous Change (2) |

Dominant Design (2)

Technological Discontinuity (1)

| Incremental Change (1) | **Variation Selection** | Discontinuous Change (1) |

Dominant Design (1)

Source: *MANAGING STRATEGIC INNOVATION* by Tushman, Anderson, O'Reilly (1997) Fig. 1-1 - Originally from *Evolutionary Dynamics of Organisation* by Rosenkopf and Tushman (1994) published by Oxford University Press © 1997 by Oxford University Press, Inc. By permission of Oxford University Press, USA.

An innovation stream begins with a **technological discontinuity**, in which a scientific advance or a unique combination of existing technologies creates a significant breakthrough in performance or function. Technological discontinuities are followed by **discontinuous change**, which is characterized by technological substitution and design competition. **Technological substitution** occurs when customers then purchase new technologies

Technological discontinuity a scientific advance or a unique combination of existing technologies creates a significant breakthrough in performance or function.

Discontinuous change the phase of a technology cycle characterized by technological substitution and design competition.

Technological substitution the purchase of new technologies to replace older ones.

Design competition competition between old and new technologies to establish a new technological standard or dominant design.

to replace older technologies—like in replacing a simple wall thermostat in your house.

Most home thermostats simply raise or lower the temperature. Advanced models can change the temperature when you leave for work and come home, but because they're difficult to program, most people just set the temperature manually, greatly reducing energy efficiency. The Nest thermostat, which was designed by the people who created the iPod, has a digital screen showing the temperature and a silver control ring that turns to adjust the temperature. But what makes Nest revolutionary is its ability to learn and program itself. Cofounder Tony Fadell says, "Think of a normal thermostat. Everyone turns it up, turns it down, a couple of times a day—that's a pattern we can infer from. Instead of changing it 1,500 times a year, do it 10 or 20 times and the Nest thermostat can learn from that."[17] Nest has motion sensors that know if you're home; links to your utility company to reduce power usage at expensive, peak energy times; and has smart phone apps to control your home's temperature even when you're not there. The Nest thermostat has been proven by third-party researchers to save people, on average, about 10–12 percent on their heating bills and about 15 percent on cooling bills.[18]

Discontinuous change is also characterized by **design competition**, in which the old technology and several different new technologies compete to establish a new technological standard or dominant design. Because

Courtesy of Nest Labs

of large investments in old technology and because the new and old technologies are often incompatible with each other, companies and consumers are reluctant to switch to a different technology during a design competition.

Discontinuous change is followed by the emergence of a **dominant design**, which becomes the new accepted market standard for technology.[19] Dominant designs emerge in several ways. The first is by achieving critical mass, meaning that a particular technology can become the dominant design simply because most people use it, for example, Blu-ray beating out HD-DVD. Critical mass will likely determine the dominant design for wireless device charging; where instead of plugging in your device to recharge you simply place it on top of a recharging station containing magnetic charging coils. Recently, three different wireless technologies were trying to become the dominant standard: the Power Matters Alliance (PMA) backing Duracell's Powermat, a Duracell and Procter & Gamble joint venture supported by Google, AT&T, Starbucks, and McDonald's; the Alliance for Wireless Power (A4WP) and its Rezence charging mats, backed by Samsung, Broadcom, Deutsche Telekom, and Texas Instruments; and the Wireless Power Consortium (WPC) and its Qi charging mats, supported by LG Electronics, Energizer, and Nokia. However, PMA and A4WP joined forces to create a new, combined standard for wireless charging devices.[20] Again, why does this matter? Because the market for wireless charging, estimated at $785 million, is projected to increase to $8.5 billion by 2018. In other words, becoming the dominant standard is worth billions to the winner.[21]

Second, a design can become dominant if it solves a practical problem. The QWERTY keyboard (named for the top left line of letters) became the dominant design for typewriters because it slowed down typists who caused mechanical typewriter keys to jam because they typed too fast. Computers can easily be switched to the DVORAK keyboard layout, which doubles typing speed and cuts typing errors by half, yet QWERTY lives on as the standard keyboard. The QWERTY keyboard solved a problem; with the advent of computers, that problem is no longer relevant, yet QWERTY remains the dominant technology because most people learned to type that way and continue to do so.

Third, dominant designs can also emerge through independent standards bodies. The International Telecommunications Union (ITU, http://www.itu.ch) is an agency of the United Nations that establishes international standards for the communications industry (i.e., Internet, telephone, satellites, radio, etc.). For example, the ITU has agreed on the new standard for 4G, or fourth-generation, service on mobile phones. "True" 4G, according to the ITU, allows

Natalia Pushchina/Shutterstock

larger amounts of data to be sent over smaller cellular bandwidth and will be much faster than the 4G LTE (or 4G Light) now offered by mobile phone companies. According to Hamadoun Touré, the ITU's secretary general, true 4G "will make the present day smart phone feel like an old dial-up Internet connection." François Rancy, who directs ITU's Radiocommunication Bureau, says that true 4G "would be like putting a fibre optic broadband connection on your mobile phone, making your phone at least 500 times faster than today's 3G smart phones."[22]

There's a new buzzword in the oil and gas industry these days, says Bob Schulz, a business strategy professor at the University of Calgary's Haskayne School of Business: *innovation*. "If prices are high and you're making money, you say, 'Oh, well, we don't really need to be too innovative,'" says Schulz. "But when the price is $50 a barrel instead of $100, well, we've got to go figure out how we're going to make things work."[23] Suncor, from Calgary, is a perennial leader in oilsands innovation, spending about $150 million each year on research and development (R&D). Now it's looking at new oil extraction methods, such as extending antennas as far as 100 metres down into the oilsands' bitumen layer to heat the hydrocarbon with radio waves before extraction. The time is ripe for anyone with new ideas on some facet of oil and gas exploration, drilling, or production that could cut costs: "Necessity is the mother of invention, so the doors could be opened. Clients could be more responsive to cost-saving technologies, services, and initiatives than they would be when things are very good. The mindset to consider and possibly adopt change is greater."[24]

No matter how it happens, the emergence of a dominant design is a key event in an innovation stream.

Dominant design a new technological design or process that becomes the accepted market standard.

Matthew Staver/Bloomberg/Getty Images

Courtesy of the James M Tour Group.

Because they are both transparent and flexible, new memory chips could allow touchscreens to double as a memory location.

First, the emergence of a dominant design indicates that there are winners and losers. Technological innovation is both competence enhancing and competence destroying. Companies that bet on the now-dominant design usually prosper. By contrast, when companies bet on the wrong design or the old technology, they may experience **technological lockout**, which occurs when a new dominant design (i.e., a significantly better technology) prevents a company from competitively selling its products or makes it difficult to do so.[25] "If you want to continue playing relatively contemporary movies, then you need digital," says Daniel Demois, general manager of a theatre in Toronto. Theatres must find anywhere from $30,000 to $100,000 to buy new equipment to replace aging projectors—or go extinct.[26] Last year, two of the largest Canadian exhibitors, Cineplex Entertainment and Empire Theatres, formed a joint venture to finance the upgrade of their combined 1,600 screens to digital. "Consumers will get a crisper image on the screen, and it also allows theatres the capacity to open up more programming," said Pat Marshall, vice president of Cineplex.[27] The economics are even more compelling for studios to encourage exhibitors to switch over. One 35-mm print could cost $1,000 versus $200 for a digital hard drive. Multiply that by 10,000 screens for a wide release film and the difference in distribution costs is staggering. In 2015, the total number of digital screens in Canada passed the halfway mark for the first time.[28] More companies are likely to go out of business in a time of discontinuous change and changing standards than in an economic recession or slowdown.

Second, the emergence of a dominant design signals a shift from design experimentation and competition to **incremental change**, a phase during which companies innovate by lowering costs and improving the performance of the dominant design. For example, manufacturing efficiencies enable Intel to cut the cost of its chips by one-half to two-thirds during a technology cycle, while doubling or tripling their speed. This focus on improving the dominant design continues until the next technological discontinuity occurs.

6-2 MANAGING INNOVATION

One consequence of technology cycles and innovation streams is that managers must be equally good at managing innovation in two very different circumstances. Unfortunately, what works well when managing

Technological lockout when a new dominant design (i.e., a significantly better technology) prevents a company from competitively selling its products or makes it difficult to do so.

Incremental change the phase of a technology cycle in which companies innovate by lowering costs and improving the functioning and performance of the dominant technological design.

innovation during discontinuous change doesn't work well when managing innovation during periods of incremental change (and vice versa). Consequently, to successfully manage innovation streams, companies need to be good at three things: 6-2a managing sources of innovation, 6-2b managing innovation during discontinuous change, and 6-2c managing innovation during incremental change.

6-2a Managing Sources of Innovation

Innovation comes from great ideas. So a starting point for managing innovation is to manage the *sources* of innovation, that is, where new ideas come from. One source of new ideas is brilliant inventors. But only a few companies have the likes of a Thomas Edison, Nikola Tesla, or Canada's own Alexander Graham Bell working for them. Given that great thinkers and inventors are in short supply, what might companies do to ensure a steady flow of good ideas?

Well, when we say that innovation begins with great ideas, we're really saying that innovation begins with creativity, the production of novel and useful ideas.[29] Although companies can't command employees to be creative ("You *will* be more creative!"), they can jump-start innovation by building **creative work environments** in which workers perceive that creative thoughts and ideas are welcomed and valued. As Exhibit 6.3 shows, creative work environments have six components that encourage creativity: challenging work, organizational encouragement, supervisory encouragement, work group encouragement, freedom, and a lack of organizational impediments.[30]

Work is *challenging* when it requires effort, demands attention and focus, and is perceived as important to others in the organization. Challenging work promotes creativity because it creates a rewarding psychological experience known as "flow." **Flow** is a psychological state of effortlessness in which you become completely absorbed in what you're doing and time seems to fly.[31] A key part of creating flow experiences, and thus creative work environments, is to achieve a balance between skills and task challenge. When workers can do more than is required of them, they become bored, and when their skills aren't sufficient to accomplish a task, they become anxious. When skills and task challenge are balanced, however, flow and creativity can occur.

A creative work environment requires three kinds of encouragement: organizational, supervisory, and work group encouragement. *Organizational encouragement*

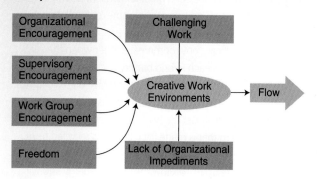

Exhibit 6.3
Components of Creative Work Environments

Source: Adapted from T. M. Amabile, R. Conti, H. Coon, J. Lanzenby, and M. Herron, "Accessing the Work Environment for Creativity," *Academy of Management Journal* 39 (1996): 1154–1184; A. Serban and A. Roberts, (2016). "Exploring Antecedents and Outcomes of Shared Leadership in a Creative Context: A Mixed-Methods Approach," *The Leadership Quarterly.*

of creativity occurs when management encourages risk taking and new ideas, supports and fairly evaluates new ideas, rewards and recognizes creativity, and encourages the sharing of new ideas throughout the company. Bring Your Own Device (BYOD) is a fact of life for much of today's workforce.[32] Employees are happier because they have the freedom to use their favourite devices and employers are adjusting to the idea. Initially spooked by the loss of control and data security risks, they're now seeing an increase in employee satisfaction and productivity. More importantly, BYOD is saving companies money.[33]

Supervisory encouragement of creativity occurs when supervisors provide clear goals, encourage open interaction with subordinates, and actively support development teams' work and ideas. *Work group encouragement* occurs when group members have diverse experience, education, and backgrounds and when the group fosters mutual openness to ideas; positive, constructive challenges to ideas; and shared commitment to ideas. CEO Marissa Mayer's decision to order Yahoo! Inc. staff to work in the company's offices was meant to enhance face time and increase creativity. This was a reversal of what the hyper-creative company had been

Creative work environments workplace cultures in which workers perceive that new ideas are welcomed, valued, and encouraged.

Flow a psychological state of effortlessness, in which you become completely absorbed in what you're doing and time seems to pass quickly.

Toyota Addresses Environmental Threat From Hybrid Car Batteries

Hybrid engines have been great for consumers and the environment. Using less gas helps prevent pollution and saves drivers money at the pump. However, the batteries represent a significant environmental danger when the car is no longer useful, as each hybrid battery pack contains nickel, which can cause irritation and cancer and give off toxic fumes as well. To prevent the potential harm of this toxic metal, Toyota has created an Electricity Management System, a backup energy system that is made from batteries recycled from its old hybrid vehicles. According to Toyota engineers, the systems will store up to 10 kilowatt-hours of energy and will provide backup or supplemental power as needed.

Source: D. King, "Toyota Recycling Old Hybrid Batteries Into Energy Storage Systems for Dealers," AutoBlogGreen, February 2, 2013, http://green.autoblog.com/2013/02/02/toyota-recycling-old-hybrid-batteries-into-energy-storage-system/.

doing since its inception. Only time will tell if she has gotten it right.[34]

The Toronto-based Automotive Parts Manufacturers' Association (APMA) believes that organizational and supervisory encouragement is critical to the future of the automobile industry in Canada, and APMA president Flavio Volpe has eagerly embraced this concept. The association is now in the second phase of a project it launched last year involving a Toyota Lexus RX350 SUV with the latest in high-end communications, infotainment, safety, operating, and lighting gear. Canadian firms that assisted with the project include Magna, Lixar, Leggett & Platt, Rogers, QNX Software Systems, the University of Waterloo Centre for Automotive Research (WatCAR), and others. Workers from the various plants are encouraged to participate and contribute and this encouragement has allowed the industry to navigate a sometimes tumultuous manufacturing era.[35]

Freedom means having autonomy over one's day-to-day work and a sense of ownership and control over one's ideas. Numerous studies have indicated that creative ideas thrive under conditions of freedom. What do NASA, Netflix, Nike, *The New Yorker*, and *New York Magazine* have in common? Besides beginning with the letter N, they're all leading companies that provide freedom for creative talent, according to the second annual survey from creative-industry talent networking platform "Working Not Working"; when work equals play, then freedom to create skyrockets.[36] 3M scientist Art Fry came up with a clever new item. He thought that if he could apply an adhesive (dreamed up by colleague Spencer Silver several years earlier) to the back of a piece of paper, he could create the perfect bookmark (instead of loose paper, which is what he had been using in his church choir's hymn book). We now call his innovation the "Post-It." What is not as well known is that Fry came up with the now iconic product during his "15 percent time, a program at 3M that allows employees to use a portion of their paid time to chase rainbows and hatch their own ideas."[37]

To foster creativity, companies may also have to *remove impediments* to creativity from the work environment. Internal conflict, power struggles, rigid management structures, and a conservative bias toward the status quo can all discourage creativity. They can also create the perception that others in the organization will decide which ideas are acceptable and deserve support.

6-2b Managing Innovation During Discontinuous Change: Experiential Approach

A study that assessed progress in innovation and knowledge management research during 1980–2014, using a sample of "highly cited" journal publications, revealed a change in research from incremental to transformative innovation. The study discussed the nature of this transformation and outlined a future agenda for the development of better design and new competencies

Exhibit 6.4
Experiential Approach to Innovation

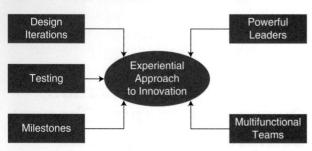

Source: Adapted by Ike Hall from K.M. Eisenhardt, "Accelerating Adaptive Processes: Product Innovation in the Global Computer Industry," *Administrative Science Quarterly* 40 (1995): 84–110. Professor Kathleen Eisenhardt is the Stanford W. Ascherman M.D. Professor and Co-Director of the Stanford Technology Ventures Program.

in theory and practice.[38] As shown in Exhibit 6.4, the **experiential approach to innovation** assumes that innovation is occurring within a highly uncertain environment and that the key to fast product innovation is to use intuition, flexible options, and hands-on experience to reduce uncertainty and accelerate learning and understanding. The experiential approach to innovation has five aspects: design iterations, testing, milestones, multifunctional teams, and powerful leaders.[39]

An "iteration" is a repetition. So a **design iteration** is a cycle of repetition in which a company tests a prototype of a new product or service, improves on the design, and then builds and tests the improved product or service prototype. A **product prototype** is a full-scale working model that is being tested for design, function, and reliability. For example, Facebook-owned Oculus VR designed virtual reality headsets (i.e., goggles) to be used in simulations and digital games. Oculus shipped 60,000 units of its first product prototype, and used the resulting product feedback to develop its second prototype, the DK2, which it pre-sold to game developers who will not only test the DK2, but provide feedback on how well the digital games they're designing perform using the DK2.[40] **Testing** is a systematic comparison of different product designs or design iterations. Companies that want to create a new dominant design following a technological discontinuity quickly build, test, improve, and retest a series of different product prototypes. One of Oculus Rift's key concerns during prototype testing was "simulator sickness," the nausea or disorientation caused by "motion blur." Thanks to testing and feedback from game developers, Oculus improved the DK2 with a faster, higher resolution display that provides greater clarity and contrast, and reduces motion blur and judder

(jagged, stuttering movement), both of which are major contributors to simulator sickness.[41]

By trying a number of very different designs or making successive improvements and changes in the same design, frequent design iterations reduce uncertainty and improve understanding. Simply put, the more prototypes you build, the more likely you are to learn what works and what doesn't. Also, when designers and engineers build a number of prototypes, they are less likely to fall in love with a particular prototype. Instead, they'll be more concerned about improving the product or technology as much as they can. Testing speeds up and improves the innovation process, too. When two very different design prototypes are tested against each other or the new design iteration is tested against the previous iteration, product design strengths and weaknesses quickly become apparent. Likewise, testing uncovers errors early in the design process, when they are easiest to correct. Finally, testing accelerates learning and understanding by forcing engineers and product designers to examine hard data about product performance. When there's hard evidence that prototypes are testing well, the confidence of the design team grows. Also, personal conflict between design team members is less likely when testing focuses on hard measurements and facts rather than personal hunches and preferences.

Milestones are formal project review points used to assess progress and performance. For example, a company that has put itself on a 12-month schedule to complete a project might schedule milestones at the three-, six-, and nine-month points on the schedule. By making people regularly assess what they're doing, how well they're performing, and whether they need to take corrective action, milestones provide structure to the general chaos that follows technological discontinuities. Milestones also shorten the innovation process by

Experiential approach to innovation an approach to innovation that assumes a highly uncertain environment and uses intuition, flexible options, and hands-on experience to reduce uncertainty and accelerate learning and understanding.

Design iteration a cycle of repetition in which a company tests a prototype of a new product or service, improves on that design, and then builds and tests the improved prototype.

Product prototype a full-scale, working model that is being tested for design, function, and reliability.

Testing the systematic comparison of different product designs or design iterations.

Milestones formal project review points used to assess progress and performance.

creating a sense of urgency that keeps everyone on task. Finally, milestones are beneficial for innovation because meeting regular milestones builds momentum by giving people a sense of accomplishment.

Multifunctional teams are work teams composed of people from different departments. Multifunctional teams accelerate learning and understanding by mixing and integrating technical, marketing, and manufacturing activities. By involving all key departments in development from the start, multifunctional teams speed innovation through early identification of new ideas or problems that would typically not have been generated or addressed until much later. The Sealy Company, a leading mattress manufacturer, had to find a way to revive its high-end Stearns & Foster brand, whose sales were declining. Sealy's solution was to redesign the entire brand through collaboration teams, or jokingly, "getting in bed together." So it brought its engineering, sales, and marketing staff together to find out directly what customers wanted by visiting their retail stores. The message? Focus on quality. Don't cut costs. Allen Platek, vice president of new product development, said, "Prior to this, what we did was in silos. Sales did their thing, marketing did their promotions and ads, R&D developed innovation, and then it was all thrown to operations. We had a disjointed effort." Sealy's multifunctional teams got the job done. Even though the redesigned Stearns & Foster mattresses cost 40 percent more, the changes produced record sales.[42]

Powerful leaders provide the vision, discipline, and motivation to keep the innovation process focused, on time, and on target. Powerful leaders are able to get resources when they are needed, are typically more experienced, have high status in the company, and are held directly responsible for the product's success or failure. On average, powerful leaders can get innovation-related projects done nine months faster than leaders with little power or influence. Tesla, the electric car manufacturer, has had its share of ups and downs as it has led the way in electric automobile innovation. In the past two years, the firm has seen some remarkable milestones: It's now sold tens of thousands of cars, employs nearly 6,000 people around the world, and has plans to double the world's supply of lithium-ion batteries. The company hasn't always looked this good, however. It nearly collapsed during the 2008 financial crisis and had to settle with one of its cofounders. A negative review from *The New York Times* prompted CEO Elon Musk to take to social media and appear on TV to defend the firm. Powerful leadership like this can't be bought.[43]

6-2c Managing Innovation During Incremental Change: Compression Approach

The experiential approach is used to manage innovation in highly *uncertain* environments during periods of *discontinuous* change; the compression approach is used to manage innovation in more *certain* environments during periods of *incremental* change. The goals of the experiential approach are significant improvements in performance and the establishment of a *new* dominant design; the goals of the compression approach are lower costs and incremental improvements in the performance and function of the *existing* dominant design.

The general strategies in each approach are different. With the experiential approach, the general strategy is to build something new, different, and substantially better. Because there's so much uncertainty—no one knows which technology will become the market leader—companies adopt a winner-take-all approach by trying to create the market-leading, dominant design. With the compression approach, the general strategy is to compress the time and steps needed to bring about small, consistent improvements in performance and functionality. Because a dominant technology design already exists, the general strategy is to continue improving the existing technology as rapidly as possible.

In short, a **compression approach to innovation** assumes that innovation is a predictable process, that incremental innovation can be planned using a series of steps, and that compressing the time it takes to complete those steps can speed up innovation. The compression approach to innovation has five aspects: planning for incremental innovation, involving suppliers, shortening the time of individual steps, using overlapping steps, and creating multifunctional teams.[44]

When *planning for incremental innovation*, the goal is to squeeze or compress development time as much as possible, and the general strategy is to create a series of planned steps to accomplish that goal. Planning for incremental innovation helps avoid unnecessary steps and enables developers to sequence steps in the right order to avoid wasted time and delays between steps.

Multifunctional teams work teams composed of people from different departments.

Powerful leaders are typically more experienced, have high status in the company, and are held directly responsible for the product's success or failure.

Compression approach to innovation an approach to innovation that assumes that incremental innovation can be planned using a series of steps and that compressing those steps can speed innovation.

Apple's Incremental Change Innovation

Apple is famous for its incremental approach to the iPhone. The iPhone 6s and 6s Plus are examples of this. There was a RAM incremental upgrade, an upgrade from a DDR3 to a DDR4, the A9 chipset, 12-megapixel rear-cameras, improved touch ID for Apple Pay, and the same Force Touch technology seen on the Apple Watch and Retina MacBook. On the exterior design front, Apple avoided a redo of the "Bendgate" phenomenon and added a rose gold colour option, (again borrowing from the Apple Watch). Apple rarely changes the form factor dramatically for "s" releases and sticks to incremental changes only, making the smaller 6s more popular than the phablet 6s Plus.

Source: L. Dormehl. "iPhone 6s Could Be Apple's Biggest 'Incremental' Upgrade of All Time," Cult of Mac, May 12, 2015, http://www.cultofmac.com/322312/iphone-6s-could-be-apples-biggest-incremental-upgrade-of-all-time/.

Planning also reduces misunderstandings and improves coordination. Most planning for incremental innovation is based on the idea of **generational change**, which occurs when incremental improvements are made to a dominant technological design such that the improved version of the technology is fully backward compatible with the older version.[45] Most computers, for instance, have USB (universal serial bus) input slots to connect and power USB thumb drives, monitors, or external hard drives used for backup storage. USB 3.1, the latest USB standard, can transfer more than 10 Gbps (gigabytes per second), compared to USB 3.0 devices, which operate at 5 Gbps, or USB 2.0 devices, which operate at roughly 0.5 Gbps.[46] What happens if you buy a new computer with USB 3.1 slots, but still own a USB 3.0 external hard drive and a USB 2.0 thumb drive? Both will work because they are backward compatible with USB 3.1, but at slower speeds.

Because the compression approach assumes that innovation can follow a series of preplanned steps, one way to shorten development time is through *involving suppliers*. Delegating some of the preplanned steps in the innovation process to outside suppliers reduces the amount of work that internal development teams must do. Plus, suppliers provide an alternative source of ideas and expertise that can lead to better designs. Supplier involvement allows Government Services Canada to meet shifting expectations from both Government of Canada clients and industry. It allows procurement to be about more than just buying goods and services. Supplier involvement is one of the key elements of the "smart procurement" approach recently announced by the Canadian government, under which suppliers can expect greater involvement in the procurement process and are asked for their expertise before a requirement is identified. Supplier involvement provides an opportunity for companies to fully understand the current industry landscape, leverage market expertise, and capitalize on innovation solutions which can ultimately save time and money.[47]

Another means of shortening development time is simply *shortening the time of individual steps* in the innovation process. A common way to do that is through computer-aided design (CAD). CAD speeds up the design process by allowing designers and engineers to make and test design changes using computer models rather than physically testing expensive prototypes. CAD also speeds innovation by making it easy to see how design changes affect engineering, purchasing, and production.

For example, 3-D design software reduces the time and cost involved in creating new products. ANSYS simulation software (ansys.com) shows how products will actually operate in the real world. Created by 600 PhD holders, it uses advanced algorithms to mirror the physics of heat, friction, fluids, loads, and stress, allowing users to simulate anything from tennis racquets to passenger jet lift coefficients during takeoffs and landings. Instead of

Generational change change based on incremental improvements to a dominant technological design such that the improved technology is fully backward compatible with the older technology.

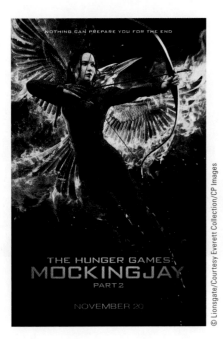

NOTHING CAN PREPARE YOU FOR THE END

THE HUNGER GAMES
MOCKINGJAY
PART 2

NOVEMBER 20

© Lionsgate/Courtesy Everett Collection/CP Images

testing dozens of mock-up products, ANSYS users save time and money by letting the software do the testing. Jim Shaikh wanted to design a baby bottle that instantly heated milk to the right temperature every time, so he used ANSYS to test different designs and plastics. The best design, according to the software, was a bottle with an internal element that heats milk as it passes through the nipple to the baby. Only after finalizing the design via thousands of tests on ANSYS did Shaikh spend $1,500 to produce a prototype of the finished product.[48]

In a sequential design process, each step must be completed before the next step begins. But sometimes multiple development steps can be performed at the same time. *Using overlapping steps* shortens the development process by reducing delays and waiting times between steps. For example, Lions Gate Entertainment used overlapping steps to reduce the time it took to make the entire series of the *Hunger Games* films. In order to capitalize on the record-breaking revenues at the box office of the first movie, Lions Gate used new directors, script writers, and production teams for each of the movies in the *Hunger Games* series so that it could begin shooting the next film while the previous one was in post-production and the one prior to that was in the theatres.[49]

> **Organizational decline** a large decrease in organizational performance that occurs when companies don't anticipate, recognize, neutralize, or adapt to the internal or external pressures that threaten their survival.

ORGANIZATIONAL DECLINE: THE RISK OF NOT CHANGING

Businesses operate in a constantly changing environment. Recognizing and adapting to internal and external changes can mean the difference between continued success and going out of business. Companies that fail to change run the risk of organizational decline.[50]

Organizational decline occurs when companies don't anticipate, recognize, neutralize, or adapt to the internal or external pressures that threaten their survival.[51] In other words, decline occurs when organizations don't recognize the need for change. General Motors (GM) Canada's loss of market share and eventual bankruptcy in late 2009 is an example of organizational decline that turned around in recent years.[52] As depicted in Exhibit 6.5, there are five stages of organizational decline: blinded, inaction, faulty action, crisis, and dissolution.[53]

In the *blinded stage*, decline begins because key managers fail to recognize the internal or external changes that will harm their organization. This "blindness" may be due to a simple lack of awareness about changes or an inability to understand their significance. It may also come from the overconfidence that can develop when a company has been successful.

In the *inaction stage*, as organizational performance problems become more visible, management may recognize the need to change but still take no action. The managers may be waiting to see if the problems will correct themselves. Or they may find it difficult to change the practices and policies that previously led to success. Possibly, too, they wrongly assume that they can easily correct the problems, so they don't recognize the situation as urgent.

In the *faulty action stage*, faced with rising costs and decreasing profits and market share, management announces "belt tightening" plans designed to cut costs, increase efficiency, and restore profits. In other words, rather than recognizing the need for fundamental changes, managers assume that if they just run it more strictly, company performance will return to previous levels.

In the *crisis stage*, bankruptcy (such as at GM) or dissolution (i.e., breaking up the company and selling its parts) is likely to occur unless the company completely reorganizes the way it does business. At this point, however, companies typically lack the resources to fully

Exhibit 6.5
Five Stages of Organizational Decline

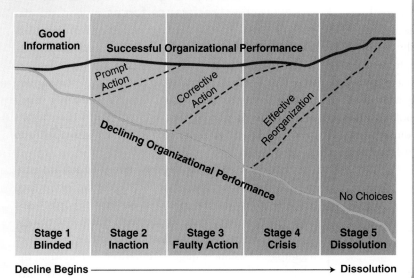

Good Information — Successful Organizational Performance

Prompt Action

Corrective Action

Effective Reorganization

Declining Organizational Performance

No Choices

| Stage 1 Blinded | Stage 2 Inaction | Stage 3 Faulty Action | Stage 4 Crisis | Stage 5 Dissolution |

Decline Begins ⟶ Dissolution

change how they run themselves. Cutbacks and layoffs will have reduced the level of talent among employees. Furthermore, talented managers who were savvy enough to see the crisis coming will have found jobs with other companies, often with competitors.

In the *dissolution stage*, after failing to make the changes needed to sustain the organization, the company is dissolved through bankruptcy proceedings or by selling assets in order to pay suppliers, banks, and creditors. At this point, a new CEO may be brought in to oversee the closing of stores, offices, and manufacturing facilities, the final layoffs of managers and employees, and the sale of assets.

Because decline is reversible at each of the first four stages, not all companies in decline reach final dissolution.

Turning BlackBerry Around

Canada's BlackBerry Ltd. has had a trend of falling revenue amid improved adjusted profit. The hardware and software maker reported a loss on revenue in 2015. Just past the midway point of a two-year restructuring, BlackBerry has sharply pared costs and has been cash flow positive this year, topping earnings estimates in each of the past four quarters. BlackBerry CEO John Chen has reaffirmed his software revenue targets, and analysts expect revenue from device sales to fall farther before things get better. Services revenues tied to handset sales are expected to continue to decline through fiscal 2016 to more than offset growth in sales from device management, messaging, and other software.

BlackBerry has registered two consecutive quarters of operating profitability; however fourth-quarter revenue declined. Chen's plan is to generate free cash flow in every quarter in fiscal 2016 and stabilize revenues to achieve sustainable profits. He believes that both the BlackBerry Passport and Classic smart phones have not yet gained traction. The Waterloo-based company had 37 million users at the end of fiscal 2015, but expects that 2016 will see a resurgence of this brilliant Canadian innovation icon.

Kevork Djansezian/Getty Images

Source: M. Lewis, "BlackBerry's Revenue Decline Expected to Continue," *The Star*, June 19, 2015. Used with permission of Torstar Syndication Services. http://www.thestar.com/business/tech_news/2015/06/19/blackberrys-revenue-decline-expected-to-continue.html.

GM aggressively cut costs, stabilized its shrinking market share, and used innovative production techniques in an effort to reverse a decline that had resulted in bankruptcy. GM in Canada made many changes to different plants, closed some assembly plants, discontinued several lines (Pontiac among them), and made new deals with unions and creditors.[54] GM had a highly successful initial public offering (IPO) after its bankruptcy and has made great leaps forward for a company that was once very much in its death throes. Looking ahead, CNBC analyst Kevin Hall has stated that "the impending impact of 23 new product introductions by 2017 seems likely to boost GM's market share, which declined to 18 percent in 2012 from 19.6 percent in 2011."[55]

6-4 MANAGING CHANGE

According to social psychologist Kurt Lewin, change is a function of the forces that promote change and the opposing forces that slow or resist change.[56] **Change forces** include:

▶ new strategic requirements (perhaps a new kind of differentiation), which are closely tied to competitor actions;

▶ competitor actions (remember Porter's Five Industry Forces analysis from Chapter 5);

▶ changes in government regulation (e.g., in trade policies, taxation, and environmental laws—remember the PESTEEL analysis from Chapter 5); and

▶ new technologies (including new manufacturing processes, new methods, and new machinery).

"The Kiss of Yes": Some of the strongest resisters may support the changes in public but then ignore them in private.

Viorika/iStockphoto

Change forces forces that produce differences in the form, quality, or condition of an organization over time.

Resistance forces forces that support the existing state of conditions in organizations.

Resistance to change opposition to change resulting from self-interest, misunderstanding and distrust, a low tolerance for change, and time and cost factors.

These forces for change quite often cause disagreement and conflict, not necessarily over the *need* for change, but over *how* change is implemented—that is, over what we actually change in our organizations.

By contrast, **resistance forces** support the status quo, that is, the existing conditions in organizations. Change is difficult under any circumstances. In a study of heart bypass patients, doctors told participants straightforwardly to change their eating and health habits or they would die. Unbelievably, a full 90 percent of participants did *not* change their habits at all![57] This fierce resistance to change also applies to organizations.

Resistance to change is caused by self-interest, misunderstanding and distrust, a general intolerance for change, and time and cost factors.[58] People resist change out of *self-interest* because they fear that change will cost or deprive them of something they value. For example, resistance might stem from a fear that the changes will result in a loss of pay, power, responsibility, or even one's job. People also resist change because of *misunderstanding and distrust*; they don't understand the change or the reasons for it, or they distrust the people—typically management—behind the change. Resistance isn't always visible at first, however. Some of the strongest resisters may initially support the changes in public, nodding and smiling their agreement, but then ignore the changes in private and do their jobs as they always have. Management consultant Michael Hammer calls this deadly form of resistance the "Kiss of Yes."[59]

Resistance may also come from a generally low tolerance for change. Some people are simply less capable of handling change than others. People with a *low tolerance for change* feel threatened by the uncertainty associated with change and worry that they won't be able to learn the new skills and behaviours they need in order to successfully negotiate change in their companies. The final factor usually falls into the *time and cost* area. People in an organization generally only accept that change is inevitable just at the point when they have the least amount of time and resources to effect the change—in other words, when it is too late!

All of the factors we've discussed are summarized in Exhibit 6.6.

Exhibit 6.6
Example of Lewin's Force Field Analysis

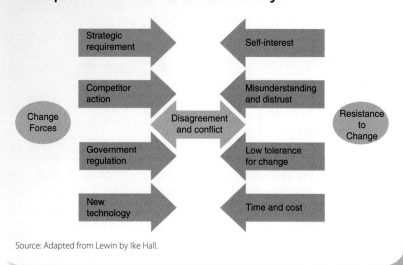

Source: Adapted from Lewin by Ike Hall.

*Because resistance to change is inevitable, successful change efforts require careful management. In this section, you will learn about **6-4a managing resistance to change, 6-4b what not to do when leading organizational change,** and **6-4c different change tools and techniques.***

6-4a Managing Resistance to Change

According to Kurt Lewin, managing organizational change is a basic process of unfreezing, change intervention, and refreezing. **Unfreezing** is getting the people affected by change to believe that change is needed. During the **change intervention** itself, workers and managers change their behaviour and work practices. **Refreezing** involves supporting and reinforcing the new changes so that they stick.

Resistance to change is an example of frozen behaviour. Given the choice between changing and not changing, most people would rather not change. Because resistance to change is natural and inevitable, managers need to unfreeze resistance to change in order to create successful change programs. The following methods can be used to manage resistance to change: education and communication, participation, negotiation, top management support, and coercion.[60]

When resistance to change is based on insufficient, incorrect, or misleading information, managers should *educate* employees about the need for change and *communicate* change-related information to them. Managers

must also supply the information and funding or other support that employees need to make changes.

Another way to reduce resistance to change is by having those affected by the change *participate* in planning and implementing the change process. Employees who participate have a better understanding of the change and the need for it. Furthermore, employee concerns about change can be addressed as they occur if employees participate in the planning and implementation process. Procter & Gamble (P&G) Canada did exactly this by involving the personnel from all levels when P&G needed to change to become more responsive to the market and more innovative. The original Swiffer duster was developed by a Japanese company that teamed up with Procter & Gamble to take the product global.[61] Innovation on a global scale is sometimes required. Tim Penner, CEO of P&G Canada, has indicated that P&G will become an innovator online and that he will be assigning as much as 20 percent of the advertising budget to digital media. Canada has often served as a testing ground for new products that P&G has eventually rolled out elsewhere in the world, such as when Penner led the launch of Swiffer WetJet in Canada a year before its American rollout.[62] P&G Canada tries to blend the best R&D practices in the world with an understanding of local Canadian markets. "We truly think globally and act locally," he says. In doing so, P&G hopes to become the fastest growing consumer products company in Canada. It plans to achieve that leadership position "through innovation in everything we do," from innovative marketing programs that foster meaningful relationships with consumers, to productive partnerships with retailers and leading workplace practices for employees.[63]

Resistance to change also decreases when change efforts receive significant *top management support*. But managers must do more than talk about the importance

Unfreezing getting the people affected by change to believe that change is needed.

Change intervention the process used to get workers and managers to change their behaviour and work practices.

Refreezing supporting and reinforcing new changes so that they stick.

of change. They must provide the training, resources, and autonomy needed to make change happen. For example, with their distinguished 70-year history of hand-drawing Hollywood's most successful animated films (*Snow White*, *Bambi*, *The Little Mermaid*, *Beauty and the Beast*), the animators at the Walt Disney Company naturally resisted the move to computer-generated (CG) animation. So Disney supported the difficult change by putting all of its animators through a six-month "CG Boot Camp," where they learned how to draw animated characters with computers.[64]

Finally, resistance to change can be managed through **coercion**, or the use of formal power and authority to force others to change. Because of the intense negative reactions it can create (e.g., fear, stress, resentment, sabotage of company products), coercion should be used only during a crisis or when all other attempts to reduce resistance to change have failed.

> Change efforts that lack vision tend to be confused, chaotic, and contradictory.

6-4b What Not to Do When Leading Organizational Change

So far, we've learned how to execute a basic change process (unfreezing, change, refreezing) and how to manage resistance to change. Harvard Business School professor John Kotter argues that, when it comes to achieving successful organizational change, knowing what *not* to do is just as important as knowing what to do.[65]

Managers commonly make certain errors when they lead change. They make the first two errors during the *unfreezing phase*. The first error is *not establishing a great enough sense of urgency*. Indeed, Kotter estimates that more than half of all change efforts fail because the people affected are not convinced that change is necessary. People will feel a greater sense of urgency if a leader in the company makes a public, candid assessment of the company's problems and weaknesses. Celestica Inc., headquartered in Toronto, produces complex printed circuit assemblies, such as PC motherboards and networking cards, flat-screen TVs, and Xbox video game systems for Microsoft. Craig Muhlhauser left the helm in late 2015, but when he took over as president

and CEO, Celestica was losing money and market share. Muhlhauser went to work right away, informing employees that the company couldn't survive if it didn't change. Within his first 30 days as CEO, he reduced staff by 35 percent, moved new people into important positions, and had the attention of everyone in the company.[66]

The second mistake that occurs in the *unfreezing phase* is *not creating a powerful enough coalition*. Change often starts with one or two people, but it has to be supported by an expanding group if it is going to build enough momentum to impact an entire department, division, or company. Besides top management, Kotter recommends that key employees, managers, board members, customers, and even union leaders be members of a *core change coalition* that guides and supports organizational change. According to Muhlhauser, in a turnaround, there are three kinds of employees—those on your side, those on the fence, and those who will never buy in. The latter have to be let go, and those on the fence should be persuaded to contribute or leave. Says Muhlhauser: "Change is difficult, and as we make change, it is important to realize that there are people who are going to resist that change. In talking to those people, the objective is to move everybody into the column of supporters. But

Errors Managers Make When Leading Change

Unfreezing

1. Not establishing a great enough sense of urgency
2. Not creating a powerful enough guiding coalition
3. Change
4. Lacking a vision
5. Undercommunicating the vision by a factor of ten
6. Not removing obstacles to the new vision
7. Not systematically planning for and creating short-term wins

Refreezing

8. Declaring victory too soon
9. Not anchoring changes in the corporation's culture

Sources: L. Bucciarelli, "A Review of Innovation and Change Management: Stage Model and Power Influences," *Universal Journal of Management* Vol. 3(1) (2015), pp. 36–42; J. P. Kotter, "Leading Change: Why Transformation Efforts Fail," *Harvard Business Review* 73, no. 2 (March–April 1995): 59.

Coercion using formal power and authority to force others to change.

that is probably unachievable."[67] It's also important to strengthen this core change coalition's resolve by periodically bringing its members together for off-site retreats.

The next four errors that managers make occur during the *change phase*, when a change intervention is used to try to get workers and managers to change their behaviour and work practices. *Lacking a vision* for change is a significant error at this point. As you learned in Chapter 4, a *vision* is a statement of a company's purpose or reason for existing. A vision for change makes clear where a company or department is headed and why the change is occurring. Change efforts that lack vision tend to be confused, chaotic, and contradictory. By contrast, change efforts guided by a vision are clear and easy to understand and can be effectively explained in five minutes or less. Procter & Gamble's beauty and grooming division accounts for one-third of its global sales. With beauty sales down 4 percent and grooming sales down 7 percent, division chief Ed Shirley has introduced a clear vision for changing the division. Said Shirley: "Our principal beauty focus has been winning with women, yet we're not broadly serving male consumers' needs outside of Gillette and fine fragrances."[68] The change, he said, "will require a cultural shift" as well as a change in the organizational structure based on gender, rather than products, "to better serve 'Him and Her.'"[69]

Undercommunicating the vision by a factor of ten is another mistake in the change phase. According to Kotter, companies mistakenly hold just one meeting to announce the vision. Or, if the new vision receives heavy emphasis in executive speeches or company newsletters, senior management then undercuts the vision by behaving in ways contrary to it. Successful communication of the vision requires that top managers link everything the company does to the new vision and that they "walk the talk" by behaving in ways consistent with the vision.

Even companies that begin change with a clear vision sometimes make the mistake of *not removing obstacles to the new vision.* They leave formidable barriers to change in place by failing to redesign jobs, pay plans, and technology to support the new way of doing things. One of Celestica's key obstacles was efficiently and effectively managing its supply chain; it worked with 4,000 suppliers around the world. The complexity of this supply chain network and the costs of uncoordinated transportation and shipping reduced the speed with which it could meet customer orders and made it difficult to keep costs low. CEO Craig Muhlhauser

and his management team removed this obstacle by implementing Liveshare, an information system that gave it and its suppliers real-time data on sales, production, inventory, and shipping for all of its products. For example, if Best Buy wanted to buy more units of a top-selling video game, it used to have to contact Celestica via phone, email, or fax to see how quickly the order could be delivered. Now, with Liveshare, it can see live, up-to-date numbers indicating how many of those video games are rolling off Celestica's production lines or are now on trucks en route to Best Buy trucking depots.[70]

Another error in the change phase is *not systematically planning for and creating short-term wins.* Most people don't have the discipline and patience to wait two years to see if the new change effort works. Change is threatening and uncomfortable, so people need to see an immediate payoff if they are to continue to support it. Kotter recommends that managers create short-term wins by choosing projects that are likely to work extremely well early in the change process. Celestica's Craig Muhlhauser understood the importance of short-term wins: "My approach was to look at the first 30 days, then at the first three months, then at the first 12 months and then I took a look at the first three years. In a turnaround, you have to take hold very quickly. You have to show relatively quick hits [i.e., short-term wins] to show your turnaround strategy is working—and then you deal with a multitude of issues in a very focused way that will allow you to continue to show improvement."[71]

The last two errors that managers make occur during the *refreezing phase*, when attempts are made to support and reinforce changes so that they stick. *Declaring victory too soon* is a tempting mistake during the refreezing phase. Managers typically declare victory right after the first large-scale success in the change process. Declaring success too early has the same effect as draining the gasoline out of a car: it stops change efforts dead in their tracks. With success declared, supporters of the change process stop pushing to make change happen. After all, why push when success has been achieved? Rather than declaring victory, managers should use the momentum from short-term wins to push for even bigger or faster changes. This maintains urgency and prevents change supporters from slacking off before the changes are frozen into the company's culture.

The last mistake that managers make is *not anchoring changes in the corporation's culture.* An *organization's culture* is the set of key values, beliefs, and attitudes shared by organizational members that determines the

Innovation at Loblaw

When you think of innovative companies, high-tech start-ups founded by Ping-Pong-playing millennials spring to mind, not a 96-year-old grocer. But Loblaw Cos. Ltd. shows that companies don't have to be young to hatch new ideas (Loblaw is also known under different "banners" as Atlantic Superstore, Dominion Stores, Real Canadian Superstore, Provigo, Valu-Mart, and many other names in different provinces throughout Canada). It's easy to overlook all the innovative concepts the business has developed. Take its President's Choice brand. Loblaw has been a world leader when it comes to creating an in-house label that is every bit as good as—if not better than—the leading national competitors, says David Soberman, national chair in strategic marketing at the Rotman School of Management. Or consider that Loblaw began developing organic foods under the PC umbrella before organic truly became mainstream. What sets the company apart is its ability to pounce on consumer trends early and its willingness to spend big to see its concepts through. Gambling on ambitious ideas is part of its DNA.

Perhaps Loblaw's boldest move was its foray into clothing with Joe Fresh. While some initially questioned the idea of selling apparel in a grocery store, no one doubts the logic today. "The idea of selling apparel in a supermarket isn't that crazy," says Soberman, yet Loblaw is still the only grocery store in Canada with an apparel section, he adds.

Expect the marriage between Loblaw and Shoppers Drug Mart to create more fertile ground to develop fresh

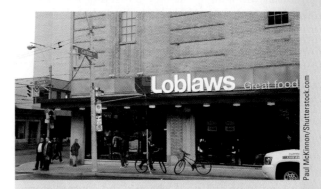

Loblaws at the former Maple Leaf Gardens

ideas. Loblaw's takeover of the drugstore chain was barely complete before it unveiled a national patient contact centre, which was developed to ensure customers are kept up to date with their prescriptions. The Shoppers patient contact centre, located in Mississauga, Ontario, is the first of its kind in Canada. It's staffed by pharmacists and pharmacy technicians who will make about 5 million calls a year, answering patients' questions and reminding them to refill their prescriptions. The idea was developed after consulting with pharmacists, who found they were spending a great deal of time calling customers to ensure they were on top of their medications.

Source: Mark Brown, "Loblaw's Merger With Shoppers Drug Mart Is Creating Crossover Innovations," *Canadian Business* (March 23, 2015). Used with permission. http://www.canadianbusiness.com/innovation/most-innovative-companies-2015-loblaw/.

"accepted way of doing things" in a company. As you learned in Chapter 2, changing cultures is extremely difficult and slow. According to Kotter, two things help anchor changes in a corporation's culture. The first is showing people that the changes have actually improved performance. At Celestica, that proof is provided by the strong sequential growth in the company's earnings.[72] The second is to make sure that the people who get promoted fit the new culture. If they don't, it's a clear sign that the changes were only temporary. At Celestica, Muhlhauser created a culture of meritocracy that rewarded managers and employees for their contributions. The rewards came in the form of promotions, pay increases, and huge bonuses. Customer satisfaction improved. With the increasing demand for consumer products such as smart phones, employees

were excited about the prospects for Celestica. "We've got some new programs in the pipeline so we're optimistic about our ability to compete in and win in that market," said Muhlhauser.[73]

6-4c Change Tools and Techniques

Imagine your boss came to you and said, "All right, genius, you wanted it. You're in charge of turning around the division." How would you start? Where would you begin? How would you encourage change-resistant managers? What would you do to include others in the change process? How would you get the change process off to a quick start? Finally, what approach would you use to promote long-term effectiveness and

Exhibit 6.7
How to Create a Results-Driven Change Program

1. Set measurable, short-term goals to improve performance.

2. Make sure your action steps are likely to improve measured performance.

3. Stress the importance of immediate improvements.

4. Solicit help from consultants and staffers to achieve quick improvements in performance.

5. Test action steps to see if they actually yield improvements. If they don't, discard them and establish new ones.

6. Use resources that you have or can easily acquire. It doesn't take much.

Sources: H. Robinson, "An Overview of Change Management: The Identification of the Critical Success Factors That Will Ensure the Survival and Progression of an Organization," (2012). University of Johannesburg, https://ujdigispace.uj.ac.za/handle/10210/7283. Reprinted by permission of *Harvard Business Review* (exhibit) from "Successful Change Programs Begin With Results," by R. H. Schaffer & H. A. Thomson, J.D, *Harvard Business Review on Change* (Boston: Harvard Business School Press, 1998), 189–213. Copyright 1998 by the Harvard Business School Publishing Corporation; all rights reserved.

performance? *Results-driven change*, the *General Electric Workout*, and *organizational development* (OD) are three change tools and techniques that can be used to address these issues.

Results-driven change emphasizes quickly measuring and improving results.[74] When Ben van Beurden became CEO of Royal Dutch Shell, one of the world's largest oil companies, he put everyone in the company on notice by proclaiming that oil refining profits were "simply too low," and that Shell needed "better operational discipline." Furthermore, he changed managers' focus from "professional excellence," which served Shell well after a serious financial scandal, to specific results-driven goals. So van Beurden split Shell into 150 performance units, each to be evaluated on its profitability, with profitable units continuing and unprofitable units closing or being sold. Likewise, managers now had to compete for additional funds for their units by submitting formal requests to a central committee, which in turn had its spending recommendations reviewed by a "challenge committee."[75] An advantage of results-driven change is that managers introduce changes in procedures, philosophy, or behaviour only if they are likely to improve measured performance.[76] In other words, changes are tested to see whether they actually make a difference. Another advantage of results-driven change is that quick, visible improvements motivate employees to continue to make additional changes to improve measured performance. Exhibit 6.7 describes the basic steps of results-driven change.

The **General Electric Workout** is a special kind of results-driven change. The "workout" involves a three-day meeting that brings together managers and employees from different levels and parts of an organization to quickly generate and act on solutions to specific business problems.[77] On the first morning, the boss discusses the agenda and targets specific business problems that the group will solve. The boss then leaves, and an outside facilitator breaks the group (typically 30 to 40 people) into five or six teams and helps them spend the next day and a half discussing and debating solutions. On day three, in what GE calls a "town meeting," the teams present specific solutions to their boss, who has been gone since day one. As each team's spokesperson makes specific suggestions, the boss has only three options: agree on the spot, say no, or ask for more information so that a decision can be made by a specific, agreed-on date.[78]

GE boss Armand Lauzon sweated his way through a town meeting. To encourage him to say yes, his workers set up the meeting room to put pressure on him. He recalled: "I was wringing wet within half an hour. They had 108 proposals, I had about a minute to say yes or no to each one, and I couldn't make eye contact with *my* boss without turning around, which would show everyone in the room that I was chicken."[79] In the end, Lauzon agreed to all but eight suggestions. Furthermore, once

Results-driven change change created quickly by focusing on the measurement and improvement of results.

General Electric Workout a three-day meeting in which managers and employees from different levels and parts of an organization quickly generate and act on solutions to specific business problems.

Exhibit 6.8
General Steps for Organizational Development Interventions

1.	Entry	A problem is discovered and the need for change becomes apparent. A search begins for someone to deal with the problem and facilitate change.
2.	Startup	A change agent enters the picture and works to clarify the problem and gain commitment to a change effort.
3.	Assessment and feedback	The change agent gathers information about the problem and provides feedback about it to decision makers and those affected by it.
4.	Action planning	The change agent works with decision makers to develop an action plan.
5.	Intervention	The action plan, or organizational development intervention, is carried out.
6.	Evaluation	The change agent helps decision makers assess the effectiveness of the intervention.
7.	Adoption	Organizational members accept ownership and responsibility for the change, which is then carried out through the entire organization.
8.	Separation	The change agent leaves the organization after first ensuring that the change intervention will continue to work.

Sources: A. H. Church, C. T. Rotolo, A. Margulies, et al. "The Role of Personality in Organization Development: A Multi-Level Framework for Applying Personality to Individual, Team, and Organizational Change," *Research in Organizational Change and Development*, Volume 23, 2015; W. J. Rothwell, R. Sullivan, and G. M. McLean, *Practicing Organizational Development: A Guide for Consultants* (San Diego: Pfeiffer & Co., 1995).

those decisions were made, no one at GE was allowed to overrule them.

Organizational development is a philosophy and collection of planned change interventions designed to improve an organization's long-term health and performance. OD takes a long-range approach to change; assumes that top management support is necessary for change to succeed; creates change by educating workers and managers to change ideas, beliefs, and behaviours so that problems can be solved in new ways; and emphasizes employee participation in diagnosing, solving, and evaluating problems.[80] As shown in Exhibit 6.8, OD interventions begin with the recognition of a problem. Then, the company designates a **change agent** to

be formally in charge of guiding the change effort. This person can be someone from the company or a professional consultant. The change agent clarifies the problem, gathers information, works with decision makers to create and implement an action plan, helps evaluate the plan's effectiveness, implements the plan throughout the company, and then leaves (if from outside the company) after making sure the change intervention will continue to work.

Organizational development interventions are aimed at changing large systems, small groups, or people.[81] More specifically, the purpose of *large system interventions* is to change the character and performance of an organization, business unit, or department. *Small group interventions* focus on assessing how a group functions and helping it work more effectively to accomplish its goals. *Person-focused interventions* are intended to increase interpersonal effectiveness by helping people become aware of their attitudes and behaviours and acquire new skills and knowledge. Exhibit 6.9 describes the most frequently used organizational development interventions for large systems, small groups, and people.

Organizational development a philosophy and collection of planned change interventions designed to improve an organization's long-term health and performance.

Change agent the person formally in charge of guiding a change effort.

Exhibit 6.9

Different Kinds of Organizational Development Interventions

LARGE SYSTEM INTERVENTIONS	
Sociotechnical systems	An intervention designed to improve how well employees use and adjust to the work technology used in an organization.
Survey feedback	An intervention that uses surveys to collect information from the members, reports the results of that survey to the members, and then uses those results to develop action plans for improvement.
SMALL GROUP INTERVENTIONS	
Team building	An intervention designed to increase the cohesion and cooperation of work group members.
Unit goal setting	An intervention designed to help a work group establish short- and long-term goals.
PERSON-FOCUSED INTERVENTIONS	
Counselling/coaching	An intervention designed so that a formal helper or coach listens to managers or employees and advises them on how to deal with work or interpersonal problems.
Training	An intervention designed to provide individuals with the knowledge, skills, or attitudes they need to become more effective at their jobs.

Source: W.J. Rothwell, R. Sullivan, and G. M. McLean, *Practicing Organizational Development: A Guide for Consultants* (San Diego: Pfeiffer & Co., 1995).

STUDY TOOLS 6

READY TO STUDY?

LOCATED IN TEXTBOOK:

☐ Rip out the Chapter Review Card at the back of the book to have a summary of the chapter and key terms handy.

LOCATED AT NELSON.COM/STUDENT:

☐ Access the eBook or use the ReadSpeaker feature to listen to the chapter on the go.

☐ Prepare for tests with practice quizzes.

☐ Review key terms with flashcards and the glossary feature.

☐ Work through key concepts with case studies and Management Decision Exercises.

☐ Explore practical examples with You Make the Decision Activities.

7 Global Management

veer/iStockphoto

LEARNING OUTCOMES

After studying this chapter, you will be able to...

7-1 Discuss the impact of global business and the trade rules and agreements that govern it.

7-2 Explain why companies choose to standardize or adapt their business procedures.

7-3 Explain the different ways that companies can organize and act ethically to do business globally.

7-4 Explain how to find a favourable business climate.

7-5 Discuss the importance of identifying and adapting to cultural differences.

7-6 Explain how to successfully prepare workers for international assignments.

After you finish this chapter, go to **PAGE 151** for **STUDY TOOLS**

An International Outlook

The wider world beckoned Marcus Fuchs long before he ended up in global business. Straight out of high school, instead of immersing himself immediately in further studies in Canada, he headed for Europe with a backpack and, when his money ran out, earned his keep as an ESL (English as a second language) teacher. These days Marcus lives in Dubai, United Arab Emirates, and his titles include managing director of Gladstone Global Alliance—a worldwide alliance of asset management and distribution groups—and partner in CEREFunds (Central European Real Estate Funds). After his year away from Canada following high school, Marcus studied at Brock University in St. Catharines, Ontario from 1997 to 2001, graduating with a BA (honours) in economics and a Distinguished Graduating Student Award (his average was 93 percent). He recalls being accepted into all the top graduate schools in Canada after that. He chose Queen's University in Kingston, Ontario, and was the recipient of both the R.S. McLaughlin Fellowship and a Queen's Graduate Scholarship. He emerged in 2002 with an MA in economics. Marcus moved back to Europe, working as a university lecturer in Prague from 2003 to 2005. He also was involved in launching CEREFunds in that period. "When CEREFunds took off, I decided to stop teaching." In 2005, he moved to Dubai.

1. How would you sum up the kind of work you do these days?

Since 2012, my work has predominantly been investment development of early stage private equity companies as well as late stage venture capital firms. I generally look to take a stake in the business and build up the firms to either commercialize their products or bridge them with funds to raise further capital. I still am approached to provide corporate finance as well as real estate consultancy, but generally take a strong position with regards to financial benefits for Gladstone's business.

2. One of the companies you're involved in has offices in four countries. How difficult is it to keep on top of different trade rules and agreements?

Each office is generally operated independently and has its own directors and board meetings. This allows for a lower overall operating cost as we essentially do not have any cost centres in the group and each office must cover its own operating expenditure.

The global alliance I am building will allow each country to build in its own service model as well as specialize in what they are good at. This allows for independence as well as bonding to allow the overall brand and group to prosper.

3. You've obviously had to adapt to major cultural differences. Is that challenging?

It can be. I would say the biggest challenge is to not "go local," by which I mean become overly involved in the local social and cultural aspects and lose sight of the global economy. It's important to maintain one's identity.

4. How important to your work is the business climate in the regions you are involved in?

It's very important that the macroeconomics of the economy can drive the overall appetite for investment development. I am generally focused on the top three industries in each jurisdiction.

There are anticyclical business opportunities that allow for a greater chance of success when there is a downturn, but overall investment development is most successful when there's a perceived growth in the economy.

5. What about political risk?

Political risk can usually be insured. I often find that private equity and venture capital do not price political risk as accurately as more efficient markets such as stock markets (i.e., liquid assets). One should practise due diligence with every market one enters, and in my case having a philosophy of partnering with a strong "local/domestic" partner greatly reduces the overall timing risk of events.

6. Has anything about global business management surprised you?

Yes! What I find the most intriguing, being a small business owner and entrepreneur, is the perception between the employee and the employer. More so, with each culture.

I often struggle to understand the perceptions between a fixed-income business and a success-based business model and maintaining a constant payroll. I also struggle with the mindset of how employees feel empowerment of a role should be linked to income within that role. I'm often confronted by talented as well as inexperienced people seeking employment who really do not understand the motives of the career or salary/income they seek.

Often, I find, people in emerging or frontier markets can be more focused than those in more developed countries when it comes to wants/needs. I've concluded it doesn't matter how much you work; it matters how successfully you work!

7. What trait or skill has served you best in your career?

Understanding how money works as a tool in the world and not as a value instrument. And seeing that in business many people are motivated by greed or fear.

For the full interview go online to nelson.com/student

Photo and interview courtesy of Marcus Fuchs

7-1 GLOBAL BUSINESS, TRADE RULES, AND TRADE AGREEMENTS

Global business is the buying and selling of goods and services by people from different countries. The Timex watch on my wrist as I write this chapter was purchased at a Walmart in Manitoba. But since it was made in the Philippines, I participated in global business when I used my debit card at the Walmart in Winnipeg, which is a wholly owned subsidiary of Walmart USA. Walmart, for its part, had already paid Timex USA Group Inc., which in turn is owned by Timex Group B.V., a Dutch holding company (the corporate parent of several watchmaking companies around the globe, including Timex Group USA Inc.). Many of Timex Far East's wristwatches are manufactured by TMX Philippines Inc. in Lapu-Lapu, the Philippines, which pays the company that employs the Filipino managers and workers who made my watch. That's quite a story for a simple watch, but it's one that illustrates today's global environment.

Companies want to go global for a number of reasons: to grow into new markets while boosting their competitiveness, to cut manufacturing costs, and other similar drivers. While the incidence of early globalization by firms was a novel concept two decades ago, today global firms are found in abundance in many countries.[1]

Global business presents its own set of challenges for managers. How can you be sure that the way you run your business in one country is the right way to run that business in another? This chapter discusses how organizations answer that question. We will start by examining global business in two ways: first, by exploring its impact on Canadian businesses and then reviewing the basic rules and agreements that govern global trade. Next, we will examine how and when companies go global by considering the trade-off between consistency and adaptation and discussing how to organize a global company. Finally, we will look at how companies decide where to expand globally, including finding the best business climate, adapting to cultural differences, and preparing employees for international assignments.

If you want a simple demonstration of the impact of global business, look at your shirt, your shoes, and your smart phone (which most of the world calls a "mobile"). Chances are that these three items were made in different places around the world. My shirt, shoes, and mobile were made in Thailand, China, and Korea, respectively. Where were yours made?

*Let's learn more about **7-1a the impact of global business, 7-1b how tariff and nontariff trade barriers have historically restricted global business, 7-1c how global and regional trade agreements today are reducing trade barriers worldwide,** and **7-1d how consumers are responding to changes in trade rules and agreements.***

7-1a The Impact of Global Business

Multinational corporations are corporations that own businesses in two or more countries. Global foreign direct investment from multinational enterprises (MNEs) declined in 2014, mostly because of the fragility of the global economy, policy uncertainty for investors, and elevated geopolitical risks.[2] Today, most multinationals (more than 70 percent of them) are based in countries such as Germany, Italy, Canada, and Japan, and more than 25 percent are based in developing countries (such as Colombia, South Africa, and Tunisia). Today, multinationals can be found by the thousands all over the world.[3]

Another way to appreciate the impact of global business is to examine investment from other countries. **Foreign direct investment** occurs when a company builds a new business or buys an existing business in a foreign country. As an example, Canada's fifth-largest independent oil producer, Calgary's Talisman Energy, was purchased by Repsol, the Spanish oil major, for $8.3 billion.[4] Companies from the United Kingdom, Japan, Germany, the Netherlands, the United States, France, Switzerland, and Luxembourg have the largest foreign direct investment in Canada. Overall, foreign companies invest more than $500 billion a year in Canada.[5]

Global business the buying and selling of goods and services by people from different countries.

Multinational corporations corporations that own businesses in two or more countries.

Foreign direct investment a method of investment in which a company builds a new business or buys an existing business in a foreign country.

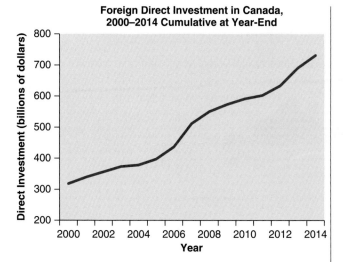

Foreign Direct Investment in Canada, 2000–2014 Cumulative at Year-End

Source: Statistics Canada. Table 376-0051, International investment position, Canadian direct investment abroad and foreign direct investment in Canada, by country, annual (dollars), (2016-04-26) CANSIM. http://www5.statcan.gc.ca/cansim/a26?lang=eng&retrLang=eng&id=3760051&&pattern=&stByVal=1&p1=1&p2=31&tabMode=dataTable&csid=. Reproduced and distributed on an "as is" basis with the permission of Statistics Canada.

But foreign direct investment in Canada is only half the picture. Canadian companies themselves have made large foreign direct investments in countries around the world. For example, in 2014, the total amount of Canadian outward investment increased almost 9 percent, while the dollar amount of Canadian outward investment to Asia increased by 11 percent. Most Canadian investment is in the United States but the United Kingdom follows close behind, and a significant amount goes to the Netherlands and Australia.[6] Note that there are many restrictions on foreign ownership in Canada. Broadcasting, aviation, liquor sales, mining, oil and gas, and pharmaceuticals are only some of the industries in which Canada restricts foreign ownership at both the provincial and the federal levels of government.[7]

Global management can be confusing. Consolidations are occurring in many industries worldwide. For example, the acquisition of Tim Hortons by Brazilian private equity group 3G Capital for $14.6 billion CDN was a transaction that combined Tim Hortons with Burger King (a 3G portfolio company) to form New York Stock Exchange-listed *Restaurant Brands International*.[8]

So whether it involves foreign companies investing in Canada or Canadian companies investing abroad, foreign direct investment is an increasingly important and common means of conducting global business.

7-1b Trade Barriers

Although today's consumers usually don't care where the products they buy come from (more on this in Section 7-1d), national governments have traditionally preferred that consumers buy domestically made products in the hope that this will strengthen domestic businesses and keep unemployment down. Indeed, governments have done much more than hope you will buy from domestic companies. In the past, governments have erected **trade barriers** to make it much more expensive or difficult (indeed, sometimes impossible) for consumers to buy or consume imported goods. For example, China places a 25 percent tax on cars imported to China. A tax is levied on almost all products; most import taxes are in the 10–20 percent range, but could be 1–40 percent.[9] The Canadian government imposes a tariff of 5 cents per litre on imported ethanol, which is blended with gasoline for use in automobiles.[10] By establishing these restrictions and taxes, the governments of China and Canada are engaging in **protectionism**, which is the use of trade barriers to protect local companies and their workers from foreign competition.

Governments have used two general kinds of trade barriers: tariff and nontariff. A **tariff** is a direct tax on imported goods. Tariffs increase the prices of imported goods relative to domestic goods. **Nontariff barriers** are nontax methods of increasing the cost or reducing the volume of imported goods. There are five types of nontariff barriers: *quotas, voluntary export restraints, government import standards, government subsidies,* and *customs valuation/classification*. Because there are so many different kinds of nontariff barriers, they can be an even more potent approach to shielding domestic industries from foreign competition.

Quotas are specific limits on the number or volume of imported products. For example, because of strict quotas, yearly imports of raw sugar cane into Canada are limited.[11] Since this is well below the demand for sugar in Canada, domestic Canadian sugar prices are much higher than sugar prices in the rest of the world.[12]

Like quotas, **voluntary export restraints** limit the amount of a product that can be imported annually.

Trade barriers government-imposed regulations that increase the cost and restrict the number of imported goods.

Protectionism a government's use of trade barriers to shield domestic companies and their workers from foreign competition.

Tariff a direct tax on imported goods.

Nontariff barriers nontax methods of increasing the cost or reducing the volume of imported goods.

Quotas limits on the number or volume of imported products.

Voluntary export restraints voluntarily imposed limits on the number or volume of products exported to a particular country.

Who Pays Tariffs?

Tariffs on foreign imports are supposed to preserve Canadian jobs, but 74 percent of shoes worn by Canadians are made outside Canada, suggesting that there aren't many Canadian jobs in the shoe industry to save. Still, Canada imposes a tax on imported shoes that can skyrocket to 32 percent, and the tariff creates $2 billion of revenue, which is more than auto tariffs. Who pays? Since low-end footwear bears the brunt of the tariff, it's mostly lower income individuals who shop at retail outlets such as Walmart Canada, where $5 of a $15 pair of tennis shoes may be a tariff.

Sources: CrossBorderShopping.ca, http://www.crossbordershopping.ca/calculators/canadian-duty-calculator; J. Davison, "New Duty-Free Limits Will Challenge Canadian Retailers," CBC News, May 31, 2012, www.cbc.ca/news/business/story/2012/05/31/f-duty-free-limits.html.

The difference is that the exporting country rather than the importing country imposes restraints. Usually, however, the "voluntary" offer to limit exports occurs because the importing country has implicitly threatened to impose quotas. According to the World Trade Organization (WTO), however, voluntary export restraints are illegal and should not be used to restrict imports (see Section 7-1c).[13]

In theory, **government import standards** are established to protect the health and safety of citizens. In reality, however, such standards are often used to restrict or ban imported goods. For example, the United States had banned the importation of nearly all Canadian beef. Ostensibly, the ban was to prevent transmission of mad cow disease (bovine spongiform encephalopathy, BSE), but the US government was actually using this government import standard to protect its own beef producers. Only after the WTO ruled that there was no scientific basis for the ban did the United States allow Canadian beef to be imported without restrictions.[14]

Many nations also use **government subsidies**—such as long-term, low-interest loans, cash grants, and tax deferments—to develop and protect companies in specific industries. Not surprisingly, businesses complain about unfair trade practices when companies receive government subsidies. For example, Embraer, the Brazilian jet airplane manufacturer, is complaining about the "investment" provided to Bombardier, the Montreal-based Canadian jet manufacturer, of about $1 billion in late 2015 (and the new Trudeau government is expected to contribute more). That particular dispute has been ongoing; the WTO has ruled on it many times. Meanwhile, the Canadian taxpayer picks up the subsidy costs.[15]

The last type of nontariff barrier is **customs valuation/classification**. When products are imported into a country, they are examined by customs agents, who must decide which of nearly 9,000 categories they fall into.[16] Classification is important because the category assigned by customs agents can greatly affect the size of the tariff and whether the item is subject to import quotas. For example, the Canadian

Government import standards standards ostensibly established to protect the health and safety of citizens but, in reality, often used to restrict imports.

Government subsidies government loans, grants, investments, and tax deferments given to domestic companies to protect them from foreign competition.

Customs valuation/classification a classification assigned to imported products by government officials that affects the size of the tariff and imposition of import quotas.

President Obama's government turned down the Keystone-XL pipeline.

Border Services Agency has several customs classifications for imported shoes. The tariff on imported leather or "nonrubber" shoes is about 10 percent, whereas the tariffs on imported rubber shoes, such as athletic footwear and waterproof shoes, are 20–84 percent.[17] The difference is large enough that some importers try to make their rubber shoes look like leather, hoping to receive the nonrubber customs classification and, it follows, the lower tariff.

7-1c Trade Agreements

Because of trade barriers, imported goods were often much more expensive than domestic goods if they could be purchased at all. A significant change occurred when 124 countries agreed to adopt the **General Agreement on Tariffs and Trade (GATT)** and make changes to encourage international trade. GATT was replaced in 1995 by the **World Trade Organization (WTO)**, which in July 2016 had 164 member countries and was headquartered in Geneva, Switzerland. It administers trade agreements, provides a forum for trade negotiations, handles trade disputes, monitors national trade policies, and offers technical assistance and training for developing countries.

In a number of ways, GATT made it much easier and cheaper for consumers in all countries to buy imported products. First, it cut tariffs by an average of 40 percent worldwide. Second, it eliminated tariffs in 10 specific industries: beer, alcohol, construction equipment, farm machinery, furniture, medical equipment, paper, pharmaceuticals, steel, and toys. Third, it placed stricter limits on government subsidies. Fourth, GATT established protections for intellectual property, such as trademarks, patents, and copyrights. Protection of intellectual property has become an increasingly important issue in global trade because of widespread product piracy. For example, 90 percent of the computer software and 95 percent of the video games in China are illegal copies.[18] Finally, trade disputes between countries are now settled by WTO arbitration panels. Countries had once been able to use their veto power to cancel a panel's decision; today, WTO rulings are final, but not binding.

The second major development to reduce trade barriers has been the creation of **regional trading zones**. By treaty or agreement, the countries within these zones reduce or eliminate tariff and nontariff barriers among themselves. The largest and most important trading zones are in Europe (Maastricht Treaty), North America (North American Free Trade Agreement, or NAFTA), Central America (Central

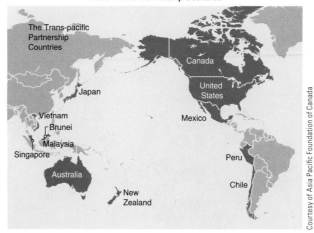

Trans-Pacific Partnership Countries

Courtesy of Asia Pacific Foundation of Canada

America Free Trade Agreement, or CAFTA-DR), South America (Union of South American Nations, or UNASUR), and Asia (Association of Southeast Asian Nations, or ASEAN, and Asia-Pacific Economic Cooperation, or APEC). Canada has just taken part in the new Trans-Pacific Partnership (TPP), the largest, most ambitious free trade initiative in history. It is a comprehensive, economic, strategic, and balanced agreement that will increase Canada's foothold in Asia-Pacific, a region that is expected to comprise two-thirds of the world's middle class by 2030, and one-half of global gross domestic product (GDP) by 2050.[19] The TPP is not without its critics and the new Liberal government of Justin Trudeau will have a rocky road instituting its far reaching policies.[20] Compare the following maps showing the TPP countries and, in Exhibit 7.1, the extent to which free trade agreements govern global trade.

The purpose of **Europe's Maastricht Treaty** was to transform all the different European economies and

General Agreement on Tariffs and Trade (GATT) a worldwide trade agreement that reduced and eliminated tariffs, limited government subsidies, and established protections for intellectual property.

World Trade Organization (WTO) the successor to GATT, the only international organization dealing with the global rules of trade between nations; its main function is to ensure that trade flows as smoothly, predictably, and freely as possible.

Regional trading zones areas in which tariff and nontariff barriers on trade between countries are reduced or eliminated.

Europe's Maastricht Treaty a regional trade agreement between most European countries.

Exhibit 7.1
Global Map of Regional Trade Agreements

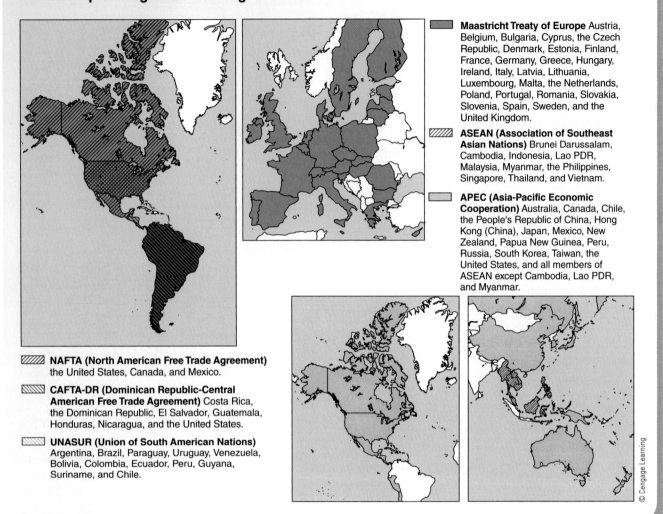

Maastricht Treaty of Europe Austria, Belgium, Bulgaria, Cyprus, the Czech Republic, Denmark, Estonia, Finland, France, Germany, Greece, Hungary, Ireland, Italy, Latvia, Lithuania, Luxembourg, Malta, the Netherlands, Poland, Portugal, Romania, Slovakia, Slovenia, Spain, Sweden, and the United Kingdom.

ASEAN (Association of Southeast Asian Nations) Brunei Darussalam, Cambodia, Indonesia, Lao PDR, Malaysia, Myanmar, the Philippines, Singapore, Thailand, and Vietnam.

APEC (Asia-Pacific Economic Cooperation) Australia, Canada, Chile, the People's Republic of China, Hong Kong (China), Japan, Mexico, New Zealand, Papua New Guinea, Peru, Russia, South Korea, Taiwan, the United States, and all members of ASEAN except Cambodia, Lao PDR, and Myanmar.

NAFTA (North American Free Trade Agreement) the United States, Canada, and Mexico.

CAFTA-DR (Dominican Republic-Central American Free Trade Agreement) Costa Rica, the Dominican Republic, El Salvador, Guatemala, Honduras, Nicaragua, and the United States.

UNASUR (Union of South American Nations) Argentina, Brazil, Paraguay, Uruguay, Venezuela, Bolivia, Colombia, Ecuador, Peru, Guyana, Suriname, and Chile.

© Cengage Learning

currencies into one common economic market, called the European Union (EU), with one common currency, the euro. As of July 2016, there are 28 countries in the EU, and Iceland, Montenegro, Serbia, and Turkey have applied and are being considered for membership.[21] Brexit (the exit of Britain from the EU) could have a major impact on the EU in the future.

Prior to the Maastricht Treaty, trucks carrying products were stopped and inspected by customs agents at each border of each country in Europe. Furthermore, since the required paperwork, tariffs, and government product specifications could be radically different in each country, companies often had to file 12 different sets of paperwork, pay 12 different tariffs, produce 12 different versions of their basic products to meet various government specifications, and exchange money in 12 different currencies. Similarly, open business travel was complicated by inspections at each border crossing. If you lived in Germany but worked in Luxembourg, your car was stopped and your passport was inspected twice every day as you travelled to and from work. Also, every business transaction required a currency exchange, for example, from German marks to Italian lira, or from French francs to Dutch guilders. Imagine all of this happening to millions of trucks, cars, and businesspeople, and you can begin to appreciate the difficulty and cost of conducting business across Europe before the Maastricht Treaty.[22]

The **North American Free Trade Agreement (NAFTA)** between the United States, Canada, and Mexico, went into effect on January 1, 1994. More than any other regional trade agreement, NAFTA has liberalized trade between countries so that businesses can plan for one market (North America) rather than for three separate ones (the United States, Canada, and Mexico). One of NAFTA's most important achievements was to eliminate most product tariffs *and* prevent Canada, the United States, and Mexico from increasing existing tariffs or introducing new ones. Mexican and Canadian exports to the United States have doubled since NAFTA went into effect. US exports to Mexico and Canada have doubled, too, which is twice as fast as US exports to any other part of the world.[23] Mexico and Canada now account for 32 percent of all US exports.[24]

The Dominican Republic–**Central America Free Trade Agreement (CAFTA–DR)** between the United States, the Dominican Republic, and the Central American countries of Costa Rica, El Salvador, Guatemala, Honduras, and Nicaragua, went into effect in August 2005. With a combined population of 51.1 million, the CAFTA-DR countries together are the twelfth-largest US export market in the world and the third-largest US export market in Latin America after Mexico. US companies export more than $20 billion in goods each year to the CAFTA-DR countries.[25]

On May 23, 2008, 12 South American countries signed the **Union of South American Nations (UNASUR)** Constitutive Treaty, uniting the former Mercosur (Argentina, Brazil, Paraguay, Uruguay, Venezuela) and Andean Community (Bolivia, Colombia, Ecuador, Peru) alliances along with Guyana, Suriname, and Chile. UNASUR aims to create a unified South America by permitting free movement between nations, creating a common infrastructure (including an inter-oceanic highway), and establishing the region as a single market by eliminating tariffs by 2019. UNASUR is one of the largest trading zones in the world, encompassing 361 million people in South America with a combined GDP of nearly $1 trillion.[26]

The **Association of Southeast Asian Nations (ASEAN)** and **Asia-Pacific Economic Cooperation (APEC)** are the two largest and most important regional trading groups in Asia. ASEAN is a trade agreement between Brunei Darussalam, Cambodia, Indonesia, Lao PDR, Malaysia, Myanmar, the Philippines, Singapore, Thailand, and Vietnam. Together, these form a market of more than 616 million people. Canadian trade with ASEAN countries exceeds $90 billion a year. In fact, Canada is ASEAN's fifth-largest trading partner (Japan is its largest), and ASEAN's member nations constitute the eighth-largest trading partner of Canada.

APEC is a broader agreement that includes Australia, Canada, Chile, the People's Republic of China, Hong Kong (China), Japan, Mexico, New Zealand, Papua New Guinea, Peru, Russia, South Korea, Taiwan, the United States, and all the members of ASEAN except Cambodia, Lao PDR, and Myanmar. APEC's 21 member countries

---

North American Free Trade Agreement (NAFTA)
a regional trade agreement between the United States, Canada, and Mexico.

Central America Free Trade Agreement (CAFTA-DR) a regional trade agreement between Costa Rica, the Dominican Republic, El Salvador, Guatemala, Honduras, Nicaragua, and the United States.

Union of South American Nations (UNASUR)
a regional trade agreement between Argentina, Brazil, Paraguay, Uruguay, Venezuela, Bolivia, Colombia, Ecuador, Peru, Guyana, Suriname, and Chile.

Association of Southeast Asian Nations (ASEAN)
a regional trade agreement between Brunei Darussalam, Cambodia, Indonesia, Lao PDR, Malaysia, Myanmar, the Philippines, Singapore, Thailand, and Vietnam.

Asia-Pacific Economic Cooperation (APEC) a regional trade agreement between Australia, Canada, Chile, the People's Republic of China, Hong Kong, Japan, Mexico, New Zealand, Papua New Guinea, Peru, Russia, South Korea, Taiwan, the United States, and all members of ASEAN, except Cambodia, Lao PDR, and Myanmar.

THE CANADIAN PRESS/Mark Spowart

contain 2.79 billion people, account for 44 percent of all global trade, and have a combined GDP of over $41 trillion.[27] APEC countries began reducing trade barriers in 2000; all the reductions will not be completely phased in until 2020.[28]

Currently, the Ambassador Bridge in Windsor, Ontario, is the busiest border crossing between Canada and the United States, carrying 25 percent of all merchandise trade between the two countries, or roughly $182 billion in annual trade going in both directions.[29] The bridge is slated to be replaced in the future, but with what, and when exactly, are unknown.

7-1d Consumers, Trade Barriers, and Trade Agreements

The average worker earns nearly $117,930 a year in Switzerland, $133,050 in Norway, $54,060 in Japan, and $66,690 in Canada. Yet, after adjusting these incomes for how much they can buy, the Norwegian income is equivalent to $65,970, the Swiss income is equivalent to just $59,600; Canada comes in at $43,400 and the Japanese income is just $37,920![30] This is the same as saying that $1 of income can buy you about 58 cents' worth of goods in Switzerland and Norway, and 88 cents' worth in Japan and about 90 cents' worth in Canada. In other words, Canadians can buy much more with their incomes than those in other countries can.[31]

One reason why Canadians get more for their money is that the Canadian marketplace has been one of the easiest for foreign companies to enter. Some Canadian industries, such as agriculture, have been heavily protected from foreign competition by trade barriers but, for the most part, Canadian consumers (and businesses) have had plentiful choices between Canadian-made and foreign-made products. More important, the high level of competition between foreign and domestic companies that has created these choices has helped keep prices low in Canada. Furthermore, it is precisely the lack of choice and the low level of competition that has kept prices higher in countries that have not been as open to foreign companies and products. For example, Japanese trade barriers are estimated to cost Japanese consumers more than $100 billion a year and amount to a 51 percent tax on food for the average Japanese family.[32]

Free trade agreements are important to consumers because they increase choices, competition, and purchasing power and thereby decrease what people pay for food, clothing, necessities, and luxuries. Accordingly, today's consumers rarely care where their products and services come from.

Free trade agreements matter to managers because, as you're about to read, while those agreements create new business opportunities, they also intensify competition, and addressing that competition is a manager's job.

7-2 CONSISTENCY OR ADAPTATION?

Once a company has decided it *will* go global, it must decide *how* it will go global. For example, if you decide to sell in Singapore, should you try to find a local business partner who speaks the language, knows the laws, and understands the customs and norms of Singapore's culture, or should you simply export your products from your home country? What do you do if you are also entering Eastern Europe, perhaps starting in Hungary? Should you use the same approach in Hungary that you used in Singapore? In this section, we return to a key issue: How can you be sure that the way you run your business in one country is the right way to run that business in another country? In other words, how can you strike the right balance between global consistency and local adaptation?

Global consistency means that when a multinational company has offices, manufacturing plants, and distribution facilities in different countries, it will use the same rules, guidelines, policies, and procedures to run those offices, plants, and facilities. Managers at company headquarters

---

Global consistency when a multinational company has offices, manufacturing plants, and distribution facilities in different countries and runs them all using the same rules, guidelines, policies, and procedures.

The Maharaja Mac is made from chicken in India

value global consistency because it simplifies decisions. By contrast, a company with a **local adaptation** policy modifies its standard operating procedures to adapt to differences in foreign customers, governments, and regulatory agencies. Local adaptation is typically more important to the local managers who are charged with making the international business successful in their countries; hamburgers don't sell all that well in India, so the "Maharaja Mac" is made from a chicken patty.[33]

If companies lean too much toward global consistency, they run the risk of using management procedures poorly suited to particular countries' markets, cultures, and employees (i.e., a lack of local adaptation). Home Depot became the biggest hardware and home improvement retailer in Canada thanks to its big-box model featuring huge stores, hundreds of suburban locations, a vast range of products, and strong customer service. But, after eight years, Home Depot closed its seven Chinese stores. Unlike Canadians, who are do-it-yourselfers (DIY) when

Annette Verschuren, former Home Depot CEO

it comes to home improvement because it saves money, the widespread availability of low-cost labour makes China more of a "do-it-for-me culture," says a Home Depot spokesperson. Furthermore, unlike Canada, where completing DIY projects is admired, there's a stigma associated with performing manual labour in China. A Chinese middle-class customer said, "Poor people are the only group in China who would bother taking on a DIY project, because they cannot afford to hire others."[34] And, unlike in Canada, where a much higher percentage of people own their homes, most Chinese, especially those with the discretionary income to afford home projects, rent small apartments in cities, which further diminished Home Depot's opportunities in China.[35] For her contribution to Canadian business, Annette Verschuren was named an Officer of the Order of Canada in 2011, the same year she stepped down from running Home Depot Canada. Verschuren led Home Depot's foray into China during 2005–2008, but things did not go well after she left.[36]

If, however, companies focus too much on local adaptation, they run the risk of losing the cost effectiveness and productivity that result from using standardized rules and procedures throughout the world. Because its French stores are nearly identical to its Canadian stores, Starbucks has never been profitable in France. As a result, says Parisian Marion Bayod, "I never go into Starbucks; it's impersonal, the coffee is mediocre, and it's expensive. For us, it's like another planet." Likewise, Parisian Laurent Pauzié says Starbucks stores "are only here to comfort tourists when they're lost." Canadian Kate Menzies, who lives in Paris, concedes that while Starbucks may not be popular for its coffee, it "is one of the few places with public toilets and free Wi-Fi in the city."[37] Starbucks, however, is now embracing local adaptation. Rather than offering strong coffee in paper cups as in Canada, its French stores will offer a lighter-tasting "blonde" espresso in glass coffee cups (because the French prefer to sit and drink) in larger redesigned stores with sumptuous wooden bars, bright chandeliers, and velvet couches, similar to traditional Parisian cafés. While Starbucks hopes these changes will attract French customers, spending tens of millions more to adapt its stores to French tastes may also sacrifice the cost effectiveness and productivity that make it profitable in Canada.[38]

Local adaptation when a multinational company modifies its rules, guidelines, policies, and procedures to adapt to differences in foreign customers, governments, and regulatory agencies.

CHAPTER 7: Global Management

7-3 FORMS OF GLOBAL BUSINESS

*In the past, companies have generally followed the phase model of globalization, shown in Exhibit 7-2. That is, they have made the transition from a domestic company to a global one in the following sequence: **7-3a exporting, 7-3b using cooperative contracts, 7-3c forming strategic alliances,** and **7-3d acquiring wholly owned affiliates.** At each phase, the company grows larger, uses the resulting resources to enter more global markets, depends less on home country sales, and becomes more committed to its global orientation. Some companies, however, do not follow the phase model of globalization.[39] Instead, they skip phases on their way to becoming more global and less domestic, **7-3e becoming global new ventures.** This section reviews these forms of global business.[40]*

7-3a Exporting

When companies produce products in their home countries and sell those products to customers in foreign countries, they are **exporting**. Exporting as a form of

Exporting selling domestically produced products to customers in foreign countries.

global business offers many advantages. It makes the company less dependent on sales in its home market and provides a greater degree of control over research, design, and production decisions. For example, while auto sales in Europe dropped 8.2 percent in 2012, the largest single-year decline in two decades, sales of Jaguars and Land Rovers, built in the United Kingdom, were up 32 percent due largely to exports to China and Asia.[41]

Though advantageous in a number of ways, exporting also has its disadvantages. The primary disadvantage is that many exported goods are subject to tariff and nontariff barriers that can substantially increase their final cost to consumers. A second disadvantage is that transportation costs can significantly increase the price of an exported product. For example, when the price of crude oil was approaching $150 a barrel, manufacturers who made everything from batteries to sofas to industrial parts started bringing manufacturing production from overseas back to Canada. Jeff Rubin, chief economist at CIBC World Markets in Toronto, said, "In a world of triple-digit oil prices, distance costs money."[42] There is a third disadvantage of exporting: companies that export depend on foreign importers for product distribution. If, for example, the foreign importer makes a mistake on the paperwork that accompanies a shipment of imported goods, those goods can be returned to the foreign manufacturer at the manufacturer's expense.

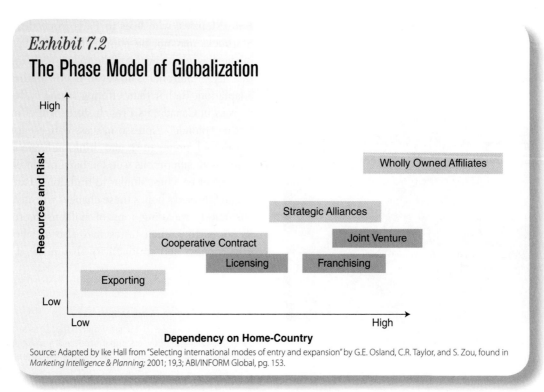

Exhibit 7.2
The Phase Model of Globalization

Source: Adapted by Ike Hall from "Selecting international modes of entry and expansion" by G.E. Osland, C.R. Taylor, and S. Zou, found in *Marketing Intelligence & Planning;* 2001; 19,3; ABI/INFORM Global, pg. 153.

Bubbly Imports

Although you can build a plant to manufacture cars, textiles, or toys virtually anywhere in the world, some products must be imported because they can only be produced in one place. Chardonnay grapes, commonly used to make sparkling wine, can be grown anywhere you can plant a vineyard, but champagne comes solely from one small region in France. Every wine has a unique characteristic called terroir, which comes from a combination of the grape variety and the soil and climate in which it is grown. The unique climate and chalky soil of the Champagne region makes champagne unique. It cannot be replicated anywhere else in the world. The name *champagne*, like *burgundy*, is legally protected in France, where it can be used only for wines from that region. Other sparkling wines from California, Spain (Cava), and the Italian Piedmont (Asti) each have their own unique terroir. Drink and enjoy, but don't call it champagne. Canada supports

Lisa S./Shutterstock

this approach to naming, mainly because it is hard to fight this logic, but also because Canada wants to claim the rights to ice wine, Canadian maple syrup, and rye whiskey (among others).

Sources: D. Vinifera, "The 2006 U. S. and European Union Wine Trade Agreement," *Wine Spectator,* November 4, 2015, http://www.winespectator.com/drvinny/show/id/5011; M. Mason, "Warning: I Hate Champagne. It's All Right to Dislike Any Other Drink. But About This One, People Have Funny Ideas," June 13, 2015, *The Spectator,* http://new .spectator.co.uk/2015/06/warning-i-hate-champagne/; L. A. Zahn, "Australia Corked Its Champagne and So Should We: Enforcing Stricter Protections for Semi-Generic Wines in the United States," *Journal of Transnational Law & Contemporary Problems,* 2015.

Canada used to be one of the most expensive places in the world to produce cars. But the fluctuating dollar and new contracts with workers are making production cheaper, prompting companies to rethink their strategies. Canadian automakers such as Chrysler are exporting Canadian-made cars to Europe, China, and Brazil. Chrysler is even moving some of its European production into Canada. Moreover, foreign companies like BMW AG are ramping up their foreign direct investment in Canada, manufacturing their cars here for export to Europe. Energy's eight-year run as Canada's biggest export is over. A Statistics Canada report in late 2015 showed that shipments of motor vehicles surpassed those of energy for the first time since 2007, as oil prices plunged and a weaker currency enhanced Canada's competitiveness.[43]

7-3b Using Cooperative Contracts

When an organization wants to expand its business globally without making a large financial commitment to do so, it may sign a **cooperative contract** with a foreign business owner, who pays the company a fee for the right to conduct that business in his or her country. There are two kinds of cooperative contracts: licensing and franchising.

Under a **licensing** agreement, a domestic company, the *licensor*, receives royalty payments for allowing another company, the *licensee*, to produce its product, sell its service, or use its brand name in a particular foreign market. For example, Labatt brews 50 different brands and is licensed to make and distribute throughout Canada the brands of Budweiser, Bud Light and PC Premium Draft. Known as the pioneer of "ice" beer, the company also brews the number-three import *into* the United States, Labatt Blue.[44] Licensing is favourable in these instances because of Canada's complex alcohol distribution system.

A key advantage of licensing is that it allows companies to earn additional profits without investing more money. As foreign sales increase, so do the royalties paid to the licensor by the foreign licensee. Moreover, it is

Cooperative contract an agreement in which a foreign business owner pays a company a fee for the right to conduct that business in his or her country.

Licensing an agreement in which a domestic company, the licensor, receives royalty payments for allowing another company, the licensee, to produce the licensor's product, sell its service, or use its brand name in a specified foreign market.

the licensee, not the licensor, who invests in production equipment and facilities to produce the licensed product. Licensing also helps companies avoid tariff and nontariff barriers. Since the licensee manufactures the product within the foreign country, tariff and nontariff barriers don't apply.

The biggest disadvantage associated with licensing is that the licensor gives up control over the quality of the product or service sold by the foreign licensee. Unless the licensing agreement contains specific restrictions, the licensee controls the entire business from production to marketing to final sales. Many licensors include inspection clauses in their licence contracts, but closely monitoring product or service quality from thousands of miles away can be difficult. An additional disadvantage is that licensees can eventually become competitors, especially when a licensing agreement includes access to important technology or proprietary business knowledge.

A **franchise** is a collection of networked firms in which the manufacturer or marketer of a product or service, the *franchisor*, licenses the entire business to another person or organization, the *franchisee*. For the price of an initial franchise fee plus royalties, franchisors provide franchisees with training, assistance with marketing and advertising, and an exclusive right to conduct business in a particular location. More than 400 companies franchise their businesses to foreign franchise partners. Overall, franchising is a way to enter foreign markets quickly. Over the past 20 years, franchisors have more than doubled their global franchises; there are now more than 100,000 global franchise units. Remember that the KFC or McDonald's restaurant in Indonesia, or Vietnam, is owned by a local business person, much the same as it is here at home in Canada.

Customizing menus to local tastes is one of the primary ways that fast-food companies can succeed in international markets. With a 40 percent market share, 4,500 locations in more than 1,050 cities, and a new restaurant opening every 18 hours, KFC, which is part of Yum! Brands, is the most successful foreign restaurant chain in China, even outperforming McDonald's, which has 16 percent of the market. Unlike McDonald's, which largely sells the same food in China as it does

testing/Shutterstock.com

in the United States, KFC China, which is run by Chinese managers hired by Yum! Brands, has focused on providing Chinese-flavoured dishes—such as the Dragon Twister, a chicken wrap with duck sauce, and tofu chicken rice—designed to reflect the spicy food found in China's Sichuan province. And, while Chinese customers will find some Western menu items like chicken and corn on the cob, they'll also find Chinese favourites like fried dough sticks, congee (rice porridge), preserved eggs, and other dishes that cater more to local tastes.[45]

Franchising has many advantages. However, franchisors face a loss of control when they sell businesses to franchisees who are thousands of kilometres away. And while there are exceptions, franchising success may be somewhat culture-bound. In other words, because most global franchisors begin by franchising their businesses in similar countries or regions (Canada is by far the first choice for American companies taking their first step into global franchising), and because 65 percent of franchisors make absolutely no change in their business for overseas franchisees, that success may not generalize to cultures with different lifestyles, values, preferences, and technological infrastructures.

7-3c Forming Strategic Alliances

Companies form a **strategic alliance** to combine key resources, costs, risks, technology, and people. Hewlett-Packard, the world's largest electronics manufacturer, with a 28 percent share of the computer server market, and Foxconn, the Taiwanese firm that assembles some of the world's most popular electronic devices, such as the iPhone and iPad, have formed a strategic alliance to co-develop large servers that can handle cloud computing and process "big data" for multinational firms.[46] The most common strategic

Franchise a collection of networked firms in which the manufacturer or marketer of a product or service, the franchisor, licenses the entire business to another person or organization, the franchisee.

Strategic alliance an agreement in which companies combine key resources, costs, risk, technology, and people.

Tim Hortons Takes on the World

Tim Hortons Inc. conjures no warm and fuzzy childhood memories or feelings of patriotic pride for Azam Shibli, a 36-year-old professional based in Abu Dhabi. "It's hard to distinguish between Tim Hortons and Starbucks and Dunkin' Donuts," Shibli said, making a comment that would probably raise eyebrows, were he to utter it in Canada. "I feel like it's maybe slightly cheaper and slightly worse."

And yet, since the Canadian coffee and doughnut chain started opening locations in his city three years ago, Shibli tends to find himself at the order counter. If there's nothing particularly memorable about it, there's nothing wrong with it, either—plus, there's a Tim's at a convenient point where Shibli stops when he makes the drive between Abu Dhabi and Dubai. And, he said, "those little Timbits are always kind of nice."

Just a few years after entering the United States, Tim Hortons has already beaten out chains like Caribou Coffee Co. Inc. that had been around for a lot longer, and it might do even better appealing to the growing demographic of Hispanic customers and lower-to-middle income groups.

Pawel Dwulit

Rohit Deshpande, a marketing professor at Harvard Business School who has studied country of origin branding, said marketing a brand's national roots is a good way to appeal to even foreign consumers looking for authenticity—think Italian sports cars, or Swiss watches.

Source: C. Brownell, "Tim Hortons Takes on the World: How Going Global Could Change the Soul of Canada's Coffee Chain," *Financial Post*, August 30, 2014. Material republished with the express permission of National Post, a division of Postmedia Network Inc. http://business.financialpost.com/news/retail-marketing/tim-hortons-takes-on-the-world-how-going-global-could-change-the-soul-of-canadas-coffee-chain.

alliance is a **joint venture**, which occurs when two existing companies collaborate to form a third company.

One advantage of global joint ventures is that, like licensing and franchising, they help companies avoid tariff and nontariff barriers to entry. Another advantage is that companies participating in a joint venture bear only part of the costs and risks of that business. Many companies find this attractive because it is expensive to enter foreign markets and develop new products.

Joint ventures can provide many benefits for Canadian companies working in China, says Paul Kim, chief financial officer of Vancouver's BioteQ Environmental Technologies Inc. "Joint ventures are a good way for small companies to begin operations," he says. A joint venture involves a partnership between Canadian and Chinese investors who share the management, profits, and losses. BioteQ, which develops custom wastewater treatment solutions for the global mining industry, operates a water treatment plant at China's Dexing Mine in a 50–50 joint venture with the Jiangxi Copper Company (JCC). The Vancouver-based business and the largest copper mining company in China are currently completing their fourth water treatment project at the mine. BioteQ's joint venture uses local employees to operate the plant with technical supervision from BioteQ in

Vancouver and assistance from the Chinese company to integrate the water treatment into the entire operation.[47]

Global joint ventures can be especially advantageous to smaller local partners, as they link up with larger, more experienced foreign firms that bring advanced management, resources, and business skills to the joint venture. Global joint ventures are not without problems, however. Because companies share costs and risks with their joint venture partners, they must also share profits. Also, managing global joint ventures can be difficult because they represent a merging of four cultures: the country and organizational cultures of the first partner and the country and organizational cultures of the second partner. Often, to be fair to all involved, each partner in the global joint venture will have equal ownership and power. But this can result in power struggles and a lack of leadership. Because of these problems, companies forming global joint ventures should carefully develop detailed contracts that specify the obligations of each party. This care is important because more than half of global joint ventures fail.[48]

> **Joint venture** a strategic alliance in which two existing companies collaborate to form a third, independent company.

7-3d Acquiring Wholly Owned Affiliates (Build or Buy)

Around one-third of multinational companies enter foreign markets through wholly owned affiliates. Unlike licensing arrangements, franchises, or joint ventures, **wholly owned affiliates** are 100 percent owned by the parent company. For example, Honda Canada Inc. and Honda of Canada Mfg. in Ontario are 100 percent owned by Honda Motor in Japan and celebrated 47 and 30 years, respectively, in Canada in 2016.

The primary advantage of wholly owned businesses is that the parent company receives all of the profits and has complete control over the foreign facilities. The biggest disadvantage is the expense of building new operations or buying existing businesses. The payoff can be enormous if a wholly owned affiliate succeeds; but the losses can be immense if it fails because the parent company assumes all of the risk.

7-3e Becoming Global New Ventures

Companies used to evolve slowly from small operations selling in their home markets to large businesses selling to foreign markets. Furthermore, as companies went global, they usually followed the phase model of globalization. Recently, however, three trends have combined to allow companies to skip the phase model when going global. First, quick and reliable air travel can transport people nearly anywhere in the world within a day. Second, low-cost communication technologies (such as international email, teleconferencing, phone conferencing, and the Internet) are making it easier to communicate with global customers, suppliers, managers, and employees. Third, there is now a critical mass of businesspeople with extensive personal experience in all aspects of global business.[49] This combination of developments has made it possible to start companies that are global from inception. **Global new ventures** are companies that are founded with an active global strategy, with sales, employees, and financing in different countries.[50]

There are several different kinds of global new ventures; all of them, though, share two factors. First,

Honda Canada CEO Jerry Chenkin is joined by Ontario premier Kathleen Wynne and minister of economic development, employment, and infrastructure Brad Duguid at an investment announcement in Alliston, Ontario.

Office of the Premier, Ontario.

the founders successfully develop and communicate their company's global vision from inception. Second, rather than going global one country at a time, new global ventures bring a product or service to market in several foreign markets at the same time.

MakerBot 3-D printers "print" items made of rigid plastic based on specifications from computer-aided design software like AutoDesk. NASA's Jet Propulsion Laboratory uses MakerBot's Replicator 2 (hat tip to *Star Trek*) to print prototype parts cheaply and quickly. Cofounder Bre Pettis believes that MakerBot can fundamentally disrupt global manufacturing and replace "two centuries of mass production" by giving anyone with an idea the tools to design their own products without a factory. Though just four years old, MakerBot, which has been global since inception, has distributors in 14 countries, including in Canada at Staples and other retailers.[51]

7-4 FINDING THE BEST BUSINESS CLIMATE

Deciding *where* to go global is just as important as deciding *how* your company will go global. Other parts of this equation include *what* to go global with (your services and your goods) and *who* to go global with (in strategic alliances, mergers, or with licensing). When deciding where to go global, companies look for countries or regions with

Wholly owned affiliates foreign offices, facilities, and manufacturing plants that are 100 percent owned by the parent company.

Global new ventures new companies that are founded with an active global strategy and have sales, employees, and financing in different countries.

Exhibit 7.3

How Consumption of Coca-Cola Varies With Purchasing Power Around the World

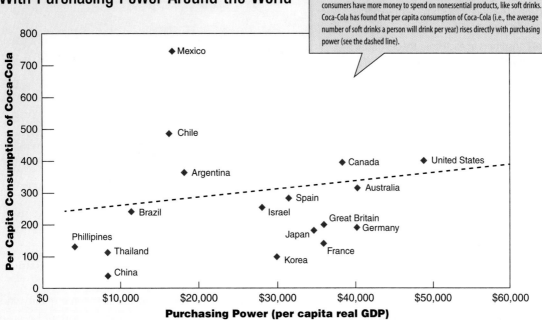

Typically, the higher the purchasing power in a country, the better that country will be for doing business. Why? Because higher purchasing power means that consumers have more money to spend on nonessential products, like soft drinks. Coca-Cola has found that per capita consumption of Coca-Cola (i.e., the average number of soft drinks a person will drink per year) rises directly with purchasing power (see the dashed line).

Per Capita Consumption of Coca-Cola (y-axis: 0 to 800)
Purchasing Power (per capita real GDP) (x-axis: $0 to $60,000)

Data points: Mexico, Chile, Argentina, Canada, United States, Australia, Spain, Israel, Great Britain, Japan, Germany, Brazil, France, Phillipines, Thailand, Korea, China

Sources: "Coca-Cola 2012 Annual Review," *Coca-Cola* Company, accessed June 10, 2013, http://www.coca-colacompany.com/annual-review/2012/year_in_review.html; "GNI Per Capita Ranking, Atlas Method and PPP Based," *The World Bank*, April 15, 2013, accessed June 10, 2013, http://data.worldbank.org/data-catalog /GNI-per-capita-Atlas-and-PPP-table.

Even Coca-Cola, which is available in more than 200 countries, still has tremendous potential for further global growth. Currently, the Coca-Cola Company gets about 80 percent of its sales from its 16 largest markets.

---

a promising business climate, promising partners, and promising markets for their products and services.

An attractive global business climate 7-4a positions the company for easy access to growing markets, 7-4b is an effective but cost-efficient place to build an office or manufacturing facility, and 7-4c minimizes the political risk to the company.

7-4a Growing Markets

The most important factor in an attractive business climate is access to a growing market. For example, no product is known and purchased by as many people throughout the world as Coca-Cola. Yet even Coke, which is available in over 200 countries, still has tremendous potential for further global growth. Coca-Cola gets 79 percent of its sales outside of North America, and emerging markets (where it has seen its fastest growth) now account for half of Coke's sales worldwide.[52] Two factors help companies

determine the growth potential of foreign markets: purchasing power and foreign competitors. **Purchasing power** is measured by comparing the relative cost of a standard set of goods and services in different countries. For example, a 600 mL bottle of Coke costs $3.79 in Oslo, Norway. Because that same Coke costs only $2.10 in Canada, the average Canadian would have more purchasing power than the average Norwegian.[53] Exhibit 7.3 illustrates the relationship between global Coke consumption and countries' purchasing power. Purchasing power is strong in countries like Mexico, India, and China, even though they have low average levels of income, because basic living expenses (such as food, shelter, and transportation) are very inexpensive in those countries. Millions of Chinese, Mexican, and

> **Purchasing power** a comparison of the relative cost of a standard set of goods and services in different countries.

Paying for a "Mac Attack"

Every year, *The Economist* magazine produces the Big Mac Index to illustrate differences in purchasing power across countries. By comparing the price of a single item—in this case, a Big Mac from McDonald's—the index shows how much (or how little) consumers in each country get for their money. According to the latest index, a Big Mac costs an average of $4.62 in the United States, $5.01 in Canada, $5.25 in Brazil, and $7.14 in Switzerland, meaning that residents of the latter countries get far less for their money than US residents do. Conversely, consumers in Russia only have to pay $2.62 for their Big Mac, while consumers in Turkey pay $3.76 and consumers in India pay only $1.54.

Source: "The Big Mac Index," *Economist*, January 23, 2014, http://www.economist.com/content/big-mac-index.

Indian consumers increasingly have extra money to spend on what they want in addition to what they need (see the box "Paying for a 'Mac Attack'").

Consequently, countries with high and growing levels of purchasing power are good choices for companies looking for attractive global markets. As Exhibit 7.3 shows, Coke has found that the per capita consumption of Coca-Cola, or the number of Cokes a person drinks per year, rises directly with purchasing power. The more purchasing power people have, the more likely they are to purchase soft drinks.

The second part of assessing the growth potential of global markets involves analyzing the degree of global competition, which is determined by the number and quality of companies that already compete in a foreign market.

7-4b Choosing an Office/Manufacturing Location

Companies do not have to establish an office or manufacturing location in each country they enter. They can license, franchise, or export to foreign markets, or they can serve a larger region from one country. But there are many reasons why a company might choose to establish a location in a foreign country. Thus, the criteria for choosing an office/manufacturing location are different from the criteria for entering a foreign market. Instead of focusing on costs alone, companies should consider both qualitative and quantitative factors.

Two key qualitative factors are workforce quality and company strategy. Workforce quality is important because it is often difficult to find workers with the specific skills, abilities, and experience that a company needs to run its business. A company's strategy is also important when it is choosing a location. For example, a company pursuing a low-cost strategy may need plentiful raw materials, low-cost transportation, and low-cost labour. A company pursuing a differentiation strategy (typically a higher priced, better product or service) may need access to high-quality materials and a highly skilled and educated workforce.

Quantitative factors such as the kind of facility being built, tariff and nontariff barriers, exchange rates, and transportation and labour costs should also be considered when choosing an office/manufacturing location.

7-4c Minimizing Political Risk

When managers think about political risk in global business, they envision burning factories and riots in the streets. Although political events such as these receive dramatic and extended coverage from the media, the political risks that most companies face usually are not covered as breaking stories on CTV and CBC. The negative consequences of *ordinary* political risk can be just as devastating to companies that fail to identify and minimize it.[54]

When conducting global business, companies should attempt to identify two types of political risk: political uncertainty and policy uncertainty.[55] **Political uncertainty** is associated with the risk of sweeping

---

Political uncertainty the risk of major changes in political regimes that can result from war, revolution, the death of a political leader, social unrest, or other influential events.

Exhibit 7.4
Overview of Political Risk in the Middle East

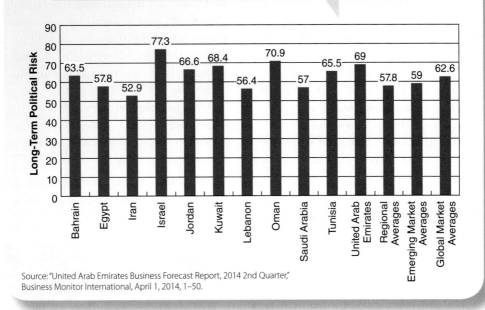

Higher scores indicate less long-term political risk, which is calculated by estimating government instability, socioeconomic conditions, internal or external conflicts, military involvement in politics, religious and ethnic tensions, foreign debt as a percent of gross domestic product, exchange rate instability, and whether there is high inflation.

Bahrain 63.5 · Egypt 57.8 · Iran 52.9 · Israel 77.3 · Jordan 66.6 · Kuwait 68.4 · Lebanon 56.4 · Oman 70.9 · Saudi Arabia 57 · Tunisia 65.5 · United Arab Emirates 69 · Regional Averages 57.8 · Emerging Market Averages 59 · Global Market Averages 62.6

Source: "United Arab Emirates Business Forecast Report, 2014 2nd Quarter," Business Monitor International, April 1, 2014, 1–50.

regime change that can result from war, revolution, the death of a political leader, social unrest, or other influential events. **Policy uncertainty** refers to the risk associated with changes in laws and government policies that directly affect how foreign companies conduct business.

Policy uncertainty is the most common, and perhaps most frustrating, form of political risk in global business, especially when changes in laws and government policies directly undercut sizable investments made by foreign companies. India is the third-largest retail market in the world behind the United States and China. The Indian government has long protected Indian retail stores by preventing foreign retailers from entering India unless they had a joint venture partner. So when India changed that policy, global retailers like Walmart (the United States), Carrefour (France), and Tesco (the United Kingdom) began making plans to enter India on their own. The Indian government, however, reversed that decision following large protests from small-business owners and politicians who feared that huge retail stores would put locally owned mom-and-pop shops out of business. Kamlesh Gupta and her husband own such a

> The political risks that most companies face usually are not covered as breaking stories on CTV and CBC.

shop, the Radha Krisna Store in Central Delhi. She said that if large retailers are allowed into India, "Everything will be over. If they sell goods cheaper than us, who will come here? Already, we have lost 20 percent of our business since Big Bazaar and Reliance [two other Indian retailers] started operating in the last two years." As a result, the only option for foreign retailers like Walmart, and it's not an attractive one, is to form joint ventures to establish "cash-and-carry" stores that sell to businesses but not consumers.[56]

Several strategies can be used to minimize or adapt to the political risk inherent in global business. An *avoidance strategy* is used when the political risks associated with a foreign country or region are viewed as too great. Firms that are already invested in high-risk areas may divest or sell their businesses. If they have not yet invested, they will likely postpone their investment until the risk shrinks. Exhibit 7.4 shows the long-term political risk for various countries in the

> **Policy uncertainty** the risk associated with changes in laws and government policies that directly affect the way foreign companies conduct business.

Middle East (higher scores indicate less political risk). The following factors, which were used to compile these ratings, indicate greater political risk: government instability, poor socioeconomic conditions, internal or external conflict, military involvement in politics, religious and ethnic tensions, high foreign debt as a percentage of GDP, exchange rate instability, and high inflation.[57] An avoidance strategy would likely be used for the riskiest countries shown in Exhibit 7.4, such as Iran and Lebanon, but would probably not be needed for the least risky countries, such as Israel, Jordan, and Oman. Risk conditions and factors change, so be sure to make risk decisions with the latest available information from resources such as the PRS Group (www.prsgroup.com), which supplies information about political risk to 80 percent of the *Fortune* 500 companies.

Control is an active strategy to prevent or reduce political risks. Firms using a control strategy lobby foreign governments or international trade agencies to change laws, regulations, or trade barriers that hurt their business in that country. Seattle-based Amazon.com, the world's largest Internet retailer, is lobbying the Indian government to change laws that prevent foreign companies from selling directly to Indian consumers. Amazon's Junglee.com is used by Indian consumers to compare prices, but it only links to Indian retailers. Ankur Bisen of Technopak, an Indian-based retail consulting firm, says, "Amazon's intent in launching Junglee.com was to have a presence in the Indian market till rules are changed to allow them to do business here." Amazon is eager to expand in India, where retail Internet sales are predicted to increase to $70 billion in 2020.[58]

Another method for dealing with political risk is *cooperation*, which involves using joint ventures and collaborative contracts such as franchising and licensing. Although cooperation does not eliminate the political risk

Emerging Markets: China

In late 2015, Canada launched the first trading hub for Chinese currency in the Americas.[59] This is the latest new rung in the ladder for Canadian businesses seizing opportunities in Asia. Canadian businesses can now shave off a significant cost in doing business with China, and reach a wider array of customers in the Asian nation—customers who do not have the resources to conduct business in foreign currencies. This is the beginning of a new era in Canada's trade and investment relationship with China, and the timing couldn't be better as the new Trans-Pacific Partnership Trade Agreement begins to kick in. Canada's exports to China—and more broadly, Asia—have long been concentrated in commodities such as coal, metals, and agricultural and forestry products, with very few exports of consumer and commercial goods and services.

What little growth in trade Canada has experienced in the last decade can largely be attributed to its relationship with Asia. While trade with the United States and Europe is expected to accelerate in the short term and remain critically important for Canada, neither region offers the growth opportunities that Asia does. Indeed, Canada's economy and living standards benefited tremendously from Asia's seemingly insatiable demand for natural resources over the last decade, and it is important to maintain this momentum. Wages are rising, making increased productivity essential if

VCG/CP Images

China is to avoid the "middle income trap" forecast by Wendy Dobson of the Rotman School of Management and other China experts. China, the world's most populous country, has had economic growth averaging about 10 percent annually for the last dozen years.[60] It is now a large consumer market. And this is another challenge—moving to a consumer-driven economy where services play a bigger role. Services are about 70 percent of Canadian GDP, versus 48 percent in China.[61] The ecommerce sector is booming, with, for example, Alibaba, the online commerce giant headed by Jack Ma (China's Bill Gates), having higher sales than eBay and Amazon combined.[62]

Sources: J. Palladini, "Canada's Big Opportunity in China Is Services, Not Just Resources," *Canadian Business*, March 18, 2015. Used with permission of the author. Found at http://www.canadianbusiness.com/blogs-and-comment/canada-china-services-export-opportunity/; A. Campbell, "Canada Has a Role to Play as China Restructures Its Economy," *Macleans*, September 12, 1015, http://www.macleans.ca/economy/economicanalysis/canada-has-a-role-to-play-as-china-restructures-its-economy/; I. Wadie, "We've Adjusted to Rising Prices; We Can Adjust to Falling Ones: For the Record, Bank of Canada Governor Stephen Poloz on Riding the Commodity Cycle," *Macleans*, September 21, 2015 http://www.macleans.ca/economy/economicanalysis/stephen-poloz-weve-adjusted-to-rising-prices-we-can-adjust-to-falling-ones/.

of doing business in a country, it can limit the risk associated with foreign ownership of a business. For example, a German company forming a joint venture with a Chinese company to do business in China may structure the joint venture contract so that the Chinese company owns 51 percent or more of the joint venture. Doing so qualifies the joint venture as a Chinese company and exempts it from Chinese laws that apply to foreign-owned businesses. However, cooperation cannot always protect against *policy risk* if a foreign government changes its laws and policies to directly affect how foreign companies conduct business.

Much has been made of most favoured nation (MFN) status as it is applied by Canada, the United States, and other countries. This designation is used to reduce tariffs, extend cooperative trading agreements, and prevent discriminatory treatment. Most WTO member countries grant MFN trading designations to one another, and this does increase trade.[63]

7-5 BECOMING AWARE OF CULTURAL DIFFERENCES

National culture refers to the shared values and beliefs that affect the perceptions, decisions, and behaviour of the people of a particular country. The first step in dealing with culture is to recognize that there are meaningful differences.

7-6 PREPARING FOR AN INTERNATIONAL ASSIGNMENT

During the 2014 Winter Olympics in Sochi, Russia, North American reporters discovered that Russians on the streets, at their hotels, or in restaurants would not return their smiles. When one reporter asked why this was, a Russian told him, "In Russia, only two types of people smile: idiots and rich people." In Russia, you only smile if you have a particularly good reason. And if you smile just to be friendly, like North Americans, Russians will think you're insincere, or maybe a bit crazy. Also, Russians typically don't smile while working because,

well, they're at work. But, at home, with friends and family, Russian smiles and laughter are as big and hearty as anyplace in the world.[64]

An **expatriate** is someone who lives and works outside his or her native country. When expatriates fail in overseas assignments, primarily it is because they find it difficult to adjust to linguistic, cultural, and social differences. The United States is the biggest destination for Canadians, with more than 1.5 million expatriates living there. The United Kingdom is the next largest destination, with almost 750,000 expats, followed by China, with 250,000. Some research has found that large numbers of expatriates return home before they have completed their overseas assignments.[65] Of those who do complete them, about one-third are judged by their companies to have been no better than marginally effective.[66] Since the average cost of sending an employee on a three-year international assignment is $1 million, failure in those assignments can be extraordinarily expensive.[67] Getting a more well rounded education is another reason people choose to become expatriates, and as a student, you might want to take advantage of opportunities to study abroad.[68]

*The chances for a successful international assignment can be increased through **7-6a language and cross-cultural training** and **7-6b consideration of spouse, family, and dual-career issues.***

7-6a Language and Cross-Cultural Training

Pre-departure language and cross-cultural training can reduce the uncertainty that expatriates feel, the misunderstandings that arise between expatriates and natives, and the inappropriate ways in which expatriates unknowingly behave when they travel to a foreign country. Indeed, simple things like using a phone, locating a public toilet, asking for directions, finding out how much things cost, exchanging greetings, or understanding what people want can become tremendously complex when expatriates don't know a foreign language or a country's customs and cultures.

For example, Bing, the name of Microsoft's search engine, means "illness" or "pancake" in Mandarin Chinese,

National culture the shared values and beliefs that affect the perceptions, decisions, and behaviour of the people of a particular country.

Expatriate someone who lives and works outside his or her native country.

so Microsoft had to change the name to "Biying" from the Chinese expression "you qui bi ying," which means, more appropriately, "seek and you shall find." Likewise, in Indonesia, an oil rig supervisor yelled to a worker to take a boat to shore. While the boss thought he was sharing instructions, the Indonesian and his workers thought he was being criticized in public, which is not done in their culture. Outraged at this behaviour, they chased the supervisor with axes.[69]

Expatriates who receive pre-departure language and cross-cultural training make faster adjustments to foreign cultures and perform better on their international assignments.[70] Unfortunately, only one-third of the managers who go on international assignments are offered any kind of pre-departure training, and only half of those actually participate in the training![71] Suzanne Bernard, director of international mobility at Bombardier Aerospace in Canada, says, "We always offer cross-cultural training, but it's very seldom used by executives leaving in a rush at the last minute."[72] This is somewhat surprising given the failure rates for expatriates and the high cost of those failures. Furthermore, with the exception of some language courses, pre-departure training is not particularly expensive or difficult to provide. Three methods can be used to prepare workers for international assignments: documentary training, cultural simulations, and field experiences.

Documentary training focuses on identifying specific critical differences between cultures. For example,

when 60 workers at Axcelis Technologies were preparing to do business in India, they learned that while North Americans make eye contact and shake hands firmly when greeting others, Indians, as a sign of respect, do just the opposite, avoiding eye contact and shaking hands limply.[73]

After learning specific critical differences through documentary training, trainees can then participate in *cultural simulations,* in which they practise adapting to cultural differences. After the workers at Axcelis Technologies learned about key differences between their culture and India, they practised adapting to those differences by role playing. Some Axcelis workers would take the roles of Indian workers, while other Axcelis workers would play themselves and try to behave in a way consistent with Indian culture. As they role played, Indian music played loudly in the background, and they were coached on what to do or not do. Axcelis human resources director Randy Longo says, "At first, I was skeptical and wondered what I'd get out of the class. But it was enlightening for me."[74]

Finally, *field experience* simulation training places trainees in an ethnic neighbourhood for three to four hours to talk to residents about cultural differences. For example, an electronics manufacturer prepared workers for assignments in South Korea by having trainees explore a nearby South Korean neighbourhood and talk to shopkeepers and people on the street about South Korean politics, family orientation, and day-to-day living practices.

MGMTFACT

Bilingualism—A Growing Trend

At least 35 percent of Canadians speak more than one language. Moreover, fewer than 2 percent of Canadians cannot speak at least one of the two official languages. Around 5.8 million people in Canada are able to speak both official languages. *Bilingual*, in Canada, generally refers to being able to speak both French and English; by this definition, however, only 17.5 percent of Canadians are bilingual. Statistics Canada, focusing on about 200 languages that make up the linguistic portrait of Canada, indicates that most of those people (almost 6 million) speak English plus an immigrant language such as Punjabi or Mandarin. More than half of Vancouverites and Torontonians were born outside Canada, and about 80 percent of immigrant-language speakers lived in Toronto, Montreal, Vancouver, Calgary, Edmonton, and Ottawa-Gatineau. This has led to a greater use of English as a second language, and also to a great deal of linguistic and cultural diversity in these places. In Europe, even more value is placed on the ability to speak multiple languages; more Europeans are multilingual, speaking three or more languages, than are bilingual. Being able to communicate in multiple languages is an important asset in any business and can help give a company the edge it needs to succeed in a competitive market.

Sources: R. Léger, "B.C. Has No Official Language," *The Vancouver Sun*, March 20, 2015, http://www.vancouversun.com/life/opinion+official+language/10907405/story.html?__lsa=c337-0321; City of Toronto, "Facts," http://www.toronto.ca/toronto_facts/diversity.htm; D. Todd, "Vancouver Teens Most Inter-Racial: Poll," *Vancouver Sun*, August 14, 2009.

FER737NG/Shutterstock

7-6b **Consideration of Spouse, Family, and Dual-Career Issues**

Not all international assignments are difficult for expatriates and their families. That said, the evidence clearly shows that how well an expatriate's spouse and family adjust to the foreign culture is the most important factor in determining the success or failure of an international assignment.[75] Indeed, a Harvard Business Review study found that 32 percent of those offered international assignments turned them down because they did not want their families to have to relocate, while 28 percent turned them down "to protect their marriages."[76] Unfortunately, despite its importance, there has been little systematic research on what does and does not help expatriates' families adapt. A number of companies, however, have found that adaptability screening and intercultural training for families can lead to more successful overseas adjustment.

Adaptability screening is used to assess how well managers and their families are likely to adjust to foreign cultures. Prudential Relocation Management's international division has developed an "Overseas Assignment Inventory" to help the Canadian International Development Agency select people who will adapt well by assessing the open-mindedness of a spouse and family, respect for others' beliefs, sense of humour, and marital communication.[77]

Only 40 percent of expatriates' families receive language and cross-cultural training, yet such training is just as important for the families of expatriates as for the expatriates themselves.[78] In fact, it may be more important because, unlike expatriates, whose professional jobs often shield them from the full force of a country's culture, spouses and children are fully immersed in foreign neighbourhoods and schools. Households must be run, shopping must be done, and bills must be paid. Facebook CEO Mark Zuckerberg stresses the importance of learning Chinese, and his mastery is so good that he spoke entirely in Chinese during his meeting with President Xi Jinping of China on a state visit. "Today I met President Xi Jinping of China at the 2015 annual US–China Internet Industry Forum in Seattle," Zuckerberg wrote on his Facebook wall. "On a personal note, this was the first time I've ever spoken with a world leader entirely in a foreign language. I consider that a meaningful personal milestone".[79] Unfortunately, expatriate spouse Laurel Larsen, despite two hours of Chinese lessons a week, hasn't learned enough of the language to communicate with the family's baby sitter. She has to phone her husband, who became fluent in Chinese in his teens, to translate. Similarly, expatriates' children must deal with different cultural beliefs and practices. While the Larsens' three daughters love the private international school they attend, they still have had difficulty adapting to the incredible differences they perceive in inner China.[80]

STUDY TOOLS **7**

READY TO STUDY?

LOCATED IN TEXTBOOK:

☐ Rip out the Chapter Review Card at the back of the book to have a summary of the chapter and key terms handy.

LOCATED AT NELSON.COM/STUDENT:

☐ Access the eBook or use the ReadSpeaker feature to listen to the chapter on the go.

☐ Prepare for tests with practice quizzes.

☐ Review key terms with flashcards and the glossary feature.

☐ Work through key concepts with case studies and Management Decision Exercises.

☐ Explore practical examples with You Make the Decision Activities.

8 Designing Adaptive Organizations

Churchill/iStockphoto

LEARNING OUTCOMES

After studying this chapter, you will be able to...

8-1 Describe the departmentalization approach to organizational structure.

8-2 Explain organizational authority.

8-3 Discuss the different methods for job design.

8-4 Explain the methods that companies are using to redesign internal organizational processes (i.e., intra-organizational processes).

8-5 Describe the methods that companies are using to redesign external organizational processes (i.e., inter-organizational processes).

After you finish this chapter, go to **PAGE 173** for **STUDY TOOLS**

Keeping Up With the Future

What are the chances that a man who built a robot in high school would own a company built along traditional lines? None, if that man is Daniel Blair, who says he was "the stereotypical nerd" and has been building computers "for as long as I could." He initially dropped out of postsecondary education but he went back, and founded the Bit Space Development technology consulting firm in his hometown of Winnipeg three months after graduating from the Business Information Technology diploma course at Red River College (RRC) in 2015. By then he had already received various awards, including the Co-operative Education Manitoba Student of the Year Award in 2014. By February 2016, at the age of 25, he had also won a Future Leaders of Manitoba (FLM) Award. Bit Space describes itself as focusing on custom web applications and services, "particularly with the purpose of gamifying education." Its flagship product at the time Dan won the FLM award was PanoPlā (pronounced PanoPlay), a virtual reality development that he says resulted from his "being given a handful of students to work with" in an RRC entrepreneurship mentoring program. PanoPlā quickly became a subsidiary of Bit Space, whose staff numbers have grown from one to ten. Dan is also an author, and he works with several community-based groups as well as mentors students.

1. First, can you explain simply what your company and its subsidiaries do?

Bit Space Development is a technology consultancy and custom development shop that helps businesses develop scalable applications. The focus of our own products is to help make virtual reality accessible.

2. Is there anything vertical about your organizational structure?

There are only vertical aspects on paper, but in operations everybody is on the same level. I'm CEO and owner, but anybody can approach me with an idea and we can collaborate on everything.

3. Does the word "organic" come to mind at all?

Although some people are brought on for their specific skills, we all grow into our positions. We have had salespeople grow into business development roles, and as we get bigger we have to make sure that we can adapt to anything, and sometimes that means our team needs to wear a few hats.

4. How centralized is your business?

We are completely set up for remote work. When we started out, most of us worked from home. It is a lot less overhead to get started as a remote company. When you don't have to worry about a fancy office, you can focus a lot more on the awesome people you want to work with.

Now, most of our staff work in our Winnipeg-based office, but we have team members in Brazil, China, and India as well.

5. What, in a nutshell, are the positives and potential negatives of all this?

Being flexible is one of the biggest positives. On the other hand, it is always nice to sit down and have a meeting, so it can be difficult to communicate with remote team members.

6. Why did you choose to become a "virtual organization," in which your company and subsidiaries share skills?

The subsidiaries were formed because there is a lot of focus on investors, but I'm here to last. If I were to sell one of my companies, I wouldn't want that to affect Bit Space.

7. Have you considered moving away from Winnipeg?

Yes, but Winnipeg is a unique place with a lot of talent that is not being utilized to its fullest. A low cost of living and amazing education institutes produces a unique environment for technology-based companies.

8. How does a typical workday start at Bit Space?

Our office has flex hours so people roll in between 6 A.M. and 10 A.M. By then we have a team stand-up, where we update everybody with what we are working on. From there you might find our team broken off into pair programming groups or collaborating with each other on ideas. No shoes allowed in the office.

9. How important are goals to you, and what kind of goals do you have?

Goals are important to everybody. If you have nothing to work towards how do you know you are going to succeed? When I was at school, I had five-year goals that I was fortunate enough to be able to meet before graduating. Now I prefer to not talk about my goals.

10. Was one of those school goals to write a book?

Yes. I wrote an electronics book called *Learning Banana Pi*, which deals mainly with open-source computing, while I was still a student. It was published physically in June 2015.

11. What's your best skill?

Finding mentors to help me through tough situations. I think that one day I would like to be a great mentor and the first step to that is being a great mentee.

For the full interview go online to nelson.com/student

8-1 DEPARTMENTALI-ZATION

Organizational structure is the vertical and horizontal configuration of departments, authority, and jobs within a company. Organizational structure is concerned with vertical questions such as "Who reports to whom?" as well as horizontal questions such as "Who does what?" and "Where is the work done?" For example, Canadian Tire Corporation (CTC) is a family of businesses with a network of approximately

Organizational structure the vertical and horizontal configuration of departments, authority, and jobs within a company.

1,700 retail outlets and gas bars across Canada, as well as a range of financial services products. In addition to having some of the most recognized retail brands in Canada, CTC is proud to report that 90 percent of Canadians live within 15 minutes of a Canadian Tire retail store and one in five Canadians has a Canadian Tire credit card. Retail operations are run under five retail banners, including Canadian Tire, PartSource, Petroleum, Mark's, and FGL Sports (which includes Sport Chek, Sports Experts, Atmosphere, and Pro Hockey Life). CTC also separates its business into key business categories to oversee different sectors of the company's business, including Automotive, Living, Fixing, Playing/Sports Goods, and Apparel.[1] Companies like Canadian Tire use organizational structure to set up departments and relationships among employees in order to make business happen. You can see Canadian Tire's organizational structure in Exhibit 8.1. In the first

Exhibit 8.1
Canadian Tire Corporation's Organizational Chart

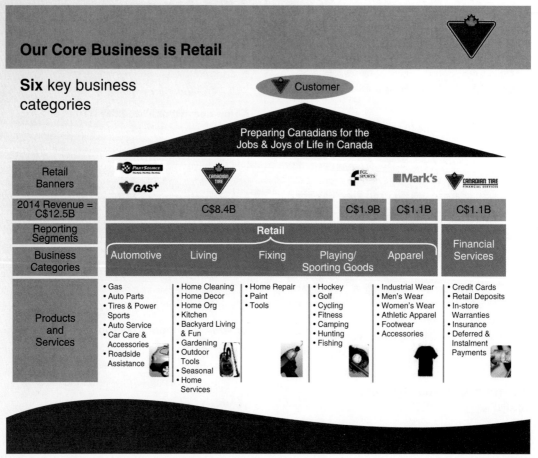

Source: Canadian Tire Corporation Investor Presentation April 2015. Used with permission. Available at: http://corp.canadiantire.ca/EN/Investors/EventsPresentations/Documents/Investor%20presentation%20-%20April%202015.pdf.

half of the chapter, you will learn about the traditional vertical and horizontal approaches to organizational structure, including departmentalization, organizational authority, and job design.

An **organizational process** is the collection of activities that transform inputs into outputs that customers value.[2] Organizational process asks: How do things get done? For example, Ubisoft, one of the world's largest independent developers of interactive entertainment products, uses basic internal and external processes to develop video games (see Exhibit 8.2). The process starts when Ubisoft gets external feedback from customers through its own website, email, social media sites, and retailers. This information helps Ubisoft understand customers' needs and problems and identify important gaming issues and needed changes and functions, as well as market trends in terms of content and format. Ubisoft then updates existing games, besides working on new games, testing these internally within the company and then externally through its beta-testing process. During beta-testing, customers who volunteer or are selected by Ubisoft give the company extensive feedback, which is then used to make improvements. After final corrections are made to a game, the company distributes and sells it to customers. Those customers then start the process again by giving Ubisoft more feedback. Organizational process is just as important as organizational structure. You'll learn about both in this chapter.

Procter & Gamble (P&G), the largest consumer packaged goods company in the world, owns some of the world's best-known brands, including Tide, Crest, Charmin, Pringles, and Pampers. P&G's product lines include 25 billion-dollar brands (i.e., brands that generate more than $1 billion in annual sales), 20 half-billion-dollar brands, and, the company's first 10-billion-dollar brand, Pampers diapers. Over the past decade, P&G has restructured its operations several times, most recently by grouping its global business units (GBUs) into four industry-based sectors: Beauty, Hair and Personal Care; Fabric and Home Care; Baby, Feminine and Family Care; and Health and Grooming. Under the leadership of a group president,

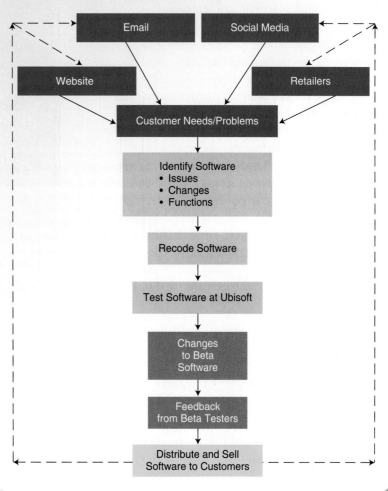

Exhibit 8.2

Process View of Ubisoft's Organization

each GBU is responsible for developing brand strategies, new product upgrades and innovations, and marketing plans for the brands within its sector. Sales and Marketing Operations supports the GBUs by developing and executing market plans at the local level and is organized under six regions: North America; Europe; Latin America; Asia Pacific; Greater China; and India, Middle East, and Africa (IMEA). P&G's organizational structure also includes Global Business Services, which provides technology, processes, and data tools to enable the GBUs and Sales and Marketing Operations

Organizational process the collection of activities that transform inputs into outputs that customers value.

Ubisoft's Gameplan

An important global player in the video game industry, Ubisoft employs more than 10,000 people worldwide, with over 3,000 employees between its Montreal and Toronto offices. According to Ubisoft Montreal CEO Yannis Mallat, the company's strong performance is a direct result of investing in new technology and in employees, while still managing costs. The company's decision to embrace the concept of larger development teams and cross-studio collaboration has led to a marked increase in productivity. Although Ubisoft employs a lean management structure, with managers charged with leading larger teams, the company prides itself on its bottom-up approach, which stimulates employee creativity and empowerment. Skill development for employees is a primary focus; it includes extensive training opportunities for employees, a group training portal, and expanded communication channels such as open forums, instant messaging, web conferencing, and the use of video to facilitate collaboration, organization, and the sharing of key

information among teams and projects. As Mallat explains, "You gather as much talent as possible, and you give them three things: trust, means, and insane challenges. Usually they come back with pretty good stuff. It's OK to invest more when you get more in return."

Sources: B. Sinclair, "No Room for B-Games' Says Ubisoft Montreal Head," *Games Industry International*, April 11, 2013, http://www.gamesindustry.biz/articles/2013-04-10-no-room-for-b-games-says-ubisoft-montreal-head; Ubisoft Financial Report 2011, https://www.ubisoftgroup.com/comsite_common/en-US/images/2467tcm9927495.pdf; Ubisoft Financial Report 2012, https://www.ubisoftgroup.com/comsite_common/en-US/images/Annual_Report_2012tcm9956562.pdf.

to better understand the business and better serve customers. According to P&G, the organizational structure plays an integral role in the company's ability to grow and to reap the benefits of its global scale as well as maintain a local focus with consumers and retail customers around the globe.[3]

Traditionally, organizational structures have been based on some form of **departmentalization**, a method of subdividing work and workers into separate units that take responsibility for completing particular tasks.[4]

Traditionally, organizational structures have been created by departmentalizing work according to five methods: 8-1a functional, 8-1b product, 8-1c customer, 8-1d geographic, and 8-1e matrix.

Departmentalization subdividing work and workers into separate organizational units responsible for completing particular tasks.

Functional departmentalization organizing work and workers into separate units responsible for particular business functions or areas of expertise.

8-1a Functional Departmentalization

The most common organizational structure is functional departmentalization. Companies tend to use this structure when they are small or just starting out. **Functional departmentalization** organizes work and workers into separate units responsible for particular business functions or areas of expertise. A common functional structure might have individuals organized into accounting, sales, marketing, production, and human resources departments.

Not all functionally departmentalized companies have the same functions. The insurance company and the advertising agency shown in Exhibit 8.3 both have sales, accounting, human resources, and information systems departments, as indicated by the orange boxes. The purple and green boxes indicate the functions that are different. As would be expected, the insurance company has separate departments for life, auto, home, and health insurance. The advertising agency has departments for artwork, creative work, print advertising, and radio advertising. So the functional departments in a company that uses functional structure depend in part on the business or industry the company is in.

Exhibit 8.3
Functional Departmentalization

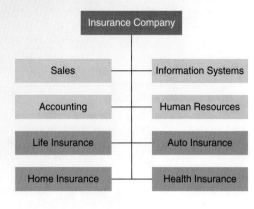

Insurance Company

Sales	Information Systems
Accounting	Human Resources
Life Insurance	Auto Insurance
Home Insurance	Health Insurance

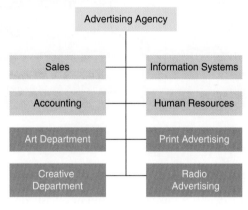

Advertising Agency

Sales	Information Systems
Accounting	Human Resources
Art Department	Print Advertising
Creative Department	Radio Advertising

Functional departmentalization has some advantages. First, it allows work to be done by highly qualified specialists. While the accountants in the accounting department take responsibility for producing accurate revenue and expense figures, the engineers in research and development can focus their efforts on designing a product that is reliable and simple to manufacture. Second, it lowers costs by reducing duplication. When the engineers in research and development come up with that fantastic new product, they don't have to worry about creating an aggressive advertising campaign to sell it. That task belongs to the advertising experts and sales representatives in marketing. Third, because everyone in the same department has similar work experience or training, communication and coordination are less problematic for departmental managers.

But functional departmentalization also has a number of disadvantages. To start, cross-department coordination can be difficult. Managers and employees are often more interested in doing what's right for their function than in doing what's right for the entire organization.

As companies grow, functional departmentalization may also lead to slower decision making and produce managers and workers with narrow experience and expertise.

8-1b Product Departmentalization

Product departmentalization organizes work and workers into separate units responsible for producing particular products or services. Exhibit 8.4 shows the product departmentalization structure used by Bombardier, the world's leading manufacturer of both planes and trains, which is organized along four different product segments: Business Aircraft, Commercial Aircraft, Aerostructures and Engineering Services, and Transportation.

One of the advantages of product departmentalization is that, like functional departmentalization, it allows managers and workers to specialize in one area. Unlike functional departmentalization, however, managers and workers develop a broader set of experiences and expertise related to an entire product line. Likewise, product departmentalization makes it easier for top managers to assess the performance of work units. For example, because of the clear separation of its four different product divisions, Bombardier's top managers can easily compare the performance of the Business Aircraft and Transportation divisions. The divisions' revenues were $7 billion for the Business Aircraft segment and $8.3 billion for Transportation; however, when you examine profitability, Transportation's profits before interest and taxes were $465 billion compared to a loss of $1.3 billion for the Business Aircraft division.[5] Finally, decision making should be faster because managers and workers are responsible for the entire product line rather than for separate functional departments. However, there are some potential disadvantages of product departmentalization. For example, if each product area maintains its own functional departments—for example, human resources, legal, accounting, purchasing—this type of duplication may result in higher costs overall. Another disadvantage involves the challenge of coordinating across different product divisions. For example, some companies may find it difficult to standardize policies and procedures for divisions that operate in very different industries.

Product departmentalization organizing work and workers into separate units responsible for producing particular products or services.

Exhibit 8.4
Product and Functional Departmentalization: Bombardier

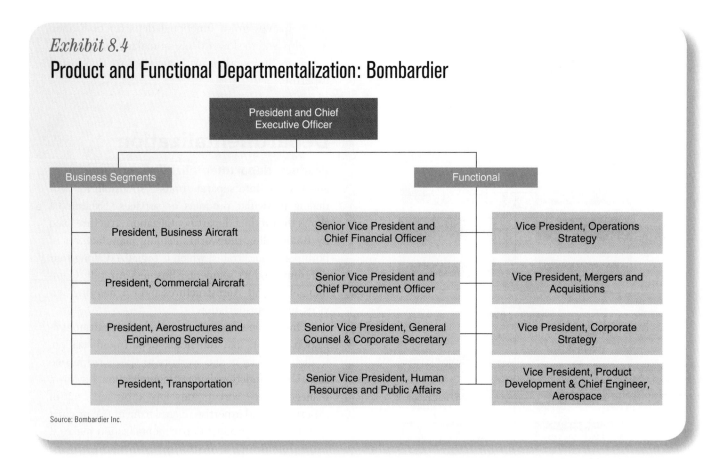

Source: Bombardier Inc.

8-1c Customer Departmentalization

Customer departmentalization organizes work and workers into separate units responsible for particular kinds of customers. For example, Exhibit 8.5 shows a distribution company that is organized into departments that cater to small and large businesses, consumers, and government customers. The primary advantage of customer departmentalization is that it focuses the organization on customer needs rather than on products or business functions. Furthermore, creating separate departments to serve specific kinds of customers allows companies to specialize and adapt their products and services to customer needs and problems.

The primary disadvantage of customer departmentalization is that, like product departmentalization, it leads to duplication of resources. Also, it can be difficult to achieve coordination across different customer departments. Finally, the emphasis on meeting customers' needs may lead workers to make decisions that please customers but hurt the business.

8-1d Geographic Departmentalization

Geographic departmentalization organizes work and workers into separate units responsible for doing business in particular geographic areas. Exhibit 8.6 shows an example of geographic departmentalization.

The primary advantage of geographic departmentalization is that it helps companies respond to the demands of different markets. This can be especially important when the company sells in different parts of the country as well as in different countries, for cultural preferences can vary widely, and so can external business environments. For example, a dairy in Canada that sells to consumers in Western Canada will find that preferences for cheeses on the Prairies will be different from those of consumers in Quebec. Geographic segregation can help address those issues. Geographic departmentalization is also useful in terms of adapting to the differences in business environments in different countries. For example, in the United States, there

Customer departmentalization organizing work and workers into separate units responsible for particular kinds of customers.

Geographic departmentalization organizing work and workers into separate units responsible for doing business in particular geographic areas.

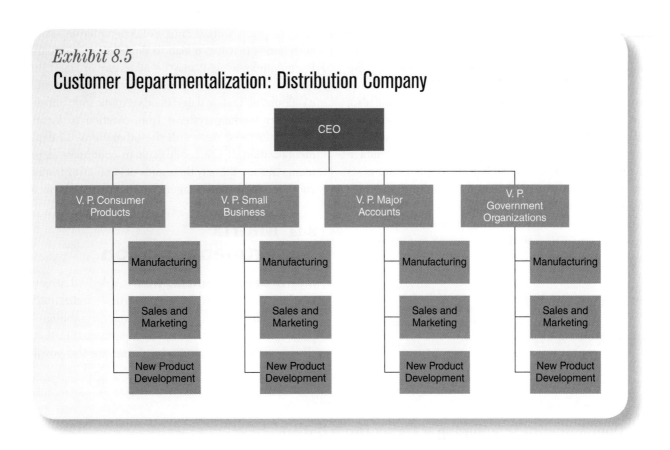

Exhibit 8.5
Customer Departmentalization: Distribution Company

CEO

- V. P. Consumer Products
  - Manufacturing
  - Sales and Marketing
  - New Product Development
- V. P. Small Business
  - Manufacturing
  - Sales and Marketing
  - New Product Development
- V. P. Major Accounts
  - Manufacturing
  - Sales and Marketing
  - New Product Development
- V. P. Government Organizations
  - Manufacturing
  - Sales and Marketing
  - New Product Development

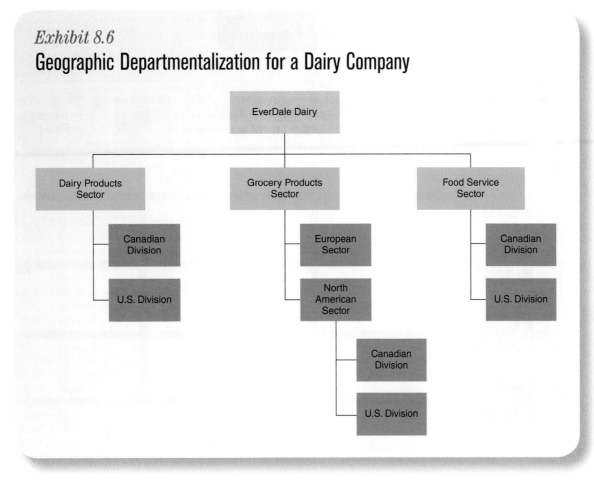

Exhibit 8.6
Geographic Departmentalization for a Dairy Company

EverDale Dairy

- Dairy Products Sector
  - Canadian Division
  - U.S. Division
- Grocery Products Sector
  - European Sector
  - North American Sector
    - Canadian Division
    - U.S. Division
- Food Service Sector
  - Canadian Division
  - U.S. Division

are extensive federal, state, and local government regulations relating to food production and the pricing of milk is based on public policy decisions. Overseas, the European Union has a multitude of food-related laws covering production, processing, and distribution; also, in Germany and the United Kingdom, standards for cheese are based on international standards overseen by the World Health Organization.[6] Another advantage is that geographic departmentalization can reduce costs by locating unique organizational resources closer to customers. For instance, it is much cheaper for a dairy to build cheese manufacturing plants in the United Kingdom than to manufacture cheese in Canada and then transport it overseas.

Matrix departmentalization a hybrid organizational structure in which two or more forms of departmentalization, most often product and functional, are used together.

The primary disadvantage of geographic departmentalization is that it can lead to duplication of resources. For example, while it may be necessary to adapt products and marketing to different geographic locations, it's doubtful that a dairy needs significantly different inventory tracking systems from location to location. Also, even more than with the other forms of departmentalization, it can be difficult to coordinate departments that are literally thousands of kilometres from one another and whose managers have very limited contact.

8-1e Matrix Departmentalization

Matrix departmentalization is a hybrid structure in which two or more forms of departmentalization are used together. The most common matrix combines the product and functional forms of departmentalization, as shown in Exhibit 8.7, but other forms are also possible.

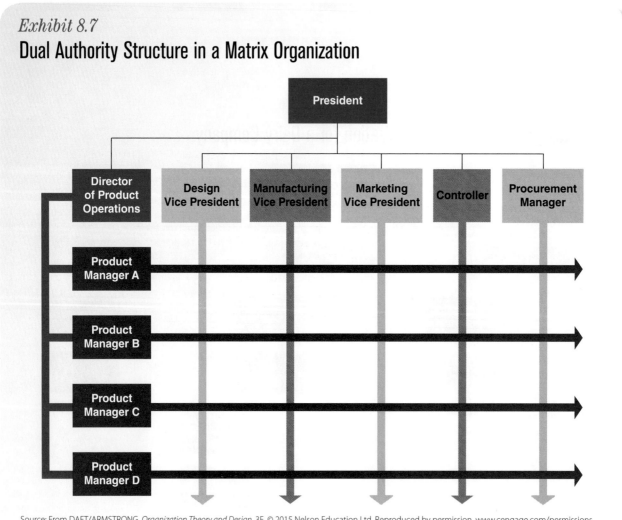

Exhibit 8.7
Dual Authority Structure in a Matrix Organization

Source: From DAFT/ARMSTRONG. *Organization Theory and Design*, 3E. © 2015 Nelson Education Ltd. Reproduced by permission. www.cengage.com/permissions.

Product managers and functional managers have equal authority within the organization, and employees report to both of them. Referring again to Exhibit 8.7, which illustrates a matrix form for a medium-sized company, each product manager relies on employees from manufacturing, design, and marketing to work on the product lines they oversee in order to serve the various markets and customers where the company's products are sold. When the manufacturing, design, and marketing functions are kept intact, employees can develop the in-depth expertise to serve all product lines efficiently. The matrix structure works best when certain conditions are met. For example, a medium-sized organization with scarce resources and a moderate number of product lines will find a matrix organization efficient in terms of allocating people and equipment across products. As well, the dual authority structure of a matrix can be useful for an organization that needs to ensure a balance between product and functional managers. Lastly, when an organization operates in a complex and unstable environment with frequent external changes, and when there is high interdependence among departments, the vertical and horizontal channels in a matrix organization can be used to better process information and facilitate coordination, for which there is a greater need.

Several things distinguish matrix departmentalization from the other traditional forms of departmentalization.[7] First, most employees report to two bosses, one from each core part of the matrix. Second, by virtue of their hybrid design, matrix structures lead to much more cross-functional interaction than other forms of departmentalization. In fact, while matrix workers are typically members of only one functional department (based on their work experience and expertise), they are also commonly members of several ongoing project, product, or customer groups. Third, because of the high level of cross-functional interaction, matrix departmentalization requires significant coordination between managers in the different parts of the matrix. In particular, managers have the complex job of tracking and managing the multiple demands (project, product, customer, or functional) on employees' time.

The primary advantage of matrix departmentalization is that it allows companies to efficiently manage large, complex tasks such as researching, developing, and marketing, or carrying out complex global businesses. Efficiency comes from avoiding duplication. For example, rather than having an entire marketing function for each project, the company simply assigns and reassigns workers from the marketing department as they are needed at various stages of product completion. More specifically, an employee from a department may simultaneously be part of five different ongoing projects, but may be actively completing work on only a few projects at a time.

Another advantage is the pool of resources available to carry out large, complex tasks. Because of the ability to quickly pull in expert help from all the functional areas of the company, matrix project managers have much more diverse expertise and experience at their disposal than do managers in the other forms of departmentalization.

The primary disadvantage of matrix departmentalization is the high level of coordination required to manage the complexities involved in running large, ongoing projects at various levels of completion. Matrix structures are notorious for confusion and conflict between project bosses in different parts of the matrix. Disagreements or misunderstandings about schedules, budgets, available resources, and the availability of employees with particular functional expertise are common. Another disadvantage is that matrix structures require much more management skill than the other forms of departmentalization.

Because of these problems, many matrix structures evolve from a **simple matrix**, in which managers in different parts of the matrix negotiate conflicts and resources directly, to a **complex matrix**, in which specialized matrix managers and departments are added to the organizational structure. In a complex matrix, managers from different parts of the matrix might report to the same matrix manager, who helps them sort out conflicts and problems.

Simple matrix a form of matrix departmentalization in which managers in different parts of the matrix negotiate conflicts and resources.

Complex matrix a form of matrix departmentalization in which managers in different parts of the matrix report to matrix managers, who help them sort out conflicts and problems.

CHAPTER 8: Designing Adaptive Organizations

8-2 ORGANIZATIONAL AUTHORITY

The second part of traditional organizational structures is **authority**—the right to give commands, take action, and make decisions to achieve organizational objectives.[8]

Traditionally, organizational authority has been characterized by the following dimensions: 8-2a chain of command, 8-2 b line versus staff authority, 8-2c delegation of authority, and 8-2d degree of centralization.

8-2a Chain of Command

Look back at Bombardier's organizational chart in Exhibit 8.4. If you place your finger on any position in the chart—say, the Purchasing department or the Commercial Aircraft division—you can trace a line upward to the company's CEO. This line, which vertically connects every job in the company to higher levels of management, represents the chain of command. The **chain of command** is the vertical line of authority that clarifies who reports to whom throughout the organization; **span of control** refers to the number of individuals who report directly to a manager or supervisor. People higher in the chain of command have the right, *if they so choose*, to give commands, take action, and make decisions concerning activities occurring anywhere below them in the chain. In the following discussion about delegation and decentralization, you will learn that managers don't always choose to exercise their authority directly.[9]

A key assumption underlying the chain of command is **unity of command**, which means that workers should report to just one boss.[10] In practical terms, this means that only one person can be in charge at a time. Matrix organizations, in which employees have two bosses, automatically violate this principle. This is one of the primary reasons why matrix organizations are difficult to manage. Unity of command serves an important purpose: to prevent the confusion that may arise when an employee receives conflicting commands from two different bosses.

8-2b Line Versus Staff Authority

A second dimension of authority is the distinction between line and staff authority. **Line authority** is the right to command immediate subordinates in the chain of command. For example, Bombardier CEO Alain Bellemare has line authority over the vice president of the Business Aircraft division of the company and can issue orders to that person and expect them to be carried out. In turn, the vice president of the Business Aircraft division can issue orders to his or her subordinates and expect them to be carried out.

Staff authority is the right to *advise* but not command others who are not subordinates in the chain of command. For example, a manager in human resources might advise the manager in charge of the operations department on a hiring decision but cannot order him or her to hire a certain applicant.

The terms *line* and *staff* are also used to describe different functions within the organization. A **line function** is an activity that contributes directly to creating or selling the company's products. So, for example, activities that take place within the manufacturing and marketing departments would be considered line functions. A **staff function**, such as accounting, human resources, or legal services, does not contribute directly to creating or selling the company's products; instead, it supports line activities. For example, marketing managers might consult with the legal staff to make sure the wording of a particular advertisement is legal.

8-2c Delegation of Authority

Managers can exercise their authority directly by completing tasks themselves, or they can choose to pass on some of their authority to subordinates.

Authority the right to give commands, take action, and make decisions to achieve organizational objectives.

Chain of command the vertical line of authority that clarifies who reports to whom throughout the organization.

Span of control the number of individuals who report directly to a manager.

Unity of command a management principle that workers should report to just one boss.

Line authority the right to command immediate subordinates in the chain of command.

Staff authority the right to advise, but not command, others who are not subordinates in the chain of command.

Line function an activity that contributes directly to creating or selling the company's products.

Staff function an activity that does not contribute directly to creating or selling the company's products, but instead supports line activities.

Exhibit 8.8
Delegation: Responsibility, Authority, and Accountability

Source: C. D. Pringle, D. F. Jennings, and J. G. Longenecker, *Managing Organizations: Functions and Behaviors* © 1990 Pearson Education, Inc. Adapted by permission of the author.

Delegation of authority is the assignment of direct authority and responsibility to a subordinate to complete tasks for which the manager is normally responsible.

When a manager delegates work, three transfers occur, as illustrated in Exhibit 8.8. First, the manager transfers full responsibility for the assignment to the subordinate. At Apple, when you've been delegated to a certain task, you become the "directly responsible individual (DRI)." As a former Apple employee explains, "Any effective meeting at Apple will have an action list. Next to each action item will be the DRI," who is, of course, responsible for completing that delegated responsibility. Furthermore, when you're trying to figure out whom to contact to get something done in Apple's corporate structure, people simply ask, "Who's the DRI on that?"[11] According to Murray Martin, former CEO of Pitney Bowes Worldwide, the higher up you rise in an organization, the more you must be willing to delegate. "I think that if you are looking at companies that have long-term, continuous success, it is with CEOs that have been able to disperse power, rather than centralize

power."[12] The challenge of delegation does not apply just to large organizations; small businesses and startup ventures can also find delegation useful to support growth. For many entrepreneurs, letting go of day-to-day operations and decision making is not easy; even so, it is often critical for them to do so if the business is past the startup phase and transitioning to growth. That is when owners need to be able to focus on developing and executing strategies for growth instead of devoting all their time to daily operations or to activities that could be carried out by others. This means that having the right people in place is vital to effective delegating. Alex Krohn, owner of Gossamer Threads Inc., a software and web-hosting company based in Vancouver, believes that recruitment and building a solid team are needed for effective delegation to occur. That in turn means you find "the right people and make sure you can trust them to deliver the same quality of service you were providing."[13] To summarize, many managers find it difficult to delegate, but "the job of the leader is to conduct the orchestra, not play all the instruments."[14]

The second transfer that occurs with delegation is that the manager gives the subordinate full authority over the budget, resources, and personnel needed to do the job. For delegation to work, delegated authority must be commensurate with delegated responsibility.

The third transfer that occurs with delegation is the transfer of accountability. The subordinate now has the authority and responsibility to do the job and in return is accountable for getting the job done.

8-2d Degree of Centralization

If you've ever contacted a company with a complaint or a special request and been told by the customer service representative, "I'll have to ask my manager" or "I'm not authorized to do that," you know that centralization of authority exists in that company. **Centralization of authority** is the location of most authority at the upper levels of the organization. In a centralized organization, managers make most decisions, even the

Delegation of authority the assignment of direct authority and responsibility to a subordinate to complete tasks for which the manager is normally responsible.

Centralization of authority the location of most authority at the upper levels of the organization.

relatively small ones. That's why the customer service representative you called couldn't make a decision without first asking the manager.

If you are lucky, however, you may have talked to a customer service representative at another company who said, "I can take care of that for you right now." In other words, the person was able to handle your problem without any input from or consultation with company management. **Decentralization** is the location of a significant amount of authority in the lower levels of the organization. An organization is decentralized if it has a high degree of delegation at all levels. In a decentralized organization, workers closest to problems are authorized to make the decisions necessary to solve the problems on their own.

Decentralization has a number of advantages, including that it develops employee capabilities throughout the company and leads to faster decision making and more satisfied customers and employees. Trillium Health Centre (THC) in Ontario has found much success with a decentralized organizational structure. THC is a merger of two hospitals, both of which had been operating under a traditional hierarchical structure, which is common in healthcare organizations. With the decentralized structure, each of the centre's 10 divisions has the ability to set its own vision, goals, and objectives and is supported by partnership councils led and chaired by staff and supported by management. The decision to employ a distributed leadership environment has been well received and has enhanced employee engagement on a collective level.[15]

With results like these, the key question is no longer *whether* companies should decentralize, but *where* they should decentralize. One rule of thumb is to stay centralized where standardization is important and to decentralize where standardization is unimportant. **Standardization** is solving problems by consistently applying the same rules, procedures, and processes. Kwik Kopy Printing Canada, a franchise business with 50 locations across Canada, uses a standardized process when recruiting and selecting potential franchisees. The company believes that selecting the right franchisees is a critical decision that affects brand awareness, the success of locations, and the company's overall financial performance. The selection process includes a series of personal interviews to assess the franchisee's skills, as well as profile testing to uncover the franchisee's strengths and weaknesses. Meetings with head office personnel and existing franchisees are also part of the selection process. In addition, potential franchisees must provide financial documentation to show they have sufficient equity to purchase the business. Brett Harding, who brought the Kwik Kopy franchise to Canada, admits that to some the selection process may seem very long and structured. But, as he puts it, "no one gets married after the first date. Good franchising is about relationships."[16]

8-3 JOB DESIGN

1. "Welcome to McDonald's. May I have your order please?"

2. Listen to the order. Repeat it for accuracy. State the total cost. "Please drive to the second window."

3. Take the money. Make change.

4. Give customers drinks, straws, and napkins.

5. Give customers food.

6. "Thank you for coming to McDonald's."

Could you stand to do the same simple tasks an average of 50 times per hour, 400 times per day, 2,000 times per week, 8,000 times per month? Few can. Fast food workers rarely stay on the job more than six months.[17] According to the National Restaurant Association, fast food restaurants have an average turnover rate of 60 percent.[18]

The shape of a job is closely related to how happy and fulfilled an employee feels doing it. In this next section, you will learn about **job design**—the number,

---

Decentralization the location of a significant amount of authority in the lower levels of the organization.

Standardization solving problems by consistently applying the same rules, procedures, and processes.

Job design the number, kind, and variety of tasks that individual workers perform in doing their jobs.

kinds, and variety of tasks that individual workers perform in doing their jobs.

*You will learn why companies continue to use **8-3a job specialization** and how **8-3b job rotation, job enlargement, and job enrichment** are being used to overcome the problems associated with job specialization.*

8-3a Job Specialization

Job specialization occurs when a job is composed of a small part of a larger task or process. Specialized jobs are characterized by simple, easy-to-learn steps, low variety, and high repetition, like the McDonald's drive-through window job just described. A clear disadvantage of specialized jobs is that, being so easy to learn, they quickly become boring. This in turn can lead to low job satisfaction and high absenteeism and employee turnover, all of which are very costly to organizations.

However, once a job has been specialized, it takes little time to learn and master, which translates into enhanced productivity, a strong economic incentive for companies to use specialization. For example, every Taco Bell has two food production lines: one for the drive-through and the other dedicated to the walk-up counter. Those lines are further broken down into distinct jobs—steamers, stuffers, and expeditors—and three prep areas—hot and cold holding areas and wrapping. The stuffer in the hot holding area follows the prescribed three-step process to stir, scoop, and tap to fill the tortillas with beef, using Taco Bell's own beef portioning tool to make sure the same quantity of beef gets placed inside the tortillas every time.[19] At most fast food restaurants like Taco Bell, every task has been engineered to make the process as simple as possible. Because the work is designed to be simple, wages can remain low, since it isn't necessary to pay high salaries to attract highly experienced, educated, or trained workers.

8-3b Job Rotation, Enlargement, and Enrichment

Because of the efficiency of specialized jobs, companies are often reluctant to eliminate them. Consequently, job redesign efforts have focused on modifying jobs to keep the benefits of specialized jobs while reducing their obvious costs and disadvantages. Three methods—job rotation, job enlargement, and job enrichment—have been used to try to improve specialized jobs.[20]

Job rotation attempts to overcome the disadvantages of job specialization by periodically moving workers from one specialized job to another to give them more variety and the opportunity to use different skills. For example, a "mirror attacher" in an automobile plant might attach mirrors in the first half of the day's work shift and then install bumpers during the second half. Because employees simply switch from one specialized job to another, job rotation allows companies to retain the economic benefits of specialized work. At the same time, the greater variety of tasks makes the work less boring and more satisfying for workers.

Another way to counter the disadvantages of specialization is to enlarge the job. **Job enlargement** increases the number of different tasks that a worker performs within one particular job. So instead of being assigned just one task, workers with enlarged jobs are given several tasks to perform. For example, an enlarged "mirror attacher" job might include attaching the mirror, checking to see that the mirror's power adjustment controls work, and then cleaning the mirror's surface. Although job enlargement increases variety, many workers report feeling more stress when their jobs are enlarged. Consequently, many workers view enlarged jobs as simply more work, especially if they are not given additional time to complete the additional tasks. In comparison, **job enrichment** attempts to overcome the deficiencies in specialized work by increasing the number of tasks and by giving workers the authority and control to make meaningful decisions about their work.[21]

MaraZe/Shutterstock

Job specialization a job composed of a small part of a larger task or process.

Job rotation periodically moving workers from one specialized job to another to give them more variety and the opportunity to use different skills.

Job enlargement increasing the number of different tasks that a worker performs within one particular job.

Job enrichment increasing the number of tasks in a particular job and giving workers the authority and control to make meaningful decisions about their work.

8-4 INTRA-ORGANIZATIONAL PROCESSES

More than 40 years ago, Tom Burns and G. M. Stalker described how two kinds of organizational designs—mechanistic and organic—are appropriate for different kinds of organizational environments.[22] **Mechanistic organizations** are characterized by specialized jobs and responsibilities; precisely defined, unchanging roles; and a rigid chain of command based on centralized authority and vertical communication. This type of organization works best in stable, unchanging business environments. By contrast, **organic organizations** are characterized by broadly defined jobs and responsibilities; loosely defined, frequently changing roles; and decentralized authority and horizontal communication based on task knowledge. This type of organization works best in dynamic, changing business environments.

The organizational design techniques described in the first half of this chapter—departmentalization, authority, and job design—are better suited for mechanistic organizations and the stable business environments that were more prevalent before 1980. In contrast, the organizational design techniques discussed next are more appropriate for organic organizations and for the increasingly dynamic environments in which today's businesses compete.

The key difference between these approaches is that mechanistic ones focus on organizational structure while organic ones focus on organizational processes—that is, on collections of activities that transform inputs into outputs valued by customers.

Mechanistic organizations organizations characterized by specialized jobs and responsibilities; precisely defined, unchanging roles; and a rigid chain of command based on centralized authority and vertical communication.

Organic organizations organizations characterized by broadly defined jobs and responsibility; loosely defined, frequently changing roles; and decentralized authority and horizontal communication based on task knowledge.

Intra-organizational process the collection of activities that take place within an organization to transform inputs into outputs that customers value.

Re-engineering fundamental rethinking and radical redesign of business processes to achieve dramatic improvements in critical measures of performance, such as cost, quality, service, and speed.

An **intra-organizational process** is the collection of activities that take place within an organization to transform inputs into outputs that customers value.

Let's take a look at how companies are using 8-4a re-engineering and 8-4b empowerment to redesign intra-organizational processes like these.

8-4a Re-engineering

In their best-selling book *Reengineering the Corporation*, Michael Hammer and James Champy define **re-engineering** as "the *fundamental* rethinking and *radical* redesign of business *processes* to achieve *dramatic* improvements in critical, contemporary measures of performance, such as cost, quality, service and speed."[23] Hammer and Champy further explain the four key words shown in italics in this definition. The first key word is *fundamental.* When re-engineering organizational designs, managers must ask themselves, "Why do we do what we do?" and "Why do we do it the way we do?" The usual answer is, "Because that's the way we've always done it." Fundamental rethinking involves getting behind "that's the way we've always done it" and pursuing answers to these questions down to the foundations so that processes are actually achieving business goals. The second key word is *radical.* Re-engineering is about significant change, about starting over by throwing out the old ways of getting work done. The third key word is *processes.* Hammer and Champy note that "most business people are not process oriented; they are focused on tasks, on jobs, on people, on structures, but not on processes." The fourth key word is *dramatic.* Re-engineering is about achieving quantum improvements in company performance.

Re-engineering is most often associated with large manufacturing businesses, however, the same concepts can be applied to service businesses as well as various sizes of businesses. McCarthy Tétrault LLP (a major Canadian law firm with offices across the country) adopted re-engineering principles to radically change the process of its business model. According to chief operating officer Tracie Crook, the legal industry has experienced a fair degree of change—including increased competition from global firms and clients who demand more efficient services and more predictable billing. As a result, the company decided to re-evaluate its business practices and embarked on a major transformation—reducing the number of support staff, adopting an open-plan workspace, and moving away from the traditional practice of billing clients by the hour. In the new model, there is one legal assistant for every four lawyers and administration tasks associated with preparing documents and handling billing are now centralized. Partners are no longer tucked away in large corner offices—partners' offices (now 10 feet by 10 feet and the same size as everyone else's offices) are now in the middle of the workspace with glass walls. The rest of the space is open concept to allow lawyers to move around and communicate with their colleagues, carrying their laptops with them and staying connected with headsets in a workspace that projects a "Starbucks" atmosphere instead of the traditional, "stuffy" corporate work environment. Not only does the new layout create a more collaborative atmosphere, but it also has saved the company money. In the Toronto office, the reduction in staff and the new office layout allowed the company to sublease one of the nine floors it previously occupied in the TD Bank Tower. An even more radical change is how the law firm deals with clients. Clients are now assigned to a client service innovation team made up of lawyers as well as administrative staff who work with the client to determine how best to bill for legal services—in some cases offering a fixed fee (versus the traditional model of charging clients for the total billable hours) or contracting out some of the work to achieve greater efficiencies and cost savings.[24]

Re-engineering changes an organization's orientation from vertical to horizontal. Instead of taking orders from upper management, lower- and middle-level managers and workers take orders from a customer, who is at the beginning and end of each process. Instead of running independent functional departments, managers and workers in different departments take ownership of cross-functional processes. Instead of simplifying work so that it becomes increasingly specialized, re-engineering complicates work by giving workers increased autonomy and responsibility for complete processes.

In essence, re-engineering changes work by changing **task interdependence**, the extent to which collective action is required to complete an entire piece of work. As shown in Exhibit 8.9, there are three kinds of task interdependence.[25] In **pooled interdependence**, each job or department independently contributes to the whole. In **sequential interdependence**, work must be performed in succession, as one group's or job's outputs become the inputs for the next group or job. Finally, in **reciprocal interdependence**, different jobs or groups work together in a back-and-forth manner to complete the process. By reducing the hand-offs between different jobs or groups, re-engineering decreases sequential interdependence. Likewise, re-engineering decreases pooled interdependence by redesigning work so that formerly independent jobs or departments now work

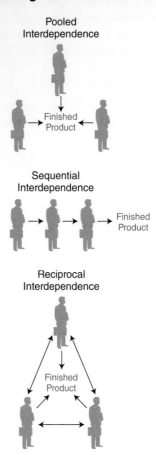

Exhibit 8.9
Re-engineering and Task Interdependence

Pooled Interdependence

Finished Product

Sequential Interdependence

Finished Product

Reciprocal Interdependence

Finished Product

together to complete processes. Finally, re-engineering increases reciprocal interdependence by making groups or individuals responsible for larger, more complete processes in which several steps may be accomplished at the same time.

As an organizational design tool, re-engineering promises big rewards, but it has also come under severe criticism. The most serious complaint is that,

Task interdependence the extent to which collective action is required to complete an entire piece of work.

Pooled interdependence work completed by having each job or department independently contribute to the whole.

Sequential interdependence work completed in succession, with one group's or job's outputs becoming the inputs for the next group or job.

Reciprocal interdependence work completed by different jobs or groups working together in a back-and-forth manner.

because it allows a few workers to do the work formerly done by many, re-engineering is simply a corporate code word for cost cutting and worker layoffs.[26] Likewise, for that reason, detractors claim that re-engineering hurts morale and performance. Today, even re-engineering gurus Hammer and Champy admit that roughly 70 percent of all re-engineering projects fail because of the effects on people in the workplace. Says Hammer, "I wasn't smart enough about that [the people issues]. I was reflecting my engineering background and was insufficiently appreciative of the human dimension. I've [now] learned that's critical."[27]

8-4b Empowerment

Another way of redesigning intra-organizational processes is through empowerment. **Empowering workers** means permanently passing decision-making authority and responsibility from managers to workers. For workers to be fully empowered, companies must give them the information and resources they need to make and carry out good decisions and then reward them for taking individual initiative.[28] Unfortunately, this doesn't happen often enough. As Michael Schrage, author and MIT researcher, wrote:

> *A warehouse employee can see on the intranet that a shipment is late but has no authority to accelerate its delivery. A project manager knows—and can mathematically demonstrate—that a seemingly minor spec change will bust both her budget and her schedule. The spec must be changed anyway. An airline reservations agent tells the Executive Platinum Premier frequent flier that first class appears wide open for an upgrade. However, the airline's yield management software won't permit any upgrades until just four hours before the flight, frequent fliers (and reservations) be damned. In all these cases, the employee has access to valuable information. Each one possesses the "knowledge" to do the job better. But the knowledge and information are irrelevant and useless. Knowledge isn't power; the ability to act on knowledge is power.*[29]

> **Empowering workers** permanently passing decision-making authority and responsibility from managers to workers by giving them the information and resources they need to make and carry out good decisions.

Hockey Night in Canada

After a security officer at the Ritz-Carlton hotel in Toronto was called to a guest's room for a second time after receiving complaints from other guests about children playing hockey in the hallway, he decided to find a creative solution to the problem. Although the children's mother apologized and promised to keep the children in the room, he thought there might be a better solution. With the help of banquet employees, he isolated space in one of the hotel's empty meeting rooms and created a hockey rink using banquet tables as the rink frame, and then visited a nearby sports store to buy two hockey nets, six sticks, and hockey balls. When the rink was ready, an invitation was delivered to the family's hotel room, letting them know that "hockey just isn't a game, it's a lifestyle" and inviting them to come and play. When the family arrived, a number of employees joined in to round out the two teams and ensure that the family had an experience they would not soon forget. When the game was over, both sides shook hands and photos were taken so the family could remember their epic game. The security officer could have

Grushin/Shutterstock

easily just knocked on the family's door and asked them to be quiet, but instead he decided to actively follow through and demonstrate one of the company's service values: "I am empowered to create unique, memorable and personal experiences for our guests." All in the name of employee empowerment and in the name of Canada's national sport.

Source: The Ritz-Carlton Leadership Center, "Seven Advantages of Employee Empowerment," November 4, 2015, http://ritzcarltonleadershipcenter.com/tag/employee-empowerment/.

When workers are given the proper information and resources and are allowed to make good decisions, they experience strong feelings of empowerment. **Empowerment** is a feeling of intrinsic motivation in which workers perceive their work to have meaning and perceive themselves to be competent, to have an impact, and to be capable of self-determination.[30] Work has meaning when it is consistent with personal standards and beliefs. Workers feel competent when they believe they can perform an activity with skill. The belief that they are having an impact comes from a feeling that they can affect work outcomes. A feeling of self-determination arises from workers' belief that they have the autonomy to choose how best to do their work.

Empowerment can lead to changes in organizational processes because meaning, competence, impact, and self-determination produce empowered employees who take active, rather than passive, roles in their work. At Ritz-Carlton Hotels, all employees are empowered to spend up to $2,000 to solve customer service issues. That's not $2,000 per year or $2,000 per day, it's $2,000 per incident. And, employees can spend that $2,000 without asking for managerial approval.[31]

8-5 INTER-ORGANIZATIONAL PROCESSES

An **inter-organizational process** is a collection of activities that occur *among companies* to transform inputs into outputs that customers value. In other words, many companies work together to create a product or service that keeps customers happy. For example, when you purchase a pair of yoga pants from a retail clothing chain like lululemon, you're not just buying from lululemon—you're also buying from a network of suppliers in other countries and from that company's sourcing team, which generates the correct fabrics and the entire line of clothing carried in lululemon stores. That team then manufactures the first product prototypes and sends them to the company's design team for final inspection and possibly last-minute changes.

In this section, you'll explore inter-organizational processes by learning about 8-5a modular organizations and 8-5b virtual organizations.

8-5a Modular Organizations

Except for the core business activities that they can perform more efficiently and effectively than others, **modular organizations** outsource all other business activities to outside companies, suppliers, specialists, or consultants. **Outsourcing**—obtaining goods and services from an outside supplier—has traditionally been associated with manufacturing businesses looking to reduce production costs by purchasing components from outside suppliers at cheaper prices than they could produce them for. **Business process outsourcing (BPO)**, the contracting of the operations of a specific business process to a third-party service provider, refers to internal business functions like accounting, human resources, and customer-related services. The term *modular* is used because the business activities purchased from outside companies can be added or dropped as needed, much like adding pieces to a three-dimensional puzzle. Exhibit 8.10 depicts a modular organization in which the company has chosen to keep training, human resources, sales, product design, manufacturing, customer service, research and development, and information technology as core business activities, but has outsourced the noncore activities of product distribution, web page design, advertising, payroll, accounting, and packaging.

Modular organizations are not limited to large companies; in fact, many small and medium-sized businesses benefit greatly from this organizational structure. The key issue is knowing which function should be accomplished by an outside company and when to do so. Companies generally prefer to remove functions that are not vital for sustaining the company's competitive advantage, allowing the organization to focus on its

Empowerment feelings of intrinsic motivation, in which workers perceive their work to have impact and meaning and perceive themselves to be competent and capable of self-determination.

Inter-organizational process a collection of activities that take place among companies to transform inputs into outputs that customers value.

Modular organizations organizations that outsource all other business activities to outside companies, suppliers, specialists, or consultants.

Outsourcing obtaining goods and services from an outside supplier.

Business process outsourcing (BPO) contracting operations of a specific business process to a third-party service provider.

Exhibit 8.10
Modular Organization

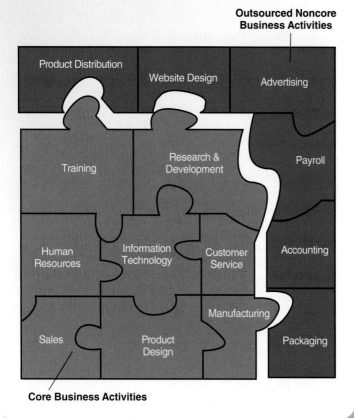

Outsourced Noncore Business Activities

Product Distribution

Website Design

Advertising

Training

Research & Development

Payroll

Human Resources

Information Technology

Customer Service

Accounting

Sales

Product Design

Manufacturing

Packaging

Core Business Activities

core activities. For example, a small bicycle shop may recognize that its repair and customization services are working well together and contributing greatly to the business's reputation and customer loyalty, however, the time spent on handling accounting functions is slowing the company down. At that point, the business should assess the benefits to outsourcing that part of the business, identifying the specific gains that would be realized relative to the drawbacks and costs associated with removing this function. The main purposes of outsourcing are reducing costs, decreasing time spent, and increasing quality of outputs.[32]

Modular organizations have several advantages. First, cost savings are gained from outsourcing and

Virtual organization groups of geographically and/or organizationally distributed participants who collaborate toward a shared goal using a combination of information and communications technologies to accomplish a task.

paying for outsourced labour, expertise, or manufacturing capabilities only when needed, meaning modular organizations can cost significantly less to run than traditional organizations. Merck, one of the world's leading pharmaceutical companies, is transforming into a modular organization. As little as two years ago, two-thirds of Merck's research budget was spent on in-house scientists and research labs that conducted expensive clinical research trials to test the drugs that Merck had in development. Today, Merck spends only one-third of its research budget on in-house clinical research. It outsources the rest to Quintiles, a company with 29,000 employees in 100 countries that specializes in conducting large-scale clinical research trials for pharmaceutical companies like Merck.[33]

Modular organizations can also benefit from increased flexibility because they can rely on the knowledge and expertise of outside companies, allowing them to focus on their business strengths and the overall business environment in order to respond and adapt to changing conditions. Outsourcing can also influence an organization's overall capabilities, as outsource supplier specialists can provide access to technology improvements, increased levels of innovation, and better management processes.[34] Modular organizations have disadvantages, too. The primary disadvantage is the loss of control that occurs when key business activities are outsourced to other companies. Modular organizations need reliable suppliers and partners they can trust and can work closely with, and can effectively communicate with to ensure that levels of quality are upheld and deadlines are adhered to. Accordingly, modular organizations would be wise to negotiate contract terms that include penalties for not meeting delivery deadlines.

Also, companies may reduce their competitive advantage in two ways if they mistakenly outsource a core business activity. First, as a result of competitive and technological change, the noncore business activities a company has outsourced may suddenly become the basis for competitive advantage. Second, related to that point, suppliers to whom work is outsourced can sometimes become competitors.

8-5b Virtual Organizations

In contrast to modular organizations, in which the interorganizational process revolves around a central company, a **virtual organization** can be defined as groups

Snapping the Pieces Into Place

Bombardier, Canada's multinational aerospace and transportation company, knows how flexible modular organizations can be. During the development of the Challenger business jet—designed to fly eight passengers comfortably from coast to coast without stopping to refuel—Bombardier broke the design of the aircraft into 12 large pieces provided by internal divisions and outside suppliers. Initially, each supplier sent teams of engineers to Bombardier's Montreal facility to examine every part of the aircraft and gain agreement on design and manufacturing specifications that would be acceptable for each company.

Drawing on the company's core competencies, Bombardier produced the cockpit and centre and forward fuselage in-house, but manufacturers spread around the globe provided the tail cone (Hawker de Havilland, Australia), stabilizers and rear fuselage (Aerospace Industrial Development, Taiwan), engines (General Electric Co., the United States), avionics (Rockwell Collins, the United States), wings (Mitsubishi, Japan), fairings to improve aerodynamics (Fischer, Austria), and lastly

Adam Rose/Invision for Bombardier/AP Images

landing gear (Messier-Dowty, Canada). It took employees in Bombardier's factory a mere four days to snap the parts together and produce a finished product. As a result of the modular approach, Bombardier was able to share development costs with its partners, drastically reduce the time required for a new product launch, and enter the market at a very competitive price point.

Sources: N. Anand and R. Daft, "What Is the Right Organizational Design?" *Organizational Dynamics*, Vol. 36, No. 4, pp. 329–344, 2007, http://citeseerx.ist.psu.edu/viewdoc/download?doi=10.1.1.453.4032&rep=rep1&type=pdf; L. MacDonald, "Bombardier's Big Bet," *Canadian Business*, June 2, 2011, http://www.canadianbusiness.com/blogs-and-comment/bombardiers-big-bet/; P. Siekman, "The Snap Together Business Jet" *Fortune*, January 21, 2002, http://faculty.msb.edu/homak/homahelpsite/webhelp/Content/Bombadier_SnapTogether_Business_Jet_Fortune_1-21-02.htm.

of geographically and/or organizationally distributed participants who collaborate toward a shared goal using a combination of information and communications technologies to accomplish a task.[35] A virtual organization might consist of a smaller group of full-time employees as well as outside professionals retained to work on a special temporary project, or it may refer to employees who work remotely from home using technology to connect with other members of the organization. Companies in the film industry follow the virtual organization model—with professionals like directors, cinematographers, screenwriters, and costume designers applying their specialized skills and moving from project to project.[36]

The composition of a virtual organization can change frequently, as the partners involved depend on the expertise needed to address a specific problem at a particular time. In this sense, the term *virtual organization* means the organization or group that exists "at the moment."

When researchers at Proctor & Gamble (P&G) discovered technologies that provided superior adhesive properties as part of ongoing product development for its diaper brands, the company recognized the opportunity to collaborate with another partner utilizing a virtual organization model. P&G initiated a special project to share its innovation and research capabilities with the Clorox Company, which contributed manufacturing knowledge and facilities that led to the introduction of the Glad Press 'N Seal line of food wrap products. The joint venture resulted in a successful collaboration; Glad sales doubled and led to more new products like ForceFlex with Febreze.[37]

Virtual organizations have a number of advantages. As in the case of P&G and Clorox, virtual organizations allow companies to take advantage of a market opportunity and also share costs. And because members can combine their efforts to meet customers' needs, tapping into each partner's strengths and specialized skills and resources, they offer much greater flexibility.

As with modular organizations, a disadvantage of virtual organizations is that once work has been outsourced, it can be difficult to control the quality of work done by partners. The greatest disadvantage, however, is that tremendous managerial skills are required to make a network of independent people or organizations work well together, especially since their relationships tend to be short and based on a single task or project.

Virtual organizations are using various methods to solve this problem, including the use of a *broker*. In traditional, hierarchical organizations, managers plan, organize, and control. But with the horizontal, inter-organizational processes that characterize virtual organizations, the job of a broker is to create and assemble the knowledge, skills, and resources from different companies for outside parties, such as customers.[38] Recently, the demand for cloud-based technology to access data and information over the internet has created a new opportunity for brokers to provide these services on behalf of business clients. *Cloud service brokerages (CSBs)* act as an intermediary between organizations wanting to purchase cloud services and cloud service providers. Brokers work with the organization to understand the work processes, budget, and data requirements, and then research and work with cloud service providers to offer cloud-based services with specific capabilities and customized services tailored to the organization's unique needs. Brokers rely on their experience and contacts with multiple cloud service providers to negotiate price breaks and additional value-added services from cloud providers, effectively saving clients time and money.[39]

Virtual Managers

In today's workplace, it is not uncommon for managers to spend much of their time leading virtually—in fact, research shows that 80 percent of managers today lead in a virtual environment. Technology has made it possible, and in some cases more cost effective, for leaders to act as virtual managers—managing employees located in other company locations, home offices, and even other countries. When Vancouver tech company Avigilon was in the market for a new chief operating officer, it did what many companies often do, and that is promote from within the organization. However, instead of physically moving the newly promoted manager to Vancouver, the executives decided to allow him to lead his team virtually from where he was currently living, which was in Texas. CEO Alexander Fernandes didn't see the need for a physical move, explaining "We're on the same computer network, we're hooked up through our video conferencing, [and] we meet up on a regular basis at various trade shows, so we're adept at running essentially a virtual organization."

Although this may be highly nontraditional for most organizations, the trend toward virtual organizations and virtual leadership has been embraced by many companies. Hootsuite's chief technology officer Ajai Sehgal was recruited from Groupon's Seattle office, and he continues to live in Seattle, telecommuting for most of the work week and travelling to Vancouver when needed.

When organizational members are geographically dispersed, it may not make sense for companies to have physical locations at all. Managers who choose to travel to

SukanPhoto/Shutterstock

meet up with members of their virtual organization can take advantage of virtual office services provided by companies like Regus Canada. Regus offers executives, managers and business owners access to a vast network of physical office spaces in every region in Canada, complete with full reception, tech support, board rooms, offices, and business lounges.

Managing a virtual workforce comes with its unique set of challenges, however. Virtual managers may find it more time consuming to manage a virtual team and more difficult to achieve consensus. In addition, virtual managers may find it more difficult to build trust and establish personal connections when their team isn't in front of them. To help overcome those difficulties, virtual managers would be wise to use face-to-face meetings strategically, to humanize the communications wherever possible, and to be clear about expectations for deadlines, availability, and communications.

Sources: T. Orton, "Bottom Line: B.C. Retains Satellite Status for Top Talent," *Business Vancouver*, September 8, 2014, https://www.biv.com/article/2014/9/bottom-line-bc-retains-satellite-status-top-talent/; K. Hedges, "Five Things Every Virtual Manager Should Do," Forbes.com, April 17, 2013, http://www.forbes.com/sites/work-in-progress/2013/04/17/five-things-every-virtual-manager-should-do/#18cb838a1826; S. White, "Virtual Offices Offer Flexibility and Freedom," *The Globe and Mail*, August 27, 2012, http://www.theglobeandmail.com/report-on-business/industry-news/property-report/virtual-offices-offer-flexibility-freedom/article4500800/.

STUDY TOOLS 8

READY TO STUDY?

LOCATED IN TEXTBOOK:

☐ Rip out the Chapter Review Card at the back of the book to have a summary of the chapter and key terms handy.

LOCATED AT NELSON.COM/STUDENT:

☐ Access the eBook or use the ReadSpeaker feature to listen to the chapter on the go.

☐ Prepare for tests with practice quizzes.

☐ Review key terms with flashcards and the glossary feature.

☐ Work through key concepts with case studies and Management Decision Exercises.

☐ Explore practical examples with You Make the Decision Activities.

9 Leading Teams

Yuri/iStockphoto

LEARNING OUTCOMES

After studying this chapter, you will be able to...

9-1 Explain the good and bad of using teams.

9-2 Recognize and understand the different kinds of teams.

9-3 Understand the general characteristics of work teams.

9-4 Explain how to enhance work team effectiveness.

After you finish this chapter, go to **PAGE 195** for **STUDY TOOLS**

Drawn to a Team Environment

When in doubt, ask for advice. That's what Devon McCubbin did before finding his career niche—working for a company where he is both a manager and a team leader. Straight out of high school, Devon studied general arts at the University of Regina (2001–03). He tried his hand at crab fishing next, then "fell in love" with Kelowna, BC, and decided to study again. But after graduating from Okanagan College with a diploma in business marketing in 2007, he was still uncertain about his future. So he contacted the coordinator of an Okanagan College program that pairs students with prospective employers and asked for advice. She suggested he visit a career fair, and that set him on the path toward working for a service and manufacturing firm that by 2016 was bringing in $4.8 billion annually. In 2007, he joined the company's staff in Kelowna. In 2015, he was asked if he would move as a now senior service manager to the relatively new company offices in Edmonton, where he started work as a "traditional service manager" in charge of a team of service and sales reps responsible for seven different "routes" or areas. The company employs more than 100 people in Edmonton. The importance of teams is stressed throughout the business.

1. It's said that people often take a moment to adjust to the thought of managing teams. Is that how it was for you?

I like to think being a leader in a team atmosphere has come naturally to me. I'll give a lot of credit to growing up in a sports environment with my close friends. I've always been outspoken and vocal when I play sports. This translated into my school dealings and then into my various workplaces. The challenging part is dealing with the constantly changing dynamic of the people you're leading. You are always adjusting as you add team members and as directives change.

2. Can you describe the kind of team you lead?

My service and sales representatives (commonly referred to as "route drivers" but they are far from being just delivery employees) are empowered to each treat their route like it's their own business. My job as their manager is to ensure they have the tools, support, and training necessary to be successful. The service and sales representatives are the face of the company to our customers, so ensuring their success enables the company to maximize profits and ultimately live by our principal objective. We hire on culture, not experience (though experience helps, of course). So in a sense, we are all cut from the same cloth. Every one of my team carries a sense of professionalism and enthusiasm.

3. How do you bring out the best in a team?

Every member of my team has different motivating factors. It's important to let them know what kind of succession plan is in place for them if they are looking to move up in their career. Equally as important is showing them how to maximize their pay plan if they are motivated by money. Consistent debriefs, training, feedback, and follow-through build the trust and ultimately keep them engaged. I'm a huge believer in leading by example as well.

4. Do your team members take responsibility for the quality of the products and services they provide?

Absolutely! The role of my service and sales representatives involves relationship building to the point where the account contact will go to them with any and all feedback on the quality of service and products.

5. What are the major advantages of using teams, in your experience?

Having a team environment really makes for an easy transition for new hires. Camaraderie is evident instantly. It allows for friendly competition. Each rep is scored on key performance metrics, so accountability for each member is on display. It really brings out the "family feel" within the organization.

6. Obviously you must have come upon disadvantages too?

Yes indeed! Keeping tenured reps motivated and engaged can definitely be a challenge. If a tenured rep doesn't agree with a new product rollout or with a corporate initiative, and they voice this opinion openly, it can easily ripple through the whole team. Also with a company that experiences significant growth, new team members are continually added. Adjusting the management time properly becomes a challenge.

7. Is there anything about leading teams that came as a surprise?

It is truly amazing how a team in a company can be very similar to a sports team. You have the "A" players: those that get you the wins, know the business, and can be counted on. Your "B" players work hard and grind it out every day. Then the rest, those that need lots of coaching and performance management: these players either get better or are not a fit for the roles they are in. This is why it's important to always have your "bench," newly hired and trained players that are eagerly awaiting more prominent roles.

OFF THE CUFF

8. You took something of a roundabout route to your career. Would you recommend that approach?

I recommend that you do what feels right and make what you believe is the right choice. Every one of my lateral peers has taken a different path. Sometimes going with your gut leads to amazing possibilities.

9. Do you have a favourite app?

Flipboard! Knowledge is power.

For the full interview go online to nelson.com/student

Photo and interview courtesy of Devon McCubbin

THE GOOD AND BAD OF USING TEAMS

Two-thirds of executives in Canada believe they significantly improve their effectiveness by establishing work teams.[1] But this has only been the case for the last 25 years. Procter & Gamble and Cummins Engine began using teams in 1962 and 1973 respectively, but many international companies—including Boeing, Caterpillar, Ford Motor Company, and General Electric—did not set up their first teams until the 1980s. Now, however, they are ubiquitous.[2] "Whether we are talking about software development, Olympic hockey, disease outbreak response, or urban warfare, teams represent the critical unit that 'gets things done' in today's world."[3] In other words, teams are a relatively new phenomenon, and there's still much for organizations to learn about managing them.

A **work team** consists of a small number of people with complementary skills who hold themselves mutually accountable for pursuing a common purpose, achieving performance goals, and improving interdependent work processes.[4] Although work teams are not the answer for every situation or organization, if the right teams are used properly and in the right settings, they can dramatically improve company performance and instill a sense of vitality in the workplace that is otherwise difficult to achieve.

*Let's begin our discussion of teams by learning about **9-1a the advantages of teams, 9-1b the disadvantages of teams,** and **9-1c when to use and not use teams.***

9-1a The Advantages of Teams (The Good)

Companies are making greater use of teams because they have been shown to improve customer satisfaction, product and service quality, employee job satisfaction, and decision making.[5] Teams help businesses increase

customer satisfaction in several ways. For example, work teams can be trained to meet the needs of specific customers. Aon Hewitt, a consulting firm with offices in Calgary, Montreal, Toronto, and Vancouver, manages benefits administration for hundreds of multinational client firms. To ensure customer satisfaction, Aon Hewitt re-engineered its customer service centre and created specific teams to handle benefits-related questions posed by employees of specific client organizations.[6] Businesses also create problem-solving teams and employee involvement teams to study ways to improve overall customer satisfaction and make recommendations for improvements. Teams like these typically meet on a weekly or monthly basis.

Teams also help firms improve *product and service quality* in several ways.[7] In contrast to traditional organizational structures where management is responsible for organizational outcomes and performance, teams take direct responsibility for the *quality* of the products and services they produce. At Whole Foods, a supermarket chain with stores in Vancouver and Toronto that sells groceries and health foods, the 10 teams that manage each store are responsible for store quality and performance (there are no departments). "Teams—and only teams—have the power to approve new hires for full-time jobs. Store leaders screen candidates and recommend them for a job on a specific team. But it takes a two-thirds vote of the team, after what is usually a 30-day trial period, for the candidate to become a full-time employee."[8]

Another reason for using teams is that teamwork often leads to increased *job satisfaction.*[9] Teamwork can be more satisfying than traditional work because it gives workers a chance to improve their skills. This is often accomplished through **cross-training**, in which team members are taught how to do all or most of the jobs performed by the other team members. The advantage for the organization is that cross-training allows a team to function normally when one member is absent, quits, or is transferred. The advantage for workers is that cross-training broadens their skills and increases their capabilities while also making their work more varied and interesting. A second reason why teamwork is satisfying is that work teams often receive proprietary business information that is available only to managers at most companies. For example, at Whole Foods, one team leader states: "If there's a new kind of cheese, everyone gets information on it and they all try it. We're always trying to bring in new kinds of produce. When the first crop of peaches comes in from Georgia, we all try it so that when the customer comes by you can say, 'I'd give 'em a week,' or, 'They're comin' in nice this year.'"[10] Team members are given full access to their

Work team a small number of people with complementary skills who hold themselves mutually accountable for pursuing a common purpose, achieving performance goals, and improving interdependent work processes.

Cross-training training team members to do all or most of the jobs performed by the other team members.

store's financial information and everyone's salaries, including those of the store manager and the CEO.[11] Team members also gain job satisfaction from unique leadership responsibilities that are not typically available in traditional organizations. For example, rotating leadership among team members can lead to more participation and cooperation in team decision making and to improved team performance.[12]

Finally, teams share many of the advantages of group decision making discussed in Chapter 4. For instance, because team members possess different knowledge, skills, abilities, and experiences, a team is able to view problems from multiple perspectives. This diversity of viewpoints increases the likelihood that team decisions will solve the underlying causes of problems and not just address the symptoms. Carol Stephenson, the former dean of the Richard Ivey School of Business, found that adding women to diversify senior teams and boards brought a different perspective to decision making. Here she quoted the poet Ezra Pound, who once said that "when two men in business always agree, one of them is unnecessary."[13]

The Great Little Box Company (GLBC) of Richmond, British Columbia, which makes corrugated boxes, custom product displays, and flexible and protective packaging for manufacturers, has an "open books" philosophy, where team members are given full access to the company's financial information. Founder Robert Meggy says, "It makes people feel more a part of the company. It instills a sense of trust. Regardless of whether the news is good or bad, people want to know and, ultimately, will try harder to make the company more profitable." After all, he says, "We want employees to run the company like their own business." Team member and customer-service representative Sandra Fung says, "If we have been profitable that month, it makes me feel good to learn that I have contributed to that." Finally, to drive home the importance of teams and teamwork, everyone receives equal monthly profit sharing cheques. Says Meggy, "When it comes to teamwork, everyone is equal here. The truck drivers, the controller, office staff, plant supervisor—everybody gets the same amount."[14] Because increased knowledge and information are available to teams, it is easier for them to generate more alternative solutions, something that is vital to improving the quality of decisions. Also, because team members are involved in decision making, they are likely to be more committed to making those decisions work. In short, teams can do a much better job than individuals in two important steps of the decision-making process: defining the problem and generating alternative solutions.

> Using teams does not guarantee positive outcomes.

9-1b The Disadvantages of Teams (The Bad)

Although teams can significantly improve customer satisfaction, product and service quality, speed and efficiency in product development, employee job satisfaction, and decision making. using teams does not guarantee these positive outcomes. In fact, if you have ever participated in an in-class team project, you are probably already aware of some of the disadvantages of work teams: initially high turnover, social loafing, and the problems associated with group decision making.

The first disadvantage of work teams is *initially high turnover.* Teams aren't for everyone, and some workers balk at the responsibility, effort, and learning required in team settings. Skills must be learned to make teams work properly, and not everyone has learned those skills.[15]

Social loafing occurs when workers withhold their efforts and fail to perform their share of the work.[16] A 19th-century French engineer named Maximilian Ringlemann first documented social loafing when he found that one person pulling on a rope alone exerted an average of 63 kilograms of force on the rope. In groups of three, the average force dropped to 53 kilograms per person. In groups of eight, the average dropped to just 31 kilograms per person. Ringlemann concluded that the larger the team, the smaller the individual effort. In fact, social loafing is more likely to occur in larger groups, where identifying and monitoring the efforts of individual team members can be difficult.[17] In other words, social loafers count on being able to blend into the background, where their lack of effort isn't easily spotted. From team-based class projects, most students in Canadian universities and colleges already know about social loafers, or "slackers," who contribute poor, little, or no work whatsoever. Not surprisingly, a study of 250 student teams found that the most talented students are typically the least satisfied with teamwork because they have to carry slackers and do a disproportionate share of their team's work. Perceptions of fairness are negatively related to the extent of social loafing within teams.[18]

Finally, teams share many of the *disadvantages of group decision making* discussed in Chapter 4, such as

> **Social loafing** behaviour in which team members withhold their efforts and fail to perform their share of the work.

Exhibit 9.1
When to Use and When Not to Use Teams

Use Teams When . . .

1. there is a clear, engaging reason or purpose.

2. the job can't be done unless people work together.

3. rewards can be provided for teamwork and team performance.

4. ample resources are available.

5. teams will have clear authority to manage and change how work gets done.

Don't Use Teams When . . .

1. there isn't a clear, engaging reason or purpose.

2. the job can be done by people working independently.

3. rewards are provided for individual effort and performance.

4. the necessary resources are not available.

5. management will continue to monitor and influence how work gets done.

Source: R. Wageman, "Critical Success Factors for Creating Superb Self-Managing Teams," *Organizational Dynamics* 26, no. 1 (1997): 49–61.

groupthink. In *groupthink*, members of highly cohesive groups feel intense pressure not to disagree with one another so that the group can approve a proposed solution. Because groupthink restricts discussion and leads to consideration of a limited number of alternative solutions, it usually results in poor decisions. Also, team decision making takes considerable time, and team meetings can often be unproductive and inefficient. Another possible pitfall is *minority domination*, where just one or two people dominate team discussions, restricting consideration of different problem definitions and alternative solutions. Finally, team members may not feel accountable for the decisions and actions taken by the team.

9-1c When to Use Teams

As the two previous subsections made clear, teams have significant advantages *and* disadvantages. Therefore, the question is not *whether* to use teams, but *when* and *where* to use them for maximum benefit and minimum cost. As Doug Johnson, associate director at the Center for the Study of Work Teams, puts it: "Teams are a means to an end, not an end in themselves."[19]

Exhibit 9.1 provides additional guidelines on when and when not to use teams.[20]

First, teams should be used when there is a clear and engaging reason or purpose for using them. Too many companies use teams because they're popular or because the companies assume that teams can fix all problems. Teams are much more likely to succeed if they know why they exist and what they are supposed to accomplish; teams are more likely to fail if they don't.

Second, teams should be used when the job can't be done unless people work together. This typically means that teams are needed when tasks are complex, require multiple perspectives, or require repeated interactions with others. If tasks are simple and don't require multiple perspectives or repeated interaction with others, teams should not be used.[21]

Is this your team at school?

Groupthink when members of highly cohesive groups feel intense pressure not to disagree with one another so that the group can approve a proposed solution.

Factors That Encourage People to Withhold Effort in Teams

1. **The presence of someone with expertise.** Team members will withhold effort when another team member is highly qualified to make a decision or comment on an issue.

2. **The presentation of a compelling argument.** Team members will withhold effort if the arguments for a course of action are very persuasive or similar to their own thinking.

3. **Lacking confidence in one's ability to contribute.** Team members will withhold effort if they are unsure about their ability to contribute to discussions, activities, or decisions. This is especially so for high-profile decisions.

4. **An unimportant or meaningless decision.** Team members will withhold effort by mentally withdrawing or adopting a "who cares" attitude if decisions don't affect them or their units, or if they don't see a connection between their efforts and their team's successes or failures.

5. **A dysfunctional decision-making climate.** Team members will withhold effort if other team members are frustrated or indifferent or if a team is floundering or disorganized.

Sources: A. Puni, C. B. Agyemang, and E. S. Asamoah (2016). "Leadership Styles, Employee Turnover Intentions and Counterproductive Work Behaviours." *International Journal of Innovation and Research (5)*1. Accessed online 12 February 2016 at http://www.ijird.com/index.php/ijird/article/view/86207; A. Powell, J. Galvin, and G. Piccoli (2006). "Antecedents to Team Member Commitment From Near and Far: A Comparison Between Collocated and Virtual Teams," *Information Technology & People* Vol. 19 Iss: 4. Check out pages 299–322 for reasons that people might have for withholding efforts using Google Docs or Drop Box for team projects in your school.

For instance, because of the enormous complexity of today's cars, you would think that auto companies routinely use interconnected design teams. After all, the typical car has 30,000 parts, 80 different computer modules, indicators sensing how close other cars are when parking or going 110 km/h, and the ability to automatically adjust braking, cornering, gas mileage, and acceleration. But auto companies actually don't routinely use interconnected design teams, as most designers are responsible for separate sections or parts of the car. Achim Badstübner, head of Audi Group design, says, "We tend to make the mistake that we all know what they're doing but the connection is not so good." Audi *does* take a team approach. Badstübner says, "I think it's very important to basically lock them in one room, literally speaking. Then there is an interaction: you talk to the guy who does seats and he tells you something about his expertise and you might take something from him that helps you develop a new wheel, for example." Badstübner says that by connecting the teams, "you get a different result because through this method you get the best of every brain. I think you can't survive if you just depend on one brain to do a complex thing like [design] a car."[22]

Third, teams should be used when rewards can be provided for teamwork and team performance. Rewards that depend on team performance rather than individual performance are the key to rewarding team behaviours and efforts. You'll read more about team rewards later in the chapter, but for now it's enough to know that if the type of reward (individual versus team) is not matched to the type of performance (individual versus team), teams won't work. Research carried out at Queen's University in Kingston, Ontario, found that team rewards for virtual teams work very effectively and should become "best practices."[23]

9-2 KINDS OF TEAMS

Let's continue our discussion of teams by learning about the different kinds of teams that companies use to make themselves more competitive. We look first at **9-2a how teams differ in terms of autonomy, which is the key dimension that makes one team different from another,** *and then at* **9-2b some special kinds of teams.**

9-2a Autonomy, the Key Dimension

Teams can be classified in a number of ways, such as permanent or temporary, functional or cross-functional. However, studies indicate that the key differences among teams relate to the amount of autonomy they possess.[24] *Autonomy* is the degree to which workers have the discretion, freedom, and independence to decide how and when to do their work.

Exhibit 9.2 shows how five kinds of teams differ in terms of autonomy. Moving left to right across the

NEL

CHAPTER 9: Leading Teams 179

Exhibit 9.2
Team Autonomy Continuum

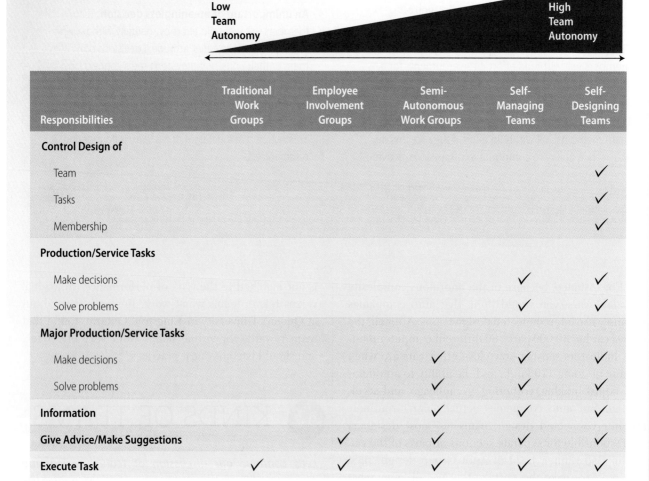

Responsibilities	Traditional Work Groups	Employee Involvement Groups	Semi-Autonomous Work Groups	Self-Managing Teams	Self-Designing Teams
Control Design of					
Team					✓
Tasks					✓
Membership					✓
Production/Service Tasks					
Make decisions				✓	✓
Solve problems				✓	✓
Major Production/Service Tasks					
Make decisions			✓	✓	✓
Solve problems			✓	✓	✓
Information			✓	✓	✓
Give Advice/Make Suggestions		✓	✓	✓	✓
Execute Task	✓	✓	✓	✓	✓

Sources: R. D. Banker, J. M. Field, R. G. Schroeder, and K. K. Sinha, "Impact of Work Teams on Manufacturing Performance: A Longitudinal Field Study," *Academy of Management Journal* 39 (1996): 867–890; J. R. Hackman, "The Psychology of Self-Management in Organizations," in *Psychology and Work: Productivity, Change, and Employment*, ed. M. S. Pallak and T. Perlof (Washington, DC: American Psychological Association), 85–136.

autonomy continuum at the top of the exhibit, traditional work groups and employee involvement groups have the least autonomy, semiautonomous work groups have more autonomy, and, finally, self-managing teams and self-designing teams have the most autonomy. Moving from bottom to top along the left side of the exhibit, note that the number of responsibilities given to each kind of

team increases directly with its autonomy. Let's review each of these kinds of teams and their autonomy and responsibilities in more detail.

The smallest amount of autonomy is found in a **traditional work group**, where two or more people work together to achieve a shared goal. In this group, workers are responsible for doing the work or executing the task, but they do not have direct responsibility for or control over their work. Workers report to managers who are responsible for their performance and who have the authority to hire and fire them, make job assignments, and control resources.

An **employee involvement team**, which has somewhat more autonomy, meets on company time on

Traditional work group a group composed of two or more people who work together to achieve a shared goal.

Employee involvement team team that provides advice or makes suggestions to management concerning specific issues.

Self-Directed Work Teams

Self-directed work teams (also known as self-managing or self-managed teams) can have a high failure rate. In a study carried out at a western Canadian university, on a team project that was worth 40 percent of the final grade, each student was required to contribute to the final self-directed team project. Each team was to design and re-engineer a workplace process. The study found that despite being told specifically that they all must contribute, several students did not perform their roles adequately, conflict was allowed to escalate to disruptive levels, and team efficiency was extremely low (does this sound like one of your student teams?).

On the other hand, research has shown that for Canadian companies such as Dofasco, Steel Case Equipment, LOF Glass, and Laurel Steel, results have been positive. These studies found increased flexibility, productivity gains, improved quality, increased commitment, and improved customer service. The key, says Michael Piczak, is to train and support management for the implementation of the new self-directed work team process. Students at university may still be learning and acquiring these valuable skills.

Sources: T. L. Rappa, L. L. Gilson, J. E. Mathieu, and T. Ruddy, (2016), "Leading Empowered Teams: An Examination of the Role of External Team Leaders and Team Coaches," *The Leadership Quarterly (27)*1, 109–123; V. Galt, "Teamwork Benefits Men, Study Says", *The Globe and Mail*, http://www.theglobeandmail.com/report-on-business/teamwork-benefits-men-study-says/article4136820/; G. H. Coetzer, and R. T. Trimble (2010), "An Empirical Examination of the Relationship Between Adult Attention Deficit, Cooperative Conflict Management and Efficacy for Working in Teams," *American Journal of Business* (25) 1, 23–33; M. W. Piczak, "Self-Directed Work Teams: An Implementation Guide," http://www.spin.mohawkcollege.ca/courses/pizcakm/oh&s&sdwts.ppt.

a weekly or monthly basis to provide advice or make suggestions to management concerning specific issues such as plant safety, customer relations, or product quality.[25] Although team members offer advice and suggestions, they do not have the authority to make decisions. Membership on these teams is often voluntary, but members may be selected because of their expertise. The idea behind employee involvement teams is that the people closest to the problem or situation are best able to recommend solutions.

A **semiautonomous work group** not only provides advice and suggestions to management but also has the authority to make decisions and solve problems related to the major tasks required to produce a product or service. Semiautonomous groups regularly receive information about budgets, work quality and performance, and competitors' products. Furthermore, members of semiautonomous work groups are typically cross-trained in a number of different skills and tasks. In short, semiautonomous work groups give employees the authority to make decisions that are typically made by supervisors and managers. That authority is not complete, however. Managers still play a role—albeit a much reduced one—in supporting the work of semiautonomous work groups.

In these groups, managers ask good questions, provide resources, and facilitate performance of group goals.

A **self-managing team** differs from a semiautonomous work group in that team members manage and control *all* of the major tasks that are *directly related* to production of a product or service without first getting approval from management. This includes managing and controlling the acquisition of materials, making a product or providing a service, and ensuring timely delivery. The use of self-managing teams has significantly increased productivity at a number of other companies, increasing quality by 12 percent at AT&T, reducing errors by 13 percent at FedEx, and helping 3M increase production by 300 percent at one of its manufacturing plants.[26] Seventy-two percent of *Fortune* 1,000 companies have at least one self-managing team.[27]

Semiautonomous work group a group that has the authority to make decisions and solve problems related to the major tasks of producing a product or service.

Self-managing team a team that manages and controls all of the major tasks of producing a product or service (also called a *self-directed work team*).

Building Cohesiveness by Eating Lunch Together

Canada is an important growing area for cranberries. Of all the cranberries harvested in Canada every year, about 60 percent are grown for Ocean Spray, the cranberry juice company. This represents as much as 20 percent of the total North American Ocean Spray cranberry crop! At Ocean Spray, no one is allowed to set a meeting during lunchtime. Why? The company sets this time aside so that employees can eat lunch together. But it's not just about eating, it's about giving everyone in the company some time to get to know each other. Leaders at Ocean Spray believe that there is no better way to find out about what is going on at work, and perhaps even to discover ways to work together, than to sit and have a conversation over lunch. It's better than emails, it's better than conference calls, and it's definitely better than cramming everyone into a conference room for five hours in the middle of the day. By encouraging everyone to eat together, the company gives people a comfortable, informal, and organic setting where they can build relationships, share knowledge and ideas, and find out what makes other people tick. And really, what's a better way to learn to trust someone—to talk to them one-on-one over lunch or to sit through another boring seminar together?

Sources: http://www.oceanspray.ca/Who-We-Are/Harvest/The-Cranberry-Harvest.aspx; M. Heffernan, "To-Do Today: Eat Lunch with a Colleague," *Inc.*, September 25, 2012, http://www.inc.com/margaret-heffernan/team-building-eat-lunch-with-a-colleague.html.

Robert Kneschke/Shutterstock

A **self-designing team** has all the characteristics of a self-managing team, but it also controls and changes the design of the team itself, the tasks it does, and how and when it does them, as well as the membership of the team.[28]

9-2b Special Kinds of Teams

Companies are increasingly using several other kinds of teams that can't easily be categorized in terms of autonomy: cross-functional teams, virtual teams, and project teams. Depending on how these teams are designed, they can be low or high in autonomy.

A **cross-functional team** is composed of employees from different functional areas of the organization.[29] Because their members have different functional backgrounds, education, and experience, these teams usually tackle problems from multiple perspectives and generate more ideas and alternative solutions, all of which are especially important when trying to innovate or do creative problem solving.[30] Cross-functional teams can be used almost anywhere in an organization and are often used in conjunction with matrix and product organizational structures (see Chapter 8). They can entail part-time/temporary team assignments or full-time/long-term ones.

A **virtual team** is a group of geographically and/or organizationally dispersed coworkers who use a

Self-designing team a team that has the characteristics of a self-managing team but also controls team design, work tasks, and team membership.

Cross-functional team a team composed of employees from different functional areas of the organization.

Virtual team a team composed of geographically and/or organizationally dispersed coworkers who use telecommunication and information technologies to accomplish an organizational task.

GOOD TIP!

Tips for Managing Successful Virtual Teams

1. Select people who are self-starters and strong communicators.
2. Keep the team focused by establishing clear, specific goals and by explaining the consequences and importance of meeting these goals.
3. Provide frequent feedback so that team members can measure their progress.
4. Keep team interactions upbeat and action-oriented by expressing appreciation for good work and completed tasks.
5. Personalize the virtual team by periodically bringing team members together and by encouraging team members to share information with one

another about their personal lives. This is especially important when the virtual team first forms.
6. Improve communication through increased telephone calls, emails, and Internet messaging, and videoconference sessions.
7. Periodically ask team members how well the team is working and what can be done to improve performance.
8. Empower virtual teams so that they have the discretion, freedom, and independence to decide how and when to accomplish their jobs.

Sources: W. F. Cascio, "Managing a Virtual Workplace," *Academy of Management Executive* 14 (2000): 81–90; B. Kirkman, B. Rosen, P. Tesluk, and C. Gibson, "The Impact of Team Empowerment on Virtual Team Performance: The Moderating Role of Face-to-Face Interaction," *Academy of Management Journal* 47 (2004): 175–192; S. Furst, M. Reeves, B. Rosen, and R. Blackburn, "Managing the Life Cycle of Virtual Teams," *Academy of Management Executive* (May 2004): 6–20; C. Solomon, "Managing Virtual Teams," *Workforce* 80 (June 2001): 60; H. Gazor, "A Literature Review on Challenges of Virtual Teams' Leadership," *Journal of Sociological Research*, Vol 3, No 2, (2012): 69–73.

combination of telecommunications and information technologies to accomplish an organizational task.[31] Virtual teams are increasingly common, and are used by 66 percent of multinational firms.[32] Members of virtual teams rarely meet face-to-face; instead, the members use email, videoconferencing, and group communication software.

Virtual teams can be employee involvement teams, self-managing teams, or nearly any kind of team discussed in this chapter. Virtual teams are often (but not necessarily) temporary teams that have been set up to accomplish a specific task.[33] Ike Hall, an adjunct professor at Athabasca University's online MBA program (the largest MBA program in Canada), indicates that team projects and interactions carried out in a virtual environment can produce excellent results. Experience working in this manner can be very useful, given that more and more Canadian businesses will require executives who can utilize virtual teams effectively.[34]

The principal advantage of virtual teams is their flexibility. Employees can work with one another regardless of physical location, time zone, or organizational affiliation.[35] Because the team members don't meet in a physical location, virtual teams also find it much easier to include other key stakeholders such as suppliers and customers. Virtual teams also have certain efficiency advantages over traditional teams. Because the teammates do not meet face-to-face, a virtual team typically requires a

smaller time commitment than a traditional team does. Moreover, employees can fulfill the responsibilities of their virtual team membership from the comfort of their own offices without the travel time or downtime typically required for face-to-face meetings.[36]

A drawback to virtual teams is that the team members must learn to express themselves in new contexts.[37] The give-and-take that naturally occurs in face-to-face meetings is more difficult to achieve through videoconferencing or other methods of virtual teaming. Indeed, several studies have shown that physical proximity enhances information processing in teams.[38] To minimize these problems, some companies bring virtual team members together physically on a regular basis.

A **project team** is created to complete specific, one-time projects or tasks within a limited time.[39] They are often used to develop new products, significantly improve existing products, roll out new information systems, or build new factories or offices. The project team is typically led by a project manager who bears the overall responsibility for planning, staffing, and managing the team, which usually includes employees from different functional areas. Effective project teams demand both

> **Project team** a team created to complete specific, one-time projects or tasks within a limited time.

individual and collective responsibility.[40] One advantage of project teams is that drawing employees from different functional areas can reduce or eliminate communication barriers. As long as team members feel free to express their ideas, thoughts, and concerns, free-flowing communication encourages cooperation among separate departments and typically speeds up the design process.[41]

Another advantage of project teams is their flexibility. When projects are finished, project team members either move on to the next project or return to their functional units. At BCIT (which stands for "Being Crammed Into Teams"), teamwork is a big deal and students take the lessons to heart. When your school project team breaks up, and you continue on other team tasks, you take good experiences of what *to do* and what *not to do* forward into other university or college student projects and, eventually, into the workplace. As another example, publication of this book required designers, editors, page compositors, and web designers, among others. When the task was finished, these people applied their skills to other textbook projects. Because of this flexibility, project teams are often used with the matrix organizational designs discussed in Chapter 8.

9-3 WORK TEAM CHARACTERISTICS

"Why did I ever let you talk me into teams? They're nothing but trouble."[42] Lots of managers have this reaction after making the move to teams. Many don't realize that this reaction is normal, both for them and for workers. In fact, such a reaction is characteristic of the *storming* stage of team development (see Section 9-3e). Managers who are familiar with these stages, and with other important characteristics of teams, will be better prepared to manage the changes that are sure to occur when companies make the switch to team-based structures. A University of Edmonton study found that a mandatory team experience, one that was case-based and that involved all of the students registered in the university's faculties of health, produced highly useful skills. The students formed interprofessional student teams (nursing, physiotherapy, medicine, and diagnostic technology), where they learned team skills and specific information about how to interact with the other professions. In this way they gained knowledge about the roles, knowledge, and contributions that could be made by professions other than their own.[43]

Understanding the characteristics of work teams is essential for making teams an effective part of an organization. Therefore, in this section you'll learn about **9-3a team norms, 9-3b team cohesiveness, 9-3c team size, 9-3d team conflict,** *and* **9-3e the stages of team development.**

9-3a Team Norms

Over time, teams develop **norms**, which are informally agreed-upon standards that regulate team behaviour.[44] Norms are valuable because they let team members know what is expected of them. Canada is setting the norm for a team approach on the world-wide stage; Michelle Cameron, Canada's ambassador to Lebanon, recently talked about Syrian refugees' deteriorating conditions and Canada's efforts to help the most vulnerable. Justin Trudeau's new Liberal government set a number of 25,000 Syrian refugees that would come from the war-torn area of the Middle East, but Ambassador Cameron never wants her team to say: "We have to get this many at all costs." It's not about Canada hitting the number, but rather "it's about the humanitarian response, and I think we really need to be focused on that. Ambassadors for other countries are coming to me and saying: 'Keep us updated. Are you moving people this quickly? How are you doing it safely? How are you doing it to protect the public health in Canada? How are you choosing refugees?' I feel like Canada is really a leader in coming out front and centre. I feel like that's the other gift that we're giving: helping other countries to say, 'Well, if Canada can do it. . . .'"[45]

Studies indicate that norms are one of the most powerful influences on work behaviour because they regulate the everyday actions that allow teams to function effectively. Effective work teams develop norms relating to the quality and timeliness of job performance, absenteeism, safety, and expression of ideas. Team norms are often associated with positive outcomes, such as stronger organizational commitment, more trust in management, and stronger job and organizational satisfaction.[46] A recent study compared business students from Canada with business students from another country and found that the norms exhibited by Canadian students demonstrated different ethical attitudes toward questionable business practices at the individual level. Social norms in Canada, compared to those of other countries, were found to be a factor.[47]

Norms informally agreed-on standards that regulate team behaviour.

Norms can also influence team behaviour in negative ways. For example, most people would agree that the following are negative behaviours: damaging organizational property; saying or doing something to hurt someone at work; intentionally doing one's work badly, incorrectly, or slowly; griping about coworkers; deliberately breaking rules; or doing something to harm the company. A study of workers from 34 teams in 20 different organizations found that teams with negative norms strongly influenced their team members to engage in these negative behaviours. In fact, the longer individuals were members of a team with negative norms and the more often they interacted with their teammates, the more likely they were to engage in negative behaviours. Since team norms typically develop early in the life of a team, these results indicate how important it is for teams to establish positive norms from the outset.[48] Results from a recent study of female MBA graduates suggest that while Canadian women have similar career profiles to men, women still lag behind their male counterparts after graduation. At the same time, women encounter intractable career barriers in the form of negative norms at both the individual level and the organizational level.[49] Negative norms are something we must continue to combat, starting in classrooms. As investment oracle Warren Buffett stated in an interview with Melinda Gates: "50 percent of the talent of the country we pushed off in a corner for almost 200 years . . . We still have a way to go."[50] His words echo findings that were presented to the World Economic Forum in the 2015 Gender Gap Report.[51] Again, we owe it to Canada, and to the female students in our schools, to ensure that these negative norms do not continue here or in the rest of the world.

9-3b Team Cohesiveness

Cohesiveness is another important characteristic of work teams. **Cohesiveness** is the extent to which team members are attracted to a team and motivated to remain in it.[52] The level of cohesiveness in a group is important for several reasons. To start, cohesive groups have a better

> Studies indicate that norms are one of the most powerful influences on work behaviour.

chance of retaining their members. As a result, cohesive groups typically experience lower turnover.[53] In addition, team cohesiveness promotes cooperative behaviour, generosity, and a willingness on the part of team members to assist one another.[54] When team cohesiveness is high, team members are more motivated to contribute to the team because they want to gain the approval of other team members. Studies have established clearly that for these reasons and others, cohesive teams consistently perform better.[55] Furthermore, cohesive teams quickly achieve high levels of performance. By contrast, teams low in cohesion take much longer to reach the same levels of performance.[56]

Watch out for situations where the team members' goals conflict with those of the organization. When this happens, team cohesiveness can lead to weak performance. Take, for instance, the recent NHL lockout and the always discussed strike possibility of Major League Soccer players.[57] The players were highly cohesive (as expected of a sports team), but their goals were very different from the owners'. The result, fully to be expected, was very low productivity—no teams played. Much the same happens with highly cohesive union groups, where productivity declines because the team's goals diverge from those of the organization.

To promote team cohesiveness, first, make sure that all team members are present at team meetings and activities. Team cohesiveness suffers when members are allowed to withdraw from the team and miss team meetings and events.[58] Second, create additional opportunities for teammates to work together by rearranging work schedules and creating common workspaces. When task interdependence is high and team members have plenty of chances to work together, team cohesiveness tends to increase.[59] Third, engaging in nonwork activities as a team can help build cohesion. At a company where teams put in extraordinarily long hours coding computer software, the software teams maintained cohesion by

NASA Goddard Space Flight Center

Cohesiveness the extent to which team members are attracted to a team and motivated to remain in it.

Teams work best when you get to know one another outside of work.

Grant Halverson/Getty Images

doing "fun stuff" together. Team leader Tammy Urban says: "We went on team outings at least once a week. We'd play darts, shoot pool. Teams work best when you get to know each other outside of work—what people's interests are, who they are. Personal connections go a long way when you're developing complex applications in our kind of time frames."[60] Finally, companies build team cohesiveness by making employees feel that they are part of a special organization. For example, all the new hires at Disney World are required to take a course titled "Traditions One," where they learn the traditions and history of the Walt Disney Company (including the names of the seven dwarves!). The purpose of Traditions One is to instill team pride in working for Disney.

9-3c Team Size

The relationship between team size and performance appears to be curvilinear. Very small or very large teams may not perform as well as medium-sized teams, and

for most teams, the right size is six to nine members.[61] This size is conducive to high team cohesion, which has a positive effect on team performance. A team of this size is small enough for the team members to get to know one another and for each member to have an opportunity to contribute in a meaningful way to the team's success. But at the same time, the team is large enough to take advantage of team members' diverse skills, knowledge, and perspectives. Finally, it is easier to instill a sense of responsibility and mutual accountability in teams of this size.[62]

By contrast, when teams get too large, team members find it difficult to get to know one another, and the team may splinter into smaller subgroups. When this occurs, subgroups sometimes argue and disagree, weakening overall team cohesion. As teams grow, there is also a greater chance of *minority domination*, where just a few team members dominate team discussions. Even if minority domination doesn't occur, larger groups may not have time for all team members to share their input.

And when team members feel that their contributions are unimportant or not needed, the result is less involvement, effort, and accountability to the team.[63] Large teams also face logistical problems such as finding an appropriate time or place to meet. Finally, social loafing is much more common in large teams.

Team performance can also suffer when a team is too small. Teams with just a few people may lack the diversity of skills and knowledge found in larger teams. Also, teams that are too small are unlikely to gain the advantages of team decision making (i.e., multiple perspectives, more ideas and alternative solutions, stronger commitment) found in larger teams.

What signs indicate that a team's size needs to be changed? If decisions are taking too long, if the team is having difficulty making decisions or taking action, if a few members dominate the team, if team members lack commitment, or if their efforts are weak, chances are the team is too big. By contrast, if a team is having difficulty coming up with ideas or generating solutions, or if the team does not have the expertise to address a specific problem, chances are the team is too small.

Overall, team size is an important characteristic of successful teams. As much as we might not like teams, learning to work with (and within) teams is required for success in the business world.[64]

9-3d Team Conflict

Conflict and disagreement are inevitable in most teams, but this shouldn't surprise anyone. From time to time, people who work together are going to disagree about what and how things get done. What causes conflict in teams? Although almost anything can lead to conflict—casual remarks that unintentionally offend a team member, or fighting over scarce resources—the primary cause of team conflict is disagreement over team goals and priorities.[65] Other common causes of team conflict include disagreements over task-related issues, interpersonal incompatibilities, and simple fatigue.

The key to dealing with team conflict is not avoiding it, but rather making sure that the team experiences the right *kind* of conflict. In Chapter 4, you learned about *c-type conflict*, or *cognitive conflict*, which focuses on problem-related differences of opinion, and *a-type conflict*, or *affective conflict*, which refers to the emotional reactions that can arise when disagreements become personal rather than professional.[66] Cognitive conflict is strongly associated with improvements in team performance, whereas affective conflict is strongly associated with decreases in team performance.[67]

With cognitive conflict, team members disagree because their different experiences and expertise lead them to different views of the problem and its solutions. Professors often require that teams come up with three alternatives and then ask students to choose the best one. We deliberately introduce conflict with such requests. Indeed, managers who participated on teams that emphasized cognitive conflict described their teammates as "smart," "team players," and the "best in the business." They described their teams as "open," "fun," and "productive." One manager summed up the positive attitude that team members had about cognitive conflict by saying, "We scream a lot, then laugh, and then resolve the issue."[68] Thus, cognitive conflict is also characterized by a willingness to examine, compare, and reconcile differences to produce the best possible solution. We need to do this to come up with the best answer. But we also must learn to do it in a constructive, diplomatic, and tactful manner. Critique is not criticism.

By contrast, affective conflict (note, again, this is not "effective" conflict—see Chapter 4 for the details) often results in hostility, anger, resentment, distrust, cynicism, and apathy. Managers who participated on teams that emphasized affective conflict described their teammates as "manipulative," "secretive," "burned out," and "political."[69] Not surprisingly, affective conflict can make people uncomfortable and cause them to withdraw or decrease their commitment to a team.[70] Affective conflict also lowers the satisfaction of team

How to Have a Good Fight

1. Work with more information to make discussion productive rather than contentious.

2. Generate several alternative solutions. Two solutions will generate debate. More than two will generate productive discussion.

3. Establish common goals.

4. Use your sense of humour.

5. Create and maintain a balance of power.

6. Do not force consensus.

Sources: P. A Lapointe and G. Cucumel, (2016). "An Alternative Typology for Teamwork," *World Review of Entrepreneurship, Management and Sustainable Development (12)*1, Université Laval, Québec QC. DOI: 10.1504/WREMSD.2016.073431; K. M. Eisenhard, J. L. Kahwajy, and L. J. Bourgeois III, "How Management Teams Can Have a Good Fight," *Harvard Business Review* 75.4 (July–August 1997): 77–85.

members, and may lead to personal hostility between coworkers and reduce team cohesiveness.[71] Cognitive conflict is beneficial; affective conflict undermines team performance by preventing teams from engaging in the kinds of activities that are vital to team effectiveness.

To handle team conflict, first, managers need to realize that emphasizing cognitive conflict alone won't be enough. Studies have found that cognitive and affective conflicts often occur together in a given team activity. Sincere attempts to reach agreement on a difficult issue can quickly deteriorate from cognitive to affective conflict if the discussion turns personal and tempers and emotions flare. While cognitive conflict is clearly the better approach to take, efforts to engage in cognitive conflict should be managed well and checked before they deteriorate and the team becomes unproductive.

Can teams disagree and still get along? Fortunately, they can. In an attempt to study this issue, researchers examined team conflict in 12 high-tech companies. In four of those companies, work teams used cognitive conflict to address problems but did so in a way that minimized the occurrence of affective conflict.

There are several ways that teams can have a good "fight".[72] First, work with more information rather than less. If data are plentiful, objective, and up-to-date, teams will focus on issues, not personalities. Second,

develop multiple alternatives to enrich debate. Focusing on multiple solutions diffuses conflict by getting the team to keep searching for a better solution. Positions and opinions are naturally more flexible when there are five alternatives rather than just two. Third, establish common goals. Remember, most team conflict arises from disagreements over team goals and priorities. It's okay to spend a lot of time arguing about which route to take to Vancouver, when someone wants to end up there, but a lot of time gets wasted in such arguments if one person secretly wants to go to Edmonton. Fourth, inject humour into the workplace. Humour relieves tension, builds cohesion, and makes being in teams fun. Fifth, maintain a balance of power by involving as many people as possible in the decision process. And sixth, resolve issues without forcing a consensus. Consensus means that everyone must agree before decisions are finalized. Also ensure you never "vote." Voting is not consensus. Consensus is discussing and agreeing. Quite often a vote is just an easy (and ineffective) way out of a tough situation. Requiring consensus gives everyone on the team veto power. Nothing gets done until everyone agrees, which, of course, is nearly impossible. As a result, insisting on consensus usually promotes affective rather than cognitive conflict. If team members can't agree after constructively discussing their options, it's better to have

> Team goals lead to much higher team performance 93 percent of the time.

the team leader make the final decision. Most team members can accept the team leader's choice if they've been thoroughly involved in the decision process.

9-3e Stages of Team Development

As teams develop and grow, they pass through four stages of development. As shown in Exhibit 9.3, those stages are forming, storming, norming, and performing.[73] Although not every team passes through each of these stages, teams that do tend to be better performers.[74] This holds true even for teams composed of seasoned executives. After a period of time, however, if a team is not managed well, its performance may start to deteriorate as the team begins a process of decline and progresses through adjourning (the stages of de-norming, de-storming, and de-forming).[75]

Forming is the initial stage of team development. This is the getting-acquainted stage, during which team members first meet one another, form initial impressions, and try to get a sense of what it will be like to be part of the team. Some of the first team norms will be established during this stage, as team members begin to find out what behaviours will and won't be accepted by the team. During this stage, team leaders should allow time for team members to get to know one another, set early ground rules, and begin to establish a preliminary team structure.

Conflicts and disagreements often characterize the second stage of team development, **storming**. As team members begin working together, different personalities and work styles may clash. Team members become more assertive at this stage and more willing to state opinions. This is also the stage when team members jockey for position and try to establish a favourable role for themselves on the team. In addition, team members are likely to disagree about what the group should do and how it should do it. Team performance is still relatively low, given that team cohesion is weak and team members are still reluctant to support one another. Since teams that get stuck in the storming stage are almost always ineffective, it is important for team leaders to focus the team on team goals and on improving team performance. Team members need to be particularly patient and tolerant with one another in this stage.

During **norming**, the third stage of team development, team members begin to settle into their roles

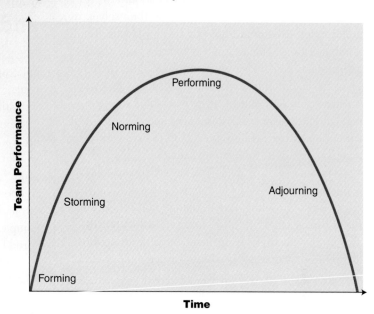

Exhibit 9.3
Stages of Team Development

Sources: J. F. McGrew, J. G. Bilotta, and J. M. Deeney, "Software Team Formation and Decay: Extending the Standard Model for Small Groups," *Small Group Research* 30, no. 2 (1999): 209–234; B. W. Tuckman, "Development Sequence in Small Groups," *Psychological Bulletin* 63, no. 6 (1965): 384–399.

as team members. Positive team norms will have developed by this stage, and teammates should know what to expect from one another. Petty differences should have been resolved, friendships will have developed, and group cohesion will be relatively strong. At this point, team members will have accepted team goals, be operating as a unit, and, as indicated by the increase in performance, be working together effectively. This stage can be very short and is often characterized by someone on the team saying, "I think things are finally coming together." Note, however, that teams may cycle back and forth between storming and norming several times before finally settling into norming.

Forming the first stage of team development, in which team members meet one another, form initial impressions, and begin to establish team norms.

Storming the second stage of development, characterized by conflict and disagreement, in which team members disagree over what the team should do and how it should do it.

Norming the third stage of team development, in which team members begin to settle into their roles, group cohesion grows, and positive team norms develop.

In one of the last stages of team development, **performing**, performance improves because the group has finally matured into an effective, fully functioning team. At this point, members should be fully committed to the team and think of themselves as members of a team and not just as employees. Team members often become intensely loyal to one another at this stage and feel mutual accountability for team successes and failures. Trivial disagreements, which can take time and energy away from the work of the team, should be rare. At this stage, teams get a lot of work done, and it is fun to be a team member. But the team should not become complacent.

Without effective management, the team's performance may begin to decline as it passes through the stages of de-norming, de-storming, and de-forming (these three stages are also known as **adjourning**).[76] *De-norming* provides team members with an opportunity to internalize what they have learned and to set out new objectives and new norms as they move on to other tasks and assignments (quite often with new teams). It enables them to adapt to new tasks. Also, team members need to celebrate their successes. In this regard, celebrations are a useful way to help them *de-storm* (this is important even in virtual teams).[77] Celebrations are not parties; rather, they are venues for recognizing the results that teams have achieved. *De-forming*, the final part of adjourning, allows team members to aim forward and create new relationships, new communication approaches, and new interactions with other members of the organization.[78]

9-4 ENHANCING WORK TEAM EFFECTIVENESS

Making teams work is a difficult challenge. Companies can increase the likelihood that teams will succeed by carefully managing 9-4a the setting of team goals and priorities

and 9-4b how work team members are selected, 9-4c trained, and 9-4d compensated and recognized.[79]

9-4a Setting Team Goals and Priorities

In Chapter 4, you learned that setting **s**pecific, **m**easurable, **a**ttainable, **r**ealistic, and **t**imely (i.e., S.M.A.R.T.) goals is one of the most effective means for improving individual job performance. Fortunately, team goals also improve team performance, especially when they are *specific* and *challenging*. In fact, team goals lead to much higher team performance 93 percent of the time.[80] For example, Whole Foods has said it wants to open 35 to 40 stores in Canada, up from its current 10, and that will take continued teamwork within the company whose success in fulfilling its vision is measured by "Team Member excellence and happiness."[81]

Setting *specific* team goals is vital to team success. One reason why is that increasing a team's performance is inherently more complex than just increasing one individual's job performance. Consider that any one team is likely to involve at least four different kinds of goals: each member's goal for the team, each member's goal for himself or herself on the team, the team's

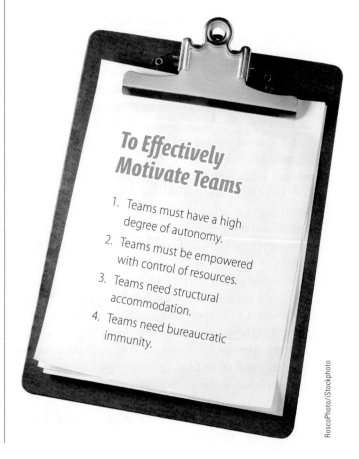

To Effectively Motivate Teams

1. Teams must have a high degree of autonomy.
2. Teams must be empowered with control of resources.
3. Teams need structural accommodation.
4. Teams need bureaucratic immunity.

RoscoPhoto/iStockphoto

goal for each member, and the team's goal for itself.[82] Without a specific, challenging goal for the team itself (the last of the four goals listed), team members may head off in all directions while pursuing these other goals. Consequently, setting a specific, challenging goal *for the team* clarifies team priorities by providing a clear focus and purpose.

The setting of challenging team goals affects how hard team members work. In particular, challenging goals greatly reduce social loafing. When faced with reasonably difficult goals, team members necessarily expect everyone to contribute. Consequently, they are much more likely to notice and complain if a teammate isn't doing his or her share. When teammates know one another well, when team goals are specific, when team communication is good, and when teams are rewarded for team performance (discussed below), there is only a 1 in 16 chance that teammates will be social loafers.[83]

Companies and teams can take steps to ensure that team goals lead to superior team performance. One increasingly popular approach is to give teams stretch goals—extremely ambitious goals that workers don't know how to reach.[84] The purpose of stretch goals is to achieve extraordinary improvements in performance by forcing managers and workers to throw away old, comfortable solutions and adopt radical solutions they have never used before.[85]

For stretch goals to motivate teams,[86] those teams must have a high degree of autonomy or control over how they achieve their goals. Also, they must be empowered with control over resources such as budgets, workspaces, computers, and whatever else they need to do their work. John Mackey, CEO of Whole Foods, was part of an executive group that discussed stretch goals that are required to "create team systems that value diversity, disagreement, and divergence as much as conformance, consensus, and cohesion."[87]

In addition, teams require **structural accommodation**, which entails providing teams with the ability to change organizational structures, policies, and practices if doing so will help them meet their stretch goals. Finally, successful teams have **bureaucratic immunity**. That is, they no longer have to go through the frustratingly slow process of multilevel reviews and sign-offs before making changes. Teams that have been granted bureaucratic immunity are shielded from the influence of various organizational groups and are accountable only to top management. As we saw in Chapter 5, Google has been reborn as Alphabet, and Google X, Google's research lab, works on "moonshots," meaning hard to accomplish projects like self-driving cars and Google Glass (eyeglasses that display email and can record videos and photos). Google X's teams work in two buildings a kilometre from Google's main campus to separate and free them from Google's main business. With bureaucratic immunity, teams can act quickly, and even experiment, with little fear of failure. Richard DeVaul says, "Google X is very consciously looking at things that Google in its right mind wouldn't do. They build the rocket pad far away from the widget factory, so if the rocket blows up, it's hopefully not disrupting the core business."[88]

9-4b Selecting People for Teamwork

Professor Edward Lawler writes that "people are very naive about how easy it is to create a team. Teams are the Ferraris of work design. They're high performance but high maintenance and expensive."[89] He adds that teams make workplaces extremely *effective*, not just fast. They are a very good use of resources (time, people, and money). That said, it's almost impossible to have an effective work team without carefully selecting people who are suited for teamwork or for working on a particular team. A focus on teamwork (individualism/collectivism), team level, and team diversity can help companies choose the right team members.[90] We may think we can always simply choose the best players, but that is not necessarily the way to success. We are hired for those high-paying jobs once we graduate from university so that we can develop teams. We are hired to take low-performance teams and turn them into higher performance teams. How do we do that? To answer that question, let's look at what makes successful team players.

Are you more comfortable working alone than with others? If you are, you may not be well suited for teamwork. Studies have found that job satisfaction is higher in teams when team members prefer working with others.[91] An indirect way to measure someone's preference for teamwork is by assessing that person's degree of individualism or collectivism. **Individualism–collectivism** refers to the degree to which a person believes that

Structural accommodation the ability to change organizational structures, policies, and practices in order to meet stretch goals.

Bureaucratic immunity the ability to make changes without first getting approval from managers or other parts of an organization.

Individualism–collectivism the degree to which a person believes that people should be self-sufficient and that loyalty to one's self is more important than loyalty to team or company.

Exhibit 9.4
The Team Player Inventory

	Strongly Disagree				Strongly Agree
1. I enjoy working on team/group projects.	1	2	3	4	5
2. Team/group project work easily allows others not to pull their weight.	1	2	3	4	5
3. Work that is done as a team/group is better than work done individually.	1	2	3	4	5
4. I do my best work alone rather than in a team/group.	1	2	3	4	5
5. Team/group work is overrated in terms of the actual results produced.	1	2	3	4	5
6. Working in a team/group gets me to think more creatively.	1	2	3	4	5
7. Teams/groups are used too often when individual work would be more effective.	1	2	3	4	5
8. My own work is enhanced when I am in a team/group situation.	1	2	3	4	5
9. My experiences working in team/group situations have been primarily negative.	1	2	3	4	5
10. More solutions/ideas are generated when working in a team/group situation than when working alone.	1	2	3	4	5

Reverse score items 2, 4, 5, 7, and 9. Then add the scores for items 1 to 10. Higher scores indicate a preference for teamwork, whereas lower total scores indicate a preference for individual work.

Source: T. J. B. Kline, "The Team Player Inventory: Reliability and Validity of a Measure of Predisposition Toward Organizational Team-Working Environments," *Journal for Specialists in Group Work* 24, no. 1 (1999): 102–112.

people should be self-sufficient and that loyalty to oneself is more important than loyalty to one's team or company.[92] *Individualists*, who put their own welfare and interests first, generally prefer independent tasks in which they work alone. *Collectivists*, who put group or team interests ahead of self-interests, generally prefer interdependent tasks in which they work with others; also, collectivists would rather cooperate than compete and are fearful of disappointing team members or of being ostracized from teams. Given these differences, it makes sense to select team members who are collectivists rather than individualists. Many companies use individualism–collectivism as an initial screening device for team members. But if team diversity is desired,

individualists may also be appropriate (see below). To determine your preference for teamwork, take the Team Player Inventory shown in Exhibit 9.4.

Team level refers to the average level of ability, experience, personality, or any other factor on a team. For example, a high level of team experience means that a team has especially experienced team members. This does not mean that every member of the team has considerable experience, but that enough team members do to significantly raise the average level of experience on the team. Team level is used to guide the selection of teammates when teams need a particular set of skills or capabilities to do their jobs well. For example, employees at Bombardier's Montreal plant are graduates of certified engineering schools in Quebec, or in other provinces, and the company's designers are registered professional engineers in the province. SAP in Vancouver employs highly trained and skilled graduates from the British Columbia Institute of Technology.[93]

Team level the average level of ability, experience, personality, or any other factor on a team.

Team diversity represents the variances in ability, experience, personality, or any other factor on a team.[94] From a practical perspective, team diversity is important. Professor John Hollenbeck explains: "Imagine if you put all the extroverts together. Everyone is talking, but nobody is listening. [By contrast,] with a team of [nothing but] introverts, you can hear the clock ticking on the wall."[95] Strong teams have talented members (i.e., team level), and in addition, those talented members vary in terms of abilities, experience, and personality. At Whole Foods the diversity is clear: "You'll work with the team and then after about a month go through a voting process. In order to officially be a part of the team, you need to have a positive two-thirds vote out of a quorum of three-fourths of the team. Once this happens, you're officially a team member."[96] For example, teams with strong team diversity on job experience have a mix of team members ranging from seasoned veterans to people with three or four years of experience to rookies with little or no experience. Team diversity is used to guide the selection of team members when teams must complete a wide range of different tasks or when tasks are especially complex.

Once the right team has been put together in terms of individualism–collectivism, team level, and team diversity, it's important to keep the team together as long as is practically possible. Interesting research by the National Transportation Safety Board found that 73 percent of the serious mistakes made by jet cockpit crews are made the very first day that a crew flies together as a team; also, of that 73 percent, 44 percent occur on their *very first flight* together that day (pilot teams fly two to three flights per day). Moreover, research has shown that fatigued pilot crews who have worked together before make significantly fewer errors than rested crews who have never worked together.[97] Their experience working together helps them overcome their fatigue and outperform new teams that have not worked together before. So, once you've created effective teams, keep them together as long as possible. Imagine the Emergency Room at St. Paul's Hospital in Vancouver. Wouldn't you feel much more confident with a team of physicians, surgeons, nurses, diagnostic technicians, and pharmacists who have worked together for a while?[98] Of course you would, which is why hospitals in Canada's major cities try to keep their teams together.

9-4c Team Training

After selecting the right people for teamwork, you need to train them. To succeed, teams need significant training in interpersonal skills, decision-making and problem-solving skills, and conflict resolution skills, in

The Rights and Wrongs of Socializing

Looking for a way to bring your team members closer together? There may be nothing better than a team outing. Whether it's dinner on a Friday night or a weekend retreat to Niagara Falls, a group outing is a great way to develop cohesiveness and interpersonal skills within a team. There are, however, certain situations to avoid. For example, you may not want to go to a bar for drinks if a team member is a recovering alcoholic. You may not want to schedule an event too late at night, or too far away, if some team members have young children at home. So do the right thing—make sure you get to know your team members, and their unique circumstances, so that you can plan team activities that everyone can participate in and enjoy.

Source: "Seven Ways to Socialize With Your Employees (Without Getting in Trouble)," *Inc.*, August 11, 2010, http://www.inc.com/guides/2010/08/7-ways-to-socialize-with-your-employees.html.

addition to technical training. Organizations that create work teams often underestimate the amount of training required to make teams effective. This mistake occurs often in successful organizations: managers assume that if employees can work effectively on their own, they can work effectively on teams. Actually, companies that use teams successfully provide thousands of hours of training to make sure their teams work. Stacy Myers, a consultant who helps companies implement teams, says: "When we help companies move to teams, we also require that employees take basic quality and business knowledge classes as well. Teams must know how their work affects the company, and how their success will be measured."[99] Quite often at business schools in Canada, we thrust people onto teams. The reason for this is to provide the training you will require once you go out into the workforce. Not every organization, however, can afford to send people to school. This is one reason why you will be valuable to your new employer: you have studied and practised team training.

Most commonly, members of work teams receive training in interpersonal skills. **Interpersonal skills**

Team diversity the variances or differences in ability, experience, personality, or any other factor on a team.

Interpersonal skills skills, such as listening, communicating, questioning, and providing feedback, that enable people to have effective working relationships with others.

such as listening, communicating, questioning, and providing feedback enable people to develop effective working relationships with others. Because of teams' autonomy and responsibility, many companies also give team members training in decision-making and problem-solving skills to help them do a better job of cutting costs and improving quality and customer service. Many organizations also teach team conflict resolution skills. Delta Faucet Canada produces plumbing and mechanical devices:

> *Teams at Delta Faucet have specific protocols for addressing conflict. For example, if an employee's behaviour is creating a problem within a team, the team is expected to work it out without involving the team leader. Two team members will meet with the "problem" team member and work toward a resolution. If this is unsuccessful, the whole team meets and confronts the issue. If necessary, the team leader can be brought in to make a decision, but . . . it is a rare occurrence for a team to reach that stage.*[100]

Firms must also provide team members with the *technical training* they need to do their jobs, particularly if they are being cross-trained to perform all of the different jobs on the team. Cross-training is less appropriate for teams of highly skilled workers. For instance, it is unlikely that a group of engineers, computer programmers, and systems analysts would be cross-trained for one another's jobs.

Team leaders need training, too, as they often feel unprepared for their new duties. New team leaders face myriad problems ranging from confusion about their new role to not knowing where to turn for help when their team has problems. The solution is extensive training.

9-4d Team Compensation and Recognition

Compensating teams correctly is very difficult. One survey found that only 37 percent of companies were satisfied with their team compensation plan and that even fewer—just 10 percent—were "very positive."[101]

Skill-based pay compensation system that pays employees for learning additional skills or knowledge.

Gainsharing a compensation system in which companies share the financial value of performance gains such as productivity, cost savings, or quality with their workers.

Syda Productions/Shutterstock

According to Susan Mohrman of the Center for Effective Organizations, one problem is that "there is a very strong set of beliefs in most organizations that people should be paid for how well they do. So when people first get put into team-based organizations, they really balk at being paid for how well the team does. It sounds illogical to them. It sounds like their individuality and their sense of self-worth are being threatened."[102] Consequently, companies need to choose a team compensation plan with care and, having done so, they must explain thoroughly to their employees how teams will be rewarded. For team compensation to work, it is vital that the type of reward (individual versus team) match the type of performance (individual versus team). The more each team member knows about rewards, the better the whole team performs.

Employees can be compensated for team participation and accomplishments in three ways: skill-based pay, gainsharing, and nonfinancial rewards. **Skill-based pay** programs pay employees for learning additional skills or knowledge.[103] These programs encourage employees to acquire the additional skills they will need to perform multiple jobs within a team, and to share that knowledge with others within their work groups.[104]

In **gainsharing** programs, companies share the financial value of performance gains such as productivity increases, cost savings, or quality improvements with their workers.[105]

Nonfinancial rewards are another means of rewarding teams for their performance. These rewards, which can range from vacation trips to T-shirts, plaques, and coffee mugs, are especially effective when coupled with management recognition, such as awards, certificates, and praise.[106] Professor Berglas notes that an A+ player "will crave praise, but unless it is sincere and tailored to them, they will suspect that it is fabricated and dismiss it out of hand." Companies want to keep the A+ players on their business teams performing for them. "Just because they think they're great doesn't mean they're not!"[107]

Nonfinancial awards tend to be most effective when teams or team-based interventions, such as total quality management (see Chapter 17), are first introduced.[108]

Which team compensation plan should your company use? In general, skill-based pay is most effective for self-managing and self-directing teams performing complex tasks. In these situations, the more each team member knows and can do, the better the whole team performs. By contrast, gainsharing works best in relatively stable environments where employees can focus on improving productivity, cost savings, or quality.

STUDY TOOLS 9

READY TO STUDY?

LOCATED IN TEXTBOOK:

☐ Rip out the Chapter Review Card at the back of the book to have a summary of the chapter and key terms handy.

LOCATED AT NELSON.COM/STUDENT:

☐ Access the eBook or use the ReadSpeaker feature to listen to the chapter on the go.

☐ Prepare for tests with practice quizzes.

☐ Review key terms with flashcards and the glossary feature.

☐ Work through key concepts with case studies and Management Decision Exercises.

☐ Explore practical examples with You Make the Decision Activities.

10 Managing Human Resource Systems

svetikd/iStockphoto

LEARNING OUTCOMES

After studying this chapter, you will be able to...

10-1 Explain how different employment laws affect human resource practice.

10-2 Explain how companies use HR planning and recruiting to find qualified job applicants.

10-3 Describe the selection techniques and procedures that companies use when deciding which applicants should receive job offers.

10-4 Describe how to determine training needs and select the appropriate training methods.

10-5 Discuss how to use performance appraisal to give meaningful performance feedback.

10-6 Describe basic compensation strategies and discuss the four kinds of employee separations.

After you finish

this chapter, go

to **PAGE 223** for

STUDY TOOLS

Passionate About People

Managing people in the radio business is a huge part of Michael Cameron's work life, since he is both general manager and general sales manager at Newcap Radio in Sudbury, Ontario. He readily admits that he loves working with people in radio, but Michael took the "scenic route," both literally and figuratively, to this kind of work. After high school, he left his home city of Ottawa and worked at a ski hill on Whistler Mountain in British Columbia. He returned to Ottawa "fat, drunk, and broke." Next, he decided to take a golf management program, but knew that wasn't for him when he was told up front that he shouldn't expect to make any money. He decided to move into marketing, where he might have more career opportunities. From 2001 to 2004, he studied at Niagara College, graduating with an advanced diploma in business administration, with marketing as his major. Since then he has worked solidly in radio, for four broadcasters in all, in 15 different formats or genres (such as country and news talk). At Newcap, his dual GM/GSM role covers two Sudbury stations: The New Hot 93.5 (a top 40/pop FM station), and Rewind 103.9 FM (which focuses on "'70s, '80s and more"). Newcap Sudbury has about 20 full-time and 12 part-time employees.

1. Human resource management is regarded as one of the most important management tasks. Is that how you see it?

Technology continues to change our world at a rapid pace. However, good people will remain at the core of any business venture. Culture is what your employees experience. Your story is what you say you do. And high morale is what happens when culture and story collide. Building your team, and your story, and continuing to cultivate both are essential to success.

2. Just how difficult is it to find, develop, and keep the right employees?

It's easy to find people. It's a task to find good people. And it's even more of a challenge to keep good people. Beyond traditional searches, you must always be actively recruiting. Find good people. Get them on the bus. Determine where they sit later.

3. Is there a unique aspect to human resource management in radio, compared with other businesses?

If you ever want to learn about radio, just ask people in radio. That's because we're passionate about radio. As much as it's a task to discuss and debate with passion, I'd rather the team be fired up than flat. Beyond passion, staff typically work odd hours, from morning show announcers arriving at 4 A.M. to promotional teams and brand cheerleaders working late in the evening and into the weekend. As a whole, we're typically operating six to seven days a week at 20 hours a day. With multiple shifts and various posts, there are constant updates re: our team and our products . . . which means managing a moving target.

4. What has been the biggest surprise for you in managing people?

People are wildly unpredictable. Those that you believe will go, stay. Those you expect to stay, go. Each day brings a unique set of circumstances because you're dealing with people and their lives. Their hopes, dreams, ambitions, and fears are all intertwined into their decision making. It's a leader's role to uncover all of those factors and work within them.

5. Is creativity important in your work?

Creative thinking is a skill that's difficult to spot and even more difficult to let loose. Often we're inundated with "policies and procedures" and they're a creativity killer. If we determine the parameters for the way people should react, then little to no thought is required, especially creative thinking. Here's to the companies that hire good people and let them do their jobs . . . with limited restrictions.

6. Would you say that your kind of work is ever-changing, with evolving awareness of workplace harassment, for example?

A healthy and safe environment is a must. Regardless of the industry. To foster that, you need to be aware of the many facets to HR—which are constantly being updated based on internal, external and precedent. Each situation is unique, because each employee's needs are unique.

7. Does working in radio mean that communication is especially important in your job?

Absolutely. There are multiple silos in radio: sales, programming, production, creative, and on-air. And each operates as a distinct entity with its own separate focus. It's imperative that those silos are broken down, that we're communicating fully—openly and honestly—and that we're all working toward the greater good of entertaining our audience and serving our clients.

8. What drew you to radio?

I grew up engaged in radio and music. It seemed like a fun environment that might provide a cool story to tell at a cocktail party. Truth is, there have been multiple job offers along the way, but my heart remains in radio.

For the full interview go online to nelson.com/student

10-1 EMPLOYMENT LEGISLATION

Human resource management (HRM), or the process of finding, developing, and keeping the right people to form a qualified workforce, is one of the most difficult and important of all management tasks. This chapter is organized around the three parts of the human resource management process shown in Exhibit 10.1: attracting, developing, and keeping a qualified workforce.

This chapter will walk you through the steps of the HRM process. HRM starts with the strategy of the corporation, as outlined in Chapter 5. The corporation's vision, mission, and strategy must be understood by the human resources manager so that the HRM plan can emulate, and help accomplish, the organization's strategic objectives. We explore how companies use recruiting and selection techniques to attract and hire qualified employees to fulfill those needs. Then we discuss how training and performance appraisal can develop the knowledge, skills, and abilities of the workforce. The chapter concludes with a review of compensation and employee separation—that is, how companies can keep their best workers through effective compensation practices and how they can manage the separation process when employees leave the organization.

Before we explore how human resource systems work, you need to better understand the complex legal environment in which they exist. So we'll begin the chapter by reviewing the federal and provincial laws that govern human resource management decisions.

Canada's employment laws rest primarily with the provinces and territories. The federal government has laws that quite often mirror those of the provinces, but human rights, employment standards, labour relations, health and safety, employment equity, and other employment-related legislation belongs to the 10 provinces and three territories. Canada's legal system is based on both British and French colonial law. The Constitution Act of 1867 (formerly known as the British North America Act) laid the foundation for our systems today. Part I of the Canadian Labour Code sets out industrial relations (bargaining rights, strikes, union certifications); Part II sets out occupational health and safety guidelines;

Human resource management (HRM) the process of finding, developing, and keeping the right people to form a qualified workforce.

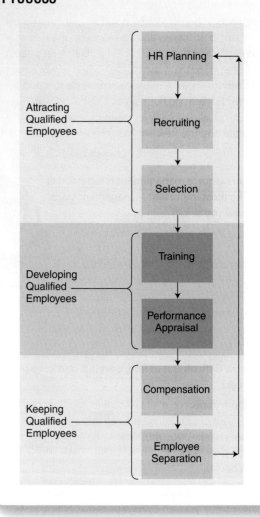

Exhibit 10.1
The Human Resource Management Process

Part III sets out standards for hours, wages, vacations, and holidays.[1]

To streamline the legal system somewhat, the governments in each jurisdiction have created special bodies, such as the British Columbia Human Rights Tribunal, to enforce compliance and to assist in the interpretation of these complex laws. "Regulations" are also drafted, and they become part of the "act" or law in Canada. Regulations also help us interpret the law.

Most provinces have an employment (labour) standards act that sets out items defined in the Canada Labour Code. Such items may be specific to a particular province (e.g., St-Jean-Baptiste Day is a paid holiday in Quebec, whereas Remembrance Day is a paid holiday in Newfoundland and Labrador). Pay equity (equal pay for equal work) is another area addressed by employment

Early Female Fire Fighters Pave Way for Future

Firefighters are brave, well respected, and looked up to in Canada. But, for many of Canada's female firefighters, there can be a dark side: bullying, harassment, and sexual assaults. Not all cases are like that. Cindy Maltman was one of the first three female firefighters hired in Burnaby in 1993. Initially, there were few modifications to the fire halls to accommodate women; over the years, as fire halls were renovated or constructed, washrooms and dorms for women were added. She said there was some tension and apprehension—not everyone thought women could do the job as well as men—but overall she felt welcomed and supported. Captain Michael Hurley, who worked with Maltman during her career, said he believes the vast majority of firefighters accepted the first

women right away. "You're a firefighter, not a woman or a man," he said. "No doubt, as you would find anywhere, there were one or two who didn't approve, but that was soon pushed aside," Hurley said. Maltman believes that she and the other women who were the "first" at their departments have made it easier for the women who came after them to focus on being firefighters. Male firefighters are now used to having women in washrooms and dorms, seeing them get in and out of their gear, and working on calls with them. "We did lay a lot of groundwork for women coming in," she said. "I think what was nice for them was they perhaps got to go through their recruit class without being that first female, without having to do that trail-blazing that we first did."

Sources: L. Mayor, "Female Firefighters Face Bullying, Sexual Harassment, Fifth Estate Finds," *CBC News*, November 6, 2015, http://www.cbc.ca/news/canada/female-firefighters-bullying-sexual-harassment-fifth-estate-1.3305509; J. Saltman, "One of B.C.'s Female Firefighting Pioneers Sees an Easier Path for Rookies," *The Province*, January 26, 2016, http://www.theprovince.com/news/female+firefighting+pioneers+sees+easier+path+rookies/11675142/story.html; Randy Shore, "Vancouver Fire and Rescue Services Has Reinvented Itself for a Post-Fire World," *Vancouver Sun*, January 5, 2016, http://www.vancouversun.com/vancouver+fire+rescue+services+reinvented+itself+post+fire+world/11625248/story.html?__lsa=3fab-c3c6.

standards acts. An employer cannot pay women differently who are performing the same work as men. The difficulty arises when we try to compare work of equal value. Should a nurse (a female-dominated job) be paid the same as a firefighter (a male-dominated job)?

The Canadian Charter of Rights and Freedoms was enacted under the government of Pierre Trudeau in 1982 (Pierre Trudeau is the father of Justin Trudeau, our current prime minister). It is part of Canada's constitution, and it covers several fundamental freedoms that affect the workplace. Section 15a of the Charter prohibits discrimination along most of the lines we are familiar with (race, creed, colour, religion, gender, sexual orientation, etc.); Yet, section 15b of the Charter allows certain hiring practices for the "amelioration" of past injustices.[2] There are some additional areas where there is a **bona fide occupational qualification (BFOQ)**. For example, if Victoria's Secret hires models for its lingerie, it probably won't be taken to task for hiring women, as being female would be seen as a BFOQ for being a women's lingerie model. But what about being female and being a firefighter? Throughout Canada there are ongoing investigations into gender discrimination against female firefighters (note that we don't use the term *fireman* anymore).[3] Testing women and men against an aerobic standard resulted in many of the female firefighters not qualifying for the job they were already doing. British Columbia's Supreme Court determined that an aerobic standard for firefighters was not a BFOQ because it was

not related to an individual's performance on the job; the same court ruled that there had been systemic discrimination on a prohibited ground.[4]

Human rights commissions in each province and territory have been established under and are responsible for enforcing the Canadian Human Rights Act. The Canadian Human Rights Commission provides guidelines and support to the various provincial agencies.[5] The provincial human rights commissions investigate and hold hearings on issues relating to complaints under the various labour acts.

*Let's explore employment legislation by reviewing **10-1a the major federal employment laws that affect human resource practice, 10-1b the concept of employment discrimination,** and **10-1c the laws regarding harassment in the workplace.***

10-1a Federal Employment Laws

Exhibit 10.2 lists some of the major federal and provincial employment laws and their websites, where you can find more detailed information. The general effect

> **Bona fide occupational qualification (BFOQ)** an exception in employment law that permits sex, age, religion, and the like to be used when making employment decisions, but only if they are "reasonably necessary to the normal operation of that particular business."

Exhibit 10.2
Some Major Federal and Provincial Employment Laws

Constitution Act (BNA) of 1867	http://laws.justice.gc.ca/en/const/index.html	Sets out basic federal and provincial responsibilities
Canadian Charter of Rights and Freedoms	http://laws.justice.gc.ca/en/charter	Sets out the 15 basic areas of freedoms in Canada
Canadian Human Rights Act	http://laws.justice.gc.ca/en/H-6/index.html	Act prohibiting discrimination on a number of grounds
Canadian Labour Code	http://laws.justice.gc.ca/eng	Lays out responsibilities of each province and provides national guidelines
Employment Equity and Pay Equity Legislation	http://laws.justice.gc.ca/en/E-5.401/index.html	Requires equal pay for equal work
Workers Compensation Act (Manitoba)	http://web2.gov.mb.ca/laws/statutes/ccsm/w200e.php	Provincial act that lays out safety standards
Ontario Employment Standards Act 2000	http://www.e-laws.gov.on.ca/html/statutes/english/elaws	Ontario's employment requirements, including written notice of termination, termination pay, and mass termination
Quebec Labour Standards Act	http://www.cnt.gouv.qc.ca/fileadmin/pdf/publications/c_0149a.pdf	Quebec's labour standards set out conditions of employment in the province

http://flaglane.com

of these laws, which are still evolving through court decisions, is that employers may not discriminate in employment decisions on the basis of gender, sexual orientation, age, religion, colour, national origin, race, or disability. The intent is to make these factors irrelevant in employment decisions. Stated another way, employment decisions should be based on factors that are "job related," "reasonably necessary," or a "business necessity" for successful job performance. The only time that gender, age, religion, and the like can be used to make employment decisions is when they are considered bona fide occupational qualifications.

Note that these laws apply to the entire HRM process and not just to selection decisions (i.e., hiring and promotion). Thus, these laws also cover all training and development activities, performance appraisals, terminations, and compensation decisions. Employers who use gender, age, race, or religion to make employment-related decisions when those factors are unrelated to an applicant's or employee's ability to perform a job may face charges of discrimination before human rights tribunals, as well as employee lawsuits.

Each province has its own act dealing with workplace safety. Requirements relating to safety equipment, accident investigation, the Workplace Hazardous Materials Information System (WHMIS), and safe work procedures are detailed in these provincial acts, which are administered by boards appointed by the provincial

and territorial governments. These boards set safety and health standards for employers and employees and conduct inspections to determine whether those standards are being met. Employers who do not meet standards may be fined.[6]

10-1b Employment Discrimination

Discrimination generally falls under one of the general headings in the Charter of Rights and Freedoms and typically leads to an investigation by a provincial or territorial human rights commission. Discrimination may be intentional or unintentional, but generally, discrimination based on race, religion, ethnic origin, and so forth is easy to see. Unintentional discrimination is harder to identify. Minimum height and weight requirements, which used to be common for police forces, can screen out females or Canadians of Asian origin, who tend to be smaller. Also, some job evaluation systems may include culturally (non–job-related) biased questions; and some job situations may discriminate against some cultures.

10-1c Workplace Harassment

Workplace harassment is prohibited by several laws, both federal and provincial. Workplace harassment does not have to be sexual in nature, although it commonly is. Harassment can also mean that someone is bullying you about your work or tormenting you simply because you are a man or a woman. Bullying is strictly prohibited under Bill 14 of the Workers Compensation Act of British Columbia (it is also covered in other provinces).[7] Expressing stereotypes about one gender or the other, for example, can be a form of harassment.[8]

In some provinces, these cases are handled by the provincial human rights commission; in other provinces, it is by a human rights tribunal. Most of these cases involve infractions of the Canada Labour Code and are dealt with under the Canadian Human Rights Act. In other cases, individuals—and employers—deal with these issues through the civil courts. *Alpaerts v. Obront* was one case that had limited success in challenging the exclusive remedial jurisdiction of the Canada Labour Code. The plaintiff alleged sexual harassment in her workplace to the point of constructive dismissal (i.e., intolerable circumstances). She sued for wrongful dismissal, alleging in part human rights violations by the employer. The case was allowed to proceed, partly on the basis that the plaintiff had a cause of action separate from the labour code violation. The court was concerned that if a code complaint had been brought at the same time, the result could have been different and a stay might have been merited.[9] None of the provinces—or, for that matter, the Canadian Human Rights Commission—will investigate without the formal filing of a complaint.

Sexual harassment occurs when employment outcomes, such as hiring, promotion, or simply keeping one's job, depend on whether an individual submits to being sexually harassed. Again, note that harassment need not be sexual in nature: "Harassment is when people make comments or actions that are unwelcome, even though they should know that what they say or do is not welcome."[10] A **hostile work environment** occurs when unwelcome and demeaning behaviour creates an intimidating, hostile, and offensive work environment. There may be no economic injury—that is, harassment isn't tied to economic outcomes—however, it can lead to psychological injury from a stressful work environment. Dora Cooke had known her eventual boss Patrice Comeau for most of her life. When Comeau and a partner opened a Sudbury, Ontario, office of HTS Engineering Ltd., they needed an assistant and Cooke was offered the job. The relationship soon soured. Dora Cooke was called an "idiot" and "pathetic." In this case, an Ontario judge ruled that when performance management is not meant to be corrective, but is designed to intimidate or insult an employee, it amounts to bullying.[11] Harassment online (via social medial such as Facebook and Twitter)

is still being sorted out. A controversial acquittal in what's believed to be Canada's first criminal harassment trial involving Twitter (where "Gregory Alan Elliott was cleared on all charges stemming from his dealings with two local women's rights activists, Stephanie Guthrie and Heather Reilly) is being hailed by some as a victory for freedom of speech and condemned by others as a green light for online attacks."[12]

Not all bullies are managers. In one B.C. case, a court sided with an employee when a coworker was consistently rude and hostile, screaming, swearing at, and belittling her, often in front of customers. Because the employer was aware of the abusive behaviour and failed to take appropriate steps to stop it, it amounted to vicarious liability against the employer for harassment.[13]

One province defines harassment as "engaging in a course of vexatious comment or conduct against a worker in a workplace that is known or ought reasonably to be known as unwelcome" (*vexatious* generally is taken as action that is distressing). In Quebec, the first province to prohibit "psychological harassment" at work, the Labour Standards Tribunal listed some examples of bullying: "rude, degrading or offensive remarks, spreading rumours, ridicule, shouting abuse, belittling employees, ignoring them or making fun of their personal choices."[14] Harassment has been endemic in some Canadian organizations, such as the Royal Canadian Mounted Police, and it will take concerted efforts of today's managers as well as future managers (the students reading this textbook) to make Canada a harassment-free place to work.[15]

What should companies do to make sure that harassment laws are not violated?[16] First, they should respond immediately when harassment is reported. A quick response encourages victims of harassment to report problems to management rather than to a lawyer or a human rights tribunal. Furthermore, a quick and fair investigation may serve as a deterrent to future harassment. Next, take the time to write a clear, understandable harassment policy that is strongly worded, gives specific examples of what constitutes workplace harassment, and spells outs sanctions and punishments, and disseminate

Sexual harassment a form of discrimination in which unwelcome sexual advances, requests for sexual favours, or other verbal or physical conduct of a sexual nature occur while performing one's job; another form of sexual harassment is when employment outcomes, such as hiring, promotion, or simply keeping one's job, depend on whether an individual submits to sexual harassment.

Hostile work environment a form of harassment in which unwelcome and demeaning behaviour creates an intimidating and offensive work environment.

dusanpetkovic/iStock/Thinkstock

it throughout the company. This lets potential harassers and victims know what will not be tolerated and how the firm will deal with harassment should it occur.

Next, establish clear reporting procedures that indicate how, where, and to whom incidents of harassment can be reported. The best procedures ensure that a complaint will receive a quick response, that impartial parties will handle the complaint, and that the privacy of the accused and accuser will be protected. Students, who quite often have to deal with harassment, can get help. The students at Simon Fraser University can go to a nonthreatening Human Rights Office representative to get help and guidance. Students at the University of British Columbia can receive help from their Equity Office in dealing with unwanted advances. The British Columbia Institute of Technology has a Harassment and Discrimination Advisory Office to help students and staff deal with these kinds of issues.[17]

Finally, managers should be aware that most provinces and many municipalities have their own employment-related laws and enforcement agencies. So compliance with federal law is often not enough. In fact, organizations can be in full compliance with federal law and at the same time be in violation of provincial or municipal harassment laws. These laws are constantly being updated, through jurisprudence established in court cases as well as through legislative authority established by the provinces.

Human resources planning an umbrella term that encompasses overarching philosophies, policies, and practices that are in line with the organization's strategy.

Recruiting the process of developing a pool of qualified job applicants.

Job analysis a purposeful, systematic process for collecting information on the important work-related aspects of a job in line with the organization's strategic direction.

HR PLANNING

Ewing Marion Kauffman, for whom the Kauffman Foundation (the foundation of entrepreneurship) is named, offered his personal twist to the talent equation with this advice to entrepreneurs: "Hire people who are smarter than you! In doing so, you prevent limiting the organization to the level of your own ability . . . and you grow the capabilities of your company." He went on to say, "If you hire people you consider smarter than you, you are more likely to listen to their thoughts and ideas, and this is the best way to expand on your own capabilities and build the strength of your company."[18]

Human resources planning ensures that the organization has the appropriate human resources to implement its chosen strategy. If the organization has adopted a strategy of customer service, for example, then the HR department must ensure that its policies, processes, and actions will help the organization realize that chosen "customer service" strategy. HR planning ensures that all parts of the HR function embrace the chosen strategy and ensures that the other functional departments (finance, manufacturing, marketing, etc.) have the human resources they need to accomplish their own strategic "customer service" objectives.

*Recruiting is the process of developing a pool of qualified job applicants. Let's examine **10-2a what job analysis is and how it is used in recruiting, 10-2b how companies use internal recruiting,** and **10-2c external recruiting to find qualified job applicants.***

10-2a Job Analysis and Recruiting

Job analysis is a "purposeful, systematic process for collecting information on the important work-related aspects of a job."[19] The information derived from job analysis is absolutely vital to effective HR planning. Typically, a job analysis collects four kinds of information:

1. work activities, such as what workers do and how, when, and why they do it;

2. the tools and equipment used to do the job;

3. the context in which the job is performed, such as the actual working conditions or schedule; and

4. the personnel requirements for performing the job, meaning the knowledge, skills, and abilities needed to do a job well.[20]

Job analysis information can be collected by having job incumbents and/or supervisors complete

Exhibit 10.3
Job Recruitment Notice for a Firefighter for the City of Calgary, Alberta

Looking for a challenging and exciting career? Firefighting may be for you . . . We're looking for physically fit men and women—motivated individuals known for integrity, professionalism, and drive. Join our team of more than 1,200 firefighters dedicated to fire education, prevention, and safety.

Professionalism

A professional firefighting career offers excellent benefits, opportunities and job security. We can offer you the opportunity to be part of a highly-skilled team whose members are admired and valued by the community they serve and protect. Recruits are trained in-house to the highest international standards. We provide numerous professional development opportunities for firefighters to enhance their knowledge and skills in the latest firefighting and rescue techniques. There are multiple support divisions—including aquatic and high-angle rescue teams, fire prevention, arson investigation, community safety, or training—where firefighters can diversify their experience and career.

The Place to Be

Calgary is a young, energetic and diverse city that offers world-class arts, entertainment and recreation opportunities. With a population of more than a million people, it is one of the fastest-growing cities in North America. Calgary provides an unsurpassed quality of life for families. Its close proximity to the Rocky Mountains guarantees year-round adventure.

Pride. Professionalism. Teamwork. Respect. These are our core values. If you share them, review the links on this website and consider joining our team.

Sources: P. Heidenreich, "Former Brit to Become Fire Chief for City of Calgary," Global News, December 12, 2014, http://globalnews.ca/news/1724553/former -brit-to-become-fire-chief-for-city-of-calgary/; City of Calgary, Firefighter Recruitment, 2010, http://content.calgary.ca/CCA/City+Hall/Business+Units/ Calgary+Fire+Department/Firefighter+Recruitment/Firefighter+Recruitment.htm. Courtesy of the City of Calgary, 2010.

Monkey Business Images/Shutterstock.com

questionnaires, by direct observation, by interviews, or by filming employees as they perform their jobs.

Job descriptions and job specifications are two of the most important results of a job analysis. A **job description** is a written description of the basic tasks, duties, and responsibilities required of an employee holding a particular job. **Job specifications**, which are often included in a separate section of a job description, summarize the qualifications needed to successfully perform the job. Exhibit 10.3 shows a job recruitment notice for a firefighter in Calgary, Alberta.

Because a job analysis specifies what a job entails as well as the knowledge, skills, and abilities that are needed to do the job well, companies must complete a job analysis *before* beginning to recruit job applicants. Job analysis, job descriptions, and job specifications comprise the foundation on which all critical human resource activities are built. They are used during recruiting and selection to match applicant qualifications with the requirements of the job. So it is critically important that job descriptions be accurate. Unfortunately, they aren't always so. Turnover is a real problem and a large reason for turnover is because job descriptions are not up to date. "Accurate, complete and up-to-date job descriptions are important to establish selection criteria for hiring, create job ads, set expectations and objectives for employees, assess performance,

Job description a written description of the basic tasks, duties, and responsibilities required of an employee holding a particular job to help the organization realize its strategy.

Job specifications a written summary of the qualifications needed to successfully perform a particular job to enable the organization to reach its organizational objectives.

assign and manage employee workload, and manage organizational changes."[21] If a job description is not up to date, then a lot of what happens can be unintentional. When we "on-board" new personnel, we need to have a written description to help that person through their introduction to the firm. They need to know what to do and what not to do on the job. As jobs change, and they always do, then we add or delete some of the functions that we need people to carry out. "When job descriptions are not kept up-to-date and do not accurately reflect what employees are actually doing, it can make them feel that they are not being appropriately recognized or rewarded for their work."[22]

Job descriptions are also used throughout the staffing process to ensure that selection devices and the decisions based on these devices are job related. The questions asked in an interview should be based on the most important work activities identified by a job analysis. Likewise, during performance appraisals (see Section 10-5), employees should be evaluated in areas that a job analysis has identified as the most important in a job.

Job analyses, job descriptions, and job specifications also help companies meet the legal requirement that their human resource decisions be job-related. To be judged *job-related*, recruitment, selection, training, performance appraisals, and employee separations must be valid and be directly related to the important aspects of the job as identified by a careful job analysis. Job requirements, if they have the potential to discriminate against members of protected groups, must then meet the standards set by the *Meiorin* decision (*BC Public Service Relations Commission vs. BCBSEU*).[23] In *Meiorin*, the Supreme Court of Canada found that an organization's new job requirements were not based on job-related information and that its job analysis was seriously flawed. Canadian human rights commissions and courts recognize the US *Uniform Guidelines for Employee Selection Procedures*. Additionally, the Canadian Society of Industrial Organizational Psychology has adapted those principles in the guidelines for developing equitable selection systems in Canada.[24] In practice, if not in law, the starting point for defensible selection is an appropriate job analysis system.

10-2b Internal Recruiting

Internal recruiting, sometimes called "promotion from within," is the process of developing a pool of qualified job applicants from people who already work in the company. Internal recruiting improves employee commitment, morale, and motivation. It also reduces recruitment startup time and costs, and because employees are already familiar with the company's culture and procedures, they are more likely to succeed in their new jobs. A university study found that external hires generally are more costly, less reliable employees. Specifically, external hires get paid 18–20 percent more than internal hires, are 61 percent more likely to be fired, and are 21 percent more likely to quit their jobs.[25] Job posting and career paths are two methods of internal recruiting.

Job posting involves advertising job openings within the company to existing employees. Typically, a job description and its requirements are posted on a bulletin board, in a company newsletter, or in a computerized job bank that only employees can access.

A *career path* is a planned sequence of jobs through which employees may advance within an organization. For example, a person who starts as a sales representative may move up to sales manager and then to district or regional sales manager. Virginia Rometty, IBM's CEO, started as a systems engineer after studying computer science in college, worked in IBM's consulting division, became general manager for IBM's Global Insurance and Financial Services sector, and then became senior vice president of IBM Global Business Services. Immediately prior to being named CEO, she served as the senior vice president of IBM's Global Sales and Distribution division and was responsible for overseeing sales in 170 global markets.[26] Career paths help employees focus on long-term goals and development; they also help companies retain employees. Career paths are useful in **succession planning**— evaluating the needs that are required in future years in terms of staffing to replace people who retire, or who may leave, and to provide personnel for needed strategic growth requirements. Succession planning is critical as employees in an organization must develop the correct strategic attributes and skills if they are to move ahead in the organization. Any organization would be wise to help its employees become more promotable.[27]

Internal recruiting the process of developing a pool of qualified job applicants from people who already work in the company.

Succession planning deals with evaluating the needs that are required in future years in terms of staffing to replace people who retire, or who may leave, and to provide personnel for needed strategic growth requirements.

10-2c External Recruiting

External recruiting involves developing a pool of qualified job applicants from outside the company. External recruitment methods include placing advertisements (newspapers, magazines, direct mail, radio, or television), generating employee referrals (asking current employees to recommend possible job applicants), encouraging walk-ins (people who apply on their own), approaching outside organizations (universities, technical/trade schools, professional societies), using employment services (provincial, federal, or private employment agencies, temporary help agencies, professional search firms), holding special events (career conferences, job fairs), and developing Internet job sites. Studies have found that for office/clerical and production/service employees, the most commonly used methods are employee referrals, walk-ins, newspaper ads, and provincial employment agencies. For professional/technical employees, the most common tools are newspaper ads and college/university recruitment services.

Realistic job previews ensure that new applicants are provided with sufficient information to arrive at an informed decision. They provide information about pay and hours of work, but they also discuss aspects of the job such as promotion rates, job progression, amount of flexibility, autonomy, stress, interaction with customers, amount of travel, and the corporate culture. Generally, job previews set out the positive and negative aspects of both the job and the organization. One quantitative meta-analysis of realistic job previews found that they led to higher performance, lower attrition, more accurate expectations of the job, and more positive affective reactions to it.[28]

When recruiting managers, organizations tend to rely most heavily on newspaper ads, employee referrals, and search firms.[29] Most students will find themselves relying more and more on web searches, utilizing sites such as Monster, Workopolis, Facebook, LinkedIn, and VancouverJobShop. In the coming decade, networking will become an increasing important tool for new graduates.[30]

Companies have been hiring nontraditional people in nontraditional ways for some time now. Companies need temporary "gurus" and "online talent platforms are increasingly connecting people to the right work opportunities."[31] Talent will migrate from company to company and they will provide top notch services to those companies that can connect with these freelance industry experts. The focal point for many of these nontraditional hires (retired executives, entrepreneurial managers,

international experts) is concentrated at the various online talent platforms available worldwide. "Such platforms include websites, like Monster.com and LinkedIn, that aggregate individual résumés with job postings from traditional employers, as well as the rapidly growing digital marketplaces of the new 'gig economy,' such as Uber and Upwork."[32]

As noted earlier, some companies are now recruiting applicants through Internet job sites such as Monster, VancouverJobShop, and BCJobs. Companies can post job openings for 30 days on one of these sites for about half the cost of running an ad just once in a Sunday newspaper. Besides that, Internet job listings generate nine times as many résumés as one ad in the Sunday newspaper.[33] And because these sites attract so many applicants and offer so many services, companies can find qualified applicants without resorting to recruitment firms, which typically charge 25 percent or more of a new hire's salary.[34]

10-3 SELECTION

After the recruitment process has produced a pool of qualified applicants, a selection process determines which applicants have the best chance of performing well on the job. **Selection** is the process of gathering information about job applicants to decide who should be offered the job. **Validation** is the process of determining how well a selection test or procedure predicts future job performance. The more accurate the prediction of future job performance, the more valid the test.

Let's examine common selection procedures, such as **10-3a application forms and résumés, 10-3b references and background checks, 10-3c selection tests, and 10-3d interviews.**

External recruiting the process of developing a pool of qualified job applicants from outside the company.

Realistic job previews a tool used to explain to potential new employees both the positive and negative aspects of a new job.

Selection the process of gathering information about job applicants to decide who should be offered a job.

Validation the process of determining how well a selection test or procedure predicts future job performance; the better or more accurate the prediction of future job performance, the more valid a test is said to be.

10-3a Application Forms and Résumés

Usually, the first selection devices that job applicants encounter are application forms and résumés. These contain similar information, such as the applicant's name, address, and job and educational history. Although an application form often asks for information already provided by the résumé, most organizations prefer to collect this information in their own format (i.e., the application form) for entry into a **human resource information system (HRIS)**. Applicants invited to Facebook's campus for onsite interviews must solve more difficult coding problems, including a take-home "hack." Facebook engineer Carlos Bueno says, "If it says 'expert in X' (on your résumé), we will try to schedule you with a proven expert in X, so be prepared. If you are not, leave it off your résumé."[35]

Employment laws apply to application forms just as they do to all selection devices. Application forms are allowed to ask applicants only for valid, job-related information. Even so, they often ask applicants for non-job-related information such as marital status, maiden name, age, or date of high school graduation. (See various websites, such as the Alberta Human Rights Commission website, www.albertahumanrights.ab.ca, for information on pre-employment questions).[36] There is quite a bit of information that companies are not permitted to request in application forms, during job interviews, or in any other part of the selection process. Courts will assume that you consider all of the information you request of applicants, even if you don't. So be sure to ask only those questions that directly relate to the candidate's ability and motivation to perform the job.

Résumés also pose problems for companies, but in a different way. Studies have found that as many as one-third of job applicants intentionally falsify some information on their résumés and that 80 percent of the information on résumés may be misleading.[37] Therefore,

managers should verify the information collected via résumés and application forms by comparing it with additional information collected during interviews and other stages of the selection process, such as references and background checks (see below).

10-3b References and Background Checks

Nearly all companies ask the applicant to provide **employment references**, such as previous employers or coworkers, whom they can contact to learn more about the candidate. **Background checks** are used to verify the truthfulness and accuracy of the information that applicants provide about themselves and to uncover negative, job-related background information not provided by applicants. Background checks are conducted by contacting "educational institutions, prior employers, court records, police and governmental agencies, and other informational sources either by telephone, mail, remote computer access, or through in-person investigations."[38]

Unfortunately, previous employers are increasingly reluctant to provide references or background check information. It is unlikely that Canadian employers will be sued for honestly providing unfavourable references. Yet at the same time, employers are quite vulnerable to being sued in cases where they knowingly hold back unfavourable information, especially if an employee is hired and subsequently causes harm to the new employer or its clients.[39] Many previous employers provide only dates of employment, positions held, and date of separation.

A former employer should not impede a former employee's job search. The Supreme Court of Canada ruled that employers have an obligation to act in good faith when an employee is terminated. In *Jack Wallace v. The United Grain Growers*, the plaintiff was awarded 24 months' salary when it was found that United Grain Growers neglected to provide a reference letter for him to secure a new job.[40]

With previous employers generally unwilling to give full and candid references, and with negligent hiring lawsuits awaiting companies that don't get such references and background information, what can companies do? To start with, they can conduct criminal record checks, especially if the job for which the person is applying involves money, drugs, control over valuable goods, or access to the elderly, children with disabilities, or people's homes.[41] According to the Society for Human Resource Management, 96 percent of companies conduct background checks and 80 percent conduct criminal record checks.[42]

Human resource information system (HRIS)
a computerized system for gathering, analyzing, storing, and disseminating information related to the HRM process.

Employment references sources such as previous employers or coworkers who can provide job-related information about job candidates.

Background checks procedures used to verify the truthfulness and accuracy of information that applicants provide about themselves and to uncover negative, job-related background information not provided by applicants.

MGMT TIP

Don't Ask (Topics to Avoid in an Interview)

1. **Gender, gender identity, gender expression, marital status, or family status.** Do not ask the applicant to specify Mr., Mrs., Miss, Ms. or other forms of address that would reveal their gender, gender identity or expression, or marital or family status.

2. **Source of income.** Any inquiry concerning source of income must be job-related. You can request information about former employment. Avoid inquiries about other sources of income that may have a stigma attached to them, such as social assistance, disability pension, or child maintenance, unless you have a job-related reason for asking.

3. **Previous names.** Asking an applicant to provide previous names can cause the applicant to indirectly disclose marital status, gender, place of origin, or ancestry. Any inquiry that requires an applicant to disclose this information would be contrary to the Alberta Human Rights Act, unless there is a business reason for doing so that is acceptable under the act.

4. **Next of kin.** Asking for names of relatives or next of kin before hiring is not recommended. Such information can reveal the gender, marital status, place of origin, or ancestry of the applicant.

5. **Dependants and child care.** Avoid inquiries about an applicant's spouse, number of children or dependants, child care arrangements, or plans to have children. The answers to these questions are usually not related to the job and can reveal gender and marital or family status. Inquiries that focus on willingness to work the required schedule, to work rotating shifts, or to relocate are clearly business-related and are acceptable.

6. **Age and date of birth.** It is not advisable to ask for the applicant's date of birth or age, unless the applicant is under 18. In employment situations where there is a legal minimum age requirement, you can verify that the applicant meets the legal age requirement.

7. **Previous address.** It is not acceptable to request a previous address, unless it is for a business-related purpose that is acceptable under the act.

8. **Citizenship.** Citizenship is not specifically dealt with in the act. However, asking the applicant to reveal citizenship could require a non-Canadian applicant to disclose place of origin, which is protected under the act. Ask questions to solicit information that is related to the specific requirements of the job to be performed. Appropriate questions could include:
Are you legally entitled to work in Canada?
Are you a Canadian citizen or landed immigrant? Yes __ No __
(Do not distinguish between the two.)

9. **Physical or mental disability.** It is not acceptable to ask questions that are not related to the specific job to be performed. With this in mind, it is contrary to the act to ask applicants to provide information about the general state of their physical or mental health, their appearance, or their height or weight.

10. **Sexual orientation.** Avoid inquiries about an applicant's sexual orientation.

11. **Workers' Compensation.** Asking if the applicant has received or is receiving Workers' Compensation indirectly requires an applicant to provide information about a physical injury or disability. This can be contrary to the act.

12. **Language ability.** It is appropriate to ask applicants if they have some proficiency in the languages that are specifically required for the job. The job description and employment advertisement should specify which languages are required. The level of language ability required should match the job requirements.

13. **Educational institutions.** You can request the names and addresses of academic, vocational, technical, and professional institutions attended and the nature and level of education received. Requiring information that reflects either the religious or racial affiliation of schools or other institutions attended is not advisable as it could reveal religious beliefs or race.

14. **Religious beliefs.** Avoid requesting information about applicants' religious beliefs, including which religious holidays and customs they observe, which church they attend, or whether their clothing is prescribed by their religion. It is permissible for an employer to specify the hours of work in a job advertisement. A job advertisement may indicate that the position will require shift, evening, or weekend work, or that it is functional 365 days per year. Courts and tribunals have said that the employer must make all efforts up to the point of undue hardship to accommodate the religious beliefs of an employee. In turn, the employee is expected to cooperate fully with the employer's efforts. Undue hardship may occur if accommodation would create the following conditions for an employer: an intolerable financial cost, serious disruption to a business or workplace, or other serious issues that cannot be overcome.

Source: Adapted from http://www.albertahumanrights.ab.ca/publications/bulletins_sheets_booklets/sheets/hr_and_employment/pre_employment_inquiries.asp with the permission of the Alberta Human Rights Commission.

Dan Tero, iStockphoto

Next, they can ask the applicant to sign a waiver that permits them to check references, run a background check, or contact anyone with knowledge of the applicant's work performance or history. Likewise, they can ask the applicant if there is anything he or she would like the company to know or if the company is likely to hear anything unusual when contacting references.[43] This is often enough to get the applicant to share information that might otherwise have been withheld. The company, once it has finished checking, should keep its findings confidential to minimize the chances of a defamation charge.

Finally, many companies are starting to perform social media background checks. Certainly, applicants should be careful about what they have posted on sites such as Facebook and Twitter. It may well make sense for a job applicant to delete anything that might be embarrassing.[44]

Susan Chiang/iStockphoto

10-3c Selection Tests

Selection tests can tell decision makers who will likely do well in a job and who won't. Applicants take a test that measures something directly or indirectly related to doing well on the job. The selection tests discussed here are specific ability tests, cognitive ability tests, personality tests, and work sample tests. We also look at assessment centres and biographical data.

Specific ability tests measure the extent to which an applicant possesses the particular abilities needed to do a job well. Specific ability tests are also called **aptitude tests** because they measure aptitude for doing a particular task well. If you decide to go on for an MBA after you have completed your undergraduate degree (and after you have worked for a few years), you will most likely be required to take the Graduate Management Admissions Test (GMAT). If you apply to law school in Canada, you will likely need to write the Law School Admissions Test (LSAT). These tests are predictors of how well students will do in those graduate schools. Specific ability tests also exist for mechanical,

clerical, sales, and physical work. For example, clerical workers have to be good at accurately reading and scanning numbers. About one-third of Canadian companies currently use formal assessments during recruitment. David Towler, president of Creative Organizational Design in Kitchener, Ontario, says that he is "gob-smacked that some companies do no testing at all. It costs only $20–$150 to make sure you have not hired someone else's reject." It can cost thousands of dollars to replace a bad hire.[45]

Cognitive ability tests measure applicants' verbal comprehension, numerical aptitude, general reasoning, and spatial aptitude. In other words, they indicate how quickly and how well people understand words, numbers, logic, and spatial dimensions. Specific ability tests predict job performance in only particular types of jobs, whereas cognitive ability tests accurately predict job performance in almost all kinds of jobs.[46] This is because people with strong cognitive or mental abilities are usually good at learning new things, processing complex information, solving problems, and making decisions—abilities that are important in almost all jobs.[47] In fact, cognitive ability tests are almost always the best predictors of job performance. If you were allowed to use just one selection test, a cognitive ability test would be the one to use.[48] (In practice, though, companies use a battery of tests because doing so leads to much more accurate selection decisions.)

Biographical data (biodata) are extensive surveys that ask applicants questions about their personal background and life experiences. The basic idea behind biodata is that past behaviour is the best predictor of future behaviour. Most biodata questionnaires have over 100 items that gather information about habits and

Specific ability tests (aptitude tests) tests that measure the extent to which an applicant possesses the particular kind of ability needed to do a job well.

Cognitive ability tests tests that measure the extent to which applicants have abilities in perceptual speed, verbal comprehension, numerical aptitude, general reasoning, and spatial aptitude.

Biographical data (biodata) extensive surveys that ask applicants questions about their personal backgrounds and life experiences.

attitudes, health, interpersonal relations, money, family life (parents, siblings, childhood years, teen years), personal habits, current home (spouse, children), hobbies, education and training, values, preferences, and work.[49] Biodata can be a very good predictor of future job performance, especially in an entry-level job.

You may have noticed that some of the information requested in biodata surveys is related to topics that employers should avoid in applications, interviews, or other parts of the selection process. This information can be requested in biodata questionnaires provided that the company can demonstrate that the information is job-related (i.e., valid) and does not have an adverse impact on protected groups of job applicants. Biodata surveys should be reviewed by HR professionals for legality, validated and tested for adverse impact, and thoroughly vetted by knowledgeable professionals before they are used to make selection decisions.[50] For example, studies have found that married Canadian military recruits have a much higher attrition rate than single recruits, yet it is illegal in Canada to discriminate against anyone on the basis of marital status.[51]

Work sample tests, also called *performance tests,* require applicants to perform tasks that are actually done on the job. Unlike specific ability, cognitive ability, biographical data, and personality tests, which are indirect predictors of job performance, work sample tests directly measure job applicants' capabilities for the job. So, for example, one computer-based work sample test in the real estate industry has applicants assume the role of a real estate agent who must decide how to interact with virtual clients in a game-like scenario. And, as in real life, the clients are variously frustrating, confused, demanding, or indecisive. In one situation, the wife loves the house but the husband hates it. The applicants, just like actual real estate agents, must demonstrate what they will do in these realistic situations.[52] This work sample simulation provides real estate companies with

direct evidence of whether applicants will be able to do the job if they are hired. Work sample tests are generally very good at predicting future job performance; however, they can be expensive to administer and can be used for only one kind of job.[53] For example, an auto dealership could not use a work sample test for mechanics as a selection test for sales representatives.

Assessment centres use a series of job-specific simulations, which are then graded by multiple trained observers to determine applicants' ability to perform managerial work. Unlike the previously described selection tests, which are commonly used for specific jobs or entry-level jobs, assessment centres are most often used to select applicants who have high potential to be good managers. Assessment centres often last two to five days and require participants to complete a number of tests and exercises that simulate managerial work.

Some of the more common assessment centre exercises are in-basket exercises, role plays, small-group presentations, and leaderless group discussions. An *in-basket exercise* is usually a computer-simulated test in which the applicant is given a manager's in-basket containing emails, memos, phone messages, VoIP messages, organizational policies, and other communications normally received by and available to managers. Applicants have a limited time to read through the in-basket, prioritize the items, and decide how to deal with each item. Experienced managers then score the applicants' decisions and recommendations. Exhibit 10.4 describes an in-basket exercise used by an assessment centre in British Columbia.

In a *leaderless group discussion*, another common assessment centre exercise, a group of six applicants is given approximately two hours to solve a problem, but no one is put in charge (hence "leaderless"). Trained observers watch and score each participant on the extent to which he or she facilitates discussion, listens, leads, persuades, and works well with others.

Tests are not perfect predictors of job performance. Some people who do well on selection tests will do poorly in their jobs. Likewise, some people who do poorly on selection tests (and therefore weren't hired) would have been very good performers. Nonetheless, valid tests minimize these selection errors (hiring people who should not have been hired and not hiring

Coprid/Shutterstock.com

Work sample tests tests that require applicants to perform tasks that are actually done on the job.

Assessment centres a series of managerial simulations, graded by trained observers, that are used to determine applicants' capability for managerial work.

people who should have been hired) while maximizing correct selection decisions. In short, tests make it more likely that you'll hire the right person for the job. While tests aren't perfect, almost nothing predicts future job performance as well as the selection tests discussed here.[54] Again, before using them, make sure they are legal in your jurisdiction.[55]

10-3d Interviews

In **interviews**, company representatives ask applicants job-related questions to determine whether they are qualified for the job. Interviews are probably the most frequently used and heavily relied upon tools for selecting among job candidates. There are several

Interviews a selection tool in which company representatives ask job applicants job-related questions to determine whether they are qualified for the job.

Unstructured interviews interviews in which interviewers are free to ask the applicants anything they want.

Structured interviews interviews in which all applicants are asked the same set of standardized questions, usually including situational, behavioural, background, and job knowledge questions.

basic kinds of interviews: unstructured, structured, and semistructured.

In **unstructured interviews**, interviewers are free to ask applicants anything they want, and studies show that they do. Because interviewers often disagree about which questions should be asked during interviews, different interviewers tend to ask applicants very different questions.[56] Furthermore, individual interviewers seem to have a tough time asking the same questions from one interview to the next. This high level of inconsistency reduces the validity of unstructured interviews as a selection device because comparing applicant responses can be difficult. As a result, unstructured interviews are about half as accurate as structured interviews at predicting which job applicants should be hired.

By contrast, with **structured interviews**, standardized interview questions are prepared ahead of time so that all applicants are asked the same job-related questions.[57] Structuring interviews ensures that interviewers ask only for important, job-related information. This approach improves the accuracy, usefulness, and validity of the interview; in addition, it is less likely that interviewers will ask questions that violate employment laws (see the "Don't Ask" box for a list of these topics).

The primary advantage of structured interviews is that comparing applicants is much easier because they are all asked the same questions. Structured interviews typically contain four types of questions: situational, behavioural, background, and job knowledge. Situational questions ask applicants how they would respond in a hypothetical situation (e.g., "What would you do if . . ."). These questions are more appropriate for hiring new graduates, who are unlikely to have encountered real work situations because of their limited experience. Behavioural questions ask applicants what they did in previous jobs that may be similar to what is required for the job for which they are applying (e.g., "In your previous jobs, tell me about . . ."). These questions are more appropriate for hiring experienced individuals. Background questions ask applicants about their work experience, education, and other qualifications (e.g., "Tell me about the training you received at . . ."). Finally, job knowledge questions ask applicants to demonstrate their job knowledge (e.g., for nurses, "Give me an example of a time when one of your patients had a severe reaction to a medication. How did you handle it?").[58]

Semistructured interviews are in between structured and unstructured interviews. A large part of the semistructured interview (perhaps as much as 80 percent) is based on structured questions, but some time is set aside

Exhibit 10.5
Guidelines for Conducting Effective Structured Interviews

Interview Stage	What to Do

Planning the Interview

- Identify and define the knowledge, skills, abilities, and other (KSAO) characteristics needed for successful job performance.
- For each essential KSAO, develop key behavioural questions that will elicit examples of past accomplishments, activities, and performance.
- For each KSAO, develop a list of things to look for in the applicant's responses to key questions.

Conducting the Interview

- Create a relaxed, nonstressful interview atmosphere.
- Review the applicant's application form, résumé, and other information.
- Allocate enough time to complete the interview without interruption.
- Put the applicant at ease; don't jump right into heavy questioning.
- Tell the applicant what to expect. Explain the interview process.
- Obtain job-related information from the applicant by asking those questions prepared for each KSAO.
- Describe the job and the organization to the applicant. Applicants need adequate information to make a selection decision about the organization.

After the Interview

- Immediately after the interview, review your notes and make sure they are complete.
- Evaluate the applicant on each essential KSAO.
- Determine each applicant's probability of success and make a hiring decision.

Sources: B. M. Farrell, "The Art and Science of Employment Interviews," *Personnel Journal 65* (1986): 91–94; V. Catano, et al. *Recruitment and Selection in Canada.* Toronto: Nelson Education, (2013), p. 431.

for unstructured interviewing to allow the interviewer to probe into ambiguous or missing information uncovered during the structured portion of the interview.

Contrary to what you've probably heard, recent evidence indicates that even unstructured interviews do a fairly good job.[59] When conducted properly, however, structured interviews can lead to much more accurate hiring decisions than unstructured ones. The validity of structured interviews can sometimes rival that of cognitive ability tests. But even more important, because interviews are especially good at assessing applicants' interpersonal skills, they work particularly well with cognitive ability tests. The combination (i.e., smart people who work well in conjunction with others) leads to even better selection decisions than using either alone.[60] Exhibit 10.5 provides guidelines for conducting effective structured employment interviews.

10-4 TRAINING

According to the Canadian Society for Training and Development, a typical investment in employee training increases productivity by an average of 17 percent, reduces employee turnover, and makes companies more profitable.[61] Giving employees the knowledge and skills they need to improve their performance is just the first step in developing employees, however. The second step—and not enough companies do this—is giving employees formal feedback about their actual job performance.

Training means providing opportunities for employees to develop the job-specific skills, experience, and knowledge they need to do their jobs or improve their performance. Canadian companies spend more than $7 billion a year on training.[62]

*To make sure those training dollars are well spent, companies need to **10-4a determine specific training needs**, **10-4b select appropriate training methods**, and **10-4c evaluate training**.*

10-4a Determining Training Needs

Needs assessment is the process of identifying and prioritizing the learning needs of employees. Needs assessments can be conducted by identifying performance deficiencies, listening to customer complaints, surveying employees and managers, or formally testing employees' skills and knowledge.

Training developing the skills, experience, and knowledge employees need to perform their jobs or improve their performance.

Needs assessment the process of identifying and prioritizing the learning needs of employees.

Note that training should never be conducted without first performing a needs assessment. Sometimes training isn't needed at all or isn't needed for all employees. Unfortunately, many organizations simply require all employees to attend training whether they need it or not. As a result, employees who aren't interested or who don't need the training may react negatively during or after training. Likewise, employees who should be sent for training but aren't may also react negatively. Consequently, a needs assessment is an important tool for deciding who should or should not attend training.

Employment law restricts employers from discriminating on the basis of age, gender, race, colour, religion, national origin, or disability when selecting training participants. Just as with hiring decisions, the selection of training participants should be based on job-related information.

Finally, if the company's technology infrastructure can support it, elearning can be much faster than traditional training methods.

10-4b Selecting Training Methods

Assume that you're a training director for a major oil company and that you're in charge of making sure all employees know how to respond effectively in case of an oil spill off the Newfoundland and Labrador coast. Keep in mind the lessons learned from the BP oil spill in the Gulf of Mexico.[63] There are a number of training methods that

The Cost of Not Training

An energy firm in Calgary was fined $250 000 over an Alberta oil pipeline breach that spilled 537,000 litres of oil emulsion in northern Alberta over a 48-day period. The Alberta energy regulator says the mixture of oil and oil well salt water leaked between December 1, 2013, and January 18, 2014, before the company became aware of the spill. Rob Borth, the regulator's director of enforcement, says in a report that the company "lacked knowledge, training and management oversight of the pipeline". He says the company had training shortcomings that would enable workers to be able to detect leaks.

British oil company BP has so far agreed to pay a total of $69 billion, up to 2016, for costs associated with the *Deepwater Horizon*, which, after a fire and explosion that killed 11 workers, spilled millions of gallons of crude into the Gulf of Mexico.

goce/iStock/Thinkstock

Sources: J. Cotter, "Pengrowth Energy Fined $250K Over Alberta Oil Pipeline Breach." The Canadian Press, January 15, 2016. Used with permission. Found at http://www.cbc.ca/news/canada/calgary/pengrowth-fined-pipeline-leak-1.3405176; "Low Oil Prices Eat Into BP's Investment Plans and Cut Potential for Profit," CBC News, July 28, 2015. Used with permission. Found at http://www.cbc.ca/news/business/bp-reports-5-8b-loss-after-setting-cash-aside-for-gulf-oil-spill-1.3170988.

Exhibit 10.6
Training Objectives and Methods

Training Objective	Training Methods
Impart Information and Knowledge	▸ *Films and videos.* Films and videos present information, illustrate problems and solutions, and effectively hold trainees' attention.
	▸ *Lectures.* Trainees listen to instructors' oral presentations.
	▸ *Planned readings.* Trainees read about concepts or ideas before attending training.
Develop Analytical and Problem-Solving Skills	▸ *Case studies.* Cases are analyzed and discussed in small groups. The cases present a specific problem or decision, and trainees develop methods for solving the problem or making the decision.
	▸ *Coaching and mentoring.* Coaching and mentoring of trainees by managers involves informal advice, suggestions, and guidance. This method is helpful for reinforcing other kinds of training and for trainees who benefit from support and personal encouragement.
	▸ *Group discussions.* Small groups of trainees actively discuss specific topics. The instructor may perform the role of discussion leader.
Practice, Learn, or Change Job Behaviours	▸ *On-the-job training.* New employees are assigned to experienced employees. The trainee learns by watching the experienced employee perform the job and eventually by working alongside the experienced employee. Gradually, the trainee is left on his or her own to perform the job.
	▸ *Role-playing.* Trainees assume job-related roles and practice new behaviours by acting out what they would do in job-related situations.
	▸ *Simulations and games.* Experiential exercises place trainees in realistic job-related situations and give them the opportunity to experience a job-related condition in a relatively low-cost setting. The trainee benefits from hands-on experience before actually performing the job, where mistakes may be more costly.
	▸ *Vestibule training.* Procedures and equipment similar to those used in the actual job are set up in a special area called a "vestibule." The trainee is then taught how to perform the job at his or her own pace without disrupting the actual flow of work, making costly mistakes, or exposing the trainee and others to dangerous conditions.
Impart Information and Knowledge; Develop Analytical and Problem-Solving Skills; and Practice, Learn, or Change Job Behaviours	▸ *Computer-based learning.* Interactive videos, software, CD-ROMs, personal computers, teleconferencing, and the Internet may be combined to present multimedia-based training.

Source: A. Fowler, "How to Decide on Training Methods," *People Management* 25, no. 1 (1995): 36.

can be used: films and videos, lectures, planned readings, case studies, coaching and mentoring, group discussions, on-the-job training, role playing, simulations and games, vestibule training, and computer-based learning. These are listed in Exhibit 10.6. Which method would be best?

When choosing the best method, consider various factors such as the number of people to be trained, the cost of training, and the objectives of the training. For instance, if the training objective is to impart information or knowledge to trainees, then you should use films and videos, lectures, and planned readings. In our example,

trainees might read a manual or attend a lecture about how to seal a shoreline to keep it from being affected by the spill.

If the objective is to develop analytical and problem-solving skills, then use case studies, coaching and mentoring, and group discussions. In our example, trainees might view a video documenting how a team handled exposure to hazardous substances, talk with first responders, and discuss what they would do in a similar situation.

If practising, learning, or changing job behaviours is the objective, then use on-the-job training, role playing,

CHAPTER 10: Managing Human Resource Systems 213

simulations and games, and vestibule training. In our example, trainees might participate in a mock shoreline (or forest) cleanup to learn what to do in the event of an oil spill. This simulation could take place in a forest or on an actual shoreline or on a video-game-like virtual shoreline.

If training is supposed to meet more than one of these objectives, then your best choice may be to combine one of the previous methods with computer-based training.

These days, many companies are adopting Internet training, or "elearning." Elearning can offer several advantages. Because employees don't need to leave their jobs, travel costs are greatly reduced. Also, because employees can take the training modules when it is convenient (in other words, they don't have to fall behind at their jobs to attend week-long training courses), workplace productivity should increase and employee stress should decrease.

There are, however, several disadvantages to elearning. First, despite its increasing popularity, it's not always the appropriate training method. Elearning can be a good way to impart information, but it isn't always as effective for changing job behaviours or for developing problem-solving and analytical skills. Second, elearning requires a significant investment in computers and high-speed Internet and network connections for all employees. Finally, although elearning can be faster, many employees find it so boring and unengaging that they may choose to do their jobs rather than complete elearning courses when sitting alone at their desks. Elearning may become more interesting, however, as more companies incorporate game-like features such as avatars and competition into their elearning courses.

10-4c Evaluating Training

After selecting a training method and conducting the training, the last step is to evaluate the training. Training can be evaluated in four ways: on *reactions* (how satisfied trainees were with the program), on *learning* (how much employees improved their knowledge or skills), on *behaviour* (how much employees actually changed their on-the-job behaviour because of training), or on *results* (how much training improved job performance—for example, how much it increased sales or quality, or decreased costs).[64] In general, if done well, training provides meaningful benefits for most companies. A study by the Canadian Society for Training and Development found that even a

small training budget can produce a 15 percent increase in sales, or a 22 percent reduction in rejected parts.[65]

10-5 PERFORMANCE APPRAISAL

Performance appraisal is the process of assessing how well employees are doing their jobs. Most employees and managers intensely dislike performance appraisals. One manager says: "I hate annual performance reviews. I hated them when I used to get them, and I hate them now that I give them. If I had to choose between performance reviews and paper cuts, I'd take paper cuts every time. I'd even take razor burns and the sound of fingernails on a blackboard."[66] Unfortunately, attitudes like this are all too common. In fact, 70 percent of employees are dissatisfied with the performance appraisal process at their company. And according to the Society for Human Resource Management, 90 percent of human resource managers are dissatisfied with their company's performance appraisal system.[67]

*Let's explore how companies can avoid some of these problems with performance appraisals by **10-5a accurately measuring job performance** and **10-5b effectively sharing performance feedback with employees.***

10-5a Accurately Measuring Job Performance

Workers often have strong doubts about the accuracy of their performance appraisals—and they may be right. For example, it's widely known that assessors are prone to errors when rating worker performance. One of the reasons managers make these errors is that they often don't spend enough time gathering or reviewing performance data. To minimize rating errors and improve the accuracy

E-learning
Online education
electronically suppor
Web-based learning
virtual classroom or
digital collaboration

Ivelin Radkov/Shutterstock.com

Performance appraisal the process of assessing how well employees are doing their jobs.

of job performance measures, two general approaches have been taken: improving performance appraisal measures themselves, and training performance raters to be more accurate.

One way for companies to improve performance appraisals is to use as many objective performance measures as possible. **Objective performance measures** are measures of performance that are easily counted or quantified. Common objective performance measures include output, scrap, waste, sales, customer complaints, and rejection rates.

But when objective measures aren't available—and frequently they aren't—subjective measures have to be used instead. Subjective performance measures require that someone judge or assess a worker's performance. The most common kind of subjective performance measure is the graphic rating scale (GRS); see Exhibit 10.7. Graphic rating scales are most widely used because they are easy to construct, but they are very susceptible to rating errors.

A popular alternative to graphic rating scales is the **behavioural observation scale (BOS)**. A BOS requires raters to rate the frequency with which workers perform specific behaviours representative of the job dimensions that are critical to successful job performance. Exhibit 10.7 shows a BOS for two important job dimensions for a retail salesperson: customer service, and money handling. Notice that each dimension lists several specific behaviours characteristic of a worker who excels in that dimension of job performance. (Normally, the scale would list seven to 12 items per dimension, not three as in the exhibit.) Notice also that the behaviours are good behaviours, meaning they indicate good performance, and that the rater is being asked to judge how frequently an employee engaged in those good

Exhibit 10.7
Subjective Performance Appraisal Scales

Graphic Rating Scale

	Very Poor	Poor	Average	Good	Very Good
Example 1: Quality of work performed is	1	2	3	4	5

	Very Poor (20% errors)	Poor (15% errors)	Average (10% errors)	Good (5% errors)	Very Good (less than 5% errors)
Example 2: Quality of work performed is	1	2	3	4	5

Behavioural Observation Scale

Dimension: Customer Service

	Almost Never				Almost Always
1. Greets customers with a smile and a "hello."	1	2	3	4	5
2. Calls other stores to help customers find merchandise that is not in stock.	1	2	3	4	5
3. Promptly handles customer concerns and complaints.	1	2	3	4	5

Dimension: Money Handling

	Almost Never				Almost Always
1. Accurately makes change from customer transactions.	1	2	3	4	5
2. Accounts balance at the end of the day, no shortages or surpluses.	1	2	3	4	5
3. Accurately records transactions in computer system.	1	2	3	4	5

Objective performance measures measures of job performance that are easily and directly counted or quantified.

Behavioural observation scale (BOS) a rating scale that indicates the frequency with which workers perform specific behaviours that are representative of the job dimensions critical to successful job performance.

Common Rating Errors

- *Central tendency error* occurs when assessors rate all workers as average or in the middle of the scale.

- *Halo error* occurs when assessors rate a particular worker as performing at the same level (good, bad, or average) in all parts of his or her job.

- *Leniency error* occurs when assessors rate all workers as performing particularly well.

wavebreakmedia/Shutterstock

behaviours. The logic behind the BOS is that better performers engage in good behaviours more often.

BOSs work well for rating critical dimensions of performance. Also, studies have found that managers strongly prefer BOSs when giving performance feedback; when differentiating between poor, average, and good workers; when identifying training needs; and when measuring performance. In response to the statement, "If I were defending a company, this rating format would be an asset to my case," lawyers strongly preferred BOSs over other kinds of subjective performance appraisal scales.[68]

Rater training training performance appraisal raters in how to avoid rating errors and increase rating accuracy.

360-degree feedback a performance appraisal process in which feedback is obtained from the boss, subordinates, peers and coworkers, and the employees themselves.

The second approach to improving the measurement of workers' job performance is **rater training**. Most effective in this regard is frame-of-reference training, in which a group of trainees learn how to conduct performance appraisals by watching a video of an employee at work. Next, they evaluate the performance of the person in the video. A trainer (i.e., subject matter expert) then shares his or her evaluations, and trainees' evaluations are compared with the expert's. The expert then explains his or her evaluations. This process is repeated until the differences in evaluations by trainees and evaluations by the expert are minimized. The logic behind frame-of-reference training is that by adopting the frame of reference used by an expert, trainees will be able to accurately observe, judge, and use the scale to evaluate performance of others.[69]

10-5b Sharing Performance Feedback With Employees

After gathering accurate performance data, the next step is to share performance feedback with employees. Unfortunately, even when performance appraisal ratings are accurate, the appraisal process often breaks down at the feedback stage. Employees become defensive and dislike hearing any negative assessments of their work, no matter how small. Managers become defensive, too, and dislike giving appraisal feedback as much as employees dislike receiving it.

What can be done to overcome the inherent difficulties in performance appraisal feedback sessions? Since performance appraisal ratings have traditionally been the judgments of just one person, the boss, one possibility is to use **360-degree feedback**. In this approach, feedback comes from four sources: the boss, subordinates, peers and coworkers, and the employees themselves. The data, which are obtained anonymously (except for the feedback from the boss), are compiled into a feedback report that compares the employee's self-ratings with those of the boss, subordinates, peers, and coworkers. Usually, a consultant or human resource specialist discusses the results with the employee. The advantage of 360-degree programs is that

Neustockimages/iStockphoto

feedback such as "You don't listen" is often more credible when it comes from several people.

Herbert Meyer, who has been studying performance appraisal feedback for more than 30 years, recommends a list of topics for discussion in performance appraisal feedback sessions (see Exhibit 10.8).[70]

How these topics are discussed in a review session is important for its success. Managers can do three things to make performance reviews as comfortable and productive as possible. First, they can separate developmental feedback, which is designed to improve future performance, from administrative feedback, which is used as a reward for past performance (e.g., raises). When managers give developmental feedback, they're acting as coaches, but when they give administrative feedback, they're acting as judges. These two roles, coaching and judging, are clearly incompatible. As coaches, managers are encouraging, pointing out opportunities for growth and improvement, and employees are typically open and receptive to feedback. But as judges, managers are evaluative, and employees are typically defensive and closed to feedback.

Second, Meyer suggests that performance appraisal feedback sessions be based on self-appraisals, in which employees carefully assess their own strengths, weaknesses, successes, and failures in writing. Because employees play an active role in the review of their performance, managers can be coaches rather than judges. Also, because the focus is on goals and development, both employees and managers are likely to be more satisfied with the process and more committed to plans and changes. And because the focus is on development and not administrative assessment, self-appraisals lead to more candid self-assessments than traditional supervisory reviews.[71] See Exhibit 10.8 for a list of topics that Meyer recommends for discussion in performance appraisal feedback sessions.

Finally, what people do with the performance feedback they receive really matters. A study of 1,361 senior managers found that managers who reviewed their 360-degree feedback with an executive coach (hired by the company) were more likely to set specific goals for improvement, ask their bosses for ways to improve, and subsequently improve their performance.[72]

Managers need to receive feedback as well as give it. HCL Technologies, an outsourcer of technology services, has team members rate their bosses, and the evaluations are made public on the company's intranet to hold top managers accountable. This was the *boss's* idea.[73] A five-year study of 252 managers found that their performance improved dramatically if they met with their subordinates to discuss their 360-degree feedback ("You don't listen") and how they were going to address it ("I'll restate what others have said before stating my opinion"). Performance was dramatically lower for managers who never discussed their 360-degree feedback with subordinates and for managers who did not routinely do so (some managers did not review their 360-degree feedback with subordinates

Exhibit 10.8
What to Discuss in a Performance Appraisal Feedback Session

✔ Overall progress—an analysis of accomplishments and shortcomings. There should be no surprises coming into the interview.

✔ Problems encountered in meeting job requirements. The discussion should also include any goals from the employee on the 360 feedback system.

✔ Opportunities to improve performance. Give employees praise and comments on their strong points. Telling them what they did wrong can be useful, but they won't necessarily know what to do right. Telling them what they did right helps them remember these behaviours.

✔ Long-range plans and opportunities— for the job and for the individual's career. This should be part of HR planning, HR training, and HR succession planning.

✔ General discussion of possible plans and goals for the coming year, again including the employee's 360 goals.

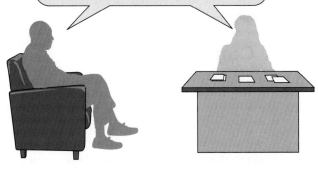

Sources: M. Cuticelli, M. Collier-Meek, and M. Coyne, "Increasing the Quality of Tier 1 Reading Instruction: Using Performance Feedback to Increase Opportunities to Respond During Implementation of a Core Reading Program," *Psychology in the Schools (53)*1 (2016): 89–105; I. M. Jawahar, "Correlates of Satisfaction With Performance Appraisal Feedback," *Journal of Labor Research* 27, no. 2 (2006): 213–236; H. H. Meyer, "A Solution to the Performance Appraisal Feedback Enigma," *Academy of Management Executive* 5, no. 1 (1991): 68–76; and S. C. Payne, M. T. Horner, W. R. Boswell, A. N. Schroeder, and K. J. Stine-Cheyne, "Comparison of Online and Traditional Performance Appraisal Systems," *Journal of Managerial Psychology* 24, no. 6 (2009): 526–544.

Performance Feedback

Next time you have to talk with someone about their performance, follow these four steps:

1. Be specific. Feedback needs to be actionable. Use concrete examples to back up your conclusions. Avoid generalized character attacks. Instead, describe the behaviour.
2. State the impact. Tell the person how his behaviour is affecting you, the team, or the organization.
3. Prescribe. Be specific about what needs to change. Often employees won't know what to change unless you tell them.
4. Do it often. Get in the habit of praising good performance and identifying troublesome behaviour.

Coaching, supporting, recognizing, and managing performance is a tough part of management, but it is an extremely important one. Organizations can only reach their strategic objectives if their personnel are coached and supported in their journey toward accomplishing their various strategic goals that add up to the organization's objectives.

Sources: Adapted from *Guide to Giving Effective Feedback*, http://hbr.org/product/guide-to-giving-effective-feedback/an/10667-PDF-ENG; C. M. Phoel, S. Grady, A. Gallo, C. Bielaszka-DuVernay, J.-F. Manzoni, T. Butler, J. L. Barsoux, T. Erickson, and P. Krattenmaker, "Guide to Giving Effective Feedback," *Harvard Business Review* (2011).

each year of the study). Why is discussing 360-degree feedback with subordinates so effective? These discussions help managers better understand their weaknesses, force them to develop a plan to improve, and demonstrate to the subordinates the managers' public commitment to improving.[74] In short, it helps to have people discuss their performance feedback with others, but it particularly helps to have them discuss their feedback with the people who provided it.

10-6 COMPENSATION AND EMPLOYEE SEPARATION

Compensation includes both the financial and the nonfinancial rewards that organizations provide to employees in exchange for their work. **Employee separation** is a broad term covering the loss of an employee for any reason. *Involuntary separation* occurs when employers decide to terminate or lay off employees. *Voluntary separation* occurs when employees decide to quit or retire. Because employee separations affect recruiting, selection, training, and compensation, organizations should forecast the number of employees they expect to lose through terminations, layoffs, turnover, or retirements when doing human resource planning. The tax rate in Canada may be a surprise to many internationally recruited workers, as may be the overtime that many employees are required to contribute to the organization.

*Let's learn more about compensation and employee separation by examining the **10-6a compensation decisions** that managers must make as well as **10-6b terminating employees, 10-6c downsizing, 10-6d retirement,** and **10-6e employee turnover.***

10-6a Compensation Decisions

There are three basic kinds of compensation decisions: pay level, pay variability, and pay structure.[75]

Pay-level decisions are decisions about whether to pay workers at a level that is below, above, or at current market wages. Companies use job evaluation to set their pay structures. **Job evaluation** determines the worth of each job by establishing the market value of the knowledge, skills, and requirements needed to perform it. After conducting a job evaluation, most companies try to pay the going rate, meaning the current market wage. There are always companies, however, whose financial

Compensation the financial and nonfinancial rewards that organizations give employees in exchange for their work.

Employee separation the voluntary or involuntary loss of an employee.

Job evaluation a process that determines the worth of each job in a company by establishing the market value of the knowledge, skills, and requirements needed to perform it.

situation causes them to pay considerably less than the current market wage.

Some companies choose to pay above-average wages to attract and keep employees. *Above-market wages* can attract a larger, more qualified pool of job applicants, increase the rate of job acceptance, decrease the time it takes to fill positions, and increase the time that employees stay.[76]

Foreign workers in many parts of the world end up in low-paying jobs that disappear at the whim of the employer, with little in the way of security or benefits. Canada has a Seasonal Agricultural Workers Program that is considered by many to be a model of well managed temporary immigration, and in the European Union, a third-country national (someone from outside the EU) who has held a legal temporary position for five years is entitled to permanent residency.[77]

Pay variability decisions concern the extent to which employees' pay varies with individual and organizational performance. Linking pay to performance is intended to increase employee motivation, effort, and job performance. Piecework, sales commissions, profit sharing, employee stock ownership plans, and stock options are common pay variability options. For instance, under **piecework** pay plans, employees are paid a set rate for each item produced up to some standard (e.g., 35 cents per item produced for output up to 100 units per day). Once productivity exceeds the standard, employees are paid a set amount for each unit of output over the standard (e.g., 45 cents for each unit above 100 units). Under a sales **commission** plan, salespeople are paid a percentage of the purchase price of items they sell. The more they sell, the more they earn.

Because pay plans such as piecework and commissions are based on individual performance, they can reduce the incentive that people have to work together. Therefore, companies also use group incentives (discussed in Chapter 9) and organizational incentives such as profit sharing, employee stock ownership plans, and stock options to encourage teamwork and cooperation.

With **profit sharing**, employees receive a portion of the organization's profits over and above their regular compensation. The more profitable the company, the more profit is shared. Employees at Proform Concrete Services Inc. of Red Deer, Alberta, share profits with the company. Proform awards 15 percent of the company's profits to its employees. The program is designed specifically to reward employees' loyalty and commitment.[78]

An **employee stock ownership plan (ESOP)** compensates employees by awarding them shares of the company in addition to their regular compensation. By contrast, **stock options** give employees the right

Top Photo Corporation/Thinkstock

to purchase shares at a set price. Proponents of stock options argue that this gives employees and managers a strong incentive to work hard to make the company successful. If they do, the company's profits increase, as does its share price, and stock options increase in value. If they don't, profits stagnate or turn into losses, and stock options decrease in value or become worthless.

The incentive has to be more than just a piece of paper, however. A study carried out by the Toronto Stock Exchange found that ESOP companies' five-year profit growth was 123 percent higher, their net profit margins were 95 percent higher, and their productivity measured by revenue per employee was 24 percent higher than for non-ESOP companies, among other benefits.[79]

Pay structure decisions are concerned with internal pay distributions—that is, the extent to which people in the company receive very different levels of pay.[80] With *hierarchical pay structures*, there are big differences from one pay level to the next. The highest pay levels are for people near the top of the pay distribution. The basic idea behind hierarchical pay structures is that large differences in pay between jobs or organizational

---

Piecework a compensation system in which employees are paid a set rate for each item they produce.

Commission a compensation system in which employees earn a percentage of each sale they make.

Profit sharing a compensation system in which a company pays a percentage of its profits to employees in addition to their regular compensation.

Employee stock ownership plan (ESOP) a compensation system that awards employees shares of company stock in addition to their regular compensation.

Stock options a compensation system that gives employees the right to purchase shares of stock at a set price, even if the value of the stock increases above that price.

How Do Options Work?

Options work like this. Let's say that you are awarded the right (or option) to buy 100 shares from the company for $5 a share. If the company's stock price rises to $15 a share, you can exercise your options and make $1,000. When you exercise your options, you pay the company $500 (100 shares at $5 a share), but because the stock is selling for $15 in the stock market, you can sell your 100 shares for $1,500 and make $1,000. Of course, as the company's profits and share values increase, stock options become even more valuable to employees. Stock options have no value, however, if the company's stock falls below the option "grant price," which is the price at which the options have been issued to you. For instance, the options you have on 100 shares of stock with a grant price of $5 aren't going to do you a lot of good if the company's stock is worth $2.50. Why exercise your stock options and pay

$5 a share for stock that sells for $2.50 a share on the stock market? (Stock options are said to be "underwater" when the grant price is lower than the market price.)

---

levels should motivate people to work harder to obtain those higher paying jobs. Many publicly owned companies have hierarchical pay structures by virtue of the huge amounts they pay their top managers and CEOs. For example, the average CEO now makes 364 times as much as the average worker. True, this is down from 525 times the pay of average workers just eight years ago. But with CEO pay packages averaging $18.8 million per year and average workers earning just $36,140, the difference is still vast and can have a significant detrimental impact on employee morale.[81]

By contrast, *compressed pay structures* typically have fewer pay levels and smaller differences in pay between levels. Pay is less dispersed and more similar across jobs in the company. The basic idea behind compressed pay structures is that similar pay levels should lead to higher levels of cooperation, feelings of fairness and common purpose, and better group and team performance.

So, should a company choose a hierarchical pay structure or a compressed one? Studies tend to indicate that there are significant problems with the hierarchical approach. The most damaging finding is that there appears to be little link between organizational performance and the pay of top managers.[82] Furthermore, studies of professional athletes indicate that hierarchical pay structures (e.g., paying superstars 40 to 50 times more than the lowest paid athlete on the team) hurt the performance of teams and individual players.[83] Likewise, managers are twice as likely to quit their jobs when their

companies have strongly hierarchical pay structures (i.e., when they're paid dramatically less than the people above them).[84] It seems that hierarchical pay structures work best for independent work, where it's easy to determine the contributions of individual performers and little coordination with others is needed to get the job done. In other words, hierarchical pay structures work best when clear links can be drawn between individual performance and individual rewards. By contrast, compressed pay structures, in which everyone receives similar pay, seem to work best for work that requires employees to work together. Some companies are pursuing a middle ground, combining hierarchical and compressed pay structures by giving ordinary workers the chance to earn more through ESOPs, stock options, and profit sharing.

10-6b Terminating Employees

Hopefully, the words "You're fired!" have never been directed at you. They are inappropriate and need to be relegated to the junkyard of antiquated business phrases. Employees are not property and should not be spoken to as if they are. No one should hear those words; there are many more professional terms to use such as downsizing, layoffs, staff reductions, redundancies (really a British term), and other more progressive terms. The *Ontario Employment Standards Act, 2000*, lists a number of expressions that are commonly used to describe termination of employment. These include "let go," "discharged," "dismissed," "fired," and "permanently laid off."[85]

During the oil crisis of 2016, more than 30,000 workers in Alberta were let go from their jobs in the first half of the year. Getting let go is a terrible thing, but many managers make it even worse by bungling the process, needlessly provoking the person who was let go and unintentionally inviting lawsuits. Although downsizing is never pleasant (and managers hate it nearly as much as employees), managers can do several things to minimize the problems inherent in laying off or discharging employees.[86]

First, in most situations, discharge should not be the first option. Instead, employees should be given a chance to change their behaviour. When problems arise, employees should have ample warning and must be specifically informed as to the nature and seriousness of the trouble they're in. After being notified, they should be given sufficient time to change. If the problems continue, the employees should again be counselled about their job performance, what could be done to improve their performance, and the possible consequences if things don't change (e.g., written reprimand, suspension without pay, or, ultimately, discharge). Sometimes this is enough to solve the problem. If the problem isn't corrected after several rounds of warnings and discussions, however, the employee may be terminated.[87]

Second, employees should be terminated only for a good reason. Employers used to hire and un-hire employees under the legal principle of employment at will, which allowed them to do so for any reason—good, bad, or none at all. Similarly, employees could quit for a good reason, a bad reason, or no reason whenever they desired. As employees began contesting their discharges in court, however, the principle of wrongful discharge developed. **Wrongful discharge** is a legal doctrine that requires employers to have a job-related reason to terminate employees. In other words, as with other major human resource decisions, termination decisions must be made on the basis of job-related factors, such as consistently poor performance or violating company rules.

10-6c Downsizing

Downsizing is the planned elimination of jobs in a company. Whether it's because of cost cutting, declining market share, previous overaggressive hiring and growth, or outsourcing, companies typically eliminate jobs every year. When Zynga terminated almost all of the employees from OMGPOP, a startup company it had acquired a year before, one of the employees tweeted, "I learned via Facebook I was laid off today and @omgpop office is closed. Thanks @zynga for again reminding me how not to operate a business."[88] Professor Marc Mentzer of the University of Saskatchewan analyzed data from 250 of Canada's largest companies, and found that downsizing is not always done for economic reasons or because the company needs to become more efficient. Contrary to common belief, decisions to downsize were unrelated to past performance. Profitable companies were no more likely to downsize than less profitable ones. Also, downsized companies were no more likely to be profitable than companies that did not downsize.[89] Two-thirds of companies that downsize will downsize a second time within a year.

Another study of downsizing, this one over 15 years, found that downsizing 10 percent of a company's workforce produced only a 1.5 percent decrease in costs; that downsized firms increased their stock price by only 4.7 percent over three years, compared to 34.3 percent for firms that did not downsize; and that profitability and productivity were generally not improved by downsizing.[90] Downsizing can also result in the loss of skilled workers who will be expensive to replace when the company grows again.[91] Clearly, the best strategy is to conduct effective human resource planning and avoid downsizing altogether. Downsizing should always be a last resort.

Companies that do find themselves having to downsize to survive should train their managers in how to break the news to downsized employees. Also, senior managers should explain in detail why downsizing is necessary and should time the announcement so that employees hear it from the company and not from other sources such as news reports.[92] Finally, companies should do everything they can to help downsized employees find other work. One of the best ways to do this is to use **outplacement services** that provide counselling for employees faced with downsizing. Outplacement services often include advice and training in preparing résumés, getting ready for job interviews, and identifying job opportunities in other companies. Sixty-nine percent of companies provide outplacement services for laid-off employees, 61 percent

Wrongful discharge a legal doctrine that requires employers to have a job-related reason to terminate employees.

Downsizing the planned elimination of jobs in a company.

Outplacement services employment-counselling services offered to employees who are losing their jobs because of downsizing.

provide extended health coverage, and most offer up to 26 weeks of severance payments.[93] Offering this kind of assistance can soften the blow from being laid off, preserve goodwill, and lower the risk of future lawsuits.[94] In all instances, layoffs should be handled with as much empathy as possible, and organizations should do everything in their power to help people through the process.

10-6d Retirement

Early retirement incentive programs (ERIPs) offer financial benefits to employees to encourage them to retire early. Companies use ERIPs to reduce the number of employees in the organization; to reduce costs by eliminating positions after employees retire; to reduce costs by replacing highly paid with lower paid, less experienced employees; or to create openings and job opportunities for people inside the company.

ERIPs can save companies money, but they can also pose a big problem for managers if they fail to accurately predict which employees—the good performers or the bad ones—and how many will retire early. Consultant Ron Nicol says: "The thing that doesn't work is just asking for volunteers. You get the wrong volunteers. Some of your best people will feel they can get a job anywhere. Or you have people who are close to retirement and are a real asset to the company."[95] A "bigger than expected" response to the University of Waterloo's cost-cutting, early retirement package resulted in the loss of 340 faculty and staff—about one-eighth of its employees, almost all of whom were senior faculty or senior administrators. This unexpected response to the ERIP offer represented a change that would normally occur over 10 years.[96]

Because of the problems associated with ERIPs, many companies are now offering **phased retirement**, in which employees transition to retirement by working reduced hours over a period of time before completely retiring. The advantage for employees is that they have more free time but continue to earn salaries and benefits without changing companies or careers. The advantage for companies is that it allows them to reduce salaries as well as hiring and training costs and retain experienced, valuable workers.[97] Phased retirement should be anticipated and become an ongoing part of the HR planning cycle, along with succession planning and employee career path development (as outlined in Section 10-2).

10-6e Employee Turnover

Employee turnover is the loss of employees who voluntarily choose to leave the company. In general, most companies try to keep the rate of employee turnover low to reduce recruiting, hiring, training, and replacement costs. Not all kinds of employee turnover are bad for organizations, however. In fact, some turnover can actually be good. For instance, **functional turnover** is the loss of poorly performing employees who choose to leave the organization.[98] Functional turnover gives the organization a chance to replace poor performers with better ones. One study found that simply replacing poorly performing leavers with average workers would increase the revenues produced by retail salespeople in an upscale department store by $112,000 per person per year.[99] By contrast, **dysfunctional turnover**, the loss of high performers who choose to leave, is a costly loss to the organization.

Employee turnover should be carefully analyzed to determine whether good or poor performers are choosing to leave the organization. If the company is losing too many high performers, managers should determine the reasons and find ways to reduce the loss of valuable employees. The company may have to raise salary levels, offer enhanced benefits, or improve working conditions to retain skilled workers. One of the best ways to influence functional and dysfunctional turnover is to link pay directly to performance. A study of four sales forces found that when pay was strongly linked to performance via sales commissions and bonuses, poor performers were much more likely to leave (i.e., functional turnover). By contrast, poor performers were much more likely to stay when paid large, guaranteed monthly salaries and small sales commissions and bonuses.[100]

Managing human resource systems is a complex and changing area. Students interested in a career in HR should check out one of the many national or

Early retirement incentive programs (ERIPs) programs that offer financial benefits to employees to encourage them to retire early.

Phased retirement employees transition to retirement by working reduced hours over a period of time before completely retiring.

Employee turnover loss of employees who voluntarily choose to leave the company.

Functional turnover loss of poorly performing employees who voluntarily choose to leave a company.

Dysfunctional turnover loss of high-performing employees who voluntarily choose to leave a company.

provincial websites (www.hrpa.ca; www.bchrma.org; www.hrpnl.ca; www.hrmam.org; etc.). Also, students should talk to their faculty about gaining student membership in their prospective provincial associations and pursuing a Certified Human Resources Professional (CHRP) designation (see www.chrp.ca). Many of the requisite knowledge areas can be covered in your courses at the university or college level to help you prepare for the national exam. In fact, starting in 2016 many colleges and universities provide the courses that except candidates from the CHRP exam.[101] The CHRP designation is a mark of distinction, and anyone interested in a career in HR should seriously consider enrolling in the program.

STUDY TOOLS 10

READY TO STUDY?

LOCATED IN TEXTBOOK:

☐ Rip out the Chapter Review Card at the back of the book to have a summary of the chapter and key terms handy.

LOCATED AT NELSON.COM/STUDENT:

☐ Access the eBook or use the ReadSpeaker feature to listen to the chapter on the go.

☐ Prepare for tests with practice quizzes.

☐ Review key terms with flashcards and the glossary feature.

☐ Work through key concepts with case studies and Management Decision Exercises.

☐ Explore practical examples with You Make the Decision Activities.

11 Managing Individuals and a Diverse Workforce

Goodluz/iStockphoto

LEARNING OUTCOMES

After studying this chapter, you will be able to...

11-1 Describe diversity and explain why it matters.

11-2 Understand the special challenges that the dimensions of surface-level diversity pose for managers.

11-3 Explain how the dimensions of deep-level diversity affect individual behaviour and interactions in the workplace.

11-4 Explain the basic principles and practices that can be used to manage diversity.

After you finish

this chapter, go

to **PAGE 243** for

STUDY TOOLS

Vive la Différence!

Taylar Sherriff works in Vancouver, a city whose population is regarded as extremely diverse. So, as an account executive for a major cosmetics company, she deals with diversity of all kinds among the scores of people she manages at any one time. Taylar manages the teams that sell products for a luxury brand of her employer's cosmetics in two major department stores with branches throughout Metro Vancouver. She is involved in both hiring and developing those teams, who do the actual selling. She was born and raised in Vancouver, and graduated (with honours) from the BC Institute of Technology in 2010 with a Bachelor of Business Administration and a Business Management Diploma. These days, Taylar divides her work time between her home office and being "out on the road, working with my teams." In 2014, she won a Western-region sales award from her company. Sales have been her work focus ever since she graduated from BCIT—she worked first in outside sales and then joined the cosmetics company, a job that she calls "a dream come true." Her mom also worked in the cosmetics field. When we interviewed Taylar, she was taking maternity leave from her account management job following the birth of her first child.

1. Is diversity of all kinds something you take for granted among the people you manage?

It depends on the day and situation. I am very lucky to work within such a richly diverse group of people who all have their own strengths to offer.

2. How important is that diversity to customers?

Extremely important. Customers want to be able to trust and relate to the beauty advisers they are purchasing from. Depending on the location, some areas have another first language. Those customers want to be able to communicate with someone who speaks their language. If, for example, we only had English-speaking beauty advisers at that specific location, it would be much harder for customers to communicate their needs and therefore it would hinder sales.

Some clients prefer more mature opinions and advice from the beauty adviser they are purchasing skincare from, or conversely, sometimes younger clients prefer a younger makeup artist to teach them tips and tricks, so we have to be very conscious of our teams' diversity to ensure we have the right dynamic to serve all customers' needs.

3. What are some of the positives for employees to such diversity?

Learning new and unique strategies to overcome obstacles and be successful at the task at hand, even learning some words in a different language! Everyone has a different perspective on how things can be done, and working within such diverse groups means the opportunities to learn are exponential.

4. Have you had to face any special challenges in regards to diversity among employees?

Sometimes, in a language-diverse region, it can be difficult for employees who speak only one language to communicate with customers. Within the teams, employees are normally helpful to one another at translating, but at times customers whose first language isn't English want to communicate easily with someone. This can cause frustration for some employees who don't speak the language because they want to help the client or make the sale.

5. Do you as a manager have any advice about how to handle diversity in general?

Embrace it and find how it will best give you an edge. There is a positive in every situation, and our job as leaders is to find what that is and maximize it. I try to look at the bigger picture and see how a diverse workforce will get me to my end goal—in my case, meeting sales goals and having happy, well balanced teams.

6. What is the most important thing you've learned about managing individuals?

Adaptability is key, and so is the ability to listen in order to find a solution that will work not only for me but also for the team.

7. What has surprised you the most about diversity in the workforce?

That success always comes down to people's attitudes.

8. How important are communication and creativity in your work?

Communication and creativity in my job are essential in order to get the job done. We deal with a lot of back and forth. Sometimes things we initially plan for can change at the drop of a hat so we must be creative and resourceful in order to make things work and get the job done.

9. What is the most important thing you learned in business school that you use to this day?

How to work smart under stress and several simultaneous deadlines.

10. What's the best advice you've ever received?

Always treat people the way you want to be treated.

11. What was your first job?

I always wanted to work! So when I was 14, I earned money outside school hours by working in a clothing store and a juice bar.

For the full interview go online to nelson.com/student

Danielle Dobson Photography

Interview courtesy of Taylar Morgan Sherriff.

11-1 DIVERSITY: DIFFERENCES THAT MATTER

Demographic projections are that Canada's population diversity will increase greatly by 2031, which will in turn have an impact on workplace diversity. In 2011, 20.6 percent of Canadians were foreign born. If immigration levels continue as they are, by 2031, roughly one in three Canadian workers will be foreign born.

Of those who arrived in Canada between 2001 and 2006, 58 percent came from Asia and the Middle East, and almost all were in the 25–54 age group, injecting youth into Canada's society, including its labour market. According to the National Housing Survey, South Asians are the largest visible minority group in Canada, followed by Chinese and Blacks and this trend

Diversity a variety of demographic, cultural, and personal differences among an organization's employees and customers.

is expected to continue, with South Asians expected to represent 28 percent of the visible minority population by 2031.[1] International immigration continues to fuel increases in Canada's population, especially in the Western provinces, signalling to managers that the face of Canada's workforce is changing and will continue to do so. Exhibit 11.1 shows the projected changes to Canada's population over the next decade. Other demographic changes continue to draw attention, including the aging of the baby boomers. The proportion of Canadians over 65 continues to increase and is expected to represent 23–25 percent of the Canadian population by 2036 (compared to 14.9 percent in 2012). This will affect the future composition of the Canadian workforce. In 2009, 69 percent of the Canadian population was considered to be working-age; by 2036, this is expected to decline to 60 percent.[2]

Diversity means variety. Therefore, **diversity** exists in an organization when there are a variety of demographic, cultural, and personal differences among the people who work there and the customers who do business there. At Xerox Research Institute of Canada (XRIC) in Mississauga, there are 100 to 150 employees from 30 different countries. "It's like a United Nations here," say Yiliang Wu, a Ph.D. who

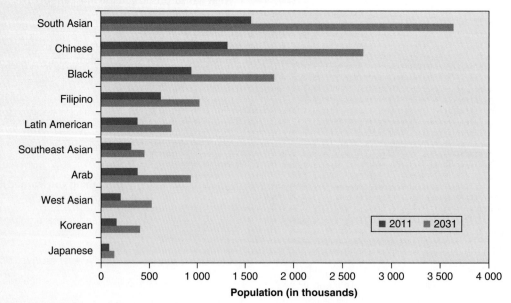

Exhibit 11.1
Visible Minority Groups in Canada, 2011 and 2031

Note(s): Data not shown for visible minority, n.i.a. and multiple visible minorities.

Source: Statistics Canada. Canadian Demographics at a Glance. Second edition (February 19, 2016), Catalogue no. 91-003-X, found at http://www.statcan.gc.ca/pub/91-003-x/2014001/section03/32-eng.htm.

came to Canada from his native China in 1999 and is now a team leader at XRIC. "It is a wonderful place to work. The diversity is exciting and embracing. What counts here is the contribution you make, not where you came from."[3]

You'll begin your exploration of diversity by learning that **11-1a diversity is not employment equity,** *and* **11-1b diversity makes good business sense,** *and how to make a business case for it.*

11-1a Diversity Is Not Employment Equity

A common misconception is that workplace diversity and employment equity are the same. However, these concepts differ in several critical ways, including their purpose, how they are practised, and the reactions they produce. In Canada, the term **employment equity** was introduced in 1984 to describe a planning process for achieving equality in all aspects of employment for four designated groups in Canada: women, Aboriginal peoples, persons with disabilities, and members of visible minorities.[4] In contrast, diversity exists in organizations where a variety of demographic, cultural, and personal differences exist among the people who work there and the customers who do business there. So, one key difference is that employment equity focuses more narrowly on demographics (gender, race, physical abilities), whereas diversity more broadly includes demographic as well as cultural and personal differences.

A second difference is that employment equity is a process for actively creating diversity; however, diversity can exist even if organizations don't take purposeful steps to create it. For example, a McDonald's restaurant located near the University of British Columbia is more likely to have a more diverse group of employees than a McDonald's in Cochrane, Alberta.

A third important difference is that in Canada, certain employers are subject to the Employment Equity Act, passed in 1986, which contains two federal employment equity programs: the Legislated Employment Equity Program (LEEP), and the Federal Contractors Program (FCP). The goal of the LEEP is to ensure that the workforce of federally regulated employers reflects the composition of the labour force in Canada. As such, by June 1 of every year, employers must submit employment equity reports that detail the representation of the designated groups within their workforce. The FCP applies to provincially regulated employers that have been awarded a federal government contract for goods and services of $1 million or more and have 100 or more employees. Under the FCP, contractors must demonstrate their commitment to employment equity by fulfilling a number of requirements, including collecting and analyzing workforce information and setting goals and making progress to achieving workplace equity.[5] By contrast, there is no federal or provincial legislation to oversee diversity; organizations that pursue diversity goals do so voluntarily.

Fourth, employment equity programs and diversity programs have different purposes. The purpose of employment equity is to

> achieve equality in the workplace so that no person shall be denied employment opportunities or benefits for reasons unrelated to ability and in the fulfillment of goals, to correct the conditions of disadvantage in employment experienced by women, Aboriginal peoples, persons with disabilities, and visible minority people by giving effect to the principle that employment equity means more than treating persons in the same way but also requires special measures and the accommodation of differences.[6]

In contrast, the general purpose of diversity programs is to create a positive work environment where no one is advantaged or disadvantaged, where "we" is everyone, where everyone can do his or her best work, where differences are respected and not ignored, and where everyone feels comfortable.

A distinction should be made between employment equity in Canada and affirmative action in the United States. **Affirmative action** refers to the purposeful steps taken by an organization to create employment opportunities for women and minorities; it includes programs that compensate for past discrimination, which was widespread before affirmative action legislation was passed. Affirmative action is required by law for private employers with 50 or more employees,

> A common misconception is that workplace diversity and employment equity are the same.

Employment equity an ongoing planning process used by an employer to eliminate barriers in an organization's employment procedures and to ensure appropriate representation of specific members of the workforce.

Affirmative action purposeful steps taken by an organization to create employment opportunities for minorities and women.

and organizations that fail to uphold these laws may be required to hire, promote, or give back pay to those not hired or promoted; reinstate those who were wrongly terminated; pay legal fees and court costs for those who bring charges against them; and/or take other actions that make individuals whole by returning them to the condition or place they would have been had it not been for discrimination.[7] Thus, affirmative action is basically a punitive approach aimed at organizations that have not achieved specific gender and race ratios in their workforces.[8]

Despite the overall success of affirmative action and employment equity in making workplaces much fairer than they used to be, the practice has drawn criticism from many, especially when it comes to admissions quotas and hiring practices in institutions of higher education; government hiring practices; and the awarding of government contracts. Those who oppose these programs argue that giving preferential treatment to some groups at the expense of others is not fair; in particular, some Americans consider it unconstitutional.

11-1b Diversity Makes Good Business Sense

Those who support the idea of diversity in organizations often ignore its business aspects altogether, claiming instead that diversity is simply the right thing to do in terms of social responsibility. However, a growing number of organizations have embraced workplace diversity because it actually makes good business sense. Sonia Kang, from the Rotman School of Management, says diverse organizations often have better employee relations, which can translate into bottom line benefits. "You typically find less absenteeism, less turnover, higher productivity, people are more committed" in a diverse organization, which means "there is a higher sense of belonging, which tends to make them better workers."[9]

Diversity experts have identified three strategic benefits of managing workplace diversity effectively:[10]

1. **Greater creativity and improved problem solving.** A workforce that has variances in demographic variables such as age, gender, and ethnicity/culture will also have diverse perspectives, skills, and talents. This aids in the performance of creative tasks and problem solving. In addition, employees who feel that diversity is supported in their organization tend to feel more valued and, as a result, tend to be more innovative. According to Marilyn Nagel, director of diversity at Cisco Systems Inc., "The link between innovation and diversity is clear. Companies that are more diverse regularly outperform companies that are not because they have stronger teamwork and a greater understanding of customers, partners, and suppliers."[11]

2. **Better insight into the needs of a diverse customer/client base.** As the market for goods and services continues to become more diverse, a diverse workforce with expanded cultural understanding becomes a competitive advantage for businesses that are intent on competing in the new global economy. Zabeen Hirji, chief human resources officer for Royal Bank of Canada (RBC), explains, "There are differences that you want to bring to the table so that you end up with more options and more of a reflection of your clients. To win in your market, you need to hire the market."[12]

3. **Enhanced ability to attract the best talent.** Companies achieve a competitive advantage when they optimize their human resources. They acquire that advantage when they hire and retain the best talent from an increasingly diverse labour market. Many companies today now understand that talented individuals are attracted to organizations that value their abilities and that respond to their unique needs; as a result, diversity has become an important part of recruitment efforts today. Diversity-friendly companies tend to attract better and more diverse job applicants.

The case for promoting workforce diversity is supported by research studies, including a *Forbes Insights* study of senior executives from companies that had in excess of $500 million in sales. That study found that 85 percent of companies agreed or strongly agreed that diversity is vital to innovation in the workplace.[13]

A national survey of Canadians found that 77 percent of workers believe that cultural diversity contributes to innovation and creates a stronger business environment. Hadi Mahabadi, vice president of the Xerox Research Centre of Canada, explains: "In the global economy of the 21st century, innovation will only thrive with the shared ideas of individuals with different backgrounds, areas of expertise and life experiences."[14]

In short, "diversity is no longer about counting heads; it's about making heads count," says Amy George, vice president of diversity and inclusion at PepsiCo.[15] Ernest Hicks, who directs Xerox's corporate diversity office, says that "because we gain a competitive advantage by drawing on the experience, insight, and creativity of a well-balanced, diverse workforce, diversity enables Xerox to attract talent from the broadest possible pool of candidates. It creates more diverse work teams—facilitating diversity of thought and more innovative ideas—and it positions Xerox to attract a wider customer base and to address the needs of diverse customers."[16]

Overall, for many businesses today, the ability to manage and harness the benefits of today's diverse workforce is vital to remaining competitive in the changing global marketplace.

11-2 SURFACE-LEVEL DIVERSITY

A survey asked managers, "What is meant by *diversity* to decision makers in your organization?" The following were most frequently mentioned: race, culture, gender, national origin, age, religion, and regional origin.[17] When managers describe workers this way, they are focusing on **surface-level diversity**—differences that are immediately observable, typically unchangeable, and easy to measure.[18] In other words, independent observers can usually agree on dimensions of surface-level diversity, such as another person's age, gender, race/ethnicity, or physical capabilities.

Most people start by using surface-level diversity to categorize or stereotype other people. But those initial categorizations typically give way to deeper impressions formed from knowledge of others' behaviour and psychological characteristics such as personality and attitudes.[19] When you think of others this way, you are focusing on **deep-level diversity**—differences that are communicated through verbal and nonverbal behav-

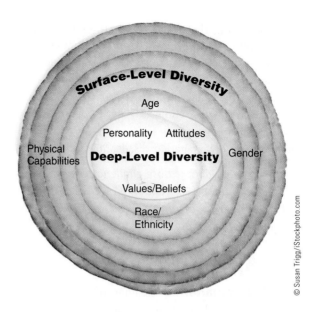

iours and that are learned only through extended interaction with others.[20] Examples of deep-level diversity include personality differences, attitudes, beliefs, and values. In other words, as people in diverse workplaces get to know one another, the initial focus on surface-level differences such as age, race/ethnicity, gender, and physical capabilities is replaced by deeper, more complex knowledge of coworkers.

If managed properly, the shift from surface- to deep-level diversity can accomplish two things.[21] First, coming to know and understand one another better can result in reduced prejudice and conflict. Second, it can lead to stronger social integration. **Social integration** is the degree to which group members are psychologically attracted to working with one another to accomplish a common objective, or, as one manager put it, "working together to get the job done."

Because age, gender, race/ethnicity, and physical capabilities are usually immediately observable, many managers and workers use these dimensions of surface-level diversity to form initial impressions and

Surface-level diversity differences such as age, gender, race/ethnicity, and physical capabilities that are observable, typically unchangeable, and easy to measure.

Deep-level diversity differences such as personality and attitudes that are communicated through verbal and nonverbal behaviours and are learned only through extended interaction with others.

Social integration the degree to which group members are psychologically attracted to working with one another to accomplish a common objective.

categorizations of coworkers, bosses, customers, or job applicants. Intentionally or not, sometimes those initial categorizations and impressions lead to decisions or behaviours that discriminate. Consequently, these dimensions of surface-level diversity pose special challenges for managers who are trying to create positive work environments where everyone feels comfortable and no one is advantaged or disadvantaged.

*Let's learn more about those challenges and the ways that **11-2a age**, **11-2b gender**, **11-2c race/ethnicity**, and **11-2d mental or physical disabilities** can affect decisions and behaviours in organizations.*

11-2a Age

Age discrimination is treating people differently (e.g., in hiring and firing, promotion, and compensation decisions) because of their age. An Ipsos-Reid survey reports that one in three Canadians believe they've been the victim of age discrimination at work in a job interview, based on perceptions associated with their age. Age discrimination can be levelled at younger as well as older workers; however, approximately three-quarters of Canadians agree that workplaces discriminate against older workers who are looking for jobs.[22] Age discrimination directed at older workers is often based on the assumption that "you can't teach an old dog new tricks," especially when it comes to technology. In addition, some have the perception that older workers won't adapt to change, are sick more often, and, in general, are more expensive to employ than younger workers.

So, what's reality and what's myth? Do older employees actually cost employers more? In some ways, they do. The older people are and the longer they stay with a company, the more the company pays for salaries, pension plans, and vacation time. However, a study by AARP Research reports that employees aged 50+ do not cost employers significantly more than younger workers and in fact are a critical component of many high-performing businesses when you consider the incremental benefits this age group often brings. The added value comes in the form of higher levels of employee engagement, lower turnover rates, greater judgment and experience, enhanced professionalism, and a stronger work ethic.[23] As for the belief that job performance declines with age, the scientific evidence clearly refutes this stereotype. Performance does not necessarily decline with age and experience can offset expected age-related physical and cognitive decline.[24]

The stereotype and perception of older workers has changed somewhat in recent years. A survey conducted with 500 hiring managers across a range of industries examined how managers view mature workers (defined as age 50 or above) and younger candidates, referred to as Millennials (i.e., born just before the millennium, from 1981 through 2000). It found that mature workers were considered more reliable (cited by 91 percent of respondents), more professional (88 percent), and better listeners (77 percent). Millennial workers, on the other hand, were thought to be more creative (74 percent), stronger networkers (73 percent) and more highly motivated (42 percent). Overall, these respondents said they were three times as likely to hire a mature worker as they were to hire a Millennial.[25]

Age will continue to be an important issue for managers as long as aging baby boomers continue to represent a substantial portion of the workforce. Those workers will be harder to replace when they exit the workforce. According to Statistics Canada, there is only one worker aged 25–34 years old for every three workers aged 55 or older; two decades ago, that ratio was reversed, at three younger workers for every older worker. As a result, employers will need to consider ways to maintain the skills of older workers, encourage older employees to stay at work, and make plans to prepare for when they leave. For example, making a commitment to provide ongoing training and development will help keep older workers engaged. It will also maintain their skills and enable them to master new skills as the economy changes. Reverse mentoring—where an experienced worker is trained by a younger mentor—can help support the professional development of both older and younger workers. Sue Black, head of human resources at Sodexo Canada, supports this practice: "We've found strong outcomes with reverse mentoring. It helps our older employees keep up with new trends, especially in technology, while also being able to share their wisdom with their younger mentor."[26] As well, allowing more part-time work and telecommuting may encourage older workers to stay on, extending their time in the workforce by placing lighter burdens on them.[27]

11-2b Gender

Gender discrimination occurs when people are treated differently because of their gender. Gender

Age discrimination treating people differently (e.g., in hiring and firing, promotion, and compensation decisions) because of their age.

Gender discrimination treating people differently because of their gender.

The Generation Gaps

Dealing with the generation gap in the workplace is not a new issue for many organizations. For many managers, that meant trying to balance the needs of two key generational groups: older, experienced workers, and younger new hires looking to move ahead in an organization. However, in today's work environment, it is not uncommon to find four or five generations working side by side. Traditionalists, Baby Boomers, Generation X, Millennials, and most recently Generation Z may find themselves coexisting in the same workplace, however, not necessarily all in perfect harmony.

Since each generation has a view of the world shaped by the culture and significant historical events of its time, there are fundamental differences in how the various generations approach the workplace, including everything from dress code, to values, to work hours, to communication. These differences can lead to tension, workplace rifts, and even more challenges for managers in charge of such diverse groups. Which generations find it toughest to work together? According to the authors of *Crucial Conversations, Tools for Talking When Stakes are High,* Baby Boomers and Millennials have the most tumultuous relationship. Baby Boomers criticize Millennials for lacking commitment, focus, and discipline and for being easily distracted.

Right back at them, Millennials complain that Boomers are resistant to change, devoid of creativity, defensive, and insensitive.

How can leaders make a multigenerational workplace more productive, efficient, and harmonious? One way is to ensure various generations are represented in project groups to capitalize on the power of diverse opinions, ideas, and skill sets. Partnering younger workers with more seasoned veterans also helps facilitate learning. By encouraging interaction among the generations, older workers may find their technology skills boosted and younger workers learn first-hand about the value of face-to-face communication. It would also be beneficial to overcome the tendency to assume more experience is always best and to downplay the importance of youthful enthusiasm and attitude—soft skills are often a key driver in moving an organization forward. Lastly, recognizing that conflict is inevitable, have processes in place whereby employees can be heard, raise issues, voice their opinion, and resolve conflict. Effective leaders can help employees work through their differences and appreciate the value different employees bring to the table.

Sources: B. Miller, "How to Bridge the Workplace Generation Gap," *Entrepreneur*, May 30, 2014, http://www.entrepreneur.com/article/234314; R. Trapp, "Leaders Need to Bridge the Generation Gap," *Forbes*, March 31, 2015, http://www.forbes.com/sites/rogertrapp/2015/03/31/leaders-need-to-bridge-the-generation-gap/#64606fc42ae2; S. Vozza, "4 Steps to Bridging the Workplace Generation Gap," *Fast Company*, March 11, 2014, http://www.fastcompany.com/3027459/leadership-now/4-steps-to-bridging-the-workplace-divide-between-baby-boomers-and-millenials; N. Fallon Taylor, "Tackling the Challenges of the Multi-Generational Workforce," BusinessNewsDaily.com, June 16, 2014, http://www.businessnewsdaily.com/6609-multigenerational-workforce-challenges.html; Team CGK, "Five Generations of Employees in Today's Workforce," *The Center for Generational Kinetics*, April 27, 2015, http://genhq.com/five-generations-of-employees-in-todays-workforce/.

discrimination and racial/ethnic discrimination (discussed in the next section) are often associated with the so-called **glass ceiling**, the invisible barrier that prevents women and minorities from advancing to the top jobs in organizations.

To what extent do women face gender discrimination in the workplace? Statistics Canada reports that, in 2012, men earned on average $988 per week while women earned $744.[28] A recent study found that, on a global basis, one in 10 businesses had a female CEO, 21 percent of senior management roles are held by women, and 34 percent of companies reported having no women in senior management at all. Although Canada's statistics are higher than the global average, with 25 percent of women occupying senior management positions, the proportion of women in the Canadian workforce is 63 percent, highlighting a serious gap in

> **Glass ceiling** the invisible barrier that prevents women and minorities from advancing to the top jobs in organizations.

the workforce.[29] "Women have made great progress in many areas of society over the past 22 years, but not in the ranks of senior management positions," says Conference Board of Canada president and CEO, Anne Golden.[30] The statistics in business ownership are more encouraging—although in Canada the proportion of self-employed individuals has been fairly flat from 2009 to 2014, self-employment among women has expanded, suggesting women are increasingly opting to pursue an entrepreneurial path.[31]

Is gender discrimination the sole reason for the gender wage gap and for the slow rate at which women have been promoted to middle and upper management? Most economists agree that wage structures reflect a variety of human capital factors (such as experience, education, and tenure) and demographic characteristics (such as marital status and presence of children), as well as job characteristics (such as union status, part-time status, occupation, industry, and firm size).[32] In some instances, the slow progress appears to be due to career and job choices. However men's career and job choices are often driven by the search for higher pay and advancement, women are more likely to choose jobs or careers that also give them a greater sense of accomplishment, more control over their work schedules, and easier movement in and out of the workplace.[33] Furthermore, women are historically much more likely than men to prioritize family over work at some point in their careers.

Beyond these reasons, however, it's likely that gender discrimination does play a role in women's slow progress into higher management. A national study of female executives found that even women who had climbed to the top of the corporate ladder believed that the glass ceiling still exists. Of those polled, 92 percent felt there was a divide in the opportunities for men and women to be promoted, and 72 percent felt that men were more likely to be given the opportunity to make important decisions.[34] As stated previously, there is an economic case for pursuing diversity in the workplace, and that includes gender diversity. According to Anne Golden, "Increasing women's representation at the senior level is not simply a matter of justice or fairness—although it is that. And it

iofoto/Shutterstock

The Golf Divide

For decades, golf has been known as the great executive pastime—the white male executive pastime. A study by Catalyst found that 6 percent of women identified "exclusion from informal networks" as being an impediment to reaching their career goals, and golf was identified as one of the leading informal networks linked to business from which women felt excluded. Although other activities are gaining popularity among executives, including cycling and running, golf still reigns as the activity of choice for many—and golf courses are considered ideal places to build and sustain business relationships. A recent survey by the Executive Women's Golf Association reported that 79 percent of respondents agree they can get to know a person better on the golf course and 73 percent say that golf has helped them to develop new relationships.

In an effort to encourage all types of businesspeople to play golf, the Professional Golf Association of America

© Don Mason/Brand X Pictures/Jupiterimages

has a program called "Golf: For Business and for Life," which sponsors courses at colleges and universities. Similarly, the Executive Women's Golf Association teaches the game to businesswomen, a growing number of whom are middle managers with executive aspirations.

Source: L. Andrews, "Nice Girls Who Play Golf Do Get the Corner Office," Forbes.com, May 4, 2012, http://www.forbes.com/sites/85broads/2012/05/04/nice-girls-who-play-golf-do-get-the-corner-office/#7a3f2f8a356d; P. Swenson, "Why More Women Should Play Golf," CNBC, June 12, 2015, http://www.cnbc.com/2015/06/12/why-more-women-should-play-golf-commentary.html; J. P. Newport and R. Adams, "Business Gold Changes Course," The Wall Street Journal, May 26–27, 2007, P1.

is not simply a 'women's issue.' Companies that fail to integrate women's perspectives into their high-level decision making risk losing market share, competitive advantage, and profits."[35]

So, what can companies do to make sure that women have the same opportunities for development and advancement as men? One strategy is mentoring, or pairing promising female executives with senior executives from whom they can seek advice and support. A vice president at a utility company says: "I think it's the single most critical piece to women advancing career-wise. In my experience you need somebody to help guide you and . . . go to bat for you."[36] In fact, 91 percent of female executives have had a mentor at some point and feel their mentor was vital to their advancement.

11-2c Race/Ethnicity

Racial and ethnic discrimination occurs when people are treated differently because of their race or ethnicity. To what extent is racial and ethnic discrimination a factor in the workplace? And how is it addressed in the Canadian workplace? In Canada, the Canadian Human Rights Commission (CHRC) administers the Canadian Human Rights Act (CHRA) and is responsible for employers' compliance under the Employment Equity Act.

As noted previously, the role of visible minorities in Canada's workplace continues to expand in the face of an aging Canadian workforce and a lower birth rate. By 2031, Canada could be home to 14.4 million people belonging to a visible minority group, more than double the 5.3 million reported in 2006. The largest visible minority group, the South Asian population, could more than double from approximately 1.3 million in 2006 to 4.1 million by 2031, followed by the Chinese population, which is projected to grow from 1.3 million to 3 million.[37]

A national survey on career satisfaction and advancement of visible minorities in corporate Canada reported that visible minorities were more likely to perceive workplace barriers and lower levels of career satisfaction compared to white/Caucasian employees. Workplace barriers included the following: a perceived lack of fairness in terms of career advancement; inequality in performance standards; and fewer high-profile assignments. Given that career satisfaction is linked to productivity, the results are especially important for Canadian businesses—another reason to embrace diversity in the workplace.[38]

What accounts for the disparity between minority groups in the general population and their representation in management positions? Some studies have found that the disparities are due to preexisting differences in training, education, and skills; when workers have similar skills, training, and education, they are much more likely to have similar jobs and salaries.[39]

Other studies, however, provide strong direct evidence of racial or ethnic discrimination in the workplace. A University of Toronto study found that employers across Toronto, Montreal, and Vancouver discriminate against applicants with common Indian and Chinese names relative to English names. Although recruiters responded that employers often view a name as an indication that an applicant may lack language or social skills, the study indicated that name-based discrimination was largely unaffected by including other indicators of language or social skills, comparing occupations that require less of these skills, and by using European names, rather than Chinese or Indian names.[40]

In another study using Canadian census data, a wide gap was identified between average employment income of university educated immigrants aged 25–44 by race. Immigrants who identified themselves as nonwhite had lower earnings than those who did not, earning only 81.4 cents for every dollar paid to non-racialized Canadians. The data also points to the fact that although racialized Canadians have slightly higher levels of labour market participation, they continue to experience higher levels of unemployment and earn less income than nonracialized Canadians.[41]

What can companies do to make sure that people of all racial and ethnic backgrounds have the same opportunities?[42] Start by looking at the numbers, comparing the hiring rates for whites to the hiring rates for racial and ethnic applicants. Then, do the same thing for promotions within the company, and see if nonwhite workers quit at higher rates than white workers. Also, survey employees to compare white and nonwhite employees' satisfaction with jobs, bosses, and the company, as well as their perceptions regarding equal treatment. Next, if the numbers indicate racial or ethnic disparities, consider employing a private firm to test the hiring system by having applicants of different races with identical qualifications apply for company jobs.[43]

Another step companies can take is to eliminate unclear selection and promotion criteria. Vague criteria allow decision makers to focus on non-job-related characteristics that may lead unintentionally to employment discrimination. Selection and promotion criteria should spell out the specific knowledge, skills, abilities, education, and experience needed to perform a job well.

Racial and ethnic discrimination treating people differently because of their race or ethnicity.

The Judy Project

For six days each spring, a group of 25 senior-level, female business executives put their demanding roles on hold and sequester themselves at an offsite venue to discuss management trends, development leadership skills and, most importantly, network. This unique gathering is part of the Judy Project, an annual workshop established in the memory of Judy Elder, a successful Toronto-based business leader who achieved great success at several large Canadian companies, including Microsoft Canada, IBM Canada, and Ogilvy One, and who passed away in 2002 at the age of 48. She was known for her passion and support of women in the business world, believing that there was plenty of room at the top for other women. The Judy Project was established in her memory, in partnership with the Joseph L. Rotman School of Management at the University of Toronto.

The annual week-long forum includes fireside chats, seminar-style discussions, and Q&A sessions where participants and leaders discuss everything from leadership styles and business ethics to juggling multiple roles and responsibilities. The cohort then stays in touch for a year after the meeting, acting as sounding boards and informal advisors to each other. The Judy Project's focus is to equip women to better navigate to the upper levels of management while addressing the realities of the challenges that they face in seeking to be leaders of large organizations. According to Colleen Moorehead, the Judy Project co-founder, "In a

Courtesy of David Powell/*Marketing Magazine*

competitive environment, organizations thrive and grow on diversity of thinking and ideas. Selecting from 100 percent of available talent will always drive better results. Companies with diversity at the top outperform their not so diverse peers where it counts, shareholder value. Corporate Canada can't afford to write-off 50 percent of its talent pool."

Sources: R. Walberg, "Executive Women Build Lifelong Professional Bonds Through Unique MBA Networking Programs," FinancialPost.com, November 26, 2012, http://business.financialpost.com/executive/business-education/unique-networking-program-builds-lifelong-professional-bonds?__lsa=e5ad-f461; M. Johne, "Dynamic Soul Inspires Program," *The Globe and Mail*, June 14, 2002; L. Bogomolny, "Melting the Glass Ceiling," *Canadian Business* Online, April 24, 2006.

Finally, as explained in Chapter 10, "Managing Human Resource Systems," it is also important to train managers and others who make hiring and promotion decisions.

11-2d Mental or Physical Disabilities

According to the Canadian Survey on Disability, about 3.8 million Canadians of working age (15–64) self-identify as having a disability, which translates into one in 10 or 13.7 percent of Canadians. People are identified as having a **disability** if they have difficulty performing tasks as a result of a long-term condition or health-related problem that causes them to experience limitation in their daily activities.[44] **Disability discrimination** occurs when people are treated differently because of their disability.

To what extent is disability discrimination a factor in the workplace? According to a 2014 Statistics Canada report, of Canadians with a disability, overall 12 percent reported having been refused a job in the previous five years as a result of their condition, and that percentage was 33 percent among 25–34-year-olds with a severe or very severe disability.[45] In *The Business Case for Accessibility*, Bill Wilkerson summarizes the human resources potential of persons with disabilities in this way: "For far too many years, people with disabilities have been ignored

Disability an activity limitation or participation restriction associated with a physical or mental condition or health problem.

Disability discrimination treating people differently because of their disabilities.

in the marketplace. Yet this significant segment of the population is made up of many dedicated and talented people with much-needed abilities that have so far been underutilized in the work environment."[46] Canadian statistics report that although 79 percent of working-age Canadians (those 25–64 years of age) were employed in 2011, only 49 percent of working-age Canadians with disabilities were.[47] In terms of income levels, individuals with disabilities earn less than people without disabilities, and women with disabilities earn far less than men with disabilities. Anna MacQuarrie, director of policy and programs for the Canadian Association for Community Living, says that "about 750,000 Canadians live with intellectual disabilities and they are predominantly among the poorest of the poor in Canada."[48]

What accounts for the disparities between the employment and income levels of able people and people with disabilities? One factor is that, as a group, individuals with disabilities often have lower levels of education than those without, and corresponding lower levels of employment. But education alone does not explain the employment and income gaps that exist. From an employer's perspective, the principal barriers to employing workers with disabilities are lack of awareness of disability and accommodation issues, concern over costs, and fear of legal liability.[49] However, studies show that as long as companies make reasonable accommodations for disabilities (e.g., changing procedures or equipment), people with disabilities perform their jobs just as well as able people. They also have better safety records and are no more likely to be absent or quit their jobs.[50]

What can companies do to make sure that people with disabilities have the same opportunities as everyone else? A good place to start is to commit to providing reasonable workplace accommodations to current and prospective employees with disabilities. Workplace modifications can be resource specific (e.g., job redesign, modified work schedules, computer aids) or physical/structural (e.g., handrails, modified workstations, accessible washrooms).[51] Accommodations for disabilities needn't be expensive. According to the Job Accommodation Network, 71 percent of accommodations cost employers $500 or less, and 20 percent of accommodations don't cost anything at all.[52]

Some of the accommodations described involve *assistive technology* that gives workers with disabilities the tools they need to overcome their disabilities. Providing workers with assistive technology is also an effective strategy for recruiting, retaining, and enhancing the productivity of people with disabilities. According to the National Council on Disability, 92 percent of workers with disabilities who use assistive technology report that

Photo by Jim Wilkes/Toronto Star via Getty Images

it helps them work faster and better, 81 percent indicate that it helps them work longer hours, and 67 percent say that it is critical to getting a job.[53]

Finally, companies should actively recruit qualified workers with disabilities. In order to do so, Canadian employers need to overcome some misconceptions related to persons with disabilities. If an employer can move beyond these myths, hiring individuals with disabilities can make economic sense based on a simple equation: employers need skilled workers; persons with disabilities are a largely untapped human resource available to meet today's growing labour and skill shortages; and persons with disabilities are a large, growing consumer market.[54]

Myth:	Persons with disabilities can't keep up with other workers.
Reality:	90 percent of people with disabilities rated average or better on job performance than their nondisabled colleagues.
Myth:	A person with a disability will miss a lot of work.
Reality:	86 percent of people with disabilities rated average or better on attendance than their nondisabled colleagues.
Myth:	A person with a disability will have more accidents on the job.
Reality:	98 percent of people with a disability rate average or better in work safety compared to their nondisabled colleagues.
Myth:	Persons with disabilities don't really want to work.
Reality:	Staff retention is 72 percent higher among persons with disabilities.

IBM Makes the Grade

IBM has consistently achieved a high ranking in Diversity Inc.'s annual survey of the Top 10 Companies for People With Disabilities. In addition to education and recruitment programs, IBM provides a wide range of accommodations for its disabled workers. Ramps and power doors are installed for employees who use wheelchairs. Captioning devices, sign language interpreters, and note takers are available for deaf employees. Software programs that read text on a computer screen and audio transcripts of company publications are available for the blind. IBM has also formed Accommodation Assessment Teams to consult with employees to continue identifying and resolving unmet accommodations. IBM's efforts in training and mentoring programs for people with disabilities began when the company found itself constantly struggling to find precision machinists who could operate lathes and milling equipment. Eventually the company was able to find a trained and willing workforce in what some would consider an unlikely place—the National Technical Institute for the Deaf. This led IBM to hire employees with disabilities in other

Huntstock/Getty Images

areas of the company. IBM's board of directors adopted a worldwide standard for the entire organization to support disabled employees as well as customers and members of the public by providing tools to enhance the ability to participate in a world where access to information is vital to daily life. The company now estimates that 4–6 percent of its workforce have disabilities.

Sources: The Diversity Inc. Top 10 Companies for People with Disabilities, http://www.diversityinc.com/top-10-companies-people-with-disabilities/; IBM.com, http://www-03.ibm.com/able/product_accessibility/ibmcommitment.html; C. Rash, "Hiring Disabled Veterans vs. Hiring Civilian Disabled People," Let's Talk About Work website, March 21, 2011, http://www.letstalkaboutwork.tv/hiring-disabled-veterans-vs-hiring-civilian-disabled-people.

11-3 DEEP-LEVEL DIVERSITY

As you learned in Section 11-2, people often use the dimensions of surface-level diversity to form initial impressions about others. Over time, however, initial impressions based on age, gender, race/ethnicity, and mental or physical disabilities give way to deeper impressions based on behaviour and psychological characteristics. When we think of others this way, we are focusing on deep-level diversity, or the differences that can be learned only through extended interaction with others—for example, differences in personality, attitudes, beliefs,

and values. In short, recognizing deep-level diversity requires that we get to know and understand one another better. And that matters because it can result in less prejudice, discrimination, and conflict in the workplace. These changes can then lead to better *social integration*, defined as the degree to which organizational or group members are psychologically attracted to working with one another to accomplish a common objective.

Stop for a second and think about your current or previous manager. What words would you use to describe him or her? Is your boss introverted or extroverted? Agreeable or disagreeable? Organized or disorganized? When you describe your manager or others in this way, you are describing dispositions and personality.

A **disposition** is the tendency to respond to situations and events in a predetermined manner. **Personality** is the relatively stable set of behaviours, attitudes, and emotions displayed over time that makes people different from one another.[55] In other words, it is the person's core personality. In the past decade, personality research conducted in different cultures, different settings, and different languages has shown that five basic dimensions of personality account for

Disposition the tendency to respond to situations and events in a predetermined manner.

Personality the relatively stable set of behaviours, attitudes, and emotions displayed over time that makes people different from one another.

The Introvert as Manager

Can introverts be effective managers? Sixty-five percent of senior managers believe that introversion prevents people from being promoted to higher management levels. But research shows that both introverts and extroverts can be successful managers. While extroverts may be more effective (and comfortable) in public roles, introverts are effective in one-on-one interactions and in involving others in decision making. Colgate-Palmolive's CEO, Ian Cook, says his listening skills helped him advance in the company. Says Cook, "I listen intently. I am extremely attentive to language and body cues." Subordinates can mistakenly view their boss's introversion as aloofness, particularly if they're quiet during meetings. When Campbell Soup Company CEO Douglas Conant was president of a division at Nabisco, "People were drawing [inaccurate] conclusions about my behavior." So, he shared with his coworkers and subordinates

that it takes him time to formulate his thoughts and responses. Conant said that helped, and "the more transparent I became, the more engaged people became."

Source: J. Lublin, "Introverted Execs Find Ways to Shine," *Wall Street Journal*, April 14, 2011, http://online.wsj.com/article/SB10001424052748703983104576263053775879800.html.

most of the differences in people's behaviours, attitudes, and emotions. The Big Five Personality Dimensions are extroversion, emotional stability, agreeableness, conscientiousness, and openness to experience.[56]

Extroversion is the degree to which someone is active, assertive, gregarious, sociable, talkative, and energized by others. In contrast to extroverts, introverts are less active, prefer to be alone, and are shy, quiet, and reserved. For the best results in the workplace, introverts and extroverts should be correctly matched to their jobs.

Emotional stability is the degree to which someone is not angry, depressed, anxious, emotional, insecure, or excitable. People who are emotionally stable respond well to stress. In other words, they can maintain a calm, problem-solving attitude in even the toughest situations (e.g., conflict, hostility, dangerous conditions, or extreme time pressures). By contrast, emotionally unstable people find it difficult to handle the most basic demands of their work under only moderately stressful situations and become distraught, tearful, self-doubting, and anxious. Emotional stability is particularly important for high-stress jobs such as police work, firefighting, emergency medical treatment, and piloting planes.

Agreeableness is the degree to which someone is cooperative, polite, flexible, forgiving, good-natured, tolerant, and trusting. Basically, agreeable people are easy to work with and be around, whereas disagreeable people are distrusting and difficult to work with and be around.

Conscientiousness is the degree to which someone is organized, hard-working, responsible, persevering, thorough, and achievement oriented. Ninety-two studies across five occupational groups (professionals, police, managers, sales, and skilled/semiskilled jobs) with a combined total of 12,893 study participants indicated that, on average, conscientious people are inherently more motivated and are better at their jobs.[57]

Openness to experience is the degree to which someone is curious, broad-minded, and open to new ideas, things, and experiences; is spontaneous; and has a high tolerance for ambiguity. People in marketing, advertising, research, and other creative jobs need to be curious, open to new ideas, and spontaneous.

Extroversion the degree to which someone is active, assertive, gregarious, sociable, talkative, and energized by others.

Emotional stability the degree to which someone is not angry, depressed, anxious, emotional, insecure, and excitable.

Agreeableness the degree to which someone is cooperative, polite, flexible, forgiving, good-natured, tolerant, and trusting.

Conscientiousness the degree to which someone is organized, hardworking, responsible, persevering, thorough, and achievement oriented.

Openness to experience the degree to which someone is curious, broad-minded, and open to new ideas, things, and experiences; is spontaneous; and has a high tolerance for ambiguity.

Which of the Big Five Personality Dimensions has the largest impact on behaviour in organizations? The cumulative results indicate that conscientiousness is related to job performance across five different occupational groups (professionals, police, managers, sales, and skilled/semi-skilled jobs).[58] In short, people "who are dependable, persistent, goal directed, and organized tend to be higher performers on virtually any job; viewed negatively, those who are careless, irresponsible, low-achievement striving, and impulsive tend to be lower performers on virtually any job."[59] The results also indicate that extroversion is related to performance in jobs, such as sales and management, that involve significant interaction with others. In people-intensive jobs like these, it helps to be sociable, assertive, and talkative and to have energy and be able to energize others. Finally, people who are extroverted and open to experience seem to do much better in training. Being curious and open to new experiences as well as sociable, assertive, talkative, and full of energy helps people perform better in learning situations.[60]

RelaxFoto.de/E+//Getty Images

11-4 MANAGING DIVERSITY

How much should companies change their standard business practices to accommodate the diversity of their workers? What do you do when a talented top executive has a drinking problem that only seems to affect his behaviour at company social events or when entertaining clients, where he has made inappropriate advances toward female employees? What do you do when, despite aggressive company policies against racial discrimination, employees continue to tell racial jokes and publicly post cartoons displaying racial humour? And, since many people confuse diversity with employment equity, what do you do to make sure that your company's diversity practices and policies are viewed as benefiting all workers and not just some workers?

Questions like these make managing diversity one of the toughest challenges that managers face.[61] Nonetheless, there are steps companies can take to begin to address these issues.

As discussed earlier, diversity programs try to create a positive work environment where no one is advantaged or disadvantaged, where "we" is everyone, where everyone can do his or her best work, where differences are respected and not ignored, and where everyone feels comfortable.

Please Remain Stable

A well-known incident in which a JetBlue flight attendant lost his cool when dealing with a rude passenger illustrates what can happen when emotional stability is lacking in stressful situations. Moments after a JetBlue flight from Pittsburgh landed at New York's John F. Kennedy International Airport, a passenger stood up to retrieve his bags from the overhead bin while the plane was still moving—before the crew gave permission. When flight attendant Steven Slater told the passenger to remain seated, he refused. Slater approached the passenger just as he was pulling his bag down, striking Slater in the head. When Slater asked for an apology, the passenger cursed at him.

© Diane Diederich/iStockphoto.com

Slater responded by cursing the passenger over the plane's public address system microphone, grabbing two beers from the beverage cart, and activating the emergency chute, which he used to slide out of the plane, head to the parking lot, and go home. Slater lost his job because of his inability to remain emotionally stable in this situation.

Source: A. Newman and R. Rivera, "Fed-Up Flight Attendant Makes Sliding Exit," *New York Times*, August 9, 2010, http://www.nytimes.com/2010/08/10/nyregion/10attendant.html.

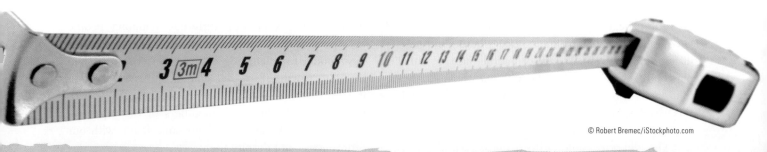

if you *don't* measure something, it *doesn't count.*

*Let's begin to address those goals by learning about **11-4a diversity paradigms, 11-4b diversity principles**, and **11-4c diversity training and practices.***

11-4a Diversity Paradigms

There are several different methods or paradigms for managing diversity: the discrimination and fairness paradigm, the access and legitimacy paradigm, and the learning and effectiveness paradigm.[62]

The *discrimination and fairness paradigm*, which is the most common method of approaching diversity, focuses on equal opportunity, fair treatment, recruitment of minorities, and strict compliance with the equal employment opportunity laws. Under this approach, success is measured by how well companies achieve recruitment, promotion, and retention goals for women, people of different racial/ethnic backgrounds, and other underrepresented groups. One manager says: "If you don't measure something, it doesn't count. You measure your market share. You measure your profitability. The same should be true for diversity. There has to be some way of measuring whether you did, in fact, cast your net widely, and whether the company is better off today in terms of the experience of people of colour than it was a few years ago. I measure my market share and my profitability. Why not this?"[63] The benefit of the discrimination and fairness paradigm is that it generally brings about fairer treatment of employees and increases demographic diversity. The limitation is that the focus of diversity remains on the surface-level dimensions of gender, race, and ethnicity.

The *access and legitimacy paradigm* focuses on the acceptance and celebration of differences to ensure the diversity within the company matches the diversity found among primary stakeholders such as customers, suppliers, and local communities. This is similar to the *business growth* advantage of diversity discussed earlier in the chapter. The basic idea behind this approach is to attract a broader customer base by creating a more diverse workforce. According to the vice president of human resources for Enterprise Rent-a-Car, "We are living in an increasingly multi-cultural country, and new ethnic groups are quickly gaining consumer power. Our company needs a demographically more diverse workforce to help us gain access to these differentiated segments."[64] Consistent with this goal, he adds, "We want people who speak the same language, literally and figuratively, as our customers. We don't set quotas. We say [to our managers], 'Reflect your local market.'"[65] The primary benefit of this approach is that it establishes a clear business reason for diversity. Like the discrimination and fairness paradigm, however, it focuses only on surface-level diversity dimensions of gender, race, and ethnicity. Furthermore, employees who are assigned responsibility for customers and stakeholders on the basis of their gender, race, or ethnicity may eventually feel frustrated and exploited.

The *learning and effectiveness paradigm* focuses on integrating deep-level diversity differences—such as personality, attitudes, beliefs, and values—into the actual work of the organization. For example, the CEO of Newton Investment Management, Helena Morrissey, admits to sometimes keeping her business opinions to herself for fear of being seen as "the annoying" woman at the table. "At a recent meeting I wasn't comfortable with a controversial point and I spoke up, but I also had a different view on the next item on the agenda but instead of speaking up I held back." Says Morrissey, "I have been conscious of feeling that where I did have different views from the rest of the [all-male] group, I may be being perceived as the 'difficult woman' rather than being listened to for what I was saying." She felt this way despite there being "no evidence that the men were actually feeling that."[66]

The learning and effectiveness paradigm is consistent with achieving organizational plurality. **Organizational plurality** describes a work environment where (1) all members are empowered to contribute in a way that maximizes the benefits to the organization, customers, and themselves, and (2) the individuality of each member is respected by not segmenting or polarizing people on the basis of their membership in a particular group.[67]

The learning and effectiveness diversity paradigm offers four benefits.[68] First, it values common ground. Dave Thomas of the Harvard Business School explains: "Like the fairness paradigm, it promotes equal opportunity for all individuals. And like the access paradigm,

it acknowledges cultural differences among people and recognizes the value in those differences. Yet this new model for managing diversity lets the organization internalize differences among employees so that it learns and grows because of them. Indeed, with the model fully in place, members of the organization can say, 'We are all on the same team, with our differences—not despite them.'"[69]

Second, this paradigm distinguishes between individual and group differences. When diversity focuses only on differences between groups, such as females versus males, large differences within groups are ignored.[70] For example, think of the women you know at work. Now, think for a second about what they have in common. After that, think about how they're different. If your situation is typical, the list of differences should be just as long as the list of commonalities if not longer. In short, managers can achieve a greater understanding of diversity and their employees by treating them as individuals and by realizing that not all employees want the same things at work.[71]

Third, because the focus is on individual differences, the learning and effectiveness paradigm is less likely to encounter the conflict, backlash, and divisiveness sometimes associated with diversity programs that focus only on group differences.

Finally, unlike other diversity paradigms that simply focus on the value of being different (primarily in terms of surface-level diversity), the learning and effectiveness

Organizational plurality a work environment where (1) all members are empowered to contribute in a way that maximizes the benefits to the organization, customers, and themselves, and (2) the individuality of each member is respected by not segmenting or polarizing people on the basis of their membership in a particular group.

"We are all on the **same team,**

paradigm focuses on bringing different talents and perspectives *together* (i.e., deep-level diversity) to make the best organizational decisions and to produce innovative, competitive products and services.

11-4b Diversity Principles

Diversity paradigms are general approaches or strategies for managing diversity. Whichever diversity paradigm is chosen, diversity principles will help managers do a better job of *managing company diversity programs*.[72]

In a study of the top 1,000 Canadian companies and employers filing employment equity reports, researchers at the Richard Ivey School of Business identified nine action areas for managing diversity.[73]

Linking diversity to strategic business goals. At Alberta-based Syncrude Canada, understanding of the strategic value of diversity is expressed by the following equation: High job satisfaction = Motivation = Going above and beyond in times of change and growth = Breakthrough business performance. In general, larger organizations are more likely to include diversity in their mission statement, to have a diversity council (that includes executives), to link diversity to business strategy, and to have a clear understanding of how diversity links to economic performance.

Including diversity in human resource planning. Organizations that understand how diversity can contribute to success will make strides to incorporate diversity in human resource planning. For example, Xerox Corporation traced the career paths—specifically, the key jobs—taken by top executives as they advanced in the company, and then set goals for placing women and visible minorities on those same paths in order to ensure diversity in future top executive candidates.

Recruiting a diverse workforce. Organizations can ensure that recruiting materials (ads, brochures, website), recruiting processes, and the pools for identifying potential hires encourage a diverse set of applicants

Selecting a diverse workforce. To facilitate diversity in the selection process, organizations should utilize structured interviews, assemble diverse teams to interview candidates, and identify ways that candidates can demonstrate job qualifications beyond traditional experiences. The University of British Columbia trains recruitment managers on employment equity in the interview process, and Corus Entertainment Inc. forwards job openings to organizations representing the disabled, such as the Canadian National Institute for the Blind.[74]

Training and developing a diverse staff. Research shows that women and visible minorities are more likely to be chosen for management positions in organizations that provide more training and development opportunities. This highlights critical elements needed for career advancement among a diverse workforce. TD Bank, for example, offers a training curriculum to help foreign-educated professionals integrate into the workforce, and also offers a mentoring and internship program.[75]

with our **differences**—not despite them."

© Robert Churchill/iStockphoto.com

© Yuri/iStockphoto.com

Monitoring the effectiveness of staffing for diversity. Organizations that fall under Canada's Employment Equity Act are required to submit statistics annually to the federal government. However, other firms may also collect data to assess the level of workforce diversity by tracking the diversity of applicants, new hires, promotions, and turnover rates.

Providing work-life flexibility and *Creating an inclusive working environment.* Organizations offering flexible organizational structures and benefits to employees create a more inclusive workplace environment for employees with a variety of family situations. An inclusive work environment has been linked to increased productivity and profitability. Flexibility benefits might include these: flexible work scheduling, work-at-home options, job sharing, reduced work hours, a compressed work week, part-time employment, and an on-site or company-supported dependant care centre.

Senior executive support for diversity. Support from senior management can be vital for creating and promoting workplace diversity. Home Depot Canada created a Diversity and Inclusion Committee, led by the VP of human resources, to measure recruitment activities in

relation to diverse groups and to increase the number of disabled employees.[76]

11-4c Diversity Training and Practices

Organizations use diversity training and several common diversity practices to manage diversity. There are two basic types of diversity training programs: *awareness training* and *skills-based diversity training*.

Awareness training is designed to raise employees' awareness of diversity issues, such as the Big Five Personality Dimensions discussed in this chapter, and to get employees to challenge underlying assumptions or stereotypes they may have about others. L'Oréal Canada has developed a training program where baby boomers and Generation X and Y employees meet to discuss their different expectations in the workplace. They also work in mixed-generation teams to learn about and appreciate one another's strengths and aptitudes.[77]

By contrast, **skills-based diversity training** teaches employees the practical skills they need for managing a diverse workforce, such as flexibility and adaptability, problem solving, negotiation tactics, and conflict resolution.[78] The retail chain Canada Safeway Limited provides employees with hands-on training materials and a resource library on the company's diversity website, which is available on the company intranet. Similarly, KPMG Canada has introduced an online diversity training program, mandatory for all employees, that includes customized modules for employees, managers, and executive-level staff.[79]

Companies also use *diversity audits*, *diversity pairing*, and *minority experiences* for top executives to better manage diversity. **Diversity audits** are formal assessments that measure employee and management attitudes, investigate the extent to which people are advantaged or disadvantaged with respect to hiring and promotions, and review companies' diversity-related policies and procedures. Saskatchewan's electricity provider, SaskPower, measures the progress of its diversity-related recruitment goals through regular reporting to senior management. Similarly, the Royal Bank of Canada ensures that the company maintains a leadership role in diversity by preparing an annual diversity progress report in addition to its annual employment equity report.[80]

Earlier in the chapter you learned that *mentoring*—pairing a junior employee with a senior employee—is a common strategy for creating learning and promotional opportunities for women. Diversity pairing is a special kind of mentoring. In **diversity pairing**, people of

---

Awareness training training designed to raise employees' awareness of diversity issues and to challenge the underlying assumptions or stereotypes they may have about others.

Skills-based diversity training training that teaches employees the practical skills they need for managing a diverse workforce, such as flexibility and adaptability, negotiation, problem solving, and conflict resolution.

Diversity audits formal assessments that measure employee and management attitudes, investigate the extent to which people are advantaged or disadvantaged with respect to hiring and promotions, and review companies' diversity-related policies and procedures.

Diversity pairing a mentoring program in which people of different cultural backgrounds, sexes, or races/ethnicities are paired together to get to know one another and change stereotypical beliefs and attitudes.

Mixed Messages

Managers need to think twice before communicating to today's diverse workforce, to ensure they consider the cultural context of the listener, as variations exist in language, tone, phonetics, and verbal and nonverbal cues across cultures. For example, in Canada, shaking your head horizontally means "no," but in India a similar gesture signifies understanding or "yes." A "thumbs-up" in Canada can mean "good job" or "good luck," but in Australia, Thailand, and Iraq it is perceived as an obscene gesture. Canadians are also known to be very even-toned in their speech, a sign of respect and professionalism; however, other cultures communicate in a much more animated and boisterous tone, which may be perceived by Canadians as anger or agitation. With workforce diversity nearing record

levels in Canada, managers must take note of cultural differences in order to reduce communication gaps and misunderstandings.

Sources: S. Tatla, "Thumbs Up Not Always a Sign of Approval," *Financial Post*, April 28, 2010, http://www.financialpost.com/Thumbs+always+sign+approval/2961001/story .html; B. Koerner, "What Does a Thumbs Up Mean in Iraq?" Slate.com, March 28, 2003, http://slate.msn.com/id/2080812.

different cultural backgrounds, sexes, or races/ethnicities are paired for mentoring. The hope is that stereotypical beliefs and attitudes will change as people get to know one another as individuals.[81] HSBC Bank Canada established an Aboriginal mentorship program that paired senior-level executives with Aboriginal employees. Ernst & Young Canada has developed a number of unique "reverse mentoring" programs, including one where junior-level LGBT (lesbian, gay, bisexual, transgendered) employees mentor senior executives on issues relating to generational differences and sexual orientation.[82]

In summary, population trends and related growth in immigration levels in Canada together suggest that managers must be aware of, and prepared to manage, the cultural diversity of the Canadian workforce. "Opportunities exist for senior managers who wish to move their firms ahead in the competition for the next generation of talent. By developing a diverse internal pipeline to build the diverse top management teams of the future, senior executives can move their companies to the forefront of the Canadian business community in the area of diversity and inclusiveness."[83]

STUDY TOOLS 11

READY TO STUDY?

LOCATED IN TEXTBOOK:

☐ Rip out the Chapter Review Card at the back of the book to have a summary of the chapter and key terms handy.

LOCATED AT NELSON.COM/STUDENT:

☐ Access the eBook or use the ReadSpeaker feature to listen to the chapter on the go.

☐ Prepare for tests with practice quizzes.

☐ Review key terms with flashcards and the glossary feature.

☐ Work through key concepts with case studies and Management Decision Exercises.

☐ Explore practical examples with You Make the Decision Activities.

12 Motivation

skynesher/iStockphoto

LEARNING OUTCOMES

After studying this chapter, you will be able to...

12-1 Explain the basics of motivation.

12-2 Use equity theory to explain how employees' perceptions of fairness affect motivation.

12-3 Use expectancy theory to describe how workers' expectations about rewards, effort, and the link between rewards and performance influence motivation.

12-4 Explain how reinforcement theory works and how it can be used to motivate.

12-5 Describe the components of goal-setting theory and how managers can use them to motivate workers.

12-6 Discuss how the entire motivation model can be used to motivate workers.

After you finish

this chapter, go

to **PAGE 266** for

STUDY TOOLS

Driven by Passion

Sareena Sharma-Nickoli calls herself a workaholic and says she wouldn't have it any other way. Passion, she says, drives her. Her father was a cofounder of City Furniture & Appliances, which today has more than 20 stores in British Columbia and Alberta, and Sareena was helping out in the Vernon, BC, store from an early age. After graduating from Okanagan Community College (OCC) in 2001 with a bachelor of business administration, marketing, she joined the Vernon outlet as a sales rep. Today she is director of purchasing and marketing, has been to Europe and China on business, and regularly travels within North America for buying shows. Sareena has also been teaching fitness classes since 1999. She fell in love with Zumba Fitness in 2008, and a year later started her own business, Zumba With Sareena. In December 2014, she opened Soul Studio, her own fitness/dance studio in Vernon, where she teaches Zumba and Booty Barre classes. By 2016, a team of 10 instructors were teaching classes there—with half of them having started out as class participants back in Sareena's early Zumba days. Sareena also has a certificate in interior decorating from OCC (where she studied again in 2002–03), and she designed City Furniture's new 30,000-sq ft showroom in Vernon. In 2015, she received the Okanagan College Alumni Association Distinguished Alumni Award.

1. In a nutshell, how important is motivation to you in your two-pronged work life?

I am a very driven individual, and motivation is what drives me. I know I am only given as much as I can handle, and whatever that may be, I have the intention of doing the best I can do. I have to constantly keep myself motivated to achieve the goals I aim for in both businesses. It's the power of positive thinking and not being afraid of failure. I call "failures" opportunities to see how I can make things better. I don't stop trying to be better than I was yesterday.

2. For the dance/fitness business you created, what part does your vision play in motivating the people who work for you?

Soul Studio is a business that was created though my passion for teaching fitness. What has kept me motivated is how I feel when I teach a class, and how my participants feel after taking the class. Those feelings have been strong enough to keep me going for all these years. My overall vision for Soul Studio is to help others feel happiness within. All of the instructors that teach at Soul Studio are driven by the same feelings I have when I teach. It's self-fulfillment that is my motivation, and that has become their motivation.

3. Would it be true to say that you need to motivate people outside your studio as well as inside?

Yes! The interesting thing about my studio is that I start the motivation process, then it spreads to people outside the studio through my team of instructors and the members! It's like a spiral effect of motivation to get people to exercise and feel good about themselves.

I believe that business relationships also require motivation. You work with so many people who are there to assist you with becoming successful. Whether it's an advertising rep or a supplier rep, it's nice to also keep everyone motivated to do the best work they can do, as ultimately the end goal is for them to help you achieve success in your business.

4. "Move, connect, belong" is your studio slogan. Is that part of your motivation toolkit?

This slogan came directly from my members, as this is what they felt like when they attended my Zumba classes before I opened the studio. These are very powerful and motivating words that have definitely helped others feel more comfortable in coming to the studio.

5. How does creativity fit in?

Creativity is just as important as motivation! The more creative you are, the easier it is for people to stay motivated. People lose interest in things pretty easily if it is the same thing over and over again.

6. Does fair treatment come into the picture?

Yes, most definitely! This is one of the first things I made clear to my team . . . that everybody will be treated fairly. It's all about having people on a common ground, so we can become successful together and at the same time motivate and help each other to do the best we can do.

7. What kind of rewards motivate people who work in a fitness/dance studio?

Self-fulfillment, feeling happy from within, and helping others achieve their fitness goals. It's so good for your soul. One of the best rewards for me has been watching my participants turn into instructors. You never know what can happen when you push yourself out of your comfort zone and the effect it will have on so many.

OFF THE CUFF

8. What's the most important thing you've learned about motivation?

That it stems from positive thinking . . . and that it's contagious, and makes people feel good, including yourself!

9. What's the best advice you've ever received?

Don't waste your time pondering a decision so much that it takes your thoughts in a full circle. Make a decision and live with it. And if it wasn't a good decision, learn from it.

10. Do you have a favourite app?

I don't really use a lot of apps.

For the full interview, go online to nelson.com/student

12-1 BASICS OF MOTIVATION

What makes people more satisfied and most productive at work? Is it money, benefits, opportunities for growth, interesting work, or something else altogether? And if people desire different things, how can a company manage to keep every different person motivated? It takes insight and hard work to motivate workers to join the company, perform well, and stay with the company. Indeed, a recent worldwide study by Gallup found that only about one-third of employees are "engaged" or motivated at work. Half are "not engaged," meaning they are unmotivated and not interested in organizational goals or outcomes. Even worse, about one-fifth of employees are "actively disengaged" and are "unhappy, unproductive, and liable to spread negativity.[1]

Motivation is the set of forces that initiates, directs, and makes people persist in their efforts to accomplish a goal.[2] *Initiation of effort* is concerned with the choices people make regarding how much effort they will put forth in their jobs ("Do I really knock myself out for these performance appraisals or

> **Motivation** the set of forces that initiates, directs, and makes people persist in their efforts to accomplish a goal.

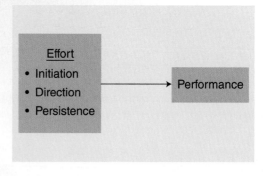

Exhibit 12.1

A Basic Model of Work Motivation and Performance

Effort
- Initiation
- Direction
- Persistence
→ Performance

just do a decent job?"). *Direction of effort* is concerned with the choices people make in deciding *where* to put forth effort in their jobs ("I should be spending time with my high-dollar accounts instead of learning this new computer system!"). *Persistence of effort* is concerned with the choices people make about how long they will put forth effort in their jobs before reducing or eliminating those efforts ("I'm only halfway through the project, and I'm exhausted. Do I plough through to the end, or just call it quits?"). Initiation, direction, and persistence are at the heart of motivation and lead to performance, as shown in Exhibit 12.1. A recent

The Path to Leadership for Some Canadians

Michael Cheng is a highly motivated entrepreneur. When he was only 23 years old, he was named Surrey's Student Entrepreneur of 2012 and had already established 11 startups, mostly in the fields of marketing and technology. One of his most recent startups is Sniply, which lets you add a custom call-to-action to every link you share, thus creating a conversion opportunity within every page. This creates a tangible return from every piece of shared content. For example, you can share a TechCrunch article and still direct traffic back to your own website.

Cheng is a graduate from Simon Fraser University Surrey's School of Interactive Arts and Technology. Cheng was also featured in *Macleans* magazine as one of Canada's Future Leaders,

in *BCBusiness* magazine as one of Top 30 Under 30, and on *24 Hours Daily* as one of the Top 24 Under 24. Michael is also a judge of the Enactus Student Entrepreneur National Competition and the SFU Entrepreneur of the Year Annual Competition.

Cheng arrived in B.C. at age seven from Hong Kong. His parents, he says, "sacrificed everything—career, language, family"—so he could avoid China's "rigid, robotic" learning. The move to B.C. pushed his parents into poverty. The fight to make it in Canada, he says, "really brought us together," and Cheng still shares a 400-square-foot, one-bedroom apartment with his parents. He can't imagine leaving them; clearly they are Cheng's motivation. "The people I care about most are still struggling," he says. "That's what gets me up every day."

Sources: N. Macdonald, "Canada's future leaders under 25, Our annual round-up of the ones to watch". Originally published in Maclean's TM magazine in April 23, 2013. Used with permission of Rogers Media Inc. All rights reserved. Found at http://www.macleans.ca/news/canada/future-leaders-under-25/#cheng; BCBusiness 30 Under 30 Winners 2014. Found at http://www.bcbusiness.ca/30under30/2014/michael-cheng#profile.

study of entrance scholarships at two Ontario universities found that they had little impact on how students performed throughout their postsecondary years. This suggests that the persistence that netted promising high school students their scholarships in the first place may not be further increased by financial aid from the university. This research provokes an interesting question: Would that persistence have been sustained in the absence of aid?[3]

Take your right hand and point the palm toward your face. Keep your thumb and pinky finger straight and bend the three middle fingers so the tips are touching your palm. Now rotate your wrist back and forth. If you were in the Regent Square Tavern, that hand signal would tell server Marjorie Landale that you wanted a Yuengling beer. Marjorie, who isn't deaf, would not have understood that sign a few years ago. But with a university for the deaf nearby, the tavern always has its share of deaf customers, so she decided on her own to take classes in signing. At first, deaf customers would signal for a pen and paper to write out their orders. But after Marjorie signalled that she was learning to sign, "their eyes [would] light up, and they [would] finger-spell their order." Word quickly spread as the students started bringing in their friends, classmates, teachers, and hearing friends as well. Says Marjorie: "The deaf customers are patient with my amateur signing. They appreciate the effort."[4]

What would motivate an employee like Marjorie to voluntarily learn sign language? And yes, sign language is every bit as much of a language as, say, French or Spanish. She wasn't paid to take classes in her free time. She chose to do it on her own. And while she undoubtedly makes more tip money with a full bar than with an empty one, it's highly unlikely that she began her classes with the objective of making more money. Just what is it that motivates employees like Marjorie Landale?

Let's learn more about motivation by building a basic model of motivation out of **12-1a effort and performance, 12-1b need satisfaction,** *and* **12-1c extrinsic and intrinsic rewards.** *Then we'll discuss* **12-1d how to motivate people** *with this basic model of motivation.*

12-1a Effort and Performance

When most people think of work motivation, they think that working hard (effort) should lead to a good job (performance). Exhibit 12.1 shows a basic model of work motivation and performance, displaying this process. The first thing to notice about Exhibit 12.1 is that this is a basic model of work motivation *and* performance. In practice, it's almost impossible to talk about one without mentioning the other. Managers often assume that motivation is the only determinant of performance. This is evidenced when they say things like "Your performance was really terrible last quarter. What's the matter? Aren't you as motivated as you used to be?"

Since job performance is a multiplicative function of motivation times ability times situational constraints, job performance will suffer if any one of these components is weak. Does this mean that motivation doesn't matter? Not at all. It just means that all the motivation in the world won't translate into high performance when you have

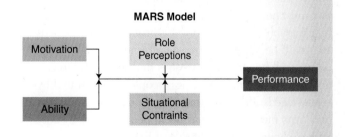

MARS Model

Motivation is just one of four primary determinants of job performance. In industrial psychology, job performance is frequently represented by the MARS model.

In this formula, job *performance* is how well someone performs the requirements of the job. *Motivation*, as defined above, is effort, the degree to which someone works hard to do the job well. *Ability* is the degree to which workers possess the knowledge, skills, and talent they need to do a job well. *Role perceptions* involve people understanding the specific tasks assigned to them, the relative importance of those tasks, and the preferred behaviours to accomplish those tasks. And

MARS Model

Motivation → ⤬
Ability → ⤬
Role Perceptions ↓
Situational Constraints ↑
→ Performance

situational constraints are factors beyond the control of individual employees, such as tools, policies, and resources that have an effect on job performance.

Exhibit 12.2
Adding Need Satisfaction to the Model

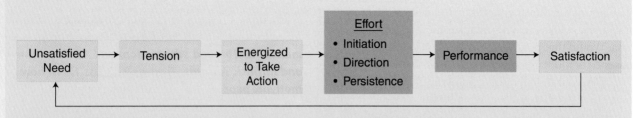

As shown on the left side of this exhibit, a person's unsatisfied need creates an uncomfortable, internal state of tension that must be resolved. So, according to needs theories, people are motivated by unmet needs. But once a need is met, it no longer motivates. When this occurs, people become satisfied, as shown on the right side of the exhibit.

little ability and high situational constraints. So, while we will spend this chapter developing a model of work motivation, it is important to remember that ability and situational constraints affect job performance as well.

12-1b Need Satisfaction

In Exhibit 12.1, we started with a very basic model of motivation in which effort leads to job performance. But managers want to know, "What leads to effort?" Determining employee needs is the first step toward answering that question.

In this section, we look at some of the basic principles of need theories as they are useful for understanding human behaviour. Then we will discuss the shortcomings of need theory. **Needs** are the physical or psychological requirements we must meet to ensure our survival and well-being.[5] As shown on the left side of Exhibit 12.2, an unmet need creates an uncomfortable state of tension that must be resolved. For example, if you normally skip breakfast but then have to work through lunch, chances are you'll be so hungry by late afternoon that the only thing you'll be motivated to do is find something to eat. So, according to need theories, people are motivated by unmet needs. It follows that a need no longer motivates once it is met. Once it has been, people become satisfied, as shown on the right side of Exhibit 12.2.

Needs the physical or psychological requirements that must be met to ensure survival and well-being.

Note: Throughout the chapter, as we build on this basic model, the parts of the model that we've already discussed will appear shaded in colour. For example, since we've already discussed the **effort** and **performance** parts of the model, those components are shown with a coloured background. When we add new parts to the model, they will have a white background.

Since we're adding need satisfaction to the model at this step, the need-satisfaction components of *unsatisfied need, tension, energized to take action*, and *satisfaction* are shown with a white background. This shading convention should make it easier to understand the work motivation model as we add to it in each section of the chapter.

Since people are motivated by unmet needs, managers must learn what those unmet needs are and address them. This is not always a straightforward task, because different needs theories suggest different needs categories. Consider three well-known needs theories. Maslow's Hierarchy of Needs suggests that people are motivated by five needs: *physiological* (food and water), *safety* (physical and economic), *belongingness* (friendship, love, social interaction), *esteem* (achievement and recognition), and *self-actualization* (realizing your full potential).[6] Alderfer's ERG Theory collapses Maslow's five needs into three: *existence* (safety and physiological needs), *relatedness* (belongingness), and *growth* (esteem and self-actualization).[7] McClelland's Learned Needs Theory suggests that people are motivated by the need for *affiliation* (to be liked and accepted), the need for *achievement* (to accomplish challenging goals), or the need for *power* (to influence others).[8]

Things become even more complicated when we consider the various predictions made by these theories. According to Maslow, needs are arranged in a hierarchy from low (physiological) to high (self-actualization), and people are motivated by their lowest unsatisfied need. As each need is met, they work their way up the hierarchy from physiological toward self-actualization needs. By contrast, Alderfer says that people can be motivated by more than one need at a time. Furthermore, he suggests that people are just as likely to move down the needs hierarchy as up, particularly when they are unable to achieve satisfaction at the next higher need level. McClelland argues that the degree to which particular needs motivate varies tremendously from person to person, with some people being motivated primarily by achievement and others by power or affiliation. McClelland also says that needs are learned, not innate. For instance, studies have found that children whose parents own a small business or hold a managerial position are much more likely to have a high need for achievement.[9]

So, with three different sets of needs and three very different ideas about how needs motivate, how do we provide a practical answer to managers who just want to know what leads to effort? Let's simplify the research

> Since people are motivated by unmet needs, managers must learn what those unmet needs are and address them.

a bit. To start, studies indicate that there are two basic needs categories.[10] As you would expect, *lower order needs* are concerned with safety and with physiological and existence requirements, whereas *higher order needs* are concerned with relationships (belongingness, relatedness, and affiliation), challenges and accomplishments (esteem, self-actualization, growth, and achievement), and influence (power). Studies generally show that there is a logical progression and that higher order needs will not motivate people as long as lower order needs remain unsatisfied.[11]

Imagine that you graduated from university six months ago and are still looking for your first job. With money running short (you're probably living on your credit cards and other people's couches) and the possibility of having to move back in with your parents looming (if that doesn't motivate you, what will?), your basic needs for food, shelter, and security drive your thoughts, behaviour, and choices at this point. But once you land that job, find a great place (of your own!) to live, and put some money in the bank, these basic needs should decrease in importance as you begin to think about making new friends and taking on challenging work assignments. In fact, once lower order needs are satisfied, it's difficult for managers to predict which higher order needs will motivate behaviour.[12] Some people will be motivated by affiliation, while others

Needs Classification of Different Theories

	MASLOW'S HIERARCHY	ALDERFER'S ERG	McCLELLAND'S LEARNED NEEDS
Higher-Order	Self-Actualization	Growth	Power
	Esteem		Achievement
	Belongingness	Relatedness	Affiliation
Lower-Order	Safety	Existence	
	Physiological		

Exhibit 12.3
Adding Rewards to the Model

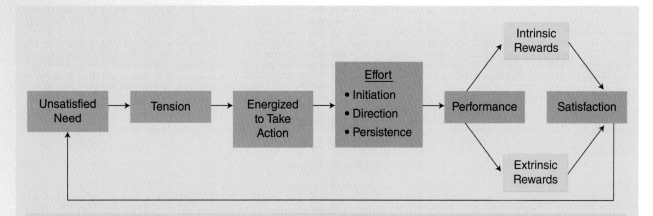

Performing a job well can be rewarding intrinsically (the job itself is fun, challenging, or interesting) or extrinsically (as you receive better pay or promotions, etc.). Intrinsic and extrinsic rewards lead to satisfaction of various needs.

will be motivated by growth or esteem. Also, the relative importance of the various needs may change over time but not necessarily in a predictable pattern.

Although popular, Maslow's needs hierarchy theory has been dismissed by most motivational experts. In general, research support for Maslow's theory is weak, mostly because it is somewhat rigid; that said, there is support for some sort of hierarchy of needs. There is disagreement about how quickly and for how long people fulfill their needs, and whether just one need is a motivator.[13] Why do we study something that is not perfect? Well, Maslow did not get everything right, but neither did he get it all wrong. Einstein did not get everything right either, but he could not have known about the boson particle. We learn more about human motivation as we progress in social sciences. Maslow deserves credit for bringing a positive approach to the study of human motivation and for laying some foundation for further topics of study, such as motivation crowding.[14] One additional thing to consider when discussing motivation is that there are some things that are seen by many to be motivators, but are defined by Frederick Herzberg (in the 1950s) as hygiene factors. He introduced the

motivator–hygiene theory to differentiate motivators (growth and esteem needs) from hygienes (poor working conditions, job security, and other lower level needs). Again, there is not much research support for this theory, but Herzberg's ideas generated new thinking about the motivational potential of the job itself.[15]

12-1c Extrinsic and Intrinsic Rewards

So, what leads to effort? In part, needs do. But rewards are also important, and no discussion of motivation would be complete without considering them. So let's add two kinds of rewards—extrinsic and intrinsic—to the model in Exhibit 12.3.[16]

Extrinsic rewards are tangible and visible to others and are given to employees contingent on the performance of specific tasks or behaviours.[17] External agents (e.g., managers) determine and control the distribution, frequency, and amount of extrinsic rewards such as pay, company stock, benefits, and promotions. Gibraltar Solutions (an IT solutions provider based in Mississauga, Ontario) provides some nice extrinsic rewards. For example, 15-year employees get an all-expenses-paid Caribbean trip. "It confirms their work is valued," says human resources director Joan Hughson. "And when employees know that, their satisfaction and productivity rises."[18] Many jobs are "dulled" by having to go into the same old office day after day. Gibraltar has

Extrinsic rewards rewards that are tangible, visible to others, and given to employees contingent on the performance of specific tasks or behaviours.

What's Better Than Cash? Try a Vacation

While no employee is going to turn down a cash bonus if offered, other incentives are worth considering. *The Journal of Economic Psychology* reports that, when given the choice between cash and noncash rewards, employees will take cash when offered in the abstract. However, when specific non-cash rewards are offered, employees tend to choose those. So, what's the best incentive? According to one study, 96 percent of employees are motivated by travel, and 72 percent who received a travel bonus expressed increased loyalty to the company. Studies also show that a good health insurance package is both a strong motivator and a good means of attracting new talent.

Source: The Build Network, "What Motivates Employees Better than Cash? A Break." *Inc.*, December 31, 2013, accessed May 14, 2014, http://www.inc.com/the-build-network/what-motivates-employees-better-than-cash.

Christian Wheatley/iStockphoto

---

nixed that dullness. Workers can work from wherever they like (home, Timmy's, Starbucks), as long as they are available by phone or text between 10 a.m. and 4 p.m. (on a mobile device of their choice that is company funded up to $2,300). These kinds of perks provide a lot of personal freedom (which seems to be a great motivator for these employees). "A lot of our work is independent, so employees appreciate that we're not looking over their shoulder all the time," says Hughson. "If we have to do that, then we have the wrong employee."

Companies offer extrinsic rewards in order to get people to do what they wouldn't otherwise do. Richard Yerema, managing editor of the Canada's Top 100 Employers project at Mediacorp Canada, says that a common thread that runs through forward-thinking companies is that they "create an ownership culture." "Money talks when it comes to attracting and retaining skilled labour," he says. "But decent wages and benefits don't form the whole bottom line when it comes to motivating employees." In fact, a motivated and productive workplace often hinges on nonfinancial strategies and incentives that boost morale, productivity, and quality of work life. So say human resources, workplace counselling, and other experts.[19]

Companies use extrinsic rewards to motivate people to perform four basic behaviours: join the organization, regularly attend their jobs, perform their jobs well, and stay with the organization.[20] Think about it. Would you show up to work every day to do the best job you can just out of the goodness of your heart? Very few people would. KPMG Canada, the accounting firm, now offers its employees paid sabbaticals, complete with benefits and a guaranteed job when they return. Deloitte &

Touche LLP has a sabbatical program that offers staff from across Canada a chance to work in Mozambique, Egypt, Ghana, and Latin America, where they will work with nonprofits on projects. The longer an employee perseveres, the greater the rewards.[21] More than 20 of the 95 top-ranked employers in the Greater Toronto Area offer bonuses to *all* their employees. These bonuses are tied to performance, and these companies give all employees an opportunity to earn them, not just managers and company veterans. For example, in the oilsands of Alberta, Suncor Energy has created an achievement culture. "We have a strong pay for performance philosophy in our compensation structure," says Don Heath, Suncor's vice president of human resources. "If you deliver, you will share in the rewards."[22] Canada's six biggest banks set aside 4.3 percent (or more) for bonuses based on performance; bonus pools at the country's largest banks climbed to $12.5 billion for the year ended October 31 2015.[23]

Intrinsic rewards are the natural rewards associated with performing a task or activity for its own sake. Setting aside the external rewards that management offers for doing something well, employees often find the activities or tasks they perform interesting and enjoyable. Examples of intrinsic rewards include a sense of accomplishment or achievement, a feeling of responsibility, the chance to learn something new or interact with others, or simply the fun that comes from performing an interesting, challenging, and engaging task.

Intrinsic reward a natural reward associated with performing a task or activity for its own sake.

VGstockstudio/Shutterstock

A number of surveys suggest that extrinsic and intrinsic rewards are both important. One survey found that the most important rewards were good benefits and health insurance, job security, a week or more of vacation (all extrinsic rewards), interesting work, the opportunity to learn new skills, and independent work situations (all intrinsic rewards). Also, employee preferences for intrinsic and extrinsic rewards appear to be relatively stable. Studies conducted over the past three decades have consistently found that employees are twice as likely to indicate that important and meaningful work matters more to them than what they are paid.[24]

With over 200 million active gamers (playing one to two hours a day on average) and 5 million "extreme" gamers (playing more than 45 hours a week), video games are a $25 billion industry in North America. Overall, we spend 3 billion hours a week on video games! Why? Because they're interesting, challenging, and engaging (i.e., intrinsically rewarding).[25] Companies are now beginning to apply "gamification"—meaning levels, points, time limits, and friendly competition—to organizational tasks like training, data entry, sales leads, car-pooling, etc. Gabe Zichermann, who organizes the Gamification Summit conference, says, "The reason why gamification is so hot is that most people's jobs are really freaking boring." Does it work? Well, if you play Guitar Hero you're more likely to actually learn to play a real guitar. Likewise, at work, people trained via video games learn more information, remember it longer, and progress to higher skill levels.[26]

12-1d Motivating With the Basics

Given the basic model of work motivation based on needs and rewards in Exhibit 12.3, what practical steps can managers take to motivate employees to increase their effort?

Well, *start by asking people what their needs are.* If managers don't know what workers' needs are, they won't be able to provide them with the opportunities and rewards that can satisfy those needs. For Kim Neutens, the director of the University of Calgary's Haskayne School of Business's Hunter Centre for Entrepreneurship and Innovation, motivation is helping develop a new generation of business innovators—"It is my dream job. It is about thinking big, being bold." Under Neutens (who has an MBA from the University of British Columbia), the centre launched one of the most popular courses on campus—Entrepreneurial Thinking, with 650 undergraduates and 150 graduates enrolled—culminating in the RBC Fast Pitch Competition. Students don't compete just for cash but, rather for ideas to kick-start their own business. Says Neutens, "That's what motivates me: others' success."[27]

Next, *satisfy lower order needs first.* Higher order needs will not motivate people as long as lower order needs remain unsatisfied. In practice, this means providing the equipment, training, and knowledge to create a safe workplace free of physical risks, as well as paying employees enough to provide financial security. Richard Yerema, from Canada's Top 100 Employers, says that most forward-thinking companies "create an ownership culture."[28] Third, managers should *expect people's needs to change.* As some needs are satisfied or situations change, what motivated people before may not motivate them now. Similarly, what motivates people to accept a job (pay and benefits) may not necessarily motivate them once they actually have the job (the job itself, opportunities for advancement). Managers should also expect needs to change as people mature.[29] For older employees, benefits are as important as pay, which is always ranked as more important by younger employees. Older employees also rank job security as more important than personal and family time, which is more important to younger employees.[30]

Finally, *as needs change and lower order needs are satisfied, create opportunities for employees to satisfy higher order needs.* Recall that intrinsic rewards such as accomplishment, achievement, learning something new, and interacting with others are the natural rewards associated with performing a task or activity for its own sake. And intrinsic rewards generally correspond quite closely to higher order needs, which are concerned with relationships (belongingness, relatedness, affiliation) and challenges and accomplishments (esteem, self-actualization, growth, achievement). Therefore, one way for managers to meet employees' higher order needs is to create opportunities for employees to experience intrinsic rewards by providing challenging work, encouraging employees to take greater responsibility for their work, and giving employees the freedom to pursue tasks and projects they find naturally interesting.

12-2 EQUITY THEORY

We've now seen that people are motivated to achieve intrinsic and extrinsic rewards. When employees believe that rewards are not fairly awarded, or when they don't believe they can achieve the performance goals the company has set for them, they won't be very motivated.

Fairness—that is, what people perceive to be fair—is a critical issue in organizations. **Equity theory** says that people will be motivated at work when they *perceive* that they are being treated fairly. In particular, equity theory stresses the importance of perceptions. So, whatever the actual level of rewards people receive, they must also perceive that they are being treated fairly relative to others.

Gwyn Morgan, chairman of SNC-Lavalin Group Inc., the Montreal-based engineering company, takes the word "group" (in the company name) to heart. "When it comes to executive compensation, the board makes a point of regularly fine-tuning its pay policy according to what it believes are fair-minded, down-to-earth principles," he says. "The next thing we're going to do is examine longer periods of holding back incentive shares and putting more emphasis on long-term performance, even more than there has been." The point of this is to ensure that people in the company feel that everyone is being recognized equitably.[31]

*Let's learn more about equity theory by examining **12-2a the components of equity theory, 12-2b how people react to perceived inequity**, and **12-2c how to motivate people using equity theory**.*

12-2a Components of Equity Theory

The basic components of equity theory are inputs, outcomes, and referents. **Inputs** are the contributions that employees make to the organization. Inputs include

> **Equity theory** a theory that states that people will be motivated when they perceive that they are being treated fairly.
>
> **Inputs** in equity theory, the contributions employees make to the organization.

Motivated to Eliminate Pollution in China

They had grown up along the banks of the poisoned Huai River and escaped to white-collar jobs in gleaming faraway city towers, but it took only one phone call to bring brothers Huo Minjie and Huo Minhao home. Their father, a tireless defender of China's storied Huai River and thorn in the side of polluting industries, had been beaten—badly.

Both sons quit their jobs. "I knew that if I decided to come back, I would likely have to lead a very poor life," said the younger son, Huo Minjie. When a government report proclaimed that cleanliness targets had been met, it was more than Huo Daishan could tolerate. "When I arrived at the Huai River, the water was still black . . . there were dead fish, and the river stunk," said Huo Daishan. "It didn't reach the standards. They lied. We needed to get the truth to the central government." But it was the deaths of his mother and 18 members of his family from cancer that motivated Huo Daishan to get to the bottom of what exactly was turning the sparkling river of his youth into a toxic mess. "It is especially the high rate of cancer that I cannot accept," Huo Daishan said.

Text and photo source: L. Zapf-Gilje, M. Wallberg, and Y. Xie, "China's Generation Green," UBC International Reporting Program, 2016. Used with permission of UBC International Reporting Program. http://projects.thestar.com/chinas-generation-green/.

education and training, intelligence, experience, effort, number of hours worked, and ability. **Outcomes** are what employees receive in exchange for their contributions to the organization. Outcomes include pay, fringe benefits, status symbols, and job titles and assignments. And, since perceptions of equity depend on comparisons, **referents** are those others with whom people compare themselves when determining whether they are being treated fairly. The referent can be a single person (comparing yourself with a coworker) or a generalized other (e.g., comparing yourself with "students in general"); it can also be yourself over time ("I was better off last year than I am this year"). Usually, people compare themselves with referents who hold the same job or a similar one, or who are otherwise similar in gender, race, age, tenure, or other characteristics.[32]

According to equity theory, employees compare their outcomes (the rewards they receive from the organization) to their inputs (their contributions to the organization). This comparison of outcomes to inputs is called the **outcome/input (O/I) ratio**.

$$\frac{\text{OUTCOMES}_{\text{SELF}}}{\text{INPUTS}_{\text{SELF}}} = \frac{\text{OUTCOMES}_{\text{REFERENT}}}{\text{INPUTS}_{\text{REFERENT}}}$$

After an *internal* comparison in which they compare their own outcomes to their own inputs, employees make an *external* comparison—that is, they compare their O/I ratio with the O/I ratio of a referent.[33] When people perceive that their O/I ratio is equal to the referent's O/I ratio, they conclude that they are being treated fairly; when people perceive that their O/I ratio is different from their referent's O/I ratio, they conclude that they are being treated inequitably or unfairly.

Inequity can take two forms: under-reward and over-reward. **Under-reward** occurs when your O/I ratio is worse than your referent's O/I ratio. In other words, you are getting fewer outcomes relative to your inputs than your referent is getting. When people perceive that they have been under-rewarded, they tend to experience anger or frustration.

By contrast, **over-reward** occurs when your O/I ratio is better than your referent's O/I ratio. In this case, you are getting more outcomes relative to your inputs than your referent is. In theory, when people perceive that they have been over-rewarded, they experience guilt. Not surprisingly, though, people have a very high tolerance for being over-rewarded. It takes a tremendous amount of overpayment before people decide that their pay or benefits are more than they deserve.

REFERENT'S OUTCOME/INPUT RATIO

MY OUTCOME/INPUT RATIO

12-2b How People React to Perceived Inequity

What happens, then, when people perceive that they have been treated inequitably at work? Exhibit 12.4 indicates that perceived inequity affects satisfaction. In the case of under-reward, this usually translates into frustration or anger; with over-reward, the reaction is guilt. These reactions lead to tension and a strong need to take action to restore equity in some way. At first, a slight inequity may not be strong enough to motivate an employee to take immediate action. But if the inequity persists or there are multiple inequities, tension may build over time until a point of intolerance is reached, and the person is energized to take action.[34]

When people perceive that they have been treated unfairly, they may try to restore equity by reducing inputs, increasing outcomes, rationalizing inputs or outcomes, changing the referent, or simply leaving. We will discuss these possible responses in terms of the inequity associated with under-reward, which is much more common than the inequity associated with over-reward.

People who perceive that they have been under-rewarded may try to restore equity by *decreasing or withholding their inputs* (i.e., effort). The City of Toronto has implemented a fair wage policy that advances the city's

Outcomes in equity theory, the rewards employees receive for their contributions to the organization.

Referents in equity theory, others with whom people compare themselves to determine if they have been treated fairly.

Outcome/input (O/I) ratio in equity theory, an employee's perception of how the rewards received from an organization compare with the employee's contributions to that organization.

Under-reward a form of inequity in which you are getting fewer outcomes relative to inputs than your referent is getting.

Over-reward a form of inequity in which you are getting more outcomes relative to inputs than your referent.

Exhibit 12.4
Adding Equity Theory to the Model

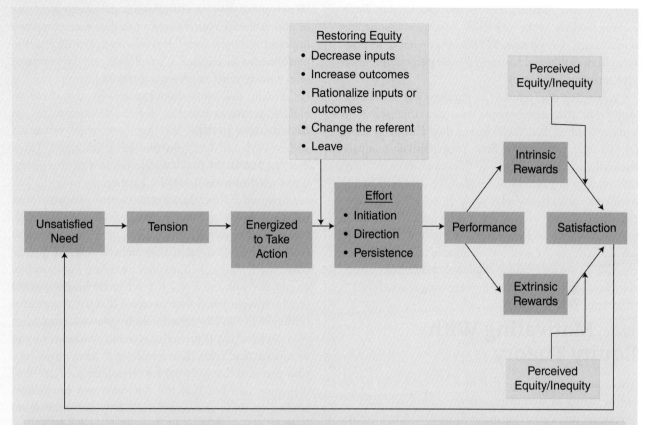

When people perceive that they have been treated inequitably at work because of the intrinsic or extrinsic rewards they receive relative to their efforts, they are dissatisfied (or frustrated or angry), their needs aren't met, and those reactions lead to tension and a strong need to take action to restore equity in some way (as explained in the "Restoring Equity" box).

commitment toward access, equity, and workers' rights by ensuring that workers on city contracts are paid a "fair wage" and are not subject to harassment or discrimination. Through the implementation of this policy, workers become aware of their rights and this is particularly important to newly arrived immigrants and other vulnerable workers. Through these efforts, workers and employers will be better informed of their rights and responsibilities.[35]

Increasing outcomes is another way people try to restore equity. This might include asking for a raise or pointing out the inequity to the boss and hoping that he or she takes care of it. Sometimes, however, employees may go to external organizations such as labour unions, federal agencies, or the courts for help in increasing outcomes to restore equity.

Another method of restoring equity is to *rationalize or distort inputs or outcomes*. Instead of decreasing

inputs or increasing outcomes, employees restore equity by making mental or emotional adjustments to their O/I ratios or the O/I ratios of their referents. Suppose that a company downsizes 10 percent of its workforce. It's likely that the survivors, the people who still have jobs, will be angry or frustrated with management because of the layoffs. If alternative jobs are difficult to find, however, these survivors may rationalize or distort their O/I ratios and conclude, "Well, things could be worse. At least I still have my job." Outcomes may be rationalized or distorted when other ways to restore equity aren't available. At TD Bank, says Teri Currie, executive vice president of human resources, "We know there's a war for talent and for us to be the best, we need to be the most attractive place for people to come to work. We want people to come to work for us and stay for their entire career." In its sales pitch to prospective employees, TD emphasizes the opportunities: "When we go into the marketplace, one of the things we talk about is that because we are such a broad North American and global organization with a number of businesses, people can have multiple careers working at the TD Bank . . . a quite compelling opportunity," Currie says. TD fills 90 percent of its positions from within and has roughly a 90 percent retention rate across its businesses.[36]

Changing the referent is another way to restore equity. In this case, people compare themselves to someone other than the referent they had been using for O/I ratio comparisons. Since people usually compare themselves to others who hold the same job or a similar one or who are otherwise similar (i.e., friends, family members, neighbours who work at other companies), they may change referents to restore equity when their personal situations change, such as a getting decrease in job status or pay.[37] Finally, when none of these methods is possible or restores equity, *employees may leave* by quitting their jobs, transferring, or increasing absenteeism.[38]

12-2c Motivating With Equity Theory

There are practical steps that managers can take to use equity theory to motivate employees. They can *start by looking for and correcting major inequities.* Among other things, equity theory makes us aware that an employee's sense of fairness is based on subjective perceptions. What one employee considers grossly unfair may not affect another employee's perceptions of equity at all. Although these different perceptions make it difficult for managers to create conditions that satisfy all employees, it's important that they do their best to take care of major inequities that can energize employees to take disruptive, costly, or harmful actions, such as decreasing inputs or leaving the company. Managers should look for major inequities and correct them whenever possible.

Second, managers can *reduce employees' inputs.* Increasing outcomes is often the first and only strategy that companies use to restore equity, yet reducing employee inputs is just as viable a strategy. In fact, with dual-career couples working 50-hour weeks, more and more employees are looking for ways to reduce stress and restore a balance between work and family. Consequently, it may make sense to ask employees to do less, not more; to have them identify and eliminate the 20 percent of their jobs that doesn't increase productivity or add value for customers; and to eliminate company-imposed requirements that really aren't critical to the performance of managers, employees, or the company (e.g., unnecessary meetings and reports).

Finally, managers should *make sure that decision-making processes are fair.* Equity theory focuses on **distributive justice**, the degree to which outcomes and rewards are fairly distributed or allocated. However, **procedural justice**, the fairness of the procedures used to make reward allocation decisions, is just as important.[39] Procedural justice matters because even when employees are unhappy with their outcomes (i.e., low pay), they're much less likely to be unhappy with company management if they believe that the procedures used to allocate outcomes were fair. For example, employees who are laid off tend to be hostile toward their employer when they perceive that the procedures leading to the layoffs were unfair. By contrast, employees who perceive layoff procedures as fair tend to continue to support and trust their employer.[40] Also, employees who perceive that outcomes were unfair (i.e., distributive injustice), but that the decisions and procedures leading to those outcomes were fair (i.e., procedural justice), are much more likely to seek constructive ways of restoring equity such as discussing these matters with their manager. By contrast, employees who perceive both distributive and procedural injustice may resort to more destructive tactics such as absenteeism, tardiness, withholding effort, or even sabotage and theft.[41] The Great Little Box Co. (GLBC), a packaging manufacturer

People who perceive that they have been under-rewarded may try to restore equity by decreasing or withholding their efforts.

Distributive justice the perceived degree to which outcomes and rewards are fairly distributed or allocated.

Procedural justice the perceived fairness of the process used to make reward allocation decisions.

with its head office in Vancouver, employs 199 people and opens its books to employees each month to offer a profit-sharing option. One novel Great Little Box program—which actually saves the company money—rewards employees who come up with company cost-savings ideas that are put into use by giving them a share of those savings. Now that's equity![42]

12-3 EXPECTANCY THEORY

One of the hardest things about motivating people is that rewards that are attractive to some employees are unattractive to others. **Expectancy theory** says that people will be motivated to the extent that they believe their efforts will lead to good performance, that good performance will be rewarded, and that they will be offered attractive rewards.[43]

Let's learn more about expectancy theory by examining **12-3a the components of expectancy theory** *and* **12-3b how to use expectancy theory as a motivational tool.**

12-3a Components of Expectancy Theory

Expectancy theory holds that people make conscious choices with regard to their motivation. The three factors that affect those choices are *valence*, *expectancy*, and *instrumentality*.

Valence is the attractiveness or desirability of various rewards or outcomes. Expectancy theory recognizes that the same reward or outcome—say, a promotion—will be highly attractive to some people, will be highly disliked by others, and will not make much difference one way or the other to still others. Accordingly, when people are deciding how much effort to put forth, expectancy theory says that they will consider the valence of all possible rewards and outcomes that they can receive from their jobs. The greater the sum of those valences, each of which can be positive, negative, or neutral, the more effort people will choose to put forth on the job.

Expectancy is the perceived relationship between effort and performance. When expectancies are strong, employees believe that their hard work and efforts will result in good performance, so they work harder. By contrast, when expectancies are weak, employees figure that no matter what they do or how hard they work, they won't be able to perform their jobs successfully, so they don't work as hard.

Instrumentality is the perceived relationship between performance and rewards. When instrumentality is strong, employees believe that improved performance will lead to more and better rewards, so they choose to work harder. When instrumentality is weak, employees don't believe that better performance will result in more or better rewards, so they choose not to work as hard.

Expectancy theory holds that for people to be highly motivated, all three variables—valence, expectancy, and instrumentality—must be high. Thus, expectancy theory can be represented by the following simple equation:

$$\text{Motivation} = \text{Valence} \times \text{Instrumentality} \times \text{Expectancy}$$

If any one of these variables (valence, expectancy, instrumentality) declines, overall motivation will decline as well.

Exhibit 12.5 incorporates the expectancy theory variables into our motivation model. Valence and instrumentality combine to affect employees' willingness to put forth effort (i.e., the degree to which they are energized to take action), while expectancy transforms intended effort ("I'm really going to work hard in this job") into actual effort. If you're offered rewards that you desire and you believe that you will in fact receive these rewards for good performance, you're highly likely to be energized to take action. However, you're not likely to actually exert effort unless you also believe that you can do the job (i.e., that your efforts will lead to successful performance).

12-3b Motivating With Expectancy Theory

Managers can take practical steps to use expectancy theory to motivate employees. First, they can *systematically gather information to find out what employees want from their jobs*. Individual managers can ask employees directly what they want from their jobs (see Section 12-1d, "Motivating With the Basics"). But in addition to that,

Expectancy theory a theory that people will be motivated to the extent to which they believe that their efforts will lead to good performance, that good performance will be rewarded, and that they will be offered attractive rewards.

Valence the attractiveness or desirability of a reward or outcome.

Expectancy the perceived relationship between effort and performance.

Instrumentality the perceived relationship between performance and rewards.

Exhibit 12.5
Adding Expectancy Theory to the Model

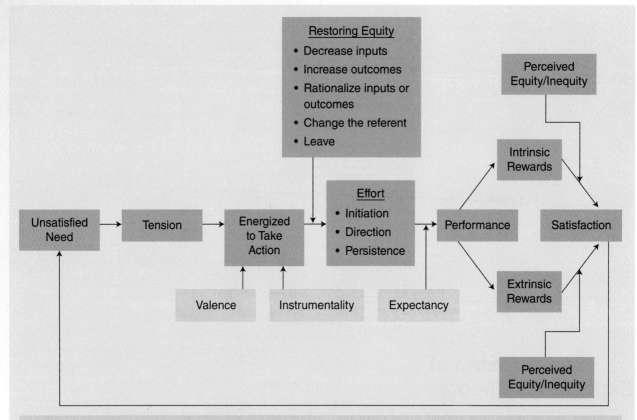

If rewards are attractive (valence) and linked to performance (instrumentality), then people are energized to take action. In other words, good performance gets them rewards that they want. Intended effort (i.e., energized to take action) turns into actual effort when people expect that their hard work and efforts will result in good performance. After all, why work hard if that hard work is wasted?

companies need to survey their employees regularly to determine their wants, needs, and dissatisfactions. Since people consider the valence of all the possible rewards and outcomes that they can receive from their jobs, regular identification of wants, needs, and dissatisfactions gives companies the chance to turn negatively valent rewards and outcomes into positively valent rewards and outcomes, thus raising overall motivation and effort. Therefore, employers should routinely survey employees not only to identify the range of rewards they value the most but also to understand the preferences of specific employees.

Second, managers can *take specific steps to link rewards to individual performance in a way that is clear and understandable to employees.* Unfortunately, most employees are extremely dissatisfied with the link between pay and performance in their organizations. In

Using Expectancy Theory to Motivate

Survey employees to identify preferred rewards.

Ensure that employees see the connection between pay and performance.

Motivate employees to take active rather than passive roles.

one study, based on a representative sample, 80 percent of the employees surveyed wanted to be paid according to a different kind of pay system. Moreover, only 32 percent of employees were satisfied with how their annual pay raises were determined, and only 22 percent were happy with the way the starting salaries for their jobs were determined.[44] One way to make sure that employees see the connection between pay and performance is for managers to publicize how pay decisions are made. This is especially important given that only 41 percent of employees know how their pay increases are determined.[45] As employees do more with less, more and more businesses are finding themselves challenged to find and retain good employees. The BC Lottery Corporation (BCLC) "doesn't participate in the seemingly endless competition to provide headline-grabbing perks for our employees. But we still have incredibly high levels of employee engagement that even rival numbers from the latest tech start-ups," states CEO Jim Lightbody. For BCLC, employee engagement is driven by cultural drivers of collaboration, embracing change, customer focus, and trust. These facets of the corporate culture are brought to life by creating opportunities for professional development for our people and by promoting from within whenever possible. "Basic, bread-and-butter initiatives like these have taken our employee engagement to 83 percent—a figure that puts us in the company of top organizations across the country, according to the Best Employers in Canada Study."[46]

Finally, managers should *empower employees to make decisions*. When valent rewards are linked to good performance, people should be energized to take action. But this works only if they also believe that their efforts will lead to good performance. One way that managers destroy the expectancy that hard work and effort will lead to good performance is by restricting what employees can do or by ignoring employees' ideas. *Empowerment* is a feeling of intrinsic motivation that arises when workers perceive their work to have meaning and perceive themselves to be competent, to have an impact, and to be capable of self-determination.[47] So if managers want workers to have strong expectancies, they should empower them to make decisions. Doing so will motivate employees to take active rather than passive roles in their work.

> If managers want workers to have strong expectancies, they should empower them to make decisions.

Charles Mann/iStockphoto

motivate employees. But leaders who focus blindly on meeting goals at all costs often find that they destroy motivation.

Reinforcement theory says that behaviour is a function of its consequences, that behaviours followed by positive consequences (i.e., that are reinforced) will occur more frequently, and that behaviours followed by negative consequences, or not followed by positive consequences, will occur less frequently.[48] More specifically, **reinforcement** is the process of changing behaviour by changing the consequences that follow behaviour.[49]

Reinforcement has two parts: reinforcement contingencies and schedules of reinforcement. **Reinforcement contingencies** are the cause-and-effect relationships between the performance of specific behaviours and specific consequences. For example, if you get docked an hour's pay for being late to work, then a reinforcement contingency exists between a behaviour (being late to work) and a consequence (losing an hour's pay). A **schedule of reinforcement** is the set of rules regarding reinforcement

12-4 REINFORCEMENT THEORY

When used properly, rewards motivate and energize employees. When used incorrectly, they can demotivate, baffle, and even anger them. Goals are also supposed to

Reinforcement theory a theory that behaviour is a function of its consequences, that behaviours followed by positive consequences will occur more frequently, and that behaviours followed by negative consequences, or not followed by positive consequences, will occur less frequently.

Reinforcement the process of changing behaviour by changing the consequences that follow behaviour.

Reinforcement contingencies cause-and-effect relationships between the performance of specific behaviours and specific consequences.

Schedule of reinforcement rules that specify which behaviours will be reinforced, which consequences will follow those behaviours, and the schedule by which those consequences will be delivered.

contingencies, such as which behaviours will be reinforced, which consequences will follow those behaviours, and the schedule by which those consequences will be delivered.[50]

Exhibit 12.6 incorporates reinforcement contingencies and reinforcement schedules into our motivation model. First, notice that extrinsic rewards and the schedules of reinforcement used to deliver them are the primary method for creating reinforcement contingencies in organizations. In turn, those reinforcement contingencies directly affect valences (the attractiveness of rewards), instrumentality (the perceived link between rewards and performance), and effort (how hard employees will work).

Let's learn more about reinforcement theory by examining **12-4a the components of reinforcement theory, 12-4b the different schedules for delivering reinforcement, and 12-4c how to motivate with reinforcement theory.**

12-4a Components of Reinforcement Theory

As just described, *reinforcement contingencies* are the cause-and-effect relationships between the performance of specific behaviours and specific consequences. There are four kinds of reinforcement

Exhibit 12.6
Adding Reinforcement Theory to the Model

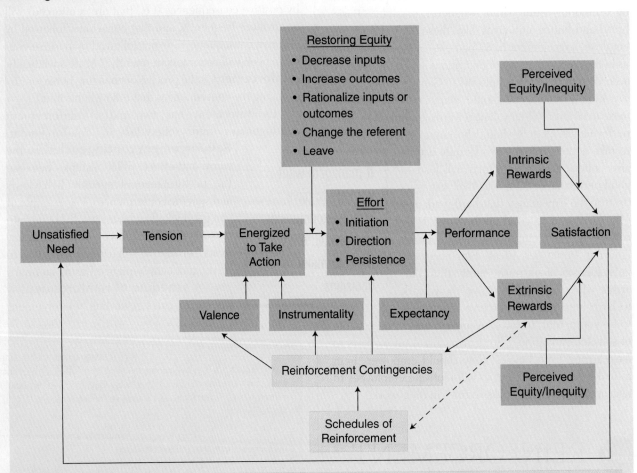

Extrinsic rewards and the schedules of reinforcement used to deliver them are the primary method for creating reinforcement contingencies in organizations. In turn, those reinforcement contingencies directly affect valences (the attractiveness of rewards), instrumentality (the perceived link between rewards and performance), and effort (how hard employees will work).

contingencies: *positive reinforcement, negative reinforcement, punishment,* and *extinction.*

Positive reinforcement strengthens behaviour (i.e., increases its frequency) by following behaviours with desirable consequences. By contrast, **negative reinforcement** strengthens behaviour by withholding an unpleasant consequence when employees perform a specific behaviour. Negative reinforcement is also called avoidance learning because workers perform a behaviour to avoid a negative consequence.

Thinking about others, and what they want, can lead to more creative and useful ideas, according to new research. This finding has important implications for reinforcement, says Adam Grant, an associate professor at the University of Pennsylvania's Wharton School: "People who focus on others tend to be more creative than those who are just out for themselves, because focusing on others forces you to consider a wider range of perspectives."[51]

By contrast, **punishment** weakens behaviour (i.e., decreases its frequency) by following behaviours with undesirable consequences. For example, the standard disciplinary or punishment process in most companies is an oral warning ("Don't ever do that again"), followed by a written warning ("This letter is to discuss the serious problem you're having with . . ."), followed by three days off without pay ("While you're at home not being paid, we want you to think hard about . . ."), followed by being dismissed ("That was your last chance"). Although punishment can weaken behaviour, managers have to be careful to avoid the backlash that sometimes occurs when employees are punished at work. Frito-Lay began getting complaints from customers that they were finding potato chips with obscene messages written on them. Frito-Lay eventually traced the problem to a potato chip plant where supervisors had dismissed 58 out of the 210 workers for disciplinary reasons over a nine-month period. The remaining employees were so angry over what they saw as unfair treatment from management that they began writing the phrases on potato chips with felt-tipped pens.[52]

Extinction is a reinforcement strategy in which a positive consequence is no longer allowed to follow a previously reinforced behaviour. By removing the positive consequence, extinction weakens the behaviour, making it less likely to occur. Based on the idea of positive reinforcement, most companies give company leaders and managers substantial financial rewards when the company performs well. Based on the idea of extinction, you would then expect that leaders and managers would not be rewarded (i.e., removing the positive consequence) when companies perform poorly. If companies really want pay to reinforce the right kinds of behaviours, then rewards have to be removed when company management doesn't produce successful performance.

12-4b Schedules for Delivering Reinforcement

As mentioned earlier, *a schedule of reinforcement* is the set of rules regarding reinforcement contingencies such as which behaviours will be reinforced, which consequences will follow those behaviours, and the schedule by which those consequences will be delivered. There are two categories of reinforcement schedules: *continuous* and *intermittent.*

With a **continuous reinforcement schedule**, a consequence follows every instance of a behaviour. For example, employees working on a piece-rate pay system earn money (consequence) for every part they manufacture (behaviour). The more they produce, the

Cartoonresource./Shutterstock.com

Positive reinforcement reinforcement that strengthens behaviour by following behaviours with desirable consequences.

Negative reinforcement reinforcement that strengthens behaviour by withholding an unpleasant consequence when employees perform a specific behaviour.

Punishment reinforcement that weakens behaviour by following behaviours with undesirable consequences.

Extinction reinforcement in which a positive consequence is no longer allowed to follow a previously reinforced behaviour, thus weakening the behaviour.

Continuous reinforcement schedule a schedule that requires a consequence to be administered following every instance of a behaviour.

Exhibit 12.7
Intermittent Reinforcement Schedules

	Fixed	Variable
Interval (Time)	Consequences follow behaviour after a fixed time has elapsed.	Consequences follow behaviour after different times, some shorter and some longer, that vary around a specific average time.
Ratio (Behaviour)	Consequences follow a specific number of behaviours.	Consequences follow a different number of behaviours, sometimes more and sometimes less, that vary around a specified average number of behaviours.

more they earn. By contrast, with an **intermittent reinforcement schedule**, consequences are delivered after a specified or average time has elapsed or after a specified or average number of behaviours has occurred. As Exhibit 12.7 shows, there are four types of intermittent reinforcement schedules. Two of these are based on time and are called *interval reinforcement schedules*, while the other two, known as *ratio schedules*, are based on behaviours.

With a **fixed interval reinforcement schedule**, consequences follow a behaviour only after a fixed time has elapsed. For example, most people receive their paycheques on a fixed interval schedule (e.g., once

Intermittent reinforcement schedule a schedule in which consequences are delivered after a specified or average time has elapsed or after a specified or average number of behaviours has occurred.

Fixed interval reinforcement schedule an intermittent schedule in which consequences follow a behaviour only after a fixed time has elapsed.

Variable interval reinforcement schedule an intermittent schedule in which the time between a behaviour and the following consequences varies around a specified average.

Fixed ratio reinforcement schedule an intermittent schedule in which consequences are delivered following a specific number of behaviours.

Variable ratio reinforcement schedule an intermittent schedule in which consequences are delivered following a different number of behaviours, sometimes more and sometimes less, that vary around a specified average number of behaviours.

or twice per month). As long as they work (behaviour) during a specified pay period (interval), they get a paycheque (consequence). With a **variable interval reinforcement schedule**, consequences follow a behaviour after different times, some shorter and some longer, that vary around a specified average time. On a 90-day variable interval reinforcement schedule, you might receive a bonus after 80 days or perhaps after 100 days, but the average interval between performing your job well (behaviour) and receiving your bonus (consequence) will be 90 days.

With a **fixed ratio reinforcement schedule**, consequences are delivered following a specific number of behaviours. For example, a car salesperson might receive a $1,000 bonus after every 10 sales. Therefore, a salesperson with only nine sales would not receive the bonus until he or she finally sold a tenth car.

With a **variable ratio reinforcement schedule**, consequences are delivered following a different number of behaviours, sometimes more and sometimes less, that vary around a specified average number of behaviours. With a 10-car variable ratio reinforcement schedule, a salesperson might receive the bonus after seven car sales, or after 12, 11, or 9 sales, but the average number of cars sold before receiving the bonus would be 10 cars.

Which reinforcement schedules work best? In the past, the standard advice was to use continuous reinforcement when employees were learning new behaviours because reinforcement after each success leads to faster learning. Similarly, the standard advice was to use intermittent reinforcement schedules to maintain behaviour after it is learned because intermittent rewards are supposed to make behaviour much less subject to extinction.[53] Research shows, however, that interval-based systems usually produce weak results, and that the continuous reinforcement, fixed ratio, and variable ratio schedules are almost equally effective.[54] In organizational settings, all three produce consistently large increases over noncontingent reward schedules. So managers should choose whichever of these three is easiest to use.

Managers are doing the best they can with the tools they have, but many of them have forgotten a tool that actually recognizes results and actions. That missing tool is acknowledgment, whichever reinforcement scheduled is used. "Managers need to simply acknowledge, in an appreciative tone, what the employee has done, without adding any judgment or any story about how it has helped the boss or the company."[55]

12-4c Motivating With Reinforcement Theory

What practical steps can managers take to use reinforcement theory to motivate employees? University business professor Fred Luthans, who has been studying the effects of reinforcement theory in organizations for more than a quarter of a century, says that there are five steps to motivating workers with reinforcement theory: *identify, measure, analyze, intervene,* and *evaluate* critical performance-related behaviours.[56]

Identify critical, observable, performance-related behaviours. These are the behaviours that are most important to successful job performance. In addition, they must also be easily observed so that they can be accurately measured. *Measure* the baseline frequencies of these behaviours. In other words, find out how often workers perform them. *Analyze* the causes and consequences of these behaviours. Analyzing the causes helps managers create the conditions that produce these critical behaviours, and analyzing the consequences helps them determine whether these behaviours produce the results they want. *Intervene* by changing the organization using positive and negative reinforcement to increase the frequency of these critical behaviours. *Evaluate* the extent to which the intervention actually changed workers' behaviour. This is done by comparing behaviour after the intervention to the original baseline of behaviour before the intervention.

In addition to these five steps, managers should remember three other key things when motivating with reinforcement theory. The first of these is *don't reinforce the wrong behaviours.* Although reinforcement theory sounds simple, it's actually very difficult to put into practice. One of the most common mistakes is accidentally reinforcing the wrong behaviours. Sometimes managers reinforce behaviours that they don't want.

Managers should also *correctly administer punishment at the appropriate time.* Many managers believe that punishment can change workers' behaviour and help them improve their job performance. Furthermore, managers believe that fairly punishing workers also lets other workers know what is or isn't acceptable.[57] A danger of using punishment is that it can produce a backlash against managers and companies. But if administered properly, punishment can weaken the frequency of undesirable behaviours without creating a backlash.[58] To be effective, the punishment must be strong enough to stop the undesired

behaviour, and it must be administered objectively (the same rules applied to everyone), impersonally (without emotion or anger), consistently and contingently (each time improper behaviour occurs), and quickly (as soon as possible following the undesirable behaviour). In addition, managers should clearly explain what the appropriate behaviour is and why the employee is being punished. Employees typically respond well when punishment is administered this way.[59]

Finally, managers should *choose the simplest and most effective schedule of reinforcement.* When choosing a schedule of reinforcement, managers need to balance effectiveness against simplicity. In fact, the more complex the schedule of reinforcement, the more likely it is to be misunderstood and resisted by managers and employees. Since continuous reinforcement, fixed ratio, and variable ratio schedules are about equally effective, continuous reinforcement schedules may be the best choice in many instances by virtue of their simplicity.

12-5 GOAL-SETTING THEORY

The basic model of motivation with which we began this chapter showed that individuals feel tension after becoming aware of an unfulfilled need. Once they experience tension, they search for and select courses of action that they believe will eliminate this tension. In other words, they direct their behaviour toward something. This something is a **goal**—a target, objective, or result that someone tries to accomplish. **Goal-setting theory** says that people will be motivated to the extent they accept specific, challenging goals and receive feedback that indicates their progress toward goal achievement.

Let's learn more about goal setting by examining 12-5a the components of goal-setting theory and 12-5b how to motivate with goal-setting theory.

> One of the simplest, most effective ways to motivate workers is to assign them specific, challenging goals.

Goal a target, objective, or result that someone tries to accomplish.

Goal-setting theory a theory that people will be motivated to the extent to which they accept specific, challenging goals and receive feedback that indicates their progress toward goal achievement.

12-5a Components of Goal-Setting Theory

The basic components of goal-setting theory are goal specificity, goal difficulty, goal acceptance, and performance feedback.[60] **Goal specificity** is the extent to which goals are detailed, exact, and unambiguous. Specific goals, such as "I'm going to have a 3.0 average this semester," are more motivating than general goals, such as "I'm going to get better grades this semester."

Goal difficulty is the extent to which a goal is hard or challenging to accomplish. Difficult goals, such as "I'm going to have a 3.5 average and make the Dean's List this semester," are more motivating than easy goals, such as "I'm going to have a 2.0 average this semester."

Goal acceptance, which is similar to the idea of goal commitment discussed in Chapter 4, is the extent to which people consciously understand and agree to goals. Accepted goals, such as "I really want to get a 3.5 average this semester to show my parents how much I've improved," are more motivating than unaccepted goals, such as "My parents really want me to get a 3.5 average this semester, but there's so much more I'd rather do on campus than study!"

Performance feedback is information about the quality or quantity of past performance and indicates whether progress is being made toward the accomplishment of a goal. Performance feedback, such as "My prof said I need a 92 on the final to get an 'A' in that class," is more motivating than no feedback—"I have no idea what my grade is in that class." In short, goal-setting theory says that people will be motivated to the extent to which they accept specific, challenging goals and receive feedback that indicates their progress toward goal achievement.

How does goal setting work? To start, challenging goals focus employees' attention (i.e., direction of effort) on the critical aspects of their work and away from unimportant ones. Goals also energize behaviour. When faced with unaccomplished goals, employees

> **Goal specificity** the extent to which goals are detailed, exact, and unambiguous.
>
> **Goal difficulty** the extent to which a goal is hard or challenging to accomplish.
>
> **Goal acceptance** the extent to which people consciously understand and agree to goals.
>
> **Performance feedback** information about the quality or quantity of past performance that indicates whether progress is being made toward the accomplishment of a goal.

© morganl/iStockphoto

Exhibit 12.8
Adding Goal-Setting Theory to the Model

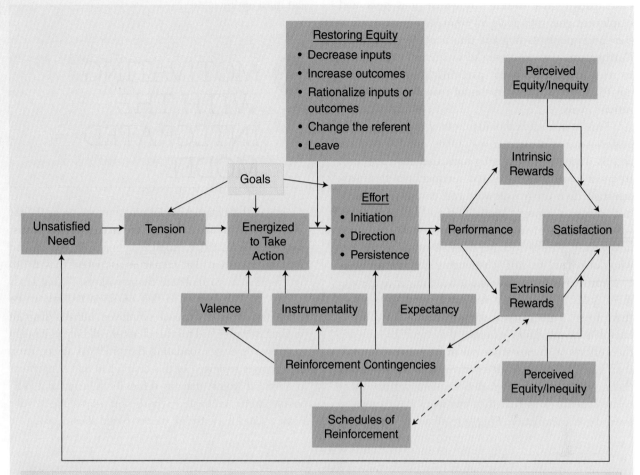

Goals create tension between the goal, which is the desired future state of affairs, and where the employee or company is now, meaning the current state of affairs. This tension can be satisfied only by achieving or abandoning the goal. Goals also energize behaviour. When faced with unaccomplished goals, employees typically develop plans and strategies to reach those goals. Finally, goals influence persistence.

typically develop plans and strategies to reach those goals. Goals also create tension between the goal (the desired future state of affairs) and where the employee or company is now (the current state of affairs). This tension can be satisfied only by achieving or abandoning the goal. Finally, goals influence persistence. Since goals only go away when they are accomplished, employees are more likely to persist in their efforts in the presence of goals. Exhibit 12.8 incorporates goals into the motivation model by showing how they directly affect tension, effort, and the extent to which employees are energized to take action.

12-5b Motivating With Goal-Setting Theory

Managers can take practical steps to use goal-setting theory to motivate employees. One of the simplest and most effective ways to motivate workers is to *assign them specific, challenging goals.*

Second, managers should *make sure that workers truly accept organizational goals.* Specific, challenging goals won't motivate workers unless they really accept, understand, and agree to the organization's goals. For this to occur, people must see the goals as fair and reasonable. They must also trust management and believe that managers are using goals to clarify what is expected from them rather than to exploit or threaten them ("If you don't achieve these goals . . ."). Participative goal setting, in which managers and employees generate goals together, can help increase trust and understanding and thus acceptance of goals. Furthermore, providing workers with training can help increase goal acceptance, particularly when workers don't believe they are capable of reaching the organization's goals.[61]

Finally, managers should *provide frequent, specific, performance-related feedback.* Once employees have accepted specific, challenging goals, they should receive frequent performance-related feedback so that they can track their progress toward goal completion. Feedback leads to stronger motivation and effort in three ways.[62] First, receiving specific feedback that indicates how well they're performing can encourage employees who don't have specific, challenging goals to set goals to improve their performance. Second, once people meet goals, performance feedback often encourages them to set higher, more difficult goals. Third, feedback lets people know whether they need to increase their efforts or change strategies in order to accomplish their goals. So, to motivate employees with goal-setting theory, make sure they receive frequent performance-related feedback so that they can track their progress toward goal completion. Simple feedback benefits from

immediacy and spontaneity. If you want to recognize an employee for going the extra mile, you need to do it immediately. Furthermore, you need to articulate to employees what it was about their performance that you most appreciated.

12-6 MOTIVATING WITH THE INTEGRATED MODEL

We began this chapter by defining motivation as the set of forces that initiates, directs, and makes people persist in their efforts to accomplish a goal. We also asked the basic question that managers ask when they try to figure out how to motivate their workers: "What leads to effort?" The answer to that question is likely to be somewhat different for each employee, but the diagram on your Review Card for this chapter will help you begin to answer it by consolidating the practical advice from the theories reviewed in this chapter in one convenient location. If you're having difficulty figuring out why people aren't motivated where you work, check your Review Card for a useful, theory-based starting point.

STUDY TOOLS 12

READY TO STUDY?

LOCATED IN TEXTBOOK:

- ☐ Rip out the Chapter Review Card at the back of the book to have a summary of the chapter and key terms handy.

LOCATED AT NELSON.COM/STUDENT:

- ☐ Access the eBook or use the ReadSpeaker feature to listen to the chapter on the go.
- ☐ Prepare for tests with practice quizzes.
- ☐ Review key terms with flashcards and the glossary feature.
- ☐ Work through key concepts with case studies and Management Decision Exercises.
- ☐ Explore practical examples with You Make the Decision Activities.

13 Leadership

skynesher/iStockphoto

LEARNING OUTCOMES

After studying this chapter, you will be able to...

13-1 Explain what leadership is.

13-2 Describe who leaders are and what effective leaders do.

13-3 Explain Fiedler's contingency theory.

13-4 Describe how path–goal theory works.

13-5 Explain the normative decision theory.

13-6 Discuss gender and leadership.

13-7 Explain how visionary leadership (i.e., charismatic and transformational leadership) helps leaders achieve strategic leadership.

After you finish this chapter, go to **PAGE 291** for **STUDY TOOLS**

Leading by Example

Jessica Clahane is manager, assurance, for the Kentville, Nova Scotia, office of Grant Thornton LLP, a major Canadian accounting and business advisory firm. Don't let her title fool you, though: Clahane sees herself as having a leadership role as well as a management one. She is a chartered professional accountant who took a step-by-step approach toward her career. First, she graduated from Nova Scotia Community College with a diploma in business administration, accounting, in 2004, and then in 2010 she enrolled at the Atlantic School of Chartered Accountancy, which she left in 2011 as a designated chartered accountant. With the changing times, her qualifications have legally become "CA, CPA." She joined Grant Thornton in 2009 as an accountant, after working as an accounting assistant and clerk elsewhere, including in the agricultural industry. She became a senior accountant in 2011 and was promoted to her current job in 2013. There are about 25 people in her office. The professional services company provides audit, tax, and advisory services to private clients and public organizations. More than 4,000 people across Canada work for both the firm, which is headquartered in Toronto, and its Quebec counterpart, Raymond Chabot Grant Thornton LLP.

1. Being a leader and being a manager can be quite different jobs. Are the two roles very different aspects of your work life?

I consider management to be the execution of specific tasks required to meet an outcome. It includes resource allocation, overseeing work performed by other team members, completing my own assigned tasks and ensuring that all the pieces come together to provide a deliverable by the assigned deadline.

Leadership, on the other hand, is how you mentor, challenge and inspire others to perform at their personal best and achieve their aspirations. I do not believe you have to manage someone in order to lead them, but you must lead them to effectively manage them.

Leadership is demonstrated in every aspect of your life. Living the values of honesty, integrity, respect and empathy in all avenues of life is critical to being an inspirational leader.

2. How would you describe your personal leadership style?

First: to lead by example. I feel strongly that it's always important to display in your own words and actions the behaviours, attitudes, and morals you expect to see in others. Equally important is investing the time to understand people as individuals—being able to identify their strengths and weakness, to understand their goals, to listen and help guide them toward success, whatever that is for them.

Last: it has to be fun. While assurance is serious business, it's important to take time to laugh and to generally enjoy the company of others.

3. Have you learned anything about leadership that took you by surprise?

I was surprised by how much other people's successes would mean to me. Being able to say "Great job" to someone often feels even better than being told the same yourself.

4. Does the nature of the assurance industry put limits on how much creativity and risk-taking a leader can encourage?

In this industry, leaders encourage people to be creative through using innovative ways to approach an issue, while still ensuring the professional standards are achieved. For example, the rapidly increasing uses of technology can impact the way we perform specific procedures.

5. Have you personally ever seen gender raising its head as an issue in leadership?

I have not personally seen gender as an issue in leadership. I have been pleased with how this issue has been recognized in recent years by large companies in terms of implementing more support programs for childcare, flexible work arrangements, maternity/parental leave, etc., to help people find balance between their parenting and careers.

As a parent, I recognize the challenge of balancing a professional career and managing family responsibilities. I do not, however, see this as a gender-specific issue, as in today's society the primary caregiver role can fall to either the mother or father, or to them both equally.

6. What advice would you give to someone about to step into a leadership role?

Truly care—about your team, your organization, your community, and yourself. Take the time to invest in each of these areas for a well balanced approach to leadership.

7. Is it fair to say that you took an unusual path to becoming a CPA?

Yes. Most professionals enter the CA/CPA program directly from university. I took a more roundabout route in order to effectively balance work, education, and family. While working, I took several university courses via correspondence. This combination of work experience and education gained me entrance into the CA program in 2009. This allowed me the opportunity to gain practical experience, earn a designation, and spend time raising my three children.

8. What attracted you to accountancy?

Accounting came very naturally to me; it was both logical, in terms of calculations, and interesting, in terms of policy choices.

For the full interview, go online to nelson.com/student

Photo and interview courtesy of Jessica Clahane

13-1 LEADERS VERSUS MANAGERS

If you've ever been in charge, or even just thought about it, chances are you've considered questions like these: "Do I have what it takes to lead? What are the most important things leaders do? How can I transform a poorly performing department, division, or company? Do I need to adjust my leadership depending on the situation and the employee? Why doesn't my leadership inspire people?" If you feel overwhelmed at the prospect of being a leader, you're not alone—millions of leaders in organizations around the world struggle with fundamental leadership issues on a daily basis.

How does an ensemble of 100 or more musicians, all playing different parts at different times on different instruments, manage to produce something as beautiful as Beethoven's Fifth Symphony? (If Gustav Mahler's Eighth Symphony—nicknamed "Symphony of a Thousand"—is on the program, a lot more people might be involved!) The conductor, like a CEO, is responsible for managing all of this complexity and ensuring great output. But conducting is about much more than keeping the beat with a baton. According to Dr. Ramona Wis, author of *The Conductor as Leader*, conductors must also build connections between people, inspire them with vision, command their trust, and persuade them to participate in the ensemble at their very best.[1]

Whether the end result is a stirring musical performance, the innovation of new products, feeding more people, or increased profits, **leadership** is the process of influencing others to achieve group or organizational goals. The knowledge and skills you'll learn in this chapter won't make the task of leadership less daunting, but they will help you navigate it.

Henri Mintzberg of Montreal's McGill University spent a lifetime trying to understand what a manager does. His seminal work, *The Manager's Job: Folk Lore and Fact*, helped define the difference between management and leadership. Managers make an endless series of decisions about doing things right. Leaders make decisions about doing the right thing.[2] In other words, leaders begin with the question, "What should we be doing?", while managers start with "How can

we do better what we're already doing?" Leaders focus on vision, mission, goals, and objectives, while managers focus on productivity and efficiency. Managers see themselves as preservers of the status quo, while leaders see themselves as promoters of change and challengers of the status quo. Leaders, consequently, encourage creativity and risk taking. Ashley Good, of Canadian Engineers Without Borders, was awarded the prestigious HBR/McKinsey Innovating Innovation Challenge with her "Fail Forward" message, referring to a "refreshing and bold practice that takes the tired mantra of 'embracing failure' and turns it into a way of life for an organization."[3] We can win by producing new products or designs that are a total embarrassment, says Good, and we need to "include phrases like 'the courage to fail' and 'learning means admitting failure'" in order to ultimately be successful.

Another difference is that managers take a relatively short-term perspective, while leaders take a long-term one. Also, managers are more concerned about *means* (that is, about *how* to get things done) while leaders are more concerned about *ends* (that is, about *what* gets done). Managers concern themselves with control and with limiting the choices of others, while leaders concern themselves with expanding people's choices and options.[4] Finally, managers solve problems so that others can do their work, while leaders inspire and motivate others to find their own solutions.

Although leaders are different from managers, organizations need both. Managers are vital to getting out the day-to-day work; leaders are vital to inspiring employees and setting the organization's long-term direction. For any organization, the key issue is whether it is properly led and properly managed. As Mintzberg said in summarizing the difference between leaders and managers, organizations are underled and overmanaged. They do not pay enough attention to doing the right thing, and they pay too much attention to doing things right.[5]

13-2 WHO LEADERS ARE AND WHAT LEADERS DO

With Suncor's 2016 purchase of Canadian Oil Sands (COS), it now owns 49 percent of Syncrude. Steve Williams, president and chief executive of Suncor, stated that, "From the outset, we've spoken about the

---

Leadership the process of influencing others to achieve group or organizational goals.

excellent value this offer creates for both Canadian Oil Sands and Suncor." Suncor spokesperson Sneh Seetal said new leaders are required for COS to be more engaged with the operational aspects of Syncrude and to work more closely with Exxon/Imperial Oil (which own 25 percent of the facility) to identify and implement operational improvements. These are heady tasks for leaders in Canada.[6]

So, what makes a good leader? Does leadership success depend on who leaders are (i.e., whether they are introverts or extroverts), or on what leaders do and how they behave? Let's learn more about who leaders are by investigating **13-2a leadership traits** *and* **13-2b leadership behaviours.**

Art Babych/Shutterstock.com

13-2a Leadership Traits

Trait theory is one way to describe who leaders are. **Trait theory** posits that effective leaders possess similar characteristics. **Traits** are relatively stable characteristics, such as abilities, psychological motives, and patterns of behaviour. For example, according to trait theory, leaders are taller and more confident and have greater physical stamina (i.e., higher energy) than nonleaders. It is noteworthy that 14.5 percent of men are 183 centimetres tall or more, yet 58 percent of *Fortune* 500 CEOs are taller than that.[7] Trait theory is also known as the "great person" theory because early versions of it stated that leaders are born, not made. In other words, you either have the right stuff to be a leader or you don't. And if you don't, there is no way to get it.

For some time, it was thought that trait theory was faulty and that there are no consistent trait differences between leaders and nonleaders or between effective and ineffective leaders. However, more recent evidence suggests that "successful leaders are not like other people"—that they are indeed different from the rest of us.[8] Specifically, leaders are different from nonleaders in the following traits: drive, the desire to lead, honesty/integrity, self-confidence, emotional stability, cognitive ability, and knowledge of the business.[9]

Drive refers to a high level of effort and is characterized by achievement, motivation, initiative, energy, and tenacity. In terms of achievement and ambition, leaders always try to make improvements or achieve success in what they're doing. They have a strong desire to promote change or solve problems. Leaders typically have more energy—they have to, given the long hours they put in and followers' expectations that they be positive and

> Organizations are underled and overmanaged.

upbeat. Leaders are also more tenacious than nonleaders and are better at overcoming obstacles and problems that would deter most of us.

Successful leaders also have a stronger *desire to lead*. They want to be in charge, and they think about ways to influence or convince others about what should or shouldn't be done. *Honesty/integrity* is also important to leaders. *Honesty*, being truthful with others, is a cornerstone of leadership. Leaders won't be trusted if they are dishonest, and when they are honest, subordinates are willing to overlook other flaws. *Integrity* is the extent to which leaders do what they say they will do. Leaders may be honest and have good intentions, but they won't be trusted if they don't consistently deliver on what they promise.

Self-confidence, believing in one's abilities, also distinguishes leaders from nonleaders. Self-confident leaders are more decisive and assertive and are more likely to gain others' confidence. Moreover, self-confident leaders will admit mistakes because they view them as learning opportunities rather than as refutations of their capacity to lead. This means that leaders are also *emotionally stable*. Even when things go wrong, they remain even-tempered and consistent in their outlook and in the way they treat

Trait theory a leadership theory that holds that effective leaders possess a similar set of traits or characteristics.

Traits relatively stable characteristics, such as abilities, psychological motives, or consistent patterns of behaviour.

others. Leaders who can't control their emotions, who anger quickly or attack and blame others for mistakes, are unlikely to be trusted. Leaders also have *emotional intelligence*—the ability of people to recognize their own and other people's emotions, to discriminate between different feelings, and to use emotional information to guide thinking and behaviour—as demonstrated by Justin Trudeau.[10] Although comedian John Oliver mocks it, saying, "Emotional intelligence is the kind of made-up quality you might find on a report card from a Montessori school," it seems obvious that John Oliver never took MGMT![11]

Leaders are also smart. They typically have strong *cognitive abilities*. This doesn't mean they are geniuses, but it does mean they have the capacity to analyze large amounts of seemingly unrelated, complex information and see patterns, opportunities, or threats where others might not. Finally, leaders know their stuff, which means they have superior technical knowledge about the businesses they run. Leaders who have a good *knowledge of the business* understand the key technological issues and challenges facing their companies. Studies indicate that more often than not, effective leaders have extensive experience in their industry.

Don't Judge a Female Leader Differently

When Facebook chief operating officer and *Lean In* author Sheryl Sandberg spoke at the 2016 World Economic Forum in Davos, Switzerland, one of Sandberg's big arguments was that gender diversity is not just a good thing to do, "it's also a smart thing to do to help your company." Companies that want to boost their bottom line should promote more women to the executive suite, a recent global survey concludes. Profitable firms that went from having no female leaders to 30 percent representation saw a 15 percent increase in their financial performance, the study by the Peterson Institute for International Economics found.

When Sheryl Sandberg spoke with Prime Minister Trudeau, she noted that women will outnumber men on what could turn out to be the most influential group of people around Trudeau and Minister of Finance Bill Morneau in 2016. The Federal Government's Advisory Council, a team that will help draw up a plan designed to get the economy out of a rut, includes a lineup of business and academic leaders that consists of eight women and six men on the Council.

Women are also filling the ranks of entrepreneurs in Canada. A recent TD Economics report found Newfoundland and Labrador led growth of self-employed women at 48 percent, followed by Saskatchewan (9 percent), Manitoba (6 percent), Prince Edward Island (6 percent), and Alberta

Jason Alden/Bloomberg via Getty Images

(5 percent). "More women are starting new enterprises, or taking over existing businesses," said Richard Truscott, Alberta director for the Canadian Federation of Independent Business.

Jeanette Sutherland, manager of workforce and productivity for Calgary Economic Development, said one factor in the rise of female entrepreneurs is the result of well established ecommerce and social media. "We also have a generation of Millennials that are very well educated and enterprising in nature. Many women from this generation are very prepared to break the mould and directly go after what they want," she said.

Sources: J. McGregor, "Sheryl Sandberg's Latest Thoughts on Women, Work and Equality," *Washington Post*, January 22, 2016, https://www.washingtonpost.com/news/on-leadership/wp/2016/01/22/sheryl-sandbergs-latest-thoughts-on-women-work-and-equality/; S. N. Talamas, K. I. Mavor, and D. I. Perrett, "Blinded by Beauty: Attractiveness Bias and Accurate Perceptions of Academic Performance," *PloS one (11)*2 (2016): e0148284; Statistics Canada, 2016, http://www.statcan.gc.ca/tables-tableaux/sum-som/l01/cst01/labor64-eng.htm; M. Toneguzzi, "More Women Have Become Self-Employed Since the Recession, But Are Still Underrepresented Among Entrepreneurs," *Calgary Herald*, January 18, 2015, http://calgaryherald.com/business/growing-number-of-women-entrepreneurs?__lsa=d2f5-db9e; D. Flavelle, "Women Executives Boost Bottom Line: Survey," *Toronto Star*, February 9, 2016, http://www.thestar.com/business/2016/02/09/women-executives-boost-bottom-line-survey.html; A. Blatchford, "Women Dominate Liberals' Economic Advisory Council," *Toronto Star*, February 28, 2016, http://www.thestar.com/news/canada/2016/03/18/women-dominate-liberals-economic-advisory-council.html.

Mary Forrest, recipient of the Women's Executive Network Scotiabank Corporate Executives award, leads a combined US and Canadian operation of Munich Reinsurance that manages more than $14.9 billion in assets and $3.9 billion in capital. Forrest's leadership and experience in the insurance market garners her considerable respect among her peers. She was recently selected as chair of the board for the Canadian Life and Health Insurance Association (CLHIA). She sees obstacles as opportunities to drive new ways of thinking. That insight has served her well on a career path that has transformed her from an actuarial student in 1991 to president and chief executive officer. "We have worked hard to prove our ability and capacity to serve life insurers in a strict regulatory environment. I am proud of my teams' achievements and our leading position in the Canadian market," says Forrest. "The insurance and reinsurance industry has changed a great deal over the years and it continues to do so today. While some are intimidated by change, change excites me. I'm optimistic that it will lead to more opportunities in the future, in a playing field that is altogether different."[12]

13-2b Leadership Behaviours

Thus far, you've read about who leaders *are*. It's hard to imagine a truly successful leader who lacks all of these qualities. But traits alone are not enough to make a successful leader. Leaders who have all of these traits (or many of them) must then take actions that encourage people to achieve group or organizational goals.[13] So we will now examine what leaders *do*, meaning the behaviours they perform or the actions they take to influence others to achieve group or organizational goals.

Rob Quinn can spot future CEOs. Quinn is a Toronto-based partner at Odgers Berndtson, an executive search firm, and he has developed an inventory of the behaviours that leaders demonstrate—curiosity, vision, and ability to relate. "With a student, those skills are not going to be as well developed," concedes Quinn. "But that potential, if honed, is going to deliver results—no question about it."[14] Quinn is one of the founders of the 'CEO for a Day' program, with the objective being to match Canada's "best and brightest" students, as he calls them, with leading Canadian CEOs, ranging from GE Canada's Elyse Allan to lululemon's Laurent Potdevin.[15] The concept behind his program is to get senior industry personnel more in touch with the new generation of future business leaders, and for today's students to get a hands-on feel for what it is that leaders really do.

Researchers at the University of Michigan, Ohio State University, and the University of Texas examined the specific behaviours that leaders use to improve the satisfaction and performance of their subordinates. Hundreds of studies were conducted and hundreds of leader behaviours were examined. At all three universities, two basic leader behaviours emerged as central to successful leadership: *initiating structure* (called *job-centred leadership* at the University of Michigan, and *concern for production* at the University of Texas), and *consideration*, or considerate leader behaviour (called *employee-centred leadership* at the University of Michigan and *concern for people* at the University of Texas).[16] These two leader behaviours form the basis for many of the leadership theories discussed in this chapter.

Initiating structure refers to the degree to which a leader structures the roles of followers by setting goals, giving directions, setting deadlines, and assigning tasks. A leader's ability to initiate structure primarily affects subordinates' job performance. The Newfoundland and Labrador Association of Public and Private Employees (NAPE) is the largest union in the province and is the recognized bargaining agent for over 25,000 public and private sector employees. NAPE president Jerry Earle was talking tough as the union began its latest convention in St. John's. "Let me be crystal clear to government and those aspiring to form government. If privatization of public services are in your plans, your best bet is to reconsider because we will be there to fight you every step of the way," said Earle, to a standing ovation. Earle told delegates that contracts expire in the next six months for 12,000 public servants, including student assistants, air services and lab and X-ray workers. "We are going into a very difficult round of bargaining," said Earle. "Our message for government, whomever that might be, and for employers that might be involved in upcoming rounds of . . . negotiations [is that] we will not come to the table with our benefits and rights that we have fought for decades to retain, up for the taking. That is not on," he stated as he hinted at a possible strike. This kind of leadership is very task oriented and high in initiating structure.[17]

> **Initiating structure** the degree to which a leader structures the roles of followers by setting goals, giving directions, setting deadlines, and assigning tasks.

GlobalStock/iStockphoto

Consideration refers to the extent to which a leader is friendly, approachable, and supportive and shows concern for employees. Consideration primarily affects subordinates' job satisfaction. Specific consideration behaviours include listening to employees' problems and concerns, consulting with employees before making decisions, and treating employees as equals.[18] Canadian Tire CEO Stephen Wetmore knows about concern for people and relations within a company. The company's relationship with dealers (store owners) has not always been smooth when it comes to implementing change.

Canadian Tire long had a reputation for moving at a snail's pace, and both head office and its store owners realized that had to change. It took two years of negotiations to hammer out an agreement, which will last until 2020, but both sides say that because of their new relationship Canadian Tire is positioned for success. According to Wetmore, "We've removed a lot of the procedural red tape that held up the speed of progress in an effort to make the relationship more streamlined

and agile." In the past, when a product line was under review, it would take more than a year to make a decision after evaluating cost structure, quality, and capability. "You'd have an argument over here, disagreements over there and end up losing sight of the customer," says Wetmore, who adds that the company has now shaved months off the process and is working to get it down even more. But, he adds, the biggest benefit of the new consideration for people deal is that it has "rebuil[t] the trust between the organization and the dealers, which had eroded over the years."[19]

Researchers at universities in Michigan, Texas, and Ohio generally agreed that initiating structure and consideration were basic leader behaviours, but they departed from one another with regard to how those two behaviours were related and which was more important. The Michigan studies indicated that the two were mutually exclusive behaviours on opposite ends of a continuum. In other words, leaders who wanted to be more considerate would have to do less initiating of structure (and vice versa). The Michigan studies also found that only considerate leader behaviours (i.e., employee-centred behaviours) were associated with successful leadership. By contrast, the researchers at Ohio and Texas found that initiating structure and showing consideration were independent behaviours—in other words, leaders could show consideration and initiate structure at the same time. Additional evidence confirms this finding.[20] The same researchers concluded that the most effective leaders excelled at both initiating structure and considerate leader behaviours.

This "high–high" approach can be seen in the upper right corner of the Blake/Mouton leadership grid, as shown in Exhibit 13.1. Blake and Mouton used two leadership behaviours—concern for people (i.e., consideration) and concern for production (i.e., initiating structure)—to categorize five different leadership styles. In the exhibit, both behaviours are rated on a nine-point scale, with 1 representing "low" and 9 representing "high." Blake and Mouton suggest that a "high–high" or 9,9 leadership style is the best. They call this style *team management* because leaders who use it display a high concern for people (9) as well as a high concern for production (9).

By contrast, leaders use a 9,1 *authority–compliance* leadership style when they have a high concern for production and a low concern for people. A 1,9 *country club* style arises when leaders care about having a friendly and enjoyable work environment and don't really pay much attention to production or performance. Worst of all,

Exhibit 13.1
Blake/Mouton Leadership Grid

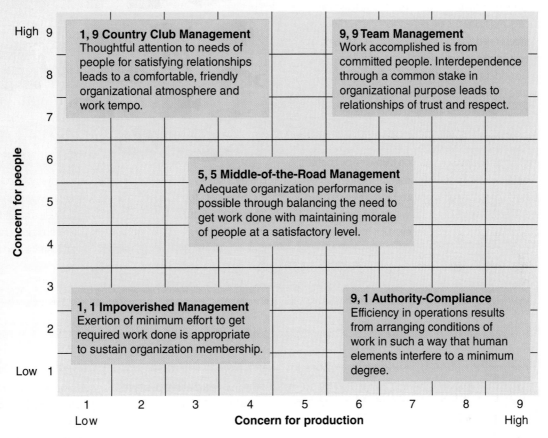

1, 9 Country Club Management
Thoughtful attention to needs of people for satisfying relationships leads to a comfortable, friendly organizational atmosphere and work tempo.

9, 9 Team Management
Work accomplished is from committed people. Interdependence through a common stake in organizational purpose leads to relationships of trust and respect.

5, 5 Middle-of-the-Road Management
Adequate organization performance is possible through balancing the need to get work done with maintaining morale of people at a satisfactory level.

1, 1 Impoverished Management
Exertion of minimum effort to get required work done is appropriate to sustain organization membership.

9, 1 Authority-Compliance
Efficiency in operations results from arranging conditions of work in such a way that human elements interfere to a minimum degree.

Concern for people — High 9 / Low 1
Concern for production — Low 1 / High 9

Source: R. R. Blake and A. A. McCanse, "The Leadership Grid," *Leadership Dilemmas—Grid Solutions* (Houston: Gulf Publishing Company), 21. Copyright © 1991, by Scientific Methods, Inc. Reproduced by permission of Grid International, Inc.

according to the grid, is the 1,1 *impoverished* leader, who shows little concern for people or production and who does the bare minimum necessary to keep his or her job. Finally, the 5,5 *middle-of-the-road* style develops when leaders show a moderate amount of concern for both people and production.

At just 42, Glen Hansman is a very young but seasoned CEO. As the president of British Columbia's 41,000 strong teachers' union, Hansman is used to the pressure that can be found in heated union contract talks. Hansman took over as president from Jim Iker, who stepped down after three terms as president. Iker calls Hansman a team leader who is very caring and articulate. "He's a very hard worker, he's friendly, and he's approachable. He likes to build consensus, and he is passionate about social justice issues," Iker said.[21]

The current president of the B.C. Federation of Labour, Irene Lanzinger, thinks he is a real team leader: "He's very calm, he's very reasonable and he is very thoughtful," Lanzinger said.[22] These are important team management 9,9 factors for a leader to possess.

Is the team management style, with its high concern for production and a high concern for people, really the best leadership style? Logically, it would seem so. Why wouldn't you want to show high concern for both people and production? Yet five decades of research indicates that there isn't one best leadership style. Rather, the best leadership style depends on the situation. In other words, there is no single combination of leadership behaviours that works well across all situations and employees.

Followers as Leaders

As more organizations become flatter, or adopt less hierarchical organizational structures, it is becoming increasingly clear that leaders and followers are dependent each other. One thing good leaders need is good followers. Barbara Kellerman of Harvard University outlines five different types of followers and urges leaders to understand what kinds of followers they have. The five types are (1) isolates, (2) bystanders, (3) participants, (4) activists, and (5) diehards. *Isolates* and *bystanders* are not invested. They just do their jobs and tend to impede change. They can be useful for leaders who want to maintain the status quo but are otherwise dead weight. Good followers, by contrast, support a leader they've invested in. Consequently, they are good assets. *Participants* are self-motivated and driven to make a difference, and *activists* are eager and will go the extra mile, while *diehards* will support their leader even if it means going down with the ship. But leaders beware: these types of followers

f9photos/Shutterstock.com

can be a liability if you have not inspired their loyalty. So followers are leaders, too. Terri Williams states that followers demand leadership and trustworthiness and are fickle. Kellerman adds that "while they may lack authority, at least in comparison with their superiors, followers do not lack power and influence."

Sources: R. Buch, G. Thompson, and B. Kuvaas, "Transactional Leader–Member Exchange Relationships and Followers' Work Performance: The Moderating Role of Leaders' Political Skill," *Journal of Leadership and Organizational Studies*, 2016; T. Williams, "What Every Leader Needs to Know About Followers," AZCentral.Com/Business & Entrepreneurship, 2013, http://yourbusiness.azcentral.com/leader-needsfollowers-17672.html; B. Kellerman, "What Every Leader Needs to Know About Followers," *Harvard Business Review* (December 2007): 84–91.

13-3 PUTTING LEADERS IN THE RIGHT SITUATION: FIEDLER'S CONTINGENCY THEORY

After leader traits and behaviours, the situational approach to leadership is the third major method used in the study of leadership. We'll review three major situational approaches to leadership: *Fiedler's contingency theory, House's path–goal theory,* and *Vroom and Yetton's normative decision model.* All assume that the effectiveness of any **leadership style** depends on the situation.[23] A study of 130 restaurants in a pizza franchise examined the interaction between how extroverted store managers were and how involved employees were in trying "to bring about improved procedures [in the store]." Profits were 16 percent above average in stores with extroverted managers and less involved employees. In those instances, the strengths of the more outgoing boss fit well with the less involved employees. By contrast, profits were 14 percent below average in stores with extroverted leaders and highly involved employees. Why? Because the extroverted leaders were less comfortable with employees who wanted a say in making improvements. Again, leadership success depends on the situation.[24]

According to situational leadership theories, there is no one best leadership style. But one of these situational theories differs from the other three in one significant way: Fiedler's contingency theory assumes that leadership styles are consistent and difficult to change, therefore, leaders must be placed in or matched to a situation that fits their leadership style. By contrast, the other three situational theories all assume that leaders are capable of adapting and adjusting their leadership styles to fit the demands of different situations. Fiedler's **contingency theory** states that, in order to maximize work group performance, leaders must be matched to

Leadership style the way a leader generally behaves toward followers.

Contingency theory a leadership theory that, in order to maximize work group performance, leaders must be matched to the situation that best fits their leadership style.

the right leadership situation.[25] The first basic assumption of Fiedler's theory is that leaders are effective when the work groups they lead perform well. So, instead of judging leaders' effectiveness by what the leaders do (i.e., initiating structure and consideration) or by who they are (i.e., trait theory), Fiedler assesses leaders in terms of the conduct and performance of the *people they are leading*. Second, Fiedler assumes that leaders are generally unable to change their style and that they are more effective when that style fits the situation. Third, he assumes that the success of a leader depends on the degree to which he or she is able to influence the behaviour of group members. Note that it is the *group* behaviour and not the *leader* behaviour we are talking about here. In other words, besides traits, behaviours, and a favourable situation, leaders need the group's "permission" to lead.

Let's learn more about Fiedler's contingency theory by examining **13-3a the least preferred coworker style, 13-3b situational favourableness,** *and* **13-3c how to match leadership styles to situations.**

13-3a Leadership Style: Least Preferred Coworker

When you are applying for a job right out of business school, your prospective employer will ask you some questions about leadership. We are going to be discussing this on a rather technical footing, but if you can master this, you will be able to tell your employer that you know and understand leadership. You will probably answer that leadership "depends on the situation." How will you explain that? Read on.

When Fiedler refers to *leadership style,* he means the way that leaders generally behave toward their followers. Do the leaders yell and scream and blame others when things go wrong? Or do they correct mistakes by listening and then quietly but directly making their point? Do they let others make their own decisions and hold them accountable for the results? Or do they micromanage, insisting that all decisions be approved first by them? Fiedler also assumes that leadership styles are tied to leaders' underlying needs and personalities. Since personality and needs are relatively stable, he assumes that leaders are generally incapable of changing their leadership styles.

How Would You Rank Your Least Preferred Coworker? He or She Is:

	8	7	6	5	4	3	2	1	
Pleasant	⑧	⑦	⑥	⑤	④	③	②	①	Unpleasant
Friendly	⑧	⑦	⑥	⑤	④	③	②	①	Unfriendly
Supportive	⑧	⑦	⑥	⑤	④	③	②	①	Hostile
Boring	①	②	③	④	⑤	⑥	⑦	⑧	Interesting
Gloomy	①	②	③	④	⑤	⑥	⑦	⑧	Cheerful
Insincere	①	②	③	④	⑤	⑥	⑦	⑧	Sincere

Source: F. E. Fiedler and M. M. Chemers, *Improving Leadership Effectiveness: The Leader Match Concept,* 2nd ed. (New York: John Wiley & Sons, 1984). Reproduced by permission of the authors.

In other words, the way that leaders treat people now is probably the way they've always treated others.

Fiedler uses a questionnaire (which uses arcane terminology—but stay with us here!) called the **Least Preferred Coworker (LPC) Scale** to measure leadership style. He instructs people who are completing that scale to consider all of the people with whom they have ever worked and then to choose the one person with whom they have worked *least* well. Fiedler explains: "This does not have to be the person you liked least well, but

Least Preferred Coworker (LPC) Scale consider (and scale or grade) all of the people with whom they have ever worked and then to choose the one person with whom they have worked least well.

should be the one person with whom you have the most trouble getting the job done."[26] How you describe this person is a clue to your own preferred leadership style—don't we all want to work with people we get along with?

Would you describe your LPC as pleasant, friendly, supportive, interesting, cheerful, and sincere? Or would you describe that person as unpleasant, unfriendly, hostile, boring, gloomy, and insincere? People who describe their LPC in a positive way (as scoring 64 and above on the full inventory of 18 oppositional pairs) have a *relationship-oriented* leadership style. After all, if they can still be positive about their least preferred coworker, they must be people-oriented. By contrast, people who describe their LPC in a negative way (as scoring 57 or below) have a *task-oriented* leadership style. Given a choice, they'll focus first on getting the job done and second on making sure everyone gets along. Finally, those with moderate scores (from 58 to 63) have a more flexible leadership style and can be somewhat relationship-oriented or somewhat task-oriented. We can see certain commonalities here with Exhibit 13.1.

13-3b Situational Favourableness

Fiedler assumes that leaders will be more effective when their leadership styles are matched to the proper situation. Specifically, he defines **situational favourableness** as the degree to which a particular situation either allows or denies a leader the chance to influence the behaviour of group members.[27] In highly favourable situations, leaders find that their actions influence followers; in highly unfavourable situations, they have little or no success influencing the people they are trying to lead.

Three situational factors determine the favourability of a situation: *leader–member relations, task structure,* and *position power.* The most important situational factor is **leader–member relations**, which refers to how well followers respect, trust, and like their leaders. When leader–member relations are good, followers trust the leader and there is a friendly work atmosphere. **Task structure** is the degree to which the requirements of a subordinate's tasks are clearly specified. With highly structured tasks, employees have clear job responsibilities, goals, and procedures. **Position power** is the degree to which leaders are able to hire, fire, reward, and punish workers. The more influence leaders have over hiring, firing, rewards, and punishments, the greater their power.

> **Situational favourableness** the degree to which a particular situation either permits or denies a leader the chance to influence the behaviour of group members.
>
> **Leader–member relations** the degree to which followers respect, trust, and like their leaders.
>
> **Task structure** the degree to which the requirements of a subordinate's tasks are clearly specified.
>
> **Position power** the degree to which leaders are able to hire, fire, reward, and punish workers.

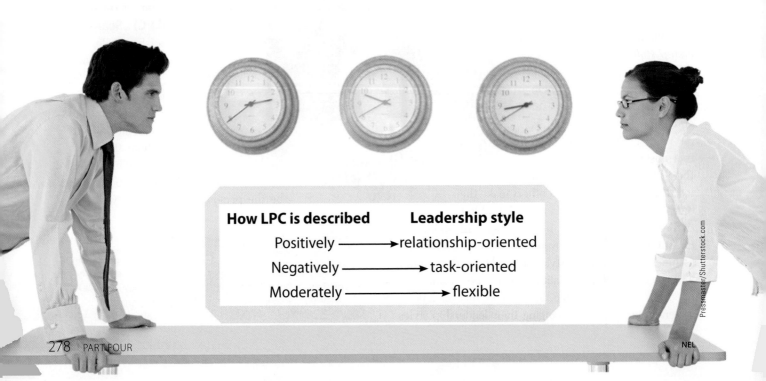

How LPC is described	Leadership style
Positively ⟶	relationship-oriented
Negatively ⟶	task-oriented
Moderately ⟶	flexible

Pressmaster/Shutterstock.com

Exhibit 13.2
Situational Favourableness

Leader–member relations	Good	Good	Good	Good	Poor	Poor	Poor	Poor
Task structure	High	High	Low	Low	High	High	Low	Low
Position power	Strong	Weak	Strong	Weak	Strong	Weak	Strong	Weak
Situation	I	II	III	IV	V	VI	VII	VIII
		Favourable			Moderately favourable			Unfavourable

Exhibit 13.2 shows how leader–member relations, task structure, and position power can be combined into eight situations that differ in their favourability to leaders. In general, Situation I, on the left side of Exhibit 13.2, is the most favourable situation for a leader. The followers like and trust their leader and know what to do because their tasks are highly structured. Also, the leader has the formal power to influence workers through hiring, firing, rewarding, and punishing them. Thus, in Situation I, it's relatively easy for the leader to influence his or her followers. By contrast, Situation VIII, on the right side of Exhibit 13.2, is the least favourable situation for a leader. The followers neither like nor trust their leader. Also, they are not sure what they're supposed to be doing because their tasks or jobs are highly unstructured. Finally, this leader finds it difficult to influence followers without the ability to hire, fire, reward, or punish them.

13-3c Matching Leadership Styles to Situations

After studying thousands of leaders and followers in hundreds of different situations, Fiedler found that the performances of relationship- and task-oriented leaders followed the pattern displayed in Exhibit 13.3.

In moderately favourable situations, relationship-oriented leaders—those with high LPC scores—were better leaders (i.e., their groups performed more effectively). In these situations, the leader is liked somewhat, tasks are somewhat structured, and the leader has some position power. In such a situation, a relationship-oriented leader improves the most important of the three situational factors, which is leader–member relations. As a consequence, morale and performance improve.

Exhibit 13.3
Matching Leadership Styles to Situations

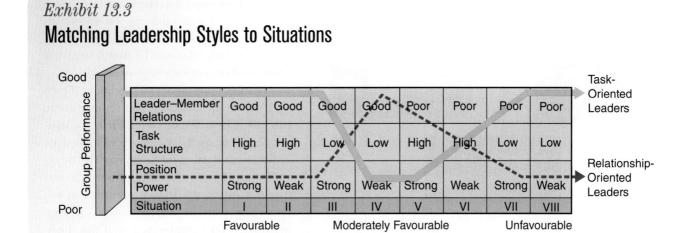

By contrast, as shown in Exhibit 13.3, task-oriented leaders—those with low LPC scores—are better leaders in highly favourable and highly unfavourable situations. Task-oriented leaders do well in favourable situations where leaders are liked, tasks are structured, and the leader has the power to hire, fire, reward, and punish. In these situations, task-oriented leaders are in effect stepping on the accelerator of a well-tuned car. Their focus on performance sets the goal for the group, which then charges forward to meet it. But task-oriented leaders also do well in unfavourable situations, those in which leaders are disliked, tasks are unstructured, and the leader doesn't have the power to hire, fire, reward, and punish. In these situations, the task-oriented leader sets goals that focus attention on performance and that clarify what needs to be done, thus overcoming low task structure. This is enough to jump-start performance even if workers don't like or trust the leader.

Finally, although not shown in Exhibit 13.3, people with moderate LPC scores (who can be somewhat relationship-oriented or somewhat task-oriented) tend to do fairly well in all situations because they can adapt (or

change) their behaviour to suit the situation. Typically, though, they don't perform quite as well as relationship-oriented or task-oriented leaders whose leadership styles are well matched to the situation.

Recall, though, that Fiedler assumes leaders to be incapable of changing their leadership style. Accordingly, the key to applying Fiedler's contingency theory in the workplace is to accurately assess leaders and then match them to what they need to do to change the situation at hand. Of course, the theory won't work as well if leaders are attempting to change situational factors to fit their perceived leadership style rather than their real leadership style.[28] You will most likely be asked about your own personal leadership style in job interviews.

Path–goal theory a leadership theory that leaders can increase subordinate satisfaction and performance by clarifying and clearing the paths to goals and by increasing the number and kinds of rewards available for goal attainment.

13-4 ADAPTING LEADER BEHAVIOUR: PATH–GOAL THEORY

In contrast to Fiedler's contingency theory, path–goal theory assumes that leaders can adapt their leadership styles to the situation at hand. Exhibit 13.4 illustrates this process. As its name suggests, **path–goal theory** (as developed by the University of Toronto's John House) also posits that leaders can increase their followers' satisfaction and performance by clarifying and clearing the paths to goals and by increasing the number and kinds of rewards available for goal attainment. Put another way, leaders need to clarify how followers can achieve organizational goals, address the problems that prevent followers from achieving those goals, and then find more and varied rewards and satisfiers to motivate followers to achieve those goals.[29] Note that rewards are not necessarily monetary—indeed, they can be many different things (here, it would be useful to review Chapter 12 on motivation).

Leaders must meet two conditions if path clarification, path clearing, and rewards are to increase followers' motivation. First, the leader's behaviour must be a source of immediate or future satisfaction for followers. The things you do as a leader must please your followers today or lead to activities or rewards that will satisfy them in the future. Second, leaders' behaviours must complement and not duplicate the characteristics of their followers' work

Exhibit 13.4
Path–Goal Theory

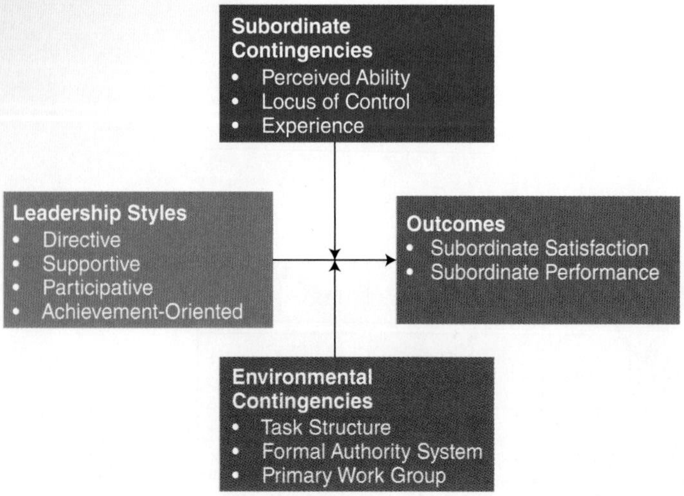

Source: R. J. House and T. R. Mitchell, "Path–Goal Theory of Leadership," *Journal of Contemporary Business* 3 (1974) 81–07.

environments. Thus, leaders' behaviours must offer something unique and valuable to followers beyond what they're already experiencing as they do their jobs and beyond what they can already do for themselves.

Let's learn more about path–goal theory by examining 13-4a the four kinds of leadership styles that leaders use, 13-4b the subordinate and environmental contingency factors that determine when different leadership styles are effective, and 13-4c the outcomes of path–goal theory in improving employee satisfaction and performance.

13-4a Leadership Styles

As illustrated in Exhibit 13.4, the four leadership styles in path–goal theory are directive, supportive, participative, and achievement-oriented.[30] **Directive leadership** involves letting employees know precisely what is expected of them, giving them specific guidelines for performing their tasks, scheduling work, setting standards of performance, and making sure that people follow rules.

Supportive leadership involves being approachable, showing concern for employees and their welfare, treating them as equals, and creating a friendly climate. Supportive leadership is very similar to Blake and Mouton's considerate leader behaviour (see Exhibit 13.1). Supportive leadership often results in employee satisfaction with the job and with leaders. This leadership style may also result in improved performance when it increases employee confidence, lowers employee job stress, or improves relations and trust between employees and leaders.[31]

Participative leadership involves asking employees for suggestions and input before making decisions. Participation in decision making should help followers understand which goals are most important and clarify the paths to accomplishing them. When people participate in decisions, they become more committed to making them work: "Those who plan the battle don't battle the plan."

Achievement-oriented leadership entails setting challenging goals, having high expectations of employees, and displaying confidence that employees will assume responsibility and put forth extraordinary effort.

Rachel Notley displays an achievement-oriented leadership style. Against all the odds, she turned Alberta's small four-person MLA NDP opposition party into a giant killer, defeating the Tory dynasty that had governed the province for almost 44 years. Since becoming the premier of Alberta, Notley has unleashed a whirlwind of achievements in the province, including "election

MGMT TIP

How to Apply Path–Goal Theory

1. Clarify paths to goals.
2. Clear paths to goals by solving problems and removing roadblocks.
3. Increase the number and kinds of rewards/satisfaction available for goal attainment.
4. Do things that satisfy followers today or that will lead to future rewards or satisfaction.
5. Offer followers something unique and valuable beyond what they're experiencing or can already do for themselves.

Source: R. J. House and T. R. Mitchell, "Path–Goal Theory of Leadership," *Journal of Contemporary Business* 3 (1974): 81–97.

promises to enact far-reaching and, in many cases, controversial revisions to government policy including a review of energy royalties, a new climate change strategy, boosting the minimum wage, hiking corporate taxes, banning political donations from corporations and unions, and introducing a provincial budget that runs a $6 billion deficit this year alone while borrowing billions to build roads, schools and hospitals."[32]

Whatever leadership style you adopt, the ability to persuade and influence others is key to your success. As business becomes more global, and as the way people work changes, organizational structures are becoming flatter, or less hierarchical. This means that leaders must cross traditional boundaries and work with peers and subordinates alike in other divisions or even in other

Directive leadership a leadership style in which the leader lets employees know precisely what is expected of them, gives them specific guidelines for performing tasks, schedules work, sets standards of performance, and makes sure that people follow standard rules and regulations.

Supportive leadership a leadership style in which the leader is friendly and approachable, shows concern for employees and their welfare, treats them as equals, and creates a friendly climate.

Participative leadership a leadership style in which the leader consults employees for their suggestions and input before making decisions.

Achievement-oriented leadership a leadership style in which the leader sets challenging goals, has high expectations of employees, and displays confidence that employees will assume responsibility and put forth extraordinary effort.

THE CANADIAN PRESS/Jason Franson

companies. Motivation is thus becoming far more important than direction. Whether you're a directive, supportive, participative, or achievement-oriented leader, your ability to bring others on board with your vision and plan is vital to good leadership.[33]

13-4b Subordinate and Environmental Contingencies

As shown in Exhibit 13.4, path–goal theory specifies that a leader's behaviours should be fitted to subordinates' characteristics. The theory identifies three kinds of contingencies relating to subordinates: perceived ability, locus of control, and experience. *Perceived ability* is simply how much ability subordinates believe they have for doing their jobs well. Subordinates who perceive they have a great deal of ability will be dissatisfied with directive leader behaviours.

Locus of control is a personality measure that indicates the extent to which people believe they have control over what happens to them in life. *Internals* believe that what happens to them, good or bad, is largely a result of their choices and actions. *Externals*, on the other hand, believe that what happens to them is caused by external forces beyond their control. Accordingly, externals are much more comfortable with a directive leadership style, while internals greatly prefer a participative leadership style because they like to have a say in what goes on at work.

Experienced employees are likely to react in a similar way. Since they already know how to do their jobs (or perceive that they do), they don't need or want close supervision. By contrast, subordinates with little experience or little perceived ability will welcome directive leadership.

Path–goal theory specifies that leader behaviours should complement rather than duplicate the characteristics of followers' work environments. In other words, a leader should use a leadership style that best responds to the characteristics of the environment as well as the characteristics of the people involved. There are three kinds of environmental contingencies: task structure, the formal authority system, and the primary work group. As in Fiedler's contingency theory, *task structure* refers to the degree to which the requirements of a subordinate's tasks are clearly specified. When task structure is low and tasks are unclear, directive leadership should be used because it complements the work environment. When task structure is high and tasks are clear, however, directive leadership is not needed because it duplicates what task structure provides. Alternatively, when tasks are stressful, frustrating, or dissatisfying, leaders should respond with supportive leadership.

The *formal authority system* is an organization's set of procedures, rules, and policies. When the formal authority system is unclear, directive leadership complements the situation by reducing uncertainty and increasing clarity. But when the formal authority system is clear, directive leadership is redundant and should not be used.

Primary work group refers to the amount of work-oriented participation or emotional support that is provided by an employee's immediate work group. Participative leadership should be used when tasks are complex and there is little existing work-oriented participation in the primary work group. When tasks are stressful, frustrating, or repetitive, supportive leadership is called for.

Finally, since keeping track of all of these subordinate and environmental contingencies can get a bit confusing, Exhibit 13.5 provides a summary of when directive, supportive, participative, and achievement-oriented leadership styles should be used. Above all, using path–goal theory means that a leader must be attuned and responsive to the sometimes changing complexities of his or her environment.

13-4c Outcomes

Does following path–goal theory improve subordinates' satisfaction and performance? Research evidence suggests that it does.[34] In particular, people who work for supportive leaders are much more satisfied with their jobs and their bosses. Likewise, people who work for directive leaders are more satisfied with their jobs and bosses (but not quite as much as when their bosses are supportive) and perform their jobs better, too. Does adapting one's leadership style to subordinate and

Exhibit 13.5

Path–Goal Theory: When to Use Directive, Supportive, Participative, or Achievement-Oriented Leadership

Directive Leadership	Supportive Leadership	Participative Leadership	Achievement-Oriented Leadership
Unstructured tasks	Structured, simple, repetitive tasks; stressful, frustrating tasks	Complex tasks	Unchallenging tasks
Workers with external locus of control	Workers lack confidence	Workers with internal locus of control	Workers with internal locus of control
Unclear formal authority system	Clear formal authority system	Workers not satisfied with rewards	
Inexperienced workers		Experienced workers	
Workers with low perceived ability		Workers with high perceived ability	Workers with high motivation

environmental characteristics improve subordinates' satisfaction and performance? At this point, because it is difficult to completely test this complex theory, it's too difficult to be 100 percent certain.[35] However, since the data clearly show that it makes sense for leaders to be both supportive *and* directive, it also makes sense that leaders could improve subordinates' satisfaction and performance by adding participative and achievement-oriented leadership styles to their capabilities as leaders.

13-5 ADAPTING LEADER BEHAVIOUR: NORMATIVE DECISION THEORY

Many people believe that making tough decisions is at the heart of leadership. Yet experienced leaders will tell you that deciding *how* to make decisions is just as important. Vroom's **normative decision theory** (also known as the Vroom–Yetton–Jago model) helps leaders decide how much employee participation (from none to letting employees make the entire decision) should be used when making decisions.[36]

Let's learn more about normative decision theory by investigating 13-5a decision styles and 13-5b decision quality and acceptance.

13-5a Decision Styles

Unlike nearly all of the other leadership theories discussed in this chapter, which have specified *leadership* styles, the normative decision theory specifies five different *decision* styles, or ways of making decisions. (Refer back to Chapter 4 for a more complete review of decision making in organizations.) As shown in Exhibit 13.6, those styles vary from *autocratic* (AI or AII) on the left, in which leaders make the decisions by themselves, to *consultative* (CI or CII), in which leaders share problems with subordinates but still make the decisions themselves, to *group* (GII) on the right, in which leaders share the problems with subordinates and then have the group make the decisions. GE Aircraft Engines uses this approach when making decisions. According to *Fast Company* magazine, "At GE/Durham, every decision is either an 'A' decision, a 'C' decision, or a 'G' decision. An 'A' decision is an Autocratic decision that the plant manager makes herself, without consulting anyone."[37] Plant manager Paula Sims says, "I don't make very many of those, and when I do make one, everyone at the plant knows it. I make maybe 10 or 12 a year."[38] "C" decisions are also made by the plant manager, but with Consultation of the people affected. "G" decisions, the most common type, are Group decisions by consensus among the people directly involved, with plenty of discussion. With "G" decisions, the

> **Normative decision theory** a theory that suggests how leaders can determine an appropriate amount of employee participation when making decisions.

Exhibit 13.6

Normative Theory, Decision Styles, and Levels of Employee Participation

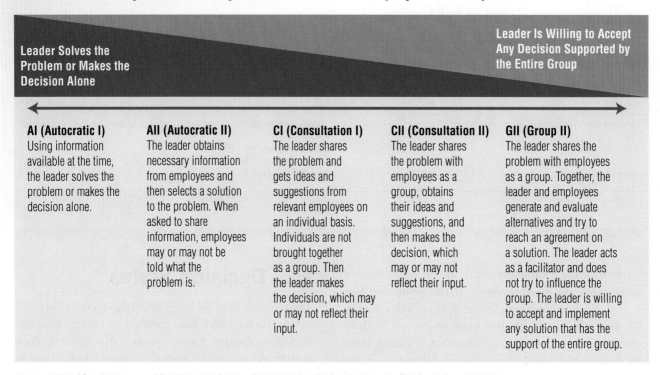

AI (Autocratic I)	AII (Autocratic II)	CI (Consultation I)	CII (Consultation II)	GII (Group II)
Using information available at the time, the leader solves the problem or makes the decision alone.	The leader obtains necessary information from employees and then selects a solution to the problem. When asked to share information, employees may or may not be told what the problem is.	The leader shares the problem and gets ideas and suggestions from relevant employees on an individual basis. Individuals are not brought together as a group. Then the leader makes the decision, which may or may not reflect their input.	The leader shares the problem with employees as a group, obtains their ideas and suggestions, and then makes the decision, which may or may not reflect their input.	The leader shares the problem with employees as a group. Together, the leader and employees generate and evaluate alternatives and try to reach an agreement on a solution. The leader acts as a facilitator and does not try to influence the group. The leader is willing to accept and implement any solution that has the support of the entire group.

Leader Solves the Problem or Makes the Decision Alone

Leader Is Willing to Accept Any Decision Supported by the Entire Group

Source: Adapted from V. H. Vroom and P. W. Yetton, *Leadership and Decision Making* (Pittsburgh: University of Pittsburgh Press, 1973), 13.

view of the plant manager doesn't necessarily carry more weight than the views of those affected."[39]

13-5b Decision Quality and Acceptance

According to normative decision theory, using the right degree of employee participation improves the quality of decisions and the extent to which employees accept and are committed to decisions. Exhibit 13.7 lists the decision rules that normative decision theory uses to increase the quality of a decision and the degree to which employees accept and commit to a decision. The quality, leader information, subordinate information, goal congruence, and problem structure rules are used to increase decision quality. For example, the leader information rule states that a leader who doesn't have enough information to make a decision on his or her own should not use an autocratic decision style.

The commitment probability, subordinate conflict, and commitment requirement rules, shown in Exhibit 13.7, are used to increase employee acceptance and commitment to decisions. For example, the commitment requirement rule says that if decision acceptance and commit-

ment are important and the subordinates share the organization's goals, then you shouldn't use an autocratic or consultative style. In other words, if followers want to do what's best for the company and you need their acceptance and commitment to make a decision work, then use a group decision style and let them make the decision. As you can see, these decision rules help leaders improve decision quality and follower acceptance and commitment by eliminating decision styles that don't fit the particular decision or situation they're facing. Normative decision theory, like path–goal theory, is situational in nature.

The abstract decision rules in Exhibit 13.7 are then framed as yes/no questions, which makes the process of applying these rules more concrete. These questions are shown in the decision tree displayed in Exhibit 13.8. You start at the left side of the model and answer the first question, "How important is the technical quality of this decision?", by choosing "high" or "low." Then you continue by answering each question as you proceed along the decision tree until you get to a recommended decision style.

Let's use the model to make the decision of whether to change from a formal business attire policy to a casual

Exhibit 13.7
Normative Theory Decision Rules

Decision Rules to Increase Decision Quality

Quality Rule. If the quality of the decision is important, then don't use an autocratic decision style.

Leader Information Rule. If the quality of the decision is important, and if the leader doesn't have enough information to make the decision on his or her own, then don't use an autocratic decision style.

Subordinate Information Rule. If the quality of the decision is important, and if the subordinates don't have enough information to make the decision themselves, then don't use a group decision style.

Goal Congruence Rule. If the quality of the decision is important, and subordinates' goals are different from the organization's goals, then don't use a group decision style.

Problem Structure Rule. If the quality of the decision is important, the leader doesn't have enough information to make the decision on his or her own, and the problem is unstructured, then don't use an autocratic decision style.

Decision Rules to Increase Decision Acceptance

Commitment Probability Rule. If having subordinates accept and commit to the decision is important, then don't use an autocratic decision style.

Subordinate Conflict Rule. If having subordinates accept the decision is important and critical to successful implementation and subordinates are likely to disagree or end up in conflict over the decision, then don't use an autocratic or consultative decision style.

Commitment Requirement Rule. If having subordinates accept the decision is absolutely required for successful implementation and subordinates share the organization's goals, then don't use an autocratic or consultative style.

Sources: Adapted from V. H. Vroom, "Leadership," in *Handbook of Industrial and Organizational Psychology,* ed. M. D. Dunnette (Chicago: Rand McNally, 1976); V. H. Vroom and A.G. Jago, *The New Leadership: Managing Participation in Organizations* (Englewood Cliffs, NJ: Prentice Hall, 1988).

Which shirt do I wear for "casual day"?

catwalker/Shutterstock.com

wear policy. The problem sounds simple, but it is actually more complex than you might think. Follow the yellow line in Exhibit 13.8 as we work through the decision in the discussion.

Problem: Change to Casual Wear?

1. *Quality requirement: How important is the technical quality of this decision?* High. This question has to do with whether there are quality differences in the alternatives and whether those quality differences matter. In other words: Is there a lot at stake in this decision? Although most people would assume that quality isn't an issue here, it really is, given the overall positive changes that generally accompany changes to casual wear.

2. *Commitment requirement: How important is subordinates' commitment to the decision?* High. Changes in culture, like dress codes, require subordinates' commitment or they fail.

3. *Leader's information: Do you have sufficient information to make a high-quality decision?* Yes. Let's assume that you've done your homework. Much has been written about casual wear, from how to

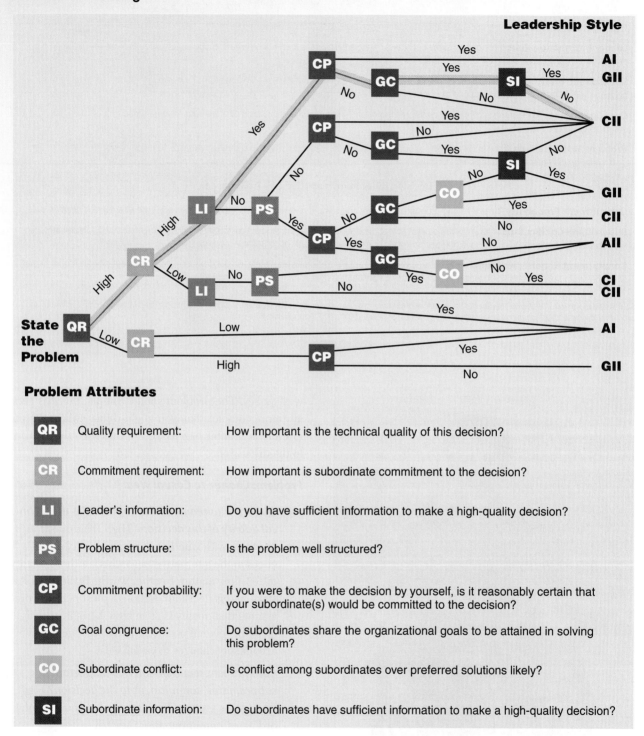

Exhibit 13.8

Normative Decision Theory Tree for Determining the Level of Participation in Decision Making

Leadership Style

State the Problem

Problem Attributes

QR	Quality requirement:	How important is the technical quality of this decision?
CR	Commitment requirement:	How important is subordinate commitment to the decision?
LI	Leader's information:	Do you have sufficient information to make a high-quality decision?
PS	Problem structure:	Is the problem well structured?
CP	Commitment probability:	If you were to make the decision by yourself, is it reasonably certain that your subordinate(s) would be committed to the decision?
GC	Goal congruence:	Do subordinates share the organizational goals to be attained in solving this problem?
CO	Subordinate conflict:	Is conflict among subordinates over preferred solutions likely?
SI	Subordinate information:	Do subordinates have sufficient information to make a high-quality decision?

Source: Figure 9.3. Decision-Process Flow Chart for Both Individual and Group Problems from *Leadership and Decision-Making*, by Victor H. Vroom and Philip W. Yetton, © 1973. All rights controlled by the University of Pittsburgh Press, Pittsburgh, PA 15260. Adapted and used by permission of University of Pittsburgh Press.

make the change to the effects it has in companies (almost all positive).

4. ***Commitment probability: If you were to make the decision by yourself, is it reasonably certain that your subordinate(s) would be committed to the decision?*** No. Studies of casual wear find that employees' reactions are almost uniformly positive. Nonetheless, employees are likely to be angry if you change something as personal as clothing policies without consulting them.

5. ***Goal congruence: Do subordinates share the organizational goals to be attained in solving this problem?*** Yes. The goals that usually accompany a change to casual dress policies are a more informal culture, better communication, and less money spent on business attire.

6. ***Subordinate information: Do subordinates have sufficient information to make a high-quality decision?*** No. Most employees know little about casual wear policies or even what constitutes casual wear in most companies. Consequently, most companies have to educate employees about casual wear practices and policies before making a decision.

7. ***CII is the answer:*** With a CII, or consultative decision process, the leader shares the problem with employees as a group, obtains their ideas and suggestions, and then makes the decision, which may or may not reflect their input. So, given the answers to these questions (remember, different managers won't necessarily answer these questions the same way), the normative decision theory recommends that leaders consult with their subordinates before deciding whether to change to a casual wear policy.

How well does the normative decision theory work? A prominent leadership scholar has described it as the best supported of all leadership theories.[40] In general, the more managers violate the decision rules in Exhibit 13.7, the less effective their decisions are, especially with respect to subordinate acceptance and commitment.[41]

13-6 GENDER AND LEADERSHIP

Is there a difference between female leadership and male leadership? This is a complex question, and we will just scratch the surface here. "Elite-level leaders in business and government make significant and far-reaching decisions [that influence] many facets of society. However, relatively few of these powerful positions are held by women."[42]

Several studies reflect how "stereotypes, prejudice, and discrimination contribute to women's under-representation in elite leadership roles by both impacting perceptions of and responses to women as well as impacting the experiences of women themselves." There is also a "lack of parity between the sexes in leadership and there is empirical research that serves to illuminate obstacles to women's progress" (the glass ceiling).[43] Although the role of traits in understanding leadership emergence and effectiveness has been a controversial issue in the literature, "the extant research reveals that traits do play an important, albeit limited, role in leadership effectiveness."[44]

One study carried out on creativity and innovation management revealed that "employees report more innovative behaviour when the transformational leadership is displayed by male in comparison with female managers, confirming our gender bias hypothesis."[45] A separate experimental study "suggests that the romance of leadership does exist for both men and women but that the process of pay allocation differs as a function of gender." Generally for a female leader, it is based on perceptions of her charisma and leadership ability rather than directly on company performance.[46] Warren Buffett of Berkshire Hathaway urges all men in business to fully employ "the talents of all its citizens … We've seen what can be accomplished when we use 50 percent of our human capacity. If you visualize what 100 percent can do, you'll join me" in promoting and supporting female leaders.[47]

13-7 VISIONARY LEADERSHIP

Strategic leadership refers to the ability to anticipate, envision, maintain flexibility, think strategically, and work with others to initiate changes that will create a positive future for an organization.[48] This form of leadership captures how leaders inspire their companies to change and their followers to make extraordinary efforts to accomplish organizational goals.

Strategic leadership the ability to anticipate, envision, maintain flexibility, think strategically, and work with others to initiate changes that will create a positive future for an organization.

In Chapter 4, we defined vision as a statement of a company's purpose or reason for existing. Similarly, **visionary leadership** creates a positive image of the future that motivates organizational members and provides direction for future planning and goal setting.[49]

*Two kinds of visionary leadership are **13-7a charismatic leadership** and **13-7b transformational leadership**.*

13-7a Charismatic Leadership

Charisma is a Greek word meaning "divine gift." The ancient Greeks saw people with charisma as inspired by the gods and as capable of incredible accomplishments. German sociologist Max Weber viewed charisma as a special bond between leaders and followers.[50] Weber wrote that the special qualities of charismatic leaders enable them to strongly influence followers. For example, Sergio Marchionne, a manager from Toronto, was the only person who could fix Fiat. It now turns out that he is the only person who can make Chrysler really drive. The young Marchionne attended the University of Toronto, then received a law degree from Osgoode Hall and an MBA from the University of Windsor. "He loves to talk, loves to gossip, can charm an audience in several languages, adores his mother, is quick with a put-down," says Eric Reguly. "These are the attributes of a transformational leader, and Marchionne must now apply them to transform Chrysler."[51] Marchionne is utterly convinced that a merger is in the best financial interests of the auto industry and he is not abandoning his view that auto makers must consolidate amid the technological change that is sweeping the industry.[52] "I would give Sergio a chance to pull off anything that he really wants. He's persistent and persuasive," said Tony Faria, co-director of the University of Windsor's Office of Automotive and Vehicle Research.[53]

The ancient Greeks saw people with charisma as inspired by the gods and capable of incredible accomplishments.

Weber also noted that charismatic leaders tend to emerge in times of crisis and that the radical solutions they propose enhance the admiration that followers feel for them. Indeed, charismatic leaders tend to have incredible influence over their followers, who may be inspired by their leaders and become fanatically devoted to them. From this perspective, charismatic leaders are often seen as larger-than-life or as more special than other employees of the company.

Charismatic leaders have strong, confident, dynamic personalities that attract followers. This enables them to create strong bonds with their followers, who in turn trust their charismatic leaders, are loyal to them, and are inspired to work toward accomplishing their vision. Followers who become devoted to charismatic leaders may go to extraordinary lengths to please them. Thus, we can define **charismatic leadership** as the behavioural tendencies and personal characteristics of leaders that create an exceptionally strong relationship between them and their followers.

Charismatic leaders also

▶ articulate a clear vision for the future that is based on strongly held values or morals;

▶ model those values by acting in ways that are consistent with the vision;

▶ communicate high performance expectations to followers; and

▶ display confidence in followers' abilities to achieve the vision.[54]

Does charismatic leadership work? Studies indicate that it often does. In general, the followers of charismatic leaders are more committed and satisfied, are better performers, are more likely to trust their leaders, and simply work harder.[55] Nonetheless, charismatic leadership also has risks that are at least as large as its benefits. The problems are likely to occur with ego-driven charismatic leaders who take advantage of fanatical followers.

In general, there are two kinds of charismatic leaders: ethical charismatics and unethical charismatics.[56] **Ethical charismatics** provide developmental opportunities for followers, are open to positive and negative feedback, recognize others' contributions, share information, and have moral standards that

Visionary leadership leadership that creates a positive image of the future that motivates organizational members and provides direction for future planning and goal setting.

Charismatic leadership the behavioural tendencies and personal characteristics of leaders that create an exceptionally strong relationship between them and their followers.

Ethical charismatics charismatic leaders who provide developmental opportunities for followers, are open to positive and negative feedback, recognize others' contributions, share information, and have moral standards that emphasize the larger interests of the group, organization, or society.

Bavorndej/Shutterstock

Exhibit 13.9
Ethical and Unethical Charismatics

Charismatic Leader Behaviours	 Ethical Charismatics	 Unethical Charismatics
Exercising power	Power is used to serve others.	Power is used to dominate or manipulate others for personal gain.
Creating the vision	Followers help develop the vision.	Vision comes solely from leader and serves his or her personal agenda.
Communicating with followers	Two-way communication: Seek out viewpoints on critical issues.	One-way communication: Not open to input and suggestions from others.
Accepting feedback	Open to feedback. Willing to learn from criticism.	Inflated ego thrives on attention and admiration of sycophants. Avoid or punish candid feedback.
Stimulating followers	Want followers to think and question status quo as well as leader's views.	Don't want followers to think. Want uncritical, intellectually unquestioning acceptance of leader's ideas.
Developing followers	Focus on developing people with whom they interact. Express confidence in them and share recognition with others.	Insensitive and unresponsive to followers' needs and aspirations.
Living by moral standards	Follow self-guided principles that may go against popular opinion. Have three virtues: courage, a sense of fairness or justice, and integrity.	Follow standards only if they satisfy immediate self-interests. Manipulate impressions so that others think they are doing the right thing. Use communication skills to manipulate others to support their personal agenda.

Source: J. M. Howell and B. J. Avolio, "The Ethics of Charismatic Leadership: Submission or Liberation?" *Academy of Management Executive* 6, no. 2 (1992): 43–54.

emphasize the larger interests of the group, organization, or society.

By contrast, **unethical charismatics** control and manipulate followers, do what is best for themselves instead of their organizations, want to hear only positive feedback, share only information that benefits themselves, and have moral standards that place their interests before everyone else's. Because followers can become just as committed to unethical as to ethical charismatics, unethical charismatics pose a tremendous risk for companies.

Exhibit 13.9 shows the stark differences between ethical and unethical charismatics with regard to several leader behaviours: exercising power, creating the vision, communicating with followers, accepting feedback, stimulating followers intellectually, developing follow-

ers, and living by moral standards. For example, ethical charismatics include followers' concerns and wishes when creating a company vision by having them participate in the development of that vision. By contrast, unethical charismatics develop a vision by themselves solely to meet their personal agendas. One unethical charismatic said that "the key thing is that it is my idea; and I am going to win with it at all costs."[57]

> **Unethical charismatics** charismatic leaders who control and manipulate followers, do what is best for themselves instead of their organizations, want to hear only positive feedback, share only information that benefits themselves, and have moral standards that put their interests before everyone else's.

Russell Wasendorf, Sr., CEO and founder of Peregrine Financial Group, a commodities trading firm, stole $215 million over the course of 20 years from his clients and the company. Wasendorf printed false bank statements to hide his theft, used some of the stolen money to falsely boost Peregrine's financial performance, and used the money to live well above his means, "hiring a 'four-star chef' to run Peregrine's cafeteria, building an expansive house with a swimming pool, and sinking investor money into ventures like an Italian restaurant—the staff of which he once flew to Italy for a vacation." The 65-year-old Wasendorf was sentenced to 50 years in prison.[58]

13-7b Transformational Leadership

Charismatic leadership involves articulating a clear vision, modelling values consistent with that vision, communicating high performance expectations, and establishing very strong relationships with followers. **Transformational leadership** goes even farther than this by generating awareness and acceptance of a group's purpose and mission and by getting employees to see beyond their own needs and self-interest for the good of the group.[59] Like charismatic leaders, transformational leaders are visionary, but they transform their organizations by getting their followers to accomplish more than they intended and even more than they thought possible.

Transformational leaders make their followers feel that they are a vital part of the organization and help them see how their jobs fit with the organization's vision. By linking individual and organizational interests, transformational leaders encourage followers to make sacrifices for the organization. Followers willingly do so do

Transformational leadership leadership that generates awareness and acceptance of a group's purpose and mission and gets employees to see beyond their own needs and self-interests for the good of the group.

so because they know they will prosper when the organization does. Transformational leadership has four components: charismatic leadership or idealized influence, inspirational motivation, intellectual stimulation, and individualized consideration.[60]

Transformational leaders practise *charismatic leadership or idealized influence* by acting as role models for their followers. Because transformational leaders put others' needs ahead of their own and share risks with their followers, they are admired, respected, and trusted, and followers want to emulate them. When Whole Foods' profit dropped 10 percent and the company needed to trim costs, CEO John Mackey voluntarily cut his pay by 67 percent. Likewise, *The Tonight Show*'s Jay Leno voluntarily took a $15 million cut in pay when NBC announced that it needed to cut $20 million in costs for the show. While 20 employees were let go, Leno's voluntary pay cut absorbed 75 percent of the needed cost reduction so that many other long-time staffers on the show could keep their jobs.[61] Thus, in contrast to purely charismatic leaders (especially unethical charismatics), transformational leaders can be counted on to do the right thing and maintain high standards of ethical and personal conduct.

Regarding *inspirational motivation,* transformational leaders motivate and inspire followers by providing meaningful and challenging work. By clearly communicating

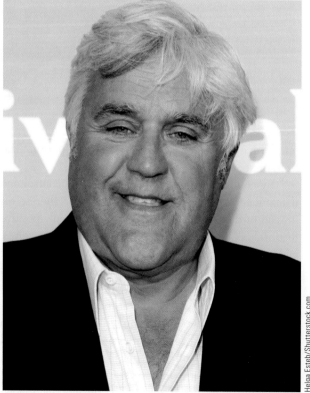

How to Reduce the Risks Associated With Unethical Charismatics

1. Have a clearly written code of conduct that is fairly and consistently enforced for all managers.
2. Recruit, select, and promote managers with high ethical standards.
3. Train leaders to value, seek, and use diverse points of view.
4. Train leaders and subordinates regarding ethical leader behaviours so that abuses can be recognized and corrected.
5. Reward people who exhibit ethical behaviours, especially ethical leader behaviours.

Sources: J. M. Burns, *Leadership* (New York: Harper & Row, 1978); B. M. Bass, "From Transactional to Transformational Leadership: Learning to Share the Vision," *Organizational Dynamics* 18 (1990): 19–36.

expectations and demonstrating commitment to goals, transformational leaders help followers envision the future. This leads to greater enthusiasm and optimism about the future. Regarding *intellectual stimulation,* transformational leaders encourage followers to be creative and innovative, to question assumptions, and to look at problems and situations in new ways even if their ideas are different from the leader's.

Individualized consideration means that transformational leaders pay special attention to followers'

individual needs by creating learning opportunities, accepting and tolerating individual differences, encouraging two-way communication, and being good listeners.

Finally, a distinction needs to be drawn between transformational leadership and transactional leadership. Transformational leaders use visionary and inspirational appeals to influence followers, whereas **transactional leadership** is based on an exchange process in which followers are rewarded for good performance and punished for poor performance. When leaders administer rewards fairly and offer followers rewards they want, followers often reciprocate with effort. A problem, however, is that transactional leaders often rely too heavily on discipline or threats to bring performance up to standards. This may work in the short run but is much less effective in the long run. Also, as discussed in Chapters 10 and 12, many leaders and organizations find it difficult to link pay practices to individual performance. That is why studies consistently show that transformational leadership is much more effective on average than transactional leadership. In Canada, Japan, the United States, and India, and at all organizational levels from first-level supervisors to upper-level executives, followers view transformational leaders as much better leaders and are much more satisfied when working for them. Furthermore, companies with transformational leaders have significantly better financial performance.[62]

Transactional leadership leadership based on an exchange process, in which followers are rewarded for good performance and punished for poor performance.

STUDY TOOLS 13

READY TO STUDY?

LOCATED IN TEXTBOOK:

☐ Rip out the Chapter Review Card at the back of the book to have a summary of the chapter and key terms handy.

LOCATED AT NELSON.COM/STUDENT:

☐ Access the eBook or use the ReadSpeaker feature to listen to the chapter on the go.

☐ Prepare for tests with practice quizzes.

☐ Review key terms with flashcards and the glossary feature.

☐ Work through key concepts with case studies and Management Decision Exercises.

☐ Explore practical examples with You Make the Decision Activities.

14 Managing Communication

Tyler Olson/Shutterstock

LEARNING OUTCOMES

After studying this chapter, you will be able to...

14-1 Explain the role that perception plays in communication and communication problems.

14-2 Describe the communication process and the various kinds of communication in organizations.

14-3 Explain how managers can manage effective one-on-one communication.

14-4 Describe how managers can manage effective organization-wide communication.

After you finish this chapter, go to **PAGE 312** for

STUDY TOOLS

Connecting With Creativity, Technology, and Your Sister

Communication is at the heart of TinyEYE Therapy Services, the groundbreaking company that Greg Sutton and his sister, Marnee Brick, cofounded in Saskatoon in 2005. It was communication, too, that originally gave Greg the idea for the business, because it was during a chat that Marnee told him she had problems travelling to all the students in her caseload as a speech language pathologist (SLP). Greg, who has a "real passion" for technology, suggested the solution: online speech therapy. TinyEYE was born, offering online speech therapy and later online occupational therapy too. SLPs evaluate and treat communication and swallowing disorders; occupational therapists help with physical, mental, and cognitive disorders. TinyEYE has grown from a small start-up into "the world leader in online speech pathology," according to the Futurpreneur Canada website, and the company has won many awards for innovation and customer service. Greg is the CEO, and Marnee the president. Greg graduated from the University of Saskatchewan in 1999 with a bachelor of commerce degree, majoring in finance and marketing, and worked in the tech industry before TinyEYE was formed. About 150 people work for TinyEYE, including therapists on contract and about 25 employees, with 95 percent of the staff working remotely. TinyEYE provides services to thousands of students in more than 20 countries, and has offices in three countries.

1. Is it fair to say that managing communication is what your business is all about?

Communication is at the heart of every business. A huge part of our business is the shared lexicon that we have developed to reflect our culture. For example, we strongly encourage debate in our meetings and, to engage in a debate, you simply say, "I would like to have safe conflict with you"—both people know that they are going to wrestle with an issue and not each other.

2. What kinds of technology does TinyEYE use for communication purposes?

We use Skype for most remote meetings and we have our own custom-build video/audio software for online therapy. We also use Google Docs for our collaboration documents and Dropbox for our shared files.

3. Which of the various kinds of communication—formal, informal, coaching/consulting, nonverbal—are part of day-to-day life in the organization?

All of the above. We have standardized communication protocols for handoffs between departments—for example, when a salesperson closes a new deal, they have a standard form for the information they need to pass on to the startup team and a protocol to follow if any of that information is missing. This reduces wasted time searching for info and allows flexibility for each customer's unique needs, as well as reducing tension between departments. As our organization grows, we find that we move from art to science or from informal to formal. Having standardized ways to communicate the basics frees up time to be creative and add value to the bigger overall process.

4. Does the nature of the company mean that you as a manager are keenly aware of the different aspects of communication, such as problems with how we perceive ourselves and others?

Yes—specifically when giving feedback. My sister and cofounder, Marnee Brick, noticed that giving performance feedback was not effective. As an SLP she looked at the many models used in her profession on giving feedback during a therapy session and she developed a framework for providing performance feedback. It starts by helping our employees understand the cognitive processes and associated feelings that happen when receiving feedback—which helps them to open up themselves to feedback and ultimately personal growth. The model that we use to deliver feedback is also very useful; it's called the KSS—what do I Keep doing, what do I Stop doing, what do I Start doing. The model is an order of magnitude better than the standard "How am I doing?"

5. In your experience, does technology have a large role in communication in most modern organizations now?

Yes, but using great technology does not improve one's ability to communicate effectively. Being able to communicate in a clear and concise manner is a skill that can be developed in anyone. Technology simply makes communicating more efficient. We often say, "Please speak in bullet points."

6. Is creativity important at all in your work?

Creativity is the essence of our work. Despite what Silicon Valley would have you believe, it is not resources that create sustainable wins on the business battleground—resourcefulness does that!

7. What is the most important thing you learned in business school that you use to this day?

I learned how to learn. As a business student, it is critical to have a lab in which you can apply your education on a daily basis. While in university, I volunteered hundreds of hours in nonprofit organizations and worked in small businesses where I got to try out my daily lessons in real-world settings and reflect on my ability to create outcomes from my knowledge.

For the full interview, go online to nelson.com/student

Photo and interview courtesy of Greg Sutton

14-1 PERCEPTION AND COMMUNICATION PROBLEMS

Communication is the process of transmitting information from one person or place to another. It's estimated that managers spend over 80 percent of their day communicating with others.[1] Indeed, much of the basic management process—planning, organizing, leading, and controlling—cannot be performed without effective communication. The shift from an industrial economy to an information society has led to greater emphasis being placed on developing the soft skills that are critical for productive performance in current and future business leaders. Research studies on this topic support this trend, including a study that found that 75 percent of long-term job success depends on people skills, while only 25 percent depends on technical knowledge. The need for effective communication skills—which include listening, following instructions, conversing, and giving feedback—becomes even more critical for employees looking to progress in their careers, particularly in management. A study that examined the critical soft skills that employers want from their employees found that, overwhelmingly, communication was one of the top two soft skills needed by employees in today's workplace.[2] Furthermore, across all industries, poor communication skills rank as the single most important reason why people do not advance in their careers.[3]

One study found that when *employees* were asked whether their supervisor gave recognition for good work, only 13 percent said their supervisor gave a pat on the back, and a mere 14 percent said their supervisor gave sincere and thorough praise. But when the *supervisors* of these employees were asked if they gave recognition for good work, 82 percent said they gave pats on the back, while 80 percent said that they gave sincere and thorough praise.[4] How could managers and employees have had such different perceptions of something as simple as praise?

*Let's learn more about perception and communication problems by examining **14-1a the basic perception**

process, 14-1b perception problems, 14-1c how we perceive others, and **14-1d how we perceive ourselves.** *We'll also consider how all of these factors make it difficult for managers to achieve effective communication.*

14-1a Basic Perception Process

As shown in Exhibit 14.1, **perception** is the process by which individuals attend to, organize, interpret, and retain information from their environments. And since communication is the process of transmitting information from one person or place to another, perception is obviously a key part of communication. Yet perception can also be a key obstacle to communication.

In today's workplace, people are often exposed to a wide variety of informational stimuli, including emails, texts, direct conversations with coworkers, rumours heard over lunch, stories about the company on social media, or a podcast of a speech from the CEO to all employees.

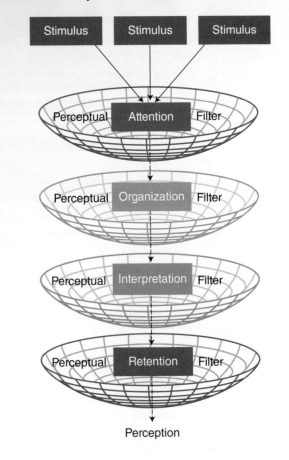

Exhibit 14.1
Basic Perception Process

Communication the process of transmitting information from one person or place to another.

Perception the process by which individuals attend to, organize, interpret, and retain information from their environments.

Just being exposed to an informational stimulus, however, is no guarantee that an individual will pay attention to that stimulus. People experience stimuli through their own **perceptual filters**—the personality-, psychology-, or experience-based differences that influence them to ignore or pay attention to particular stimuli. Because of filtering, people exposed to the same information will often have different opinions on what they saw or heard. For example, a store manager may say to her employees, "The regional manager is coming to talk to us tomorrow." One of the employees may perceive that she said, "The regional manager is coming tomorrow to break some bad news to us." Another employee may think, "Head office must have noticed our sales are up, and the regional manager is coming to congratulate us." Yet another employee may interpret this as, "The regional manager is really difficult to understand; he always seems to use jargon and obscure examples to try and get his point across." As shown in Exhibit 14.1, perceptual filters affect each part of the *perception process:* attention, organization, interpretation, and retention.

Attention is the process of noticing or becoming aware of particular stimuli. Because of perceptual filters, we attend to some stimuli and not others. *Organization* is the process of incorporating new information (from the stimuli that you notice) into your existing knowledge. Because of perceptual filters, we are more likely to incorporate new knowledge that is consistent with what we already know or believe. *Interpretation* is the process of attaching meaning to new knowledge. Because of perceptual filters, our preferences and beliefs strongly influence the meaning we attach to new information (e.g., "This must mean that top management supports our project"). Finally, *retention* is the process of remembering interpreted information. In other words, retention is what we recall and commit to memory after we have perceived something. Of course, perceptual filters also affect retention, that is, what we're likely to remember in the end.

In short, because of perception and perceptual filters, even when people are exposed to the same communications (e.g., emails or discussions with managers or customers), they can end up with very different perceptions and understandings. This is why communication can be so difficult and frustrating for managers. Let's review some of the communication problems created by perception and perceptual filters.

14-1b Perception Problems

Two of the most common perception problems in organizations are *selective perception* and *closure*. Employees are constantly bombarded with sensory stimuli while at work—ringing phones, computers that ding as new email arrives, people talking in the background, cellphones signalling new text or email messages, and so on. As "limited processors," we cannot possibly notice, receive, and interpret all of this information. So we attend to and accept some stimuli, while screening out and rejecting others. **Selective perception** is the tendency to notice and accept objects and information consistent with our values, beliefs, and expectations while ignoring or screening out inconsistent information. A classic case of selective perception occurred when Apple introduced the iPhone 4, which had a metal antenna circling its edge. Since touching an antenna reduces signal reception, customers immediately began complaining about poor phone reception. Apple hadn't encountered this problem in real-world testing, however, because it always cloaked its new phones in covers (so that they couldn't be photographed before product launch). Those covers prevented testers from touching the phone's antenna and experiencing the problem. Within days, "Antennagate" had become a public relations crisis for Apple as media sources began reporting the problem. In fact, after conducting lab tests, *Consumer Reports* magazine recommended that customers not buy the iPhone 4.[5] What made matters worse was that Apple denied the problem. Then-CEO Steve Jobs said, "This has been blown so out of proportion that it's incredible. There is no Antennagate." The iPhone 4, he said, was "perhaps the best product made by Apple."[6] Furthermore, Jobs, who didn't think there was an issue (i.e., selective perception), instructed customers who emailed him about the issue to "avoid gripping it in the lower left corner in a way that covers both sides of the black strip in the metal [antenna] band, or simply use one of many available cases." The problem continued to snowball until even Jobs couldn't ignore it, however, and within 10 days, Apple offered each of its iPhone 4 customers a free "bumper" (or case) that solved the problem by preventing contact with the antenna.[7]

Once we have initial information about a person, event, or process, **closure** is the tendency to fill in the

Perceptual filters the personality-, psychology-, or experience-based differences that influence people to ignore or pay attention to particular stimuli.

Selective perception the tendency to notice and accept objects and information consistent with our values, beliefs, and expectations while ignoring or screening out or not accepting inconsistent information.

Closure the tendency to fill in gaps of missing information by assuming that what we don't know is consistent with what we already know.

gaps where information is missing, that is, to assume that what we don't know is consistent with what we already know. If employees are told that budgets must be cut by 10 percent, they may automatically assume that 10 percent of employees will lose their jobs, too, even if that isn't the case. Not surprisingly, when closure occurs, people sometimes fill in the gaps with inaccurate information. Needless to say, this can create problems for organizations.

14-1c Perceptions of Others

Attribution theory says that we all have a basic need to understand and explain the causes of other people's behaviour.[8] In other words, we need to know why people do what they do. According to attribution theory, we use two general reasons or attributions to explain people's behaviour: an *internal attribution,* in which behaviour is thought to be voluntary or under the control of the individual, and an *external attribution,* in which behaviour is thought to be involuntary and outside of the control of the individual.

For example, have you ever seen someone changing a flat tire on the side of the road and thought to yourself, "What bad luck—somebody's having an awful day"? If you did, you perceived the person through an external attribution known as the defensive bias. The **defensive bias** is the tendency for people to perceive themselves as personally and situationally similar to someone who is having difficulty or trouble.[9] And when we identify with the person in a situation, we tend to use external attributions (i.e., the situation) to explain the person's behaviour. For instance, since flat tires are common, it's easy to perceive ourselves in that same situation and to put the blame on external causes such as running over a nail.

Now, let's assume a different situation, this time in the workplace: A utility company worker places a ladder against a utility pole and then climbs up to do his work. As he's doing his work, he falls from the ladder and seriously injures himself.[10] Answer this question: Who or what caused the accident?

If you thought, "It's not the worker's fault; anybody could fall from a tall ladder," then you interpreted the incident with a defensive bias in which you saw yourself as personally and situationally similar to someone who is having difficulty or trouble. In other words, you have made an external attribution by attributing the accident to an external cause, meaning the situation.

Most accident investigations, however, initially blame the worker (i.e., an internal attribution) and not the situation (i.e., an external attribution). Typically, 60–80 percent of workplace accidents each year are blamed on "operator error," that is, on the employees themselves. In reality, more complete investigations usually show that workers are responsible for only 30–40 percent of all workplace accidents.[11] Why are accident investigators so quick to blame workers? The reason is that they are committing the **fundamental attribution error**, which is the tendency to ignore external causes of behaviour and to attribute other people's actions to internal causes.[12] In other words, when investigators examine the possible causes of an accident, they're much more likely to assume that the accident was a function of the person and not the situation.

Which attribution—the defensive bias or the fundamental attribution error—are workers likely to choose when something goes wrong? In general, employees and coworkers are more likely to perceive events and explain behaviour from a defensive bias. Because they do the work themselves and see themselves as similar to others who make mistakes, have accidents, or are otherwise held responsible for things that go wrong at work, employees and coworkers are likely to attribute problems to external causes such as failed machinery, poor

Attribution theory a theory that we all have a basic need to understand and explain the causes of other people's behaviour.

Defensive bias the tendency for people to perceive themselves as personally and situationally similar to someone who is having difficulty or trouble.

Fundamental attribution error the tendency to ignore external causes of behaviour and to attribute other people's actions to internal causes.

support, or inadequate training. By contrast, because they are typically observers (who don't do the work themselves) and see themselves as situationally and personally different from workers, managers (i.e., bosses) tend to commit the fundamental attribution error and blame mistakes, accidents, and other things that go wrong on workers (i.e., an internal attribution).

Consequently, workers and managers in most workplaces can be expected to take opposite views when things go wrong. Therefore, together, the defensive bias, which is typically used by workers, and the fundamental attribution error, which is typically made by managers, present a significant challenge to effective communication and understanding in organizations.

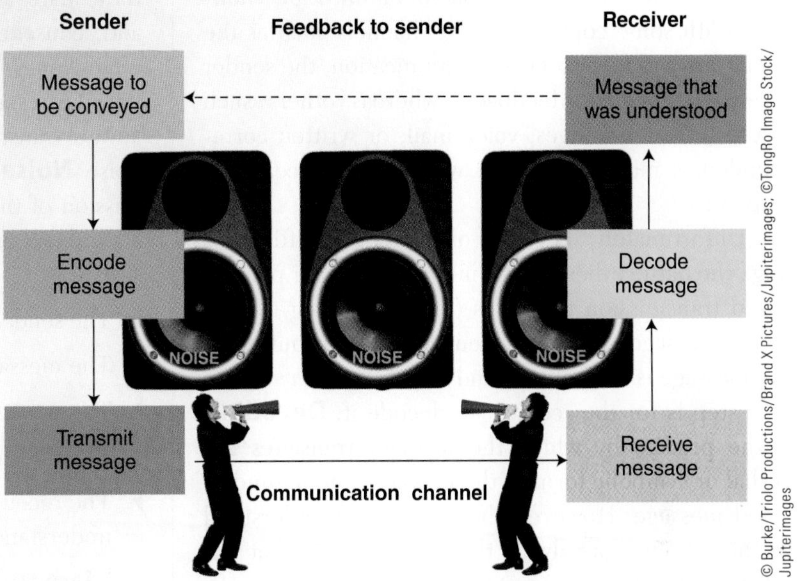

14-1d **Self-Perception**

The **self-serving bias** is the tendency to overestimate our value by attributing successes to ourselves (internal causes) and attributing failures to others or the environment (external causes).[13] The self-serving bias can make it especially difficult for managers to talk to employees about performance problems. In general, people have a need to maintain a positive self-image. This need is so strong that when people seek feedback at work, they typically want verification of their worth (rather than information about performance deficiencies) or assurance that mistakes or problems weren't their fault.[14] And when managerial communication threatens people's positive self-image, they can become defensive and emotional. They quit listening, and communication becomes ineffective. In the second half of this chapter, which focuses on improving communication, we'll explain ways in which managers can minimize this self-serving bias and improve effective one-on-one communication with employees.

14-2 KINDS OF COMMUNICATION

There are many kinds of communication—formal, informal, coaching/counselling, and nonverbal—but they all follow the same fundamental process.

Exhibit 14.2

The Interpersonal Communication Process

© Burke/Triolo Productions/Brand X Pictures/Jupiterimages; ©TongRo Image Stock/Jupiterimages

Let's learn more about the different kinds of communication by examining **14-2a the communication process, 14-2b formal communication channels, 14-2c informal communication channels, 14-2d coaching and counselling, or one-on-one communication,** and **14-2e nonverbal communication.**

14-2a **The Communication Process**

Earlier in the chapter, we defined *communication* as the process of transmitting information from one person or place to another. Exhibit 14.2 displays a model of the communication process and its major components: the sender (message to be conveyed, encoding the message, transmitting the message); the receiver (receiving message, decoding the message, and the message that was understood); and noise, which interferes with the communication process.

The communication process begins when a *sender* thinks of a message he or she wants to convey to

Self-serving bias the tendency to overestimate our value by attributing successes to ourselves (internal causes) and attributing failures to others or the environment (external causes).

another person. The next step is to encode the message. **Encoding** means putting a message into a verbal (written or spoken) or symbolic form that can be recognized and understood by the receiver. The sender then *transmits the message* via *communication channels*. With some communication channels such as the telephone and face-to-face communication, the sender receives immediate feedback, whereas others such as email, text messages, voice mail, or written correspondence, make the sender wait for the receiver to respond.

Unfortunately, because of technical difficulties (e.g., the battery dies in your mobile phone) or people-based transmission problems (e.g., forgetting to pass on the message), messages aren't always transmitted. If the message is transmitted and received, however, the next step is for the receiver to decode it. **Decoding** is the process by which the receiver translates the verbal or symbolic form of the message into an understood message. However, the message as understood by the receiver isn't always the same message that was intended by the sender. Because of different experiences or perceptual filters, receivers may attach a completely different meaning to a message than was intended.

The last step of the communication process occurs when the receiver gives the sender feedback. **Feedback to sender** is a return message to the sender that indicates the receiver's understanding of the message (of what the receiver was supposed to know, to do, or not to do). Feedback makes senders aware of possible miscommunications and enables them to continue communicating until the receiver understands the intended message.

Unfortunately, feedback doesn't always occur in the communication process. Complacency and overconfidence about the ease and simplicity of communication can lead senders and receivers to simply assume that they share a common understanding of the message and, consequently, not use feedback to improve the effectiveness of their communication. This is a serious mistake, especially since messages and feedback are always transmitted with and against a background of noise. **Noise** is anything that interferes with the transmission of the intended message, much like a pop-up ad online. Noise can occur in any of the following situations:

▶ The sender isn't sure what message to communicate.

▶ The message is not clearly encoded.

▶ The wrong communication channel is chosen.

▶ The message is not received or decoded properly.

▶ The receiver doesn't have the experience or time to understand the message.

Jargon, which is vocabulary particular to a profession or group, is another form of noise that interferes with communication in the workplace. For example, do you have any idea what "rightsizing," "unsiloing," "pain points," and "drilling down" mean? *Rightsizing* means laying off workers. *Unsiloing* means getting workers in different parts of the company (i.e., different vertical silos) to work with others outside their own areas. *Pain points* are customer problems that represent opportunities for businesses to fix. *Drilling down* is moving from a general analysis to a more specific, in-depth focus with greater detail.[15] According to Carol Hymowitz of the *Wall Street Journal*, "a new crop of buzzwords usually sprouts every three to five years, or about the same length of time many top executives have to prove themselves. Although some of these words become overused and annoying, some can be useful in swiftly communicating, and spreading, new business concepts."

14-2b Formal Communication Channels

An organization's **formal communication channel** is the system of official channels that carry organizationally approved messages and information. Organizational objectives, rules, policies, procedures, instructions, commands, and requests for information are all transmitted via the formal communication system or "channel." There are three formal communication channels: *downward communication, upward communication,* and *horizontal communication.*[16]

Encoding putting a message into a written, verbal, or symbolic form that can be recognized and understood by the receiver.

Decoding the process by which the receiver translates the written, verbal, or symbolic form of a message into an understood message.

Feedback to sender in the communication process, a return message to the sender that indicates the receiver's understanding of the message.

Noise anything that interferes with the transmission of the intended message.

Jargon vocabulary particular to a profession or group.

Formal communication channel the system of official channels that carry organizationally approved messages and information.

Annoying Business Jargon

It seems that every few years, new business jargon and buzz-words make the rounds. Some become increasingly annoying through overuse; others are destined to make their users sound hopelessly outdated. Here are some of the most common business terms, jargon, and clichés, and what they really mean.

▶ **Bandwidth.** One's availability and workload.

▶ **Low hanging fruit.** Goals that don't require much effort to achieve.

▶ **Take it offline.** Have a private discussion

▶ **Pull the oars.** Focus 100 percent on a specific task or project.

▶ **Drill down.** Diagnose the root cause of an issue.

▶ **Scalable.** A business or activity that requires minimal effort or cost in order to gain additional output.

▶ **Leverage.** How a situation or environment can be controlled or manipulated to a company's advantage.

▶ **Think outside the box.** Approach a problem from a unique or unconventional perspective.

Business communication should be clear, straightforward, and devoid of industry jargon because when terms are overused, they lose their effectiveness. Case in point: the phrase "think outside the box"—a hall of famer—is considered by many to be so overused that it can lead to the opposite effect. As Daisy Yu, a Canadian business lawyer, points out, "It really doesn't encourage you to think outside the box when someone tells you that."

Igor Dutina/Shutterstock.com

Sources: J. Smith, "20 Annoying Phrases You Should Stop Saying at Work," BusinessInsider.com, April 29, 2015, http://www.businessinsider.com/most-overused-office-buzzwords-2015-4; M. Mallet, B. Nelson, and C. Steiner, "The Most Annoying, Pretentious, and Useless Business Jargon," *Forbes*, January 26, 2012, http://www.forbes.com/sites/groupthink/2012/01/26/the-most-annoying-pretentious-and-useless-business-jargon; J. Schott, "The Most Annoying Corporate Buzzwords," *CEB Marketing and Communications*, August 13, 2012, http://www.executiveboard.com/marketing-blog/the-most-annoying-corporate-buzzwords.

Downward communication flows from higher to lower levels in an organization. Downward communication is used to issue orders down the organizational hierarchy, to give organizational members job-related information, to give managers and workers performance reviews from upper managers, and to clarify organizational objectives and goals.[17] Harvard professor Michael Beer says, "You can never overcommunicate. When you think you've communicated well, go out three or four more times and communicate again." Beer's consulting firm, TruePoint, studied 40 CEOs whose companies have been above-average performers for over a decade. He found that those remarkable leaders spend an enormous amount of time in communicating downward. They have a simple story, and that story gets out every place they go."[18]

Upward communication flows from lower levels to higher levels in an organization. Upward communication is used to give higher level managers feedback about operations, issues, and problems; to help higher level managers assess organizational performance and effectiveness; to encourage lower level managers and employees to participate in organizational decision making; and to give those at lower levels the chance to share their concerns with higher level authorities. As important as upward communication is, however, it is sometimes a challenge to get employees to voice their opinions or communicate to supervisors, managers, and higher-ups in the organization. A recent Canadian online poll found that about 44 percent of employees did not feel comfortable speaking their mind to their bosses.[19] This is unfortunate, since employee feedback is often vital to helping managers understand how they are being perceived and to creating a positive work environment.

Horizontal communication flows among managers and workers who are at the same organizational level, such as when a day shift nurse comes in at 7:30 A.M. for a half-hour discussion with the night nurse supervisor who leaves at 8:00 A.M. Horizontal communication helps facilitate coordination and cooperation between

Downward communication communication that flows from higher to lower levels in an organization.

Upward communication communication that flows from lower to higher levels in an organization.

Horizontal communication communication that flows among managers and workers who are at the same organizational level.

different parts of a company and allows coworkers to share relevant information. It also helps people at the same level resolve conflicts and solve problems without involving high levels of management. Studies show that communication breakdowns—which occur most often during horizontal communication, such as when patients are handed over from one nurse or doctor to another—are the largest source of medical errors in hospitals.[20]

In general, what can managers do to improve formal communication? First, decrease reliance on downward communication. Second, increase chances for upward communication by increasing personal contact with lower-level managers and workers. Third, encourage much better use of horizontal communication.

14-2c Informal Communication Channels

An organization's **informal communication channel**, sometimes called the *grapevine* or the *rumour mill*, is the transmission of messages from employee to employee outside of formal communication channels. The grapevine arises out of curiosity, that is, the need to know what is going on in an organization and how it might affect you or others. In some organizations, the grapevine is often fed in the absence of reliable information or effective communication as people fill the void by speculating or passing on incomplete or inaccurate information. Consider what happens often in organizations—a new initiative is underway, but management is still working out the details so decides not to share any specifics and keep it "confidential" until everything is finalized, not wanting to share incomplete information. However, invariably employees will start to pick up on the fact that something is in the works, and in the absence of any formal communication or reliable data, the rumour mill kicks into high gear, with all kinds of worst-case scenarios being discussed among employees. As time goes on, the misinformation may snowball and what management may find is what they were trying to avoid: incomplete information has now become reality, and they must work to reassure employees and correct the misinformation. The office water cooler or lunchroom has long been considered the best place to learn company news and to swap stories

Andersen Ross/Blend Images/Jupiterimages

with coworkers—including rumours and office gossip. However, in today's work environments, text messages, social media, and email are often relied on to transmit information through the grapevine.

Some believe that grapevines are a waste of employees' time, that they promote gossip and rumours that fuel political speculation, and that they are sources of highly unreliable, inaccurate information. Cy Charney, a management consultant and author of *The Instant Manager*, believes that for some employees, office gossip is a way to blow off steam. Thus, it fills a need in the workplace.[21] Others believe that gossip can lead to a sense of camaraderie and create closer team relationships in a workplace, as coworkers who trade nonofficial knowledge often bond better. Studies clearly show that grapevines are highly accurate sources of information for a number of reasons.[22] First, because grapevines typically carry "juicy" information that is interesting and timely, information spreads rapidly. Second, since information is typically spread by face-to-face conversation, receivers can send feedback to make sure they understand the message that is being communicated. This reduces misunderstandings and increases accuracy. Third, since most of the information in a company moves along the grapevine rather than formal communication channels, people can usually verify the accuracy of information by checking it out with others.

What can managers do to manage organizational grapevines? Often the worst thing they can do is withhold information or try to punish those who share information with others. A better strategy is to embrace the grapevine and keep employees informed about possible changes and strategies. If it is partial or preliminary information, preface the release of information by commenting that plans have not been finalized. The vast

---

Informal communication channel the transmission of messages from employee to employee outside of formal communication channels; sometimes called "the grapevine" or "the rumour mill".

majority of employees understand that information may be subject to change and will be prepared to accept changes later, which is far better than speculating and spreading misinformation.

Another strategy is to harness the power of the grapevine by strategically communicating information to select individuals in the organization's grapevine who are known to be skilled at circulating information through the network. In this way, the transmission of information can be expedited and you will have a greater chance of accurate information being circulated.

Lastly, in addition to using the grapevine to communicate with others, managers should not overlook the grapevine as a tremendous source of valuable information and feedback. In fact, information flowing through organizational grapevines is estimated to be 75–95 percent accurate.

14-2d Coaching and Counselling: One-on-One Communication

When the Wyatt Company surveyed 531 US companies undergoing major changes and restructuring, it asked the CEOs, "If you could go back and change one thing, what would it be?" The answer: "The way we communicated with our employees." The CEOs said that instead of flashy videos, printed materials, or formal meetings, they would make greater use of one-on-one communication, especially with employees' immediate supervisors instead of with higher-level executives whom employees didn't know.[23] There are a variety of opportunities for one-on-one communication within an organization, including *coaching, mentoring,* and *counselling.*

Coaching is communicating with someone for the direct purpose of improving the person's on-the-job performance or behaviour.[24] Coaching is also a valuable tool for retaining employees, however, managers sometimes make mistakes when it comes to coaching employees. First, they wait for a problem to arise before coaching. Jim Concelman, manager for leadership development at Development Dimensions International, says, "Of course, a boss has to coach an employee if a mistake has been made, but they shouldn't be waiting for the error. While it is a lot easier to see a mistake and correct it, people learn more through success than through failure, so bosses should ensure that employees are experiencing as many successes as possible. Successful employees lead to a more successful organization."[25] Second, when mistakes *are* made, managers wait much too long before

talking to the employee about the problem. Management professor Ray Hilgert says, "A manager must respond as soon as possible after an incident of poor performance. Don't bury your head. When employees are told nothing, they assume everything is okay."[26] Jack Welch, who was CEO at General Electric for two decades, says, "I've spoken to more than 500,000 people around the world and I always ask audiences, 'How many of you know where you stand in your organization?'" He says, "Typically no more than 10 percent raise their hands. That's criminal! As a manager, you owe candor to your people. They must not be guessing about what the organization thinks of them. My experience is that most employees appreciate this reality check, and today's 'Millennials' practically demand it."[27]

Coaching can be a manager within the organization acting as an internal coach or it may be an outside professional hired to function as an external coach to provide managers with additional training to assist with employee coaching. According to Patty Prosser of Oi Partners, a talent management consulting company, "providing coaching in how to become better managers is as important a signal of investing in career development as are salary and benefit increases."[28] Tribute Communities, an Ontario-based home-building company, hired a workplace coach to help improve the quality of decision making, teamwork, and communication throughout the company. Eileen Chadnick, a certified coach, began by involving all employees in the development of a set of core values for the company; she then helped the company put those values in place through a year-long coaching initiative.[29] According to a Pricewaterhouse Coopers Global survey, the return on investment for companies who invest in coaching is seven times the initial investment.

Similar to coaching, mentorship focuses on employee development, however, mentoring programs have a longer time line as **mentorship** concentrates on career development and knowledge transfer versus individual skill development or immediate performance improvement. Mentoring can be a valuable tool for employees within an organization to help them prepare for new roles, take on new responsibilities, and build confidence in terms of career development.

Coaching communicating with someone for the direct purpose of improving the person's on-the-job performance or behaviour.

Mentorship communicating with someone with a focus on career development and knowledge transfer versus individual skill development or immediate performance improvement.

Mentoring is often used to help people transition between different career stages or opportunities, and to support individuals who are being accelerated into leadership roles as it can focus on developing overall management skills.

There are various types of mentor programs, including *non-directive mentoring* where a mentor acts as a sounding board and perhaps a role model; as well as a *sponsor model*, where typically a senior person promotes, oversees, and takes control over a junior employee's career path. However, there are also *reverse mentoring* programs where junior employees take on the role of mentor for someone at the executive level. Reverse mentoring started a decade ago at General Electric Co. (GE), when then-CEO Jack Welch asked hundreds of the company's seasoned managers to connect with younger employees. The concept was simple: pass ideas, expertise, and knowledge up the corporate ladder instead of the other way. Reverse mentoring can provide valuable benefits to both groups—senior employees often find themselves feeling reenergized and more motivated because of the interaction, younger workers appreciate the increased visibility it gives them among senior management, and overall it can help engage and improve relationships between different generations in the workplace. The biggest challenge in implementing reverse mentorship is getting senior employees, particularly senior-level managers, to accept the role reversal and learn how to be a follower instead of a leader. In addition to reverse mentoring, organizations are also developing mentor programs geared toward women and minorities to help support diversity initiatives within the workplace. Exhibit 14.3 compares coaching and mentoring.

In contrast to coaching and mentoring, **counselling** is communicating with someone about non-job-related issues such as stress, childcare, health issues, retirement planning, or legal issues that may be affecting or interfering with the person's performance. Counselling does not mean that managers should try to be clinicians, even though an estimated 20 percent of employees are dealing with personal problems at any given time. Instead, managers should discuss specific performance problems, listen if the employee chooses to share personal issues, and then

Counselling communicating with someone about non-job-related issues that may be affecting or interfering with the person's performance.

Exhibit 14.3
Coaching vs. Mentoring Programs

COACHING VS. MENTORING PROGRAMS

COACHING PROGRAMS

✓ Shorter term: week, month

✓ Session-based

✓ One-way: coach to employee

✓ Good for specific skill development, such as management training or other job-related skills

✓ Good for performance improvement in areas such as diversity training

MENTORING PROGRAMS

✓ Longer term: months, years

✓ Relationship-based

✓ Multiple ways: peer-to-peer, senior to junior, junior to senior

✓ Good for whole person development, such as overall career development or high potential employee development

✓ Good for knowledge sharing and role modelling between employees

Source: Lis Merrick, *How Coaching & Mentoring Can Drive Success In Your Organization*, Chronus. Used with permission. Found at http://chronus.com/wp-content/uploads/2013/11/How-Coaching-Mentoring-Can-Drive-Success-in-Your-Organization.pdf.

recommend that the employee call the company's Employee Assistance Program (EAP). EAPs are typically free when provided as part of a company's benefit package. In emergencies or times of crisis, EAPs can offer immediate counselling and support and provide referrals to organizations and professionals that can help employees and their family members address personal issues.

Role Reversal

Reverse mentorship—where younger workers take on the role of advisor to more experienced employees—is a trend that is gaining momentum. and not just in large corporate organizations. In British Columbia, which has the highest percentage of small businesses in Canada, Mentorship BC was started by the provincial government to help encourage business owners to connect with reverse mentors. When Deborah Richardson, owner of a small retail boutique, offered a recent fashion school graduate an internship, she also gained a mentor. Her young intern was able to teach Deborah the digital tools she needed to integrate social media into her marketing plan. "I had no social media skills, but she got me on HootSuite and Twitter and helped me to set up a blog about Canadian fashion. Now I'm the social media queen."

For Andrew Graff, an advertising executive who participated in a reverse mentoring program, his 23-year-old mentor provided him with input on everything from the latest

michaeljung/iStock/Thinkstock

smartphone apps to the layout for his new office. Graff also gained insight into the Millennial mindset, which led to some changes like allowing employees to work unconventional hours and check in from home or a coffee shop.

Sources: T. Wanless, "Mentoring Now a Two-Way Street: Tech-Savy Young People Have Plenty to Offer," *Financial Post*, February 5, 2014, http://business.financialpost.com/entrepreneur/mentoring-now-a-two-way-street-tech-savvy-young-people-have-plenty-to-offer; D. Wood, "Reverse Mentoring Gives Gen Y Workers Boost of Confidence," *The Globe and Mail*, January 22, 2014, http://www.theglobeandmail.com/report-on-business/small-business/sb-managing/reverse-mentoring-gives-gen-y-workers-boost-of-confidence/article16437897/; L. Kwoh, "Reverse Mentoring Cracks Workplace," *Wall Street Journal*, November 28, 2011, http://www.wsj.com/articles/SB10001424052970203764804577060051461094004.

14-2e Nonverbal Communication

Nonverbal communication is any communication that doesn't involve words. Nonverbal communication almost always accompanies verbal communication and may either support and reinforce the verbal message or contradict it. The importance of nonverbal communication is well established. Researchers have estimated that as much as 93 percent of any message is transmitted nonverbally, with 55 percent coming from body language and facial expressions and 38 percent coming from the tone and pitch of the voice.[30] Since many nonverbal cues are unintentional, receivers often consider nonverbal communication to be a more accurate representation of what senders are thinking and feeling than the words they use.

Kinesics and paralanguage are two kinds of nonverbal communication.[31] **Kinesics** (from the Greek word *kinesis*, meaning "movement") are movements of the body and face.[32] These movements include arm and hand gestures, facial expressions, eye contact, folding arms, crossing legs, and leaning toward or away from another person. For example, people tend to avoid eye contact when they are embarrassed or unsure of the message they are sending. Crossed arms or legs usually indicate defensiveness or that the person is not receptive to the message or the sender. Also, people tend to smile frequently when they are seeking someone's approval. Unfortunately, not making or maintaining eye contact is an increasingly frequent occurrence in today's workplace. To form positive connections when speaking to others, you should maintain eye contact 60–70 percent of the time. Consultant Suzanne Bates, author of *Speak Like a CEO*, says that some of her CEO clients check their phones so much during appointments that "it's the equivalent of not showing up for half of the meeting." And that, she says, breeds resentment in others who think, "I'm just as busy as the CEO. I just have different things to juggle."[33]

Paralanguage includes the pitch, rate, tone, volume, and speaking pattern (use of silences, pauses,

---

Nonverbal communication any communication that doesn't involve words.

Kinesics movements of the body and face.

Paralanguage the pitch, rate, tone, volume, and speaking pattern (use of silences, pauses, or hesitations) of one's voice.

or hesitations) of one's voice. When people are unsure of what to say, for example, they tend to decrease their communication effectiveness by speaking softly. When people are nervous, they tend to speak faster and louder. How much does paralanguage matter? A study in which 1,000 people listened to 120 different speeches found that the tone of the speaker's voice accounted for 23 percent of the difference in listeners' evaluations of the speech, compared to speech content, which accounted for only 11 percent.[34] So paralanguage was twice as important as what was actually said. In short, because nonverbal communication is so informative, especially when it contradicts verbal communication, managers need to learn how to monitor and control their nonverbal behaviour.

14-3 MANAGING ONE-ON-ONE COMMUNICATION

When it comes to improving communication, managers face two primary tasks: managing one-on-one communication and managing organization-wide communication. On average, first-line managers spend 57 percent of their time with people; for middle managers, it is 63 percent, and for top managers, it's as much as 78 percent.[35] Clearly, managers spend a great deal of time in one-on-one communication with others.

Learn more about managing one-on-one communication by reading about how to **14-3a choose the right communication medium, 14-3b be a good listener,** *and* **14-3c give effective feedback.**

14-3a Choosing the Right Communication Medium

Sometimes messages are poorly communicated simply because they are delivered using the wrong **communication medium**, which is the method used to deliver a message. There are two general kinds of communication media: oral and written.

Communication medium the method used to deliver an oral or written message.

Oral communication includes face-to-face and group meetings either in person or through telephone calls, videoconferencing, or any other means of sending and receiving spoken messages. Studies show that managers generally prefer oral communication over written because it provides the opportunity to ask questions about parts of the message they don't understand. Oral communication is also a rich communication medium because it allows managers to receive and assess the nonverbal communication that accompanies spoken messages (i.e., body language, facial expressions, and the voice characteristics associated with paralanguage. However, it has been suggested that voice mail and email have made managers less willing to engage in meaningful, face-to-face oral communication than before. In fact, 67 percent of managers admit to using email as a substitute for face-to-face conversations.

Written communication includes letters, memos, emails and texts. The convenience and speed of email has changed how managers communicate with workers, customers, and one another. For instance, because people read six times faster than they can listen, they usually can read 30 email messages in 10–15 minutes.[36] By contrast, dealing with voice messages can take a considerable amount of time.

Furthermore, with email accessible at the office, at home, and on the road (by laptop computer, cellphone, or web-based email), managers can use email to stay in touch from anywhere at almost any time. And since email and other written communications don't have to be sent and received simultaneously, messages can be sent and stored for reading at any time. Consequently, managers can send and receive many more messages using email than using oral communication, which requires people to get together in person or by phone or videoconference.

Email has its own drawbacks, however. One disadvantage is that it lacks the formality of paper memos and letters. It is easy to fire off an email that is not well written or fully thought out. Another drawback to email is that it lacks nonverbal cues, making emails very easy to misinterpret. Kristin Byron, assistant professor of management at Syracuse University, says that "people perceive emails as more negative than they are intended to be, and even emails that are intended to be positive can be misinterpreted as more neutral. You get an email that's really short, with no greeting, no closing; it's probably because they were very rushed, or maybe they're not very skilled typists. But because of those things, people have a tendency to perceive the message as negative."[37]

Is Texting the New Normal in Business?

Texting has become the preferred mode of communication for many individuals when it comes to personal interactions, but what about the workplace? It may be surprising for some to know that texting was actually developed by a software programmer trying to develop an internal paging system for employees at his company. His first text message contained just two words: "Merry Christmas."

Tech-savvy teens and millennials embraced this new form of communication and it quickly spread to other demographic groups, charting new territory for how people communicate in their personal lives. For many, texting is a quick and casual way to exchange information with little thought—and not much attention to punctuation or grammar! However, texting can also be an effective communication tool for businesses—for internal employee communications as well as business partners—in that it can be instantaneously responsive as well as more personalized.

For organizations that conduct business with other countries where getting access to the internet can be a problem, text messaging via mobile phones can be a way to maintain an efficient communication channel. Of course, the safety and security of information being transmitted should be a consideration for businesses electing to use texting as a

GaudiLab/Shutterstock

form of business communication. Other things to consider when texting for business: before hitting "send," be sure to check your text for auto-correct errors, avoid texting a last-minute change to a meeting time or venue in case the person doesn't check their phone in time, avoid overly casual abbreviations like "u" (you) or "np" (no problem), and lastly, avoid texting in relation to serious topics or bad news since those types of conversations are better delivered using a communication channel that will allow you to communicate the appropriate tone.

Sources: J. Whitmore, "Five Rules for Texting Anyone You Do Business With," Entrepreneur.com, February 17, 2014, https://www.entrepreneur.com/article/231379; L. Dishman, "Texting Is the New Email—Does Your Company Do It Right?" FastCompany.com, May 30, 2013, http://www.fastcompany.com/3010237/bottom-line/texting-is-the-new-email-does-your-company-do-it-right; N. Gupta, "Texting, the Great Untapped Business Resource," FastCompany.com, March 11, 2013, http://www.fastcompany.com/3006745/texting-great-untapped-business-resource; V. Gang, "Five Rules of Texting Etiquette Every Professional Needs to Know," BusinessInsider.com, September 20, 2013, http://www.businessinsider.com/texting-etiquette-rules-every-professional-needs-to-know-2013-9.

In addition, more and more organizations are relying on new communication forms, like social media, to complement traditional communication channels both for communicating "out" to employees and for receiving information.

14-3b Listening

Are you a good listener? You probably think so. But, in fact, most people (including managers) are terrible listeners, retaining only about 25 percent of what they hear.[38] You qualify as a poor listener if you frequently interrupt others, jump to conclusions about what people will say before they've said it, hurry the speaker to finish his or her point, are a passive listener (not actively working at your listening), or simply don't pay attention to what people are saying.[39] On this last point—attentiveness—college students were periodically asked

to record their thoughts during a psychology course. On average, 20 percent of the students were paying attention (only 12 percent were actively working at being good listeners), 20 percent were thinking about sex, 20 percent were thinking about things they had done before class, and the remaining 40 percent were thinking about other things unrelated to the class.[40]

For a manager, how important is it to be a good listener? According to Jim Treliving, chair of Boston Pizza International Inc., understanding and listening are the skills most responsible for his business success. With over 340 restaurants across Canada and annual sales over $1 billion, Treliving is a successful Canadian entrepreneur who believes that "if you are going to hire and work with a person, you have to have the ability to listen to them."[41] In general, about 45 percent of the total time you spend communicating with others is spent listening. Furthermore, listening

is important for managerial and business success, even for those at the top of an organization. Listening is a more important skill for managers than ever, since Generation X and Millennial employees tend to expect a high level of interaction with their supervisors. They want feedback on their performance, but they also want to offer feedback and know that it is heard.[42] In fact, managers with good listening skills are rated as better managers by their employees and are much more likely to be promoted.[43]

So, what can you do to improve your listening ability? First, understand the difference between hearing and listening. According to *Webster's New World Dictionary*, **hearing** is the act or process of perceiving sounds, whereas **listening** is making a conscious effort to hear. In other words, we react to sounds, such as bottles breaking or music being played too loud, because hearing is an involuntary physiological process. By contrast, listening is a voluntary behaviour. So if you want to be a good listener, you have to *choose* to be a good listener. Typically, that means choosing to be an active, empathetic listener.[44]

Active listening means assuming some of the responsibility for successful communication by making

> Most people (including managers) are terrible listeners, retaining only about 25 percent of what they hear.

it clear from your behaviour that you are listening carefully to what the speaker has to say. In terms of physical cues or body language, active listeners maintain eye contact, avoid distracting actions or gestures, and show the speaker that they are attentively listening by nodding and making appropriate facial expressions.

Several other strategies can help you be a better active listener. First, clarify responses by asking the speaker questions about confusing or ambiguous statements. Second, when there are natural breaks in the speaker's delivery, use this time to paraphrase or summarize what has been said. Paraphrasing and summarizing give the speaker the chance to correct the message if the active listener has attached the wrong meaning to it, and also show the speaker the listener is interested in the speaker's message. Active listeners also avoid interrupting the speaker and, when they do engage the speaker by asking clarifying questions or paraphrasing, they avoid overtalking. Lastly, active listening may also include **empathetic listening**, which means showing your desire to understand and to reflect people's feelings by giving them sufficient time to talk before responding or interrupting. Empathetic listening is just as important as active listening, especially for managers, because it helps build rapport and trust with others. Exhibit 14.4 lists some active listening behaviours that improve communication.

Hearing the act or process of perceiving sounds.

Listening making a conscious effort to hear.

Active listening assuming half the responsibility for successful communication by actively giving the speaker nonjudgmental feedback that shows you've accurately heard what he or she said.

Empathetic listening understanding the speaker's perspective and personal frame of reference and giving feedback that conveys that understanding to the speaker.

Exhibit 14.4
Active Listening Behaviours

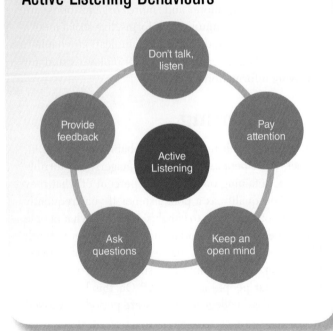

14-3c Giving Feedback

In Chapter 10, you learned that performance appraisal feedback (i.e., judging) should be separated from developmental feedback (i.e., coaching).[45] We can now focus on the steps needed to communicate feedback one-on-one to employees.

To start, managers need to recognize that feedback can be constructive or destructive. **Destructive feedback** is disapproving without any intention of being helpful and almost always causes a negative or defensive reaction in the recipient. By contrast, **constructive feedback** is intended to be helpful, corrective, and/or encouraging. It is aimed at correcting performance deficiencies and motivating employees. For feedback to be constructive rather than destructive, it must be immediate, focused on specific behaviours, and problem-oriented. Immediate feedback is much more effective than delayed feedback because manager and worker can recall the mistake or incident more accurately and discuss it in detail. For example, if a worker is rude to a customer and the customer immediately reports the incident to management, and if the manager, in turn, immediately discusses the incident with the employee, there should be little disagreement over what was said or done. By contrast, it's unlikely that either the manager or the worker will be able to accurately remember the specifics of what occurred if the manager waits several weeks to discuss the incident. When that happens, it's usually too late to have a meaningful conversation.

Specific feedback focuses on particular acts or incidents that are clearly under the control of the employee. For instance, instead of telling an employee that he or she is "always late for work," it's much more constructive to say, "In the last three weeks, you have been 30 minutes late on four occasions and more than an hour late on two others." Furthermore, specific feedback isn't very helpful unless employees have control over the problems that the feedback addresses. Giving negative feedback about behaviours beyond someone's control is likely to be seen as unfair. Similarly, giving positive feedback about behaviours beyond someone's control may be viewed as insincere.

Last, *problem-oriented feedback* focuses on the problems or incidents associated with the poor performance rather than on the worker or the worker's personality. Giving feedback does not give managers

> **Destructive feedback** feedback that disapproves without any intention of being helpful and almost always causes a negative or defensive reaction in the recipient.
>
> **Constructive feedback** feedback intended to be helpful, corrective, and/or encouraging.

Coaching a Small Team

When the topic of executive coaching comes up, many assume this is an activity only used by large companies but this is not the case. Business coach Agnes Cserhait works with many small and medium sized businesses and the feedback she receives from her clients is that coaching can create a huge competitive advantage. She explains that for entrepreneurs and small business owners, "Coaching can be critical to the survival of the early days, and similarly during the growth phase, especially for high-growth businesses. It shortens the decision-making process, enabling action to be taken much sooner—a key to survival in a fast-moving entrepreneur world. By increasing the business owner's confidence and their professionalism in the way that they conduct business, it has a positive impact on customer satisfaction and, ultimately, business growth." As with the benefit associated with employee

Keith A Frith/Shutterstock

development in a large organization, business owners can learn to develop habits that they can transfer to any future business, or continue to use when business grows.

Source: A. Coleman, "Secrets to Success: Would You Benefit From a Business Coach," *The Guardian*, April 10, 2014, http://www.theguardian.com/small-business-network/2014/apr/10/business-coach-sme-growth-planning. Copyright Guardian News & Media Ltd. 2016.

the right to personally attack workers. Managers may be frustrated by a worker's poor performance, but the point of problem-oriented feedback is to draw attention to the problem in a nonjudgmental way so that the employee has enough information to correct it.

 MANAGING ORGANIZATION-WIDE COMMUNICATION

Although managing one-on-one communication is important, managers must also know how to communicate effectively with a larger number of people throughout an organization. According to studies by Watson Wyatt Research, there is a strong correlation between effective employee communication and financial success. Organizations that are highly effective in communication and change management are 2.5 times as likely to significantly outperform their peers as organizations that are not as highly effective in either of these areas.[46]

Learn more about organization-wide communication by reading the following sections about **14-4a improving transmission by getting the message out** *and* **14-4b improving reception by finding ways to hear what others feel and think.**

14-4a Improving Transmission: Getting the Message Out

In today's work environment, technology allows individuals within an organization to communicate quickly and efficiently with each other, as well as with individuals outside the organization. Having access to more information in a shorter amount of time can improve the pace of decision making and also improve the turnaround time for many tasks within an organization. Technology has also provided greater opportunities for collaboration, allowing for ideas, information, and feedback to be shared at any time and anywhere. For some managers, technology has also enhanced the ability to monitor individual employee performance as well as team efforts. Let's examine some of the most important developments in information technology that have had the most significant impact on organizational communication.

Text-based communication; which includes email, instant messaging, and text messages, is the most popular category of communication used by organizations today. Within that category, email is the most prevalent form of communication technology used in the workplace, because of the convenience of being able to share information quickly, having a record of the information shared that can be referenced when needed, and the fact that email forces individuals to write things down which can encourage users to be specific and provide greater detail. Although we normally think of email as a means of one-on-one communication, it also plays an important role in organization-wide communication, allowing managers to keep employees up-to-date on changes and developments.

However, email has its challenges in terms of its effectiveness when you consider timing and volume. According to Phil Simon, author of *Message Not Received*, the average person receives 120 to 150 emails per day, and while message delivery is typically reliable, it's very likely that the person will misplace, delete, or not even see a specific email, and therefore could miss a crucial piece of communication. Employees can easily and quickly become overwhelmed by the amount of information they are expected to process through their inboxes and the "always-on" nature of email messages, as we rely so much on our mobile devices today that we are never far away from our in-box. Suggestions to improve email overload include limiting the number of internal emails wherever possible, and embracing other communication methods (like corporate intranet platforms) to improve the overall level of internal communication.

Business communication tools are also increasingly becoming web-based. In addition to email, *instant messaging* is now available as a business communication tool, operating within a company's computer network or cloud-based system or through cellular networks operating as a mobile application. Many instant messaging systems also offer organizations additional communication features like offline messaging, group chat, voice transmission, and video chat, similar to what many are used to in their own personal mobile communications.

Organization-wide communication can also be facilitated through the use of *online collaboration tools* which allow people to work together over the Internet. Using online collaboration tools like Google Docs or wikis, individuals can work together on documents and presentations, sharing knowledge and communicating ideas back and forth. Similarly, *web or video conferencing* allows people to meet online in real time much like a face-to-face meeting, facilitating the exchange of information, the brainstorming of ideas, and the presentation of material—all without having to be in the same room together. For companies that would ordinarily have to incur travel costs to get employees to a central meeting location, substantial savings can be realized using this method of communication. In particular, the use of web real-time communication (WebRTC) has been gaining popularity within the global business community because it allows users to hold audio or video calls within their browser or app—using open and free Internet technologies and without the need for plugins or additional software.

Along with the increased use of digital and web-based technology, organizations are exploring new communication platforms including systems hosted by *cloud-based servers*, storing and accessing data and programs over the Internet instead of on a hard drive or a server. For organizations, there are many benefits of being "in the cloud," including reduced capital investment in information technology, ability to alter capacity during seasonal periods, and the ability to provide access to applications and data to users anywhere there is Internet access.

14-4b Improving Reception: Hearing What Others Feel and Think

When people think of "organization-wide" communication, they think of the CEO and top managers getting their message out to people in the company.

Knowledge Hiding

One of the most frustrating practices related to communication—or more like a lack of communication—is what professor Catherine Connolley refers to as knowledge hiding. Similar to organizational silence, employees withhold information—however, knowledge hiding is deliberately withholding knowledge, in response to a request, not because employees are afraid of the consequences or don't feel their voice will be heard.

Why would someone participate in knowledge hiding? Some employees might be more likely to do so when they feel rushed or pressed for time, and spending the time to provide information will take them away from tasks they need to complete in their own job. In addition, some employees may distrust certain coworkers and question what the employee will do with the information provided. In her research, Connolly identifies three strategies used in knowledge hiding.

1. **Rationalized hiding:** When someone is asked for specific information and doesn't want to share it, the person instead explains why they can't provide the knowledge. For example, someone is asked if they know who is being transferred to another department, and the individual responds that they can't disclose the information until they speak to all the individuals that will be affected.

2. **Evasive hiding:** In this scenario, the "hider" only provides a limited amount of information. They may say, "I'm not really sure" or "I'll get back to you on that" (and never do), or

Diego Cervo/Shutterstock

they may gloss over the question and tell you, "It's really simple" and "I'm sure you'll be able to figure it out."

3. **Playing dumb:** This is often the most frustrating strategy—when the "hider" pretends not to have the knowledge at all. In this situation, they may suggest you ask someone else or simply say, "I'm sorry, I have no idea."

For organizations, knowledge hiding can lead to unnecessary time and resources spent trying to come up with a solution or answer that someone else already has. In addition, it can damage relationships between coworkers, leading to distrust and weakened credibility. In order to minimize knowledge hiding, managers can set good examples by sharing as much information as possible, using online collaboration technology to facilitate sharing information, and ensuring there are enough informal opportunities for employees to communicate and get to know each other.

Sources: C. Connelly, "What are your organizations hiding? Knowledge hiding in organizations," DeGroote School of Business, McMaster University, October 7, 2015. Used with permission of the author. Available at: http://www.degroote.mcmaster.ca/articles/employees-hiding-knowledge-hiding-organizations/; Connelly, C.E., Turel, O., Ford, D., Gallupe, B. & Zweig, D. (2014). I'm busy (and competitive)! Antecedents of knowledge sharing under pressure. Knowledge Management Research & Practice. 12, 74–85; C. Connelly, D. Zweig, J. Webster, J.P. Trougakos, "Knowledge Hiding in Organizations," Journal of Organizational Behavior, Vol. 33, Issue 1, pgs. 64-88, January 2012.

But organization-wide communication also means finding ways to hear what people throughout the organization are feeling and thinking. This is important because often employees and managers are reluctant to share their thoughts and feelings with top managers. Surveys indicate that only 29 percent of first-level managers feel that their companies encourage employees to express their opinions openly. Another study of 22 companies found that 70 percent of the people surveyed were afraid to speak up about problems they knew existed at work.

Withholding information about organizational problems or issues is called **organizational silence**. Organizational silence occurs when employees believe that telling management won't make a difference or that they'll be punished or hurt in some way for sharing the information.[47] Since employees are regarded as a major source of information, learning, and innovation (all critical factors to success), organizational silence can be particularly detrimental to an organization when employees elect to stay silent and not voice their opinions. Through organizational silence,

> **Organizational silence** when employees withhold information about organizational problems or issues.

Social Media in the Workplace

Social media has changed the way people communicate, not only at home but also at work. Social media applications have now provided employers with opportunities to use these tools for internal and external communication, recruiting, training and development, and collaboration. Here are some current examples of social media platforms used by organizations:

Facebook: Organizations can create Facebook pages or, even better, a Facebook group where all members will receive personal notifications of activity within the group network and can download any notes or documents uploaded by the organization. A nice benefit is the fact that the organization can see and track real-time statistics of how many people have actually seen any given update.

Yammer: This chat service acts as an internal communications platform that allows the sharing of information socially using online forums which can be accessed online or through a mobile app.

Twitter: Employers can choose to tweet publicly or privately, sharing short bursts of information with employees or a wider audience using this quick and easy channel.

LinkedIn: With a LinkedIn group, a business can create its own company intranet by managing a group for employees and using the platform to share internal event information and announcements.

Company blogs: Companies can use blogs to do a variety of things to support communications, such as posting updates on information regarding benefits, sharing survey results, or conducting Q&A sessions with employees.

Live-streaming apps: Social media platforms like Periscope and Meerkat can train employees remotely in real time, allowing employees to watch video live as it is happening.

YouTube: Video broadcasts can also be used to help with employee training, using a private YouTube channel which can be used to archive content for future use—including videos produced in-house or posted from third-party vendor sites.

Snapchat: This video messaging application allows the communication of content that has a one-day lifespan. With its focus on visual content and its 10-second window to post content, Snapchat forces users to keep communication simple and succinct, relying on what many consider the best way to communicate, storytelling.

Instagram: This photography-based social networking site has been embraced by many as their favoured personal social media platform, allowing users to take pictures and videos, and share them publicly or privately, as well as through other social networking platforms such as Facebook and Twitter. Due to its popularity, organizations have started to harness the power of Instagram to communicate to employees by, for example, promoting workplace wellness initiatives or recognizing employee efforts.

Sources: L. Taurasi, "Seven Ways to Use Social Media for Employee Communication," Care.com/careatwork, July 6, 2015, http://workplace.care.com/7-ways-to-use-social-media-for-employee-communications; "Five Reasons Why Instagram Is a Winner When It Comes to Employee Engagement," Ovationbenefits.com. July 2, 2013, http://www.ovationbenefits.com/blog/2013/07/5-reasons-why-instagram-is-a-winner-when-it-comes-to-employee-engagement/; "Managing and Leveraging Workplace Use of Social Media," *Society for Human Resource Management*, December 5, 2012, available at https://www.shrm.org/templatestools/toolkits/pages/managingsocialmedia.aspx.

some employees may withhold personal struggles as well as organizational issues; this is a concern for managers as well as the organization as a whole. In order to address organizational silence, management may elect to use *company hotlines or websites, surveys, informal meetings,* and *social media* to deal with this communication roadblock.[48]

Various types of organizations have established *company hotlines or websites* that anyone in the company can use to anonymously share information with upper management. For example, global professional services firm Deloitte Touche Tohmatsu has a toll-free hotline for employees to call to report any kind of problem or issue within the company. Hotlines are particularly important because 44 percent of employees will not report misconduct. Why not? The reason is two-fold: they don't believe anything will be done, and they "fear that the report will not be kept confidential."[49]

Internal *surveys* can collect valuable information from organization members, which can then be compiled, disseminated, and used to develop action plans for improvement. At Four Seasons Hotels and Resorts, an employee opinion survey is conducted once a year to ensure that management keeps its finger on the pulse of what it considers one of its greatest

assets, its corporate culture.[50] Similarly, FedEx utilizes an online survey, which is completely anonymous, to enable all employees to evaluate their managers and the overall environment at FedEx, including benefits, incentives, and working conditions. The results are compiled and then given back to each FedEx work group to decide where changes and improvements need to be made and to develop specific action plans to address those problems.

Frequent *informal meetings* between top managers and lower-level employees are means of letting managers hear what others feel and think. Many people assume that top managers are at the centre of everything that goes on in organizations, but top managers commonly feel isolated from most of their lower level managers and employees. Consequently, more and more top managers are scheduling frequent informal meetings with people throughout their companies.

Social media platforms are another means of hearing what people are thinking and saying both inside and outside the organization. The grocery chain SUPERVALU has embraced the concept of social media for external as well as internal communication. Each store brand has its own Facebook page, and store directors use Twitter accounts to communicate with customers about individual stores. However, customers aren't the only audience for social media. Through the social media platform Yammer, store directors, corporate executives, and other employees within the organization are able to share best practices in real time, and a Twitter feed is used to share organizational news with investors, media bloggers, and others. As Jeff Swanson, director of external communications, explains, "There are blurring lines on what social media means today. We see it as part marketing, part communications, part customer service."[51] Prior to using social media, there were limited opportunities for employees to send ideas upward to higher levels of management, and in cases where information was being shared, it was at a slow place and often filtered along the way. With Yammer, higher executives, including the CEO, are pleased with the quick turnaround of information, even when it is used to pose tough questions to company executives. Wayne Shurts, chief information officer, explains: "One of the biggest lessons we learned: never underestimate the need for an employee to be heard and the value of listening."[52]

STUDY TOOLS 14

READY TO STUDY?

LOCATED IN TEXTBOOK:

☐ Rip out the Chapter Review Card at the back of the book to have a summary of the chapter and key terms handy.

LOCATED AT NELSON.COM/STUDENT:

☐ Access the eBook or use the ReadSpeaker feature to listen to the chapter on the go.

☐ Prepare for tests with practice quizzes.

☐ Review key terms with flashcards and the glossary feature.

☐ Work through key concepts with case studies and Management Decision Exercises.

☐ Explore practical examples with You Make the Decision Activities.

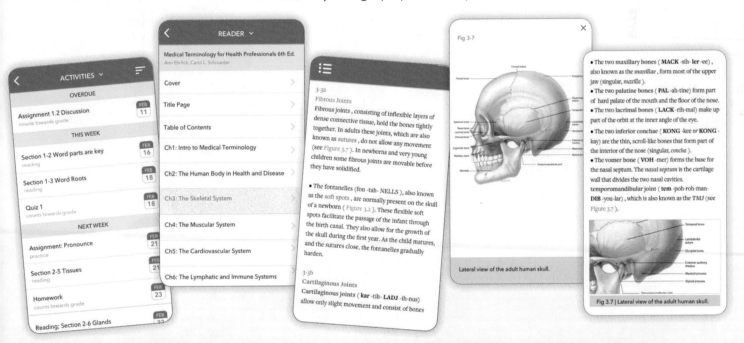

15 Control

kristian sekulic /iStockphoto

LEARNING OUTCOMES

After studying this chapter, you will be able to...

15-1 Describe the basic control process.

15-2 Discuss the various methods that managers can use to maintain control.

15-3 Describe the behaviours, processes, and outcomes that today's managers are choosing to control in their organizations.

After you finish

this chapter, go

to **PAGE 333** for

STUDY TOOLS

Keeping Up Standards

Because accountancy involves business finance, it's a field where standards—and control—are especially important. Accountancy has held great appeal for Rosa Gomez for decades, and working as an accountant in Canada has been a case of returning to something familiar. She grew up in Ecuador and that's where she first worked as an accountant, for two years around the time she graduated from the University of Cuenca in 1993 with a bachelor's degree in commerce. She moved to Canada in 1997, then to the United States for a while, and then returned to Canada. By that point she had experience in fields such as import–export and co-owning a jewellery business, and she also had three children. She decided to return to something she knew, enrolled at George Brown College in Toronto, and in 2013 graduated with an advanced diploma in accounting (honours). She joined the staff of Trowbridge Professional Corporation as a tax associate, and then in January 2016 started work as an accountant in international taxes at the Toronto offices of MNP LLP, a large full-service chartered accounting and business advisory firm. And she has a new personal goal: to become a chartered professional accountant.

1. How important is control—including standards and company goals—in your day-to-day work?

Very important! Everything I do will contribute toward achieving not only the company's goals but also my own personal goals, as I follow standards established for aspects of the company's vision such as leadership, client service excellence, and technical skills.

2. How can you personally help meet company goals?

By performing my duties as expected, and for that I need to communicate my personal goals within the company, which will be aligned to the company's goals. Then I can personally follow a plan during the year that eventually will be measured during my annual performance evaluation.

3. Do the employees play a part in setting the standards or goals?

On the one hand, I think that employees are chosen or hired based on how they will fit within an organization and how they can contribute toward achieving company goals and following the company's established standards. On the other hand, I think employees can play a part in setting standards or goals based on their ability to provide ideas to improve some of the procedures.

4. What have you learned about control that surprised you the most?

I have learned that control is one of the functions that companies will pay a lot of attention to and that it is a tool used for making sure that all actions and procedures applied will contribute to the main goal or goals.

In my case as an employee, my annual performance evaluation is taken seriously, for measuring and comparing my actual performance against the expected one. This evaluation can provide me with the opportunity to be rewarded. The performance evaluation tests me in terms of my attitude toward work, my skills, and the knowledge required to meet expectations in my position. If my performance was not meeting expectations, corrections would need to be made and suggestions would be given for ways to improve.

5. What trait or skill do you think serves you best when it comes to control?

I certainly believe that work ethics have helped me to achieve what I wanted to achieve. Attitude or ethics at work cannot be taught—they are personal attributes, while technical skills can be acquired through training and knowledge and can be learned at school.

6. What do you love best about your job?

I really love that my job offers me the opportunity to learn something new every day. It is dynamic and it challenges me always, due to the changes in the rules and regulations that need to be applied in the area of international taxation.

7. How important is your goal to become a CPA?

This is very important because it is my long-term goal, and not only will it challenge me to coordinate my time among full-time work, my family, and my studies, but it can also help me to be promoted and, as a result, could increase my income.

8. What's the most important thing you learned as a student?

As a student, I always appreciated the opportunity to talk to my teachers, not only to get a better understanding of a subject but also to learn more about the real world. Teachers were the resource I turned to in order to determine what it would take to succeed after graduation.

I also the had the opportunity to participate in a co-op program, which helped me to get a co-op position at KPMG LLP, one of the Big Four accounting firms in the world, and later another opportunity in a small accounting firm. In both instances, this helped me to determine the path I would follow within the accounting industry.

For the full interview, go online to nelson.com/student

15-1 THE CONTROL PROCESS

For all companies, past success is no guarantee of future success. Even successful companies fall short, face challenges, and have to make changes. **Control** is a regulatory process of establishing standards to achieve organizational goals, comparing actual performance to the standards, and taking corrective action when necessary to restore performance to those standards. Control is not telling people what to do; it is working out, with the people in the firm, what the company goals should be. Control is achieved when behaviour and work procedures conform to standards and company goals are accomplished.[1] Control is not just an after-the-fact process, however. Preventive measures are also a form of control.

Nothing is more central to our economy than the banking system, but it has come under continuing criticism with respect to control. Banks operating from Hong Kong, London, and other tax havens facilitate flows out of China and elsewhere into Canada. According to *Financial Post* journalist Diane Francis, "The G20 and G7 have each paid lip service to cracking down on tax havens but nothing substantive has occurred."[2] Canada's top banking regulator has found that "money-laundering controls at the country's banks failed on numerous occasions" in a recent five year-period, according to a document obtained by *The Wall Street Journal*.[3] Canada has been facing growing pressure to step up efforts to fight money laundering, in line with efforts of regulators and law-enforcement agencies globally. Canada's Department of Finance rated the vulnerabilities of deposit-taking institutions as "high to very high" in a report entitled "Assessment of Inherent Risks of Money Laundering and Terrorist Financing in Canada." Indeed, the Financial Transactions and Reports Analysis Centre of Canada (Fintrac) recently fined an unnamed bank $1.1 million for "failing to report a suspicious transaction and various other transfers."[4] There will be increased emphasis on controls needed to "undo" the harm caused by banks' reputations if they are "dragged into" the global tax evasion controversy connected to the so-called Panama Papers

data leak tied to the Panamanian law firm Mossack Fonseca, which is at the heart of the scandal.[5]

*The basic control process begins with **15-1a establishing clear standards of performance**; involves **15-1b comparing performance to those standards** and **15-1c taking corrective action**, if needed, to repair performance deficiencies. Control is a **15-1d dynamic, cybernetic process**, and consists of three basic methods: **15-1e feedback control, concurrent control, and feedforward control**. However, as much as managers would like it to be, **15-1f control isn't always worthwhile or possible**.*

15-1a Establishing Standards

The control process begins when managers set goals, such as satisfying 90 percent of customers or increasing sales by 5 percent. Companies then specify the performance standards that must be met to accomplish those goals. **Standards** are a basis of comparison for measuring the extent to which organizational performance is satisfactory or unsatisfactory. For example, many pizzerias use 30–40 minutes as the standard for delivery times. Since anything longer is viewed as unsatisfactory, they'll typically reduce the price if they can't deliver a hot pizza to you within that time period.

So how do managers set standards? How do they decide which levels of performance are satisfactory and which are not? To start with, a good standard must enable goal achievement. If you're meeting the standard but still not achieving company goals, the standard may have to be changed. There are many approaches to "standards." The Standards Council of Canada (SCC) is a federal Crown corporation whose mandate is to promote efficient and effective standardization in Canada. It oversees Canada's National Standards System. Located in Ottawa, the SCC reports to Parliament through the Minister of Industry. It is also part of the International Organization for Standardization (ISO), which has 163 member countries. Because "International Organization for Standardization" would have different initialisms in different languages ("IOS" in English, "OIN" in French for *Organisation internationale de normalisation*, etc.), its founders decided to also give it a short, all-purpose name. They chose "ISO," derived from the Greek *isos*, meaning "equal." Whatever the country, whatever the language, the short form of the organization's name is always ISO.[6]

Companies also determine standards by listening to customers' comments, complaints, and suggestions, or by observing competitors' products and services. Standards are also sometimes set by government authorities. Although the Canadian Food Inspection Agency

Control a regulatory process of establishing standards to achieve organizational goals, comparing actual performance to the standards, and taking corrective action when necessary.

Standards a basis of comparison for measuring the extent to which various kinds of organizational performance are satisfactory or unsatisfactory.

typically establishes food standards, some companies are not satisfied with the government's slow response to food safety concerns. In order to monitor and enforce quality standards, they have turned to private regulators such as GlobalGap. This organization is an offshoot of a Canadian program, Canada GAP. GlobalGap focuses on safety and sustainability for primary producers, including the agriculture, livestock, and aquaculture supply chains. GlobalGap has more than 130,000 producers representing 300 fruit products alone. BC Hothouse in Vancouver is a registered producer. Most meat packing plants in Alberta and Ontario are also producer-members of GlobalGap. With private regulators, companies can move more quickly to prompt growers to comply with the standards, thereby improving food quality through the entire system.[7]

Standards can also be determined by benchmarking other companies. **Benchmarking** is the process of determining how well other companies (and not just competitors) are performing business functions or tasks. In other words, benchmarking is the process of determining other companies' standards. When setting standards by benchmarking, the first step is to determine what to benchmark. Companies can benchmark anything from cycle time (how fast) to quality (how well) to price (how much). The next step is to identify the companies against which to benchmark your standards. The last step is to collect data to determine other companies' performance standards.

15-1b Comparing Performance to Standards

The next step in the control process is to compare actual performance to performance standards. The quality of the comparison largely depends on the measurement and information systems a company uses to keep track of performance. The better the system, the easier it is for companies to track their progress and identify problems that need to be fixed. One way for retailers to verify that performance standards are being met is to use mystery shoppers—that is, individuals who visit stores pretending to be customers but are really there to determine whether employees provide helpful customer service. The Canadian federal government has sent mystery shoppers to major airports to see how bilingual they are. Official Languages Commissioner Graham Fraser says that his office has used undercover observers to conduct checks. "People are uncertain about what bilingual services they can expect," Fraser said.[8]

15-1c Taking Corrective Action

The next step in the control process is to identify performance deviations, analyze those deviations, and then develop and implement programs to correct them.

Beta versions of software programs are a classic tool that developers use to monitor deviations from the standard. They can then take tive action *before* the product is the market. Microsoft has an program called Software Quality Metrics (SQM) that company software developers use when creating new releases. SQM helps the developers determine how each change in the software code will affect the functionality of the program. It uses a system of comparison charts to show how the changes will affect users of new software.[9]

15-1d Dynamic, Cybernetic Process

As shown in Exhibit 15.1, control is a continuous, dynamic, cybernetic process. Control begins by setting standards, measuring performance, and then comparing performance to the standards. If the performance deviates from the standards, then managers and employees analyze the deviations and develop and implement corrective programs that (hopefully) achieve the desired performance by meeting the standards. Managers must repeat the entire process again and again in an endless feedback loop. Thus, control is not a one-time achievement or result. Rather, it continues over time (i.e., it is dynamic) and requires daily, weekly, and monthly attention from managers if performance levels are to be maintained at the standard. This constant attention is what makes control a cybernetic process. **Cybernetic** derives from the Greek word *kubernetes*, meaning "steersman"—that is, one who steers or keeps on course.[10] The control process shown in Exhibit 15.1 is cybernetic because constant attention to the feedback loop is necessary to keep the company's activities on course.

Benchmarking the process of identifying outstanding practices, processes, and standards in other companies and adapting them to your company.

Cybernetic the process of steering or keeping on course.

Exhibit 15.1
Cybernetic Control Process

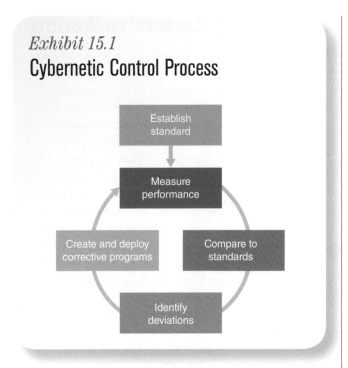

Establish standard → Measure performance → Compare to standards → Identify deviations → Create and deploy corrective programs

Alvov/Shutterstock.com

15-1e Feedback, Concurrent, and Feedforward Control

The three basic control methods are feedback control, concurrent control, and feedforward control.

Feedback control is a mechanism for gathering information about performance deficiencies after they occur. This information is then used to correct performance deficiencies or prevent future deficiencies. Study after study has shown that feedback improves both individual and organizational performance. In most instances, any feedback is better than no feedback. If feedback has a downside, it's that it always occurs after the fact, after performance deficiencies have already occurred. Control can minimize the effects, but the damage is already done. The Canadian aircraft maintenance engineer (AME) licensing and approved training organization (ATO) systems are set by Transport Canada for private firms. This government organization is responsible for

controls, regulations, standards, policies, and procedures for aircraft in Canada. Private firms then carry out maintenance work under a feedback control system.[11]

Concurrent control addresses the problems inherent in feedback control by gathering information about performance deficiencies as they occur. Instead of continuing to sell the Nike+ GPS running watch and FuelBand fitness tracker, Nike has chosen to refine its app offerings for smart phones and smart watches. These apps track distance, pace, time, and calories burned with GPS, providing audio feedback as you run. Along with the ability to record the time, distance and map of your run, the Nike+ Running app has coaching, challenge, social features and device/third-party integrations. After a run, it automatically uploads data via a smartphone to Nikeplus.com or Facebook so that friends can see the runs, including the route and elevation. Runners can actually track their efforts every moment of their run and make changes on the fly.[12] Concurrent control is an improvement over feedback because it attempts to eliminate or shorten the delay between performance and feedback about the performance.

Feedforward control is a mechanism for gathering information about performance deficiencies *before* they occur. In contrast to feedback and concurrent

Feedback control a mechanism for gathering information about performance deficiencies after they occur.

Concurrent control a mechanism for gathering information about performance deficiencies as they occur, thereby eliminating or shortening the delay between performance and feedback.

Feedforward control a mechanism for monitoring performance inputs rather than outputs to prevent or minimize performance deficiencies before they occur.

Guidelines for Using Feedforward Control

1. Plan and analyze thoroughly.
2. Be discriminating as you select input variables.
3. Keep the feedforward system dynamic. Don't let it become a matter of habit.
4. Develop a model of the control system.
5. Collect data on input variables regularly.
6. Assess data on input variables regularly.
7. Take action on what you learn.

Sources: S. Guerreiro, R. P. Marques, and K. Gaaloul, "Optimizing Business Processes Compliance Using an Evolvable Risk-Based Approach," 2016 49th Hawaii International Conference on System Sciences (HICSS), IEEE, 2016; H. Koontz and R. W. Bradspies, "Managing Through Feedforward Control: A Future Directed View," *Business Horizons* 15 (June 1972): 25–36.

control, which provide feedback on the basis of outcomes and results, feedforward control provides information about performance deficiencies by monitoring inputs, not outputs. Microsoft uses feedforward controls to try to prevent software problems before they occur. For example, when developing the latest version of its Windows 10 operating system, Microsoft taught all of its experienced programmers new methods for writing more reliable software code *before* asking them to develop new features for the software. Microsoft has also developed new software testing tools that let the programmers thoroughly test the code they've written (i.e., input) before passing the code on to others to be used in beta testing and then in final products. To summarize, feedforward control seeks to prevent or minimize performance deficiencies before they happen.[13]

15-1f Control Isn't Always Worthwhile or Possible

Control is achieved when behaviour and work procedures conform to standards and goals. By contrast, **control loss** occurs when behaviour and work procedures do not conform to standards.[14] Maintaining control is important because loss of control prevents organizations from achieving their goals. When control loss occurs, managers need to find out what, if anything, they could have done to prevent it. Usually, as discussed above, that means identifying deviations from standard performance, analyzing the causes of

those deviations, and taking corrective action. Even so, implementing controls isn't always worthwhile or possible. Let's look at regulation costs and cybernetic feasibility to see why.

To determine whether control is worthwhile, managers need to carefully assess **regulation costs**, which are the costs associated with implementing or maintaining control. If a control process costs more than an organization gains from its benefits, it may not be worthwhile. Thanks to technology, however, companies are finding it easier (i.e., more feasible) to control many more processes. For example, handwritten prescriptions can be difficult for pharmacists to read, but digital technology can be used to control the accuracy of prescriptions. Doctors can send prescriptions to the pharmacy electronically, and software can alert them to interactions with other drugs that might be harmful to a patient. Newfoundland and Labrador has started to link up 190 pharmacies in a provincial health department project. "A lot of drugs now do have serious interaction between them, and you obviously work with the pharmacy and doctors to try to avoid those," says St. John's pharmacist Chris Hollett. Remembers St. John's pharmacist Tom Healy: "We got a call from a drugstore in Conception Bay North that is also on the same health information network, and he had a customer there who was trying to purchase a codeine product. But the prescription was also dispensed three days before, so we prevented a narcotic from being overdispensed." An Ontario pharmacy assistant discovered that chemotherapy drugs administered to more than 1,200 cancer patients in Ontario and New Brunswick were diluted. He had noticed that the electronic worksheet for calculating the dose for each patient was using the final concentration indicated on an old label. "It's just part of the process, it's part of our job, and it just happens that this check that we made had a broader impact than we certainly would have anticipated," Craig Woudsma said.[15]

Another factor to consider is **cybernetic feasibility**, which is the extent to which it is possible to implement each of the three steps in the control process. If one or more steps cannot be implemented, then maintaining effective control may be difficult or impossible.

Control loss the situation in which behaviour and work procedures do not conform to standards.

Regulation costs the costs associated with implementing or maintaining control.

Cybernetic feasibility the extent to which it is possible to implement each step in the control process.

15-2 CONTROL METHODS

Soon after becoming CEO of Yahoo!, Marissa Mayer told her 14,500 employees to start driving in to work every day—otherwise they could be terminated. Yoav Schwartz, CEO of Uberflip, understood immediately why she set this new policy. Uberflip, a 20-person startup based in downtown Toronto, instituted a no-home-office policy just two years after founding the PDF-sharing technology company. "Over time, we noticed that people working from home were getting out of touch, or the outside developers were not keeping up-to-date with the changes in the organization," he says.[16]

However, not all companies agree. "Mobile workers can be among a company's more productive workers because they often work at different locations within the company or at a client's site," says Michael Thornburrow,

> **Bureaucratic control** the use of hierarchical authority to influence employee behaviour by rewarding or punishing employees for compliance or noncompliance with organizational policies, rules, and procedures.

senior vice president of corporate real estate at BMO Financial Group. However, Richard Branson, the head of Virgin Group PLC, has said on the company's blog that not letting employees work outside the office is "old school thinking."[17] Firms like 37Signals, Mozilla, UpWorthy, Universal Mind, StackExchange, GitHub, and Treehouse are known for having fully or largely distributed teams from day one—and they use that to their advantage in recruiting the best talent wherever they live. "More and more people want the freedom to decide where, when, how, and with whom they work," states Nathaniel Koloc in a recent *Harvard Business Review* Article.[18]

When you become a manager, what approach will you take to controlling your employees' behaviour?

*Managers can use five different methods to achieve control in their organizations: **15-2a bureaucratic, 15-2b objective, 15-2c normative, 15-2d concertive,** and **15-2e self-control.***

15-2a Bureaucratic Control

Most people, when they think of managerial control, have in mind bureaucratic control. **Bureaucratic control** is top-down control—in other words, managers

Be Careful What You Say on Facebook

When a clothing retailer was made aware that one of its employees posted negative comments on his Facebook page about the death of Amanda Todd (the teen from Port Coquitlam, BC, who committed suicide after being bullied on the Internet), it didn't hesitate to take action. The man was fired from his job at a London, Ontario, outlet of Mr. Big and Tall. The company CEO said that the firm was taking the action it felt was appropriate.

Similarly, in Regina, a Prince Albert nurse who made a Facebook post about her grandfather's care was given a disciplinary hearing by the Saskatchewan Registered Nurses Association and charged with professional misconduct. The post said some staff were not "up to speed" on end-of-life care and also suggested that family members of facility residents "keep an eye on things and report anything you do not like," and that staff would do well to have some refresher training.

"The vast majority of people believe that what they say outside of the workplace is none of the employer's business,"

© Marcin Winnicki/Dreamstime.com

states David Doorey, associate professor of labour and employment law at York University's School of Human Resource Management in Toronto. "But that's not true," he continues. "The employer can always fire you for whatever you say. In a private workplace, there is no right to free expression."

Sources: A. Martin, "Saskatchewan Nurse Has Disciplinary Hearing Over Facebook Comments About Grandpa's Care," *Regina Leader Post*, February 11, 2016, http://leaderpost.com/news/local-news/nurse-has-disciplinary-hearing-over-facebook-comments-about-grandpas-care; J. Davidson, "How an Online Posting Can Cost You Your Job," CBC News, October 18, 2012, http://www.cbc.ca/news/technology/how-an-online-posting-can-cost-you-your-job-1.1289054.

try to influence their employees' behaviour by rewarding (or punishing) them for complying (or not) with organizational policies, rules, and procedures. Most employees, though, would argue that bureaucratic managers emphasize punishment for noncompliance much more than rewards for compliance.

Yet, as you learned in Chapter 2, bureaucratic management and control were created to prevent precisely this type of managerial behaviour. By encouraging managers to apply well-thought-out rules, policies, and procedures in an impartial, consistent manner to everyone in the organization, bureaucratic control is supposed to make companies more efficient, effective, and fair. Ironically, it often has just the opposite effect: managers who use bureaucratic control often emphasize following the rules above all else.

Another characteristic of bureaucratically controlled companies is that because of their rule- and policy-driven decision making, they are highly resistant to change and slow to respond to customers and competitors. Max Weber, the German sociologist who popularized the bureaucratic ideal, referred to bureaucracy as the "iron cage." He wrote that "once fully established, bureaucracy is among those social structures which are the hardest to destroy."[19]

15-2b Objective Control

In many companies, bureaucratic control has evolved into **objective control**, which is the use of observable measures of employee behaviour or output to assess performance and influence behaviour. Bureaucratic control focuses on whether policies and rules are followed, whereas objective control focuses on observing and measuring worker behaviour or output. There are two kinds of objective control: behaviour control and output control.

Behaviour control involves regulating behaviours and actions that people perform on the job. The basic assumption of behaviour control is that if you do the right things (i.e., perform the right behaviours) every day, then those things should lead to goal achievement. Behaviour control is still management-based, however, which means that managers are responsible for monitoring and rewarding employees for exhibiting desired behaviours and helping people overcome undesired behaviours. Companies that use global positioning satellite (GPS) technology to track where their employees are and what they're doing are using behaviour control.

GPS can be used in a multitude of ways. In Winnipeg, youths with multiple car-theft convictions were ordered by the court to wear ankle bracelets. In the

© Marmaduke St. John/Alamy Stock Photo

first three years of the program, those ankle bracelets were tampered with 39 times. In one case, two chronic offenders stole a vehicle, cut off their GPS-tracking bracelets, and threw them out the window. One of the bracelets landed in the back seat of the stolen car, however, providing the police with their location.[20]

Instead of measuring what managers and employees do, **output control** measures the results of their efforts. Behaviour control regulates, guides, and measures how employees behave on the job; by contrast, output control

Objective control the use of observable measures of worker behaviour or outputs to assess performance and influence behaviour.

Behaviour control the regulation of the behaviours and actions that employees perform on the job.

Output control the regulation of employees' results or outputs through rewards and incentives.

gives managers and employees the freedom to behave as they see fit as long as they accomplish pre-specified, measurable results. Output control is often coupled with rewards and incentives.

There are three preconditions for output control and rewards to lead to improved business results. First, the output control measures must be reliable, fair, and accurate. Second, employees and managers must believe they can produce the desired results. If they don't, then the output controls won't affect their behaviour. Third, the rewards or incentives tied to output control measures must truly depend on achieving established standards of performance. This kind of output control can also be applied to CEOs. Before he became Ontario's Deputy Minister of Health, Robert Bell, former CEO of Toronto's sprawling University Health Network, had part of his salary tied to a list of performance measures. His comment as the time was, "My compensation is dramatically at risk. If we don't accomplish what the board thinks we should accomplish, I don't get as much salary."[21]

15-2c Normative Control

Another way to control what goes on in an organization involves shaping the beliefs and values of its people. With **normative control**, a company's widely shared values and beliefs guide employees' behaviour and decisions. High-end retailer Nordstrom—with stores in Ottawa, Calgary, and Vancouver, plus two in Toronto—has one value that permeates the entire workforce from top to bottom: extraordinary customer service.[22] On their very first day at Nordstrom, trainees begin their transformation to the "Nordstrom way" by reading the employee handbook. Sounds boring, doesn't it? But Nordstrom's handbook is printed on *one side* of a 3-by-5-inch note card (see Exhibit 15.2). That's it. No lengthy rules. No specifics about what behaviour is or is not appropriate. Just use your judgment.[23]

Companies that use normative control are very careful about whom they hire. Many companies screen job applicants on the basis of their abilities; normatively controlled companies are just as likely to screen them for their attitudes and values. For example, before building

---

Exhibit 15.2
Nordstrom's Employee Handbook

Our number one goal is to provide outstanding customer service. Set both your personal and professional goals high. We have great confidence in your ability to achieve them so our employee handbook is very simple. We have only one rule…

Our one rule:
Use good judgement in all situations.

Please feel free to ask your department manager, store manager or Human Resources any questions at any time.

Sources: Used with permission of Nordstrom.

---

stores in a new city, Nordstrom sends its human resource team into town to interview prospective employees. In a few cities, the company cancelled its expansion plans when it could not find enough applicants who embodied the service attitudes and values for which Nordstrom is known.[24]

Also, with normative control, both managers and employees learn what they should and should not do by observing experienced employees and by listening to the stories they tell about the company. At Nordstrom, many of these stories—which employees call "heroics"—have been inspired by the company motto, "Respond to Unreasonable Customer Requests!"[25] "Nordies," as Nordstrom employees call themselves, like to tell the story about a customer who just had to have a pair of burgundy Donna Karan slacks that had gone on sale, but she could not find her size. The sales associate who was helping her contacted five nearby Nordstrom stores, but none had the customer's size. So rather than leave the customer dissatisfied with her shopping experience, the sales associate went to her manager for petty cash and then went across the street and paid full price for the slacks at a competitor's store. She then resold them to the customer at Nordstrom's lower sale price.[26] Obviously, Nordstrom would quickly go out of business if this were the norm. Nevertheless, this story makes clear the attitude that drives employee performance at Nordstrom in ways that rules, behavioural guidelines, or output controls could not.

15-2d Concertive Control

Although normative control is based on beliefs that are strongly held and widely shared throughout a company, **concertive control** is based on beliefs that are shaped and negotiated by work groups.[27] However, normative control is driven by strong organizational cultures, concertive control usually arises when companies give independent work groups complete autonomy and responsibility for task completion. The most autonomous groups operate without managers and are completely responsible for controlling work group processes, outputs, and behaviour. Such groups do their own hiring, firing, worker discipline, work schedules, materials ordering, budget making and meeting, and decision making.

Concertive control is not established overnight. Highly autonomous work groups go through two phases as they develop concertive control. In the first phase, group members learn to work with one another, supervise one another's work, and develop the values and beliefs that will guide and control their behaviour. And because they develop these values and beliefs themselves, work group members feel strongly about following them. In the steel industry, Nucor, which operates in Canada as the Harris Steel Canada Group, was long considered an upstart compared to the largest steel firms. Yet Nucor has managed to outlast many other mills; indeed, it has bought out many other mills in recent years. Nucor has a unique culture that gives real power to employees on the line and that fosters teamwork throughout the organization. This type of teamwork can be a difficult thing for a newly acquired group of employees to get used to, however. For example, at Nucor's first big acquisition, David Hutchins is a front-line supervisor or "lead man" in the rolling mill, where steel from the furnace is spread thin enough to be cut into sheets. Under the plant's previous ownership, if the guys doing the cutting got backed up, the guys doing the rolling—including Hutchins—would just take a break. He says, "We'd sit back, have a cup of coffee, and complain: 'Those guys stink.'" It took six months to convince the employees at the plant that the Nucor teamwork way was better than the old way. Now, Hutchins says, "At Nucor, we're not 'you guys' and 'us guys.' It's all of us guys. Wherever the bottleneck is, we go there, and everyone works on it."[28]

The second phase in the development of concertive control is the emergence and formalization of objective rules to guide and control behaviour. The beliefs and values developed in the first phase usually become more objective rules as new members join teams. The clearer those rules are, the easier it becomes for new members to figure out how and how not to behave.

Ironically, concertive control may lead to even higher expectations on employees than bureaucratic control. Under bureaucratic control, most employees only have to worry about pleasing the boss. But with concertive control, their behaviour has to satisfy the rest of the team. One team member says, "I don't have to sit there and look for the boss to be around; and if the boss is not around, I can sit there and talk to my neighbour or do what I want. Now the whole team is around me and the whole team is observing what I'm doing."[29] In addition, with concertive control, team members have a second, much more stressful role to perform—that of making sure their team members adhere to team values and rules.

15-2e Self-Control

Self-control (or self-management) is a control system in which managers and employees control their own behaviour.[30] Self-control does not result in anarchy, or a state in which everyone gets to do whatever he or she wants. In self-control or self-management, leaders and managers provide employees with clear boundaries within which they may guide and control their own goals and behaviours.[31] Leaders and managers also contribute to self-control by teaching others the skills they need to maximize and monitor their own work effectiveness. In turn, individuals who manage and lead themselves establish self-control by setting their own goals, monitoring their own progress, rewarding or punishing themselves for achieving or for not achieving their self-set goals, and constructing positive thought patterns that remind them of the importance of their goals and their ability to accomplish them.[32]

If you control for just one thing, such as costs, then other dimensions—like marketing, customer service, and quality—are likely to suffer. For example, let's assume you need to do a better job of praising and recognizing the good work that your staff does for you. You can use goal setting, self-observation, and self-reward to self-manage this behaviour. For self-observation, use a memory app on your mobile smart device for

---

Concertive control the regulation of employees' behaviour and decisions through work group values and beliefs.

Self-control (or self-management) a control system in which managers and employees control their own behaviour by setting their own goals, monitoring their own progress, and rewarding themselves for goal achievement.

"praise/recognition." Put an annotation or note on the app each time you praise or recognize someone (wait until the person has left before you do this). Keep track for a week. This serves as your baseline or starting point. Simply keeping track will probably increase how often you do this. After a week, assess your baseline or starting point, and then set a specific goal. For instance, if your baseline was twice a day, you might set a specific goal to praise or recognize others' work five times a day. Continue monitoring your performance with your app. Once you've achieved your goal every day for a week, give yourself a reward (perhaps a movie or lunch with a friend at a new restaurant) for achieving your goal.[33]

The components of self-management—self-set goals, self-observation, and self-reward—have their roots in the motivation theories you read about in Chapter 12. The key difference is that the goals, feedback, and rewards originate from employees themselves and not from their managers or organizations.

15-3 WHAT TO CONTROL?

In Section 15-1, we discussed the basics of the control process and that control isn't always worthwhile or possible. In Section 15-2, we looked at the various ways in which control can be obtained. In this third and final section, we address an equally important issue: "What should managers and the rest of the employees control?" The way a firm answers this question has important implications for most businesses.

Again, if you control for just one thing, then other dimensions are likely to suffer. If you try to control for too many things, then managers and employees become confused about what's really important. In the end, successful companies find a balance that comes from doing three or four things right, such as managing costs, providing value, and keeping customers and employees satisfied.

The Triple Bottom Line (people, planet, and profits) is similar in purpose to the Balanced Scorecard and gives a long-term perspective and a measure of

Balanced Scorecard measurement of organizational performance from four equally important perspectives: customer, internal, and innovation and learning, and financial.

an achievement toward corporate goals in different arenas. Additionally, many firms use a Total Quality Management (TQM) approach and programs like General Electric's Six Sigma and Lean to control in some of the more technical areas of their firms. They are very worthwhile, and you may wish to delve into these areas yourself.[34]

After reading this section, you should be able to explain **15-3a the Balanced Scorecard** *approach to control and how companies can achieve balanced control of company performance from* **15-3b the financial perspective: controlling budgets, cash flows, and economic value added;** **15-3c the customer perspective: controlling customer defections;** **15-3d the internal perspective: controlling quality;** *and* **15-3e the innovation and learning perspective: controlling waste and pollution.**

15-3a The Balanced Scorecard

Most companies measure performance using standard financial and accounting measures such as return on capital, return on assets, return on investments, cash flow, net income, and net margins. The **Balanced Scorecard** encourages managers to look beyond traditional financial measures to four different perspectives on company performance:

1. The customer perspective—How do customers see us?

2. The internal perspective—What must we excel at?

3. The innovation and learning perspective—Can we continue to improve and create value?

4. The financial perspective—How do we look to shareholders?[35]

The Balanced Scorecard has several advantages over traditional control processes that rely solely on financial measures. First, it forces managers at each level of the company to set specific goals and measure performance in each of the four areas. For example, Exhibit 15.3 shows that Nova Scotia Power Inc. uses different measures, at different levels in its organization, to determine whether it is meeting the standards it has set for itself from the financial, customer, internal, and learning and growth perspectives. *Financial* perspectives are very common in businesses: they include ROI, profitability ratios, debt ratios, and so forth. The *customer* perspectives include items such as getting 100 percent power 100 percent of the time—in other words, "What is the power outage rate, and how long do outages last?" *Internal* measures include items such as preventive maintenance; on-time performance; on-time, on-budget capital construction;

Exhibit 15.3
Nova Scotia Power Inc.'s Balanced Scorecard

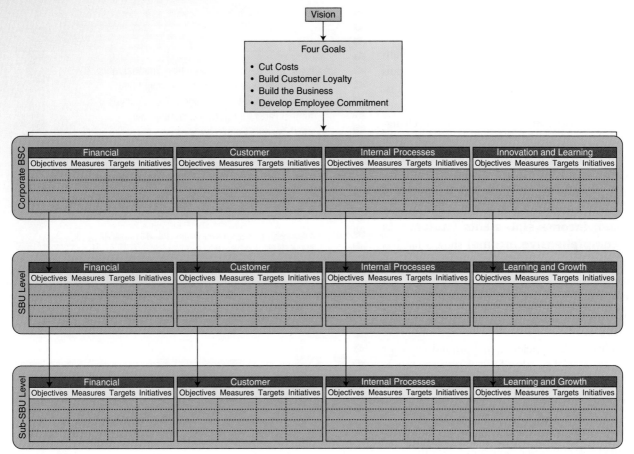

Source: P. Niven, "Cascading the Balanced Scorecard: A Case Study on Nova Scotia Power, Inc.," 2006, http://www.scribd.com/doc/3489336/Cascading-the-Balanced-Scorecard-A-Case-Study-on-Nova-Scotia-Power. Reprinted by permission.

and power frequency boundaries. *Learning and growth* perspectives deal with employee training, work-safe practices, innovations, and employee–management relations. Each of the corporation's strategic subunit (SBU), and subSBU (department) goals measures the four perspectives along the lines of the overall goals of Nova Scotia Power, which are to (1) cut costs, (2) build customer loyalty, (3) build the business, and (4) develop employee commitment.

The second major advantage of the Balanced Scorecard approach to control is that it minimizes the chances of **suboptimization**, which occurs when performance improves in one area but simultaneously decreases in others. As an example, Jon Meliones, chief medical director at a major children's hospital, says: "We could increase productivity by assigning more patients to a nurse, but doing so would raise the likelihood of errors— an unacceptable trade-off."[36]

Let's examine some of the ways in which companies are controlling the four basic parts of the Balanced Scorecard: the financial perspective (budgets, cash flows, economic value added [EVA]); the customer perspective (customer defections); the internal perspective (total quality management); and the innovation and learning perspective (waste and pollution).

> **Suboptimization** performance improvement in one part of an organization at the expense of decreased performance in another part.

15-3b The Financial Perspective: Controlling Budgets, Cash Flows, and Economic Value Added

The traditional approach to controlling financial performance focuses on accounting tools such as cash flow analysis, balance sheets, income statements, financial ratios, and budgets. **Cash flow analysis** predicts how changes in a business will affect its ability to take in more cash than it pays out. **Balance sheets (statements of financial position)** provide a snapshot of a company's financial position at a particular point in time (but not the future). **Income statements (statements of comprehensive income)** show what has happened to an organization's income, expenses, and net profit (income less expenses) over a period of time (these were also traditionally called *profit and loss statements*). **Financial ratios** are typically used to track a business's liquidity (cash), efficiency, and profitability over time compared to other businesses in its industry. Finally, **budgets** are used to project costs and revenues, prioritize and control spending, and ensure that expenses don't exceed available funds and revenues. The Financial Review Card bound in the back of this book contains tables that (a) show the basic steps or parts for cash flow analyses, balance sheets, and income statements; (b) list a few of the most common financial ratios and explain how they are calculated, what they mean, and when to use them; and (c) review

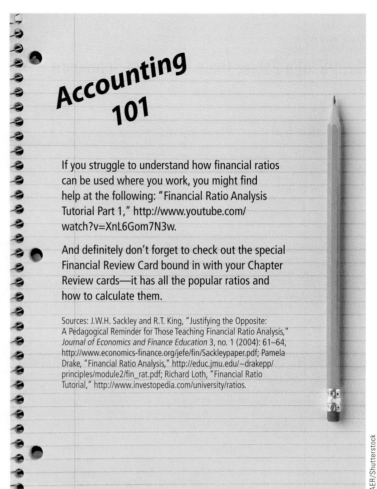

Accounting 101

If you struggle to understand how financial ratios can be used where you work, you might find help at the following: "Financial Ratio Analysis Tutorial Part 1," http://www.youtube.com/watch?v=XnL6Gom7N3w.

And definitely don't forget to check out the special Financial Review Card bound in with your Chapter Review cards—it has all the popular ratios and how to calculate them.

Sources: J.W.H. Sackley and R.T. King, "Justifying the Opposite: A Pedagogical Reminder for Those Teaching Financial Ratio Analysis," *Journal of Economics and Finance Education* 3, no. 1 (2004): 61–64, http://www.economics-finance.org/jefe/fin/Sackleypaper.pdf; Pamela Drake, "Financial Ratio Analysis," http://educ.jmu.edu/~drakepp/principles/module2/fin_rat.pdf; Richard Loth, "Financial Ratio Tutorial," http://www.investopedia.com/university/ratios.

AER/Shutterstock

the different kinds of budgets that managers can use to track and control company finances.

By themselves, none of these tools—cash flow analysis, balance sheets, income statements, financial ratios, or budgets—tells the whole financial story of a business. They must be used together when assessing a company's financial performance. Since these tools are reviewed in detail in your accounting and finance classes, only a brief overview is provided here. Still, these are necessary tools for controlling organizational finances and expenses, and they should be part of your business toolbox.

Though no one would dispute the importance of these four accounting tools, accounting research also indicates that the complexity and sheer amount of information contained in them can shut down the brain and glaze over the eyes of even the most experienced manager.[37] Sometimes there's simply too much information to make sense of. The Balanced Scorecard simplifies things by focusing on one simple question when it comes to finances: How do we look to shareholders? One way to answer that question is through something called *economic value added*.

Cash flow analysis a type of analysis that predicts how changes in a business will affect its ability to take in more cash than it pays out.

Balance sheets (statements of financial position) accounting statements that provide a snapshot of a company's financial position at a particular point in time.

Income statements (statements of comprehensive income) accounting statements that show what has happened to an organization's income, expenses, and net profit over a period of time (also historically called *profit and loss statements*).

Financial ratios calculations typically used to track a business's liquidity (cash), efficiency, and profitability over time compared to other businesses in its industry.

Budgets quantitative plans through which managers decide how to allocate available money to best accomplish company goals.

Exhibit 15.4
Calculating Economic Value Added (EVA)

1. Calculate net operating profit after taxes (NOPAT).	$3,500,000
2. Identify how much capital the company has invested (i.e., spent).	$16,800,000
3. Determine the cost (i.e., rate) paid for capital (usually between 5% and 13%).	10%
4. Multiply capital used (Step 2) times cost of capital (Step 3).	(10% × $16,800,000) = $1,680,000
5. Subtract the total dollar cost of capital from net profit after taxes.	$3,500,000 NOPAT − $1,680,000 Total cost of capital $1,820,000 Economic value added

Conceptually, **economic value added (EVA)** is not the same thing as profits. It is the amount by which profits exceed the cost of capital in a given year. It is based on the simple idea that capital is necessary to run a business and that capital comes at a cost. Although most people think of capital as cash, once it is invested (i.e., spent), capital is more likely to be found in a business in the form of computers, manufacturing plants, employees, raw materials, and so forth. And just as with the interest that a homeowner pays on a mortgage or that a college student pays on a student loan, there is a cost to that capital.

The most common costs of capital are the interest paid on long-term bank loans used to buy all those resources, the interest paid to bondholders (who lend organizations their money), and the dividends (cash payments) and growth in stock value that accrue to shareholders. EVA is positive when company profits (revenues minus expenses minus taxes) exceed the cost of capital in a given year. In other words, if a business is to truly grow, its revenues must be large enough to cover both short-term costs (annual expenses and taxes) and long-term costs (the cost of borrowing capital from bondholders and shareholders). If you're a bit confused, Clay Gillespie, portfolio manager with Vancouver-based Rogers Group Financial, states that when considering debt, "I would only recommend its use if your normal cash flow can pay the debt. Most individuals who use leverage get in trouble when they assume the investment can always pay the debt. This will not always be the case."[38]

Exhibit 15.4 shows how to calculate EVA.

▸ First, starting with a company's income statement, you calculate the net operating profit after taxes (NOPAT) by subtracting taxes owed from income from operations. (Remember, a quick review of an income statement is on the Financial Review Card bound at the back of your book.) The NOPAT shown in Exhibit 15.4 is $3,500,000.

▸ Second, identify how much capital the company has invested (i.e., spent). Total liabilities (what the company owes) less accounts payable and less accrued expenses (neither of which you pay interest on), provides a rough approximation of this amount. In Exhibit 15.4, total capital invested is $16,800,000.

▸ Third, calculate the cost (i.e., rate) paid for capital by determining the interest paid to bondholders (who lend organizations their money), which is usually 5–8 percent, and the return that shareholders want in terms of dividends and stock price appreciation, which is historically about 13 percent. Take a weighted average of the two to determine the overall cost of capital. In your finance classes in future years you will learn more about the weighted average cost of capital, but these two facets (bond and dividends) will suffice for our example. In Exhibit 15.4, the cost of capital is 10 percent.

▸ Fourth, multiply the total capital ($16,800,000) from Step 2 by the cost of capital (10 percent) from Step 3. In Exhibit 15.4, this amount is $1,680,000.

Economic value added (EVA) the amount by which company profits (revenues, minus expenses, minus taxes) exceed the cost of capital in a given year.

Fifth, subtract the total dollar cost of capital in Step 4 from the NOPAT in Step 1. In Exhibit 15.4, this value is $1,820,000, which means that our example company has created economic value or wealth this year. If our EVA number had been negative, meaning that the company didn't make enough profit to cover the cost of capital from bondholders and shareholders, then the company would have destroyed economic value or wealth by taking in more money than it returned.[39]

Why is EVA so important? First and most important, because it includes the cost of capital, it shows whether a business, division, department, profit centre, or product is really paying for itself. The key is to make sure that managers and employees can see how their choices and behaviour affect the company's EVA.

Second, because EVA can easily be determined for subsets of a company such as divisions, regional offices, manufacturing plants, and sometimes even departments, it makes managers and employees at all levels pay much closer attention to their own segments of the business. For example, because of EVA training and information systems, factory workers at Herman Miller, a leading office furniture manufacturer, understand that using more efficient materials (such as less expensive wood-dust board instead of real wood sheeting) contributes an extra dollar of EVA from each desk the company makes. On its website, Herman Miller explains, "Under the terms of the EVA plan, we shifted our focus from budget performance to long-term continuous improvements and the creation of economic value. When we make plans for improvements around here, we include an EVA analysis. When we make decisions to add or cut programs, we look at the impact on EVA. Every month we study our performance in terms of EVA, and this measurement system is one of the first things new recruits to the company learn."[40] In other words, EVA motivates managers and employees to think like small business owners who must scramble to contain costs and generate enough business to meet their bills each month. And, unlike many kinds of financial

Customer defections a performance assessment in which companies identify which customers are leaving and measure the rate at which they are leaving.

controls, EVA doesn't specify what should or should not be done to improve performance. Thus, it encourages managers and employees to be creative in looking for ways to improve EVA performance.

If you want an eye-opener, just google EVA for Apple, Inc.—it is greater than many countries' gross domestic product.[41]

15-3c The Customer Perspective: Controlling Customer Defections

The second aspect of organizational performance that the Balanced Scorecard helps managers monitor is customers, which it does by forcing managers to address this question: "How do customers see us?" Unfortunately, most companies try to answer the question through customer satisfaction surveys, but these are often misleadingly positive. Most customers are reluctant to talk about their problems because they don't know who to complain to or think that complaining will not do any good. Companies are beginning to realize that social media, including chat groups and Facebook, are a source for gut reaction comments about them.[42]

Customer satisfaction surveys can be misleading because even very satisfied customers often switch to competitors. Studies indicate that companies may be farther ahead monitoring **customer defections**—that is, by identifying which customers are abandoning them and at what rate. After all, customer defections have a great effect on profits.

Very few managers realize that landing a new customer costs 10 times as much as keeping a current one. In fact, the cost of replacing old customers with new ones is so great that most companies could double their profits by increasing their customer retention rates by just 5–10 percent per year.[43] And if a company can keep a customer for life, the benefits are even greater. According to Stew Leonard, owner of the Connecticut-based Stew Leonard's grocery store chain: "The lifetime value of a customer in a supermarket is about $246,000. Every time a customer comes through our front door I see, stamped on their forehead in big red numbers, '$246,000.' I'm never going to make that person unhappy with me. Or lose her to the competition."[44]

The second reason to study customer defections is that customers who have left are much more likely

Courtesy Herman Miller, Inc.

than current customers to tell you what you were doing wrong. Finally, companies that understand why customers leave not only can take steps to fix ongoing problems, but also can identify which customers are likely to leave and make changes to prevent them from leaving.

15-3d The Internal Perspective: Controlling Quality

The third part of the Balanced Scorecard, the internal perspective, relates to the processes, decisions, and actions that managers and employees make within the organization. The internal perspective asks this question: "What must we excel at?" For McDonald's, it could be processes and systems that enable the company to provide consistent, quick, low-cost food. For Toyota, it could be reliability—when you turn your key in the ignition, the car starts, no matter whether the car has 20,000 or 200,000 kilometres on it. Yet, no matter what area a company chooses, the key is to excel in that area. Consequently, the internal perspective of the Balanced Scorecard usually leads managers to a focus on quality.

Quality is typically defined and measured in three ways: excellence, value, and conformance to specifications.[45] When the company defines its quality goal as *excellence,* managers must try to produce a product or service of unsurpassed performance and features. For example, Singapore Airlines is the best airline in the world by almost any standard. It has also received various "best airline" awards from the Pacific Asia Travel Association, *Travel+Leisure, Business Traveller, Condé Nast Traveller,* and *Fortune.*[46] Many airlines try to cram passengers into every available inch on a plane; by contrast, Singapore Airlines delivers creature comforts to encourage repeat business and customers willing to pay premium prices. On its newer planes, the first-class cabin is divided into eight private mini-rooms, each with an unusually wide leather seat that folds down flat for sleeping, a 23-inch LCD TV that doubles as a computer monitor, and an adjustable table. These amenities and services are common in private jets but truly unique in the commercial airline industry.[47] Singapore Airlines was the first airline, in the 1970s, to introduce a choice of meals, complimentary drinks, and earphones in coach class. It was also the first to introduce worldwide video, news, telephone, and fax services and the first to feature personal video monitors for movies, news, documentaries, and games. Singapore Airlines has had AC power for laptop computers for some time, and recently it became the first airline to introduce on-board high-speed Internet access.

Value is the customer's perception that a product's quality is excellent for the price offered. At a higher price, customers may perceive the same product to be less of a value. When a company emphasizes value as its quality goal, managers must simultaneously control excellence, price, durability, and other features of a product or service that customers strongly associate with value. Loblaw currently operates under more than 22 different banners—including Independent, Zehrs, Superstore, T&T, Wholesale Club, Valu-mart, No Frills, Maxi, Loblaws, Provigo, and its newly acquired (at $12.4 billion) Shoppers Drug Mart—and all of these operate on the principle of bringing maximum value to customers. Loblaw has always been known for the quality, innovation, and value of its food offerings. Just a short while ago,

Value customer perception that the product quality is excellent for the price offered.

Niloo/Shutterstock.com

however, executive chairman Galen Weston said: "We are not delivering the right value for money. Our actual prices relative to Walmart are significantly higher than we thought." Loblaw had to turn that around, and it did. It now offers Canada's strongest control label program (private label), one that includes President's Choice, No Name, and PC Decadent items. People will pay extra for a product that has a high value but that, technically, is not a name brand. President's Choice has consistently beaten name brand rivals in taste and quality. In remarks accompanying recent record earnings, Weston said that thanks to this simple "value" approach to business, "our fresh-led, customer-focused strategy is delivering results."[48] Loblaw planned to build 50 new stores and renovate or improve more than 150 existing stores in 2016.[49]

When a company defines its quality goal as *conformance to specifications*, employees must base their decisions and actions on whether the services and products they offer measure up to the standard. In contrast to excellence and value-based definitions of quality, which can be somewhat ambiguous, measuring whether products and services are "in spec" is relatively easy. Although conformance to specifications (i.e., precise tolerances for a part's weight or thickness) is usually associated with manufacturing, it can be used equally well to control quality in nonmanufacturing jobs. For example, Exhibit 15.5 shows a checklist that a cook or restaurant owner would use to ensure quality when buying fresh fish.

The way in which a company defines quality affects the methods and measures that employees use to control quality. Exhibit 15.6 shows the advantages and disadvantages associated with the excellence, value, and conformance-to-specification definitions of quality.

15-3e The Innovation and Learning Perspective: Controlling Waste and Pollution

The last part of the Balanced Scorecard, the innovation and learning perspective, addresses this question: "Can we continue to improve and create value?"

Exhibit 15.5
Conformance to Specifications Checklist for Buying Fresh Fish

LUNAMARINA/iStock/Thinkstock

Quality Checklist For Buying Fresh Fish		
Fresh Whole Fish	**Acceptable**	**Not Acceptable**
Gills	✓ bright red, free of slime, clear mucus	✗ brown to greyish, thick, yellow mucus
Eyes	✓ clear, bright, bulging, black pupils	✗ dull, sunken, cloudy, grey pupils
Smell	✓ inoffensive, slight ocean smell	✗ ammonia, putrid smell
Skin	✓ opalescent sheen, scales adhere tightly to skin	✗ dull or faded colour, scales missing or easily removed
Flesh	✓ firm and elastic to touch, tight to the bone	✗ soft and flabby, separating from the bone
Belly cavity	✓ no viscera or blood visible, lining intact, no bone protruding	✗ incomplete evisceration, cuts or protruding bones, off-odour

Sources: "A Closer Look: Buy It Fresh, Keep It Fresh," Consumer Reports Online, June 20, 2005, http://www.seagrant.sunysb.edu/SeafoodTechnology/SeafoodMedia/cR02 -2001/CR-SeafoodII020101.htm; "How to Purchase: Buying Fish," AboutSeaFood, June 20, 2005, http://www.aboutseafood.com/faqs/purchase1.html.

Exhibit 15.6
Advantages and Disadvantages of Different Measures of Quality

Quality Measure	Advantages	Disadvantages
Excellence	Promotes clear organizational vision.	Provides little practical guidance for managers.
	Being/providing the "best" motivates and inspires managers and employees.	Excellence is ambiguous. What is it? Who defines it?
Value	Appeals to customers, who "know excellence when they see it."	Difficult to measure and control.
	Customers recognize differences in value.	Can be difficult to determine what factors influence whether a product/service is seen as having value.
	Easier to measure and compare whether products/services differ in value.	Controlling the balance between excellence and cost (i.e., affordable excellence) can be difficult.
Conformance to Specifications	If specifications can be written, conformance to specifications is usually measurable.	Many products/services cannot be easily evaluated in terms of conformance to specifications.
	Should lead to increased efficiency.	Promotes standardization, so may hurt performance when adapting to changes is more important.
	Promotes consistency in quality.	May be less appropriate for services, which are dependent on a high degree of human contact.

Source: C. A. Reeves and D. A. Bednar, "Defining Quality: Alternatives and Implications," *Academy of Management Review* 19 (1994): 419–445.

Thus, the innovation and learning perspective involves continuous improvement in ongoing products and services (see Chapter 17); relearning and redesigning the processes by which products and services are created (see Chapter 6); and even things like waste and pollution minimization, an increasingly important area of innovation.

Exhibit 15.7 shows the four levels of *waste minimization* ranging from Level 1: Waste Disposal (which produces the smallest minimization of waste), to Level 4: Waste Prevention and Reduction (which produces the greatest minimization).[50]

At Level 1, *Waste Disposal*, wastes that cannot be prevented, reduced, recycled, reused, or treated should be safely disposed of in processing plants or in environmentally secure landfills that prevent leakage and contamination of soil and underground water supplies. For example, with the average computer lasting just three years, approximately 60 million computers come out of service each year. But because of the lead in the monitors, toxic metals in the circuit boards,

paint-coated plastic, and metal coatings that can contaminate ground water, old computers, tablets, and phones can't just be thrown away.[51] Annual retail sales of consumer electronics have jumped to $283 billion according to the Consumer Technology Association, and this generates more than 6.5 million tonnes of unwanted electronics each year.[52] While electronics powerhouse Best Buy is counting on its recycling program to lure shoppers into its stores—no easy feat these days with the popularity of online shopping—"that benefit may not be significant enough to offset the expenses of running the recycling program. A retailer or a collector must either charge the customer, or subsidize the recycling themselves, or it won't be properly recycled."[53]

At Level 2, *Waste Treatment*, companies use biological, chemical, and other processes to turn potentially harmful wastes into harmless compounds or useful byproducts. Usually supermarkets throw away the food they don't sell, but in the United Kingdom, several supermarket chains are using warm water and

Exhibit 15.7
Waste Minimization

Waste Prevention and Reduction	• Prevent waste and pollution before they occur • Reduce when waste occurs
Waste Reuse and Recycling	• Reuse materials for as long as possible • Collect materials for recycling
Waste Treatment	• Biological, chemical, and other processes turn waste into harmless compounds or useful by products
Waste Disposal	• Safely dispose of waste in processing plants or in environmentally secure landfills

bacteria to convert food waste to a methane-rich biogas that powers electricity plants. Because the supermarkets are taxed $98 for every ton of trash that goes into landfills, Marks & Spencer now sends 89 percent of its food waste for biogas conversion, saving the company $163 million a year.[54]

At Level 3, *Waste Reuse and Recycling*, wastes are reduced by reusing materials as long as possible or by collecting materials for on- or off-site recycling. A growing trend in recycling is *design for disassembly*, where products are designed from the start for easy disassembly, recycling, and reuse once they are no longer usable. The province of Alberta has been doing a lot to recycle. Albertans recycle standard-sized beer bottles (which are reused rather than recycled) and all other beverage containers. Containers are collected at privately owned for-profit bottle depots. Most of Alberta's larger municipalities have Blue Box recycling programs for which curbside recycling of newsprint, cardboard, plastic packaging, and other nonfood household wastes is a municipal respon-sibility. Edmonton has citywide curbside recycling for single-family houses; it also recycles Christmas trees and construction waste. Higher levels of processing including large-scale composting and capturing methane to produce energy. Collection includes multifamily buildings and businesses. Edmonton now diverts approximately 90 percent of its waste from landfills.[55] By contrast, Calgary currently collects recyclables only at private houses, and has no plans to introduce collection at condominium and apartment buildings.[56]

The goal at the top, Level 4, *Waste Prevention and Reduction*, is to prevent waste and pollution from occurring and to reduce them when they do occur. As an example of how much of a problem waste and pollution have become, the global oceans have amassed more than 5.25 trillion plastic particles, weighing about 240,000 tonnes,[57] and it is not just in garbage patches: the plastic is "dispersed throughout the water, resting on the ocean floor and trapped in Arctic ice."[58] Aquatic animals also ingest or become ensnared in

Bakalusha/Shutterstock.com

this highly polluted plastic, harming or killing them. Companies are increasingly taking notice of the environmental impact of their products and business practices, and using three strategies for waste prevention and reduction:

1. *Good housekeeping.* Examples of this include performing regularly scheduled preventive maintenance for offices and plants and making sure that machines are running properly so that they don't use more fuel than necessary.

2. *Material/product substitution.* Examples include replacing toxic or hazardous materials with less harmful ones. As part of its Pollution Prevention Pays program, 3M Canada participates in the 2025 sustainability goals that "reflect 3M's commitment to improving our business, our planet and every life," said Gayle Schueller, 3M vice president, global sustainability.[59]

3. *Process modification.* Examples include changing steps or procedures to eliminate or reduce waste.

STUDY TOOLS 15

READY TO STUDY?

LOCATED IN TEXTBOOK:

☐ Rip out the Chapter Review Card at the back of the book to have a summary of the chapter and key terms handy.

LOCATED AT NELSON.COM/STUDENT:

☐ Access the eBook or use the ReadSpeaker feature to listen to the chapter on the go.

☐ Prepare for tests with practice quizzes.

☐ Review key terms with flashcards and the glossary feature.

☐ Work through key concepts with case studies and Management Decision Exercises.

☐ Explore practical examples with You Make the Decision Activities.

16 Managing Information in a Global World

GlobalStock/iStockphoto

LEARNING OUTCOMES

After studying this chapter, you will be able to...

16-1 Explain the strategic importance of information.

16-2 Describe the characteristics of useful information (i.e., its value and costs).

16-3 Explain the basics of capturing, processing, and protecting information.

16-4 Describe how companies can access and share information and knowledge.

After you finish
this chapter, go
to **PAGE 354** for
STUDY TOOLS

Treading a New Virtual Path

With international borders often reduced to virtual reality these days, Elizabeth Lee works out of the Vancouver head office of Hootsuite but deals with the United States, European, and Australian clients as well as Canadians. In 2014, she became a customer success manager for Hootsuite, which describes itself as a social relationship platform (SRP). Elizabeth says her job is similar to that of an account manager and that she handles troubleshooting, strategizing with domestic and international clients, aligning products with client objectives, and ensuring the success of her clients. She obtained her business education at the BC Institute of Technology (BCIT), graduating with both a diploma in marketing communications (2008–10) and a bachelor of business administration degree in marketing management (2010–11). Hootsuite traces its start to the year she first entered BCIT. Ryan Holmes started the social media platform in 2008, and within six years it was boasting more than 10 million users; by 2016 it had more than 500 staff in its nine offices around the world, and was being used in more than 175 countries. It's a "freemium" company in that casual social media users can make use of the platform for free, but it also has major paying clients. Hootsuite is known for its signature dashboard, which allows clients to manage various social media accounts from one place.

1. Would it be true to say that the company you work for has always been a good candidate to use the very tool it offers others?

Yes. Hootsuite has revolutionized how we as a company engage with our audience. Having the ability to bring all of our social networks into one dashboard enables us to connect with our audience and aggregate data on those interactions in real time.

2. Just how important do you think information management is around the world these days?

Information management is absolutely crucial to the longevity of any company. In Roman times one needed brute strength to succeed (or privilege via birth); now one needs information. Data, big data, google alerts, analytics . . . it is our job—as in everyone, not just those in the tech sector—to find out what information is important, create a strategy, and execute accordingly. If there is a kink in the chain connecting decision makers to vital information, that company will not survive.

3. Is it exhilarating or scary to work in what might be seen as a cutting-edge business?

Scary is what's making business these days exhilarating. People are scared of the unknown. It is those who are willing to embrace that fear who will find something more. For example, my role! Customer success manager is a new position. This field has no roadmap telling us what success is. There are no experts. We have the ability to pave our own road and be those experts. Personally, I find that scary and exhilarating, which tells me I am doing what I am supposed to be doing.

4. What trait or skill do you think has served you the best in this kind of work?

In a word, adaptability. Technology is ever changing and so are the roles surrounding it. If you want a nine-to-five, and return home to your white picket fence, you can, or you can work remote from your terrace in Spain. Just as long as you can adapt to your surroundings, you can succeed.

5. Do you ever get surprised by aspects of business information management?

Always. Information moulds the way we do business and information is more readily available than it ever has been before. What do we do with this information? What's important? What tool do we use to help us aggregate this information? All of us have been tasked with internalizing mass amounts of data. Since the answers to the aforementioned questions are always changing, so is information management, which definitely keeps us all on our toes.

6. Do you get to see the good side of information management in your work?

Definitely. Leveraging information to understand your clientele or the competitive environment or to draw conclusions as to what the future holds is fantastic! Information makes companies agile. It's agile companies that make it for the long haul. Think P&G.

7. Obviously you must hear about the less fun side, too—would security threats be a prime example?

We are in a hyper-growth industry. Which means growing pains are inevitable. Security would be one of those pains. The best part is the discovery of the solution.

8. What do you love best about your job?

The best part about my job is how new it is. As I mentioned earlier, the ability to pave my own way and have the opportunity to be an expert is incredibly exciting to me. I am in a unique situation that allows me to interact with those who are older than I and be seen as an equal. Technology is just getting started!

For the full interview, go online to nelson.com/student

Photo and interview courtesy of Elizabeth Lee

16-1 STRATEGIC IMPORTANCE OF INFORMATION

A generation ago, computer hardware and software had little to do with managing business information. Instead of storing information on hard drives, managers stored it in filing cabinets. Instead of uploading daily sales and inventory levels by satellite to corporate headquarters, they mailed hardcopy summaries to headquarters in Toronto at the end of each month. There were no word processors, so reports were typed on an electric typewriter.

There were no spreadsheets, so calculations were made on adding machines. Managers communicated by sticky notes, not email. Phone messages were written down by assistants and coworkers, not left on voice mail. Workers did not use desktop or laptop computers as a daily tool to get work done. Instead, they scheduled limited access time to run batch jobs on the mainframe computer (and prayed that the batch job computer code they wrote would work).

Today, a generation later, computers are integral to managing business information. This is due mainly to something called *Moore's law*. Gordon Moore was one of the founders of Intel Corporation, which today makes 75 percent of the integrated processors used in personal computers. Way back in 1965, in what has become known as **Moore's law**, Moore predicted that computer-processing power would double and its cost would drop by 50 percent about every two years.[1] As Exhibit 16.1 shows, he was right. Computer power, as measured by the number of transistors per

Moore's law the prediction that the cost of computing will drop by 50 percent every 18 months as computer-processing power doubles.

Exhibit 16.1
Moore's Law

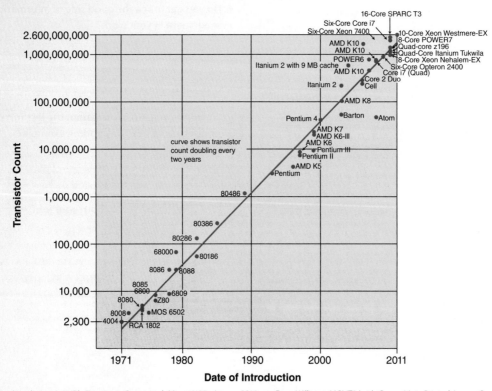

Sources: http://en.wikipedia/org/wiji/File:Transistor_Count_and_Moore%27s_Law_-_2011.svg. From Williams. *MGMT5* (with CourseMate Printed Access Card), 5E. © 2013 SouthWestern, a part of Cengage Learning, Inc. Reproduced by permission. www.cengage.com/permissions.

computer chip, *has* more than doubled every few years. Consequently, the device sitting on your lap or on your desk or in your pocket is not only smaller but also much cheaper and more powerful than the large mainframe computers used by *Fortune* 500 companies 30 years ago. For instance, your iPhone replaces 13 of the 15 items, such as a desktop computer, mobile phone, CD player, camcorder, etc., commonly sold by Radio Shack in 1991, items that would have cost you $3,071.21 then, or, after adjusting for inflation, $5,374.46 today. So your $600 iPhone not only replaces a trunkful of 1991 electronics gear, it does so for only 11 percent of the cost.[2] That's Moore's law in action. Will Moore's law eventually fail and technological progress eventually slow? Perhaps, but it's not likely in your lifetime. Intel's vice president of technology and manufacturing, Mike Mayberry, says, "If you're only using the same technology, then in principle you run into limits. The truth is we've been modifying the technology every five or seven years for forty years, and there's no end in sight for being able to do that."[3]

Raw data are facts and figures. For example, 11, $752, 32, and 26,100 are some data that I used the day I wrote this section of the chapter. However, facts and figures aren't particularly useful unless they have meaning. You probably can't guess what these four pieces of raw data represent, can you? And if you can't, they are useless. That's why researchers make the distinction between raw data and information. Although raw data consist of facts and figures, **information** is useful data that can influence someone's choices and behaviour. Data have no context; information does have context.

So what did those four pieces of data mean to me? Well, 11 stands for Channel 11, the local CBC affiliate on which I watched part of the NHL finals (those darn Canucks!). $752 is how much it will cost me to rent a minivan for a week if I go skiing over spring break at Whistler. 32 is for the 32-gigabyte storage card that I want to insert in my digital camera (prices are so low I'll probably buy two, although, to be truthful, my smart phone takes better pictures!). And 26,100 kilometres tells me that it's time to go to Canadian Tire and get the oil changed in my car.

In today's hypercompetitive business environment, information is as important as capital (i.e., money) for business success, whether it relates to furniture delivery, product inventory, pricing, or costs. It takes money to get a business started, but a business can't survive and grow without the right information. Information has strategic importance for organizations because it can be used to **16-1a obtain**

first-mover advantage and 16-1b sustain a competitive advantage once it has been created.

16-1a Obtaining First-Mover Advantage

First-mover advantage is the strategic advantage that companies earn by being the first in an industry to use new information technology to substantially lower costs or to differentiate a product or service from that of competitors. Pandora, for example, pioneered music streaming and leads this highly competitive market with a 9.13 percent share of the total US radio listening market (which includes all radio stations and streaming services), up from 7.29 percent a year earlier. Pandora, which is free to listeners because it makes money via advertising, had 81 million active listeners per month as of December 31, 2015.[4] While first-mover advantage typically leads to above average profits and market share, it doesn't immunize a company from competition. Pandora already faces three primary competitors: Spotify (40 million listeners, 10 million subscribers), Deezer (12 million listeners, 5 million subscribers), and Apple's iTunes Radio (free/ad-based, 40 million listeners). Two other music streaming sources—Amazon's Prime Music, which is free for Amazon's 10 million

ManuelBurgos/iStockphoto

Raw data facts and figures.

Information useful data that can influence people's choices and behaviour.

First-mover advantage the strategic advantage that companies earn by being the first to use new information technology to substantially lower costs or to make a product or service different from that of competitors.

Prime members (who pay $99 a year for Prime membership which includes two-day shipping and a number of other benefits), and Apple's Beats Music (250,000 subscribers)—represent new, serious threats to Pandora.[5]

16-1b Sustaining a Competitive Advantage

As described above, a company that uses information technology (IT) to establish first-mover advantage usually enjoys a higher market share as well as higher profits. According to the resource-based view of IT (as shown in Exhibit 16.2), companies need to address three critical questions in order to sustain a competitive advantage through IT.

1. *Does the IT create value for the firm by lowering costs or providing a better product or service?* If the IT doesn't add value, then investing in it will put the firm at a competitive *dis*advantage relative to companies that choose IT that does add value.

2. *Is the IT the same or different across competing firms?* If all firms have access to the same IT and use it in the same way, then no firm has an advantage over another (i.e., there is competitive parity).

3. *Is it difficult for other companies to create or buy the IT they use?* If it is, then the firm that *has* acquired the IT has established a sustainable competitive advantage over its competitors. If it is not, then the competitive advantage is only temporary, and competitors should eventually be able to duplicate the advantages that the leading firm has gained from IT. (For more about sustainable competitive advantage and its sources, see Chapter 5, "Organizational Strategy.")

In short, the key to sustaining a competitive advantage is not faster computers, more memory, and larger hard drives. The key is using IT to continuously improve and support the business's core functions.

Savvy businesses use social media to improve customer service. The staff of leading hotels search for any mention of their hotel on Twitter, Facebook, Tumblr, and websites like TripAdvisor. When they find a complaint they offer an immediate apology and, more often than not, perks like a room upgrade or a free meal as compensation.[6] Many pet owners have complained about problems they encounter when travelling with their pets. "You can check in, but you'll be sleeping in the smelly room across from the ice machine on the ground floor." In Sault Ste. Marie, Ontario, for instance, "our pet-friendly hotel room had tufts of fur on the pillowcase when I turned

down the bedspread. I called the front desk to complain, and we got moved to a new room where our cat disappeared into a hole in the drywall behind the toilet." People will go out of their way to check into pet-friendly hotels that present none of these problems.[7]

Companies that achieve first-mover advantage with IT and then sustain it with continued investment create a moving target that competitors have difficulty hitting.

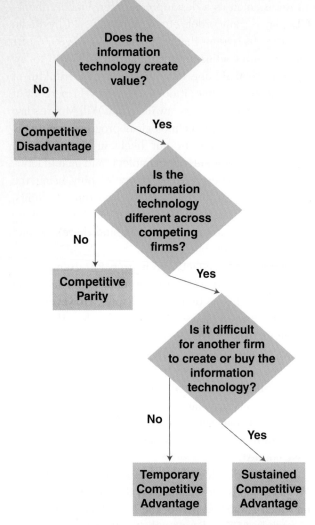

Exhibit 16.2
Using Information Technology to Sustain a Competitive Advantage

Does the information technology create value?
No → Competitive Disadvantage
Yes → Is the information technology different across competing firms?
No → Competitive Parity
Yes → Is it difficult for another firm to create or buy the information technology?
No → Temporary Competitive Advantage
Yes → Sustained Competitive Advantage

Source: Adapted from F. J. Mata, W. L. Fuerst, and J. B. Barney, "Information Technology and Sustained Competitive Advantage: A Resource-Based Analysis," *MIS Quarterly 19*, no. 4 (December 1995): 487–505. Copyright © 1995, Regents of the University of Minnesota. Reprinted by permission.

16-2 CHARACTERISTICS AND COSTS OF USEFUL INFORMATION

Toronto is a major business, travel, and tourism hub (besides being home to more than 6 million Canadians). To handle the crush of commuters and visitors, Toronto has 9,300 Toronto Transit Commission (TTC) bus stops in the city and there are another 800 stops in the Greater Toronto Area. TTC passengers can use a real-time GPS-tracking website to find out when their next bus will arrive. The site uses "satellite technology and advanced computer modeling" to track TTC buses along their routes. Passengers can also use trip planning software or download one of several available apps to determine which bus route to take. In Ontario, the Guelph and Thunder Bay transit systems use this same service; so do some areas in Quebec, Alberta, New Brunswick, and Manitoba.[8]

*Information is useful when it is **16-2a accurate**, **16-2b complete**, **16-2c relevant**, and **16-2d timely**. However, there can be significant **16-2e acquisition**, **16-2f processing**, **16-2g storage**, **16-2h retrieval**, and **16-2i communication costs** associated with useful information.*

16-2a Accurate Information

Information is useful when it is accurate. Before relying on information to make decisions, you must know that the information is correct. But what if it isn't? Many retailers use customer satisfaction surveys to determine what they need to improve, and checkout wait times are always near the top of the list. But asking customers about checkout wait times can produce inaccurate data. Shoppers accurately estimate wait times of three minutes or less but overestimate four-minute waits, which they report as five or six minutes, and completely misestimate five-minute waits, which they report as 10 minutes. Typically, retailers relying on these data overestimate checkout wait time and can end up hiring too many cashiers to solve the problem.[9] Kroger, a US grocery giant that has been eyeing Canada for years, gets more accurate data from infrared cameras that count the number of customers in the store and waiting at checkout registers. These data showed Kroger that its stores had many customers at lunch and in the morning buying just a few items, which would be better served by express lanes, so Kroger added 2,000 more to its stores. As a result of these changes, made on the basis of more accurate information, the average wait at Kroger has dropped from four minutes to 26 seconds.[10]

16-2b Complete Information

Information is useful when it is complete. Incomplete or missing information makes it difficult to recognize problems and identify potential solutions. Following an airplane crash, investigators recover critical information from the plane's black box recordings. If the black box is lost or damaged, then investigators may never understand what happened. "Everyone talks about the black box on an airplane," says Vic Charlebois, vice president of flight operations at Canadian airline First Air, "but it is permanently installed on an airplane, and if the airplane goes missing so does the black box."[11] Indeed, when Malaysia Airlines Flight 370 disappeared en route from Kuala Lumpur to Beijing in March 2014, investigators were left guessing as to the cause because the plane and its black box are still missing more than two years later.[12]

Regulators have long suggested putting live data systems on planes to transmit real-time in-flight data, but airlines have hesitated because of costs estimated at $100,000 per plane.[13] Canadian-based First Air is installing a live data streaming service that can provide much more complete and useful information. Made by Canadian-based Flyht, First Air's FLYHTStream system can be preprogrammed to automatically transmit live data under certain conditions, or it can be manually activated by the pilot or ground-based flight controllers. First Air's Vic Charlebois says, "Let's take the case of the Malaysian aircraft. If it was being monitored through satellites and a dispatcher did see it wander off course somewhere, the procedure would be to activate

Kiev.Victor/Shutterstock.com

the FLYHTStream and then contact the crew to see what was going on."[14]

16-2c Relevant Information

You can have complete, accurate information, but it's not very useful if it doesn't pertain to the problems you're facing. For instance, if you're unlucky enough to contract bullous pemphigoid, a rare skin condition resulting in large, watery blisters on your inner thighs and upper arms, chances are the dermatologist you visit won't have any relevant experience with this condition to be able to recognize and treat it. And that's exactly what happened to Dr. Kavita Mariwalla, who was stumped when a patient came in with these problems. So she turned to Modernizing Medicine, an iPad-based medical records system to obtain the relevant information needed to determine what was wrong. Modernizing Medicine is a web-based database, containing information from more than 14 million patient visits compiled by 3,700 doctors, that uses the same kind of data mining and artificial intelligence used by websites like Amazon.com. Dr. Eric Horvitz, Microsoft's managing director of research, says, "Electronic health records [are] like large quarries where there's lots of gold, and we're just beginning to mine them."[15] Dr. Mariwalla was able to quickly access similar cases on Modernizing Medicine's database and find drugs that had been effective in those cases. Dr. Mariwalla said that Modernizing Medicine "gives you access to data, and data is king. It's been very helpful, especially in clinically challenging situations."[16]

16-2d Timely Information

Finally, information is useful when it is timely. News that your bus passed the stop 10 minutes ago is not helpful in getting you where you want to go. To be timely, the information must be available when needed to define a problem or to begin to identify possible solutions. If you've ever thought, "I wish I had known that earlier," then you understand the importance of timely information and the opportunity cost of not having it.

What could be more Canadian than maple syrup? Maple sap used to make syrup used to be collected in buckets hanging from taps bored into trees. Instead of buckets, modern maple syrup production uses long flexible plastic tubes to transport the sap kilometres away to sugar-storage houses. When the sap stops flowing because of leaks, it can take workers days to walk the lines to locate them. And with a short four- to six-week season, fixing leaks quickly is critical. Meadowbrook Maple Syrup has 5,000 taps and 30 kilometres of tubes spread out over 40 hectares. To reduce the time spent looking for leaks, Meadowbrook installed a Tap Track system that uses solar-powered sensors to monitor line pressure at each tree. When the system detects a drop in pressure (indicating a leak), it sends an alert to company computers and smart phones. Eric Sorkin, of Thunder Basin Maple Works, described how the Tap Track system directed his workers to a porcupine-caused leak. Just as they fixed that leak, the system alerted them to one nearby. Sorkin said, "You could follow the porcupine right to the next line where he'd cut it. Otherwise, it would have been a few more days before we found those two lines."[17]

16-2e Acquisition Costs

Acquisition cost is the cost of obtaining data that you don't have. For example, Acxiom, a billion-dollar company with a major data centre in Toronto, gathers and processes data for direct-mail marketing companies. If you've received an unsolicited, preapproved credit card application recently (and who hasn't?), chances are Acxiom helped the credit card company gather information about you. Where does Acxiom get that information? Mainly from companies that sell consumer credit reports at a wholesale cost of $1 each. Acxiom also obtains information from retailers. Each time you use your credit card, checkout scanners gather information about your spending habits and product preferences. Many retailers sell this information to companies like Acxiom that use it for market research. So why pay for this information? The reason is that acquiring it can help credit card companies do a better job of identifying who will mail back a signed credit card application and who will simply

Paul Johnson/iStockphoto

Acquisition cost the cost of obtaining data that you don't have.

shred it. The ability to target likely customers saves the companies money and effort in the end.

For example, Nordstrom would find it worthwhile to advertise to "Apple Pie Families," who are usually defined as married homeowners between the ages of 46 and 65 who live in urban areas, earn $100,000 to $500,000, and have school-age children. Likewise, Walmart is better off advertising to "Trucks and Trailers," who might be defined as people between the ages of 30 and 45 who earn less than $100,000 and live in rural areas. Paying Acxiom to acquire this kind of data significantly increases the return that retailers and credit card companies get from advertising and direct marketing.

16-2f Processing Costs

Companies often have massive amounts of data but not in the form or combination they need. **Processing cost** is the cost of turning raw data into usable information. While Google offers a wide range of online services, most of its revenues come from search-related ads. But those ads are effective only when Google serves up accurate searches that help people find what they're looking for. In an effort to provide more precise searches, Google is now connecting and linking the information that users "leave behind" as they use Google search, YouTube, Gmail, other Google services, and their Android phones. For example, Google says that these additional data can help it determine if a user searching for "jaguar" is looking for a cat or a car. Of course, turning all of that data into meaningful information to improve

search accuracy requires massive computing power. Thus, Google operates 10 extraordinarily expensive data centres around the world. Google's data centre in Finland, for example, cost $273 million; the one in Hong Kong, $300 million; and the one in Singapore, $120 million. And that is just the up-front cost; the cost of staffing and maintaining the centres for years to come will be millions more.[18]

16-2g Storage Costs

Storage cost is the cost of physically or electronically archiving information for later use and retrieval. Canadian winters are pretty challenging for most of us, but they have their advantages. In addition to producing the world's best hockey players, Canada has become host to a growing number of data centres that take advantage of the cold climate to mitigate the extensive costs of cooling their server infrastructure. "The advantage Canada has is it's far cheaper and easier to bring data to power sources, and vice versa," says Mike O'Neil, president of IT research firm IT Market Dynamics. "It's much cheaper to stick your data centre next to a hydro dam." This unique weather and inexpensive power puts

> **Processing cost** the cost of turning raw data into usable information.
>
> **Storage cost** the cost of physically or electronically archiving information for later use and retrieval.

Jaguar   OR   Jaguar

Ammit Jack/Shutterstock; Paolo Cipriani/iStockphoto

Canada in a similar league with Sweden and Finland, which have recently become the hosts of huge data centres built by Facebook and Google.[19] Many believe these facilities are only the beginning. In the increasingly common cloud computing scenario, companies are outsourcing their computing to remote providers, and Canadian data centres are able to serve markets anywhere in the world.

16-2h Retrieval Costs

Retrieval cost is the cost of accessing information that has already been stored and processed. One of the most common misunderstandings about information is that it is easy and cheap to retrieve once the company has it. Not so. First, you have to find the information. Then you've got to convince whoever has it to share it with you. Then the information has to be processed into a form that is useful for you.

For example, more organizations are moving toward the paperless office. One challenge this move presents is how employees will retrieve various kinds of data that exist across a company, whether they come from an email, a file record, a website, a word processing document, or an image. With this variety of information, how do you quickly find what you need? Canada is emerging as a world centre for data retrieval. This country has yet another advantage besides cheap power, cold weather, and plentiful water (needed for cooling systems): Canada's Privacy Act appeals to European and international companies looking to locate data centres. "Canadian law, which doesn't allow a government institution to collect personal information unless it relates directly to an operating program or activity of that institution, tends to be better aligned with European regulations than the Patriot Act [in the United States], which makes data accessible to any parties of government," says Michel Cartier of the University of Quebec–Montreal. "Most companies coming into Canada aren't a Yahoo or Google type of company. We're seeing large, global co-locators with customers

Companies often have massive amounts of data, but not in the form or combination they need.

based in Europe and Asia who want to bring operations to North America but need regulations that protect the customer's privacy."[20]

16-2i Communication Costs

Communication cost is the cost of transmitting information from one place to another. The most important information that a company like BC Hydro collects each month is the information from the meter attached to the side of your house. For many years, electricity companies employed meter readers to walk from house to house to gather information, which was then entered into company computers. Now, however, companies like BC Hydro are using electric meters that contain radio frequency (RF) transmitters (see Section 16-3a). The transmitters turn on when a meter reader drives by the house in a utility company van, which has a laptop computer specially equipped to receive the RF signals. Such a van, travelling at legal speeds, can read 12,000 to 13,000 meters in an eight-hour day. The RF signal lasts about 1.4 seconds. By contrast, a meter reader on foot would record data from 500 meters per day.[21]

Retrieval cost the cost of accessing already stored and processed information.

Communication cost the cost of transmitting information from one place to another.

Getting and Sharing Information

In 1907, Metropolitan Life Insurance, which now owns MetLife Canada, built a huge office building for its brand new, state-of-the-art IT system. What was this great breakthrough in information technology? Card files. That's right, the same card file system that every library in Canada used before computers. Metropolitan Life's IT consisted of 20,000 separate file drawers that sat in hundreds of file cabinets more than five metres tall. This filing system held 20 million insurance applications, 700,000 accounting books, and 500,000 death certificates. Metropolitan Life employed 61 workers who did nothing but sort, file, and climb ladders to pull files as needed.[22]

How we get and share information has clearly changed. Today, if a storm, a fire, or an accident damages a policyholder's property, the insurance company writes a cheque on the spot to cover the loss. When a policyholder buys a car, she calls her Insurance Corporation of British Columbia (ICBC) agent from the dealership to activate her insurance before driving off in her new car. Today, even provincial Crown corporations like ICBC are marketing their products and services to customers directly from the Internet.

Carsten/Hulton Archive/Getty Images

16-3 CAPTURING, PROCESSING, AND PROTECTING INFORMATION

*In this section, you will learn about the information technologies that companies use to **16-3a capture, 16-3b process,** and **16-3c protect information**.*

16-3a Capturing Information

There are two basic methods for capturing information: manual and electronic. Manual capture of information is a slow, costly, labour-intensive process that entails recording and entering data by hand into a data storage device. Consequently, companies are relying more on electronic capture. They use electronic storage devices such as *bar codes, radio frequency identification tags,* and *electronic scanners* to capture and record data electronically.

Bar codes represent numerical data by varying the thickness and pattern of vertical bars. The primary advantage of bar codes is that the data they represent can be read and recorded in an instant with a handheld or pen-type scanner. Bar codes cut checkout times in half, reduce data entry errors by 75 percent, and save stores money because stockers don't have to go through the labour-intensive process of putting a price tag on each item in the store.[23]

Radio frequency identification (RFID) tags contain microchips and minuscule antennae that transmit information via radio waves.[24] Unlike bar codes, which require direct line-of-sight scanning, RFID tags are read by turning on an RFID reader that, like a radio, tunes into a specific frequency to determine the number *and* location of products, parts, or anything else to which the RFID tags are attached. Turn on an RFID reader, and every RFID tag within the reader's range (from several hundred to several thousand metres) is accounted for.

Bar codes visual patterns that represent numerical data by varying the thickness and pattern of vertical bars.

Radio frequency identification (RFID) tags tags containing minuscule microchips that transmit information via radio waves and can be used to track the number and location of the objects into which the tags have been inserted.

Loblaw's has a new, 81,300-square-metre distribution centre in Ajax, just east of Toronto (it's about the size of 13 football fields). Keeping track of 7,196 different products and 67,000 pallets is no small feat. Before Loblaw's opened this large centre, a container of Yoplait yogurt travelled from an Ultima Foods plant to a Loblaw regional distribution warehouse and then on to a store. Along the way, the yogurt bided its time in trucks and on warehouse pallets until, finally, it found its way into a store and onto a shelf. By the time the yogurt made it to a dairy fridge, its month-long shelf life had ticked down to just 13 days, and no profits had been made in the first 17 days (although plenty of costs had been incurred).

According to Rand Russell, the Ajax facility's general manager, a big innovation is called Vocollect. Order selectors driving "pallet jack" vehicles receive instructions from the central computer via wireless headsets. "Leaving the workers' hands free has increased their efficiency by 10–15 percent," estimates Russell.[25]

Electronic scanners, which convert printed text and pictures into digital images, have become an increasingly popular means of capturing data electronically because they are inexpensive and easy to use. The first requirement for a good scanner is a *document feeder* that automatically feeds document pages into the scanner (or turns the pages—often with a puff of air—if books or bound documents are being scanned). Text that has been digitized cannot be searched or edited like the regular text in your word processing software, however, so the second requirement for a good scanner is

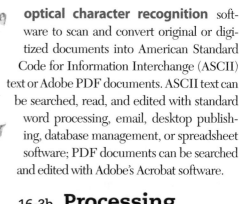

optical character recognition software to scan and convert original or digitized documents into American Standard Code for Information Interchange (ASCII) text or Adobe PDF documents. ASCII text can be searched, read, and edited with standard word processing, email, desktop publishing, database management, or spreadsheet software; PDF documents can be searched and edited with Adobe's Acrobat software.

16-3b Processing Information

Processing information means transforming raw data into meaningful information that can be applied to business decision making. Evaluating sales data to determine the best- and worst-selling products, examining repair records to determine product reliability, and monitoring the cost of long-distance phone calls are all examples of processing raw data into meaningful information. With automated, electronic capture of data, increased processing power, and cheaper and more plentiful ways to store data, managers no longer worry about getting data. Instead, they scratch their heads about how to use the overwhelming amount of data pouring into their businesses every day. Most managers know little about statistics and have neither the time nor the inclination to learn how to use them to analyze data.

One promising tool for helping managers dig out from under the avalanche of data is **data mining**—the process of discovering patterns and relationships in large amounts of data.[26] Data mining works by applying complex algorithms such as neural networks, rule induction, and decision trees. If you don't know what those are, that's okay. With data mining, you don't have to. Most

Electronic scanner an electronic device that converts printed text and pictures into digital images.

Optical character recognition the ability of software to convert digitized documents into American Standard Code for Information Interchange (ASCII) text or PDF documents that can be searched, read, and edited by word processing and other kinds of software.

Processing information transforming raw data into meaningful information.

Data mining the process of discovering patterns and relationships in large amounts of data.

 pairs well with

. . . if you're a dad in a hurry after work.

managers only need to know that data mining looks for patterns that are already in the data but are too complex for them to spot on their own.

Data mining typically splits a data set in half, finds patterns in one half, and then tests the validity of those patterns by trying to find them again in the second half of the data set. The data typically come from a **data warehouse** that stores huge amounts of data that have been prepared for data mining analysis by being cleaned of errors and redundancies. The data in a data warehouse can then be analyzed using two kinds of data mining: *supervised* and *unsupervised*. **Supervised data mining** usually begins with the user telling the data mining software to look and test for specific patterns and relationships in a data set. Typically, this is done through a series of "What if . . .?" questions or statements. For instance, a grocery store manager might instruct the data mining software to determine whether coupons placed in the Sunday paper increase or decrease sales. By contrast, with **unsupervised data mining**, the user simply tells the data mining software to uncover whatever patterns and relationships it can find in a data set. Unsupervised data mining is especially good at identifying *association or affinity patterns, sequence patterns,* and *predictive patterns*. It can also identify what data mining technicians call *data clusters*.

Association or affinity patterns arise when two or more database elements tend to occur together in a significant way. Surprisingly, one company found that beer and diapers tended to be bought together between 5 P.M. and 7 P.M. The question, of course, was "why?" The answer, on further review, was fairly straightforward: fathers, who were told by their wives to buy some diapers on their way home, decided to pick up a six-pack for themselves, too.[27]

Sequence patterns occur when two or more database elements occur together in a significant pattern in which one of the elements precedes the other.

StratBridge provides data mining capability to professional sports teams so that they can analyze their ticket sales in real time. Its StratTix software can help a team view up-to-the-minute seating charts to see which seats are selling and which are not. It also provides information about the people purchasing the tickets—for example, their geographic area and which source they used to purchase them (Ticketmaster, etc.). And it helps teams find the best time to market and promote games, and tells them which prices (at which times) will provide the best revenues. StratBridge has deals with most teams in the National Hockey League, so when you go to the Rogers Arena in Vancouver to watch the Canucks, you know you are getting the best seat at the best price.[28]

Predictive patterns are the opposite of association or affinity patterns. Association or affinity patterns look for database elements that seem to go together, whereas **predictive patterns** help identify database elements that are different.

Data warehouse stores huge amounts of data that have been prepared for data mining analysis by being cleaned of errors and redundancy.

Supervised data mining the process when the user tells the data mining software to look and test for specific patterns and relationships in a data set.

Unsupervised data mining the process when the user simply tells the data mining software to uncover whatever patterns and relationships it can find in a data set.

Association or affinity patterns when two or more database elements tend to occur together in a significant way.

Sequence patterns when two or more database elements occur together in a significant pattern, but one of the elements precedes the other.

Predictive patterns patterns that help identify database elements that are different.

David Cooper/Toronto Star via Getty Images

The Hudson's Bay Company (HBC), Canada's oldest company, generates a tremendous amount of data, but for a long time it was spread across a number of operational systems. The implementation of a centralized data warehouse for its 500 stores, combined with database query manager programs, turned out to be an excellent investment. HBC is now able to ensure that the right inventory is in the right location at the right time. In addition, it is now making inventory and buying decisions based on analyses of detailed transaction data, and market basket analysis has uncovered product affinities that have led to more effective promotions. The new system has also cut down on fraud against the company.[29]

Data clusters occur when three or more database elements converge in a significant way. After analyzing several years' worth of repair and warranty claims, Ford Motor Company might find that, compared to cars built in its Mississauga plant, the cars it builds in Oakville (first element) are more likely to have problems with over-tightened fan belts (second element) that break (third element) and result in overheated engines (fourth element), ruined radiators (fifth element), and payments for tow trucks (sixth element), which are paid for by Ford's three-year, 60,000 kilometre[30] warranty.

Data mining services and analyses are much more affordable than they used to be, within reach of most companies' budgets. And if it follows the path of most technologies, it will become even easier and cheaper to use in the future.

16-3c Protecting Information

Protecting information is the process of ensuring that data are reliably and consistently retrievable in a usable format for authorized users but no one else. Customers who purchase prescription medicines at CanadaDrugs.com, an online drugstore and health aid retailer, want to be confident that their medical and credit card information is available only to them, their pharmacist, and their doctor. Visit CanadaDrugs.com and click "Privacy Policy" (https://www.canadadrugs.com/privacy).

Companies like CanadaDrugs.com find it necessary to protect information because of the many security threats to data listed in Exhibit 16.3. People inside and

Data clusters when three or more database elements occur together (i.e., cluster) in a significant way.

Protecting information the process of ensuring that data are reliably and consistently retrievable in a usable format for authorized users but no one else.

Exhibit 16.3
Security Threats to Data and Data Networks

Security Problem	Source	Affects	Severity	The Threat	The Solution
Denial of service, web server attacks, and corporate network attacks	Internet hackers	All servers	High	Loss of data, disruption of service, theft of service.	Implement firewall, password control, server-side review, threat monitoring, bug fixes; turn PCs off when not in use.
Password cracking software and unauthorized access to PCs	Local area network, Internet	All users, especially digital subscriber line and cable Internet users	High	Hackers take over PCs. Privacy can be invaded. Corporate users' systems are exposed to other machines on the network.	Close ports and firewalls, disable file and print sharing, and use strong passwords.
Viruses, worms, Trojan horses, and rootkits	Email, downloaded and distributed software	All users	Moderate to high	Monitor activities and cause data loss and file deletion. Compromise security by sometimes concealing their presence.	Use antivirus software and firewalls; control Internet access.
Spyware, adware, malicious scripts, and applets	Rogue web pages	All users	Moderate to high	Invade privacy, intercept passwords, and damage files or file system.	Disable browser script support; use security, blocking, and spyware/adware software.
Email snooping	Hackers on your network and the Internet	All users	Moderate to high	People read your email from intermediate servers or packets, or they physically access your machine.	Encrypt message, ensure strong password protection, and limit physical access to machines.
Keystroke monitoring	Trojan horses, people with direct access to PCs	All users	High	Records everything typed at the keyboard and intercepts keystrokes before password masking or encryption occurs.	Use antivirus software to catch Trojan horses, control Internet access to transmission, and implement system monitoring and physical access control.
Phishing	Hackers on your network and the Internet	All users, including customers	High	Fake, but real-looking, emails and websites that trick users into sharing personal information on what they wrongly thought was the company's website. This leads to unauthorized account.	Educate and warn users and customers about the dangers. Encourage both not to click on potentially fake URLs, which might take them to phishing websites. Instead, have them type your company's URL into the web browser.
Spam	Email	All users and corporations	Mild to high	Clogs and overloads email servers and inboxes with junk mail. HTML-based spam may be used for profiling and identifying users.	Filter known spam sources and senders on email servers; have users create further lists of approved and unapproved senders on their personal computers.
Cookies	Websites you visit	Individual users	Mild to moderate	Trace web usage and permit the creation of personalized web pages that track behaviour and interest profiles.	Use cookie managers to control and edit cookies, and use ad blockers.

Sources: "Top 10 Security Threats," *PC Magazine*, April 10, 2007, 66; M. Sarrel, "Master End-User Security," *PC Magazine*, May 2008, 101; K. Bannan, "Look Out: Watching You, Watching Me," *PC Magazine*, July 2002, 99; A. Dragoon, "Fighting Phish, Fakes, and Frauds," *CIO*, September 1, 2004, 33; B. Glass, "Are You Being Watched?" *PC Magazine*, April 23, 2002, 54.

outside companies can steal or destroy company data in various ways. For example, denial-of-service web server attacks have brought down some of the busiest and best-run sites on the Internet; viruses and spyware/adware can spread quickly and result in data loss and business disruption; keystroke monitoring observes and stores every mouse click and keystroke you make and sends that information to unauthorized users; and password-cracking software steals supposedly secure passwords. Finally, there is phishing, where fake but real-looking emails and websites trick users into sharing personal information (usernames, passwords, or account numbers).

Authentication making sure potential users are who they claim to be.

Authorization granting authenticated users approved access to data, software, and systems.

Biometrics identifying users by unique, measurable body features, such as fingerprint recognition or iris scanning.

Malware infects 30 percent of computers. A recently released report on computer viruses indicated that 48 percent of the 22 million computers scanned for the study were infected with malware. Over 1.5 million were infected with crimeware or banker trojans. Also, only one-third were running behind a protected firewall (see below). Studies have found that the threats listed in Exhibit 16.3 are so widespread that automatic attacks will begin on an unprotected computer just 15 seconds after it connects to the Internet.[31]

As shown in the right-hand column of Exhibit 16.3, many steps can be taken to secure data and data networks. Some of the most important involve authentication and authorization, firewalls, antivirus software for PCs and email servers, data encryption, and virtual private networks. We will review those steps and then finish this section with a brief review of the dangers of wireless networks, which are exploding in popularity.

Two critical steps are required to ensure that data can be accessed by authorized users and no one else. One is **authentication**, that is, making sure users are who they claim to be.[32] The other is **authorization**,

No More Passwords?

Passwords are one of the biggest inconveniences when going online. If you pick a password that's too simple, you might get hacked. If you pick a complicated password, it's too hard to remember. Many technology companies are looking for new ways to improve security, such as the use of **biometrics**. Many laptops have built-in fingerprint readers, and Apple's iPhone 5S introduced a fingerprint sensor to Apple's smartphones. Microsoft designed Windows 10 with a fingerprint-based biometric ID system as well. Some analysts believe that smart phones and other mobile devices could actually help provide better security, as most of them have built-in cameras and microphones that could be used for voice- and facial-recognition applications. "We think that biometric authentication is going to be significantly more popular," says Ant Allan, research vice president at Gartner Inc., "and the driver and enabler of this is mobile computing." Allan explains that, for large companies, installing new hardware for every employee would be very expensive. Using existing technologies that everyone already has, Allan says, could have great economic advantages.

Source: A. Blackman, "Say Goodbye to the Password," *Wall Street Journal*, September 15, 2013, http://online.wsj.com/news/articles/SB10001424127887323585604579008620509295960?mg=reno64-wsj.

that is, granting authenticated users approved access to data, software, and systems.[33] When an automated teller machine prompts you to enter your personal identification number (PIN), the bank is authenticating that you are you. Once you've been authenticated, you are authorized to access your own funds and no one else's. Of course, as anyone who has lost a PIN or password or had one stolen knows, user authentication systems are not foolproof. In particular, users create security risks by not changing their default account passwords (such as birth dates) or by using weak passwords such as names ("Larry") or complete words ("football"), which are quickly guessed by password cracker software.[34]

This is why many companies are now turning to **two-factor authentication**, which is based on what users know, such as a password, and what they have in their possession, such as a secure ID card, their phone, or unique information that only they would know. When logging in, users are first asked for their password. But then they must provide a second authentication factor, such as an answer to a security question (i.e., unique information) or a validation code that has been sent to their mobile phone. Google, for example, requires two-factor authentication for its Google Apps (Gmail, Calendar, Drive, Docs, etc.). After entering their password, users can use either the code sent via text to their phone, or a code generated by Google's Authenticator app. Google Authenticator works via your mobile phone connection or Wi-Fi, gives you the ability to generate authentication codes for multiple accounts (including non-Google accounts), and generates codes that are only good for 60 seconds.[35]

Unfortunately, stolen or cracked passwords are not the only means by which hackers and electronic thieves gain access to an organization's computer resources. Unless special safeguards are put in place, every time corporate users are online there's literally nothing between their personal computer and the Internet (home users with high-speed DSL or cable Internet access face the same risks). Hackers can access files, run programs, and control key parts of computers if precautions aren't taken. To reduce these risks, companies use **firewalls**, which are hardware or software devices that sit between the computers in an internal organizational network and outside networks such as the Internet. Firewalls filter and check incoming and outgoing data. They also prevent company insiders from accessing unauthorized sites or from sending confidential company information to people outside the company. Firewalls also prevent outsiders from identifying and gaining access to company computers and data. If a firewall is working properly, the computers behind the company firewall literally cannot be detected or accessed by outsiders.

A **virus** is a program or piece of code that, without your knowledge, attaches itself to other programs on your computer and can trigger anything from a harmless flashing message to the reformatting of your hard drive to a system-wide network shutdown. You used to have to do or run something to get a virus—for example, double click on an infected email attachment. Today's viruses are much more threatening. In fact, with some viruses, just being connected to a network can infect your computer. *Antivirus software for personal computers* scans email, downloaded files, and computer hard drives, disk drives, and memory to detect and stop computer viruses from doing damage. However, this software is effective only to the extent that users of individual computers have and use up-to-date versions. With new viruses appearing all the time, users should update their antivirus software weekly or, even better, configure their virus software to automatically check for, download, and install updates. *Corporate antivirus software* automatically scans email attachments such as Microsoft Word documents, graphics, and text files as they come across the company email server. It also monitors and scans all file downloads across company databases and network servers. So, while antivirus software for personal computers prevents individual computers from being infected, corporate antivirus software for email servers, databases, and network servers adds another layer of protection by preventing infected files from multiplying and being sent to others.

Another way of protecting information is to encrypt sensitive data. **Data encryption** transforms data into complex, scrambled digital codes that can be unencrypted only by authorized users who possess unique decryption keys. There is nothing like having the freedom to take your information with you. We take for granted that we can hop on a plane with our laptop, visit a major client in a distant city, and wow them with our

Two-factor authentication authentication based on what users know, such as a password, and what they have in their possession, such as a secure ID card or key.

Firewalls protective hardware or software devices that sit between the computers in an internal organizational network and outside networks, such as the Internet.

Virus a program or piece of code that, against your wishes, attaches itself to other programs on your computer and can trigger anything from a harmless flashing message to the reformatting of your hard drive to a system-wide network shutdown.

Data encryption the transformation of data into complex, scrambled digital codes that can be unencrypted only by authorized users who possess unique decryption keys.

comprehensive full-colour presentation. But wait a minute—what if we relax in the supposed safety of a private airport lounge, look away for only a second, and our laptop disappears? Canada's privacy laws require that businesses protect personal information in their possession from unauthorized access or disclosure by taking appropriate security measures. Across Canada, the number of reported break-and-enters into businesses continues to rise. Mercantile Mergers & Acquisitions Corporation of Toronto couldn't take that chance. As a brokerage firm specializing in the merger business in Canada, it needed encryption software to protect sensitive client information. Mercantile evaluated five commercial encryption software packages and picked one that suited its purposes, was within its budget, and provided a cost-effective solution.[36]

And with people increasingly gaining unauthorized access to email messages—email snooping—it's also important to encrypt sensitive email messages and file attachments. You can use a system called "public key encryption" to do so. First, give copies of your "public key" to anyone who sends you files or email. Have the sender use the public key, which is actually a piece of software, to encrypt files before sending them to you. The only way to decrypt the files is with a companion "private key" that you keep to yourself.

Although firewalls can protect personal computers and network servers connected to the corporate network, people away from their offices (e.g., salespeople, business travellers, telecommuters who work at home) who interact with their company networks via the Internet face a security risk. Because Internet data are not encrypted, packet sniffer software (see Exhibit 16.3) easily allows hackers to read everything sent or received except files that have been encrypted before sending. Previously, the only practical solution was to have employees dial in to secure company phone lines for direct access to the company network. Of course, with international and long-distance phone calls, the costs quickly added up. Now, a **virtual private network (VPN)** solves this problem by using software to encrypt all Internet data at both ends of the transmission process. Instead of making long-distance calls, employees connect to the Internet. But, unlike typical Internet connections in which Internet data packets are unencrypted, the VPN encrypts the data sent by employees outside the company computer network, decrypts the data when they arrive within the company network, and does the same when data are sent back to the computer outside the network. If your employer or university doesn't provide a VPN, you can purchase VPN services for personal use and protection from well known providers, such as AnchorFree Hotspot Shield (www.anchorfree.com) or Cloak VPN (www.getcloak.com), for about $3 a month. VPN services should be used when connected to public Wi-Fi systems, such as in hotels, airports, or coffee shops, where anyone on the public network can monitor or spy on what you're doing.

Alternatively, many companies are now adopting web-based **secure sockets layer (SSL) encryption** to provide secure off-site access to data and programs. If you've ever entered your credit card in a web browser to make an online purchase, you've used SSL technology to encrypt and protect that information. You can tell if SSL encryption is being used on a website if you see a padlock icon (gold in Internet Explorer or Firefox, green in Google Chrome, silver in Safari) or if the URL begins with "https." SSL encryption works the same way in the workplace. Managers and employees who aren't at the office simply connect to the Internet, open a web browser, and then enter a user name and password to gain access to SSL-encrypted data and programs.

Many companies now have wireless networks, which make it possible for anybody with a laptop and a wireless card to access the company network from anywhere in the office. Although wireless networks come equipped with security and encryption capabilities that, in theory, permit only authorized users to access the wireless network, those capabilities are easily bypassed with the right tools. Compounding the problem, many wireless networks are shipped with their security and encryption capabilities turned off for ease of installation.[37] Caution is important even when encryption is turned on because the WEP (Wired Equivalent Privacy) security protocol is easily compromised. If you work at home or are working on the go, extra care is critical because Wi-Fi networks in homes and public places such as hotel lobbies are among the most targeted by hackers.[38] See the Wi-Fi Alliance website at www.wi-fi.org for the latest information on wireless security and encryption protocols, which provide much stronger protection for your company's wireless network.

Virtual private network (VPN) software that securely encrypts data sent by employees outside the company network, decrypts the data when they arrive within the company computer network, and does the same when data are sent back to employees outside the network.

Secure sockets layer (SSL) encryption Internet browser–based encryption that provides secure off-site Web access to some data and programs.

Companies are combating security threats by hiring "white hat hackers," so-called good guys who test security weak points in information systems so that they can be fixed. While this is typically done using traditional hacking tools, as discussed in Exhibit 16.3, white hat hackers also test security via social engineering, in which they trick people into giving up passwords and authentication protocols or unknowingly providing unauthorized access to company computers. One test involves emailing a picture of a cat with a purple mohawk and the subject line, "Check out these kitties!" to employees with a link to "more cute kitty photos." When you click the embedded link to "more cute kitty photos," you're taken to a company website warning about the dangers of phishing scams. While everyone thinks that *they* wouldn't fall for this, 48 percent of employees receiving this email actually click the link.[39]

16-4 ACCESSING AND SHARING INFORMATION AND KNOWLEDGE

Today, information technologies allow companies to communicate data, share data, and provide data access to workers, managers, suppliers, and customers in ways that were unthinkable just a few years ago.

*After reading this section, you should be able to explain how companies use IT to improve **16-4a internal access and sharing of information, 16-4b external access and sharing of information,** and **16-4c the sharing of knowledge and expertise.***

16-4a Internal Access and Sharing of Information

Executives, managers, and workers inside a company use three kinds of IT to access and share information: executive information systems, intranets, and portals. An **executive information system (EIS)** uses internal and external sources of data to provide managers and executives with the information they require to monitor

and analyze organizational performance.[40] The purpose of an EIS is to provide accurate, complete, relevant, and timely information to managers.

Managers at Colgate-Palmolive Canada—which makes toothpaste, soap, and other home care products, as well as pet foods—use the company EIS, which they call the "dashboard," to see how well their company is running. Ruben Panizza, Colgate's global IT director of business intelligence, says that "these real-time dashboards are a change for people who are used to seeing a lot of numbers with their data. But they quickly realize they can use the information as it's presented in the dashboards to make faster decisions. In the past, executives relied on other people to get custom reports and data. Now, they can look at the information themselves. They see the real data as it is in the system much more easily and quickly. For the first time, many of the company's business leaders are running BI [business intelligence] tools—in this case, dashboards—to monitor the business to see what's going on at a high level."[41]

Intranets are private company networks that allow employees to access, share, and publish information using Internet software. Intranet websites are just like external websites, but the firewall separating the internal company network from the Internet permits only authorized internal access.[42] Companies typically use intranets to share information (e.g., about benefits) and to replace paper forms with online forms. Many company intranets are built on the web model as it existed a decade ago. With more than 5,500 employees at its corporate head office and 475 retail outlets nationwide, Canadian Tire was looking to refresh its intranet site, known as inTIREnet. "Our employees require the ability to obtain information quickly and easily to make timely and well-informed decisions," says Laura Sousa, vice president of enterprise IT and governance at Canadian Tire. "Our new system ensures we have the most up-to-date and relevant information at our fingertips." Canadian Tire employees can now search documents, share information across the network, and

rustamank/Shutterstock

Intranets Are Evolving to Include:

▶ collaboration tools, like wikis, where team members can post all relevant information for a project they're working on together

▶ customizable email accounts

▶ presence awareness (whether someone you are looking for on the network is in the office, in a meeting, working from home, etc.)

▶ instant messaging

▶ simultaneous access to files for virtual team members

receive daily corporate news updates. The new intranet has helped Canadian Tire increase communication among employees in the home office, while offering greater security measures and access to internal documents.[43]

Finally, a **corporate portal** is a hybrid of executive information systems and intranets. An EIS provides managers and executives with the information they need to monitor and analyze organizational performance, and intranets help companies distribute and publish information *and* forms within the company, whereas corporate portals allow company managers and employees to access customized information and complete specialized transactions using a web browser.

16-4b External Access and Sharing of Information

Historically, companies have been unable or reluctant to let outside groups have access to corporate information. Now, however, a number of information technologies—extranets, electronic data interchange, web services, and the Internet—are making it easier to share company data with external groups like suppliers and customers. They're also reducing costs, increasing productivity by eliminating manual information processing (70 percent of the data output from one company, like a purchase order, ends up as data input at another company, such as a sales invoice or shipping order), reducing data entry errors, improving customer service, and speeding communications. As a result, managers are scrambling to adopt these technologies. With **extranets**, companies' networks allow information to be exchanged and transactions to be conducted with outsiders by providing them direct, web-based access to authorized parts of a company's intranet or information system. With **electronic data interchange (EDI)**, two companies convert purchase and ordering information to a standardized format to enable direct electronic transmission of that information from one company's computer system to the other company's. For example, when an Apple Store associate drags an Apple iPod across the checkout scanner at the West Edmonton Mall, the store's computerized inventory system automatically reorders another iPod through the direct EDI connection that its computer has with Apple's manufacturing and shipping computer. No one at Apple or at Apple's main supplier, Foxconn, fills out paperwork. No one makes a phone call. There are no delays to wait to find out whether Apple has the iPod in stock. The transaction takes place instantly and automatically because the data from Apple and all of its manufacturing companies like Foxconn have been translated into a standardized, shareable, compatible format.

Web services are another way for companies to directly and automatically transmit purchase and ordering data from one company's computer system to another company's computer system. Web services use standardized protocols to describe and transfer data from one company in such a way that those data can automatically be read, understood, transcribed, and processed by different computer systems in another company.[44] RouteOne, which helps automobile dealers process loans for car buyers, was started by the financing companies of DaimlerChrysler, Ford, General Motors, and Toyota. Not surprisingly, each auto company had a different computer system with different operating systems, different programs, and different data structures. RouteOne relies on web services to connect these different computer systems to the wide variety of different databases and software used by various auto dealers, credit bureaus, banks, and other auto financing companies. Without web services, there's no way these different companies and systems could share information.[45]

Corporate portal a hybrid of executive information systems and intranets that allows managers and employees to use a web browser to gain access to customized company information and to complete specialized transactions.

Extranets networks that allow companies to exchange information and conduct transactions with outsiders by providing them direct, web-based access to authorized parts of a company's intranet or information system.

Electronic data interchange (EDI) when two companies convert their purchase and ordering information to a standardized format to enable the direct electronic transmission of that information from one company's computer system to the other company's computer system.

16-4c Sharing Knowledge and Expertise

At the beginning of the chapter, we distinguished between raw data, which consist of facts and figures, and information, which consists of useful data that influence someone's choices and behaviour. One more important distinction needs to be made—namely, data and information are not the same as knowledge. **Knowledge** is the understanding that one gains from information. Importantly, knowledge does not reside in information; it resides in people. That's why companies hire consultants and why family doctors refer patients to specialists. Unfortunately, it can be quite expensive to employ consultants, specialists, and experts, so companies have begun using two information technologies to capture and share these people's knowledge with other managers and workers: *decision support systems* and *expert systems.*

However, an executive information system (EIS) speeds up and simplifies the acquisition of information, a **decision support system (DSS)** helps managers understand problems and potential solutions by analyzing information using sophisticated models and tools.[46] Furthermore, whereas EIS programs are broad in scope and permit managers to retrieve all kinds of information about a company, DSS programs are usually narrow in scope and targeted toward helping managers solve specific kinds of problems. DSS programs have been developed to help managers pick the shortest and most efficient routes for delivery trucks, select the best combinations of stocks for investors, and schedule the flow of inventory through complex manufacturing facilities.

It's important to understand that DSS programs don't replace managerial decision making; they *improve* it by furthering managers' and workers' understanding of the problems they face and the solutions that might work. Although used by just 2 percent of physicians, medical DSS programs hold the promise of helping doctors make more accurate patient diagnoses. A British study of 88 cases misdiagnosed or initially misdiagnosed (to be correctly diagnosed much later) found that a medical DSS made the right diagnosis 69 percent of the time.[47] With a medical DSS, doctors enter patient data, such as age, gender, weight, and medical symptoms. The medical DSS then produces a list of diseases and conditions, ranked by probability, low or high, or by medical specialty, such as cardiology or oncology. For instance, when emergency room physician Dr. Harold Cross treated a 10-year-old boy who had been ill with nausea and dizziness for two weeks, he wasn't sure what was wrong because the boy had a healthy appetite, no abdominal pain, and just one brief headache. However, when the medical DSS that Dr. Cross used suggested a possible problem in the back of the boy's brain, he ordered an MRI scan that revealed a tumour, which was successfully removed two days later. Says Dr. Cross: "My personal knowledge of the literature and physical findings would not have prompted me to suspect a brain tumor."[48]

An **expert system** is created by capturing the specialized knowledge and decision rules used by experts and experienced decision makers. It permits nonexpert employees to draw on this expert knowledge base to make decisions. Most expert systems work by using a collection of "if–then" rules to sort through information and recommend a course of action. For example, let's say that you're using your Bank of Montreal MasterCard or your TD Visa card to help your spouse celebrate a promotion. After dinner and a movie, the two of you stroll by a travel office with a Montreal poster in its window. Thirty minutes later, caught up in the moment, you find yourselves at the airport ticket counter trying

> **Knowledge** the understanding that one gains from information.
>
> **Decision support system (DSS)** an information system that helps managers understand specific kinds of problems and potential solutions and analyze the impact of different decision options using "what if" scenarios.
>
> **Expert system** an information system that contains the specialized knowledge and decision rules used by experts and experienced decision makers so that nonexperts can draw on this knowledge base to make decisions.

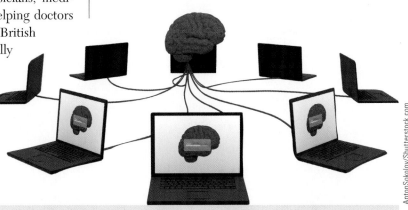

People have knowledge. Computers contain data and information.

AntonSokolov/Shutterstock.com

to purchase last-minute tickets to Montreal. But there's just one problem. VISA didn't approve your purchase. In fact, the ticket counter agent is now on the phone with a VISA customer service agent.

What brought your weekend escape to Montreal to a temporary halt? It was an expert system that VISA calls "Authorizer's Assistant."[49] The first "if–then" rule that prevented your purchase was the rule "*if* a purchase is much larger than the cardholder's regular spending habits, *then* deny approval of the purchase." This if–then rule, just one of 3,000, is built into Royal Bank's VISA transaction-processing system, which handles thousands of purchase requests per second. Now that the VISA customer service agent is on the line, he or she is prompted by the Authorizer's Assistant to ask the ticket counter agent to examine your identification. You hand over your photo I.D. and another credit card to prove that you're you. Finally, your ticket purchase is approved. Why? Because you met the last series of "if–then" rules: *if* the purchaser can provide proof of identity and *if* the purchaser can provide personal information that isn't common knowledge, *then* approve the purchase.

STUDY TOOLS 16

READY TO STUDY?

LOCATED IN TEXTBOOK:

☐ Rip out the Chapter Review Card at the back of the book to have a summary of the chapter and key terms handy.

LOCATED AT NELSON.COM/STUDENT:

☐ Access the eBook or use the ReadSpeaker feature to listen to the chapter on the go.

☐ Prepare for tests with practice quizzes.

☐ Review key terms with flashcards and the glossary feature.

☐ Work through key concepts with case studies and Management Decision Exercises.

☐ Explore practical examples with You Make the Decision Activities.

Education has changed; your textbook should too.

4LTR PRESS

nelson.com/student

17 Managing Service and Manufacturing Operations

monkeybusinessimages/iStock/Thinkstock

LEARNING OUTCOMES

After studying this chapter, you will be able to...

17-1 Discuss the kinds of productivity and their importance in managing operations.

17-2 Explain the role that quality plays in managing operations.

17-3 Explain the essentials of managing a service business.

17-4 Describe the different kinds of manufacturing operations.

17-5 Explain why and how companies should manage inventory levels.

After you finish this chapter, go to **PAGE 374** for

STUDY TOOLS

A Positive Approach

Quick: What could working on a rig in the Alberta oil patch teach an 18-year-old that might help him run a cutting-edge, high-tech-related Vancouver business in his twenties? In the more isolated environment of northern Alberta, "I learned that no matter what the problem, you could solve it if you tried," Adrian Duke says. He moved West to study business, and graduated from the BC Institute of Technology with a marketing management diploma in 2009. Three years later, he and Lance Fisher cofounded Skyturtle Technologies, a futuristic operation tied to the waterpark industry that has both service and manufacturing aspects. Adrian is the CEO. Company designs include a unique vertical freefall waterslide with a completely vertical loop that sells for around $1.5 million and is built in the United States, where equal partner company Avalanche Waterslides does the major manufacturing for Skyturtle. A Skyturtle sister company, Immmersive Environments (and yes, the three *M*'s in the name are correct), creates futuristic adventures aimed mainly at the business community. Adrian started life in Saskatchewan, as a descendant of the Muscowpetung First Nation; by the age of 28 he was on *BCBusiness Magazine's* 2015 "30 Under 30" list of those "who will lead business in this province for years to come." Adrian also goes out of his way to be a positive presence in the lives of Indigenous youth.

1. Can you briefly describe the kind of service and manufacturing setup you have?

We provide engineering, design, installation, commissioning, and maintenance services for the technology products that we manufacture, which include ride safety and control systems, interactive amusement features, and machine to machine systems.

2. Is quality of special importance for products that a lot of children get to use?

Quality is very important, but nothing trumps safety. Safety and quality are in many ways connected, however when designing and manufacturing products that people, especially children, interact with, we explore every possible use and outcome to ensure our design is 100 percent safe and built to last.

3. Do you use ISO certification and if so, why?

We use ISO 13849 certification because it holds our products to the highest performance level required for carrying out safety functions specific to control systems.

4. Do you use the total quality management approach to management?

Yes . . . because it ensures that we are consistently looking for ways to improve and utilize our team in the most effective way possible.

5. Do you have an inventory at all?

We maintain a very limited inventory of supplies because the proliferation of online purchasing and one- to two-day shipping times has reduced the benefit of having a large stock of products. We build to order.

6. Does your design firm have any Canadian clients, and if not, why work from Vancouver?

We have a very limited client base in Canada due to the fact that it is a very small market for water park attractions. We work out of Vancouver because of its international accessibility and we love the mountains.

7. How important in general are creativity, problem solving, and communication to you?

Without a doubt, problem solving is the number one asset we look for in a team member. If someone focuses on problems rather than solutions, they will not fit well with our culture. Everyone is creative in their own way and to varying degrees. We look to have a diverse set of mindsets on the team to balance creativity with the many other important factors in designing new and innovative products.

Good communication is critical to the success of any team. We utilize a number of communication tools to allow us to have open and ongoing dialogue about every aspect of our business. We encourage everyone on our team to contribute their thoughts openly because some of the best ideas can come from the most unlikely of sources.

8. Is that positive attitude something you've fostered?

It is. For example, in 2010, I studied for a certificate from a Dale Carnegie Business Group communication course. Fostering a positive attitude has been essential to my success in entrepreneurship. Learning to stay positive and focus on the solution rather than the problem is something I learned at both BCIT and the Dale Carnegie Business Group.

9. How important is your work with Indigenous youth?

To me, working with Indigenous youth is extremely important. Today, Aboriginal youth represent Canada's youngest and fastest growing population. By 2020, an additional 400,000 young Aboriginal people will enter the workforce, which will provide a massive wave of talent into the Canadian economy if we properly allocate the time and resources to education. Every little bit of effort helps, so I jump at every opportunity I get to engage with young Aboriginal people.

10. What's the most important thing you learned in business school that helps you today?

Critical thinking was the single most important skill I developed in business school: learning how to objectively analyze a situation and the possible outcomes so that I can make a decision and move forward confidently.

For the full interview go online to nelson.com/student

Photo and interview courtesy of Adrian Duke

17-1 PRODUCTIVITY

Furniture manufacturers, hospitals, restaurants, automakers, airlines, and many other kinds of businesses struggle to find ways to produce quality products and services efficiently and then deliver them in a timely manner. Managing the daily production of goods and services, or operations management, is a key part of a manager's job. But an organization's success depends on the quality of its products and services as well as on its productivity.

Take the airline industry as an example. An airline's profitability rests on being able to achieve a delicate balance: filling seats to achieve as close to capacity as possible, and increasing the utilization of aircraft by flying them more hours in the day, all the while keeping costs as low as possible without sacrificing safety or quality. Canada's WestJet has made a name for itself as Canada's low-cost airline and is now this country's second largest carrier. The company has modelled itself on US-based Southwest Airlines. Its success can be attributed to its commitment to cost control, high-growth revenue, and customer service. WestJet keeps its costs low by primarily flying a single type of aircraft (the Boeing 737), creating cost efficiencies in employee training, maintenance, and purchasing, and keeping ground-handling charges low through subcontracting. WestJet's strategy has been to focus wherever possible on airports with competitive cost terms, as well as on niche routes where it is the only carrier to offer nonstop service and short-haul flights. This has allowed it to reduce some costly in-flight amenities.[1] Want a meal on your short haul flight? You can buy snacks à la carte or, better yet, pack your own meal. Need earbuds or a blanket? These are options items you can purchase. Want to visit the airport lounge? For $30 you can enter one of the open access lounges that WestJet has partnered with across the country.[2] WestJet also looks closely at labour costs—its nonunionized employees can allocate 20 percent of their paycheques into a share purchase plan which the company matches, effectively reducing the amount of cash paid out and enhancing employees' commitment to maintaining high quality service and productivity.[3]

As a result of its strategy, WestJet's costs are an estimated 36 percent lower on domestic flights than those of its rival, Air Canada. Thus, WestJet has been able to do more for less and to benefit from higher productivity.[4] In 2015, WestJet reported its fourth consecutive year of record net earnings and also marked its eleventh consecutive year of profitability. WestJet has also consistently been ranked in *Aviation Week*'s top 10 list of international airlines—an airline industry ranking that compares airline performance in five major operational categories.[5] Recently, WestJet expanded its fleet to include some widebody planes for exploring more international routes, including flights to Europe and Hawaii. Industry observers will be watching with interest to see how WestJet's strategy will accommodate the additional costs for maintenance and pilot training that comes with the decision to expand.[6]

At their core, organizations are production systems. Companies combine inputs such as labour, raw materials, capital, and knowledge to produce outputs in the form of finished products or services. **Productivity** is a measure of performance that indicates how efficiently goods and services are produced or how many inputs it takes to produce or create an output.

$$\text{Productivity} = \frac{\text{Outputs}}{\text{Inputs}}$$

The fewer inputs it takes to create an output (or the greater the output from one input), the higher the productivity. For example, productivity in the steel industry is measured in terms of man-hours per ton of steel. The fewer the man-hours it takes to produce a ton of steel, the higher the productivity. In North America, average productivity is two man-hours per ton, with some steel mills able to produce a ton of steel in less than one hour. This is a marked improvement compared to the 10 hours on average it took in the 1980s.[7]

Let's examine **17-1a why productivity matters** and **17-1b the different kinds of productivity**.

17-1a Why Productivity Matters

Why does productivity matter? For companies, higher productivity—that is, doing more with less—can lead to lower costs for the company, lower prices to customers, faster service, higher market share, and higher profits. Boeing has incorporated a series of changes to its assembly line to increase the rate at which it produces its wide-body 777 jets. For example, since each airline configures the floor layout of the planes it buys from Boeing a little differently, floor panels had to be drilled by hand (to attach seats, kitchens, walls, lavatories, etc.) to accommodate those design differences. Boeing,

---

Productivity a measure of performance that indicates how efficiently goods and services are produced.

Stephen Brashear/Getty Images

however, bought automated floor-drilling equipment, which completes each airplane floor three to four times faster while also increasing quality. Jason Clark, Boeing's director of manufacturing for the 777, says, "The day we opened the box [for automated floor drilling equipment] and put it on the airplane...we got a 93 percent improvement in hole quality."[8]

Boeing also switched from hand-spraying its wings, which only sprays paint in four-foot widths, to an automated 19-axis painting process that sprays paint in 18-foot widths. As a result, the amount of time it takes to spray a 777 wing has dropped from 4.5 hours to just 24 minutes. Likewise, the quality and consistency with which the paint is applied to the wing has reduced the weight of each pair of wings by 50–60 pounds. Together, changes like this have increased productivity at Boeing's 777 production line from 84 planes per year to 100 per year. With the average 777 selling for $288 million, the extra 16 planes that Boeing can make every year thanks to higher productivity yields an additional $4.6 billion in revenue.[9]

Productivity also matters when you consider the impact it can have on a country's standard of living and quality of life. A more productive worker is a more profitable one as increased productivity means increased output and increased sales revenue. Since profits generated by each worker increase, companies will often decide to hire more workers to keep boosting profits. In a competitive labour market, the increase in the demand for labour places upward pressure on wages, and an increase in output supplied to a competitive goods market will drive prices down.[10] For households, that translates into additional income without loss of purchasing power. For businesses, higher productivity means profit growth; for governments, additional tax revenues can support

healthcare, education, and/or social services.[11] For the country as a whole, productivity makes products more affordable or better. The richest countries are the ones that manufacture products and deliver services most effectively.[12]

Small improvements in productivity sustained for an extended time can result in significant increases in living standards, which is why economists and the business community closely monitor changes in productivity levels and productivity growth.[13] In 2012, the Conference Board of Canada reported that Canada ranked 13th among its 16 peer countries in labour productivity. Canada's productivity level had fallen to 80 percent of the US level, after reaching a high of 91 percent in the mid-1980s.[14] In terms of labour productivity growth, Canada ranked fifth among the 16 countries, earning a "B" grade. However, with a growth rate of only 0.8 percent, Canada's performance was not impressive by historical standards and Canada's ranking improved because other countries did relatively worse.[15]

17-1b Kinds of Productivity

Two common measures of productivity are partial productivity and multifactor productivity.

Partial productivity indicates how much of a particular kind of input it takes to produce an output:

$$\text{Partial productivity} = \frac{\text{Outputs}}{\text{Single kind of input}}$$

Labour is one kind of input that is often used when determining partial productivity. *Labour productivity* typically indicates the cost of the labour it takes to produce an output (or the number of hours of labour). In other words, the lower the labour cost per unit of output, or the less labour time it takes to produce a unit of output, the higher the labour productivity. Automakers often measure labour productivity by determining the average number of hours of labour it takes to completely assemble a car. Lower labour costs give automakers an average cost advantage, which is important in this highly competitive industry.

Partial productivity assesses how efficiently companies use only one input, such as labour, when creating outputs. *Multifactor productivity* is an overall measure of productivity; it assesses how efficiently companies use *all* the inputs it takes to make outputs.

Partial productivity a measure of performance that indicates how much of a particular kind of input it takes to produce an output.

Want to Be More Productive? Stop Multitasking!

Multitasking may seem like the answer to increasing productivity, but experts say it isn't so. Individuals who believe they are multitasking are simply switching tasks. According to author Devora Zack, multitasking is a myth. "The brain cannot be in two places at once, so what people are referencing as multitasking is actually what neuroscientists call task switching and that means rapidly moving back and forth between different tasks." According to the *Harvard Business Review*, multitaskers often accomplish less, miss information, and reduce their efficiency by as much as 40 percent. It takes an average of 15 minutes for a person to reorient to a task after being distracted by another, and often, the result is that tasks do not get completed before people move on to the next one, which causes a ripple effect as workers get off track and miss deadlines.

Here are some tips from the experts on how best to improve your productivity at work.

▸ *Employ the 20-minute rule.* Dedicate a 20-minute chunk of time to a single task, then switch to the next one.

▸ *Cluster-task emails.* Instead of checking email throughout the day, limit yourself to checking three times a day (in the morning, after lunch, and before leaving at the end of the day). This means email will take up less of your day and al-

alphaspirit/Shutterstock

low you to be more focused and productive during the other tasks you have to do, instead of splitting your time into tiny pieces all day long.

▸ *Practise quiet reflection.* Carve out 15 minutes a day to be alone with your thoughts and give your brain a break from the information overload that surrounds you. A Harvard Business School study found that this can increase your performance by an average of 23 percent.

Sources: Issie Lapowsky, "Don't Multitask: Your Brain Will Thank You," *Time Magazine*, April 17, 2013, http://business.time.com/2013/04/17/dont-multitask-your-brain-will-thank-you/; L. Evans, "Forget Multitasking. Real Productivity Comes From Singletasking," *Entrepreneur*, July 1, 2015, http://www.entrepreneur.com/article/247833; D. Gulati, "Multitasking's Real Victims," *Harvard Business Review*, July 18, 2012, http://blogs.hbr.org/cs/2012/07/multitaskings_real_victims.html; C. Deeb, "Multitasking Effects on a Worker's Performance," *Small Business Chronicle*, http://smallbusiness.chron.com/multitasking-effectsworkers-performance-32339.html; P. Atchley, "You Can't Multitask, So Stop Trying," *Harvard Business Review*, December 21, 2010, https://hbr.org/2010/12/you-cant-multi-task-so-stop-tr/.

Specifically, **multifactor productivity** indicates how much labour, capital, materials, and energy it takes to produce an output.[16]

$$\frac{\text{Multifactor}}{\text{productivity}} = \frac{\text{Outputs}}{(\text{Labour} + \text{Capital} + \text{Materials} + \text{Energy})}$$

In assessing multifactor productivity (MFP) in Canada, once again, the United States is used for comparison. Until 1984, Canadian productivity was closing in on US levels, however, since then it has steadily declined. As of 2012, Canadian productivity (including private and public sectors) was 24 percent lower than that of the US economy.[17] Between 1961 and 2008, there

was essentially no growth in Canadian MFP. Statistics Canada reports that "the slowdown in labour productivity after 2000 was almost entirely accounted for by the factors that determine multifactor growth—technology, innovation, firm organization, scale and capacity utilization effect." Industries that contributed to declines in business MFP were mining, oil and gas extraction, and manufacturing; those associated with growth included finance, insurance, and real estate.[18]

17-2 QUALITY

With the average new car costing more than $30,000, buyers want to make sure they're getting good quality for their money. J.D. Power and Associates conducts an annual quality study based on the problems experienced by vehicle owners during the first 90 days of

Multifactor productivity an overall measure of performance that indicates how much labour, capital, materials, and energy it takes to produce an output.

ownership. Initial quality is determined by the number of problems experienced per 100 vehicles (PP100), with a lower score reflecting higher quality. Over the years, the overall quality of vehicles has improved dramatically, as indicated by the number of problems per 100 cars (PP100). In 1981, Japanese cars averaged 240 PP100, while General Motors cars averaged 670, Ford 740, and Chrysler 870. In other words, as measured by PP100, the quality of North American cars was two to three times poorer than that of Japanese cars. The most recent J.D. Power and Associates Survey of initial car quality reported an overall industry average of 112 PP100 (a 3 percent improvement over the previous year). A number of manufacturers had scores under 100, meaning less than one problem per car. The study also noted another change, as Korean brands led the industry in initial quality by the widest margin ever, averaging 90 PP100 and, for the first time in the study's history, European brands surpassed Japanese brands, while North American automakers equalled the Japanese for a second time. The top five "winners" included Porsche (80 PP100), Kia (86 PP100), Jaguar (93 PP100), Hyundai (95 PP100), and Infiniti (97 PP100). According to Renee Stephens from J.D. Power, "Japanese brands have been viewed by many as the gold standard in vehicle quality. While the Japanese automakers continue to make improvements, we're seeing other brands, most notably Korean makes, really accelerating the rate of improvement."[19]

Canadian productivity was also recognized in the J.D. Power Study, as Toyota Canada's assembly plant in Cambridge, Ontario, was once again the recipient of several J.D. Power Quality Awards, including the Gold Plant Quality Award, the first Toyota plant outside of Japan to win the global top honour.[20]

The American Society for Quality offers two meanings for **quality**. It can mean a product or service free of deficiencies, or a product or service that satisfies customer needs.[21] Today's cars are of higher quality than those produced 20 years ago in both senses. Not only do they have fewer problems per 100 cars, but they also have a larger number of standard features (air bags, anti-lock brakes, power windows and locks, cruise control, and air conditioning), as well as a plethora of available options (GPS navigational systems, satellite radio, Bluetooth and USB connectivity, backup cameras, and blind spot monitoring) to address the changing needs of today's drivers.

In this part of the chapter, you will learn about 17-2a quality-related characteristics for products and services, 17-2b international standards ISO 9000 and 14000, and 17-2c total quality management.

17-2a Quality-Related Characteristics for Products and Services

Quality products usually have three characteristics: reliability, serviceability, and durability.[22] A breakdown occurs when a product stops working or doesn't do what it was designed to do. The longer it takes for a product to break down, or the longer the time between breakdowns, the more reliable the product. Consequently, many companies define product *reliability* in terms of the average time between breakdowns.

Serviceability refers to how easy or difficult it is to fix a product. The easier it is to maintain a working product or fix a broken product, the more serviceable that product is. Western Digital sells the WD RE4 2TB hard drive, an extremely fast two-terabyte hard drive that customers can use for gaming, multimedia, and video applications. This particular product is so reliable that the estimated mean time between breakdowns is 1.2 million hours, or more than 137 years.[23]

A product breakdown assumes that a product can be repaired. However, some products don't break down—they fail. *Product failure* means that products can't be repaired, only replaced. *Durability* is defined as the mean time to failure. A typical incandescent light bulb, for example, has a mean time of failure of 1,000 hours. By contrast, LED bulbs, which use the same technology that lights up HDTVs and cellphone screens, have a mean time to failure of 20–25 years. Furthermore, the energy savings from one $10 LED bulb means it will pay for itself within two years and then provide 20 more years of lighting, while saving $149 in energy costs over the longer lifetime of the bulb.[24]

While high-quality products are characterized by reliability, serviceability, and durability, services are different. For example, once a lawn service has mown your lawn, the job is done until they return the next week to do it again. Also, services don't have serviceability—that is, they can't be maintained or fixed. If a service wasn't performed correctly, all you can do is have it performed again. Finally, the quality of service often depends on how the service provider interacts with the customer. Was the service provider friendly, rude, helpful? Five characteristics typically distinguish a quality service: reliability, tangibles, responsiveness, assurance, and empathy.[25]

Quality a product or service free of deficiencies, or the characteristics of a product or service that satisfy customer needs.

Service reliability is the ability to consistently perform a service well. Studies have found that *service reliability* matters more to customers than anything else when they are buying services. If your dry cleaner gives you back perfectly clean and pressed clothes every time, it's providing a reliable service.

Also, although services themselves are not tangible (you can't see or touch them), they are provided in tangible places. *Tangibles* relate to the offices, equipment, and personnel involved with the delivery of a service. One of the best examples of the effect of tangibles on perceptions of quality is the restroom. When you eat at a fancy restaurant, you expect clean, if not upscale, restrooms. How different is your perception of a business—say, a gas station—if it has clean restrooms rather than filthy ones?

Responsiveness refers to the promptness and willingness with which service providers give good service (your dry cleaner returning your laundry perfectly clean and pressed in a day or an hour). *Assurance* refers to the customer's confidence that service providers will be knowledgeable, courteous, and trustworthy. *Empathy* is the extent to which service providers give individual attention and care to customers' concerns and problems.

When Apple first launched its retail stores, they were widely predicted to fail given all of the locations already available where consumers could buy computer and electronics equipment. Those predictions were wrong, however, as the more than 400 Apple stores worldwide attract more than 1 million visitors per day. Why? Because the stores are great at delivering responsiveness, assurance, and empathy. At Apple stores, responsiveness manifests itself in a sales philosophy of not selling. Instead, Apple store employees are trained to help customers solve problems. An Apple training manual says, "Your job is to understand all of your customers' needs—some of which they may not even realize they have." David Ambrose, a former Apple store employee, says, "You were never trying to close a sale. It was about finding solutions for a customer and finding their pain points."

Apple store employees demonstrate assurance through the high level of training that they receive. Apple "geniuses," who staff the Genius Bar in each Apple store, are trained at Apple headquarters and, according to Apple's website, "can take care of everything from troubleshooting your problems to actual repairs." Geniuses are regularly tested on their knowledge and problem-solving skills to maintain their certification. Other Apple store employees are highly trained, too, and are not allowed to help customers until they've spent two to four weeks shadowing experienced store employees.

The acronym APPLE reminds employees how to empathetically engage with customers: "Approach customers with a personalized warm welcome," "Probe politely to understand all the customer's needs," "Present a solution for the customer to take home today," "Listen for and resolve any issues or concerns," and "End with a fond farewell and an invitation to return." And when customers are frustrated and become emotional, the advice is to "listen and limit your responses to simple reassurances that you are doing so. 'Uh-huh,' 'I understand,' etc."

The results from Apple's retail approach speak for themselves, as Apple retail sales average $4,551 per square foot, higher than Tiffany & Co. jewellery stores ($3,043) and luxury retailer Coach ($1,532).[26]

17-2b International Standards ISO 9000 and 14000

ISO, pronounced *eye-so*, comes from the Greek word *isos*, meaning "equal, similar, alike, or identical" and is also a standard universal acronym for the International Organization for Standardization, an independent, non-governmental organization that publishes standards that facilitate the international exchange of goods and services. An international standard is a document containing practical information and best practices, often describing an agreed way of doing something or a solution to a global problem.[27] ISO develops and publishes standards for products, services, and systems covering almost every category and industry—including information security, healthcare, general management, food safety, and energy management. ISO standards help make products and systems compatible so they fit and work well with each other, ensure safety issues are addressed, and allow the sharing of technological know-how and best practices. In addition, ISO standards can increase the potential for international trade by improving compatibility, product information, and measurement. For example, ISO standards for paper sizes make life easier for printer, photocopier, and office supplies manufacturers, because they know their products will work with available paper formats.[28]

One of the most popular standards is the **ISO 9000** family of standards that focus on quality management, providing guidance and tools for organizations who want to ensure their products and services consistently meet customer requirements and that quality is consistently improved.[29] The ISO 9000 standards don't describe how to make a better-quality car, computer, or widget; instead, they describe how companies can extensively document (and thus standardize) the steps they take to create and improve the quality of their products. The **ISO 14000** family of standards provides organizations with tools and systems to help manage environmental responsibilities.[30]

A study commissioned by the Conference Board of Canada examined the impact of standardization on the Canadian economy, and found that standards play a key role in enhancing labour productivity. In addition, study participants indicated that standardization was the basis for continuous improvement, innovation, and new product development, and helped establish a level playing field for business. Without quality management standards that bolster and validate credibility, many would not be in business. The chief economist of the Canadian Manufacturers and Exporters Association explains, "In some cases if you don't meet the standard, you don't do business, so one could argue that 100 percent of your business depends on your ability to meet that standard." For example, some large companies require ISO 9001 registration before they will use a company as a supplier. In other situations, Canadian companies wanting to sell products to the US marketplace are required to meet US Food and Drug Administration (FDA) standards before their products can be approved for the American marketplace.[31]

To become ISO certified (a process that can take months), a company must show that it is following its own procedures for improving production, updating design plans and specifications, keeping machinery in top condition, educating and training workers, and satisfactorily dealing with customer complaints.[32] An accredited third party oversees ISO certification, in much the same way that a certified public accountant verifies that a company's financial accounts are up-to-date and accurate. Once a company has been certified as ISO compliant, the accredited third party issues an ISO certificate, which the company can use in its advertising and publications.[33] Continued ISO certification is not guaranteed, however. Accredited third parties conduct periodic audits to ensure that the company is still following quality procedures. If it is not, its certification is suspended or cancelled.

17-2c Total Quality Management

Total quality management (TQM) is an integrated, organization-wide strategy for improving product and service quality.[34] TQM is not a specific tool or technique, but rather a philosophy or overall approach to management. It is based on three principles: *customer focus and satisfaction, continuous improvement,* and *teamwork.*[35]

Although most economists, accountants, and financiers argue that companies exist to earn profits for shareholders, TQM suggests that customer focus and customer satisfaction should be a company's primary goals. **Customer focus** means that the entire organization, from top to bottom, should be focused on meeting customers' needs. The result of that customer focus should be **customer satisfaction**, which occurs when the company's products or services meet or exceed customers' expectations.

At companies where TQM is taken seriously, such as Enterprise Rent-a-Car, paycheques and promotions depend on keeping customers satisfied. Enterprise measures customer satisfaction with a simple but effective survey called the Enterprise Service Quality index (ESQi), developed and refined over the years to find out specifically what makes loyal customers and who the loyal customers are. The survey is based on two key questions: 1. How would you rate your last Enterprise experience? (This is ranked on a scale from 'completely satisfied' to 'completely dissatisfied.') 2. Would you rent from Enterprise again? The survey allows the company to concentrate on its key driver—making loyal customers; which leads to profitable growth. Enterprise not only ranks each branch office by operating profits and customer satisfaction, but also makes promotions to higher-paying

ISO 9000 a series of international standards for achieving consistency in quality management and quality assurance in companies throughout the world.

ISO 14000 a series of international standards for managing, monitoring, and minimizing an organization's harmful effects on the environment.

Total quality management (TQM) an integrated, principle-based, organization-wide strategy for improving product and service quality.

Customer focus an organizational goal to concentrate on meeting customers' needs at all levels of the organization.

Customer satisfaction an organizational goal to provide products or services that meet or exceed customers' expectations.

Who You Gonna Call? Germ Busters!

In terms of quality management, reducing the risk of germs and the spread of infectious diseases is critical in a hospital, particularly when potentially deadly bugs such as *C. difficile* and the norovirus pose a serious threat to vulnerable patients, visitors, and healthcare workers. Increased incidences of these bugs as well as even more terrifying outbreaks, like the Ebola virus, have signalled the need for more effective methods of sterilization and led to the development of an important new weapon in the healthcare industry.

At the St. Joseph Hospital, this weapon is nicknamed "Gigi," and she and her kind are "Xenex Germ-Zapping Robots," devices made by Xenex Disinfection Services that emit ultraviolet light 25,000 times more powerful than sunlight in killing contagion. Once a room has been cleaned using standard cleaning procedures, Gigi is wheeled in to finish the job. Once activated, the robot blasts powerful UV light that can clean even the hard-to-reach areas, like under a bed or between the folds of curtains. The robot only takes about five or ten minutes to kill off the germs and prevent them from replicating their harmful DNA. According to hospital experts, manual cleaning using cleansers and bleach can kill off about 85 percent of harmful bacteria and viruses. The Xenex robot has the advantage that it does not use chemicals as part of the cleaning process, just high-intensity ultraviolet light, yet it kills 99.9 percent of harmful germs invisible to the naked eye.

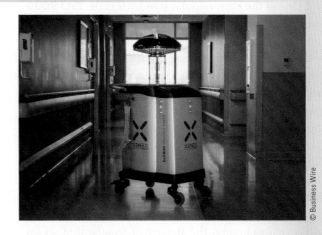

© Business Wire

Xenex Disinfection Services sells its robots to hospitals across North America, at a price tag of approximately $104,000 each, which works out to a cost on average of about $3.00 per patient. The Dallas hospital where the first Ebola patient in the United States was treated has purchased two Xenex robots. In addition to hospitals and healthcare facilities, the company also hopes to also sell to airlines, especially considering that air travel makes the spread of disease so easy and quick. Interestingly, the healthcare facilities that purchase the devices often name their robots, as Gigi was named by the St. Joseph Hospital—perhaps there is still a need to feel there is a "personal" touch being used in providing this service.

Sources: M. Martinez, P. Vercammen, and J. Hannah, "Germ-Zapping Robot Gigi Sets Its Sights on Ebola," CNN, October 16, 2014, http://www.cnn.com/2014/10/16/us/germ-zapping-robot-ebola/; "Martin Health System Unveils Xenex Germ-Zapping Robot," BusinessWire.com, December 22, 2015, http://www.businesswire.com/news/home/20151222005673/en/Martin-Health-System-Unveils-Xenex-Germ-Zapping-Robot%E2%84%A2; E. Augenbraun, "Germ-Zapping Robot Enlisted to Fight Hospital Infections," CBC News, October 8, 2014, http://www.cbsnews.com/news/germ-zapping-robot-combats-hospital-infections/.

jobs contingent on above-average customer satisfaction scores. Employees cannot seek promotion unless their branch ESQi is at or above the company average. This stems from company founder Jack Taylor's belief that if you look after your customers, the profits will look after themselves.[36]

Continuous improvement an organization's ongoing commitment to constantly assess and improve the processes and procedures used to create products and services.

Variation a deviation in the form, condition, or appearance of a product from the quality standard for that product.

Six Sigma a data-driven approach and methodology that strives to eliminate defects from products and services with a goal of having no more than 3.4 defects per million units or procedures.

Continuous improvement refers to an ongoing commitment to increasing product and service quality by constantly assessing and improving the processes and procedures used to create those products and services. Besides higher customer satisfaction, continuous improvement is usually associated with reduced variation. **Variation** is a deviation in the form, condition, or appearance of a product from the quality standard for that product. The less a product varies from the quality standard, or the more consistently a company's products meet a quality standard, the higher the quality. A quality improvement program most associated with continuous improvement is **Six Sigma**, a data-driven approach and methodology that strives to eliminate defects from products and services with a goal of having no more than 3.4 defects per million units or procedures—in other words, as close to zero defects as possible. Manufacturing and

service industries alike have embraced the concept of quality improvement programs like Six Sigma, In fact, people trained in Six Sigma earn credentials as "green belts" or "black belts" that make them sought after as managers or outside consultants. According to the Six Sigma Academy, black belts save companies approximately $230,000 per project and can complete four to six projects per year.[37]

The third principle of TQM is **teamwork**—collaboration between managers and non-managers, across business functions, and between the company and its customers and suppliers. At Toronto's Sunnybrook Hospital, teamwork has been the key to success in a number of departments, including the Odette Cancer Centre and the Department of Medical Imaging. Health care teams in these areas include surgeons, nurses, technicians, and administrative assistants, all of whom focus on achieving an important goal—reducing wait times for cancer surgery patients. Team members work together to ensure that the process is as efficient as possible; for example, a special "nurse navigator" acts as a sort of traffic control centre for cancer care. All aspects of the diagnostic imaging process are studied, including the booking process and no-show rates, to ensure that all available imaging slots are being utilized. As a result of these efforts, wait times at Sunnybrook Hospital are now well below the provincial average.[38]

Customer focus and satisfaction, continuous improvement, and teamwork mutually reinforce one another to improve quality throughout a company. Customer-focused continuous improvement is necessary to increase customer satisfaction. At the same time, continuous improvement depends on teamwork from different functional and hierarchical parts of the company.

17-3 SERVICE OPERATIONS

At the start of this chapter, you learned that operations management focuses on the daily production of goods and services. Then you learned that, to manage production, you must oversee the factors that affect produc-

tivity and quality. In this part of the chapter, you will learn about managing operations in service and manufacturing businesses. The chapter ends with a discussion of inventory management, which is a key factor in a company's profitability.

Imagine that your laptop suddenly stops working just as you head into the last month of your semester. You've got two choices: you can run to the closest Best Buy and buy a new laptop, or you can try to have it fixed in Best Buy's Geek Squad repair department. Either way, you hope to end up with the same thing—a working laptop. However, the first choice—getting a new laptop—involves buying a physical product (a good); whereas the second—dealing with the repair department—involves buying a service.

Services differ from goods in several ways. First, goods are produced or made, whereas services are performed. In other words, services are almost always labour-intensive: someone has to perform the service for you. A repair shop could sell you the parts you need to repair your laptop, but you would still need someone to actually perform the repair. Second, goods are tangible, but services are intangible. You can touch and see that new laptop, but you can't touch or see the service provided by the technician who fixed your computer. All you can "see" is that the laptop is working again. Third, services are perishable and not storable. If you don't use them when they're available, they're wasted. If the computer repair department is backlogged or your machine has to be sent away to another service area, you'll have to wait to get your laptop repaired. You can't store an unused service and use it when you like. By contrast, you can purchase a good, such as computer paper, and store it until you're ready to use it.

*Because services are different from goods, managing a service operation is different from managing a manufacturing or production operation. Let's look at **17-3a the service–profit chain** and **17-3b service recovery and empowerment.***

17-3a The Service–Profit Chain

A key assumption in the service business is that success depends on how well employees—that is, service providers—deliver their services to customers. But success actually begins with how well management

Teamwork collaboration between managers and non-managers, across business functions, and between companies, customers, and suppliers.

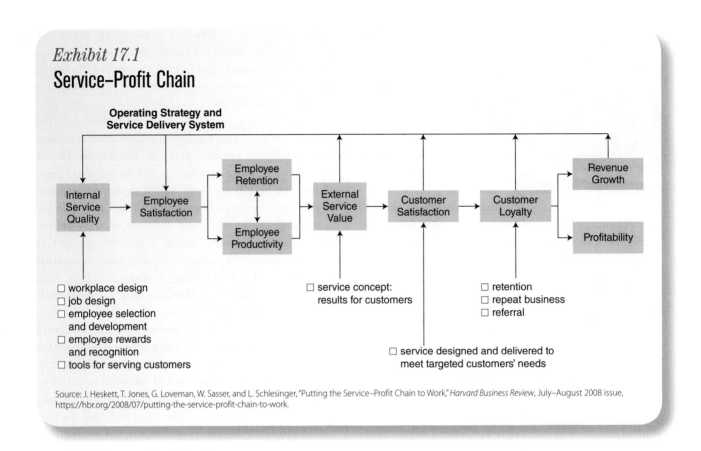

Exhibit 17.1
Service–Profit Chain

Operating Strategy and Service Delivery System

Internal Service Quality → Employee Satisfaction → Employee Retention / Employee Productivity → External Service Value → Customer Satisfaction → Customer Loyalty → Revenue Growth / Profitability

- ☐ workplace design
- ☐ job design
- ☐ employee selection and development
- ☐ employee rewards and recognition
- ☐ tools for serving customers

- ☐ service concept: results for customers

- ☐ retention
- ☐ repeat business
- ☐ referral

- ☐ service designed and delivered to meet targeted customers' needs

Source: J. Heskett, T. Jones, G. Loveman, W. Sasser, and L. Schlesinger, "Putting the Service–Profit Chain to Work," *Harvard Business Review*, July–August 2008 issue, https://hbr.org/2008/07/putting-the-service-profit-chain-to-work.

treats service employees, as illustrated in the service–profit chain in Exhibit 17.1. The service–profit chain establishes relationships between profitability, customer loyalty, and employee satisfaction, loyalty, and productivity. The links in the chain are as follows: Profitability and revenue growth are stimulated primarily by customer loyalty, which is a direct result of customer satisfaction. Customer satisfaction is largely influenced by the value of services provided to customers. Value is created by satisfied, loyal, and productive employees. Employee satisfaction, in turn, results primarily from high-quality support services and policies that enable employees to deliver results to customers.[39] The driving factor behind the service–profit chain is *internal service quality*, meaning the quality of treatment that employees receive from a company's internal service providers in areas such as workplace and job design, employee selection and development, employee rewards and recognition, and tools for servicing customers. Successful service managers pay attention to the factors that drive profitability in this new service paradigm: investment in people, technology that supports frontline workers, revamped recruiting and training practices, and compensation linked to performance from employees at every level.[40]

Vancouver City Savings Credit Union (or Vancity, as it is better known), is Canada's largest credit union and an organization that believes strongly that success starts with employees. Recognized as one of Canada's Top 100 Employers in 2016 (and for the tenth time since 2001), Vancity earned top marks in key categories like employee engagement, work atmosphere and employee communications, financial benefits and compensation, training and skill development, and physical workplace. One of Vancity's unique initiatives is a week-long employee onboarding program at the end of which new hires are given a choice to bow out of the organization (receiving $1500 for their trouble) if they decide it isn't for them. Vancity senior executives participate in the immersion week, as new hires learn about the organization's business model and values and visit community partners and social enterprises supported by the credit union. Vancity also offers employees perks at its unique head office location (atop Vancouver's SkyTrain rapid transit system) including a rooftop garden patio (with employee-led sessions for those looking to develop their gardening skills); pilates, yoga, and kick boxing classes; as well as shower facilities and a nap room. At Vancity, the connection between employees and success is so important that one of the key performance measures determining compensation for top executives relates to results from employee surveys.[41] Employees are not an afterthought; instead, they are a key group that the organization strives to impress every day.

As depicted in Exhibit 17.1, internal service quality relates to employee satisfaction which then influences external service value for customers. *Employee satisfaction* is influenced by how companies treat employees and is directly related to *employee retention* and *employee productivity*. In other words, the better employees are treated, the more satisfied they are, and the more likely they are to believe that they can and ought to provide high-value service to customers.

High *external value service* leads to *customer satisfaction* and *customer loyalty*, which, in turn, lead to *revenue growth and profitability*. What's the link between customer satisfaction and loyalty, on the one hand, and profits, on the other? To start, the average business keeps only 70–90 percent of its existing customers each year. No big deal, you say? Just replace leaving customers with new customers? Well, there's one significant problem with that solution: it costs 10 times as much to find a new customer as it does to keep an existing customer. Also, new customers typically buy only 20 percent as much as established customers. In fact, keeping existing customers is so cost-effective that most businesses could double their profits simply by keeping 5 percent more customers per year![42] How does this work? Imagine that keeping more of your customers turns some of those customers into customers for life. How much of a difference would that make to company profits? Consider that just one lifetime customer spends $8,000 on pizza and over $330,000 on luxury cars![43]

17-3b Service Recovery and Empowerment

When mistakes are made, when problems occur, and when customers become dissatisfied with the service they've received, service businesses must switch from the process of service delivery to the process of **service recovery**, or restoring customer satisfaction to strongly dissatisfied customers.[44] Service recovery sometimes requires service employees not only to fix whatever mistake was made but also to perform service acts that delight highly dissatisfied customers by far surpassing their expectations of fair treatment. For example, an executor of a family estate called a Vancouver branch of Vancity Credit Union requesting access to a deceased family member's safety deposit box. The executor lived on Vancouver Island, so an appointment was made to have the box removed. However, on the day of the appointment, the branch kept the executor waiting more than 40 minutes only to discover that the safety deposit box was located at another branch. Needless to say, the executor was not happy about what he thought was a wasted trip. The manager, however, recognizing that the branch was entirely at fault, refunded the executor $100 to cover ferry costs and his wasted time as well as the $140 in administrative costs for removing the security box.[45]

Unfortunately, when mistakes occur, service employees often don't have the discretion to resolve customer complaints. Customers who want service employees to correct or make up for poor service are often told, "I'm not allowed to do that," "I'm just following company rules," or "I'm sorry, only managers are allowed to make changes of any kind." In other words, company rules prevent them from engaging in acts of service recovery meant to turn dissatisfied customers back into satisfied customers. The result is frustration for customers and service employees and lost customers for the company.

Now, however, many companies are empowering their service employees.[46] In Chapter 8, you learned that *empowering workers* means permanently passing decision-making authority and responsibility from managers to workers. With respect to service recovery, empowering workers means giving service employees the authority and responsibility to make decisions that immediately solve customer problems.[47] As part of Vancity's Service Recovery Program, employees are encouraged to "own" complaints and are empowered to take action and make decisions. Customer complaints

> Success begins with how well management treats service employees.

Africa Studio/Shutterstock

Service recovery restoring customer satisfaction to strongly dissatisfied customers.

and their resolution are tracked electronically and, each quarter, the Sales and Outstanding Service Committee reviews the feedback.[48] Empowering service workers does entail some costs, but these are usually less than the company's savings from retaining customers.

17-4 MANUFACTURING OPERATIONS

Toyota manufactures cars, and Apple makes computers. Shell produces gasoline, Bombardier makes aircraft, and Molson makes beer. The *manufacturing operations* of these companies all produce physical goods. But not all manufacturing operations, especially these, are the same.

*Let's learn how various manufacturing operations differ in terms of **17-4a the amount of processing that is done to produce and assemble a product** and **17-4b the flexibility to change the number, kind, and characteristics of products that are produced.***

Make-to-order operation a manufacturing operation that does not start processing or assembling products until a customer order is received.

Assemble-to-order operation a manufacturing operation that divides manufacturing processes into separate parts or modules that are combined to create semi-customized products.

17-4a Amount of Processing in Manufacturing Operations

Manufacturing operations can be classified according to the amount of processing or assembly that occurs after a customer order is received.

The highest degree of processing occurs in make-to-order operations. A **make-to-order operation** does not start processing or assembling products until it receives a customer order. In fact, some make-to-order operations may not even order parts until a customer order is received. Not surprisingly, make-to-order operations produce or assemble highly specialized or customized products for customers. The John Deere 8R tractor, for example, comes with thousands of options that can be customized to the needs of a wheat farmer in Alberta or a rice farmer in India. Buyers choose from six types of axles, five transmissions, 13 types of rear hitches, and 54 different wheel and tire configurations. There are 354 option bundles for the basic tractor and 114 option bundles for attachments. Thanks to so many option combinations, Deere produced 7,800 unique 8R tractors in a single year. On average, each tractor configuration was built just 1.5 times, and over half of the configurations were built just once—truly a make-to-order operation.[49]

A moderate degree of processing occurs in assemble-to-order operations. A company using an **assemble-to-order operation** divides its manufacturing or assembly process into separate parts or modules. The company orders parts and assembles modules ahead of

Electric Cars, Made to Order

Typically, when consumers purchase cars, they have to go to a dealer and choose one from the inventory that the dealer has on hand. To sell its new Focus Electric, however, Ford is using a build-to-order model, similar to what Dell used successfully to sell computers.

Instead of a big inventory of cars, dealers will only carry one demonstration model of the Focus Electric. After trying out the model, customers can then place an order for their own Focus Electric, selecting whatever colours, interior fabric, options, and accessories they wish. So, if someone wants a silver Focus Electric with a dark grey leather interior, rear-view camera, Bluetooth connectivity, and a power sunroof, all she has to do is order one, instead of hoping that the dealer has one in the inventory. In about six weeks, the car will be delivered straight from the factory.

Source: J. Murray, "Ford Focus Electric Will Use 'Build-to-Order, Sales Model," *The Guardian*, March 29, 2012, http://www.guardian.co.uk/environment/2012/mar/29/ford-focus-electric-dell-build.

customer orders. Then, based on actual customer orders or on research forecasting what customers will want, those modules are combined to create semi-customized products.

The lowest degree of processing occurs in a **make-to-stock operation** (also called *build-to-stock*). Because the products are standardized, meaning each product is exactly the same as the next, a company using a make-to-stock operation starts ordering parts and assembling finished products before receiving customer orders. Customers then purchase these standardized products—such as Rubbermaid storage containers, microwave ovens, and vacuum cleaners—at retail stores or directly from the manufacturer. Because parts are ordered and products are assembled before customers order the products, make-to-stock operations are highly dependent on the accuracy of sales forecasts. If sales forecasts are incorrect, make-to-stock operations may end up building too many or too few products, or they may make products with the wrong features or without the features that customers want. These disadvantages are leading many companies to move from make-to-stock to assemble-to-order systems.

17-4b Flexibility of Manufacturing Operations

A second way to categorize manufacturing operations is by **manufacturing flexibility**, meaning the degree to which manufacturing operations can easily and quickly change the number, kind, and characteristics of products they produce. Flexibility allows companies to respond quickly to changes in the marketplace (i.e., competitors and customers) and to reduce the lead time between ordering and final delivery of products. There is often a tradeoff between flexibility and cost, however, with the most flexible manufacturing operations frequently having higher costs per unit and the least flexible operations having lower costs per unit.[50] Some common manufacturing operations, arranged in order from least flexible to most flexible, are *continuous-flow production, line-flow production, batch production,* and *job shops.*

Most production processes generate finished products at a discrete rate. A product is completed, and then—perhaps a few seconds, minutes, or hours later—another is completed, and so on. By contrast, in **continuous-flow production**, products are produced continuously rather than discretely. Like a water hose that is never turned off and just keeps on flowing, production of the final product never stops.

Line-flow production processes are pre-established, occur in a serial or linear manner, and are dedicated to making one type of product. Line-flow production processes are inflexible because, typically, they are dedicated to manufacturing one kind of product. For example, the production process for Tesla Motors' Model S car starts with large rolls of aluminum, which are flattened, cut, and then stamped into the shapes of the car's body panels (i.e. roof, trunk, left front). Stamped panels are then moved to the body shop, where the car's underbody, sides, and front are joined via robotic welding machines. Once the shell of the car is formed, it is primed, painted, and moved to the assembly line. There, 3,000 workers and 160 robots install the battery, motor, wiring, interior, seats, and the rest of the car's 30,000-plus parts. The assembly process for a car takes three to five days. In total, Tesla's Model S factory produces about 400 cars per week.[51]

Batch production involves the manufacture of large batches of different products in standard lot sizes. This production method is being used increasingly by restaurant chains. To ensure consistency in the taste and quality of their products, many restaurants have central kitchens, or commissaries, that produce batches of food such as mashed potatoes, stuffing, macaroni and cheese, rice, quiche filling, and chili, in volumes ranging from 10 to 200 litres. These batches are then delivered to restaurants, which serve the food to customers.

Finally, **job shops** are small manufacturing operations that handle special manufacturing processes or jobs. In contrast to batch production, which handles large batches of different products, job shops typically

---

Make-to-stock operation a manufacturing operation that orders parts and assembles standardized products before receiving customer orders.

Manufacturing flexibility the degree to which manufacturing operations can easily and quickly change the number, kind, and characteristics of products they produce.

Continuous-flow production a manufacturing operation that produces goods at a continuous rate, rather than a discrete rate.

Line-flow production manufacturing processes that are pre-established, occur in a serial or linear manner, and are dedicated to making one type of product.

Batch production a manufacturing operation that produces goods in large batches in standard lot sizes.

Job shops manufacturing operations that handle custom orders or small batch jobs.

handle very small batches, some as small as one product or process per batch. Basically, each job in a job shop is different, and once a job is done, the job shop moves on to a completely different job or manufacturing process, most likely for a different customer.

17-5 INVENTORY

Inventory is the amount and number of raw materials, parts, and finished products a company has in its possession. Over the past few years, growing concern over reports of drug shortages in Canada has prompted the Canadian Medical Association and Health Canada to investigate the limited access to medications. Health Canada reports that drug shortages are a global problem, linked to various possible causes including production issues, unexpected surges in demand, and difficulties accessing raw supplies. In addition, health analysts point to some specific areas of concern, such as pharmaceutical companies that outsource production to countries overseas where variances in quality control mean active ingredients needed to product a particular drug sometimes become contaminated and then can't be used, leading to production backups. In addition, some of the drugs in short supply are generic, indicating that some companies are reducing or ceasing production to focus on drugs that provide higher profit margins. Working with the pharmaceutical industry, the government of Canada now supports a website where pharmaceutical companies are required to post when a drug is in short supply so information is readily available to Canadians and individuals in the healthcare system.[52]

*In this section, you will learn about **17-5a how to measure inventory levels, 17-5b the costs of maintaining an inventory,** and **17-5c the different systems for managing inventory.***

17-5a Measuring Inventory

As you'll learn below, uncontrolled inventory can generate huge costs for a manufacturing operation. Consequently, managers need good measures of inventory to prevent inventory costs from becoming too large. Three basic measures of inventory are *average aggregate inventory, weeks of supply,* and *inventory turnover.*

If you ever worked in a retail store and had to take inventory, you probably weren't too excited about the process of counting every item in the store and storeroom. It's an extensive task that's a bit easier today because of bar codes that mark items and computers that can count and track them. Nonetheless, inventories still differ from day to day depending on when in the month or week they're taken. Because of such differences, companies often measure **average aggregate inventory**, which is the average overall inventory during a particular time period. Average aggregate inventory for a month can be determined by simply averaging the inventory counts at the end of each business day for that month. One way companies know whether they're carrying too much or too little inventory is to compare their average aggregate inventory to the industry average for aggregate inventory.

Inventory is also measured in terms of **weeks of supply**, meaning the number of weeks it would take for a company to run out of its current supply of inventory. In general, there is an acceptable number of weeks of inventory for a particular kind of business. Too few weeks of inventory on hand, and a company risks a **stockout**—running out of inventory.

Another common inventory measure, **inventory turnover**, is the number of times per year that a company sells or "turns over" its average inventory. For example, if a company keeps an average of 100 finished products in inventory each month, and it sells 1,000 products this year, then it has turned its inventory 10 times this year. In general, the higher the number of inventory turns, the better. In practice, a high turnover means that

Inventory the amount and number of raw materials, parts, and finished products that a company has in its possession.

Average aggregate inventory average overall inventory during a particular time period.

Weeks of supply the number of weeks it would take for a company to run out of its current supply of inventory.

Stockout the situation when a company runs out of finished product.

Inventory turnover the number of times per year that a company sells or "turns over" its average inventory.

a company can continue its daily operations with just a small amount of inventory on hand.[53]

In the consumer technology industry, competition is fierce and effective supply chain management—in particular, inventory turnover—can make or break a company. Recently, Gartner Inc., a global information technology research company, published its list of the top 25 supply chain companies. Apple Computer was ranked the number one supply chain in the world, turning over its inventory 74 times in a year—an astonishing once every five days. For a company that sells hundreds of millions of products all over the globe, this is a major competitive advantage, since the company does not need to stockpile goods in any large quantities. The next two companies in Apple's category were Dell and Samsung, which turned over their inventory approximately once every 10 and 21 days, respectively.[54]

17-5b Costs of Maintaining an Inventory

Maintaining an inventory results in four kinds of costs: *ordering, setup, holding,* and *stockout.*

Ordering cost is not the cost of the inventory itself but the costs associated with ordering the inventory. It includes the costs of completing paperwork, manually entering data into a computer, sending emails, getting competing bids, correcting mistakes, and simply determining when and how much new inventory should be reordered. For example, ordering costs are relatively high in the restaurant business because 80 percent of food service orders (which is how restaurants reorder food supplies) are processed manually. It's estimated that the food industry could save $14.3 billion if all restaurants converted to electronic data interchange in which purchase and ordering information from one company's computer system is automatically relayed to another company's computer system. Toward that end, an industry-wide effort, Efficient Foodservice Response, is underway to improve efficiencies in the food service supply chain.[55]

Setup cost is the cost of changing or adjusting a machine so that it can produce a different kind of inventory.[56] For example, 3M uses the same production machinery to make several kinds of industrial tape, and it must adjust the machines whenever it switches from one kind of tape to another.

Holding cost, also known as *carrying* or *storage cost,* is the cost of keeping inventory until it is used or sold. Holding cost includes the cost of storage facilities, insurance to protect inventory from damage or theft, inventory taxes, and obsolescence (i.e., the cost of holding inventory that is no longer useful to the company), as well as the opportunity cost of spending money on inventory that could have been spent elsewhere in the company. It's estimated that US airlines have a total of $44 billion worth of airplane parts in stock for maintenance, repair, and overhauling their planes at any one time. The holding cost for managing, storing, and purchasing these parts is nearly $11 billion—or roughly one-fourth of the cost of the parts themselves.[57]

Stockout costs are the costs incurred when a company runs out of a product, as happened to Nintendo when it failed to have enough XBox Ones for the holiday shopping season. There are two basic kinds of stockout costs. First, the company incurs the transaction costs of overtime work, shipping, and the like in trying to quickly replace out-of-stock inventories with new inventories. The second and perhaps more damaging cost is the loss of customers' goodwill when a company cannot deliver the products it promised.

17-5c Managing Inventory

Inventory management has two basic goals. The first is to avoid running out of stock and thus angering and dissatisfying customers; this goal seeks to increase inventory to a safe level that won't risk stockouts. The second is to efficiently reduce inventory levels and costs as much as possible without impairing daily operations; this goal seeks a minimal level of inventory. The following inventory management techniques—*economic order quantity (EOQ), just-in-time inventory (JIT),* and

lucato/iStockphoto

Ordering cost the costs associated with ordering inventory, including the cost of data entry, phone calls, obtaining bids, correcting mistakes, and determining when and how much inventory to order.

Setup cost the costs of downtime and lost efficiency that occur when a machine is changed or adjusted to produce a different kind of inventory.

Holding cost the cost of keeping inventory until it is used or sold, including storage, insurance, taxes, obsolescence, and opportunity costs.

Stockout costs the costs incurred when a company runs out of a product, including transaction costs to replace inventory and the loss of customers' goodwill.

The New Industrial Revolution

Additive manufacturing, commonly known as 3D printing, is changing the process by which products are created. Additive manufacturing can dramatically reduce the need for assembly, improve the consistency of each part produced, and reduce material waste and labour costs. General Electric's next-generation jet engine, the LEAP, has a fuel nozzle that would require the assembly of 18 separate parts if produced using traditional casting methods. Using 3D printing technology, however, GE can create the nozzle in a single piece, which both saves on costs and makes it five times more durable.

Nike has also begun applying these technologies to the shoemaking process. Shoe assembly is typically a serial process, whereby workers along an assembly line put shoes together one piece at a time. Nike's Flyknit shoe, however, is made by a single machine that knits the upper portion of the shoe in a single piece; design software instructs it to change materials or perform specific adjustments as it goes. The shoe is constructed using only a few pieces and a few steps, and waste is cut down by 80 percent.

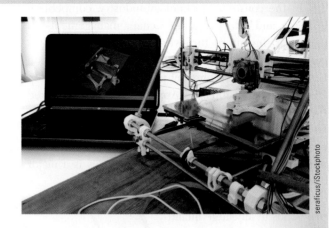

seraficus/iStockphoto

In addition to changing the manufacturing process, additive manufacturing could also change where companies locate their manufacturing operations. Since additive manufacturing is reducing labour costs, it could become increasingly advantageous for companies to build manufacturing facilities closer to end markets rather than in places where labour costs are low.

Source: J. Koten, "A Revolution in the Making," *Wall Street Journal*, June 10, 2013, http://online.wsj.com/news/articles/SB10001424127887324063304578522812684722382?KEYWORDS=advanced+manufacturing+new+industrial&mg=reno64-wsj.

materials requirement planning (MRP)—are different ways of balancing these competing goals.

Economic order quantity (EOQ) is a system of formulas that together help determine how much and how often inventory should be ordered. EOQ takes into account the overall demand (D) for a product while trying to minimize ordering costs (O) and holding costs (H). The formula for EOQ is

$$EOQ = \sqrt{\frac{2DO}{H}}$$

For example, if a factory uses 40,000 litres of paint a year (D), ordering costs (O) are \$75 per order, and holding costs (H) are \$4 per litre, then the optimal quantity to order is 1,225 litres:

$$EOQ = \sqrt{\frac{2(40,000)(75)}{4}} = 1,225$$

And, with 40,000 litres of paint being used per year, the factory uses approximately 110 litres per day:

$$\frac{40,000 \text{ litres}}{365 \text{ days}} = 110$$

Consequently, the factory would order 1,225 new litres of paint approximately every 11 days:

$$\frac{1,225 \text{ litres}}{110 \text{ litres per day}} = 11.1 \text{ days}$$

In general, EOQ formulas do a good job of letting managers know what size or amount of inventory they should reorder to minimize ordering and holding costs. Mark Lore, CEO of Diapers.com, explains how his company uses EOQ formulas to decide precisely how much inventory to keep on hand. He says, "We built software with computational algorithms to determine what the optimal number of boxes to have in the warehouse is and what the sizes of those boxes should be. Should we stock five different kinds of boxes to ship product in? Twenty kinds? Fifty kinds? And what size should those boxes be? Right now, it's twenty-three box sizes, given what we sell, in order to minimize the cost of dunnage (those little plastic air-filled bags or peanuts), the cost of corrugated

Economic order quantity (EOQ) a system of formulas that minimizes ordering and holding costs and helps determine how much and how often inventory should be ordered.

boxes, and the cost of shipping. We rerun the simulation every quarter."[58] As this examples makes clear, EOQ formulas and models can become much more complex as adjustments are made for price changes, quantity discounts, setup costs, and many other factors.[59]

While EOQ formulas try to minimize holding and ordering costs, the just-in-time (JIT) approach to inventory management attempts to eliminate holding costs by reducing inventory levels to near zero. With a **just-in-time (JIT) inventory system**, component parts arrive from suppliers just as they are needed at each stage of production. When parts arrive just in time, the manufacturer has little inventory on hand and thus avoids the costs associated with holding it. Thanks to its strict JIT inventory system, Apple carries the smallest amount of inventory among technology companies, averaging just five days of inventory of iPhones, iPads, and MacBook Pros waiting to be shipped. That five days of inventory is equivalent to an inventory turn of 74.1 times a year (remember, more turns are better). Dell was next with 35.6 turns a year, followed by Samsung with 17.1 turns a year and Amazon by 10.[60]

To have just the right amount of inventory arrive at just the right time requires a tremendous amount of coordination between manufacturers and suppliers. One way to promote tight coordination under JIT is close proximity. Most parts suppliers for Toyota's JIT system at its Georgetown, Kentucky, plant are located within 300 kilometres of the plant. Furthermore, parts are picked up from suppliers and delivered to Toyota as often as 16 times a day.[61] A second way to promote close coordination under JIT is to have a shared information system that allows a manufacturer and its suppliers to know the quantity and kinds of parts inventory each has in stock. Generally, factories and suppliers facilitate information sharing by using the same part numbers and names. Ford's seat supplier accomplishes this by sticking a bar code on each seat, and Ford then uses the sticker to route the seat through its factory. Manufacturing operations and their parts suppliers can also facilitate close coordination by using the Japanese system of kanban. **Kanban**, which is Japanese for "sign," is a simple ticket-based system that indicates when it is time to reorder inventory. Suppliers attach kanban cards to batches of parts. Then, when an assembly-line worker uses the first part out of a batch, the kanban card is removed. The cards are then collected, sorted, and quickly returned to the supplier, who begins resupplying the factory with parts that match the order information on the kanban cards. Because prices and batch sizes are typically agreed to ahead of time, kanban tickets greatly reduce paperwork and ordering costs.[62]

© Anderson Ross/Brand X Pictures/Jupiterimages

A third method for managing inventory is **materials requirement planning (MRP)**—a production and inventory system that, from beginning to end, precisely determines the production schedule, production batch sizes, and inventories needed to complete final products. The three key parts of MRP systems are the master production schedule, the bill of materials, and inventory records. The *master production schedule* is a detailed schedule that indicates the quantity of each item to be produced, the planned delivery dates for those items, and the time by which each step of the production process must be completed in order to meet those delivery

Just-in-time (JIT) inventory system an inventory system in which component parts arrive from suppliers just as they are needed at each stage of production.

Kanban a ticket-based JIT system that indicates when to reorder inventory.

Materials requirement planning (MRP) a production and inventory system that determines the production schedule, production batch sizes, and inventory needed to complete final products.

dates. Based on the quantity and kind of products set forth in the master production schedule, the *bill of materials* identifies all the necessary parts and inventory, the quantity or volume of inventory to be ordered, and the order in which the parts and inventory should be assembled. *Inventory records* indicate the kind, quantity, and location of inventory that is on hand or that has been ordered. When inventory records are combined with the bill of materials, the resulting report indicates what to buy, when to buy it, and what it will cost to order.

Independent demand system an inventory system in which the level of one kind of inventory does not depend on another.

Dependent demand system an inventory system in which the level of inventory depends on the number of finished units to be produced.

Today, nearly all MRP systems are available in the form of powerful, flexible computer software.[63]

Which inventory management system should you use? EOQ formulas are intended for use with an **independent demand system**, in which the level of one kind of inventory does not depend on another. For example, because inventory levels for automobile tires are unrelated to the inventory levels of women's shoes, Sears could use EOQ formulas to calculate separate optimal order quantities for shoes and tires. By contrast, JIT and MRP are used with a **dependent demand system**, in which the level of inventory depends on the number of finished units to be produced. For example, if Yamaha makes 1,000 motorcycles a day, then it will need 1,000 seats, 1,000 gas tanks, and 2,000 wheels and tires each day. So, when optimal inventory levels depend on the number of products to be produced, use a JIT or MRP management system.

STUDY TOOLS 17

READY TO STUDY?

LOCATED IN TEXTBOOK:

☐ Rip out the Chapter Review Card at the back of the book to have a summary of the chapter and key terms handy.

LOCATED AT NELSON.COM/STUDENT:

☐ Access the eBook or use the ReadSpeaker feature to listen to the chapter on the go.

☐ Prepare for tests with practice quizzes.

☐ Review key terms with flashcards and the glossary feature.

☐ Work through key concepts with case studies and Management Decision Exercises.

☐ Explore practical examples with You Make the Decision Activities.

Endnotes

1

1. J. Johnson, "Dunkin' Donuts Ordered to Pay $16.4 Million to Quebec Franchisees," *Financial Post*, June 25, 2012, http://business.financialpost .com/2012/06/25/dunkin-donuts-ordered-to-pay -16-4m-to-quebec-franchisees; Canadian Press, "Dunkin' Donuts to Appeal Verdict Giving ex-Quebec Franchisees $16.4 million," *Canadian Business*, June 25, 2012, http://www.canadianbusiness .com/article/88919–dunkin-donuts-to-appeal -verdict-giving-ex-quebec-franchisees-16-4-million, http://thechronicleherald.ca/business/110859 -dunkin-donuts-to-appeal-verdict-giving-franchisees -164-million; S. Silcoff, "Court Rules in Favour of Dunkin' Donuts Franchisees," *Globe and Mail*, June 25, 2012, http://www.theglobeandmail.com/ report-on-business/court-rules-in-favour-of-dunkin -donuts-franchisees/article4369753.

2. D. Dale, "Jim Treliving: The Loving Dragon," *Toronto Star*, March 15, 2010, http://www.thestar .com/business/article/779809–jim-treliving-the -loving-dragon; H. Schachter, "Dragon's Den Co-star Says Use Your Head—and Your Heart—to Make Decisions," *Globe and Mail*, September 25, 2012, http://www.theglobeandmail.com/report-on-business/ careers/management/dragons-den-co-star-says-use -your-head-and-your-heart-to-make-decisions/ article4567463; http://www.bpincomefund.com/ Files/Documents/jimbio.pdf.

3. *Shouldice Hernia Center Newsletter* 11, no. 1, http://www.shouldice.com/newsletter.htm.

4. G. Bensinger and L. Stevens, "Amazon, in Threat to UPS, Tries Its Own Deliveries. An Alternative to Shippers Like FedEx and UPS, New Service Could Deliver Goods the Same Day as Purchased," *Wall Street Journal Online*, April 24, 2014, accessed August 8, 2015, http://www.wsj.com/ articles/SB10001424052702304788404579521522 792859890; S. Banzo, S. Kapner, S. Ng, and L. Stevens, "Late Surge in Web Buying Blindsides UPS, Retailers," *Wall Street Journal*, December 25, 2013, accessed August 17, 2015.

5. D.A. Wren, A.G. Bedeian, and J.D. Breeze, "The Foundations of Henri Fayol's Administrative Theory," *Management Decision* 40 (2002): 906–18.

6. A. Bryant, "Google's Quest to Build a Better Boss," *The New York Times*, March 13, 2011, BU1, accessed August 18, 2015, http://www.nytimes.com/ 2011/03/13/business/13hire.html?_r=1; W. Chen, "Why Google's Best Leaders Aren't Stanford Grads with Perfect SATs," *Inc.com*, July 17, 2014, accessed August 18, 2015, http://www.inc.com/walter-chen/ google-isn-8217-t-looking-for-stanford-and-mit -grads-it-8217-s-looking-for-this-.html; B. Hall, "Google's Project Oxygen Pumps Fresh Air Into Management," *TheStreet.com*, February 11, 2014, accessed August 18, 2015, http://www.thestreet.com/ story/12328981/1/googles-project-oxygen-pumps -fresh-air-into-management.html.

7. H. Fayol, *General and Industrial Management* (London: Pittman and Sons, 1949).

8. R. Stagner, "Corporate Decision Making," *Journal of Applied Psychology* 53 (1969): 1–13.

9. D.W. Bray, R.J. Campbell, and D.L. Grant, *Formative Years in Business: A Long-Term AT&T Study of Managerial Lives* (New York: Wiley, 1993).

10. A. Tsotsis, "Instagram Founders: Instagram Is a 'New Entertainment Platform,'" *TechCrunch.com*, April 2, 2011, accessed August 18, 2015, http:// techcrunch.com/2011/04/02/instagram-2/.

11. M. Lewis, "Rogers Reworks the Executive Suite," *The Toronto Star*, May 23, 2014, accessed August 25, 2015, http://www.thestar.com/business/ tech_news/2014/05/23/rogers_reworks_the _executive_suite.html; J. Castaldo, "Rogers CEO Guy Laurence Says Sweeping Restructuring Is Aimed at Improving Customer Service," *Canadian Business*, May 24, 2014, accessed August 25, 2015, http://www.canadianbusiness.com/companies-and -industries/guy-laurence-rogers-3/; Rogers.com, Company Results 2014, accessed August 25, 2015, http://www.rogers.com/web/ir/overview/yearly -results.

12. "Our History," The Running Room, accessed August 18, 2015, http://www.runningroom.com/hm/ inside.php?lang=1&id=3036; "Three Things—John Stanton," *Report on Business, The Globe and Mail*, July 29, 2010, accessed August 18, 2015, http:// www.theglobeandmail.com/report-on-business/ small-business/sb-tools/sb-how-to/john-stanton/ article600034/; C. Cornell, "Running Room Goes South," *Profit Magazine*, April 2004, http://www .profitguide.com/mranage-grow/success-stories/ running-room-goes-south-28444.

13. J. Beer, "MEC Without the Mountain," *Canadian Business*, October 22, 2013, accessed August 19, 2015, http://www.canadianbusiness .com/companies-and-industries/mec-without-the -mountain/.

14. H.S. Jonas III, R.E. Fry, and S. Srivastva, "The Office of the CEO: Understanding the Executive Experience," *Academy of Management Executives* 4 (1990): 36–47.

15. N. Carlson, "Groupon CEO Andrew Mason's Honest, Charming Goodbye Memo: I Was Fired Today." *BusinessInsider.com*, February 28, 2013, accessed August 21, 2015, http://www.businessinsider .com/groupon-ceo-andrew-masons-honest-charming -goodbye-memo-i-was-fired-today-2013-2; S. Guston, "Groupon Fired CEO Andrew Mason: The Rise and Fall of Tech's Enfant Terrible," Time.com, March 1, 2013, accessed August 21, 2015, http://business .time.com/2013/03/01/groupon-fires-ceo-andrew -mason-the-rise-and-fall-of-techs-enfant-terrible/

16. M.S. Rao, "Action Plan for New CEOs During First 100 Days," *Training Magazine*, October 8, 2014, accessed August 18, 2015, http://www .trainingmag.com/action-plan-new-ceos-during -first-100-days.

17. M. Porter, J. Lorsch, and N. Nohria, "Seven Surprises for New CEOS," *Harvard Business Review* (October 2004): 62.

18. M. Murray, "As Huge Firms Keep Growing, CEOs Struggle to Keep Pace," *Wall Street Journal*, February 8, 2001, A1.

19. Q. Huy, "In Praise of Middle Managers," *Harvard Business Review* (September 2001): 72–79.

20. Coalition for Secure and Trade-Efficient Borders, Canadian Manufacturers, and Exporters (CME), "Rethinking Our Borders: A New North American Partnership," http://www.cme-mec.ca/ pdf/Coalition_Report0705_Final.pdf; University of Waterloo, Department of Economics, and Wilfrid Laurier University, Department of Economics (2011), "Border Delays Reemerging Priority: Within-Country Dimensions for Canada," *Canadian Public Policy*, http://utpjournals.metapress.com/ content/r2278402k31t6436/fulltext.pdf; "New International Trade Crossing Study: Border Delays Cost U.S. and Canada $30 billion Every Year" (April 2011), http://www.mirsnews.com/pdfs/pdfs/ Press_Releases/1304089398_Dric2.pdf; Alexander Moens and Nachum Gabler, "Measuring the Costs of the Canada–US border (August 2012), http:// www.fraserinstitute.org/uploadedFiles/fraser-ca/ Content/research-news/research/publications/ measuring-the-costs-of-the-canada-us-border.pdf.

21. K. Liyakasa, "Harry Rosen Mobilizes Luxury Menswear," *CRM Magazine*, October 2012 issue, accessed August 21, 2015, http://www.destinationcrm .com/Articles/Columns-Departments/REAL-ROI/ Harry-Rosen-Mobilizes-Luxury-Menswear-85139 .aspx, http://www.hp.com/canada/portal/smb/success _stories/stories/harry_rosen.html.

22. T. Seideman, "Harnessing the Giant," *World Trade* 15 (2002): 28–29.

23. J. Ray, "Your Favorite Restaurant's Secret Ingredient: Data, and Lots of It," Wired.com, May 3, 2012, accessed August 22, 2015, http://www .wired.com/2012/05/restaurant-moneyball/

24. S. Tully, "What Team Leaders Need to Know," *Fortune*, February 20, 1995, 93.

25. A. De Smet, M. McGurk, and M. Vinson, "Unlocking the Potential of Front-Line Managers," McKinsey and Company, August 2009, http://www .mckinsey.com/business-functions/organization/ our-insights/unlocking-the-potential-of-frontline -managers.

26. S. Zieger, "Team Leader vs. Supervisor Responsibilities," Small Business Chronicles, accessed August 23, 2015, http://smallbusiness.chron.com/ team-leader-vs-supervisor-responsibilities-35723 .html; L. Liu and A. McMurray, "Frontline Leaders: The Entry Point for Leadership Development in the Manufacturing Industry," *Journal of European Industrial Training* 28, nos. 2–4 (2004): 339–52.

27. L. Landro, "The Informed Patient: Bringing Surgeons Down to Earth—New Programs Aim to Curb Fear That Prevents Nurses from Flagging Problems," *Wall Street Journal*, November 16, 2005, D1.

28. H. Mintzberg, *The Nature of Managerial Work* (New York: Harper and Row, 1973).

29. P. Hales, "What Do Managers Do? A Critical Review of the Evidence," *Journal of Management Studies* 23, no. 1 (1986): 88–115.

30. D. Shaughnessy, "Pete Frates Story Continues to Inspire," *The Boston Globe*, March 3, 2015, accessed August 25, 2015, https://www.bostonglobe .com/sports/2015/03/03/the-amazing-pete-frates -story-continues-inspire/vDfnJSntd5Wjcx8urvsizL/ story.html; C. Gallo, "How Pete Frates Found His Calling and Launched the Ice Bucket Challenge," Forbes.com, September 5, 2014, accessed August 25, 2015, http://www.forbes.com/sites/carminegallo/ 2014/09/05/how-pete-frates-found-his-calling-and -launched-the-ice-bucket-challenge/.

31. B. Francella, "In a Day's Work," *Convenience Store News*, September 25, 2001, 7.

32. M. Wohlsen, "Jeff Bezos Says Amazon Is Seriously Serious About Drone Deliveries," Wired, April 11, 2014, accessed June 13, 2014, http://www.wired.com/2014/04/amazon-delivery-drones/. No author, "Amazon Tests Drones for Same-Day Parcel Delivery, Bezos Says," Bloomberg News, December 2, 2013, accessed June 13, 2014, http://www.bloomberg.com/news/2013-12-02/amazon-testing-octocopters-for-delivery-ceo-tells-60-minutes-.html.

33. M. Langley, "Changing Gears," Wall Street Journal, December 22, 2006, A1.

34. M. Ramsey, "Fuel Goal Tests Ford's Mettle," Wall Street Journal, January 13, 2014, B1.

35. S. Brown, "Iron Man 3 Gets Remixed for China," CNN, May 3, 2013, accessed May 14, 2013, http://edition.cnn.com/2013/05/03/business/iron-man-china; S. Montlake, "Hollywood's China Fixer," Forbes, November 19, 2012, 127–130.

36. L.A. Hill, Becoming a Manager: Mastery of a New Identity (Boston: Harvard Business School Press, 1992).

37. R.L. Katz, "Skills of an Effective Administrator," Harvard Business Review (September–October 1974): 90–102.

38. C.A. Bartlett and S. Ghoshal, "Changing the Role of Top Management: Beyond Systems to People," Harvard Business Review (May–June 1995): 132–142.

39. F.L. Schmidt and J.E. Hunter, "Development of a Causal Model of Process Determining Job Performance," Current Directions in Psychological Science 1 (1992): 89–92.

2

1. L. Fleisher, "Thousands of Taxi Drivers Protest Uber Across Europe," Wall Street Journal, June 12, 2014, B2; S. Goodyear, "Uber vs. the World: How Cities Are Dealing with Ride-Hailing Technology," CBC News, October 2, 2015, http://www.cbc.ca/news/business/uber-versus-the-world-1.3252096; A. Bosanac, "Montreal Is at War with Uber. Which Side Will Surrender?" Canadian Business Online, May 22, 2015, accessed October 11, 2015, http://www.canadianbusiness.com/innovation/montreal-declares-war-on-uber/.

2. "Industry Profile: Food Distributors," First Research, January 24, 2011, accessed February 2, 2011, http://www.firstresearch.com/Focus-Research/Food-Distributors.html.

3. S. Ovide and D. Wakabayashi, "Apple's Share of Smartphone Industry's Profits Soars to 92%," Wall Street Journal, July 12, 2015, accessed October 5, 2015, http://www.wsj.com/articles/apples-share-of-smartphone-industrys-profits-soars-to-92-1436727458; T. Danova, "These Are the Software and Hardware Trends that Will Drive Future Growth in the Smartphone Market," Business Insider Online, January 12, 2014, accessed October 5, 2015, http://www.businessinsider.com/the-state-of-the-smartphone-industry-2014-9.

4. E. Romanelli and M.L. Tushman, "Organizational Transformation as Punctuated Equilibrium: An Empirical Test," Academy of Management Journal 37 (1994): 1141–66.

5. C. Williams, A. Kondra, and C. Vibert, Management, 2nd Canadian Ed. (Toronto: Nelson, 2008); K. Owram, "Losing the 'WestJet Effect': How the Once-Scrappy Upstart Carrier's Culture Is Changing as It Expands Globally," Financial Post Online, October 2, 2015, http://business.financialpost.com/news/transportation/losing-the-westjet-effect-how-the-once-scrappy-upstart-carriers-culture-is-changing-as-it-expands-globally; T. Johnson, "WestJet Pilots Begin Union Vote—What's at Stake? Experts Say Unionization Could Change the Corporate Culture at Freewheeling Low-Cost Airline," CBCNews Online, July 20, 2015, accessed September 24, 2015, http://www.cbc.ca/news/business/westjet-pilots-begin-union-vote-what-s-at-stake-1.3128631.

6. Government of Canada, Canadian Dairy Information Centre, http://www.dairyinfo.gc.ca/pdf/histprod_e.pdf.

7. S. Rosenbaum, "The Craigslist Economy Is Booming," Forbes.com, January 26, 2015, accessed September 20, 2015, http://www.forbes.com/sites/stevenrosenbaum/2015/01/26/the-craigslist-economy-is-booming/.

8. J. Falls, "What the Wall Street Journal Has, Few Will Match," Social Media Explorer, October 30, 2009; 2010, http://www.socialmediaexplorer.com/2009/10/30/what-the-wall-street-journal-has-few-will-match; S. Ladurantaye, "Slow Online Ad Sales Hurt Publishers," Globe and Mail.com, May 10, 2012, https://secure.globeadvisor.com/servlet/articlenews/story/gam/20120510/rbnewspapersdigitalladurantayeatl.

9. S. Shah, "Power Outages Hobble Pakistan's Biggest Exporters," Wall Street Journal, November 29, 2013, accessed June 4, 2014, http://online.wsj.com/news/articles/SB10001424052702304795804579097620793610020?KEYWORDS=power+outages+hobble&mg=reno64-wsj.

10. L. Strapageil, "Tim Horton's to Increase Price of Coffee and Breakfast Sandwiches," OCanada.com, November 19, 2014, accessed October 15, 2015, http://o.canada.com/business/tim-hortons-to-increase-price-of-a-coffee-breakfast-sandwiches; J. Sturgeon, "Coffee Prices Stay Higher as Bean Prices Fall Back to Earth," GlobalNews.ca, January 5, 2015, accessed October 16, http://globalnews.ca/news/1755254/coffee-prices-stay-higher-as-bean-costs-fall-back-to-earth/.

11. Conference Board of Canada, "Economics Blog," http://www2.conferenceboard.ca/weblinx/ibc/Default.htm.

12. Dr. S. Shaw, "Who Wants to Go Shopping?" TechlifeMag.ca, November 2007, http://www.techlifemag.ca/728.htm; VIP Concierge and Errand Service, http://www.vipedmonton.net/corporate concierge.htm; J. Bond, C. Thompson, E. Galinsky, and D. Prottas, "Highlights of the National Study of the Changing Workforce," Families and Work Institute, 2002, http://www.familiesandwork.org/site/research/summary/nscw2002summ.pdf.

13. B. Auld, "Bill 14 is here," BCJobs.ca, July 31, 2012, accessed October 23, 2015, https://www.bcjobs.ca/hr-advice/bill-14-is-here/; G. T. Clarke and A. Rennebohm, "Canada: Bill 14: The New Bullying Law in BC—Is Your Workplace Prepared?" Mondaq.com, July 12, 2012, accessed October 22, 2015, http://www.mondaq.com/canada/x/186376/employee+rights+labour+relations/bill+14+the+new+bullying+law+in+bc+is+your+workplace+prepared.

14. V. Ferreira, "Ontario to Restrict E-Cigarettes, Ban Flavoured Tobacco and Require Calorie Counts in Restaurants," National Post Online, May 27, 2015, accessed October 22, 2015, http://news.nationalpost.com/news/canada/ontario-to-restrict-e-cigarettes-ban-flavoured-tobacco-and-require-calorie-counts-in-restaurants; R. Benzie, "Ontario Bans Flavoured Tobacco, Forces Calorie Count on Fast-Food Menus," TheStarNewsOnline, May 26, 2015, accessed October 22, 2015, http://www.thestar.com/news/queenspark/2015/05/26/ontario-mpps-ban-flavoured-tobacco-force-calorie-count-on-fast-food-menus.html.

15. J. Koop and D. Kirby, "Canada: Increase in Climate Change Litigation in the U.S. Courts Could Spill Over into Canada," Mondaq, November 24, 2009, http://www.mondaq.com/canada/article.asp?articleid=89816; P. Webster, "The (Legal) Heat Is On: Why Companies Should Reveal Climate Impact," Canadian Business Online, March 26, 2007, http://www.canadianbusiness.com/after_hours/lifestyle_activities/article.jsp?content=20070326_85382_85382.

16. "Macaroni Grill Case Study," Listen 360, accessed May 15, 2013, http://www.listen360.com/assets/macaronigrill_listen360casestudy_07.24.12.pdf; "Constructive Criticism," Entrepreneur, April 2012, 112.

17. R. Johnston and S. Mehra, "Best-Practice Complaint Management," Academy of Management Experience 16 (November 2002): 145–54.

18. R. Sawheney, "Broken Guitar Has United Playing the Blues to the Tune of $180 million," FastCompany.com, July 30, 2009, http://www.fastcompany.com/1320152/broken-guitar-has-united-playing-blues-tune-180-million; R. Dooley, "Why Ignoring Social Media Complaints Is a Huge Mistake," Forbes.com, September 18, 2012, accessed October 8, 2015, http://www.forbes.com/sites/rogerdooley/2012/09/18/complaints/.

19. K. Rosman, "Weather Channel Now Also Forecasts What You'll Buy," Wall Street Journal, August 14, 2013, accessed October 18, 2015, http://www.wsj.com/articles/SB10001424124127887323639704579012674092402660.

20. M. Frazier, "You Suck: Dyson, Hoover, and Oreck Trade Accusations in Court, on TV as Brit Upstart Leaves Rivals in Dust," Advertising Age, July 25, 2005, 1.

21. M. Rekei, "Waiting for Target: Canadian Retailers Retrench," Macleans.ca, October 30, 2012, http://www2.macleans.ca/2012/10/30/retailers-retrench/; H. Shaw, "Are Sears Canada's Days Numbered? Poor Results Could Have U.S. Retailers Circling Soon," Financial Post, January 8, 2012, http://business.financialpost.com/2013/01/08/are-sears-canadas-days-numbered-poor-results-could-have-u-s-retailers-circling-soon; M. Strauss, "Retailers Reap Rewards After Target's Failed Canadian Expansion," The Globe and Mail, February 26, 2015, accessed October 3, 2015, http://www.theglobeandmail.com/report-on-business/retailers-reap-rewards-after-targets-failed-canada-expansion/article23221477/.

22. J. Lessin, L. Luk, and J. Osawa, "Apple Finds It Difficult to Divorce Samsung," Wall Street Journal, June 29, 2013, A1.

23. P. Ziminisky, "A Diamond Market No Longer Controlled by De Beers," Kitco.com, June 6, 2013, accessed October 5, 2015, http://www.kitco.com/ind/Zimnisky/2013-06-06-A-Diamond-Market-No-Longer-Controlled-By-De-Beers.html; C. Jamasmie, "De Beers Market Share Set to Pick up on Canadian Mine Opening," Mining.com, November 4, 2014, accessed October 3, 2015, http://www.mining.com/de-beers-market-share-set-to-pick-up-on-canadian-mine-opening-57663/.

24. J. McCracken and P. Glader, "New Detroit Woe: Makers of Parts Won't Cut Prices: Some Can't Afford to," Wall Street Journal, March 2, 2007, A1, A15.

25. D. Birch, "Staying on Good Terms," Supply Management, April 12, 2001, 36.

26. S. Parker and C. Axtell, "Seeing Another Viewpoint: Antecedents and Outcomes of Employee Perspective Taking," Academy of Management Journal 44 (2001): 1085–1100; B. K. Pilling, L. A. Crosby, and D. W. Jackson, "Relational Bonds in Industrial Exchange: An Experimental Test of the Transaction Cost Economic Framework," Journal of Business Research 30 (1994): 237–51.

27. M. Hickens, "CIO Journal: H-P Reinvents Itself," Wall Street Journal, April 25, 2013, B5.

28. K. O'Brien, "DreamWorks Animation Data Center On-Site," *Storage Review*, October 24, 2012, accessed June 16, 2014, http://storagereview.com.dreamworks_animation_data_center_onsite.

29. Health Canada, "Toy Safety," http://www.hc-sc.gc.ca/hl-vs/iyh-vsv/prod/toys-jouets-eng.php; Government of Canada, "Regulations Amending the Hazardous Products (Toys) Regulations," *Canada Gazette*, http://www.gazette.gc.ca/rp-pr/p1/2009/2009-06-20/html/reg5-eng.html; Canadian Toy Association, http://www.cdntoyassn.com/index.cfm.

30. B. Clarkson, "LCBO Campaign Tackles Elephant in the Room," *Toronto Sun*, December 10, 2009, http://www.torontosun.com/news/torontoandgta/2009/12/10/12104056-sun.html; http://www.torontosun.com/news/torontoandgta/2009/12/09/12098991.html; M. Kuburas, "LCBO Deflates Elephant in the Room," *Media in Canada*, December 2, 2009, http://ads.strategyonline.ca/articles/news/20091207/lcboelephant.html.

31. Canadian Press, "Environmental Group Seeks Forest Product Boycott," *Business Edge* 1, no. 11 (May 27, 2004), http://www.businessedge.ca/archives/article.cfm/environmental-group-seeks-forest-product-boycott-6108; M. DeSouza, CanWest Global News Service, "Greenpeace Blasts Boreal Forest Destruction," September 25, 2008, http://www.theprovince.com/Greenpeace+blasts+boreal+forest+destruction/836502/story.html.

32. C. Mims, "Amid Stratospheric Valuations, Google Unearths a Deal with Skybox," *Wall Street Journal*, June 15, 2014, accessed October 19, 2015, http://www.wsj.com/articles/amid-stratospheric-valuations-google-unearths-a-deal-with-skybox-1402864823.

33. "China's Unsafe Water Is Nestlé's Opportunity," *Bloomberg Businessweek*, January 28–February 3, 2013, 19–20.

34. B. Thomas, S. M. Clark, and D. A. Gioia, "Strategic Sensemaking and Organizational Performance: Linkages Among Scanning, Interpretation, Action, and Outcomes," *Academy of Management Journal* 36 (1993): 239–270.

35. R. Daft, J. Sormunen, and D. Parks, "Chief Executive Scanning, Environmental Characteristics, and Company Performance: An Empirical Study," *Strategic Management Journal* 9 (1988): 123–139; V. Garg, B. Walters, and R. Priem, "Chief Executive Scanning Emphases, Environmental Dynamism, and Manufacturing Firm Performance," *Strategic Management Journal* 24 (2003): 725–744; D. Miller and P. H. Friesen, "Strategy-Making and Environment: The Third Link," *Strategic Management Journal* 4 (1983): 221–235.

36. A. Hui, "Full Stop on the Revolution: Why Toronto's Food Truck Scene Keeps Falling 50 Metres Short," *The Globe and Mail Online*, April 17, 2015, accessed October 24, 2015, http://www.theglobeandmail.com/news/toronto/full-stop-on-the-revolution-why-torontos-food-truck-scene-keeps-falling-50-metres-short/article24014861/.

37. E. Hyatt, "Targeting Boomers and Seniors to Drive Restaurant Traffic," *RestaurantCentral.ca*, July 23, 2014, accessed October 3, 2015, http://restaurantcentral.ca/Targetingboomersandseniors.aspx.

38. A. Harrington, N. Hira, and C. Tkaczyk, "Hall of Fame: If Making the 100 Best List Is an Enormous Accomplishment, Consider How Tough It Is to Repeat the Feat Every Single Year," *Fortune*, January 24, 2005, 94; "SAS Makes the *Fortune* 'Hall of Fame,'" http://www.sas.com/news/fortune2011.html.

39. P. Elmer-DeWitt, "Mine, All Mine; Bill Gates Wants a Piece of Everybody's Action, But Can He Get It?" *Time*, June 5, 1995.

40. D. M. Boje, "The Storytelling Organization: A Study of Story Performance in an Office-Supply Firm," *Administrative Science Quarterly* 36 (1991): 106–26.

41. S. Walton and J. Huey, *Sam Walton: Made in America* (New York: Doubleday, 1992).

42. M. Solomon, "Four Seasons Leader Isadore Sharpe: Treat Employees Right So They Treat Customers Right," *Forbes.com*, August 17, 2015, accessed October 24, 2015,

http://www.forbes.com/sites/micahsolomon/2015/08/17/four-seasons-leader-isadore-sharp-treat-employees-right-so-they-treat-customers-right/.

43. R. Ford and M. Sturman, "Harnessing The Power of Your Culture for Outstanding Service" *Cornell University School of Hotel Administration*, *The Scholarly Commons*, 2011, accessed October 22, 2015, http://scholarship.sha.cornell.edu/articles/240.

44. Davis, "Sky High"; J. Kirby, "WestJet's Plan to Crush Air Canada," *Maclean's*, April 30, 2009, http://www2.macleans.ca/2009/04/30/westjet%E2%80%99s-plan-to-crush-air-canada.

45. "Most Admired Corporates: #2—Four Seasons," *Financial Post*, December 3, 2008, http://www.financialpost.com/working/story.html?id=1024072.

46. D. Gilbert, R. Gold, "As Big Drillers Move in, Safety Goes up," *Wall Street Journal*, April 2, 2013, A1; "Shell Code of Conduct: How to Live by the Shell General Business Principles," *Shell*, accessed May 16, 2013, http://s06.static-shell.com/content/dam./shell/static/public/downloads/corporate-pkg/code-of-conduct-english.pdf.

47. E. Schein, *Organizational Culture and Leadership*, 2nd ed. (San Francisco: Jossey-Bass, 1992).

48. J. Costaldo, "A Lesson in Scaling Up and Phasing Out," *ProfitGuide.com*, September 8, 2014, accessed October 28, 2015, http://www.profitguide.com/manage-grow/strategy-operations/a-lesson-in-scaling-up-and-phasing-out-69025; M. Parker, "M&A and Corporate Culture," *Canadian Business Online*, July 4, 2007, http://www.canadianbusiness.com/columnists/marty_parker/article.jsp?content=20070619_150029_6476; C. Leung, "Book Values," *Canadian Business Online*, October 10, 2005, http://www.canadianbusiness.com/companies/article.jsp?content=20051010_71494_71494; "Employer Review: Yellow Pages Group Co.," Eluta.ca; M. Parker, "Creating a Responsive and Adaptive Culture," *Canadian Business Online*, July 18, 2007, http://www.canadianbusiness.com/columnists/marty_parker/article.jsp?content=20070710_125841_4696.

49. M. Parker, "M&A and Corporate Culture," *Canadian Business Online*, July 4, 2007, http://www.canadianbusiness.com/columnists/marty_parker/article.jsp?content=20070619_150029_6476; S. Islam, "Execs See Link to Bottom Line," *Vancouver Sun*, September 25, 2009, http://www.vancouversun.com/business/execs+link+bottom+line/1177050/story.html; A. Wahl, "Culture Shock: A Survey of Canadian Executives Reveals That Corporate Culture Is in Need of Improvement," http://www.waterstonehc.com/node/168; see also http://www.waterstonehc.com/news-events/news/canadas-10-most-admired-corporate-cultures-2011-announced-today.

3

1. T. Tedesco, "Canadians See Misconduct in the Workplace, But Few are Reported: Study," *FinancialPostOnline*, July 4, 2013, http://business.financialpost.com/news/fp-street/canadians-see-misconduct-in-workplace-but-few-are-reported-study; "Four in Ten (42%) Employed Canadians Have Observed Some Form of Workplace Misconduct; One in Five (17%) Cite Witnessing Privacy Violations," Ipsos, July 3, 2013, http://www.ipsos-na.com/news-polls/pressrelease.aspx?id=6187.

2. Ethics Research Center, *2011 National Business Ethics Survey. Workplace Ethics in Transition*, www.hreonline.com/pdfs/02012012Extra_EthicsReport.pdf.

3. Ethics Research Center, *2011 National Business Ethics Survey*.

4. Deloitte LLP, "Social Networking and Reputational Risk in the Workplace: 2009 Ethics and Workplace Survey," http://www.slideshare.net/opinionwatch/social-networking-and-reputational-risk-in-the-workplace-deloitte-survey-july-09.

5. LRN, "LRN Ethics Study: Employee Engagement," 2007, http://www.ethics.org/files/u5/LRNEmployeeEngagement.pdf.

6. Deloitte LLP, "Trust in the WorkPlace: 2010 Ethics and Workplace Survey," http://www.deloitte.com/view/en_US/us/About/Ethics-Independence/8aa3cb51ed812210VgnVCM100000ba42f00aRCRD.htm.

7. Association of Certified Fraud Examiners, "Report to the Nations on Occupational Fraud and Abuse, 2012 Global Fraud Survey," http://www.acfe.com/uploadedFiles/ACFE_Website/Content/rttn/2012-report-to-nations.pdf.

8. S.L. Robinson and R.J. Bennett, "A Typology of Deviant Workplace Behaviors: A Multidimensional Scaling Study," *Academy of Management Journal* 38 (1995): 555–72.

9. "Challenger March Madness Report," Challenger, Gray & Christmas, Inc., March 11, 2014, accessed June 19, 2014, https://www.challengergray.com/press/press-releases/march-madness-could-cost-employers-12b.

10. J. Norman, "Cultivating a Culture of Honesty," *Orange County Register*, October 23, 2006.

11. Norman, "Cultivating a Culture of Honesty."

12. Centre for Retail Research, "The First Worldwide Shrinkage Survey," http://www.retailresearch.org/grtb_globaltrends.php; H. Shaw, "Workers Steal 33% of All Goods That Go Missing at Retailers: Survey," *Financial Post*, 31 October 2012, http://business.financialpost.com/2012/10/31/workers-steal-33-of-all-goods-that-go-missing-at-retailers-survey.

13. Association of Certified Fraud Examiners, "Report to the Nations on Occupational Fraud and Abuse, 2012 Global Fraud Survey," http://www.acfe.com/uploadedFiles/ACFE_Website/Content/rttn/2012-report-to-nations.pdf.

14. Retail Council of Canada, "The New Face of Organized Crime," *Retail Organized Crime Report and Recommendations*, 2008, http://members.retailcouncil.org/advocacy/lp/issues/asr/2008_ROC_Report.pdf.

15. CBC News, "Almost 1 in 5 Violent Incidents Occurs in Workplace: StatsCan," February 16, 2007; Statistics Canada, Canadian Centre for Justice Statistics Profile Series, *Criminal Victimization in the Workplace* by Sylvain Leseleuc (Ottawa: Statistics Canada, 2007).

16. CBC News, "Almost 1 in 5 Violent Incidents Occurs in Workplace: StatsCan," February 16, 2007; Statistics Canada, Canadian Centre for Justice Statistics Profile Series, *Criminal Victimization in the Workplace* by Sylvain Leseleuc (Ottawa: Statistics Canada, 2007).

17. A. Fass, "One Year Later, TheIpact of Sarbanes-Oxley," *Forbes.com*, July 22, 2003, http://www.forbes.com/2003/07/22/cz_af_0722sarbanes.html.

18. T. Gray, "Canadian Response to the U.S. Sarbanes-Oxley Act of 2002: New Directions for Corporate Governance," *Parliament of Canada*, October 4, 2005, http://www.parl.gc.ca/content/lop/researchpublications/prb0537-e.htm.

19. W. Cragg and K. McKague, "Compendium of Ethics Codes and Instruments of Corporate Responsibility," Schulich School of Business, York University, Toronto, 2003; http://www.yorku.ca/csr/_files/file.php?fileid=fileCDOICwJiei&filename=file_Codes_Compendium_Jan_2007.pdf.

20. "1991 Federal Sentencing Guidelines as a Paradigm for Ethics Training," *Journal of Business Ethics* 29, nos. 1–2 (2001): 77–84.

21. K. Tyler, "Do the Right Thing: Ethics Training Programs Help Employees Deal with Ethical Dilemmas," *HR Magazine* 50 (February 2005), http://www.highbeam.com/doc/1G1-129557302.html, http://www.shrm.org/hrmagazine/articles/0205/0205tyler.asp.

22. S. Morris and R. McDonald, "The Role of Moral Intensity in Moral Judgments: An Empirical Investigation," *Journal of Business Ethics* 14 (1995): 715–26; B. Flannery and D. May, "Environmental Ethical Decision Making in the U.S. Metal Finishing Industry," *Academy of Management Journal* 43 (2000): 642–62.

23. L. Kohlberg, "Stage and Sequence: The Cognitive Developmental Approach to Socialization," in *Handbook of Socialization Theory and Research*, ed. D.A. Goslin (Chicago: Rand McNally, 1969); L. Trevino, "Moral Reasoning and Business Ethics: Implications for Research, Education, and Management," *Journal of Business Ethics* 11 (1992): 445–59.

24. L. Trevino and M. Brown, "Managing to Be Ethical: Debunking Five Business Ethics Myths," *Academy of Management Executive* 18 (May 2004): 69–81.

25. L.T. Hosmer, "Trust: The Connecting Link Between Organizational Theory and Philosophical Ethics," *Academy of Management Review* 20 (1995): 379–403.

26. M.R. Cunningham, D.T. Wong, and A.P. Barbee, "Self Presentation Dynamics on Overt Integrity Tests: Experimental Studies of the Reid Report," *Journal of Applied Psychology* 79 (1994): 643–58; J. Wanek, P. Sackett, and D. Ones, "Toward an Understanding of Integrity Test Similarities and Differences: An Item Level Analysis of Seven Tests," *Personnel Psychology* 56 (Winter 2003): 873–94.

27. H.J. Bernardin, "Validity of an Honesty Test in Predicting Theft Among Convenience Store Employees," *Academy of Management Journal* 36 (1993): 1097–108.

28. J.M. Collins and F.L. Schmidt, "Personality, Integrity, and White Collar Crime: A Construct Validity Study," *Personnel Psychology* (1993): 295–311.

29. W.C. Borman, M.A. Hanson, and J.W. Hedge, "Personnel Selection," *Annual Review of Psychology* 48 (1997): 299–337.

30. P.E. Murphy, "Corporate Ethics Statements: Current Status and Future Prospects," *Journal of Business Ethics* 14 (1995): 727–40.

31. Canadian Tire, "Our Code of Business Conduct," http://corp.canadiantire.ca/EN/AboutUs/Documents/code_of_business_conduct.pdf.

32. S.J. Harrington, "What Corporate America Is Teaching About Ethics," *Academy of Management Executive* 5 (1991): 21–30.

33. L. Bogomolny, "Good Housekeeping: How to Ensure Your Code of Ethics Is Effective," *Canadian Business Online*, March 1, 2004, http://www.canadianbusiness.com/article.jsp?content=20040301_58731_58731.

34. L.A. Berger, "Train All Employees to Solve Ethical Dilemmas," *Best's Review—Life Health Insurance Edition* 95 (1995): 70–80.

35. Lockheed Martin, "Leaders Guide 2013, Lockheed Martin 2013 Ethics Awareness Training," http://www.lockheedmartin.ca/content/dam/lockheed/data/corporate/documents/ethics/2013-EAT-Leaders-Guide.pdf, http://www.lockheedmartin.com/data/assets/corporate/documents/ethics/2008_EAT_Leaders_Guide.pdf.

36. L. Trevino, G. Weaver, D. Gibson, and B. Toffler, "Managing Ethics and Legal Compliance: What Works and What Hurts," *California Management Review* 41, no. 2 (1999): 131–51.

37. Boeing, "Ethics and Business Conduct Home," http://www.boeing.com/companyoffices/aboutus/ethics/hotline.html#howto.

38. Trevino, et al., "Managing Ethics."

39. Bogomolny, "Good Housekeeping."

40. Ethics Research Center, *2011 National Business Ethics Survey:* "Workplace Ethics in Transition, http://www.ethics.org/nbes/files/FinalNBES-web.pdf.

41. Ethics Research Center, "2009 National Business Ethics Survey," http://www.ethics.org/nbes/files/nbes-final.pdf.

42. 2011 National Business Ethics Survey, "Workplace Ethics in Transition."

43. G. Weaver and L. Trevino, "Integrated and Decoupled Corporate Social Performance: Management Commitments, External Pressures, and Corporate Ethics Practices," *Academy of Management Journal* 42 (1999): 539–52; G. Weaver, L. Trevino, and P. Cochran, "Corporate Ethics Programs as Control Systems: Influences of Executive Commitment and Environmental Factors," *Academy of Management Journal* 42 (1999): 41–57.

44. J. Salopek, "Do the Right Thing," *Training and Development* 55 (July 2001): 38–44.

45. Ethics Research Center, 2011 National Business Ethics Survey, http://www.ethics.org/nbes/files/FinalNBES-web.pdf; Ethics Research Center, 2009 National Business Ethics Survey, http://www.ethics.org/nbes/files/nbes-final.pdf.

46. M.P. Miceli and J.P. Near, "Whistleblowing: Reaping the Benefits," *Academy of Management Executive* 8 (1994): 65–72.

47. M. Master and E. Heresniak, "The Disconnect in Ethics Training," *Across the Board* 39 (September 2002): 51–52.

48. H.R. Bower, *Social Responsibilities of the Businessman* (New York: Harper and Row, 1953).

49. "Beyond the Green Corporation," *Business-Week*, January 29, 2007.

50. S.L. Wartick and P.L. Cochran, "The Evolution of the Corporate Social Performance Model," *Academy of Management Review* 10 (1985): 758–69.

51. J. Nocera, "The Paradox of Businesses as Do-Gooders," *New York Times*, February 3, 2007, C1.

52. S. Waddock, C. Bodwell, and S. Graves, "Responsibility: The New Business Imperative," *Academy of Management Executive* 16 (2002): 132–48.

53. T. Donaldson and L.E. Preston, "The Stakeholder Theory of the Corporation: Concepts, Evidence, and Implications," *Academy of Management Review* 20 (1995): 65–91.

54. M.B.E. Clarkson, "A Stakeholder Framework for Analyzing and Evaluating Corporate Social Performance," *Academy of Management Review* 20 (1995): 92–117.

55. B. Agle, R. Mitchell, and J. Sonnenfeld, "Who Matters to CEOs? An Investigation of Stakeholder Attributes and Salience, Corporate Performance, and CEO Values," *Academy of Management Journal* 42 (1999): 507–25.

56. Fierce Opposition from Green Groups," *US News & World Report*, March 7, 2013, accessed May 22, 2013, http://www.usnews.com/news/articles/2013/03/07/keystone-still-faces-delays-fierce-opposition-from-green-groups; P. Vieira, "Survey Finds Majority Backs Keystone Pipeline," *Wall Street Journal*, April 22, 2013, accessed May 22, 2013, http://online.wsj.com/article/SB10001424127887323735604578438471635120616.html.

57. A.B. Carroll, "A Three-Dimensional Conceptual Model of Corporate Performance," *Academy of Management Review* 4 (1979): 497–505.

58. J. Lublin and M. Murrary, "CEOs Leave Faster Than Ever Before as Boards, Investors Lose Patience," *Wall Street Journal Interactive*, October 27, 2000.

59. L. Cameron, "Rumble at the Tim's Drive-Thru," *Canadian Business*, January 18, 2010, 13.

60. T. Howard, "Low-Carb Message Not Popular, but Sales Are Up," *USA Today*, December 8, 2003, 10B.

61. "JPMorgan Chase Offers Relief Following Hurricane Sandy," *Business Wire*, November 1, 2012, accessed May 22, 2013, http://www.businesswire.com/news/home/20121101006246/en/JPMorgan-Chase-Offers-Relief-Hurricane-Sandy; G. Szalai, "Time Warner to Donate $1 Million for Hurricane Sandy Relief Efforts," *The Hollywood Reporter*, November 2, 2012, accessed May 22, 2013, http://www.hollywoodreporter.com/news/hurricane-sandy-time-warner-donates-million-401982; A. Stonich, "How Outdoor Gear Companies Helped Hurricane Sandy Relief Efforts," *Beyond the Edge-National Geographic Adventure Blog*, December 13, 2012, accessed May 22, 2013, http://adventureblog.nationalgeographic.com/2012/12/13/how-outdoor-gear-companies-helped-hurricane-sandy-relief-efforts/.

62. R. Spence, "What a Bargain: Do Successful Entrepreneurs Owe a Debt to the World?" *Profit Magazine*, December 2009.

63. J. Bennett, "GM Now Says It Detected Ignition Switch Problem Back in 2001," *Wall Street Journal*, March 12, 2014, accessed June 4, 2014, http://online.wsj.com/news/articles/SB10001424052702304914904579435171004763740?KEYWORDS.

64. J. Bennett, "GM Now Says It Detected Ignition Switch Problem Back in 2001," *Wall Street Journal*, March 12, 2014, accessed June 4, 2014, http://online.wsj.com/news/articles/SB10001424052702304914904579435171004763740?KEYWORDS.

65. J. Bennett and S. Hughes, "New Details Emerge in GM Cobalt Recall," *Wall Street Journal*, March 24, 2014, accessed June 4, 2014, http://online.wsj.com/news/articles/SB10001424052702303949704579459783108376974?KEYWORDS=jeff+bennett&mg=reno64-wsj.

66. J. Bennett, "GM Now Says It Detected Ignition Switch Problem Back in 2001," *Wall Street Journal*, March 12, 2014, accessed June 4, 2014, http://online.wsj.com/news/articles/SB10001424052702304914904579435171004763740?KEYWORDS; J. White and J. Bennett, "Some at GM Brass Told of Cobalt Woe," *Wall Street Journal*, April 11, 2014, accessed June 4, 2014, http://online.wsj.com/news/articles/SB10001424052702303873604579455929011143598?KEYWORDS=jeff+bennett&mg=reno64-wsj.

67. C. Duhigg, "In China, Human Costs Are Built into an iPad," *New York Times*, January 25, 2012, accessed February 28, 2012, http://www.nytimes.com/2012/01/26/business/ieconomy-apples-ipad-and-the-human-costs-for-workers-in-china.html?pagewanted=all; H. Perlberg and T. Culpan, "Apple Says Fair Labor Association Began Foxconn Inspection," *Bloomberg Businessweek*, February 14, 2012,

accessed February 28, 2012, http://www.bloomberg
.com/news/2012-02-13/apple-says-fair-labor
-association-will-inspect-suppliers-including-foxconn
.html; J. Stern, "Foxconn, Apple, and the Fair
Labor Association Respond to ABC News'
Exclusive Report," *ABCNews*, February 22, 2012,
accessed February 28, 2012, http://abcnews.go.com/
blogs/technology/2012/02/foxconn-apple-and
-the-fair-labors-association-respond-to-abc-news
-exclusive-report/.

68. "Micro-Plastics," Unilever, accessed June
22, 2014, http://www.unilever.com/sustainable-
living-2014/our-approach-to-sustainability/
responding-to-stakeholder-concerns/micro-
plastics/index.aspx.

69. A. McWilliams and D. Siegel, "Corporate Social
Responsibility: A Theory of the Firm Perspective,"
Academy of Management Review 26, no. 1 (2001):
117–27; H. Haines, "Noah Joins Ranks of Socially
Responsible Funds," *Dow Jones News Service*, October 13, 1995. A meta-analysis of 41 different studies
also found no relationship between corporate social
responsibility and profitability. Though not reported
in the meta-analysis, when confidence intervals are
placed around its average sample-weighted correlation of 0.06, the lower confidence interval includes
zero, leading to the conclusion that there is no
relationship between corporate social responsibility
and profitability. See M. Orlitzky, "Does Firm Size
Confound the Relationship Between Corporate Social Responsibility and Firm Performance?" *Journal
of Business Ethics* 33 (2001): 167–80; S. Ambec and
P. Lanoie, "Does It Pay to Be Green? A Systematic
Overview," *Academy of Management Perspectives*, 22
(2008): 45–62.

70. M. Orlitzky, "Payoffs to Social and Environmental Performance," *Journal of Investing* 14
(2005): 48–51.

71. M. Orlitzky, F. Schmidt, and S. Rynes,
"Corporate Social and Financial Performance:
A Meta-analysis," *Organization Studies* 24 (2003):
403–41.

72. Orlitzky, "Payoffs to Social and Environmental
Performance."

73. "Patagonia's Common Threads Partnership to
Reduce our Environmental Footprint," Patagonia,
accessed May 24, 2013, http://www.patagonia.com/
us/common-threads.

74. S. Stevenson, "Patagonia's Founder Is America's
Most Unlikely Business Guru," *WSJ Magazine*,
April 26, 2012, accessed May 24, 2013, http://online
.wsj.com/article/SB1000142405270230351340457735
2221465986612.html.

75. M. Orlitzky, F. Schmidt, and S. Rynes,
"Corporate Social and Financial Performance:
A Meta-analysis," *Organization Studies* 24 (2003):
403–441.

76. "GM Offers Big Discounts to Boost Volt Sales,"
Fox News, September 24, 2012, accessed May 24,
2013, http://www.foxnews.com/leisure/2012/09/24/
gm-offers-big-discounts-to-boost-volt-sales;
P. Lienert & B. Woodall, "GM Planning Lower-
Priced Version of 2016 Chevy Volt," *Reuters*,
April 8, 2014, accessed June 22, 2014, http://www
.reuters.com/article/2014/04/08/us-autos-gm
-voltidUSBREA371XW20140408; M. Maynard,
"Stunner: GM May Be Losing $50,000 on Each
Chevrolet Volt," *Forbes*, September 10, 2012,
accessed May 24, 2013, http://www.forbes.com/
sites/michelinemaynard/2012/09/10/stunner-gm
-may-be-losing-50000-on-each-chevrolet-volt/;
B. Woodall, P. Lienert, and B. Klayman, "Insight:
GM's Volt: The Ugly Math of Low Sales, High
Costs," *Reuters*, September 10, 2012, accessed
May 24, 2013, http://www.reuters.com/article/
2012/09/10/us-generalmotors-autos-volt-idUSBRE
88904J20120910.

4

1. L.A. Hill, *Becoming a Manager: Master a New
Identity* (Boston: Harvard Business School Press,
1992).

2. E. Atkins, "Maple Leaf Foods Expects
Restructuring to Pay Off," *The Globe and Mail*,
October 27, 2013, http://www.theglobeandmail
.com/report-on-business/maple-leaf-expects
-restructuring-to-pay-off/article15108078/; The
Canadian Press, "Maple Leaf Foods Trims Fat
With Five Year Plan" October 6, 2010, http://
www.cbc.ca/news/business/maple-leaf-foods
-trims-fat-with-5-year-plan-1.900621; Maple Leaf
Foods 2011 Company News Releases, October
19, 2011, http://www.mapleleaffoods.com/news/
maple-leaf-foods-proceeding-with-final-phase
-of-value-creation-plan/; Maple Leaf Foods 2015
Annual Report, http://www.mapleleaffoods.com/
investors-information/investor-material/.

3. I. Wladawsky-Berger, "Managing Innovation
Requires Unique Leaders and Goals," *Wall Street
Journal*, August 25, 2013, accessed June 5, 2014,
http://blogs.wsj.com/cio/2013/08/25/managing
-innovation-requires-unique-leaders-and-goals/?KE
YWORDS=achieving+goals.

4. E.A. Locke and G.P. Latham, *A Theory of Goal
Setting and Task Performance* (Englewood Cliffs:
Prentice Hall, 1990).

5. M.E. Tubbs, "Goal-Setting: A Meta-Analytic
Examination of the Empirical Evidence," *Journal of
Applied Psychology* 71 (1986): 474–83.

6. C.C. Miller, "Strategic Planning and Firm
Performance: A Synthesis of More Than Two
Decades of Research," *Academy of Management
Performance* 37 (1994): 1649–65.

7. H. Mintzberg, "Rethinking Strategic Planning," *Long Range Planning* 27 (1994): 12–30;
H. Mintzberg, "The Pitfalls of Strategic Planning," *California Management Review* 36 (1993):
32–47.

8. J.D. Stoll, "GM Sees Brighter Future," *Wall
Street Journal*, January 18, 2008, A3; D. Welch,
"Live Green or Die," *BusinessWeek*, May 26, 2008,
36–41; L. Greenemeier, "GM's Chevy Volt to Hit
the Streets of San Francisco and Washington D.C.,"
60-Second Science Blog, February 5, 2009, http://
www.scientificamerican.com; "Electric Vehicles
Expected in the Next Two Years [photos]" CNET,
July 16, 2010, http://news.cnet. com/2300-11128
_3-10004136.html?tag=mncol.

9. H. Mintzberg, "Rethinking Strategic Planning," *Long Range Planning* 27 (1994): 12–30;
H. Mintzberg, "The Pitfalls of Strategic Planning," *California Management Review* 36 (1993):
32–47.

10. E.A. Locke and G.P. Latham, *A Theory of Goal
Setting and Task Performance* (Englewood Cliffs:
Prentice Hall, 1990).

11. City of Vancouver Greenest City Action Plan
2020 Part Two: 2015–2020.

12. A. King, B. Oliver, B. Sloop, and K. Vaverek,
*Planning and Goal Setting for Improved Perfor-
mance: Participant's Guide* (Cincinnati: Thomson
Executive, 1995).

13. City of Vancouver Greenest City Action Plan
2020 Part Two: 2015–2020.

14. City of Vancouver Greenest City Action Plan
2020 Part Two: 2015–2020.

15. City of Vancouver Greenest City Action Plan
2020 Part Two: 2015–2020.

16. H. Klein and M. Wesson, "Goal and Commit-
ment and the Goal-Setting Process: Conceptual
Clarification and Empirical Synthesis," *Journal of
Applied Psychology* 84 (1999): 885–86.

17. B. Scudamore, "Simplicity Breeds Success,"
Profit Magazine, October 2008, http://www
.profitguide.com/manage-grow/strategy-operations/
simplicity-breeds-success-29454.

18. B. Scudamore, "Simplicity Breeds Success."

19. L. Chappell and H. Greimel, "Nissan's Ghosn
Says Missing Margin Goals Carries Consequences,"
Automotive News, November 2, 2015, http://www
.autonews.com/article/20151102/OEM02/3110
29968/nissans-ghosn-says-missing-margin-goal
-carries-consequences.

20. Nissan Motor Corporation Midterm Plan,
http://www.nissan-global.com/en/ir/midtermplan/.

21. M.J. Neubert, "The Value of Feedback and
Goal Setting Over Goal Setting Alone and Potential
Moderators of This Effect: A Meta-Analysis,"
Human Performance 11 (1998): 321–35.

22. E.H. Bowman and D. Hurry, "Strategy
Through the Option Lens: An Integrated View of
Resource Investments and the Incremental-Choice
Process," *Academy of Management Review* 18
(1993): 760–82.

23. M. Lawson, "In Praise of Slack: Time Is of the
Essence," *Academy of Management Executive* 15
(2000): 125–35.

24. "Google's Mission Is to Organize the World's
Information and Make It Universally Accessible
and Useful," http://www.google.sh/intl/en/
corporate.

25. D. Forest and F. David, "It's Time to Redraft
Your Mission Statement," *Journal of Business
Strategy*, January–February 2003, 11–14, http://
www.esf.edu/for/germain/David_8_12.pdf.

26. Starbucks, http://www.starbucks.com/about-us/
company-information/mission-statement.

27. "Our Mission Statement," http://www
.lululemon.com/about/culture; "Legion Mission
Statement," http://legion.ca/Home/mission_e.cfm.

28. V. Walt, "Amazon Invades India," *Fortune*,
January 1, 2016, http://fortune.com/amazon-india
-jeff-bezos/.

29. Industry Canada, Small Business Policy
Branch, "Blue Falls Manufacturing: Turning
Market Knowledge into a Competitive Edge,"
November 2006, http://www.ic.gc.ca/eic/site/061
.nsf/eng/..%5Cvwapj%5Cbluefallsmanufacturing
_eng.pdf%5C$file%5Cbluefallsmanufacturing
_eng.pdf.

30. CBC News, "61% of Companies Monitor
Workers' Web Surfing: Survey," April 19, 2007,
http://www.cbc.ca/technology/story/2007/04/19/
work-websurfing.html?ref=rss.

31. Adapted from quality procedure at G & G
Manufacturing, Cincinnati, Ohio.

32. N. Humphrey, "References a Tricky Issue for
Both Sides," *Nashville Business Journal* 11 (May 8,
1995), 1A.

33. K.R. MacCrimmon, R.N. Taylor, and E.A.
Locke, "Decision Making and Problem Solving,"
in *Handbook of Industrial and Organizational
Psychology*, ed. M.D. Dunnette (Chicago: Rand
McNally, 1976), 1397–453.

34. J. Jargon, "As Profit Cools, Starbucks Plans
Price Campaign," *Wall Street Journal*, April 30,
2009, B3.

35. J. Jargon, "As Profit Cools, Starbucks Plans
Price Campaign."

36. Cushman & Wakefield Healy & Baker,
"European Cities Monitor" (2010), http://www
.berlinpartner.de/fileadmin/chefredaktion/
documents/pdf_Presse/European_Investment
_Monitor_2007.pdf; European Cities Monitor 2010,
http://www.europeancitiesmonitor.eu/wp-content/
uploads/2010/10/ECM-2010-Full-Version.pdf.

37. K. Blanchard, "The Critical Role of Teams," March 2006, http://www.kenblanchard.com/img/pub/pdf_critical_role_teams.pdf.

38. L. Pelled, K. Eisenhardt, and K. Xin, "Exploring the Black Box: An Analysis of Work Group Diversity, Conflict, and Performance," *Administrative Science Quarterly* 44, no. 1 (March 1, 1999): 1.

39. I.L. Janis, *Groupthink* (Boston: Houghton Mifflin, 1983).

40. C.P. Neck and C.C. Manz, "From Groupthink to Teamthink: Toward the Creation of Constructive Thought Patterns in Self-Managing Work Teams," *Human Relations* 47 (1994): 929–52; J. Schwartz and M.L. Wald, "'Groupthink' Is 30 Years Old, and Still Going Strong," *New York Times,* March 9, 2003, 5.

41. C. Ferraris and R. Carveth, "NASA and the *Columbia* Disaster: Decision-Making by Groupthink?", Proceedings of the 2003 Association for Business Communication Annual Convention, http://businesscommunication.org/wp-content/uploads/2011/04/03ABC03.pdf.

42. C. Gallo, "How to Run a Meeting Like Google," *Business Week Online,* September 8, 2006, 15; P. Cohan, "4 Reasons Marissa Mayer's No-At-Home-Work Policy Is an Epic Fail," *Forbes,* February 26, 2013, http://www.forbes.com/sites/petercohan/2013/02/26/4-reasons-marissa-mayers-no-at-home-work-policy-is-an-epic-fail.

43. A. Mason, W.A. Hochwarter, and K.R. Thompson, "Conflict: An Important Dimension in Successful Management Teams," *Organizational Dynamics* 24 (1995): 20.

44. C. Olofson, "So Many Decisions, So Little Time: What's Your Problem?" *Fast Company*, 1 October 1999, 62.

45. R. Cosier and C.R. Schwenk, "Agreement and Thinking Alike: Ingredients for Poor Decisions," *Academy of Management Executive* 4 (1990): 69–74.

46. K. Jenn and E. Mannix, "The Dynamic Nature of Conflict: A Longitudinal Study of Intragroup Conflict and Group Performance," *Academy of Management Journal* 44, no. 2 (2001): 238–51; R.L. Priem, D.A. Harrison, and N.K. Muir, "Structured Conflict and Consensus Outcomes in Group Decision Making," *Journal of Management* 21 (1995): 691–710.

47. A. Van De Ven and A.L. Delbecq, "Nominal Versus Interacting Group Processes for Committee Decision Making Effectiveness," *Academy of Management Journal* 14 (1971): 203–12.

48. A.R. Dennis and J.S. Valicich, "Group, Sub-Group, and Nominal Group Idea Generation: New Rules for a New Media?", *Journal of Management* 20 (1994): 723–36.

49. R.B. Gallupe and W.H. Cooper, "Brainstorming Electronically," *Sloan Management Review,* Fall 1993, 27–36.

5

1. D. Travlos, "The iPad Will Mirror the iPod's Market Dominance: Here's Why and Why It Matters," *Forbes,* July 13, 2012, http://www.forbes.com/sites/darcytravlos/2012/07/13/the-ipad-will-mirror-the-ipods-market-dominance-heres-why-and-why-it-matters; E. Spence, "BlackBerry Must Ignore Market Share," *Forbes,* January 30, 2013, http://www.forbes.com/sites/ewanspence/2013/01/30/blackberry-must-ignore-market-share.

2. http://appleinsider.com/articles/13/12/19/apples-ipod-continues-to-lead-an-ever-shrinking-market-of-portable-media-players

3. http://www.macrumors.com/roundup/ipad-pro/

4. http://www.forbes.com/sites/samanthasharf/2015/08/10/goodbye-google-search-giant-changing-its-name/

5. http://www.wired.com/2015/08/new-company-called-alphabet-owns-google/

6. http://www.wired.com/2015/08/new-company-called-alphabet-owns-google/

7. A. Barr and R. Winkler, "Google Creates Parent Company Called Alphabet in Restructuring," *Wall Street Journal,* http://www.wsj.com/articles/google-creates-new-company-alphabet-1439240645; http://www.businessinsider.com/what-is-alphabet-googles-new-company-2015-8#ixzz3kQbrCWbK

8. L. Kahney, "Inside Look at the Birth of the iPod," *Wired,* July 21, 2004, http://www.wired.com/news/culture/0,64286-0.html; http://www.apple-history.com/?page=gallery&model=ipod; K. Hall, "Sony's iPod Assault Is No Threat to Apple," *BusinessWeek,* March 13, 2006, 53; N. Wingfield, "SanDisk Raises Music-Player Stakes," *Wall Street Journal,* August 21, 2006, B4; "Growing Louder: Microsoft Plods After iPod Like a Giant—Poweful, Determined, Untiring," *Winston-Salem Journal,* November 15, 2006, D1–D2; A. Athavaley and R.A. Guth, "How the Zune Is Faring So Far With Consumers," *Wall Street Journal,* December 12, 2006, D1, D7; P. Cruz, "US Top Selling Computer Hardware for January 2007," Bloomberg.com, http://www.blooberg.com/apps/news?pid=conewsstory&refer=conews&tkr=AAPL:US&sid=ap0bqJw2VpwI; J. Raphael, "Motorola's 2 GHz Android Phone Means Business," *PCWorld,* June 11,2010, http://www.pcworld.com/businesscenter/article/198636/motorolas_2ghz_android_phone_means_business.html; I. Fried, "Microsoft Claims Android Steps on Its Patents," CNET News, April 27, 2010, http://news.cnet.com/8301-13860_3-20003602-56.html; M. Ruhfass, "Bell Canada Now Offering RIM BlackBerry Pearl 3G 9100," Mobile-burn.com, June 5, 2010, http://www.mobileburn.com/news.jsp?Id=9631.

9. J. Barney, "Firm Resources and Sustained Competitive Advantage," *Journal of Management* 17 (1991): 99–120; J. Barney, "Looking Inside for Competitive Advantage," *Academy of Management Executive* 9 (1995): 49–61.

10. J. Snell, "Apple's Home Run," *Macworld,* November 2006, 7.

11. https://www.spotify.com/ca-en/

12. http://www.apple.com/ca/music/?itscg=1001&at=1000lGN&ct=CA-google&cid=wwa-ca-kwg-music

13. Lovejoy, B., 2015. 9to5 Mac. http://9to5mac.com/2015/06/12/opinion-spotify-apple-music/

14. http://www.apple.com/ios/carplay/

15. J. B. Barney, "Looking Inside for Competitive Advantage," *Academy of Management Executives* 9(4), 1995, 49–61; J. Sullivan, "How Google Became the #3 Most Valuable Firm by Using People Analytics to Reinvent HR," February 25, 2013, http://www.ere.net/2013/02/25/how-google-became-the-3-most-valuable-firm-by-using-people-analytics-to-reinvent-hr/.

16. D. Etherington, "Charting the iTunes Store's Path to 25 Billion Songs Sold, 40 Billion Apps Downloaded and Beyond," Techcrunch.com, February 6, 2013, http://techcrunch.com/2013/02/06/charting-the-itunes-stores-path-to-25-billion-songs-sold-40-billion-apps-downloaded-and-beyond.

17. http://www.statista.com/statistics/263794/number-of-downloads-from-the-apple-app-store/.

18. F. T. Rothaermel, (2012). *Strategic Management: Concepts and Cases.* McGraw-Hill/Irwin, p. 91.

19. S. Hart and C. Banbury, "How Strategy-Making Processes Can Make a Difference," *Strategic Management Journal* 15 (1994): 251–69.

20. R. A. Burgelman, "Fading Memories: A Process Theory of Strategic Business Exit in Dynamic Environments," *Administrative Science Quarterly* 39 (1994): 24–56; R. A. Burgelman and A. S. Grove, "Strategic Dissonance," *California Management Review* 38 (1996): 8–28.

21. R. Burgelman and A. Grove, "Strategic Dissonance," *California Management Review* (Winter 1996): 8–28.

22. A. Fiegenbaum, S. Hart, and D. Schendel, "Strategic Reference Point Theory," *Strategic Management Journal* 17 (1996): 219–35.

23. L. Barth, "Most and Least Reliable Brands," *Consumer Reports,* October 31, 2012, http://www.consumerreports.org/cro/news/2012/10/most-and-least-reliable-new-cars-by-brand/index.htm.

24. S. Segan and E. Griffith, "The Best (and Worst) Tech Support in America," *PC Magazine,* July 29, 2008, http://www.pcmag.com/article2/0,2817,2326603,00.asp.

25. D. J. Collis, "Research Note: How Valuable Are Organizational Capabilities?", *Strategic Management Journal* 15 (1994): 143–52.

26. CBC News, "Ottawa T & T Supermarket Opens to Huge Crowds," October 28, 2009, http://www.cbc.ca/canada/ottawa/story/2009/10/28/ottawa-091028.html.

27. H. Thomas, "An Analysis of the Environment and Competitive Dynamics of Management Education," *Journal of Management Development* 26, no. 1 (2007): 9–21, http://www.emeraldinsight.com/journals.htm?articleid=1585399&show=abstract.

28. G. C. Peng and M. E. Nunes, "Using PEST Analysis as a Tool for Refining and Focusing Contexts for Information Systems Research," 6th European Conference on Research Methodology for Business and Management Studies, Lisbon, Portugal, 2007, 229–36, http://ssrn.com/abstract=1417274

29. N. Pupo, *The Shifting Landscape of Work* (2010), http://books.google.ca/books?hl=en&lr=&id=Y0x9eqhJsUgC&oi=fnd&pg=.

30. "Canadian Tire Releases Business Sustainability Results for Third Quarter of 2012," http://corp.canadiantire.ca/EN/MAD/BusinessSustainability/Documents/Q3% 20Business%20Sustainability%20Online%20Report_FINAL%20ENG.pdf; F. Kopun, "Canadian Tire Adds Bling," *Toronto Star,* December 10, 2012, http://www.thestar.com/life/homes/2012/12/10/canadian_tire_adds_bling.html.

31. M. Lubatkin, "Value-Creating Mergers: Fact or Folklore?", *Academy of Management Executive* 2 (1988): 295–302; M. H. Lubatkin and P. J. Lane, "Psst . . . The Merger Mavens Still Have It Wrong!" *Academy of Management Executive* 10 (1996): 21–39.

32. M. Lubatkin and S. Chatterjee, "Extending Modern Portfolio Theory Into the Domain of Corporate Diversification: Does It Apply?" *Academy of Management Journal* 37 (1994), 109–36.

33. "About Samsung," http://www.samsung.com/us/aboutsamsung/index.html.

34. M. Swider, (2015). "World of Tech," Techradar.com, http://www.techradar.com/us/news/world-of-tech/what-is-alphabet-google-s-new-parent-company-explained-1301513.

35. J. A. Pearce II, "Selecting Among Alternative Grand Strategies," *California Management Review* (Spring 1982): 23–31.

36. G. B. Cunningham (2012), "Examining the Relationship Among Miles and Snow's Strategic Types and Measures of Organizational Effectiveness,"

International Management Review, 3(2), 23–37; P. M. Swiercz, (2016), "Late to the Party: HR's Contribution to Contemporary Theories of Strategy" Neostrategic Management, 203–222; S. Idris and I. Primiana (2015), "Effect of Competitive Strategy and Partnership: Strategy for Small Industry Performance," International Journal of Economics, Commerce and Management 3(4), 1–18.

37. W. M. Bulkeley, "Staples Offers $3.6 Billion for Dutch Rival," Wall Street Journal, February 20, 2008, A8.

38. "Subaru Archives Homepage," Cars101.com, http://www.cars101.com/subaru_archives.html.

39. J. A. Pearce II, "Retrenchment Remains the Foundation of Business Turnaround," Strategic Management Journal 15 (1994): 407–17.

40. E. Taylor and C. Rauwald, "Daimler Scores Profit on Its Own," Wall Street Journal, February 15, 2008, C7.

41. S. Krashinsky, "Labatt Strikes Back Against Molson With Hockey Night Deal," Globe and Mail, January 18, 2013, http://www.theglobeandmail.com/report-on-business/industry-news/marketing/labatt-strikes-back-against-molson-with-hockey-night-deal/article7499966.

42. K. Gallinger, "An Ex-Car Salesman Asks: Is My Old Job Ethical?", Toronto Star, November 17, 2012, http://www.thestar.com/life/2012/11/17/an_excar_salesman_asks_is_my_old_job_ethical.html.

43. M. Hartley, "A Tale of Two Video Game Industries—Quebec vs. British Columbia," Financial Post, October 12, 2012, http://business.financialpost.com/2012/10/15/a-tale-of-two-video-game-industries/?__lsa=8b7a-9259.

44. P. Wonacott, "Wal-Mart, Others Demand Lowest Prices, Managers Scramble to Slash Costs," Wall Street Journal, November 13, 2003, A1.

45. J. H. Block, K. Kohn, D. Miller, and K. Ullrich (2015), "Necessity Entrepreneurship and Competitive Strategy," Small Business Economics, 44(1), 37–54.

46. M. Veverka, "Bigger and Better: Costco's Costly Expansion Is About to Pay Off—for Shoppers and Shareholders," Barron's, May 12, 2003, 28.

47. L. Tischler, "The Price Is Right," Fast Company, November 1, 2003, 83.

48. B. Ibrahim (2015), "Strategy Types and Small Firms' Performance: An Empirical Investigation," Journal of Small Business Strategy, 4(1), 9–15; Y-K. Leea, S-H. Kimb, M-K. Seoc, and S. K. Hight (2015), "Market Orientation and Business Performance: Evidence From the Franchising Industry" International Journal of Hospitality Management 44 (1), 28–37.

49. M. Chen, "Competitor Analysis and Interfirm Rivalry: Toward a Theoretical Integration," Academy of Management Review 21 (1996): 100–34; J. C. Baum and H. J. Korn, "Competitive Dynamics of Interfirm Rivalry," Academy of Management Journal 39 (1996): 255–91.

50. J. C. Baum and H. J. Korn, "Competitive Dynamics of Interfirm Rivalry," Academy of Management Journal 39 (1996): 255–91.

51. S. Leung, "Wendy's Sees Green in Salad Offerings—More Sophistication, Ethnic Flavors Appeal to Women, Crucial to Building Market Share," Wall Street Journal, April 24, 2003, B2.

52. M. Stopa, "Wendy's New-Fashioned Growth: Buy Hardee's," Crain's Detroit Business, October 21, 1996.

53. https://bostonpizza.com/en; K. Crowe and H. Shachter, "The Paradox of the Canadian Diet," CBC News, January 20, 2004, http://www.cbc.ca/news/background/food/paradox.html.

54. V. Wong and S. Davidson (2015), "Subway at 40,000: Fast Food's Global King Keeps Growing," Bloomberg Business, http://www.bloomberg.com/bw/articles/2013-08-26/subway-at-40-000-fast-foods-global-king-keeps-growing; J. Jargon (2011), "Subway Runs Past McDonald's Chain," Wall Street Journal (Online), March 8, 2011, http://online.wsj.com/article/SB100014240527487033867045761864_32177464052.html.

55. "Frequently Asked Questions, Subway Restaurants," http://www.subway.com/ContactUs/CustServFAQs.aspx.

56. S. Leung, "Fast Food Budgets Don't Buy Consumer Loyalty," Wall Street Journal, July 24, 2010, B4.

57. D. Ketchen, Jr., C. Snow, and V. Street, "Improving Firm Performance by Matching Strategic Decision-Making Processes to Competitive Dynamics," Academy of Management Executive 18 (2004): 29–43.

58. J. Hagerty and K. Linebaugh, "GE, Caterpillar Face Off in Hot Locomotive Market, Wall Street Journal, April 2013.

59. K. Linebaugh, "GE to Cut Back Trains," Wall Street Journal, June 2013.

6

1. B. Dachis, "Canadian Innovation Is More Than Just Oil: Globe and Mail Op-Ed," Globe and Mail, December 5, 2014, https://www.cdhowe.org/canadian-innovation-more-just-oil-globe-and-mail-op-ed.

2. J. Balsillie, "Canada Needs More Than Talking Points to Spur an Innovation Economy," Globe and Mail, October 3, 2015, http://www.theglobeandmail.com/report-on-business/rob-commentary/canada-needs-more-than-talking-points-to-spur-an-innovation-economy/article26636556/.

3. J. Balsillie, "Canada Needs More Than Talking Points to Spur an Innovation Economy."

4. R. Kozlowski and M. Matejun, "Characteristic Features of Project Management in Small and Medium-Sized Enterprises," Economics and Management (19)3: 33–48; S. Ghafoor and H. Shaukat, "Trends and Opportunities for Social Entrepreneurs Around the Globe," Asian Research Journal of Business Management (3)3; 98–111.

5. T. M. Amabile, R. Conti, H. Coon, J. Lazenby, and M. Herron, "Assessing the Work Environment for Creativity," Academy of Management Journal 39 (1996): 1154–84.

6. Amabile et al., "Assessing the Work Environment."

7. A. H. Van de Ven and M. S. Poole, "Explaining Development and Change in Organizations," Academy of Management Review 20 (1995): 510–40.

8. Amabile et al., "Assessing the Work Environment."

9. G. Athanassakos, "Can Canada Go the Way of Greece?" Globe and Mail, September 6, 2012, http://m.theglobeandmail.com/globe-investor/investment-ideas/can-canada-go-the-way-of-greece/article4179962/?service=mobile.

10. P. Anderson and M. L. Tushman, "Managing Through Cycles of Technological Change," Research/Technology Management, May–June 1991, 26–31.

11. R. N. Foster, Innovation: The Attacker's Advantage (New York: Summitt, 1986).

12. "The Evolution of a Revolution," Intel, http://dowload,intel.com/pressroom/kits/IntelProcessorHistory.pdf; T. Smith, "Inside Intel's Haswell: What Do 1.4 BEELION Transistors Get You?" The Register, June 3, 2013, http://www.therester.co.uk/2013/06/03feature_inside_haswell_intel_4g_core/.

13. D. Wakabayashi, "The Point-and-Shoot Camera Faces Its Existential Moment," Wall Street Journal, July 30, 2013, http://online.wsj.com/news/articles/BS10014212787322515.

14. J. Osawa, "Phones Imperil Fancy Cameras," Wall Street Journal, November 7, 2013, http://onlin.wsj.com/news/articles/SB100014252712304678.

15. "HTC Talks Camera Tech: DSLR-Destroying Optical Zooming 18 Months Away," Official Vodafone UK blog, April 18, 2014, http://blog.vodafone.co.uk/2014/04/18/htc-talks-camera-tech-optical-zooming.

16. M. L. Tushman, P. C. Anderson, and C. O'Reilly, "Technology Cycles, Innovation Streams, and Ambidextrous Organizations: Organization Renewal Through Innovation Streams and Strategic Change," in Managing Strategic Innovation and Change, ed. M. L. Tushman and P. Anderson (New York: Oxford University Press, 1997), 3–23.

17. S. Levy, "Nest's Plan to Stop Brownouts Before They Start," Wired.com, April 22, 2012, http://www.wired.com/business/2013/04/nest-energy-services.

18. T. Simonite, "Nest's Smarter Home," MIT Technology Review, February 15, 2013, http://technologyreview.com/featuredstory/511086/how-nests-control-freaks-reinvented-the-thermostat/.

19. W. Abernathy and J. Utterback, "Patterns of Industrial Innovation," Technology Review 2 (1978): 40–47.

20. D. Howley, "Wireless Charging Standard Gets One Step Closer," Laptop Magazine, February 1, 2014, http://www.techhive.com/article/2096802/wireless-charging-alliances-teaming-up-to-work-toward-a-cable-free-world.html.

21. "Wireless Charging Surge Seen," Investor's Business Daily, March 24, 2014, A02.

22. M. Ramsay, "'Real' 4G Standards Ratified by ITU," Wireless Week, January 19, 2012, http://wirelessweek.com/News/2012/01/Technologies-Real-4G-Standards-Ratified-ITU-Wireless-Networks/.

23. CB Staff, "The 15 Most Innovative Canadian Companies of 2015," Canadian Business, August 15, 2015, http://www.canadianbusiness.com/innovation/the-joy-of-cheap-oil/.

24. D. Yager, "11 Ways to Survive and Thrive in the Age of Cheap Oil," Canadian Business, July 12, 2015, http://www.canadianbusiness.com/innovation/the-joy-of-cheap-oil/.

25. R. Verrier, "Small-Town Movie Theaters Threatened by Shift to Digital Cinema," Los Angeles Times, May 4, 2013, http://articles.latimes.com/print/2013/may/04/entertainment/la-et-ct-last-picture-show-20130504.

26. T. Wong, "Movie Theatres Go Digital or Go Bust," Toronto Star, January 5, 2012, http://www.thestar.com/entertainment/2012/01/05/movie_theatres_go_digital_or_go_bust.html.

27. T. Wong, "Movie Theatres Go Digital or Go Bust."

28. D. Hancock, 2015, https://www.ihs.com/experts/david-hancock.html.

29. Amabile et al., "Assessing the Work Environment."

30. Amabile et al., "Assessing the Work Environment."

31. M. Csikszentmihalyi, Flow: The Psychology of Optimal Experience (New York: Harper and Row, 1990).

32. M. Finneran, "Research: 2013 State of Mobile Security," Information Week, June 2, 2013, http://v5.reports.informationweek.com/abstract/18/10935/Mobility-Wireless/research-2013-state-of-mobile-security-.html.

33. P. White, "BYOS Is Here to Stay, and That's a Good Thing" Wired.com, October 2013, http://www.wired.com/insights/2013/10/byos-is-here-to-stay-and-thats-a-good-thing/.

34. A. Oreskovic, "Yahoo's Work-from-Home Ban Squanders Benefits Spurred by Telecommuting," *Financial Post,* March 13, 2013, http://business.financialpost.com/2013/03/15/yahoo-work-from-home-ban.

35. N. Hendley, "Automotive Manufacturing Report: Do High-Tech Vehicles + Booming Mexican Production = Opportunity?" http://www.canadianmetalworking.com/features/automotive-manufacturing-report/.

36. A. C. Diaz. "See the Top Companies Creatives Will Give up Their Freedom for (in 2015); Working Not Working Releases Second Annual Survey," September 21, 2015, http://adage.com/article/advertising/top-companies-creatives-give-freedom-2015/300465/.

37. K. Goetz, "How 3M Gave Everyone Days Off and Created an Innovation Dynamo," *Fast Company,* June 6, 2011, http://www.fastcodesign.com/1663137/how-3m-gave-everyone-days-off-and-created-an-innovation-dynamo.

38. W. O'Donohue, "Progress in Innovation and Knowledge Management Research: From Incremental to Transformative Innovation," *Journal of Business Research,* Volume 69, Issue 5, May 2016, pp. 1610–1614, http://www.sciencedirect.com/science/article/pii/S014829631500449X.

39. K.M. Eisenhardt, "Accelerating Adaptive Processes: Product Innovation in the Global Computer Industry," *Administrative Science Quarterly* 40 (1995): 84–110.

40. R. Fleming, "Oculus Rift Has Sold Over 85,000 Prototypes," *Digital Trends,* April 16, 2014, http://www.digitaltrends.com/gaming/oculus-rift-sold-85000-prototypes/#!YqqBJ.

41. D. Poeter, "Hands on With the Oculus Rift DK2," *PCMag,* March 20, 2014, http://www.pcmag.com/article2/0,2817,2455180,00.asp.

42. D. Roberts, "Sealy Goes to the Mattresses," *Fortune,* September 17, 2012, http://management.fortune.cnn.com/2012/09/17/sealy-executive-dream-team/.

43. M. Badkar and R. Wile, "How Tesla Went From Near Failure to Stunning Profitability in Just a Few Years," *Business Insider,* August 1, 2014, http://www.businessinsider.com/the-complete-tesla-story-2014-7.

44. L. Kraar, "25 Who Help the U.S. Win: Innovators Everywhere Are Generating Ideas to Make America a Stronger Competitor," *Fortune,* March 22, 1991.

45. M.W. Lawless and P.C. Anderson, "Generational Technological Change: Effects of Innovation and Local Rivalry on Performance," *Academy of Management Journal* 39 (1996): 1185–217.

46. "USB.org—Hi-Speed FAQ," USB Implementers Forum, accessed July 1, 2014, http://www.usb.org/developers/usb20/faq20/; "USB.org—SuperSpeed USB," USB Implementers Forum, http://www.usb.org/developers/ssusb/.

47. Government of Canada, "Benefits of Smart Procurement," 2015, https://buyandsell.gc.ca/initiatives-and-programs/smart-procurement/benefits-of-smart-procurement.

48. A. Vance, "ANSYS Aids Innovation With Its Simulation Software," Bloomberg Businessweek, March 7, 2013, http://www.businessweek.com/articles/2013-03-07/ansys-aids-innovation-with-its-simulation-software.

49. B. Child, "Final *Hunger Games* Movie 'More Anticipated' Than New *Star Wars* Film," *The Guardian,* September 24, 2015, http://www.theguardian.com/film/2015/sep/24/hunger-games-movie-more-anticipated-new-star-wars-film-the-force-awakens.

50. P. Strebel, "Choosing the Right Change Path," *California Management Review* (Winter 1994): 29–51.

51. W. Weitzel and E. Jonsson, "Reversing the Downward Spiral: Lessons From W.T. Grant and Sears Roebuck," *Academy of Management Executive* 5 (1991): 7–22.

52. Associated Press, "General Motors, UAW Reach Tentative Deal on New Contract," *CBC News,* October 26, 2015, http://www.cbc.ca/news/business/united-auto-workers-gm-cba-1.3288287.

53. Weitzel and Jonsson, "Reversing the Downward Spiral."

54. Associated Press, "General Motors, UAW Reach Tentative Deal on New Contract," *CBC News,* October 26, 2015, http://www.cbc.ca/news/business/united-auto-workers-gm-cba-1.3288287; T. Van Alphen, "Unions Must Change Quickly to Survive, Says Secret Report by CEP/CAW," *Toronto Star,* January 26, 2012, http://www.thestar.com/news/gta/2012/01/26/unions_must_change_quickly_to_survive_says_secret_report_by_cepcaw.html.

55. Associated Press, "General Motors, UAW Reach Tentative Deal on New Contract," *CBC News,* October 26, 2015, http://www.cbc.ca/news/business/united-auto-workers-gm-cba-1.3288287; T. Reed, "What's Wrong With Ford and GM Shares?," CNBC, March 13, 2013, http://www.cnbc.com/id/100549938.

56. K. Lewin, *Field Theory in Social Science: Selected Theoretical Papers* (New York: Harper, 1951).

57. Lewin, *Field Theory in Social Science.*

58. Lewin, *Field Theory in Social Science.*

59. J. P. Kotter and L. A. Schlesinger, "Choosing Strategies for Change," *Harvard Business Review* (March–April 1979): 106–14; Harvard Business School Press, *Managing Change to Reduce Resistance* (Cambridge, MA: Harvard Business School Press, 2005).

60. A. B. Fisher, "Making Change Stick," *Fortune,* April 17, 1995, 121.

61. D. Sewell, "P&G Open to Outside Ideas, but No Kitty Swiffers," *Report on Business,* January 4, 2010, http://www.eternalcode.com/pg-open-to-outside-ideas-but-no-kitty-swiffers/.

62. J. Neff, "P&G (Canada) Will Put 'up to' 20% of Budget in Digital in the Great North," May 21, 2008, http://customerlistening.typepad.com/customer_listening/2008/05/pg-canada-will.html.

63. PG.com, "Management Perspectives," July 18, 2013, http://www.pg.com/en_CA/company/who_we_are/letter_penner.shtml.

64. B. Orwall, "Disney Decides It Must Draw Artists Into Computer Age," *Wall Street Journal,* October 23, 2003, A1.

65. J. P. Kotter, "Leading Change: Why Transformation Efforts Fail," *Harvard Business Review* 73, no. 2 (March–April 1995): 59.

66. The Canadian Press, "Celestica Names Robert Mionis as New CEO; Takes Over From Craig Muhlhauser," *Canadian Business,* July 8, 2015, http://www.canadianbusiness.com/business-news/celestica-names-robert-mionis-as-new-ceo-takes-over-from-craig-muhlhauser/.

67. H. Miller, "Celestica Fills BlackBerry Gap With Aerospace," *Bloomberg News,* 2013, http://www.bloomberg.com/news/2013-04-24/celestica-fills-blackberry-gap-with-aerospace-corporate-canada.html.

68. B. Brown and S. Anthony, "How P&G Tripled Its Innovation Success Rate," *Harvard Business Review,* June 2011, https://hbr.org/2011/06/how-pg-tripled-its-innovation-success-rate; E. Byron, "P&G Makes a Bigger Play for Men," *Wall Street Journal,* August 28, 2009, http://online.wsj.com/article/SB124096436192766099.html.

69. B. Brown and S. Anthony, "How P&G Tripled Its Innovation Success Rate"; E. Byron, "P&G Makes a Bigger Play."

70. L. La Rose, "As Online Shopping Picks Up, Delivery Times Shorten," *The Star,* September 17, 2015, http://www.thestar.com/business/2015/09/17/as-online-shopping-picks-up-delivery-times-shorten.html; P. Engardio and J. McGregor, "Lean and Mean Gets Extreme," *Business Week,* March 23, 2009, 60, http://www.thefreelibrary.com/+LEAN+AND+MEAN+GETS+EXTREME-a01611821658.

71. Miller, "Celestica Fills BlackBerry Gap With Aerospace."

72. PRNewswire, "Strong Sequential Growth—Report on Celestica Inc," COMTEX, July 31, 2015, http://www.marketwatch.com/story/strong-sequential-growth--report-on-celestica-inc-2015-07-31.

73. W. Dabrowski, "Celestica Buoyed by Smartphone Market Potential," *Toronto Star,* April 24, 2009, B4, http://www.thestar.com/business/2009/04/24/celestica_buoyed_by_smartphone_market_potential.html.

74. Harvard Business School Press, *The Results-Driven Manager: Getting People on Board* (Cambridge, MA: Harvard Business School Press, 2005).

75. J. Scheck, "New Shell CEO Van Beurden Lays Out Turnaround Plan," *Wall Street Journal,* April 27, 2014, http://online.wsj.com/news/articles/SB10001424052702304163604579527952790186 8370442?KEYWORDS=Ben+van+Beurden+CEO+Royal+Dutch+Shell&mg=reno64-wsj.

76. Harvard Business School Press, *The Results-Driven Manager.*

77. R. N. Ashkenas and T. D. Jick, "From Dialogue to Action in GE WorkOut: Developmental Learning in a Change Process," in *Research in Organizational Change and Development* 6th ed. W.A. Pasmore and R.W. Woodman (Greenwich: JAI, 1992), 267–87.

78. T. Stewart, "GE Keeps Those Ideas Coming," *Fortune,* August 12, 1991, 40.

79. Stewart, "GE Keeps Those Ideas Coming."

80. Rothwell, Sullivan, and McLean, *Practicing Organizational Development.*

81. Rothwell, Sullivan, and McLean, *Practicing Organizational Development.*

7

1. S. T. Cavusgil and G. Knight, 2014. "The Born Global Firm: An Entrepreneurial and Capabilities Perspective on Early and Rapid Internationalization," *Journal of International Business Studies* 46, 3–16.

2. UNCTAD, *World Investment Report 2015: United Nations Conference on Trade and Development,* http://unctad.org/en/PublicationsLibrary/wir2015_en.pdf.

3. UNCTAD, *World Investment Report 2015: United Nations Conference on Trade and Development,* http://unctad.org/en/PublicationsLibrary/wir2015_en.pdf.

4. The Canadian Press, "Talisman Agrees to $15.1B Cdn Takeover by Spain's Repsol," *CBC News,* December 16, 2014, http://www.cbc.ca/news/business/talisman-agrees-to-15-1b-cdn-takeover-by-spain-s-repsol-1.2874486.

5. UNCTAD, *World Investment Report 2015: United Nations Conference on Trade and Development*, http://unctad.org/en/PublicationsLibrary/wir2015_en.pdf.

6. Asia Pacific Foundation of Canada, 2015, "Canadian Outward Foreign Direct Investment to the World," https://www.asiapacific.ca/statistics/investment/outward-foreign-direct-investment/canadian-outward-foreign-direct-investment-0.

7. Government of Manitoba, "Sectoral Limitations on Foreign Ownership of Canadian Businesses," 2015 http://www.gov.mb.ca/jec/invest/busfacts/govt/f_ownership.html.

8. R. M. Yalden, E. Pressman, and J. Fraiberg, "The Mergers and Acquisitions Review: Canada (Ninth Edition)," August 2015, https://www.osler.com/en/resources/regulations/2015/the-mergers-acquisitions-review-canada-ninth-e.

9. Government of Canada, "What Tariffs and Taxes Can Canadian Exporters Expect to Pay China Customs?" 2015, http://www.tradecommissioner.gc.ca/eng/document.jsp?did=111093.

10. Government of Canada, "Excise Taxes and Special Levies Memoranda X3.1 Goods Subject to Excise Tax," 2015, http://www.cra-arc.gc.ca/E/pub/et/x3-1/x3-1-e.html.

11. Government of Canada, "The Canadian Cane and Beet Sugar Industry (1 of 2)," (2015), http://www.agr.gc.ca/eng/industry-markets-and-trade/statistics-and-market-information/by-product-sector/processed-food-and-beverages/the-canadian-cane-and-beet-sugar-industry-1-of-2/?id=1248362081340.

12. S. Coff, "Bitter Battle Rages Over Canada's Sugar Industry," *The Globe and Mail*, June 24, 2014, http://www.theglobeandmail.com/report-on-business/international-business/european-business/bitter-battle-rages-over-canadas-sugar-industry/article4366870/.

13. World Trade Organization, "Understanding the WTO," https://www.wto.org/english/thewto_e/whatis_e/tif_e/agrm9_e.htm.

14. United States Department of Agriculture, 2015, http://www.ers.usda.gov/topics/animal-products/cattle-beef/trade.aspx; D. Poulin and K. Boame, "Mad Cow Disease and Beef Trade," November 12, 2009, http://www.statcan.gc.ca/pub/11-621-m/11-621-m2003005-eng.htm; S. Kosinski, "Canada Imports Into the US," June 21, 2010, http://www.foragebeef.ca/app33/foragebeef/index_body.jsp.

15. N. Macdonald, "Bombardier's Strange Chokehold on the Public Purse," *CBC News*, November 3, 2015, http://www.cbc.ca/news/business/bombardier-bailout-neil-macdonald-1.3300764.

16. See the Official Harmonized Tariff Schedule of Canada at www.cbsa-asfc.gc.ca/trade-commerce/tariff-tarif for more information.

17. Government of Canada, "What Tariffs and Taxes Can Canadian Exporters Expect to Pay China Customs?" http://www.tradecommissioner.gc.ca/eng/document.jsp?did=111093.

18. R. D. Atkinson and S. J. Ezell, (2012). *Innovation Economics: The Race for Global Advantage*, Yale University Press: New Haven.

19. Government of Canada, "Trans-Pacific Partnership (TPP)," 2015, http://www.international.gc.ca/trade-agreements-accords-commerciaux/agr-acc/tpp-ptp/index.aspx?lang=eng.

20. E. Obourn, "Critics Cry Foul as New Trans-Pacific Partnership Details Emerge: Devil Is in the Details Say Critics of Trade Deal's Newly Revealed Fine Print," *CBC News*, November 6, 2015, http://www.cbc.ca/news/business/trans-pacific-partnership-details-1.3308248.

21. Government of Great Britain, "Countries in the EU and EEA," 2015, https://www.gov.uk/eu-eea.

22. For more information about the Maastricht Treaty, and the EU, see http://eur-lex.europa.eu/homepage.html.

23. M. A. Villarreal and I. F. Fergusson (2015). *The North American Free Trade Agreement (NAFTA)*. Congressional Research Service, 7-5700, www.crs.gov, R42965, https://www.fas.org/sgp/crs/row/R42965.pdf.

24. WTO Publications, "International Trade Statistics 2014," 2015. https://www.wto.org/english/res_e/statis_e/its2014_e/its2014_e.pdf.

25. Office of the United States Trade Representative, "CAFTA-DR (Dominican Republic–Central America FTA)," http://www.export.gov/%5C/FTA/cafta-dr/index.asp.

26. UNASUR, Union of South American Nations, http://www.unasursg.org/en.

27. "StatsAPEC—Data for the Asia-Pacific Region—Economic and Social Statistics and Bilateral Trade and Investment Flows," StatsAPEC, http://statistics.apec.org/.

28. "Frequently Asked Questions," *Asia-Pacific Economic Cooperation*, http://www.apec.org/FAQ.aspx/.

29. L. Ch. Savage, "Why Canada Is Paying $4 Billion for a New Detroit–Windsor Bridge," *Canadian Business,* May 22, 2015, http://www.canadianbusiness.com/economy/4-billion-detroit-windsor-bridge/; CBC News, (2015). "Ambassador Bridge Fire Stops Traffic, International Trade, Cause of Blaze Remains Undetermined, as Traffic Halted on North America's Busiest Crossing," *CBC News,* April 14, 2015, http://www.cbc.ca/news/canada/windsor/ambassador-bridge-fire-stops-traffic-international-trade-1.3032424.

30. "The Big Mac Index," *The Economist*, http://www.economist.com/blogs/dailychart/2011/07/big-mac-index.

31. "Gross National Income Per Capita 2014, Atlas Method and PPP Based," *The World Bank*, April 15, 2015, http://databank.worldbank.org/data/download/GNIPC.pdf.

32. "Cost of Living in Toronto Compared to Tokyo," 2015, https://www.expatistan.com/cost-of-living/comparison/toronto/tokyo;

World Trade Organization, "Freer Trade Cuts the Cost of Living," http://www.wto.org/english/thewto_e/whatis_e/10ben_e/10b04_e.htm.

33. V. Muzumdar, "Why Does McDonald's Not Serve the Big Mac Burger in India Even Though It Is the World's Most Popular Burger?" *Quora*, 2015, https://www.quora.com/Why-does-McDonalds-not-serve-the-big-mac-burger-in-India-even-though-it-is-the-worlds-most-popular-burger.

34. M. Gao, "Culture Determines Business Models: Analyzing Home Depot's Failure Case in China for International Retailers From a Communication Perspective," *Thunderbird International Business Review*, March/April 2013: 173–191.

35. L. Burkitt, "Home Depot to Shut Seven China Stores, Take $160 Mln Charge," *WSJ*, September 14, 2012, http://www.wsj.com/articles/SB10000872396390444709004577650512492181658; L. Burkitt, "Home Depot Learns Chinese Prefer 'Do-It-for-Me,'" *WSJ*, September 14, 2012, http://www.wsj.com/articles/SB1000087239639044443350457765107291154602.

36. Z. McKnight, "Having Built out Home Depot Canada, Annette Verschuren Turns to Energy Storage," *Financial Post*, October 28, 2014, http://business.financialpost.com/entrepreneur/having-built-out-home-depot-canada-verschuren-turns-her-attention-to-energy-storage.

37. K. Englehart, "Starbucks Go Home," *Macleans*, January 25, 2013, http://www.macleans.ca/news/world/starbucks-go-home/.

38. A. Sundaram and J. S. Black, "The Environment and Internal Organization of Multinational Enterprises," *Academy of Management Review 17* (1992): 729–757.

39. H.S. James, Jr., and M. Weidenbaum, *When Businesses Cross International Borders: Strategic Alliances and Their Alternatives* (Westport: Praeger, 1993).

40. H. S. James, Jr., and M. Weidenbaum, *When Businesses Cross International Borders: Strategic Alliances and Their Alternatives* (Westport: Praeger, 1993).

41. P. Marsh, "UK Car Exports Drive Industry's Revival," *Financial Times*, January 17, 2013, http://www.ft.com/cms/s/0/579a5da2-6097-11e2-a31a-00144feab49a.html#axzz3qxJHhSQe.

42. T. Aeppel, "Oil Shocker: Stung by Soaring Transportation Cost, Factories Bring Jobs Home Again," *Wall Street Journal*, June 13, 2014, A1, http://www.wsj.com/articles/SB121331934552070357.

43. T. Argitis and E. Hertzberg, "Canada a Petro-Economy No More as Car Exports Surpass Energy," *Bloomberg*, September 3, 2015, http://www.bnn.ca/News/2015/9/3/Canada-a-petro-economy-no-more-as-car-exports-Surpass-energy.aspx.

44. S. Davidson, "There Is a Quiet Revolution Currently Growing in the Beer Industry," *Food & Beverage Canada*, Summer 2014, http://www.foodandbeveragecanada.com/index.php/featured-content/28-labatt.

45. A. Lutz, "KFC Has One Huge Problem That's Killing Business." *Business Insider*, July 16, 2015, http://www.businessinsider.com/kfc-sales-in-china-are-tanking-2015-7; W. Mellor, "McDonald's No Match for KFC in China as Colonel Rules Fast Food," *Bloomberg Businessweek,* January 26, 2011, http://www.bloomberg.com/news/articles/2011-01-26/mcdonald-s-no-match-for-kfc-in-china-where-colonel-sanders-rules-fast-food; D. Bell and M. L. Shelman, "KFC's Radical Approach to China," *Harvard Business Review*, November 2011, https://hbr.org/2011/11/kfcs-radical-approach-to-china.

46. E. Dou, "Hewlett-Packard, Foxconn Launch Joint Server Venture," *Wall Street Journal*, April 30, 2014, http://www.wsj.com/articles/SB10001424052702303948104579533080961860334.

47. Government of Canada, "A Joint Venture May Be Your Best Bet in China," *The Canadian Trade Commissioner Service*, 2015, http://www.tradecommissioner.gc.ca/eng/canadexport/document.jsp?did=146275.

48. M. Zineldin, H. Fujimoto, Y. Li, H. Kassean, and V. Vasicheva, "Why Do Both Marriages and Strategic Alliances Have Over 50% Failure Rate? A Study of Relationship Quality of Strategic Alliances in China, Japan and Mauritius," *International Journal of Strategic Business Alliances*, Vol 4, No 1, 2015, http://www.inderscienceonline.com/doi/abs/10.1504/IJSBA.2015.069305.

49. M. W. Hordes, J. A. Clancy, and J. Baddaley, "A Primer for Global Start-Ups," *Academy of Management Executive* (May 1995): 7–11.

50. D. Pavlos, J. Johnson, J. Slow, and S. Young, "Micromultinationals: New Types of Firms for the Global Competitive Landscape," *European Management Journal* 21, no. 2 (April 2003): 164; B. M. Oviatt and P. P. McDougall, "Toward a Theory of International New Ventures," *Journal of International Business Studies* (Spring 1994): 45; S. Zahra, "A Theory of International New Ventures: A Decade of Research," *Journal of International Business Studies* (January 2005): 20–28.

51. B. Keplesky, "MakerBot's Bre Pettis on the Next Industrial Revolution," *Entrepreneur*, March 9, 2013, http://www.entrepreneur.com/article/226044; M. Wolf, "How 3D Printing Is Now Helping NASA Get to Space," *Forbes*, January 12, 2013, http://www.forbes.com/sites/michaelwolf/2013/01/12/how-3d-printing-is-now-helping-nasa-get-to-space/; "Official International MakerBot Distributors," MakerBot, http://www.makerbot.com/resellers.

52. The Coca-Cola Company: SEC Filings Form 10-Q on 10/28/2015. "Worldwide Unit Case Volume Geographic Mix," Coca-Cola, http://www.coca-colacompany.com/.

53. "Coca-Cola Single Bottle (20oz/600ml)," HuMuch? http://www.humuch.com/prices/CocaCola-Bottle-500ml/___KZT_/40#.VkAz8rerS70.

54. P. W. Beamish and N. C. Lupton, "Cooperative Strategies in International Business and Management: Reflections on the Past 50 Years and Future Directions," *Journal of World Business*, January 2016, http://www.sciencedirect.com/science/article/pii/S1090951615000668; S. Kraus, T. C. Ambos, F. Eggers, and B. Cesinger, "Distance and Perceptions of Risk in Internationalization Decisions," *Journal of Business Research*, Volume 68, Issue 7, July 2015, pp. 1501–1505, http://www.sciencedirect.com/science/article/pii/S0148296315000557.

55. K. D. Miller, "A Framework for Integrated Risk Management in International Business," *Journal of International Business Studies* (2nd Quarter 1992): 311.

56. P. Beckett, "Honeywell Chairman: Foreign Firms Scared of India Now," *Wall Street Journal*, May 2, 2012, http://www.wsj.com/articles/SB10001424052702304743704577379453791550164.

57. "United Arab Emirates Business Forecast Report, 2014, 2nd Quarter," *Business Monitor International*, April 1, 2014, 1–50.

58. R. Roy, "Foreign Online Retailers Ask India to Allow Direct Sales," *Wall Street Journal*, February 12, 2013, http://www.wsj.com/articles/SB10001424127887324880504578299454251603948.

59. E. J. Blanchard, "A Shifting Mandate: International Ownership, Global Fragmentation, and a Case for Deeper Integration Under the WTO," *World Trade Review*, Vol. 14, No. 01, January 2015, pp. 87–99, http://journals.cambridge.org/action/displayAbstract?fromPage=online&aid=9494515&fileId=S1474745614000408.

60. A. Campbell, "Canada Has a Role to Play as China Restructures Its Economy," *Macleans*, September 12, 2015, http://www.macleans.ca/economy/economicanalysis/canada-has-a-role-to-play-as-china-restructures-its-economy/.

61. I. Wadie, "We've Adjusted to Rising Prices; We Can Adjust to Falling Ones: For the Record, Bank of Canada Governor Stephen Poloz on Riding the Commodity Cycle," *Macleans*, September 21, 2015, http://www.macleans.ca/economy/economicanalysis/stephen-poloz-weve-adjusted-to-rising-prices-we-can-adjust-to-falling-ones/.

62. A. Campbell, "Canada Has a Role to Play as China Restructures Its Economy," *Macleans*, September 12, 1015, http://www.macleans.ca/economy/economicanalysis/canada-has-a-role-to-play-as-china-restructures-its-economy/. 63. J. Palladini, "Canada's Big Opportunity in China Is Services, Not Just Resources," *Canadian Business*, March 18, 2015, http://www.canadianbusiness.com/blogs-and-comment/canada-china-services-export-opportunity/.

64. M. Koren, "Why Russians Aren't Smiling at You in Sochi," *National Journal*, February 7, 2014, http://www.nationaljournal.com/politics/2014/02/07/why-russians-arent-smiling-you-sochi.

65. D. Petrucci, "7 Things Canadians Need to Know Before Moving to the UK," *Huffington Post*, December 3, 2014, http://www.huffingtonpost.ca/diana-petrucci/canadians-in-uk_b_5925168.html.

66. W. W. Maddux, A. D. Galinsky, and C. T. Tadmor, "Be a Better Manager: Live Abroad," *Harvard Business Review*, September 9, 2010.

67. C. Joinson, "No Returns," *HR Magazine*, November 2002, 70.

68. M. Mackinnon, "I Am Canadian—But Now Not as Much as I Used to Be," *The Globe and Mail*, July 24, 2015, http://www.theglobeandmail.com/globe-debate/i-am-canadian-but-now-not-as-much-as-i-used-to-be/article25666787/.

69. R. Feintzeig, "After Stints Abroad, Re-Entry Can Be Hard," *Wall Street Journal*, September 17, 2013, http://www.wsj.com/articles/SB10001424127873233424045790813827818095274.

70. J. S. Black and M. Mendenhall, "Cross-Cultural Training Effectiveness: A Review and Theoretical Framework for Future Research," *Academy of Management Review* 15 (1990): 113–36.

71. J. Kidner, "Why More Corporate Executives Now Have Extensive Legal Training," *The Globe and Mail*, August 11, 2015, http://www.theglobeandmail.com/report-on-business/rob-commentary/why-more-corporate-executives-now-have-extensive-legal-training/article25907740/.

72. K. Essick, "Executive Education: Transferees Prep for Life, Work in Far-Flung Lands," *Wall Street Journal*, November 12, 2014, A6.

73. P. W. Tam, "Culture Course—'Awareness Training' Helps U.S. Workers Better Know Their Counterparts in India," *Wall Street Journal*, May 25, 2004, B1.

74. J. Rothlauf, *A Global View on Intercultural Management: Challenges in a Globalized World*, De Gruyter Gmb: Berlin.

75. W. Arthur, Jr., and W. Bennett, Jr., "The International Assignee: The Relative Importance of Factors Perceived to Contribute to Success," *Personnel Psychology* 48 (1995): 99–114; B. Cheng, "Home Truths About Foreign Postings; To Make an Overseas Assignment Work, Employers Need More Than an Eager Exec With a Suitcase," *BusinessWeek Online*, July 14, 2002, http://www.businessweek.com/careers/content/jul2002/ca20020715_9110.htm.

76. B. Groysberg and R. Abrahams, "Manage Your Work, Manage Your Life," *Harvard Business Review*, March 2014, https://hbr.org/2014/03/manage-your-work-manage-your-life.

77. Prudential Real Estate and Relocation Services Intercultural Group, "OAI: Overseas Assignment Inventory," May 11, 2011, http://www.prudential.com/view/page/public/14394.

78. D. Eschbach, G. Parker, and P. Stoeberl, "American Repatriate Employees' Retrospective Assessments of the Effects of Cross-Cultural Training on Their Adaptation to International Assignments," *International Journal of Human Resource Management* 12 (2001): 270–87; "Culture Training: How to Prepare Your Expatriate Employees for Cross-Cultural Work Environments," *Managing Training & Development*, February 1, 2005.

79. E. Kim, "Facebook CEO Mark Zuckerberg's Chinese Is So Good, He Didn't Speak a Word of English With Chinese President Xi Jinping," *Business Insider*, September 24, 2015, http://www.businessinsider.com/facebook-ceo-mark-zuckerberg-chinese-2015-9.

80. J. Ardedy, "Deep Inside China, American Family Struggles to Cope," *Wall Street Journal*, August 2, 2005, A1.

8

1. Canadian Tire Corporation Investor Presentation April 2015, page 12, http://corp.canadiantire.ca/EN/Investors/EventsPresentations/Documents/Investor%20presentation%20-%20April%202015.pdf.

2. M. Hammer and J. Champy, *Reengineering the Corporation: A Manifesto for Business Revolution* (New York: Harper and Row, 1993).

3. Procter & Gamble, 2015 Annual Report, http://www.pginvestor.com/Cache/1001201800.PDF?O=PDF&T=&Y=&D=&FID=1001201800&iid=4004124; Procter & Gamble, "Corporate Structure," http://www.pg.com/en_US/company/global_structure_operations/corporate_structure.shtml; Procter & Gamble, "Pampers: The Birth of P&G's First 10-Billion-Dollar Brand," June 27, 2012, http://news.pg.com/blog/10-billion-dollar-brand/pampers-birth-pgs-first-10-billion-dollar-brand; A. Alexander, "P&G Reorganizes Global Business Units Into Industry-Based Sectors," *Drugstore News*, June 6, 2013, http://drugstorenews.com/article/pg-reorganizes-global-business-units-industry-based-sectors; Procter & Gamble, "Procter & Gamble Announces Organization Changes," http://news.pg.com/press-release/pg-corporate-announcements/procter-gamble-announces-organization-changes.

4. J. G. March and H. A. Simon, *Organizations* (New York: John Wiley, 1958).

5. Bombardier 2015 Financial Report, http://ir.bombardier.com/modules/misc/documents/30/01/04/59/14/Bombardier-Financial-Report-2015-en2.pdf; United Technologies Corporation, 2012 Annual Report.

6. Saputo, "Annual Information Form," June 7, 2011, http://www.saputo.com/uploadedFiles/Saputo/investors-and-medias/financial-documents/AIF_EN_2011.pdf.

7. L. R. Burns, "Adoption and Abandonment of Matrix Management Programs: Effects of Organizational Characteristics and Interorganizational Networks," *Academy of Management Journal* 36 (1993): 106–38.

8. H. Fayol, *General and Industrial Management*, trans. C. Storrs (London: Pitman, 1949).

9. M. Weber, *The Theory of Social and Economic Organization*, trans. and ed. A. M. Henderson and T. Parsons (New York: Free Press, 1947).

10. Fayol, *General and Industrial Management*.

11. Lashinsky, "Inside Apple, From Steve Jobs Down to the Janitor: How America's Most Successful—and Most Secretive—Big Company Really Works," *Fortune*, May 23, 2011, 125–134.

12. K. Moore, "Murray Martin Talks to Karl Moore," *Globe and Mail*, April 6, 2010, http://www.theglobeandmail.com/report-on-business/murray-martin-talks-to-karl-moore/article1525148.

13. A. Lopez-Pacheco, "Letting Go of the Day-to-Day: It Starts With Building the Right Team," *Financial Post*, May 16, 2010, http://www.financialpost.com/Letting+starts+with+building+right+team/3038099/story.html.

14. M. Stern, "10 Worst Leadership Habits," *Canadian Business*, May 1, 2008: 63–65, http://www.michaelstern.com/coaching/10_Worst_Leadership_Habits.pdf; http://www.canadianbusiness.com/managing/career/article.jsp?content=20080312_198703_198703.

15. S. Bowness, "Healthy Leadership: Trillium Motivates From the Ground Up," *Canadian Business Online*, January 8, 2007, http://www.canadianbusiness.com/technology-news/healthy-leadership-trillium-motivates-from-the-ground-up.

16. B. Harding, "Globe and Mail Update," *Globe and Mail*, April 7, 2009, http://m.theglobeandmail.com/report-on-business/brett-harding/article884122/?service=mobile.

17. J. Jargon, "McDonald's Tackles Repair of 'Broken' Service," *Wall Street Journal*, April 10, 2013, http://online.wsj.com/article/SB10001424127887324010704578414901710175648.html.

18. S. Curry, "Retention Getters," *Incentive*, April 1, 2005.

19. B. Duffy, "Fast and Furious," *Bloomberg Business Week*, May 9, 2011, http://www.businessweek.com/magazine/content/11_20/b4228064581642.htm.

20. R. W. Griffin, *Task Design* (Glenview: Scott, Foresman, 1982).

21. F. Herzberg, *Work and the Nature of Man* (Cleveland: World Press, 1966).

22. T. Burns and G. M. Stalker, *The Management of Innovation* (London: Tavistock, 1961).

23. M. Hammer and J. Champy, *Reengineering the Corporation*.

24. J. Gray, "McCarthy Tetrault's Tracie Crook Leading Firm's Radical Transformation," *The Globe and Mail*, December 27, 2015, http://www.theglobeandmail.com/report-on-business/industry-news/the-law-page/mccarthy-tetraults-tracie-crook-leading-firms-radical-transformation/article27941227/.

25. J.D. Thompson, *Organizations in Action* (New York: McGraw-Hill, 1967).

26. J.B. White, "'Next Big Thing': Re-Engineering Gurus Take Steps to Remodel Their Stalling Vehicles," *Wall Street Journal Interactive*, November 26, 1996.

27. M. Hammer and J. Champy, *Reengineering the Corporation*.

28. G. M. Spreitzer, "Individual Empowerment in the Workplace: Dimensions, Measurement, and Validation," *Academy of Management Journal* 38 (1995): 1442–65.

29. M. Schrage, "I Know What You Mean: And I Can't Do Anything about It," *Fortune*, April 2, 2001, 186.

30. K. W. Thomas and B. A. Velthouse, "Cognitive Elements of Empowerment," *Academy of Management Review* 15 (1990): 666–81.

31. O. Dogerlioglu, "Outsourcing Versus In-House: A Modular Organization Perspective," *The Journal of International Management Studies*, Vol. 7, No. 1, April 2012, http://www.jimsjournal.org/4%20Ozgur%20Dogerlioglu.pdf.

32. O. Dogerlioglu, "Outsourcing Versus In-House: A Modular Organization Perspective."

33. H. Thomas, "Pharma Companies' Cost Cuts Could Be a Tonic for Quintiles," *Wall Street Journal*, December 21, 2013, B14; C. C. Snow, R. E. Miles, and H. J. Coleman, Jr., "Managing 21st Century Network Organizations," *Organizational Dynamics* (Winter 1992): 5–20.

34. O. Dogerlioglu, "Outsourcing Versus In-House: A Modular Organization Perspective."

35. P. Weimann, C. Hinz, E. Scott, and M. Pollock, "Changing the Communication Culture of Distributed Teams in a World Where Communication is Neither Perfect nor Complete," *The Electronic Journal Information Systems Evaluation*, Volume 13, Issue 2, 2010, pp. 187–196.

36. "Virtual Organizations—Avatars and the Business World," June 8, 2011, 899ALK, https://899alk.wordpress.com/2011/06/28/virtual-organizations-avatars-and-the-business-world/.

37. P&G, Connect + Develop, Open Innovation Stories, October 10, 2012, http://www.pgconnectdevelop.com/home/stories/jvs-joint-ventures/20121010-glad-forceflex-and-glad-pressnseal.html.

38. D. Truxillo, T. N. Bauer, and B. Erdogan, "Psychology and Work: Perspectives on Industrial and Organizational Psychology," Routledge Publishers, November 23, 2015, pp. 535–536.

39. R. Cohen, "Accenture's Cloud Business Already at $1 Billion-a-Year, Aims to Become Industry's Cloud Broker," *Forbes*, April 29, 2013, http://www.forbes.com/sites/reuvencohen/2013/04/29/accentures-cloud-business-already-at-1-billion-a-year-aims-to-become-industrys-cloud-broker/#4f937afddaac; D. Plummer, "Cloud Services Brokerage: A Must-Have for Most Organizations," *Forbes*, March 22, 2012, http://www.forbes.com/sites/gartnergroup/2012/03/22/cloud-services-brokerage-a-must-have-for-most-organizations/#3777994d52aa.

9

1. B. Dumaine, "The Trouble With Teams," *Fortune*, September 5, 1994, 86–92; G. M. Parker, *Team Players and Teamwork: New Strategies for Developing Successful Collaborations* (San Francisco: Jossey-Bass, 2010).

2. J. Hoerr, "The Payoff From Teamwork—the Gains in Quality Are Substantial—So Why Isn't It Spreading Faster?" *BusinessWeek*, July 10, 1989, 56.

3. A. Murray, "What Do Managers Do?" Adapted from *The Wall Street Journal Guide to Management*. *Wall Street Journal*, http://guides.wsj.com/management/developing-a-leadership-style/what-do-managers-do/.

4. J. R. Katzenback and D. K. Smith, *The Wisdom of Teams* (Boston: Harvard Business School Press, 1993).

5. E. Lesser and L. Ban, "How Leading Companies Practice Software Development and Delivery to Achieve a Competitive Edge," *Strategy & Leadership* 44, 1 (2016): 41–47; S. E. Gross, *Compensation for Teams* (New York: American Management Association, 1995); B. L. Kirkman and B. Rosen, "Beyond Self-Management: Antecedents and Consequences of Team Empowerment," *Academy of Management Journal* 42 (1999): 58–74; G. Stalk and T. M. Hout, *Competing Against Time: How Time-Based Competition Is Reshaping Global Markets* (New York: Free Press, 1990); S. C. Wheelwright and K. B. Clark, *Revolutionizing New Product Development* (New York: Free Press, 1992).

6. "Aon Hewitt Adds to Vancouver Team," BenefitsCanada.com, April 22, 2015, http://www.benefitscanada.com/news/aon-hewitt-adds-to-vancouver-team-65839; J. Marquez, "Hewitt-BP Split May Signal End of 'Lift and Shift' Deals," *Workforce Management*, December 29, 2006, 3.

7. R. D. Banker, J. M. Field, R. G. Schroeder, and K. K. Sinha, "Impact of Work Teams on Manufacturing Performance: A Longitudinal Field Study," *Academy of Management Journal* 39 (1996): 867–90.

8. A. Cuenllas, "Whole Foods Case Study: A Benchmark Model of Management for Hospitality," HospitalityNet, February 11, 2013, http://www.hospitalitynet.org/news/4059396.html; C. Fishman, "The Anarchist's Cookbook: John Mackey's Approach to Management Is Equal Parts Star Trek and 1970s Flashback," *Fast Company*, July 1, 2004, 70.

9. T. L. Rappa, L. L. Gilson, J. E. Mathieu, and T. Ruddy, "Leading Empowered Teams: An Examination of the Role of External Team Leaders and Team Coaches," *The Leadership Quarterly* (27)1 (2016): 109–123; J. L. Cordery, W. S. Mueller, and L. M. Smith, "Attitudinal and Behavioral Effects of Autonomous Group Working: A Longitudinal Field Study," *Academy of Management Journal* 34 (1991): 464–76; T. D. Wall, N. J. Kemp, P. R. Jackson, and C. W. Clegg, "Outcomes of Autonomous Workgroups: A Long-Term Field Experiment," *Academy of Management Journal* 29 (1986): 280–304.

10. M. Sturdevant, "Top Large Employer: Whole Foods Teamwork Is a Natural," *Hartford Courant*, September 21, 2014, http://www.courant.com/business/top-workplaces/hc-tw14-whole-foods-20140921-story.html; Whole Foods Market, "Declaration of Interdependence," http://www.wholefoodsmarket.com/mission-values/core-values/declaration-interdependence.

11. Whole Foods Market, "Declaration of Interdependence."

12. J. Gu, Z. Chen, Q. Huang, H. Liu, and S. Huang, "A Multilevel Analysis of the Relationship Between Shared Leadership and Creativity in Inter-Organizational Teams," *The Journal of Creative Behavior*, (2016): 17–23. DOI: 10.1002/jocb.135; A. Erez, J. Lepine, and H. Elms, "Effects of Rotated Leadership and Peer Evaluation on the Functioning and Effectiveness of Self-Managed Teams: A Quasi-Experiment," *Personnel Psychology* 55, no. 4 (2002): 929.

13. C. Stephenson, "Leveraging Diversity to Maximum Advantage: The Business Case for Appointing More Women to Boards," *Ivey Business Journal*, September–October 2004, 1–5.

14. "Great Little Box Company: A Team Approach to Success," *Industry Canada*, May 7, 2012, https://www.ic.gc.ca/eic/site/061.nsf/eng/.%5Cvwapj%5Cgreatlittlebox_company_eng.pdf%5C$file%5Cgreatlittlebox_company_eng.pdf.

15. M. Täksa, P. Tynjäläb, and H. Kukemelka, "Engineering Students' Conceptions of Entrepreneurial Learning as Part of Their Education," *European Journal of Engineering Education* (41)1 (2015): 53–69.

16. B. Meyera, C. C. Schermuly, and S. Kauffeld, "That's Not My Place: The Interacting Effects of Faultlines, Subgroup Size, and Social Competence on Social Loafing Behaviour in Work Groups," *European Journal of Work and Organizational Psychology* (25)1 (2016): 31–49. DOI:10.1080/1359432X.2014.996554; R. Liden, S. Wayne, R. Jaworski, and N. Bennett, "Social Loafing: A Field Investigation," *Journal of Management* 30 (2004): 285–304.

17. J. George, "Extrinsic and Intrinsic Origins of Perceived Social Loafing in Organizations," *Academy of Management Journal* 35 (1992): 191–202.

18. S. A. Conroy and N. Gupta, "Team Pay-for-Performance: The Devil Is in the Details," *Group Organization Management* (41)1 (2016): 32–65; T. T. Baldwin, M. D. Bedell, and J. L. Johnson, "The Social Fabric of a Team-Based M.B.A. Program: Network Effects on Student Satisfaction and Performance," *Academy of Management Journal* 40 (1997): 1369–97.

19. D. Johnson, "Teams at Work," *HRMagazine*, May 1, 1999, 30.

20. R. Wageman, "Critical Success Factors for Creating Superb Self-Managing Teams," *Organizational Dynamics* 26, no. 1 (1997): 49–61.

21. D. A. Harrison, S. Mohammed, J. E. McGrath, A. T. Florey, and S. W. Vanderstoep, "Time Matters in Team Performance: Effects of Member Familiarity, Entrainment, and Task Discontinuity on Speed and Quality," *Personnel Psychology* 56, no. 3 (August 2003): 633–69.

22. R. Etherington, "Audi Announces New Design Strategy," *Dezeen*, December 19, 2012, http://www.dezeen.com/2012/12/19/audi-announces-new-car-design-strategy/.

23. D. S. Staples, I. K. Wong, and A. F. Cameron, "Best Practices for Virtual Team Effectiveness," *Virtual Teams: Projects, Protocols, and Processes* (2004): 160–85.

24. Kirkman and Rosen, "Beyond Self-Management."

25. S. Easton and G. Porter, "Selecting the Right Team Structure to Work in Your Organization," in *Handbook of Best Practices for Teams*, vol. 1, ed. G.M. Parker (Amherst: Irwin, 1996).

26. T. M. Welbourne, and T. A. Paterson, "Advancing a Richer View of Identity at Work: The Role-Based Identity Scale," *Personnel Psychology* (69)1 (2016), doi: 10.1111/peps.12150; R. Williams, "Self-Directed Work Teams: A Competitive Advantage," *Quality Digest*.

27. R. M. Yandrick, "SMWT's: A Team Effort—The Promise Of Teams Isn't Achieved Without Attention to Skills and Training," *Team Builders Plus*.

28. G. Jian, "Leader–Member Exchange Theory," (2016), DOI: 10.1002/9781118540190.wbeic195.

29. M. Zhanga, X. Zhaob, C. Voss, and G. Zhue, "Innovating Through Services, Co-Creation and Supplier Integration: Cases From China," *International Journal of Production Economics* (171)2 (2016): 289–300; R. J. Recardo, D. Wade, C.A. Mention, and J. Jolly, *Teams* (Houston: Gulf, 1996).

30. D. R. Denison, S. L. Hart, and J. A. Kahn, "From Chimneys to Cross-Functional Teams: Developing and Validating a Diagnostic Model," *Academy of Management Journal* 39, no. 4 (1996): 1005–23.

31. B. E. Brewer, A. Mitchell, R. Sanders, and P. Wallace, "Teaching and Learning in Cross-Disciplinary Virtual Teams," *Professional Communication, IEEE Transactions* (58) 2 (2015): 208–229, http://ieeexplore.ieee.org/xpls/abs_all.jsp?arnumber=7108078&tag=1; A. M. Townsend, S. M. DeMarie, and A. R. Hendrickson, "Virtual Teams: Technology and the Workplace of the Future," *Academy of Management Executive* 13, no. 3 (1998): 17–29.

32. F. Rendón, "Understanding the Proliferation of Virtual Teams in the Global Economy," *Huffington Post*, April 28, 2014, http://www.huffingtonpost.com/frankie-rendon/understanding-the-prolife_b_5212366.html.

33. A. M. Townsend, S. M. DeMarie, and A. R. Hendrickson, "Are You Ready for Virtual Teams?" *HR Magazine* 41, no. 9 (1996): 122–26.

34. J. B. Arbaugh, "Do Undergraduates and MBAs Differ Online?: Initial Conclusions From the Literature," *Journal of Leadership and Organizational Studies*, May 1, 2010: 129–42.

35. R. S. Wellins, W. C. Byham, and G. R. Dixon, *Inside Teams* (San Francisco: Jossey-Bass, 1994).

36. Townsend, DeMarie, and Hendrickson, "Virtual Teams."

37. W. F. Cascio, "Managing a Virtual Workplace," *Academy of Management Executive* 14 (2000): 81–90.

38. R. Katz, "The Effects of Group Longevity on Project Communication and Performance," *Administrative Science Quarterly* 27 (1982): 245–82.

39. D. Mankin, S. G. Cohen, and T. K. Bikson, *Teams and Technology: Fulfilling the Promise of the New Organization* (Cambridge, MA: Harvard Business School Press, 1996).

40. A. P. Ammeter and J. M. Dukerich, "Leadership, Team Building, and Team Member Characteristics in High Performance Project Teams," *Engineering Management* 14, no. 4 (2002): 3–11.

41. K. Lovelace, D. Shapiro, and L. Weingart, "Maximizing Cross-Functional New Product Teams' Innovativeness and Constraint Adherence: A Conflict Communications Perspective," *Academy of Management Journal* 44 (2001): 779–93.

42. L. Holpp and H. P. Phillips, "When Is a Team Its Own Worst Enemy?" *Training*, September 1, 1995, 71.

43. D. A. Cook, "Models of Interprofessional Learning in Canada," *Journal of Interprofessional Care* 19, no. 1 (2005): 107–15

44. S. Asche, "Opinions and Social Pressure," *Scientific American* 193 (1995): 31–35.

45. M. Friscolanti, "Canada in Lebanon: 'Canadian values in action,'" *Macleans*, December 2015, http://www.macleans.ca/news/world/canadas-ambassador-to-lebanon-it-truly-is-canadian-values-in-action/.

46. S. G. Cohen, G. E. Ledford, and G. M. Spreitzer, "A Predictive Model of Self-Managing Work Team Effectiveness," *Human Relations* 49, no. 5 (1996): 643–76.

47. P. Dunn and A. Shome, "Cultural Crossvergence and Social Desirability Bias: Ethical Evaluations by Chinese and Canadian Business Students," *Journal of Business Ethics* 85, no. 4 (2009): 527–43.

48. K. Bettenhausen and J. K. Murnighan, "The Emergence of Norms in Competitive Decision-Making Groups," *Administrative Science Quarterly* 30 (1985): 350–72.

49. R. Simpson, J. Sturges, A. Woods, and Y. Altman, "Career Progress and Career Barriers: Women MBA Graduates in Canada and the UK," *Career Development International* 9, no. 5 (2004): 459–77.

50. G. T. Lemmon, "Malala, Others on Front Lines in Fight for Women," CNN, January 10, 2013, http://www.cnn.com/2013/01/09/opinion/lemmon-malala-girls-rights/index.html.

51. World Economic Forum, "The Global Gender Gap Report 2015," http://www.weforum.org/reports/global-gender-gap-report-2015.

52. M. E. Shaw, *Group Dynamics* (New York: McGraw-Hill, 1981).

53. S. E. Jackson, "The Consequences of Diversity in Multidisciplinary Work Teams," in *Handbook of Work Group Psychology*, ed. M.A. West (Chichester: Wiley, 1996).

54. A. M. Isen and R. A. Baron, "Positive Affect as a Factor in Organizational Behavior," in *Research in Organizational Behavior* 13, ed. L. L. Cummings and B. M. Staw (Greenwich: JAI, 1991), 1–53.

55. C. R. Evans and K. L. Dion, "Group Cohesion and Performance: A Meta Analysis," *Small Group Research* 22, no. 2 (1991): 175–86.

56. R. Stankiewicsz, "The Effectiveness of Research Groups in Six Countries," in *Scientific Productivity*, ed. F. M. Andrews (Cambridge: Cambridge University Press, 1979), 191–221.

57. A. Proteau, "NHLPA Boss Don Fehr: Owners Likely To Lock Out Players Again," *The Hockey News*, December 18, 2014, http://www.thehockeynews.com/blog/nhlpa-boss-don-fehr-owners-likely-to-lock-out-players-again/; T. Booth, "Major League Soccer Players Want New Deal That Closes Salary Inequity," *The Globe and Mail*, March 4, 2015, http://www.theglobeandmail.com/sports/soccer/major-league-soccer-on-brink-of-players-strike/article23278443/; "A-League Player Strike Fear After FFA Withdraws Recognition of PFA," *The Guardian*, August 12, 2015, http://www.theguardian.com/football/2015/aug/12/a-league-player-strike-fear-after-ffa-withdraws-recognition-of-pfa.

58. F. Rees, *Teamwork From Start to Finish* (San Francisco: Jossey-Bass, 1997).

59. R. E. Silverman, "Tracking Sensors Invade the Workplace," *Wall Street Journal*, March 7, 2013, http://www.wsj.com/articles/SB10001424127887324034804578344303429080678; S. M. Gully, D. S. Devine, and D. J. Whitney, "A Meta-Analysis of Cohesion and Performance: Effects of Level of Analysis and Task Interdependence," *Small Group Research* 26, no. 4 (1995): 497–520.

60. E. Matson, "Four Rules for Fast Teams," *Fast Company*, August 1996, 87.

61. F. Tschan and M. V. Cranach, "Group Task Structure, Processes and Outcomes," in *Handbook of Work Group Psychology*, ed. M. A. West (Chichester: Wiley, 1996).

62. D. E. Yeatts and C. Hyten, *High Performance Self Managed Teams* (Thousand Oaks: Sage, 1998); H. M. Guttman and R. S. Hawkes, "New Rules for Strategic Development," *Journal of Business Strategy* 25, no. 1 (2004): 34–39.

63. M. Bhardwaj and A. Rana, "Key Software Metrics and Its Impact on Each Other for Software Development Projects," *International Journal of Electrical Computer and Engineering* (6)1 (2016): 242–248; Yeatts and Hyten, *High Performance Self Managed Teams*; Guttman and Hawkes, "New Rules"; J. Colquitt, R. Noe, and C. Jackson, "Justice in Teams: Antecedents and Consequences of Procedural Justice Climate," *Personnel Psychology*, April 1, 2002, 83.

64. A. Rassuli and J. P. Manzer, "'Teach Us to Learn': Multivariate Analysis of Perception of Success in Team Learning," *Journal of Education for Business* 81, no. 1 (2005): 21–27.

65. D. S. Kezsbom, "Re-opening Pandora's Box: Sources of Project Team Conflict in the '90s," *Industrial Engineering* 24, no. 5 (1992): 54–59.

66. A. C. Amason, W. A. Hochwarter, and K. R. Thompson, "Conflict: An Important Dimension in Successful Management Teams," *Organizational Dynamics* 24 (1995): 20.

67. A. C. Amason, "Distinguishing the Effects of Functional and Dysfunctional Conflict on Strategic Decision Making: Resolving a Paradox for Top Management Teams," *Academy of Management Journal* 39, no. 1 (1996): 123–48.

68. K. M. Eisenhardt, J. L. Kahwajy, and L. J. Bourgeois III, "How Management Teams Can Have a Good Fight," *Harvard Business Review* 75, no. 4 (July–August 1997): 77–85.

69. Eisenhardt et al., "How Management Teams."

70. C. Nemeth and P. Owens, "Making Work Groups More Effective: The Value of Minority Dissent," in *Handbook of Work Group Psychology*, ed. M.A. West (Chichester: Wiley, 1996).

71. J. M. Levin and R. L. Moreland, "Progress in Small Group Research," *Annual Review of Psychology* 9 (1990): 72–78; S. E. Jackson, "Team Composition in Organizational Settings: Issues in Managing a Diverse Work Force," in *Group Processes and Productivity*, ed. S. Worchel, W. Wood, and J. Simpson (Beverly Hills: Sage, 1992).

72. P. A. Lapointe and G. Cucumel, "An Alternative Typology for Teamwork," *World Review of Entrepreneurship, Management and Sustainable Development* (12)1 (2016), Université Laval, Québec QC. DOI: 10.1504/WREMSD.2016.073431; Eisenhardt, et al., "How Management Teams."

73. B. W. Tuckman, "Development Sequence in Small Groups," *Psychological Bulletin* 63, no. 6 (1965): 384–99.

74. Gross, *Compensation for Teams*.

75. J. F. McGrew, J. G. Bilotta, and J. M. Deeney, "Software Team Formation and Decay: Extending the Standard Model for Small Groups," *Small Group Research* 30, no. 2 (1999): 209–34.

76. McGrew et al., "Software Team Formation."

77. L. Lee-Kelley, J. Crossman, and A. Cannings, "A Social Interaction Approach to Managing the 'Invisibles' of Virtual Teams," *Industrial Management and Data Systems* 104, no. 8 (2004): 650–57.

78. McGrew et al., "Software Team Formation."

79. J. R. Hackman, "The Psychology of Self-Management in Organizations," in *Psychology and Work: Productivity, Change, and Employment*, ed. M. S. Pallak and R. Perloff (Washington: APA, 1986), 85–136.

80. A. O'Leary-Kelly, J. J. Martocchio, and D. D. Frink, "A Review of the Influence of Group Goals on Group Performance," *Academy of Management Journal* 37, no. 5 (1994): 1285–301.

81. A. Cuenllas, "Whole Foods Case Study: A Benchmark Model of Management for Hospitality," HospitalityNet, February 11, 2013, http://www.hospitalitynet.org/news/4059396.html; J. Lee-Young, "Recruiters Find 'Very Good Candidates' Available to Fill Positions at New Stores," April 20, 2015, *Vancouver Sun*, http://www.vancouversun.com/business/commercial-real-estate/Store+closings+sales+managerial+talent+market/10988650/story.html#ixzz40lvlcVpk.

82. A. Zander, "The Origins and Consequences of Group Goals," in *Retrospections on Social Psychology,* ed. L. Festinger (New York: Oxford University Press, 1980), 205–35.

83. M. Erez and A. Somech, "Is Group Productivity Loss the Rule or the Exception? Effects of Culture and Group-Based Motivation," *Academy of Management Journal* 39, no. 6 (1996): 1513–37.

84. S. Sherman, "Stretch Goals: The Dark Side of Asking for Miracles," *Fortune,* 13 November 1995, 231.

85. S. Kerr and S. Landauer, "Using Stretch Goals to Promote Organizational Effectiveness and Personal Growth: General Electric and Goldman Sachs," *Academy of Management Executive* (November 2004): 134–38.

86. K. R. Thompson, W. A. Hochwarter, and N. J. Mathys, "Stretch Targets: What Makes Them Effective?" *Academy of Management Executive* 11, no. 3 (1997): 48–60.

87. G. Hamel, "25 Stretch Goals for Management," *Harvard Business Review,* February 25, 2009, https://hbr.org/2009/02/25-stretch-goals-for-managemen/; Parker, *Team Players and Teamwork.*

88. B. Stone, "Inside Google's Secret Lab," *BloombergBusiness,* May 22, 2013, http://www.bloomberg.com/bw/articles/2013-05-22/inside-googles-secret-lab.

89. Dumaine, "The Trouble with Teams."

90. G. A. Neuman, S. H. Wagner, and N. D. Christiansen, "The Relationship Between Work-Team Personality Composition and the Job Performance of Teams," *Group and Organization Management* 24, no. 1 (1999): 28–45.

91. M. A. Campion, G. J. Medsker, and A. C. Higgs, "Relations Between Work Group Characteristics and Effectiveness: Implications for Designing Effective Work Groups," *Personnel Psychology* 46, no. 4 (1993): 823–50.

92. B. L. Kirkman and D. L. Shapiro, "The Impact of Cultural Values on Employee Resistance to Teams: Toward a Model of Globalized Self-Managing Work Team Effectiveness," *Academy of Management Review* 22, no. 3 (1997): 730–57.

93. M. Hoffart, "Marketing Week at BCIT," British Columbia Institute of Technology, October 17, 2015, http://commons.bcit.ca/update/2015/10/marketing-week-at-bcit/; "SAP Salaries in Vancouver, BC," Glassdoor.ca, https://www.glassdoor.ca/Salary/SAP-Vancouver-Salaries-EI_IE10471.0,3_IL.4,13_IM972.htm; C. Fishman, "Engines of Democracy," *Fast Company,* October 1, 1999, 174.

94. J. Bunderson and K. Sutcliffe, "Comparing Alternative Conceptualizations of Functional Diversity in Management Teams: Process and Performance Effects," *Academy of Management Journal* 45 (2002): 875–93.

95. J. Barbian, "Getting to Know You," *Training,* June 2001: 60–63.

96. J. Smith, "What It's REALLY Like to Work at Whole Foods?" *Business Insider,* April 9, 2015, http://www.businessinsider.com/what-its-really-like-to-work-at-whole-foods-market-2015-4.

97. J. Hackman, "New Rules for Team Building—the Times Are Changing," *Optimize,* July 1, 2002, 50.

98. J. Christenson, G. Innes, D. McKnight, and B. Boychuk, "Safety and Efficiency of Emergency Department Assessment of Chest Discomfort," *Canadian Medical Association Journal* 170, no. 1 (2004): 1803–7; C. S. Burke, E. Salas, K. Wilson-Donnelly, and H. Priest, "How to Turn a Team of Experts Into an Expert Medical Team: Guidance From the Aviation and Military Communities," *British Medical Journal* 13, no. 1 (2004): 96–104.

99. Joinson, "Teams at Work."

100. K. Mollica, "Stay Above the Fray: Protect Your Time—and Your Sanity—by Coaching Employees to Deal With Interpersonal Conflicts on Their Own," *HRMagazine,* April 2005, 111.

101. S. Caudron, "Tie Individual Pay to Team Success," *Personnel Journal* 73, no. 10 (October 1994): 40.

102. S. W. J. Kozlowski, G. T. Chao, and C. H. Chan, "Team Dynamics: Using 'Big Data' to Advance the Science of Team Effectiveness," in *Big Data at Work; The Data Science Revolution and Organizational Psychology* (New York, N.Y.: Routledge Academic, 2016); Caudron, "Tie Individual Pay."

103. Gross, *Compensation for Teams,* 85.

104. G. Ledford, "Three Case Studies on Skill-Based Pay: An Overview," *Compensation and Benefits Review* 23, no. 2 (1991): 11–24.

105. J. R. Schuster and P. K. Zingheim, *The New Pay: Linking Employee and Organizational Performance* (New York: Lexington, 1992).

106. S. G. Cohen and D. E. Bailey, "What Makes Teams Work: Group Effectiveness Research From the Shop Floor to the Executive Suite," *Journal of Management* 23, no. 3 (1997): 239–90.

107. S. Berglas, "How to Keep 'A' Players Productive," *Harvard Business Review,* September 2006, 1–8.

108. R. Allen and R. Kilmann, "Aligning Reward Practices in Support of Total Quality Management," *Business Horizons* 44 (May 2001): 77–85.

10

1. Canada, Department of Justice, Canada Labour Code, http://laws-lois.justice.gc.ca/eng/acts/L-2.

2. Government of Canada, *Canadian Charter of Rights and Freedoms,* 2010, http://laws.justice.gc.ca/en/charter.

3. L. Mayor, "Female Firefighters Face Bullying, Sexual Harassment, *Fifth Estate* Finds," CBC News, November 6, 2015, http://www.cbc.ca/news/canada/female-firefighters-bullying-sexual-harassment-fifth-estate-1.3305509; W. Chow, "Fire Hall 6 to Be Renovated to Accommodate Firefighters," *Burnaby NewsLeader,* 2011, http://www.burnabynewsleader.com/news/124782979.html; "Female Firefighters All Off the Job," *Vancouver Province,* March 22, 2006, http://www.canada.com/theprovince/news/story.html?id=7817f631-f71c-4f55-8630-8589aebd718b; "Female Firefighters Walk Off Job in B.C. City, Alleging Harassment," CBC News, March 21, 2006, http://www.cbc.ca/canada/story/2006/03/21/firefighters-richmond060321.html#ixzz0sZm4R3eU; K. Bryce, "Nanaimo Fire Department Hires Its First Professional Female Firefighter," *Nanaimo Daily News,* May 27, 2010, http://www2.canada.com/nanaimodailynews/news/story.html?id=e43e59e9-2a9d-448f-8775-84d6d2c6734c.

4. Women's Legal Education and Action Fund, "Supreme Court Decides Fitness Test Discriminates Against B.C. Woman Firefighter," September 9, 1999, http://www.leaf.ca/media/releases/BCGSEU_Media_Release_September_9_1999.pdf.

5. Government of Canada, Canadian Human Rights Commission, http://www.chrc-ccdp.gc.ca/eng.

6. Province of British Columbia, "Work-Safe BC: Regulation and Related Materials," 2016, http://www2.worksafebc.com/publications/ohsregulation/regulation.asp.

7. G. T. Clarke and A. Rennebohm, "Canada: Bill 14: The New Bullying Law in BC—Is Your Workplace Prepared?" 2014, http://www.mondaq.com/canada/x/186376/employee+rights+labour+relations/BILL+14+THE+NEW+BULLYING+LAW+IN+BC+IS+YOUR+WORKPLACE+PREPARED.

8. Canadian Bar Association, B.C. Branch, "Sexual Harassment," 2013, http://cbabc.org/For-the-Public/Dial-A-Law/Scripts/Employment-and-Social-Benefits/271.

9. B. Etherington, ed., "Systematic Inequality and Workplace Culture: Challenging the Institutionalization of Sexual Harassment," *Canadian Labour and Employment Law Journal* 3 (1993), http://personnel.mcgill.ca/files/colleen.sheppard/Systemic_Inequality_Workplace.pdf; *Alpaerts v. Obront* [1993] OJ #732 (QL) (OCJGD), http://www.isthatlegal.ca/index.php?name=jurisdiction2.small_claims_court_law_ontario.

10. Ontario Human Rights Commission, 2016, http://www.ohrc.on.ca/en/learning/what-discrimination/harassment.

11. D. A. Lubin, "Courts Won't Tolerate Toxic Management," *Metro Canada,* February 17, 2010, http://metronews.ca/news/178046/courts-wont-tolerate-toxic-management.

12. P. Loriggio, January. 22, 2016. "Toronto Man Found Not Guilty in Twitter Harassment Trial," *The Globe and Mail–The Canadian Press,* http://www.theglobeandmail.com/news/toronto/verdict-expected-today-in-twitter-harassment-trial/article28334101/.

13. D. A. Lublin, "Is Your Boss Just Tough, or a Bully?", *Globe and Mail,* August 8, 2012, http://www.theglobeandmail.com/report-on-business/careers/career-advice/life-at-work/is-your-boss-just-tough-or-a-bully/article4469548.

14. Lublin, "Is Your Boss Just Tough, or a Bully?"

15. J. P. Tasker and A. Crawford, February 19, 2016. "Latest RCMP Harassment Allegations an 'Embarrassment,' Public Safety Minister Says," CBC News, http://www.cbc.ca/news/politics/ralph-goodale-rcmp-harassment-1.3455802; N. Clancy, "Ralph Goodale to Review Harassment Cases of B.C. Women Suing RCMP," CBC News, November 7, 2015, http://www.cbc.ca/news/canada/british-columbia/public-safety-minister-to-review-cases-of-rcmp-harassment-1.3309491; A. Sagan, "Defence Team in RCMP Harassment Case Plans to Strike Down Discrimination Claims," August 2, 2012, http://www.theglobeandmail.com/news/british-columbia/defence-team-in-rcmp-harassment-case-plans-to-strike-down-discrimination-claims/article4459487/.

16. Preventing Harassment, Discrimination and Violence in the Legal Workplace, (2012). *The Law Society of Upper Canada,* http://www.lsuc.on.ca/WorkArea/DownloadAsset.aspx?id=2147487137; E. Peirce, C.A. Smolinski, and B. Rosen, "Why Sexual Harassment Complaints Fall on Deaf Ears," *Academy of Management Executive* 12, no. 3 (1998): 41–54.; H. Burnett-Nichols, "Sexual Harassment Best Practices: University Community as Partners," March 8, 2010, http://www.universityaffairs.ca/sexual-hrassment-best-practices.aspx; "BCIT

Harassment and Discrimination Policies," 2010, http://www.bcit.ca/harassment; "SFU Human Rights Policy," 2013, http://www.sfu.ca/humanrights.html; UBC Equity Office, http://equity.ubc.ca/who/message-from-the-associate-vice-president-equity.

17. "Campus Sexual Assault Reports," *CBC News*, February 9, 2015, http://www.cbc.ca/news/multimedia/interactive-campus-sexual-assault-reports-1.2944538; Province of Ontario, "The New Mandate of the Ontario Human Rights Commission," http://www.ohrc.on.ca/en/ontario-human-right s-commission-200910%E2%80%93201112-business -plan/mandate; http://www.isthatlegal.ca/index.php?name=jurisdiction2.small_claims_court_law_ontario; Simon Fraser University, "Protocol for Investigation: Human Rights Policy (GP18)," April 30, 2008, http://www.sfu.ca/humanrights/guides-protocols/investigation-protocol.html; S. Katz, "Sexual Relations Between Students and Faculty: A Look at the Sexual Harassment Policies at Canadian Universities," January 10, 2010, http://www.universityaffairs.ca/sexual-relations-between-students-faculty.aspx.

18. A. Muller, "Build a Great Team: Then Plan to Grow," *Entrepreneurs, Forbes*, 2016, http://www.forbes.com/sites/kauffman/2012/06/22/build-a -great-team-then-plan-to-grow/#697f758644fe.

19. R. D. Gatewood and H. S. Field, *Human Resource Selection* (Fort Worth: Dryden, 1998).

20. Gatewood and Field, *Human Resource Selection*.

21. Human Resources, "Total Compensation—Other Duties as Assigned: The Importance of Keeping Up-To-Date Job Descriptions," Ryerson University, http://www.ryerson.ca/hr/yourHR/total -comp/job_descriptions.html.

22. Human Resources, "Total Compensation—Other Duties as Assigned: The Importance of Keeping Up-To-Date Job Descriptions," Ryerson University, http://www.ryerson.ca/hr/yourHR/total -comp/job_descriptions.html.

23. *British Columbia (Public Service Employee Relations Commission) v. BCGSEU*, [1999] 3 S.C.R. 3 9 September 1999, http://scc.lexum.org/decisia -scc-csc/scc-csc/scc-csc/en/item/1724/index.do.

24. V. M. Catano, W. H. Wiesner, and R. D. Hackett, *Recruitment and Selection in Canada, Fifth Edition* (Toronto: Nelson Education, 2013), 125; Canadian Human Rights Commission, "I Want to Know More About Human Rights," 2016, http://www.chrc-ccdp.gc.ca/eng/content/i-want-know -more-about-human-rights.

25. R. Silverman and L. Weber, "An Inside Job: More Firms Opt to Recruit from Within," *Wall Street Journal*, May 29, 2012, http://www.wsj.com/articles/SB10001424052702303395604577434563715828218.

26. M. Lev-Ram, "IBM CEO Ginni Rometty Gets Past the Big Blues" *Fortune*, September 18, 2014, http://fortune.com/2014/09/18/ginni-rometty-ibm/.

27. M. Belcourt, K. J. McBey, Y. Hong, and M. Yap, *Strategic Human Resource Planning*, 6th ed. (Nelson: Toronto, 2016).

28. H. M. Chehade and S. T. El Hajjar, "An Empirical Study to Examine the Effect of Realistic Job Preview on Expectancies, Personal Goals and Performance," *International Journal of Business and Management (11)*2 (2016): 164.

29. J. Breaugh and M. Starke, "Research on Employee Recruitment: So Many Studies, So Many Remaining Questions," *Journal of Management* 26 (2000): 405–34.

30. J. A. Hoek, P. O'Kane, and M. McCracken, "Publishing Personal Information Online: How Employers Access, Observe and Utilise Social Networking Sites Within Selection Procedures," *Personnel Review (45)*1 (2016); M. Granovetter, "Optimal Social-Networking Strategy Is a Function of Socioeconomic Conditions," *Psychological Science* 74, no. 5 (2012).

31. J. Manyika, S. Lund, K. Robinson, J. Valentino, and R. Dobbs, "Connecting Talent With Opportunity in the Digital Age," McKinsey Global Institute–McKinsey & Company, 2015, http://www.mckinsey.com/global-themes/employment-and-growth/connecting-talent-with-opportunity-in-the-digital-age.

32. Manyika et al., "Connecting Talent With Opportunity in the Digital Age."

33. K. Sundheim, "The Internet's Profound Impact on the Recruiting Industry," *Forbes*, April 2, 2013, http://www.forbes.com/sites/kensundheim/2013/04/02/the-internets-profound-impact-on-the -recruiting-industry/#520695316459; "Internet Recruitment Report," NAS Insights, http://www.nasrecruitment.com/our-thinking/nas-insights/.

34. K. Sundheim, "A Guide to Hiring Recruitment Firms," *Forbes*, September 19, 2013, http://www.forbes.com/sites/kensundheim/2013/09/19/331/#4a59ee637825.

35. C. Gordon, "Getting a Job at Facebook: Inside the 'Meritocratic' Hiring Process," AOL Jobs, October 5, 2012, http://jobs.aol.com/articles/2012/10/05/want-to-get-a-job-at-facebook-weve -demystified-the-hiring-proc/.

36. Government of Alberta, Human Rights Commission, "A Recommended Guide for Pre-Employment Inquiries," 2013, http://www.albertahumanrights.ab.ca/publications/bulletins _sheets_booklets/sheets/hr_and_employment/pre_employment_inquiries_guide.asp.

37. I. Dichev, J. Graham, C. R. Harvey, and S. Rajgopal, "The Misrepresentation of Earnings," *Financial Analysts Journal, (72)*1 (2016); M. N. Wexler, "Successful Résumé Fraud: Conjectures on the Origins of Amorality in the Workplace," *Journal of Human Values* 12, no. 2 (2006): 137–52.

38. S. Adler, "Verifying a Job Candidate's Background: The State of Practice in a Vital Human Resources Activity," *Review of Business* 15, no. 2 (1993–94): 3–8.

39. S. McMurray, et al., "Employer Demands From Business Graduates," *Education+ Training* 58.1 (2016); V. M. Catano, W. H. Wiesner, and R. D. Hackett, *Recruitment and Selection in Canada, Fifth Edition,* (Toronto: Nelson Education, 2013), 325.

40. *Wallace v. United Grain Growers Ltd.,* [1997] 3 S.C.R. 701, http://scc.lexum.org/decisia-scc-csc/scc-csc/scc-csc/en/item/1557/index.do.

41. Public Works and Government Services Canada, "How to Complete the Personnel Screening, Consent and Authorization Form (TBS/SCT 330-23)—Industrial Security Program—Public Works and Government Services Canada (PWGSC)," 2016, http://ssi-iss.tpsgc-pwgsc.gc.ca/outils-tools/330-23-eng.html; M. Le, T. Nguyen, and B. Kleiner, "Legal Counsel: Don't Be Sued for Negligent Hiring," *Nonprofit World*, May 1, 2003, 14–15.

42. E.A. Fattah, ed. *From Crime Policy to Victim Policy: Reorienting the Justice System.* (Springer, 2016); "Why It's Critical to Set a Policy on Background Checks for New Hires," *Managing Accounts Payable*, September 2004, 6; J. Schramm, "Future Focus: Background Checking," *HR Magazine*, January 2005.

43. D. Arms, and T. Bercik, "10 Hiring Mistakes to Avoid," *Strategic Finance (97)*7 (2016), p. 46; C. Cohen, "Reference Checks," *CA Magazine*, November 2004, 41.

44. J. Teitel, "Fired Over Facebook: The Consequences of Discussing Work Online," *Western Journal of Legal Studies* 2, no. 2 (2012): 1–22; M. Shaw, "Air Canada Workers May Be Fired Over Facebook Comments," *Toronto Sun*, February 12, 2013, http://www.torontosun.com/2013/02/13/air-canada -workers-may-be-fired-over-facebook-comments; A. Frank, "Your Facebook Status Can Cost You Your Job," Monster.ca, 2013, http://career-advice.monster.ca/in-the-workplace/leaving-a-job/fired -over–facebook-comments-canada/article.aspx; M. Fitzgibbon, "Social Media and Background Checks," September 3, 2009, http://www.slaw.ca/2009/09/03/social-media-background-checks; Back-Check, "Criminal Record Check for Employment Screening," 2010, http://www.backcheck.ca; CBC News, "NDP Candidate in B.C. Election Quits Over Racy Photos in Facebook," April 20, 2009, http://www.cbc.ca/canada/bcvotes2009/story/2009/04/20/bc-election-lam-facebook.html.

45. R. Blackwell, "Answering the Hiring Question With Psychological Testing," *Globe and Mail*, November 1, 2011, http://www.theglobeandmail.com/report-on-business/careers/answering-the-hiring -question-with-psychological-testing/article4199936.

46. P. R. Sackett, et al., "Predictor Content Matters for Knowledge Testing: Evidence Supporting Content Validation," *Human Performance (29)*1 (2016): 54–71; J. Hunter, "Cognitive Ability, Cognitive Aptitudes, Job Knowledge, and Job Performance," *Journal of Vocational Behavior* 29 (1986): 340–62.

47. F. L. Schmidt, "The Role of General Cognitive Ability and Job Performance: Why There Cannot Be a Debate," *Human Performance* 15 (2002): 187–210.

48. K. Murphy, "Can Conflicting Perspectives on the Role of g in Personnel Selection Be Resolved?", *Human Performance* 15 (2002): 173–86.

49. "Army Air Force Elimination Board and Assembling Objects Test AO," *Applied Measurement: Industrial Psychology in Human Resources Management (2)* (2016): 415; J. R. Glennon, L. E. Albright, and W. A. Owens, *A Catalog of Life History Items* (Greensboro: Richardson Foundation, 1966).

50. Gatewood and Field, *Human Resource Selection*.

51. I. Kotlyar and K. Ades, "HR Technology: Assessment Technology Can Help Match the Best Applicant to the Right Job," *HR Magazine*, May 1, 2002, 97.

52. F. Kuschnereit, "Improving the Accuracy of Biodata Questionnaires" (Saint John: University of New Brunswick, 2001), http://dspace.hil.unb.ca:8080/xmlui/bitstream/handle/1882/42937/MQ68253.pdf?sequence=1.

53. A. Wilkinson and S. Johnstone, eds., *Encyclopedia of Human Resource Management* (Melbourne: Edward Elgar Publishing, 2016).

54. E. M. Berman, et al., *Human Resource Management in Public Service: Paradoxes, Processes, and Problems.* Sage Publications; R. Gatewood, H. Feild, and M. Barrick *Human Resource Selection,* (Toronto: Nelson Education, 2015); T. T. Pittinsky and B. Welle, "Negative Outgroup Leader Actions Increase Liking for Ingroup Leaders: An Experimental Test of Intergroup Leader-Enhancement Effects," *Group Processes Intergroup Relations* 11, no. 4 (2008): 513–23; G. G. Manley, J. Benavidez, and K. Dunn, "Development of a Personality Biodata Measure to Predict Ethical Decision Making," *Journal of Managerial Psychology* 22, no. 7 (2007): 664–82.

55. A. Furnham, *The Psychology of Behaviour at Work: The Individual and the Organization*, 2nd ed. (New York: Psychology Press, 2012); A. Furnham, *Personality and Intelligence at Work: Exploring and Explaining Individual differences at Work* (New York: Psychology Press, 2008).

56. P. V. Ingold., et al., "Why Do Situational Interviews Predict Job Performance? The Role of Interviewees' Ability to Identify Criteria," *Journal of Business and Psychology (30)*2 (2015): 387–398; M. S. Taylor and J. A. Sniezek,

"The College Recruitment Interview: Topical Content and Applicant Reactions," *Journal of Occupational Psychology* 57 (1984): 157–68.

57. R. Burnett, C. Fan, S. J. Motowidlo, and T. DeGroot, "Interview Notes and Validity," *Personnel Psychology* 51, no. 10 (1998): 375–96; M. A. Campion, D. K. Palmer, and J. E. Campion, "A Review of Structure in the Selection Interview," *Personnel Psychology* 50, no. 3 (1997): 655–702.

58. Campion et al., "A Review of Structure in the Selection Interview."

59. T. Judge, "The Employment Interview: A Review of Recent Research and Recommendations for Future Research," *Human Resource Management Review* 10, no. 4 (2000): 383–406.

60. J. Cortina, N. Goldstein, S. Payne, K. Davison, and S. Gilliland, "The Incremental Validity of Interview Scores Over and Above Cognitive Ability and Conscientiousness Scores," *Personnel Psychology* 53, no. 2 (2000): 325–51.

61. F. Méndez and F. Sepúlveda, "A Comparative Study of Training in the Private and Public Sectors: Evidence From the United Kingdom and the United States," *Contemporary Economic Policy (34)*1 (2016): 107–118; "How Top Companies Make The ROI Case For Employee Training," December 1, 2014, http://www.skilledup.com/insights/how-top-companies-make-the-roi-case-for-employee-training; S. Livingston, T. W. Gerdel, M. Hill, B. Yerak, C. Melvin, and B. Lubinger, "Ohio's Strongest Companies All Agree That Training Is Vital to Their Success," *Cleveland Plain Dealer*, May 21, 1997, 30S; Rigzone, "Today's Trends: U.S., Canadian E&P Spending Estimates Rise," June 18, 2010, http://www.rigzone.com/news/article.asp?a_id=94873; Canadian Society for Training and Development, "Investing in People," 2010, http://c.ymcdn.com/sites/www.cstd.ca/resource/resmgr/iip/metastudy.pdf.

62. Conference Board of Canada, "Canadian Organizations Spending More on Staff Training: A Step in the Right Direction," February 25, 2014, http://www.conferenceboard.ca/press/newsrelease/14-02-25/canadian_organizations_spending_more_on_staff_training_a_step_in_the_right_direction.aspx.

63. Oil Spill Training Company, http://the-oil-spill-training-company.software.informer.com; CBC News , "BP Oil Spill Price Tag Hits $2 Billion," June 21, 2010, http://www.cbc.ca/world/story/2010/06/21/bp-oil-well-cost.html.

64. D. L. Kirkpatrick, "Four Steps to Measuring Training Effectiveness," *Personnel Administrator* 28 (1983): 19–25.

65. L. Gills and A. Bailey, "ROI Case Study Methodology: Putting the Pieces Together," *Canadian Society for Training and Development*, 2009, http://c.ymcdn.com/sites/www.cstd.ca/resource/resmgr/iip/metastudy.pdf.

66. J. Stack, "The Curse of the Annual Performance Review," *Inc.*, March 1, 1997, 39.

67. M. Ikramullah, et al., "Effectiveness of Performance Appraisal: Developing a Conceptual Framework Using Competing Values Approach," *Personnel Review* (2016); D. Murphy, "Are Performance Appraisals Worse Than a Waste of Time? Book Derides Unintended Consequences," *San Francisco Chronicle*, September 9, 2001, W1.

68. J. Shields, et al., *Managing Employee Performance & Reward: Concepts, Practices, Strategies* (Cambridge University Press, 2015); U. J. Wiersma and G. P. Latham, "The Practicality of Behavioral Observation Scales, Behavioral Expectation Scales, and Trait Scales," *Personnel Psychology* 39 (1986): 619–28; U. J. Wiersma, P. T. Van Den Berg, and G. P. Latham, "Dutch Reactions to Behavioral Observation, Behavioral Expectation, and Trait Scales," *Group and Organization Management* 20 (1995): 297–309.

69. J. K. Ellington and M. A. Wilson, "The Performance Appraisal Milieu: A Multilevel Analysis of Context Effects in Performance Ratings," *Journal of Business and Psychology*, (2016): 1–14; N. P. Sharma, T. Sharma, and M. N. Agarwal., "Measuring Employee Perception of Performance Management System Effectiveness: Conceptualization and Scale Development," *Employee Relations: The International Journal (38)*2 (2016); D. J. Schleicher, D. V. Day, B. T. Mayes, and R. E. Riggio, "A New Frame for Frame-of-Reference Training: Enhancing the Construct Validity of Assessment Centers," *Journal of Applied Psychology* (August 2002): 735–46.

70. M. Cuticelli, M. Collier-Meek, and M. Coyne, "Increasing the Quality of Tier 1 Reading Instruction: Using Performance Feedback to Increase Opportunities to Respond During Implementation of a Core Reading Program," *Psychology in the Schools (53)*1 (2016): 89–105; H. H. Meyer, "A Solution to the Performance Appraisal Feedback Enigma," *Academy of Management Executive* 5, no. 1 (1991): 68–76; G. C. Thornton, "Psychometric Properties of Self-Appraisals of Job Performance," *Personnel Psychology* 33 (1980): 263–71.

71. A. Waldman, L. E. Atwater, and D. Antonioni, "Has 360 Feedback Gone Amok?", *Academy of Management Executive* 12, no. 2 (1998): 86–94.

72. J. Smither, M. London, R. Flautt, Y. Vargas, and I. Kucine, "Can Working With an Executive Coach Improve Multisource Feedback Ratings Over Time? A Quasi-Experimental Field Study," *Personnel Psychology* (Spring 2003): 21–43.

73. J. McGregor, "The Employee Is Always Right," *BusinessWeek*, November 8, 2007, http://www.businessweek.com/globalbiz/content/nov2007/gb2007118_541063.htm.

74. A. Walker and J. Smither, "A Five-Year Study of Upward Feedback: What Managers Do With Their Results Matters," *Personnel Psychology* (Summer 1999): 393–422.

75. G. T. Milkovich and J. M. Newman, *Compensation*, 4th ed. (Homewood: Irwin, 1993).

76. D. S. Gilchrist, M. Luca, and D. Malhotra, "When 3+ 1> 4: Gift Structure and Reciprocity in the Field," *Management Science* (2016); M. L. Williams and G. F. Dreher, "Compensation System Attributes and Applicant Pool Characteristics," *Academy of Management Journal* 35, no. 3 (1992): 571–95.

77. S. Kossoudji, "Migration and the Labor Force," *The Wiley Blackwell Encyclopedia of Race, Ethnicity, and Nationalism* (2016); J. H. Carens, "Live-in Domestics, Seasonal Workers, and Others Hard to Locate on the Map of Democracy," *Journal of Political Philosophy—Special Issue: Philosophy, Politics, and* Society 16, no. 4 (2008): 419–45.

78. Proform Concrete Services Inc., "Profit Sharing Retirement Savings Program (PSRSP)," http://www.proformconcrete.com/.

79. J. A. Harrison, P. Singh, and S. Frawley, "What Does Employee Ownership Effectiveness Look Like? The Case of a Canadian-Based Firm," *Canadian Journal of Administrative Sciences/ Revue Canadienne des Sciences de l'Administration* (2016); C. Jensen, "Research and Legislation on ESOPs Could Have Positive Effects for Canada," *Axiom News*, January 19, 2009, http://www.axiomnews.ca/node/457.

80. M. Humphery-Jenner, et al. "Executive Overconfidence and Compensation Structure," *Journal of Financial Economics* (2016); J. Seo, et al., "The Role of CEO Relative Standing in Acquisition Behavior and CEO Pay," *Strategic Management Journal (37)*2 (2016): 425; M. Bloom, "The Performance Effects of Pay Dispersion on Individuals and Organizations," *Academy of Management Journal* 42, no. 1 (1999): 25–40.

81. O. V. Petrenko, et al., "Corporate Social Responsibility or CEO Narcissism? CSR Motivations and Organizational Performance," *Strategic Management Journal (37)*2 (2016): 262–279; D. B. Grusky and A. MacLean, "The Social Fallout of a High-Inequality Regime," *The Annals of the American Academy of Political and Social Science (663)*1 (2016): 33–52; AFL-CIO, "2007 Trends in CEO Pay," http://www.aflcio.org/Corporate-Watch/CEO-Pay-and-You; C. Hymowitz, "Pay Gap Fuels Worker Woes," *Wall Street Journal*, April 28, 2008, B8.

82. K. van Veen, and R. Wittek, "Relational Signalling and the Rise of CEO Compensation: '. . . It Is Not Just About Money, It Is About What the Money Says. . .,'" *Long Range Planning* (2016); M. Hayek, C. H. Thomas, and M. M. Novicevic, "Contextualizing Human Capital Theory in a Non-Western Setting: Testing the Pay-for-Performance Assumption," *Journal of Business Research (69)*2 (2016): 928–935; I. Dichev, J. Graham, and C. R. Harvey, "The Misrepresentation of Earnings," *Financial Analysts Journal (72)*1 (2016): 22–35; W. Grossman and R. E. Hoskisson, "CEO Pay at the Crossroads of Wall Street and Main: Toward the Strategic Design of Executive Compensation," *Academy of Management Executive* 12, no. 1 (1998): 43–57.

83. M. Bloom, "Performance Effects," 2010, http://www.keepjobsincanada.ca; "Canada Lost 129,000 Jobs in January: StatsCan," CBC News, February 6, 2009, http://www.cbc.ca/money/story/2009/02/06/januaryjobs.html#ixzz0sbRAATYf.M.

84. M. Bloom and J. G. Michel, "The Relationships Among Organizational Context, Pay Dispersion, and Managerial Turnover," *Academy of Management Journal* 45 (2002): 33–42.

85. *Ontario Employment Standards Act 2000,* http://www.e-laws.gov.on.ca/html/statutes/english/elaws_statutes_00e41_e.htm; Ontario Ministry of Labour, "Termination of Employment Defined," http://www.labour.gov.on.ca/english/es/pubs/poster_text.php.

86. R. Younglai, "Alberta's Blue-Collar Workers Worst Off in Oil Slump," *The Globe and Mail*, January 17, 2016, http://www.theglobeandmail.com/report-on-business/economy/jobs/albertas-lower-income-earners-blue-collar-workers-hit-hardest-by-oil-slump/article28233859/; R. Younglai, "Alberta Has Twice as Many EI Recipients as a Year Ago," The *Globe and Mail*, November 19, 2015, http://www.theglobeandmail.com/report-on-business/ei-recipients-in-alberta-at-highest-level-since-2010/article27364247/; M. Toneguzzi, "Group Layoffs in Alberta Close 2015 at More Than 17,000 People—Up 134% From 2014," *The Calgary Herald*, January 7, 2016, http://calgaryherald.com/business/energy/group-layoffs-in-alberta-close-2015-at-more-than-17000-people-up-134-from-2014.

87. L. M. Bernard, *The Employers' Guide to Termination Law in Ontario: Termination Payments Under Ontario Law: The Employment Standards Act ("ESA") and the Common Law* (2016); P. Michal-Johnson, *Saying Good-Bye: A Manager's Guide to Employee Dismissal* (Glenview: Scott, Foresman, 1985).

88. J. Strickland, "Zynga Layoffs: The Aftermath," *Inc.*, June 3, 2013, http://www.inc.com/julie-strickland/zynga-lay-off-eighteen-percent-staff-close-three-offices.html.

89. L. Ryser, S. Markey, and G. Halseth, "The Workers' Perspective: The Impacts of Long Distance Labour Commuting in a Northern Canadian Small Town," *The Extractive Industries and Society* (2016); G. Friebel, M. Heinz, and N. Zubanov, *The Effect of Announced Downsizing on Workplace Performance: Evidence From a Retail Chain*

(2016); M. Mentzer, "Study Suggests Downsizing Is a Fad That Does More Damage Than Good," *Canadian Journal of Administrative Sciences* 8, no. 12 (1996): 23–42, https://www.questia.com/library/journal/1P3-10317987/corporate-downsizing-and-profitability-in-canada.

90. B. Jung, B. Kim, W. J. Lee, and C. Y. Yoo, "Are Layoff Decisions of American Corporations Efficient?" *KAIST College of Business Working Paper Series 2016-001* (2016); J. R. Morris, W. F. Cascio, and C. E. Young, "Downsizing After All These Years: Questions and Answers About Who Did It, How Many Did It, and Who Benefited from It," *Organizational Dynamics* 27, no. 3 (1999): 78–87.

91. R. Darmon, "Profit and Opportunity Cost Outcomes of Sales Force Turnover and Recruiting Strategies Upon Various Performance Segments," *Marketing Challenges in a Turbulent Business Environment* (Springer International Publishing, 2016): 665–669; M. A. Sanjeev, N. Abidi, and A. V. Surya, "Functionality of Turnover Intention and Management Strategies for Sales Force: An Empirical Investigation," *International Journal of Management Practice (9)*1 (2016): 24–39; K. Maher, "Hiring Freezes Cushion New Layoffs," *Wall Street Journal*, January 24, 2008, A13.

92. J. Jung, "Through the Contested Terrain Implementation of Downsizing Announcements by Large US Firms, 1984 to 2005," *American Sociological Review* (2016); K. E. Mishra, G. M. Spreitzer, and A. K. Mishra, "Preserving Employee Morale During Downsizing," *Sloan Management Review* 39, no. 2 (1998): 83–95.

93. L. Weber and R. Feintzeig, "Assistance for Laid-Off Workers Gets Downsized," *Wall Street Journal*, February 18, 2014, http://www.wsj.com/articles/SB10001424052702304899704579391254047535652.

94. W. F. Cascio, "Employment Downsizing and Its Alternatives: Strategies for Long-Term Success," *SHRM Foundation's Effective Practice Guideline Series, Society for Human Resource Management Foundation*, https://www.shrm.org/about/foundation/products/documents/downsizing%20epg-%20final.pdf.

95. J. Hilsenrath, "Adventures in Cost Cutting," *Wall Street Journal*, May 10, 2004, R1.

96. University of Waterloo, "Early Retirement for 340," 2010, http://newsrelease.uwaterloo.ca/news.php?id=521.

97. M. Willett, "Early Retirement and Phased Retirement Programs for the Public Sector," *Benefits and Compensation Digest*, April 2005, 31.

98. J. Curtis and J. McMullin, "Older Workers and the Diminishing Return of Employment: Changes in Age-Based Income Inequality in Canada, 1996–2011," *Work, Aging and Retirement waw003* (2016); D. R. Dalton, W. D. Todor, and D. M. Krackhardt, "Turnover Overstated: The Functional Taxonomy," *Academy of Management Review* 7 (1982): 117–23.

99. R. Y. Darmon, "Profit and Opportunity Cost Outcomes of Sales Force Turnover and Recruiting Strategies Upon Various Performance Segments," *Marketing Challenges in a Turbulent Business Environment* (Springer International Publishing, 2016): 665–669; J. R. Hollenbeck and C. R. Williams, "Turnover Functionality Versus Turnover Frequency: A Note on Work Attitudes and Organizational Effectiveness," *Journal of Applied Psychology* 71 (1986): 606–11.

100. C. R. Williams, "Reward Contingency, Unemployment, and Functional Turnover," *Human Resource Management Review* 9 (1999): 549–76.

101. http://www.hrpa.ca/OfficeOfTheRegistrar/Pages/ExamRequirement.aspx.

11

1. Statistics Canada, "Canadian Demographics at a Glance, 2nd Edition," February 19, 2016, http://www.statcan.gc.ca/pub/91-003-x/91-003-x2014001-eng.pdf; Statistics Canada, "Projections of the Diversity of the Canadian Population (91-551-X)," http://www.statcan.gc.ca/pub/91-551-x/2010001/hl-fs-eng.htm; Statistics Canada, "Study: Projected Trends to 2031 for the Canadian Labour Force," August 17, 2011, http://www.statcan.gc.ca/daily-quotidien/110817/dq110817b-eng.htm; Statistics Canada, "Canada Year Book 2011," Cat. no. 11-402-X, http://www.statcan.gc.ca/pub/11-402-x/2011000/pdf/ethnic-ethnique-eng.pdf.

2. Statistics Canada, "Population Count and Population Growth in Canada," http://www.statcan.gc.ca/pub/91-520-x/2010001/aftertoc-aprestdm1-eng.htm; Statistics Canada, "Population Projections for Canada, Provinces, and Territories 2009 to 2036," http://www.statcan.gc.ca/pub/91-520-x/91-520-x2010001-eng.pdf.

3. T. Belford, "Corporations Embrace Canada's Diverse Workforce," Can-West News Service, December 4, 2009, http://www.ottawacitizen.com/about-ottawa-citizen/Newcomers+strive+speak+office/2725088/Corporations+embrace+Canada+diverse+worceforce/2286018/story.html.

4. Human Resources and Skills Development Canada, "What Is Employment Equity?", http://www.chrc-ccdp.ca/eng/content/employment-equity#1.

5. "Employment Equity Act Annual Report 2014," http://www.esdc.gc.ca/en/reports/labour_standards/employment_equity_2014.page#h2.5; "Federal Contractors Program," http://www.esdc.gc.ca/en/jobs/workplace/human_rights/employment_equity/federal_contractor_program.page.

6. *"Employment Equity Act* Annual Report—2014."

7. Equal Employment Opportunity Commission, "Federal Laws Prohibiting Job Discrimination Questions and Answers," http://www.eeoc.gov/facts/qanda.html.

8. A. P. Carnevale and S. C. Stone, *The American Mosaic: An In-Depth Report on the Future of Diversity at Work* (New York: McGraw-Hill, 1995).

9. J. Stoller, "Workplace Diversity: 'To Win in Your Market, You Need to Hire the Market," *The Globe and Mail*, October 24, 2015, http://www.theglobeandmail.com/report-on-business/careers/business-education/workplace-diversity-to-win-in-your-market-you-need-to-hire-the-market/article15039793/.

10. A. Konrad, "Managing for Diversity and Inclusiveness: Results of the 2004–05 Ivey Strategic Diversity and Inclusiveness Survey," Richard Ivey School of Business, http://www.ivey.uwo.ca/cmsmedia/35546/Konrad_Report_07.pdf.

11. T. Worth, "The Business Case for Diversity: How Companies Keep Their Competitive Edge," *California Diversity*, November 2009, http://www.californiadiversitymagazine.org/the-business-case-for-diversity/#respond.

12. Stoller, "Workplace Diversity."

13. "Global Diversity and Inclusion Fostering Innovation Through a Diverse Workforce," *Forbes Insights*, July 2011, http://images.forbes.com/forbesinsights/StudyPDFs/Innovation_Through_Diversity.pdf.

14. Xerox News Room, "Canadians Name Diversity as Key Ingredient in Formula for Innovation Success," September 25, 2007, http://en-news.xerox.ca/news/CAN_News_9_25_2007.

15. R. Rodriguez, "Diversity Finds Its Place: More Organizations Are Dedicating Senior-Level Executives to Drive Diversity Initiatives for Bottom-Line

Effect," *HR Magazine*, August 2006; Society for Human Resource Management, http://www.shrm.org.

16. "Diversity at Work: Public Relations Make a Difference for Global Giants," *Public Relations Society of America*, October 1, 2010, http://www.prsa.org/Intelligence/Tactics/Articles/view/8828/1021/Diversity_at_work_Public_relations_makes_a_difference.

17. M. R. Carrell and E. E. Mann, "Defining Workplace Diversity Programs and Practices in Organizations," *Labor Law Journal* 44 (1993): 743–64.

18. D. A. Harrison, K. H. Price, and M. P. Bell, "Beyond Relational Demography: Time and the Effects of Surface- and Deep-Level Diversity on Work Group Cohesion," *Academy of Management Journal* 41 (1998): 96–107.

19. D. Harrison, K. Price, J. Gavin, and A. Florey, "Time, Teams, and Task Performance: Changing Effects of Surface- and Deep-Level Diversity on Group Functioning," *Academy of Management Journal* 45 (2002): 1029–45.

20. Harrison, Price, and Bell, "Beyond Relational Demography."

21. Harrison, Price, and Bell, "Beyond Relational Demography."

22. "Young Canadians Most Likely to Say They've Been the Victim of Age Discrimination at Work or in an Interview," July 23, 2012, http://www.ipsos-na.com/download/pr.aspx?id=11807.

23. A. Hewitt, "A Business Case for Workers Aged 50+: A Look at the Value of Experience 2015," AARP Research, April 2015, http://www.aarp.org/research/topics/economics/info-2015/business-case-older-workers.html.

24. D. Timar, "The Dynamic Relationship Between Aging and Job Performance—A Case Study," *Agora Psycho-Pragmatica*, Full Issue, Vol 8 No. 2 (2014), http://www.uav.ro/jour/index.php/app/article/view/416; G. M. McEvoy and W. F. Cascio, "Cumulative Evidence of the Relationship Between Employee Age and Job Performance," *Journal of Applied Psychology* 74 (1989): 11–17.

25. A. Bednarz, "Hiring Preferences Favor Mature Workers Over Millennials: Study," *Network World*, October 9, 2012, http://www.networkworld.com/news/2012/100912-mature-workers-263193.html?page=.

26. M. Johne, "Don't Sweep Older Workers Under the Rug," *Globe and* Mail, June 27, 2012, http://www.theglobeandmail.com/report-on-business/careers/business-education/dont-sweep-older-workers-under-the-rug/article4374579.

27. D. Bloom and D. Canning, "How Companies Must Adapt for an Aging Workforce," *Harvard Business Review, HBR Blog Network*, December 3, 2012, http://blogs.hbr.org/cs/2012/12/how_companies_must_adapt_for_a.html.

28. Government of Canada, "Indicators of Well Being in Canada. Work–Weekly Earnings," http://well-being.esdc.gc.ca/misme-iowb/.3ndic.1t.4r@-eng.jsp?iid=18.

29. "Number of Women in Senior Management Falls in Canada, Rises in Europe," *CNW Canada*, March 15, 2012, http://www.newswire.ca/news-releases/number-of-women-in-senior-management-falls-in-canada-rises-in-europe-509817981.html.

30. L. Chenier and E. Wohlbold, "Women in Senior Management: Where Are They?", Conference Board of Canada, August 11, 2011, http://www.conferenceboard.ca/e-library/abstract.aspx?did=4416; R. Wright, "Women in Senior Management: Progress Is Glacial," November 10, 2011, http://www.conferenceboard.ca/insideedge/2011/nov2011/nov10-womenseniormgmnt.aspx; "Women

Still Missing in Action From Senior Management Positions in Canadian Organizations," News Release, Conference Board of Canada, December 29, 2012, http://www.conferenceboard.ca/press/newsrlease/11-08-31/women_still_missing_in_action_from_senior_management_positions_in_canadian_organizations.aspx.

31. "Canadian Women Leading the Charge Into Entrepreneurship," Special Report TD Economics, January 16, 2015, https://www.td.com/document/PDF/economics/special/WomenEntrepreneurs.pdf; "Majority Female Owned Small and Medium Sized Businesses, Special Edition: Key Small Business Statistics," Industry Canada, May 2015, https://www.ic.gc.ca/eic/site/061.nsf/vwapj/MFOSMEs_KSBS-PMEDMF_PSRPE_2015-05_eng.pdf.

32. J. Cool, "Wage Gap Between Women and Men," Library of Parliament, July 29, 2010, http://www.parl.gc.ca/Content/LOP/ResearchPublications/2010-30-e.htm.

33. J. R. Hollenbeck, D. R. Ilgen, C. Ostroff, and J. B. Vancouver, "Sex Differences in Occupational Choice, Pay, and Worth: A Supply-Side Approach to Understanding the Male–Female Wage Gap," Personnel Psychology 40 (1987): 715–44.

34. Y. Zacharias, "Women Execs Believe Glass Ceiling Still an Impediment in Canada: Study," Vancouver Sun, December 11, 2012, http://www.vancouversun.com/business/Women+execs+believe+glass+ceiling+still+impediment+Canada+study/7684710/story.html.

35. "Women's Glass Ceiling Remains," CBC News, August, 31, 2011, http://www.cbc.ca/news/business/story/2011/08/31/women-executive-conference-board.html.

36. B. R. Ragins, B. Townsend, and M. Mattis, "Gender Gap in the Executive Suite: CEOs and Female Executives Report on Breaking the Glass Ceiling," Academy of Management Executive 12 (1998): 28–42.

37. L. Whittington, "Visible Minorities Increasing in Canada," Toronto Star, May 17, 2012, http://www.thestar.com/news/canada/2012/05/17/visible_minorities_increasing_in_canada.html.

38. Ryerson University Media Release, "Catalyst and Ryerson University Release New Study of More Than 17,000 Seasoned Professionals," June 28, 2007, http://www.catalyst.org/media/catalyst-and-ryerson-university-release-new-study-more-17000-seasoned-professionals.

39. D. A. Neal and W. R. Johnson, "The Role of Premarket Factors in Black–White Wage Differences," Journal of Political Economy 104, no. 5 (1996): 869–95.

40. P. Oreopoulos, D. Dechief, "Why Do Some Employers Prefer to Interview Matthew, But Not Samir?" Metropolis British Columbia, September 2011, http://mbc.metropolis.net/assets/uploads/files/wp/2011/WP11-13.pdf.

41. S. Block and G. Galabuzi, "Whatever You Call It, Discrimination Is Alive and Well in The Workplace," The Globe and Mail, June 13, 2015, http://www.theglobeandmail.com/opinion/whatever-you-call-it-discrimination-is-alive-and-well-in-the-workplace/article12513864/; S. Block and G. Galabuzi, "Canada's Colour Coded Labour Market: The Gap for Racialized Workers," The Wellesley Institute, March 2011, http://www.wellesleyinstitute.com/wp-content/uploads/2011/03/Colour_Coded_Labour_MarketFINAL.pdf.

42. A. P. Brief, R. T. Buttram, R. M. Reizenstein, and S. D. Pugh, "Beyond Good Intentions: The Next Steps Toward Racial Equality in the American Workplace," Academy of Management Executive 11 (1997): 59–72.

43. L. E. Wynter, "Business and Race: Federal Agencies, Spurred on by Nonprofit Groups, Are Increasingly Embracing the Use of Undercover Investigators to Identify Discrimination in the Marketplace," Wall Street Journal, July 1, 1998, B1.

44. Canadian Survey on Disability 2012, Statistics Canada, December 3, 2013, http://www.statcan.gc.ca/daily-quotidien/131203/dq131203a-eng.htm.

45. M. Turcotte, "Insights on Canadian Society: Persons With Disabilities and Employment," Statistics Canada, December 3, 2014, http://www.statcan.gc.ca/pub/75-006-x/2014001/article/14115-eng.pdf.

46. B. Wilkerson, The Business Case for Accessibility (Toronto: Queen's Printer, November 2001), http://www.ilcanada.ca/upload/documents/information_sheet_2007_1of4.pdf.

47. M. Turcotte, "Insights on Canadian Society."

48. Canadian Press, "More Disabled People in Canada."

49. S. H. Kaye, L. H. Jans, and E. C. Jones, "Why Don't Employers Hire and Retain Workers With Disabilities?" Journal of Occupational Rehabilitation, Vol. 21, no. 4 (2011): 526–536.

50. R. Greenwood and V. A. Johnson, "Employer Perspectives on Workers With Disabilities," Journal of Rehabilitation 53 (1987): 37–45.

51. Greenwood and Johnson, "Employer Perspectives."

52. Office of Disability Employment Policy, "Low Cost Accommodation Solutions," http://www.hreonline.com/HRE/view/story.jhtml?id=26670972.

53. National Council on Disability, "Study on the Financing of Assistive Technology Devices and Services for Individuals With Disabilities: A Report to the President and the Congress of the United States," http://www.ncd.gov/publications/1993/Mar41993.

54. Government of British Columbia, "Workable Solutions: An Initiative of the Minister's Council on Employment for Persons with Disabilities," http://www.mhr.gov.bc.ca/epwd/docs/Handbook.pdf.

55. R. B. Cattell, "Personality Pinned Down," Psychology Today 7 (1973): 40–46; C. S. Carver and M. F. Scheier, Perspectives on Personality (Boston: Allyn and Bacon, 1992).

56. J. M. Digman, "Personality Structure: Emergence of the Five-Factor Model," Annual Review of Psychology 41 (1990): 417–40; M. R. Barrick and M. K. Mount, "The Big Five Personality Dimensions and Job Performance: A Meta-Analysis," Personnel Psychology 44 (1991): 1–26.

57. Barrick and Mount, "The Big Five Personality Dimensions"; M. K. Mount and M. R. Barrick, "The Big Five Personality Dimensions: Implications for Research and Practice in Human Resource Management," Research in Personnel and Human Resources Management 13 (1995): 153–200; M. K. Mount and M. R. Barrick, "Five Reasons Why the 'Big Five' Article Has Been Frequently Cited," Personnel Psychology 51 (1998): 849–57; D. S. Ones, M. K. Mount, M. R. Barrick, and J. E. Hunter, "Personality and Job Performance: A Critique of the Tett, Jackson, and Rothstein (1991) Meta-Analysis," Personnel Psychology 47 (1994): 147–56.

58. Barrick and Mount, "The Big Five Personality Dimensions and Job Performance."

59. Mount and Barrick, "Five Reasons Why."

60. Mount and Barrick, "Five Reasons Why."

61. Staff, "The Diverse Work Force," Inc., January 1993, 33.

62. D. A. Thomas and R. J. Ely, "Making Differences Matter: A New Paradigm for Managing Diversity," Harvard Business Review 74 (September–October 1996): 79–90.

63. D. A. Thomas and S. Wetlaufer, "A Question of Color: A Debate on Race in the U.S. Workplace," Harvard Business Review 75 (September–October 1997), 118–32.

64. Thomas and Ely, "Making Differences Matter."

65. A. Fisher, "How You Can Do Better on Diversity," Fortune, November 15, 2004, 60.

66. J. Espinoza, "Working to Prove Benefits of More Women at the Top," Wall Street Journal, February 27, 2011, http://www.wsj.com/articles/SB10001424052748704150604576166483012821352.

67. J. R. Norton and R. E. Fox, The Change Equation: Capitalizing on Diversity for Effective Organizational Change (Washington: APA, 1997).

68. Norton and Fox, The Change Equation.

69. Thomas and Ely, "Making Differences Matter."

70. R. R. Thomas, Jr., Beyond Race and Gender: Unleashing the Power of Your Total Workforce by Managing Diversity (New York: AMACOM, 1991).

71. Thomas, Beyond Race and Gender.

72. L. S. Gottfredson, "Dilemmas in Developing Diversity Programs," in Diversity in the Workplace, ed. S.E. Jackson and Associates (New York: Guildford, 1992).

73. A. Konrad, C. Maurer, and Y. Yang, "Managing for Diversity and Inclusiveness: Results of the 2004–5 Ivey Strategic Diversity and Inclusiveness Survey," Richard Ivey School of Business, University of Western Ontario, http://www.ivey.uwo.ca/faculty/Konrad_Report_07.pdf.

74. R. Caballero and R. Yerema, "Canada's Best Diversity Employers," March 23, 2010; UBC Employer Review, http://www.eluta.ca/diversity-at-university-of-british-columbia; http://www.eluta.ca/diversity-at-corus-entertainment.

75. "Forest Company Keys Into Aboriginal Workforce," Vancouver Sun.

76. Caballero and Yerema, "Canada's Best Diversity Employers."

77. Caballero and Yerema, "Canada's Best Diversity Employers."

78. Carnevale and Stone, The American Mosaic.

79. Caballero and Yerema, "Canada's Best Diversity Employers."

80. Caballero and Yerema, "Canada's Best Diversity Employers."

81. J. R. Joplin and C. S. Daus, "Challenges of Leading a Diverse Workforce," Academy of Management Executive 11 (1997): 32–47.

82. Caballero and Yerema, "Canada's Best Diversity Employers."

83. Konrad, Maurer, and Yang, "Managing for Diversity and Inclusiveness."

12

1. A. Adkins, "Majority of U.S. Employees Not Engaged Despite Gains in 2014," Gallup Employee Engagement, January 28, 2015, http://www.gallup.com/poll/181289/majority-employees-not-engaged-despite-gains-2014.aspx.

2. J. P. Campbell and R.D. Pritchard, "Motivation Theory in Industrial and Organizational Psychology," in Handbook of Industrial and Organizational Psychology, ed. M. D. Dunnette (Chicago: Rand McNally, 1976); E. T. Rolls, "Motivation Explained: Ultimate and Proximate Accounts of Hunger and Appetite," Advances in Motivation Science (2016).

3. M. D. Dooley, A. A. Payne, and A. L. Robb, "The Impact of Scholarships and Bursaries on Persistence and Academic Success in University," Higher Education Quality Council of Ontario, January 7, 2013, http://www.heqco.ca/en-CA/Pages/Home.aspx.

4. P. Thomas, "Waitress Makes the Difference in Bringing Deaf to Pittsburgh," *Wall Street Journal Interactive Edition*, March 2, 1999.

5. E. A. Locke, "The Nature and Causes of Job Satisfaction," in *Handbook of Industrial and Organizational Psychology*, ed. M. D. Dunnette (Chicago: Rand McNally, 1976); M. Shayganfar, C. Rich, and C. Sidner, "An Overview of Affective Motivational Collaboration Theory," *Proceedings of the AAAI Workshop on Symbiotic Cognitive Systems 2016*.

6. A. H. Maslow, "A Theory of Human Motivation," *Psychological Review* 50 (1943): 370–96; T. Kaya and H. Bicen, "The Effects of Social Media on Students' Behaviors; Facebook as a Case Study," *Computers in Human Behavior* 59 (2016): 374–379.

7. C. P. Alderfer, *Existence, Relatedness, and Growth: Human Needs in Organizational Settings* (New York: Free Press, 1972); K. L. Proudford, L. Karen, J. P. Porter, G. Javadian, and N. Dane, "Navigating the Circle of Trust: Building and Rebuilding Authentic Relationships Among Women," *Gender, Race, and Ethnicity in the Workplace: Emerging Issues and Enduring Challenges* (2016): 201–227.

8. D. C. McClelland, "Toward a Theory of Motive Acquisition," *American Psychologist* 20 (1965): 321–33; D. C. McClelland and D. H. Burnham, "Power Is the Great Motivator," *Harvard Business Review* 54, no. 2 (1976): 100–110; T. Pervaiz and O. Ahmed, "Sustaining the Growth of Employee: Motivation and Career Development in Organization," https://mpra.ub.uni-muenchen.de/69728/; A. Kaplan and H. Patrick, "Learning Environments and Motivation," *Handbook of Motivation at School*, R. K. Wentzel and D. B. Meile, (Eds.), Routledge, New York: New York, 251–278.

9. J. H. Turner, "Entrepreneurial Environments and the Emergence of Achievement Motivation in Adolescent Males," *Sociometry* 33 (1970): 147–165; K. Helker and M. Wosnitza, "The Interplay of Students' and Parents' Responsibility Judgements in the School Context and Their Associations With Student Motivation and Achievement," *International Journal of Educational Research (76)*: 34–49.

10. L. W. Porter, E. E. Lawler III, and J. R. Hackman, *Behavior in Organizations* (New York: McGraw-Hill, 1975).

11. C. Ajila, "Maslow's Hierarchy of Needs Theory: Applicability to the Nigerian Industrial Setting," *IFE Psychology* (1997): 162–74.

12. M. A. Wahba and L. B. Birdwell, "Maslow Reconsidered: A Review of Research on the Need Hierarchy Theory," *Organizational Behavior and Human Performance* 15 (1976): 212–40; J. Rauschenberger, N. Schmitt, and J.E. Hunter, "A Test of the Need Hierarchy Concept by a Markov Model of Change in Need Strength," *Administrative Science Quarterly* 25 (1980): 654–70.

13. K. Dye, A. J. Mills, and T. G. Weatherbee, "Maslow: Man Interrupted: Reading Management Theory in Context," *Management Decisions* 43, no.10 (2005): 1375–95; C. P. Alderfer, R. E. Kaplan, and K. K. Smith, "The Effect of Relatedness Need Satisfaction on Relatedness Desires," *Administrative Science Quarterly*, 19 (1974): 507–32; M. A. Wahba and L. B. Bridwell, "Maslow Reconsidered: A Review of Research on the Need Hierarchy Theory," *Organizational Behavior and Human Performance* 15 (1976): 212–40; J. Rauschenberger, N. Schmitt, and J. E. Hunter, "A Test of the Need Hierarchy Concept by a Markov Model of Change in Need Strength," *Administrative Science Quarterly* 25 (1980): 654–70.

14. B. Irlenbusch and D. Sliwka, "Incentives, Decision Frames, and Motivation Crowding Out—An Experimental Investigation," *IZA Discussion Paper No. 1758*, September 2005, http://papers.ssrn.com/sol3/papers.cfm?abstract_id=822866; A. M. Bertelli, "Motivation Crowding and the Federal Civil Servant: Evidence from the US Internal Revenue Service," *International Public Management Journal* 9, no. 1 (2006), http://www.tandfonline.com/doi/abs/10.1080/10967490600625191.

15. R. Herzberg, B. Mausner, and B. B. Snyderman, *The Motivation to Work. Vol. 1.* (Transaction Publishers, 2011); R. Herzberg, "Motivation–Hygiene Theory," *J. Miner, Organizational Behavior I: Essential Theories of Motivation and Leadership*: 61–74.

16. E. E. Lawler III and L. W. Porter, "The Effect of Performance on Job Satisfaction," *Industrial Relations* 7 (1967): 20–28; P. Kampkötter, "Performance Appraisals and Job Satisfaction," *The International Journal of Human Resource Management* (2016): 1–25.

17. Porter, Lawler, and Hackman, *Behavior in Organizations*.

18. M. Nguyen, "What Canada's Best Small Employers Do to Engage Their Employees," *ProfitGuide.com*, November 5, 2015, http://www.profitguide.com/manage-grow/human-resources/what-canadas-best-small-employers-do-to-engage-their-employees-94481.

19. M. Habib, "Motivation Without Money? You Bet," *Globe and Mail*, November 23, 2010, http://www.theglobeandmail.com/report-on-business/small-business/sb-managing/human-resources/motivation-without-money-you-bet/article1315526.

20. Porter, Lawler, and Hackman, *Behavior in Organizations*.

21. "Working at KPMG," http://www.kpmg.com/ca/en/careers/working-at-kpmg/benefits/pages/total-rewards.aspx; "Join Deloitte: Benefits and Rewards," http://www2.deloitte.com/us/en/pages/careers/articles/life-at-deloitte-benefits-and-rewards.html; J. S. Lublin, "Creative Compensation: A CEO Talks About His Company's Innovative Pay Ideas—Free Ice Cream, Anyone?", *Wall Street Journal*, April 10, 2006, R6; Tavia Grant, "Worst of Times Might Be Best of Times to Take Off," *Globe and Mail*, April 4, 2009, http://yoursabbatical.com/2009/04/04/worst-of-times-might-be-best-of-times-to-take-off; T. Amabile and S. Kramer, "What Makes Work Worth Doing?", *HBR Blog Network/HBS Faculty*, August 31, 2012, http://blogs.hbr.org/hbsfaculty/2012/08/what-makes-work-worth-doing.html.

22. Canada's Top 100 Employers for 2016, *Financial Post*, http://www.financialpost.com/story.html?id=734aceda-d1ed-4c3d-941d-0aeb47fa58c0&k=21172.

23. D. Alexander, "Canadian Banks Plan Smaller Increase in Compensation Bonuses This Year," Bloomberg News, *Globe and Mail*, December 3, 2015, http://www.theglobeandmail.com/report-on-business/canadian-banks-plan-smaller-increase-in-compensation-bonuses-this-year/article27588957/; B. Smith, "Bonuses That Are Available to All Motivate Staff," *Globe and Mail*, November 19, 2012, http://www.theglobeandmail.com/report-on-business/careers/top-employers/bonuses-that-are-available-to-all-motivate-staff/article5434755.

24. C. Caggiano, "What Do Workers Want?", *Inc.*, November 1992, 101–4; Families and Work Institute, "National Study of the Changing Workforce," http://www.familiesandwork.org/3w/research/downloads/3wes.pdf.

25. J. McGonigal, "Be a Gamer, Save the World," *Wall Street Journal*, January 22, 2011, C3; IsosMediaCT, "2014 Essential Facts About the Computer and Video Game Industry," *Entertainment Software Association (ESA)*, April 2014, http://www.theesa.com/wp-content/uploads/2014/10/ESA_EF_2014.pdf.

26. R. Silverman, "Latest Game Theory: Mixing Work and Play," *Wall Street Journal*, October 10, 2011, http://www.wsj.com/articles/SB10001424052970204294504576615371783795248.

27. "Compelling Calgarians: 20 People You'll Want to Watch in 2016," *Calgary Herald,* January 2, 2016, http://calgaryherald.com/storyline/compelling-calgarians-20-people-youll-want-to-watch-in-2016.

28. Habib, "Compensation: Motivation Without Money?"

29. R. Kanfer and P. Ackerman, "Aging, Adult Development, and Work Motivation," *Academy of Management Review* (2004): 440–58.

30. E. White, "The New Recruits: Older Workers," *Wall Street Journal*, January 14, 2008, B3.

31. T. Krisher, "GM CEO's Compensation Rises 44 per cent in 2012 to $11.1 Million as Automaker Changes Pay Mix," *Canadian Business*, April 25, 2013, http://www.canadianbusiness.com/business-news/gm-ceos-compensation-rises-44-per-cent-in-2012-to-11-1-million-with-bigger-stock-awards; B. Marotte, "SNC-Lavalin: Engineering a Fair-Minded Pay Policy," *Globe and Mail*, August 23, 2012, http://m.theglobeandmail.com/report-on-business/careers/management/board-games/snc-lavalin-engineering-a-fair-minded-pay-policy/article4330684/?service=mobile.

32. C. T. Kulik and M. L. Ambrose, "Personal and Situational Determinants of Referent Choice," *Academy of Management Review* 17 (1992): 212–37.

33. J. S. Adams, "Toward an Understanding of Inequity," *Journal of Abnormal Social Psychology* 67 (1963): 422–36; S. A. Conroy and N. Gupta, "Team Pay-for-Performance The Devil Is in the Details," *Group & Organization Management (41)*1 (2016): 32–65.

34. R. A. Cosier and D. R. Dalton, "Equity Theory and Time: A Reformulation," *Academy of Management Review* 8 (1983): 311–19; M. R. Carrell and J. E. Dittrich, "Equity Theory: The Recent Literature, Methodological Considerations, and New Directions," *Academy of Management Review* 3 (1978): 202–9.

35. M. Piplica, Fair Wage Office—2014 Annual Report, (2015), http://www1.toronto.ca/City%20Of%20Toronto/Purchasing%20and%20Materials%20Management/Selling%20to%20the%20City/Fair%20Wage%20Office/Annual%20Reports/backgroundfile-83194.pdf.

36. Canada's Top 100 Employers for 2016, *Financial Post*, http://www.financialpost.com/story.html?id=734aceda-d1ed-4c3d-941d-0aeb47fa58c0&k=21172.

37. C. Chen, J. Choi, and S. Chi, "Making Justice Sense of Local–Expatriate Compensation Disparity," *Academy of Management Journal* (2002): 807–17; S. Marasi and R. J. Bennett, "Pay Communication: Where Do We Go From Here?" *Human Resource Management Review (26)*1 (2016): 50–58.

38. L. He and J. Fang. "CEO Overpayment and Dismissal: The Role of Attribution and Attention," *Corporate Governance: An International Review (24)*1: 24–41; K. Aquino, R. W. Griffeth, D. G. Allen, and P. W. Hom, "Integrating Justice Constructs Into the Turnover Process: A Test of a Referent Cognitions Model," *Academy of Management Journal* 40, no. 5 (1997): 1208–27.

39. R. Folger and M. A. Konovsky, "Effects of Procedural and Distributive Justice on Reactions to Pay Raise Decisions," *Academy of Management Journal* 32 (1989): 115–30; M. A. Konovsky, "Understanding Procedural Justice and Its Impact on Business Organizations," *Journal of Management* 26 (2000): 489–512.

40. E. Barret-Howard and T. R. Tyler, "Procedural Justice as a Criterion in Allocation Decisions," *Journal of Personality and Social Psychology* 50

(1986): 296–305; Folger and Konovsky, "Effects of Procedural and Distributive Justice."

41. R. Folger and J. Greenberg, "Procedural Justice: An Interpretive Analysis of Personnel Systems," in *Research in Personnel and Human Resources Management*, Vol. 3, ed. K. Rowland and G. Ferris (Greenwich: JAI, 1985); R. Folger, D. Rosenfield, J. Grove, and L. Corkran, "Effects of 'Voice' and Peer Opinions on Responses to Inequity," *Journal of Personality and Social Psychology* 37 (1979): 2253–61; E. A. Lind and T. R. Tyler, *The Social Psychology of Procedural Justice* (New York: Plenum, 1988); Konovsky, "Understanding Procedural Justice."

42. D. Jermyn, "Canada's Top 100 Employers Make Their Workplaces Exceptional," *Globe and Mail*, November 4, 2014, http://www.theglobeandmail.com/report-on-business/careers/top-employers/canadas-top-100-employers-make-their-workplaces-exceptional/article21427767/.

43. M. S. Salihu, T. S. Mei, and M. H. R. Joarder, "Moderating Role of Ethical Climates on HRM Practices and Organizational Performance: A Proposed Conceptual Model," *Mediterranean Journal of Social Sciences (7)*1 (2016): 291; V. H. Vroom, *Work and Motivation* (New York: Wiley, 1964); L. W. Porter and E. E. Lawler III, *Managerial Attitudes and Performance* (Homewood: Dorsey Press and Richard D. Irwin, 1968).

44. P. V. LeBlanc and P. W. Mulvey, "How American Workers See the Rewards of Work," *Compensation and Benefits Review* 30 (February 1998): 24–28.

45. A. Fox, "Companies Can Benefit When They Disclose Pay Processes to Employees," *HR Magazine* 47 (July 2002): 25.

46. J. Lightbody, "You Don't Need Fancy Perks to Motivate Employees," *Globe and Mail*, February 9, 2016, http://www.theglobeandmail.com/report-on-business/careers/leadership-lab/you-dont-need-fancy-perks-to-motivate-employees/article28654297/.

47. A. Erhan, "Interrogating Women's Leadership and Empowerment," *Gender in Management: An International Journal (31)*2; K. W. Thomas and B. A. Velthouse, "Cognitive Elements of Empowerment," *Academy of Management Review* 15 (1990): 666–81.

48. E. L. Thorndike, *Animal Intelligence* (New York: Macmillan, 1911).

49. B. F. Skinner, *Science and Human Behavior* (New York: Macmillan, 1954); B. F. Skinner, *Beyond Freedom and Dignity* (New York: Bantam, 1971); B. F. Skinner, *A Matter of Consequences* (New York: NYU Press, 1984).

50. A. M. Dickinson and A. D. Poling, "Schedules of Monetary Reinforcement in Organizational Behavior Management: Latham and Huber Revisited," *Journal of Organizational Behavior Management* 16, no. 1 (1992): 71–91.

51. W. Immen, "Want to Be Really Creative? Stop Thinking About Yourself," *Globe and Mail*, March 18, 2011, http://www.theglobeandmail.com/report-on-business/careers/career-advice/want-to-be-really-creative-stop-thinking-about-yourself/article573600.

52. D. Grote, "Manager's Journal: Discipline Without Punishment," *Wall Street Journal*, May 23, 1994, A14.

53. J. B. Miner, *Theories of Organizational Behavior* (Hinsdale: Dryden, 1980).

54. Dickinson and Poling, "Schedules of Monetary Reinforcement."

55. H. Schachter, "Making Your Words of Praise Heard," *Globe and Mail*, January 27, 2013, http://www.theglobeandmail.com/report-on-business/careers/management/making-your-words-of-praise-heard/article7868035.

56. F. Luthans and A. D. Stajkovic, "Reinforce for Performance: The Need to Go Beyond Pay and Even Rewards," *Academy of Management Executive* 13, no. 2 (1999): 49–57.

57. K. D. Butterfield, L. K. Trevino, and G. A. Ball, "Punishment From the Manager's Perspective: A Grounded Investigation and Inductive Model," *Academy of Management Journal* 39 (1996): 1479–512.

58. R. D. Arvey and J. M. Ivancevich, "Punishment in Organizations: A Review, Propositions, and Research Suggestions," *Academy of Management Review* 5 (1980): 123–132.

59. R. D. Arvey, G. A. Davis, and S. M. Nelson, "Use of Discipline in an Organization: A Field Study," *Journal of Applied Psychology* 69 (1984): 448–60; M. E. Schnake, "Vicarious Punishment in a Work Setting," *Journal of Applied Psychology* 71 (1986): 343–45.

60. E. A. Locke and G. P. Latham, *Goal Setting: A Motivational Technique That Works* (Englewood Cliffs: Prentice Hall, 1984); E. A. Locke and G. P. Latham, *A Theory of Goal Setting and Task Performance* (Englewood Cliffs: Prentice Hall, 1990).

61. G. P. Latham and E. A. Locke, "Goal Setting—A Motivational Technique That Works," *Organizational Dynamics* 8, no. 2 (1979): 68.

62. Latham and Locke, "Goal Setting."

13

1. G. Beau, "Beyond the Leader-Centric Approach: Leadership Phenomena and Aesthetics in a Conductorless Orchestra." *Society and Business Review (11)*1 (2016); R. Wis, *The Conductor as Leader: Principles of Leadership Applied to Life on the Podium* (Napierville: GIA, 2006); C. W. Elkins, *Conducting Her Destiny: The Making of a Maestra*, A Dissertation Submitted to the Faculty at the Graduate School at The University of North Carolina at Greensboro in Partial Fulfillment of the Requirements for the Degree Doctor of Musical Arts, 2008, https://libres.uncg.edu/ir/uncg/f/umi-uncg-1539.pdf.

2. W. Bennis, "Why Leaders Can't Lead," *Training and Development Journal* 43, no. 4 (1989); H. Mintzberg, "The Manager's Job: Folklore and Fact," in *Managing People and Organizations,* ed. John J. Garbarro (Cambridge: Harvard Business School Publications, 1992), http://www.uu.edu/personal/bnance/318/mintz.html; "The Man Who Invented Management: Why Peter Drucker's Ideas Still Matter," *Business Week*, November 2005, http://www.businessweek.com/magazine/content/05_48/b3961001.htm; H. Mintzberg, *Managers, Not MBAs: A Hard Look at the Soft Practice of Managing and Management Development* (San Francisco: Berrett-Koehler, 2006); H. Mintzberg, "Proven Models: 10 Managerial Roles," 2010, http://www.provenmodels.com/88/ten-managerial-roles/mintzberg,-henry.

3. A. Good, "Fail Forward Wins the HBR/McKinsey Innovating Innovation Challenge," 2013, http://failforward.org/author/ashleygood; L. Buchanan, "How the Creative Stay Creative," *Inc.*, June 2008, 102–3.

4. A. Zaleznik, "Managers and Leaders: Are They Different?" *Harvard Business Review* 55 (1977): 76–78; A. Zaleznik, "The Leadership Gap," *Washington Quarterly* 6 (1983): 32–39.

5. Bennis, "Why Leaders Can't Lead."

6. D. Healing, "After Takeover Victory, Suncor Names New Management for Canadian Oil Sands," *Calgary Herald,* February 8, 2016, http://calgaryherald.com/business/energy/suncor-names-new-canadian-oil-sands-leaders-extends-share-offer-until-feb-22; "Suncor Reaches $6.6-Billion Deal To Acquire Canadian Oil Sands," *Calgary Herald*, January 18, 2016, http://calgaryherald.com/business/energy/suncor-reaches-6-6-billion-deal-to-acquire-canadian-oil-sands.

7. R. J. Bennett, "The Kaleidoscope Called Leadership," *Industrial and Commercial Training (48)*2 (2016); M. Gladwell, "Why Do We Love Tall Men?" Gladwell.Com, http://gladwell.com/blink/why-do-we-love-tall-men/.

8. R. J. House and R. M. Aditya, "The Social Scientific Study of Leadership: Quo Vadis?", *Journal of Management* 23 (1997): 409–73; T. Judge, R. Illies, J. Bono, and M. Gerhardt, "Personality and Leadership: A Qualitative and Quantitative Review," *Journal of Applied Psychology* (August 2002): 765–82; S. A. Kirkpatrick and E. A. Locke, "Leadership: Do Traits Matter?", *Academy of Management Executive* 5, no. 2 (1991): 48–60.

9. House and Aditya, "The Social Scientific Study"; Kirkpatrick and Locke, "Leadership: Do Traits Matter?"

10. M. Gagnon, "Justin Trudeau's Rise Shows the Benefits of Being Underestimated," CBC News, October 7, 2015, http://www.cbc.ca/news/politics/canada-election-2015-justin-trudeau-michelle-gagnon-1.3259553; R. Gwyn, "The Contender: The Appeal of Justin Trudeau's Emotional Intelligence," *National News Watch*, July 19, 2013, http://www.nationalnewswatch.com/2013/07/19/the-contender-the-appeal-of-justin-trudeaus-emotional-intelligence/#.VwyJ3OIrLq4.

11. S. Houpt, "Comedian John Oliver Appears to Flout Law by Urging Canadians Not to Vote for Harper," *The Globe and Mail*, October 19, 2015, http://www.theglobeandmail.com/arts/television/john-olivers-plead-to-canadians-not-to-vote-for-harper-was-illegal/article26870383/.

12. "Innovations Drives Her Success Story," *Financial Post*, November 27, 2015, http://business.financialpost.com/women-of-power/innovations-drives-her-success-story#!/?__lsa=db44-1d06.

13. Kirkpatrick and Locke, "Leadership: Do Traits Matter?"

14. C. Gault, "Here's What It Takes to Be a CEO, According to Somebody Who Gets Them Hired," *Financial Post*, March 24, 2015, http://business.financialpost.com/executive/leadership/heres-what-it-takes-to-be-a-ceo-according-to-somebody-who-gets-them-hired?__lsa=db44-1d06.

15. Gault, "Here's What It Takes to Be a CEO."

16. E. A. Fleishman, "The Description of Supervisory Behavior," *Journal of Applied Psychology* 37 (1953): 1–6; L. R. Katz, *New Patterns of Management* (New York: McGraw-Hill, 1961).

17. "NAPE Ready to Do Battle for Jobs, Services: Union Leader Predicts Tough Round of Bargaining," *CBC News*, October 22, 2015, http://www.cbc.ca/news/canada/newfoundland-labrador/nape-convention-jerry-earle-1.3283745.

18. K. Miller, *Organizational Communication: Approaches and Processes*, 6th ed. (Wadsworth: Boston, 2011).

19. J. Beer, "I500: Canadian Tire Rolls Out New Focus on Innovation," *Canadian Business*, May 12, 2013, http://www.canadianbusiness.com/list-and-rankings/canadian-tire-rolls-out-new-focus-on-innovation.

20. P. Weissenberg and M. H. Kavanagh, "The Independence of Initiating Structure and Consideration: A Review of the Evidence," *Personnel Psychology* 25 (1972): 119–30.

21. T. Sherlock, "Youthful Incoming BCTF President Has Experience on His Side: Glen Hansman's Approachability and Strong Sense of Social Justice Seen as Assets in Tough Position," *Vancouver Sun*, March 19, 2016, http://www.vancouversun.com/

news/Youthful+incoming+BCTF+president+experience+side/11794893/story.html#ixzz44GjkaWjj.

22. Sherlock, "Youthful Incoming BCTF President."

23. R. J. House and T. R. Mitchell, "Path–Goal Theory of Leadership," *Journal of Contemporary Business 3* (1974): 81–97; F. E. Fiedler, "A Contingency Model of Leadership Effectiveness," in *Advances in Experimental Social Psychology*, ed. L. Berkowitz (New York: Academic Press, 1964); V. H. Vroom and P. W. Yetton, *Leadership and Decision Making* (Pittsburgh: University of Pittsburgh Press, 1973); P. Hersey and K. H. Blanchard, *The Management of Organizational Behavior*, 4th ed. (Englewood Cliffs: Prentice Hall, 1984); S. Kerr and J. M. Jermier, "Substitutes for Leadership: Their Meaning and Measurement," *Organizational Behavior and Human Performance 22* (1978): 375–403.

24. A. Grant, F. Gino, and D. Hofmann, "The Hidden Advantage of Quiet Bosses," *Harvard Business Review (88)*12 (2010): 28, https://hbr.org/2010/12/the-hidden-advantages-of-quiet-bosses.

25. F. E. Fiedler and M. M. Chemers, *Leadership and Effective Management* (Glenview: Scott, Foresman, 1974); F. E. Fiedler and M. M. Chemers, *Improving Leadership Effectiveness: The Leader Match Concept*, 2nd ed. (New York: John Wiley, 1984).

26. Fiedler and Chemers, *Improving Leadership Effectiveness*.

27. F. E. Fiedler, "The Effects of Leadership Training and Experience: A Contingency Model Interpretation," *Administrative Science Quarterly 17*, no. 4 (1972): 455; F. E. Fiedler, *A Theory of Leadership Effectiveness* (New York: McGraw-Hill, 1967).

28. L. S. Csoka and F. E. Fiedler, "The Effect of Military Leadership Training: A Test of the Contingency Model," *Organizational Behavior and Human Performance 8* (1972): 395–407.

29. House and Mitchell, "Path–Goal Theory of Leadership."

30. House and Mitchell, "Path–Goal Theory of Leadership."

31. B. M. Fisher and J. E. Edwards, "Consideration and Initiating Structure and Their Relationships With Leader Effectiveness: A Meta-Analysis," *Proceedings of the Academy of Management*, August 1988, 201–5.

32. M. Goodhand, "Edmonton's Power 30: Who's Who in 2015?" *Edmonton Journal*, November 28, 2015, http://edmontonjournal.com/news/insight/edmonton-power-30-list-2015.

33. E. White, "Art of Persuasion Becomes Key," *Wall Street Journal*, May 19, 2008, B5.

34. J. C. Wofford and L. Z. Liska, "Path–Goal Theories of Leadership: A Meta-Analysis," *Journal of Management 19* (1993): 857–76.

35. House and Aditya, "The Social Scientific Study of Leadership."

36. V. H. Vroom and A. G. Jago, *The New Leadership: Managing Participation in Organizations* (Englewood Cliffs: Prentice Hall, 1988).

37. C. Fishman, "How Teamwork Took Flight: This Team Built a Commercial Engine—and Self-Managing GE Plant—From Scratch," *Fast Company*, October 1, 1999, 188.

38. Fishman, "How Teamwork Took Flight."

39. Fishman, "How Teamwork Took Flight."

40. G.A . Yukl, *Leadership in Organizations*, 3rd ed. (Englewood Cliffs: Prentice Hall, 1995).

41. B. M. Bass, *Bass and Stogdill's Handbook of Leadership: Theory, Research, and Managerial Applications* (New York: Free Press, 1990).

42. A. A. Perryman, G. D. Fernando, and A. Tripathy, "Do Gender Differences Persist? An Examination of Gender Diversity on Firm Performance, Risk, and Executive Compensation." *Journal of Business Research (69)*2 (2016): 579–586; C. L. Hoyt, "Women, Men, and Leadership: Exploring the Gender Gap at the Top," *Social and Personality Psychology Compass 4*, no. 7 (2010): 484–98.

43. C. Glass and A. Cook, "Leading at the Top: Understanding Women's Challenges Above the Glass Ceiling," *The Leadership Quarterly (27)*1 (2016): 51–63; C. L. Hoyt, "Women, Men, and Leadership: Exploring the Gender Gap at the Top," *Social and Personality Psychology Compass 4*, no. 7 (2010): 484–98.

44. S. J. Zaccaro, L. M. V. Gulick, and V. P. Khare, "Personality and Leadership," in *Leadership at the Crossroads: Leadership and Psychology*, Vol. 1, ed. C. L. Hoyt, G. R. Goethals, and D. R. Forsyth (Westport: Praeger, 2008), 1–10.

45. M. Reuvers, M. L. Van Engen, C. J. Vinkenburg, and E. Wilson-Evered, "Transformational Leadership and Innovative Work Behaviour: Exploring the Relevance of Gender Differences," *Creativity and Innovation Management 17*, no. 3 (2008): 227–44.

46. C. Kulich, M. K. Ryan, and S. A. Haslam, "Where Is the Romance for Women Leaders? The Effects of Gender on Leadership Attributions and Performance-Based Pay," *Applied Psychology 56*, no. 4 (2007): 582–601.

47. W. Buffett, "Warren Buffett Is Bullish . . . on Women," *Fortune*, May 2, 2013, http://money.cnn.com/2013/05/02/leadership/warren-buffett-women.pr.fortune/index.html; A. Steinbrecher, "Warren Buffett Says We Need More Women in Business, and a New Study Shows He's Right," News.Mic, May 6, 2013, http://www.policymic.com/articles/42421/warren-buffett-says-we-need-more-women-in-business-and-a-new-study-shows-he-s-right.

48. R. D. Ireland and M. A. Hitt, "Achieving and Maintaining Strategic Competitiveness in the 21st Century: The Role of Strategic Leadership," *Academy of Management Executive 13*, no. 1 (1999): 43–57.

49. P. Thoms and D. B. Greenberger, "Training Business Leaders to Create Positive Organizational Visions of the Future: Is It Successful?", *Academy of Management Journal* (Best Papers and Proceedings 1995): 212–16.

50. M. Weber, *The Theory of Social and Economic Organizations*, trans. R.A. Henderson and T. Parsons (New York: Free Press, 1947).

51. D. Buss, "Profit Drop Is 'One-Off Event' for Chrysler, Marchionne Says," *Forbes*, April 29, 2013, http://www.forbes.com/sites/dalebuss/2013/04/29/chrysler-profit-tumble-reminds-that-every-launch-is-important; "Why Marchionne Should Fold Fiat Into Chrysler," *Globe and Mail*, April 25, 2013; Eric Reguly, *Globe and Mail*, http://www.theglobeandmail.com/report-on-business/rob-magazine/ceo-of-the-year/article1375887.

52. G. Keenan, "Envisioning a Consolidated Future, Fiat Chrysler Shifts Focus to Debt Reduction" *The Globe and Mail*, January 11, 2016, http://www.theglobeandmail.com/report-on-business/industry-news/envisioning-a-consolidated-future-fiat-chrysler-shifts-focus-to-debt-reduction/article28117751/.

53. K. Owram, "Fiat Chrysler–GM merger Would Lead to 'Cataclysmic Changes,' But Not in Canadian Auto Industry: Marchionne," *Financial Post*, August 31, 2015, http://business.financialpost.com/news/transportation/fiat-chrysler-gm-merger-would-lead-to-cataclysmic-changes-but-not-in-canadian-auto-industry-marchionne.

54. D. A. Waldman and F. J. Yammarino, "CEO Charismatic Leadership: Levels-of-Management

and Levels-of-Analysis Effects," *Academy of Management Review 24*, no. 2 (1999): 266–85.

55. K. B. Lowe, K. G. Kroeck, and N. Sivasubramaniam, "Effectiveness Correlates of Transformational and Transactional Leadership: A Meta-Analytic Review of the MLQ Literature," *Leadership Quarterly 7* (1996): 385–425.

56. J. M. Howell and B. J. Avolio, "The Ethics of Charismatic Leadership: Submission or Liberation?", *Academy of Management Executive 6*, no. 2 (1992): 43–54.

57. Howell and Avolio, "The Ethics of Charismatic Leadership."

58. J. Bunge, "Peregrine Founder Hit With 50 Years," *Wall Street Journal*, February 1, 2013, C1; T. Polansek and R. Schlader, "Peregrine CEO Pleads Guilty to Fraud; To Stay in Jail," Reuters, September 17, 2012, http://www.reuters.com/article/2012/09/17/us-peregrine-wasendorf-idUSBRE88G16U2 0120917

59. B. M. Bass, "From Transactional to Transformational Leadership: Learning to Share the Vision," *Organizational Dynamics 4*, no. 8 (1991): 19–31, http://strandtheory.org/images/From_transactional_to_transformational_-_Bass.pdf.

60. A. Deutschman, "Is Your Boss a Psychopath?", *Fast Company*, July 2005, 44.

61. CNN Wire Staff, "Network: Leno Took 50% Pay Cut to Reduce *Tonight Show* Layoffs," CNN, September 7, 2012, http://www.cnn.com/2012/09/07/showbiz/jay-leno-tonight-show/; A. Farnham, "Bosses Who Volunteer for Pay Cuts," ABC News, September 11, 2012, http://abcnews.go.com/Business/bosses-pay-cuts/story?id=17209062.

62. B. M. Bass, "From Transactional to Transformational Leadership."

14

1. E. E. Lawler III, L. W. Porter, and A. Tannenbaum, "Managers' Attitudes Toward Interaction Episodes," *Journal of Applied Psychology 52* (1968): 423–39; H. Mintzberg, *The Nature of Managerial Work* (New York: Harper and Row, 1973).

2. M. M. Robles, "Executive Perceptions of the Top 10 Soft Skills Needed in Today's Workplace," *Business Communication Quarterly 75* no. 4 (December 2012): 453–65.

3. Robles, "Executive Perceptions of the Top 10 Soft Skills Needed in Today's Workplace."

4. E. E. Jones and K. E. Davis, "From Acts to Dispositions: The Attribution Process in Person Perception," in *Advances in Experimental and Social Psychology 2*, ed. L. Berkowitz (New York: Academic Press, 1965), 219–66; R. G. Lord and J. E. Smith, "Theoretical, Information-Processing, and Situational Factors Affecting Attribution Theory Models of Organizational Behavior," *Academy of Management Review 8* (1983): 50–60.

5. "Lab Tests: Why Consumer Reports Can't Recommend the iPhone 4," *Consumer Reports*, July 12, 2010, http://news.consumerreports.org/electronics/2010/07/apple-iphone-4-antenna-issues-signal-strength-att-network-gsm.html.

6. G. Fowler and I. Sherr, "A Defiant Steve Jobs Confronts 'Antennagate,'" *Wall Street Journal*, July 17, 2010, B1.

7. J. Topolsky, "Apple Responds to iPhone 4 Reception Issues: You're Holding the Phone the Wrong Way," Engadget.com, June 24, 2010, http://www.engadget.com/2010/06/24/apple-responds-over-iphone-4-reception-issues-youre-holding-the/.

8. H. H. Kelly, *Attribution in Social Interaction* (Morristown: General Learning, 1971).

9. J. M. Burger, "Motivational Biases in the Attribution of Responsibility for an Accident: A Meta-Analysis of the Defensive-Attribution Hypothesis," *Psychological Bulletin* 90 (1981): 496–512.

10. D. A. Hofmann and A. Stetzer, "The Role of Safety Climate and Communication in Accident Interpretation: Implications for Learning From Negative Events," *Academy of Management Journal* 41, no. 6 (1998): 644–57.

11. C. Perrow, *Normal Accidents: Living With High-Risk Technologies* (New York: Basic, 1984).

12. A. G. Miller and T. Lawson, "The Effect of an Informational Opinion on the Fundamental Attribution Error," *Journal of Personality and Social Psychology* 47 (1989): 873–96; J. M. Burger, "Changes in Attribution Errors Over Time: The Ephemeral Fundamental Attribution Error," *Social Cognition* 9 (1991): 182–93.

13. F. Heider, *The Psychology of Interpersonal Relations* (New York: Wiley, 1958); D. T. Miller and M. Ross, "Self-Serving Biases in Attribution of Causality: Fact or Fiction?" *Psychological Bulletin* 82 (1975): 213–25.

14. J. R. Larson, Jr., "The Dynamic Interplay Between Employees' Feedback-Seeking Strategies and Supervisors' Delivery of Performance Feedback," *Academy of Management Review* 14, no. 3 (1989): 408–22.

15. E. Green, "The Origins of Office Speak," *The Atlantic*, April 24, 2014, http://www.theatlantic.com/features/archive/2014/04/the-origins-of-office-speak/361135/.

16. G. L. Kreps, *Organizational Communication: Theory and Practice* (New York: Longman, 1990).

17. Kreps, *Organizational Communication.*

18. J. Jusko, "A Little More Communication," *Industry Week*, March 1, 2010, 19.

19. E. Beaton, "Frankly Speaking: Why It Pays to Tell Your Bosses What You Really Think of Them," *Globe and Mail*, March 19, 2010, http://www.theglobeandmail.com/report-on-business/frankly-speaking/article1505364.

20. L. Landro, "The Informed Patient: Hospitals Combat Errors at the 'Hand-Off,'" *Wall Street Journal*, June 28, 2006, D1.

21. D. Therrien, "Rid Your Office of Backstabbers: How Good Managers Can Control Counterproductive Workplace Gossip," *Canadian Business*, November 22, 2004, http://www.canadianbusiness.com/business-strategy/rid-your-office-of-backstabbershow-good-managers-can-control-counterproductiveworkplace-gossip.

22. J. Sandberg, "Ruthless Rumors and the Managers Who Enable Them," *Wall Street Journal*, October 29, 2003, B1.

23. W. C. Redding, *Communication Within the Organization: An Interpretive View of Theory and Research* (New York: Industrial Communication Council, 1972).

24. D. T. Hall, K. L. Otazo, and G. P. Hollenbeck, "Behind Closed Doors: What Really Happens in Executive Coaching," *Organizational Dynamics* 27, no. 3 (1999): 39–53.

25. J. Kelly, "Blowing the Whistle on the Boss," *PR Newswire*, November 15, 2004, http://www.prnewswire.com.

26. R. McGarvey, "Lords of Discipline," *Entrepreneur Magazine*, January 1, 2000.

27. J. Welch, "'Rank-and-Yank'? That's Not How It's Done," *Wall Street Journal*, November 15, 2013, A.15.

28. J. Hollon, "Half of Companies Report Higher Turnover Than Last Year," *TLTN*, May 23, 2013, http://www.tlnt.com/2013/05/23/survey-half-of-companies-reporthigher-turnover-than-last-year; W. Immen, "Hanging On to the Best and Brightest in Lean Times," *Globe and Mail*, August 23, 2012, http://m.theglobeandmail.com/report-on-business/careers/career-advice/hanging-on-to-the-best-and-brightest-in-lean-times/article4325562/?service=mobile.

29. V. Galt, "Managing Change: Coach Them, Don't Boss Them," *Globe and Mail*, September 15, 2007, B17.

30. A. Mehrabian, "Communication Without Words," *Psychology Today* 3 (1968): 53; A. Mehrabian, *Silent Messages* (Belmont: Wadsworth, 1971); R. Harrison, *Beyond Words: An Introduction to Nonverbal Communication* (Upper Saddle River: Prentice Hall, 1974); A. Mehrabian, *Non-Verbal Communication* (Chicago: Aldine, 1972).

31. M. L. Knapp, *Nonverbal Communication in Human Interaction*, 2nd ed. (New York: Holt, Rinehart & Winston, 1978).

32. H. M. Rosenfeld, "Instrumental Affiliative Functions of Facial and Gestural Expressions," *Journal of Personality & Social Psychology* 24 (1966): 65–72; P. Ekman, "Differential Communication of Affect by Head and Body Cues," *Journal of Personality & Social Psychology* 23 (1965): 726–735; A. Mehrabian, "Significance of Posture and Position in the Communication of Attitude and Status Relationships," *Psychological Bulletin* 71 (1969): 359–372.

33. S. Shellenbarger, "Just Look Me in the Eye Already," *Wall Street Journal*, May 28, 2013, http://online.wsj.com/news/articles/SB10001424127887324809804578511290822228174.

34. S. Shellenbarger, "Is This How You Really Talk?" *Wall Street Journal*, April 23, 2013, http://online.wsj.com/news/articles/SB10001424127887323735604578440851083674898.

35. A. Joyce, "Confidentiality as a Valued Benefit; Loose Lips Can Defeat the Purpose of an Employee Assistance Program," *The Washington Post*, May 11, 2003, F05.

36. T. Andrews, "E-Mail Empowers, Voice-Mail Enslaves," *PC Week*, April 10, 1995, E11.

37. J. Fry, "When Talk Isn't Cheap: Is Emailing Colleagues Who Sit Feet Away a Sign of Office Dysfunction, or a Wise Move?" *Wall Street Journal*, November 28, 2005, http://online.wsj.com.

38. R. G. Nichols, "Do We Know How to Listen? Practical Helps in a Modern Age," in *Communication Concepts and Processes*, ed. J. DeVitor (Englewood Cliffs: Prentice Hall, 1971); P. V. Lewis, *Organizational Communication: The Essence of Effective Management* (Columbus: Grid, 1975).

39. Nichols, "Do We Know How to Listen? Practical Helps in a Modern Age."

40. E. Atwater, *I Hear You*, rev. ed. (New York: Walker, 1992).

41. T. Pittaway, "*Dragons' Den*: Fly Like a Dragon," *Profit Magazine*, October 2008, http://www.profitguide.com/manage-grow/success-stories/dragons-den-fly-like-adragon-29444; "Boston Pizza Quick Facts," http://www.bostonpizza.com/assets/mediacentre/documents/pdf/Boston_Pizza_Quick_Facts.pdf.

42. C. Gallo, "Why Leadership Means Listening," *BusinessWeek*, January 31, 2007, http://www.businessweek.com/smallbiz/content/jan2007/sb20070131_192848.htm.

43. B. D. Seyber, R. N. Bostrom, and J. H. Seibert, "Listening, Communication Abilities, and Success at Work," *Journal of Business Communication* 26 (1989): 293–303.

44. E. Atwater, *I Hear You*, rev. ed. (New York: Walker, 1992).

45. H. H. Meyer, "A Solution to the Performance Appraisal Feedback Enigma," *Academy of Management Executive* 5, no. 1 (1991): 68–76.

46. "The 2011–2012 Change and Communication ROI Study Report—Clear Direction in a Complex World: How Top Companies Create Clarity, Confidence, and Community to Build Sustainable Performance," Willis Towers Watson, January 2012, http://www.towerswatson.com/en/Insights/IC-Types/Survey-Research-Results/2012/01/2011-2012-Change-and-Communication-ROI-Study-Report.

47. L. Gurkow, "The Art of Active Listening," *Jerusalem Post*, May 11, 2014, http://www.jpost.com/Jewish-World/Judaism/Active-listening-351878.

48. M. Beheshtifar, H. Borhani, and M. Nekoie. Moghadam, "Destructive Role of Employee Silence in Organizational Success," *International Journal of Academic Research in Business and Social Sciences*, Vol. 2, No. 11 (November 2012), ISSN: 2222-6990, http://www.hrmars.com/admin/pics/1314.pdf; A. Akbarian, M. Esmail Ansari, A. Shaemi, and N. Keshtiaray, "Review Organizational Silence Factors," *Journal of Scientific Research and Development* 2 (1) (2015): 178–181, http://jsrad.org/wp-content/2015/Issue%201,%202015/31%202015-2-1-178-181.pdf.

49. K. Maher, "Global Companies Face Reality of Instituting Ethics Programs," *Wall Street Journal*, November 9, 2004, B8.

50. "Four Seasons Hotels and Resorts Named to FORTUNE List of the '100 Best Companies to Work For,'" Reuters, January 16, 2008, http://www.reuters.com/article/2013/01/16/four-seasons-hotelsidUSnPnCG43386+160+PRN20130116.

51. D. Orgel, "Supervalu's Strategic Approach to Social Media," *Supermarket News*, November 7, 2011, http://supermarketnews.com/viewpoints/supervalu_strategic_1107.

52. P. Desmond, "CIO 100: Supervalu Uses Social Media to Connect with Employees and Spur Turnaround," NTT Communications, August 12, 2012, http://www.nttcom.tv/2012/08/22/supervaluuses-social-media-to-connect-with-employees-and-spurturnaround.

15

1. E. K. Macdonald, M. Kleinaltenkamp, and H. N. Wilson, "How Business Customers Judge Solutions: Solution Quality and Value-in-Use," *Journal of Marketing*, (2016); Y. Ueki, "Customer Pressure, Customer–Manufacturer–Supplier Relationships, and Quality Control Performance," *Journal of Business Research*, 69(6) (June 1, 2016): 2233–2238; R. Leifer and P. K. Mills, "An Information Processing Approach for Deciding Upon Control Strategies and Reducing Control Loss in Emerging Organizations," *Journal of Management* 22 (1996): 113–37.

2. D. Francis, "Lip Service to Money Laundering: Failure to Apply Controls a Serious Threat to Global Economy," *Financial Post*, September 25, 2015, http://business.financialpost.com/diane-francis/lip-service-to-money-laundering-failure-to-apply-controls-a-serious-threat-to-global-economy.

3. R. Trichur and A. MacDonald, "Canadian Banks' Money-Laundering Controls Failed: Canada's Banking Regulator Found 72 Failures of Anti-Money-Laundering Controls Between 2009 and 2014," *The Wall Street Journal*, August 6, 2015, http://www.wsj.com/articles/canadian-banks-money-laundering-controls-failed-1438904411.

4. S. Freeman, "Anti-Money Laundering Watchdog's Secrecy a Disservice to Canadian Banking

Industry, Advocate Says," *Toronto Star*, April 7, 2016, http://www.thestar.com/news/canada/2016/04/07/anti-money-laundering-watchdogs-secrecy-a-disservice-to-canadian-banking-industry-advocate-says.html.

5. Freeman, "Anti-Money Laundering."

6. "About the Standards Council of Canada," https://www.scc.ca/en/about-scc.

7. Global Food Safety Resource, http://globalfoodsafetyresource.com; B. Muirhead, "The Trans Pacific Partnership: Implications for Supply Management and the Canadian Dairy Industry," University of Alberta: The 34th Western Canadian Dairy Seminar March 8–11, 2016, http://www.wcds.ca/proc/2013/Manuscripts/p%20113%20-%20128%20Muirhead.pdf; GlobalGAP, http://www1.globalgap.org/north-america/front_content.php?idcat=249; J.W. Miller, "Private Food Standards Gain Favor," *Wall Street Journal*, March 11, 2008, B1; "GlobalGap Passes Producer Landmark," May 27, 2010, http://www.fruitnet.com/content.aspx?ttid=14&cid=6819; CBC News, "BC Hot House Changes Labeling on Mexican Produce," April 23, 2008, http://www.cbc.ca/canada/british-columbia/story/2008/04/23/bc-bchothouse-mexican-brand.html#ixzz0sHTUArJ0.

8. J. Hume, "Canadian Airports Need to Be More Bilingual: Languages Commissioner," *The Toronto Sun*, January 8, 2014, http://www.torontosun.com/2014/01/08/canadian-airports-need-to-be-more-bilingual-languages-commissioner.

9. A. Miranskyy, A. Hamou-Lhadj, E. Cialini, and A. Larsson, "Operational-Log Analysis for Big Data Systems: Challenges and Solutions," *IEEE Software* (33)2 (2016): 52–59; [MS-SQMCS2]: Software Quality Metrics (SQM) Client-to-Service Version 2 Protocol (2013), "No Changes to the Meaning, Language, or Formatting of the Technical Content," http://msdn.microsoft.com/en-us/library/hh554414.aspx.

10. N. Wiener, *Cybernetics; or Control and Communication in the Animal and the Machine* (New York: Wiley, 1948).

11. AME Licensing and Training, 2016, https://www.tc.gc.ca/eng/civilaviation/standards/maintenance-aarpb-ame-basic-529.htm.

12. J. McDannald, "Tech Trends: A Deeper Dive Into the Nike+ Running App," Running.Competitor.com, January 19, 2016, http://running.competitor.com/2016/01/shoes-and-gear/tech-trends-a-deeper-dive-into-the-nike-running-app_143702#Weg0t27iUUwSwcuM.99; "More From Your Run," http://nikeplus.nike.com/plus/products/gps_app.

13. D. Brandl, "Microsoft Windows 10 Features May Help Manufacturers More Than Recent Releases," *Control Engineering*, April 3, 2015, http://www.controleng.com/single-article/microsoft-windows-10-features-may-help-manufacturers-more-than-recent-releases/370c85ff232ddf13ebf2a0d718950181.html.

14. V. A. Thompson, N. H. Therriault, and I. R. Newman, "Meta-reasoning: Monitoring and Control of Reasoning, Decision Making, and Problem Solving," *Cognitive Unconscious and Human Rationality*, (Cambridge, Massachusetts: MIT Press, 2016): 275; R. Leifer and P. K. Mills, "An Information Processing Approach for Deciding Upon Control Strategies and Reducing Control Loss in Emerging Organizations," *Journal of Management* (22)1 (2013):113–37.

15. G. Richard, V. Ojala, A. Ojala, S. K. Bowles, and H. L. Banh, "Monitoring Programs for Drugs With Potential for Abuse or Misuse in Canada," *Canadian Pharmacy Journal* (145)4 (2012): 168–171; "Tamper Resistant Prescription Drug Pad Program," NFLD Department of Health and Community Services, 2016, http://www.health.gov

.nl.ca/health/prescription/hcp_tamperresistantdrugpad.html; "Newfoundland and Labrador Pharmacy Network to Limit Drug Errors, Abuse," CBC News, May 27, 2010, http://www.cbc.ca/news/canada/newfoundland-labrador/story/2010/05/27/nl-pharmacy-network-527.html; M. Babbage, "Ontario Pharmacy Assistant Who Found Chemo Errors 'Not a Hero,' He Says," *Globe and Mail*, May 7, 2013, http://www.theglobeandmail.com/news/national/ontario-pharmacy-assistant-who-found-chemo-errors-not-a-hero-he-says/article11773549/.

16. L. Kane, "Examining the Work-From-Home Debate," *Toronto Star*, http://www.thestar.com/business/personal_finance/2013/03/01/examing_the_workfromhome_debate.html; http://get.uberflip.com/press-yoav-schwartz/.

17. B. Marotte, "Out of Office Reply: Canadian Firms Split on Value of Telecommuting," *Globe and Mail*, April 26, 2013, http://www.theglobeandmail.com/report-on-business/careers/the-future-of-work/out-of-office-reply-canadian-firms-split-on-value-of-telecommuting/article11566700/.

18. N. Koloc, "Let Employees Choose When, Where, and How to Work," *Harvard Business Review*, November 10, 2014, https://hbr.org/2014/11/let-employees-choose-when-where-and-how-to-work; S. Dominus, "Rethinking the Work-Life Equation: It Takes More Than Just Policies to Make a Workplace Truly Flexible. The Whole Office Culture Has to Change," *New York Times Magazine*. February 25, 2016, http://www.nytimes.com/2016/02/28/magazine/rethinking-the-work-life-equation.html?_r=0.

19. M. Weber, *The Protestant Ethic and the Spirit of Capitalism* (New York: Scribner's, 1958).

20. K. Ramlakhan and L. Peterson, "Car Thieves Try to Break Leash: 39 Cases of Tampering With GPS Bracelet Since 2008," *Winnipeg Free Press*, January 2, 2012, http://www.winnipegfreepress.com/special/opensecrets/car-thieves-try-to-break-leash-39-cases-of-tampering-with-gps-bracelet-since-2008-136526038.html; "GPS Bracelets Lead to Arrests of 2 Chronic Car Thieves," *CBC News*, December 22, 2009, http://www.cbc.ca/canada/manitoba/story/2009/12/22/mb-police-chase-winnipeg.html#ixzz0sHg4DPzz.

21. K. Grant, "University Health Network Boss New Ontario Deputy Health Minister," *The Globe and Mail*, March 26, 2014, http://www.theglobeandmail.com/news/politics/university-health-network-boss-new-ontario-deputy-health-minister/article17690775/; *CBC, The Fifth Estate*, "Reaction to 'Rate My Hospital' in Toronto," April 12, 2013, http://www.cbc.ca/fifth/2012-2013/2013/04/reaction-to-rate-my-hospital-in-toronto.html; J. McFarland, "Hospitals Raise Caution Over Uniform Pay-for-Performance Rules," *Globe and Mail*, April 29, 2010, http://www.theglobeandmail.com/news/national/hospitals-raise-caution-over-uniform-pay-for-performance-rules/article1529878.

22. F. Kopun, "Nordstrom Begins Hiring for Toronto Stores," *Toronto Star*, February 25, 2016, http://www.thestar.com/business/2016/02/25/nordstrom-begins-hiring-for-toronto-stores.html.

23. Canadian Press, "Toronto to Get Second Nordstrom Location in Canadian Expansion," *Financial Post*, April 8, 2013, http://business.financialpost.com/2013/04/08/nordstrom-canada-toronto; "Nordstrom Expands Canadian Footprint to Yorkdale Mall," *CBC News*, April 8, 2013, http://www.cbc.ca/news/business/story/2013/04/08/business-nordstrom-yorkdale.html; A. DeFelice, "A Century of Customer Love: Nordstrom Is the Gold Standard for Customer Service Excellence," *CRM Magazine*, June 1, 2005, 42, http://www.destinationcrm.com/

Articles/Editorial/Magazine-Features/A-Century-of-Customer-Love-42958.aspx; Nordstrom, "International Shopping," http://shop.nordstrom.com/c/6025407/. . .6pbo%3D6008488.

24. R. T. Pascale, "Nordstrom: Respond to Unreasonable Customer Requests!" *Planning Review* 2 (May–June 1994): 17.

25. Pascale, "Nordstrom."

26. Pascale, "Nordstrom."

27. Y. van Nuenen, "Playing the Panopticon Procedural Surveillance in Dark Souls," *Games and Culture*, February 10, 2015, http://gac.sagepub.com/content/early/2015/02/10/1555412015570967.full.pdf+html; T. Carton, "Burnout as Alienation in the Counselling Field: The Descent From Homo-Faber to Homo-Economous," *Sociology Mind* (6)2: 33 (2016); J. R. Barker, "Tightening the Iron Cage: Concertive Control in Self-Managing Teams," *Administrative Science Quarterly* 38 (1993): 408–37.

28. N. Byrnes, "The Art of Motivation," *Business Week*, May 1, 2006, 56–62; D. Crofts and R. Delaney, "Nucor Buys Canada's Harris Steel for $1.07 Billion," *Bloomberg News*, January 3, 2007, http://www.bloomberg.com/apps/news?pid=newsarchive&sid=atc7t4wqgN1Q&refer=us.

29. Barker, "Tightening the Iron Cage."

30. R. A. Baron, B. A. Mueller, and M. T. Wolfe. "Self-Efficacy and Entrepreneurs' Adoption Of Unattainable Goals: The Restraining Effects of Self-Control," *Journal of Business Venturing* (31)1 (2016): 55–71; H. Rachlin, "Self-Control Based on Soft Commitment," *The Behavior Analyst* (2016): 1–10; S. F. Premeaux and A. G. Bedeian, "Breaking the Silence: The Moderating Effects of Self-Monitoring in Predicting Speaking Up in the Workplace," *Journal of Management Studies* 40, no. 6 (2003): 1537–62; C. Manz and H. Sims, "Leading Workers to Lead Themselves: The External Leadership of Self-Managed Work Teams," *Administrative Science Quarterly* 32 (1987): 106–28.

31. P. L. Nesbit, "The Role of Self-Reflection, Emotional Management of Feedback, and -Regulation Processes in Self-Directed Leadership Development," *Human Resource Development Review* 11, no. 2 (2012): 203–22; J. Slocum and H. A. Sims, "Typology for Integrating Technology, Organization, and Job Design," *Human Relations* 33 (1980): 193–212.

32. V. Giolito and D. Van Dierendonck, "Servant Leadership: Influence on Financial Business-Unit Performance and Employees' Well-Being," *Academy of Management Proceedings*, (2015); C. C. Manz and H. P. Sims, Jr., "Self-Management as a Substitute for Leadership: A Social Learning Perspective," *Academy of Management Review* 5 (1980): 361–67.

33. E. Zolfagharifard, "Why You SHOULD Eat That Cupcake: Self-Control Can Sap Your Memory, Claims Study," *The Daily Mail*, August 27, 2015, http://www.dailymail.co.uk/sciencetech/article-3213509/Why-eat-cupcake-Self-control-sap-memory-claims-study.html; A. Moritz, "Five Apps That Help Improve Memory and Overall Cognition," *Brainscape*, September 8, 2012, http://blog.brainscape.com/2012/08/apps-memory-cognition; C. Parker, "Best Android Apps for Improving Memory," *Android Authority*, May 9, 2012, http://www.androidauthority.com/best-android-apps-improving-memory-83632/; C. Manz and C. Neck, *Mastering Self-Leadership*, 3rd ed. (Upper Saddle River: Pearson, Prentice Hall, 2004).

34. "What Is Six Sigma?", General Electric, http://www.ge.com/en/company/companyinfo/quality/whatis.htm; B. Power, "How GE Applies Lean

Startup Practices," *Harvard Business Review*, April 2014, https://hbr.org/2014/04/how-ge-applies-lean-startup-practices/; J. Kalra and A. Kopargaonkar, "Quality Improvement in Clinical Laboratories: A Six Sigma Concept," *Pathology Laboratory Medicine Open Journal (1)*1 (2016):11–20, University of Saskatchewan.

35. R. S. Kaplan and D. P. Norton, "Using the Balanced Scorecard as a Strategic Management System," *Harvard Business Review* (January–February 1996): 75–85; R. S. Kaplan and D. P. Norton, "The Balanced Scorecard: Measures That Drive Performance," *Harvard Business Review* (January–February 1992): 71–79; P. Niven, "Cascading the Balanced Scorecard: A Case Study on Nova Scotia Power, Inc.," 2016, http://www.scribd.com/doc/3489336/Cascading-the-Balanced-Scorecard-A-Case-Study-on-Nova-Scotia-Power.

36. J. Meliones, "Saving Money, Saving Lives," *Harvard Business Review* (November–December 2000): 57–65.

37. M. H. Stocks and A. Harrell, "The Impact of an Increase in Accounting Information Level on the Judgment Quality of Individuals and Groups," *Accounting, Organizations, and Society*, October–November 1995, 685–700.

38. J. Chevreau, "When Does It Pay to Borrow to Invest?", *Financial Post* (2013), http://www.financialpost.com/money/wealthyboomer/story.html?id=a251451b-7717-42a0-962f-b1b30a0c3b74.

39. G. Colvin, "America's Best and Worst Wealth Creators: The Real Champions Aren't Always Who You Think," *Fortune*, December 18, 2000, 207; "Introducing the Wealth Added Framework (Relative Wealth Added (RWA) and Wealth Added Index (WAI)," Stern Stewart, August 2009, http://sternstewart.com/rankings/SSGlobal1000/Introducing%20the%20Wealth%20Added%20Framework.pdf.

40. "About Herman Miller: Operational Excellence," Herman Miller, http://www.hermanmiller.com/about-us/our-values-in-action/operational-excellence.html.

41. EVA for Apple, Inc., http://ftalphaville.ft.com/2015/01/28/2103622/if-apple-were-a-country/.

42. B. Turnbull, "Tweet for Satisfaction," *Toronto Star*, July 15, 2009, http://www.thestar.com/life/2009/07/15/tweet_for_satisfaction.html.

43. B. C. Holtom and T. C. Burch, "A Model of Turnover-Based Disruption in Customer Services," *Human Resource Management Review (26)*1 (2016): 25–36; A. Rao, "From Brand to Customer." *Journal of Creating Value*: 2394964315627253; C. B. Furlong, "12 Rules for Customer Retention," *Bank Marketing* 5 (January 1993): 14.

44. M. I. Valdés, and J. Beniflah, "Estimating the Value of the US Multicultural Shopper in the Independent Retail Channel: An In-Culture™ analysis," *Journal of Cultural Marketing Strategy (1)*2 (2016): 138–147; 49; K. G. Atkins, A. Kumar, and Y-K. Kim, "Smart Grocery Shopper Segments," *Journal of International Consumer Marketing (28)*1: 42–53; M. Raphel, "Vanished Customers are Valuable Customers," *Art Business News*, June 2002, 46.

45. E. E. Bowen, B. D. Bowen, and D. E. Headley, "Development of a Model of Airline Consumer Satisfaction," *Aviation Technology Faculty and Staff Publications*, Purdue University, 2013, http://docs.lib.purdue.edu/authors.html; C. A. Reeves and D. A. Bednar, "Defining Quality: Alternatives and Implications," *Academy of Management Review* 19 (1994): 419–45.

46. A. Schofield, "Mixing Models: Singapore Airlines Refines the Formula for Low-Cost Carrier Ownership," *Aviation Week & Space Technology* (2016); J. Wang, "Multimodal Narratives in SIA's 'Singapore Girl' TV Advertisements—From Branding With Femininity to Branding With

Provenance And Authenticity?" *Social Semiotics (26)*2: 208-225; Singapore Airlines, https://www.singaporeair.com/htdocs/.../sia-equal-access-plan.doc; Singapore Airlines, http://www.singaporeair.com/en_UK/ca/home.

47. S. Holmes, "Creature Comforts at 30,000 feet," *Business Week*, December 18, 2006, 138.

48. H. Shaw, "Loblaw Execs Reveal Company Problems," *Financial Post*, 2009, http://www.financialpost.com/story.html?id=65573c81-1600-48e0-88fb-8ca878b8c87c&k=0; "Loblaw Profit Soars, Vows More Aid to Bangladesh Victims," *CBC News*, May 1, 2013, http://www.cbc.ca/news/business/story/2013/05/01/business-loblaws-profit.html; Loblaw, http://www.weston.ca/en/Loblaw-Companies-Ltd.aspx; "Loblaw Net Earnings Soar in Q1," *Montreal Gazette*, May 1, 2013, http://www.montrealgazette.com/business/Loblaw+earnings+soar/8320448/story.html#ixzz2Tru3CQsq; "Loblaw Net Profits Soar 40% in Q1, Raises Dividend," *Ottawa Citizen*, http://www.ottawacitizen.com/business/Loblaw+profits+soar+raises+dividend/8320590/story.html#ixzz2TrvKCqFf.

49. A. Sagan, "Loblaw to Open 50 New Stores This Year," *The Toronto Sun*, April 12, 2016, http://www.torontosun.com/2016/04/12/loblaw-store-expansion-to-create-20000-jobs-this-year.

50. D. R. May and B. L. Flannery, "Cutting Waste With Employee Involvement Teams," *Business Horizons*, September–October 1995, 28–38.

51. Intel, "The End of the Road: Schools and Computer Recycling," http://www.intel.com/education/recycling_computers/recycling.htm.

52. A. Moodie, "Best Buy's e-Cycle Program Is Ambitious, Successful and Financially Unsustainable," *The Guardian*, February 23, 2016. http://www.theguardian.com/sustainable-business/2016/feb/23/best-buy-walmart-staples-ewaste-recycling-environment-landfill-electronics.

53. Moodie, "Best Buy's e-Cycle Program."

54. L. Downing, "British Retailers Turn Waste Into Power," *Bloomberg Businessweek*, June 14, 2012, http://www.bloomberg.com/news/articles/2012-06-14/british-retailers-turn-waste-into-power.

55. City of Edmonton, "Waste-to-Biofuels Facility Turning Garbage Into Fuel," http://www.edmonton.ca/for_residents/garbage_recycling/biofuels-facility.aspx.

56. "Recycling at Calgary Condos Grows Niche Company," *CBC News*, May 12, 2013, http://www.cbc.ca/news/canada/calgary/story/2010/10/20/calgary-condominium-recycling-company.html.

57. M. Eriksen, L. Lebreton, H. S. Carson, M. Thiel, C. J. Moore, and J. C. Borerro, "Plastic Pollution in the World's Oceans: More than 5 Trillion Plastic Pieces Weighing over 250,000 Tons Afloat at Sea," *PLoS ONE* 9(12) (2014): e111913. doi:10.1371/journal.pone.0111913.

58. A. Merkl, "A New Approach to Ocean Pollution," *Forbes*, December 17, 2014, http://www.forbes.com/sites/skollworldforum/2014/12/17/a-new-approach-to-ocean-pollution/#77eb98c93e3e.

59. "3M Announces New 2025 Sustainability Goals," Canadian Office Products Association, June 9, 2015, http://www.copa.ca/3m-announces-new-2025-sustainability-goals.

16

1. R. Lenzner, "The Reluctant Entrepreneur," *Forbes*, September 11, 1995, 162–66.

2. "Inflation Calculator: Find US Dollar's Value From 1913–2014," US Inflation Calculator, April 18, 2016, http://www.usinflationcalculator.com/; T. Lee, "Today's iPhone Is More Useful Than $3,000 Worth of Gadgets From a 1991 Radio

Shack," *The Washington Post*, January 31, 2014, https://www.washingtonpost.com/news/the-switch/wp/2014/01/31/todays-iphone-is-more-useful-than-3000-worth-of-gadgets-from-a-1991-radio-shack/.

3. S. Shankland, "Moore's Law: The Rule That Really Matters in Tech," *CNET*, October 15, 2012, http://www.cnet.com/news/moores-law-the-rule-that-really-matters-in-tech/.

4. Zacks Equity Research, "Pandora Listener Hours Up in May—Analyst Blog," nasdaq.com, June 5, 2014, http://www.nasdaq.com/article/pandora-listener-hours-up-in-may-analyst-blog-cm359420; Pandora Media Inc. SEC Filing, December 31, 2015, http://secfilings.nasdaq.com/edgar_conv_html%2f2016%2f02%2f18%2f0001230276-16-000057.html#FIS_BUSINESS.

5. H. Michael, "Updated Numbers: Beats Music Now Has 250,000 Subscribers," *PhoneArena*, May 29, 2014, http://www.phonearena.com/news/Updated-numbers-Beats-Music-now-has-250000-subscribers_id56644; H. Karp and A. Barr, "Apple Taps Tastemakers to Regain Music Mojo," *Wall Street Journal*, May 29, 2014, A1, http://www.wsj.com/articles/apple-to-buy-beats-1401308971.

6. S. Nassauer, "'I Hate My Room,' the Traveler Tweeted, Ka-Boom! An Upgrade!" *Wall Street Journal*, June 24, 2010, http://www.wsj.com/articles/SB10001424052748704256304575320730977161348.

7. J. McKinnell, "Hotel for Pets, and People Too," *Maclean's*, January 30, 2013, http://www2.macleans.ca/2013/01/30/hotel-for-pets-and-people-too.

8. T. Khandaker, "A Guide to Toronto's Best Transit Apps," *The Toronto Star*, December 27, 2014, http://www.thestar.com/news/gta/2014/12/27/a_guide_to_torontos_best_transit_apps.html; A. Donnelly, "Updated: NextBus Lets TTC Riders Track Buses by GPS," *National Post*, July 11, 2011, http://news.nationalpost.com/2011/07/11/nextbus-lets-ttc-riders-track-buses-by-gps.

9. R. Smith, "Find the Best Checkout Line—Retailers Try to Speed Up; What Works, What Adds to Shopper Aggravation," *Wall Street Journal*, December 8, 2011, http://www.wsj.com/articles/SB10001424052970204770404577082933921432686.

10. J. Jargon, "Kroger's New Weapon: Infrared Cameras—Technology Helps Kroger Reduce Wait Times to 26 Seconds," *Wall Street Journal*, May 2, 2013, B4, http://www.wsj.com/articles/SB10001424127887323798104578453293807869744.

11. N. Bogart, "Canadian Airline First Air to Live Stream Black Box Data," Global News, May 6, 2014, http://globalnews.ca/news/1314398/canadian-airline-first-air-to-live-stream-black-box-data/.

12. D. Stacey and G. Raghuvanshi, "Malaysia Airlines Flight 370: Contractor Will Get 300 Days to Complete Search," *Wall Street Journal*, June 4, 2014, http://www.wsj.com/articles/contractor-will-get-300-days-to-complete-malaysia-airlines-flight-370-search-1401849756.

13. A. Pasztor and J. Ostrower, "Missing Malaysia Jet Adds Fuel to 'Live Black Box' Debate," *Wall Street Journal*, March 9, 2014, http://www.wsj.com/articles/SB10001424052702304020104579429233516692014.

14. Bogart, "Canadian Airline First Air to Live Stream Black Box Data."

15. D. Hernandez, "Artificial Intelligence Is Now Telling Doctors How to Treat You," *Wired*, June 2, 2014, http://www.wired.com/2014/06/ai-healthcare/.

16. Hernandez, "Artificial Intelligence Is Now Telling Doctors How to Treat You."

17. Associated Press, "Syrup-Makers Go High-Tech With Wireless Monitoring," *Wall Street Journal*, April 1, 2014, http://www.15minutenews.com/business/2014/04/01/.

18. C. Kang, "Experts: Google Privacy Shift Will Have Greater Impact on Android Users,"

The Washington Post, January 25, 2012, https://www.washingtonpost.com/business/technology/google-sees-profit-in-tracking-users/2012/01/25/gIQAfDJVRQ_story.html; "Google Invests $300 Million in Hong Kong Datacenter," *PCWorld*, December 11, 2011, http://www.pcworld.com/article/245982/google_invests_300_million_in_hong_kong_datacenter.html; S. Grundberg and N. Rolander, "For Data Center, Google Goes for the Cold," *Wall Street Journal*, September 12, 2011, http://www.wsj.com/articles/SB10001424053111904836104576560551005570810; S. Mahtani, "Google to Invest $120 Million in Singapore Data Center," *Wall Street Journal*, December 15, 2011, http://allthingsd.com/20111215/google-to-invest-120-million-in-singapore-data-center/.

19. J. Stroller, "Why Cold Canada Is Becoming a Hot Spot for Data Centres," *Globe and Mail*, December 20, 2012, http://www.theglobeandmail.com/report-on-business/economy/canada-competes/why-cold-canada-is-becoming-a-hot-spot-for-data-centres/article6598555.

20. V. Beal, "Why Putting Your Data Center in Canada Makes Sense," *CIO.com*, October 8, 2012, http://www.cio.com/article/718251/Why_Putting_Your_Data_Center_in_Canada_Makes_Sense.

21. G. Murphy, "B.C. Hydro Responds to Attack on Its Smart Meter Technology," *Victoria News*, February 22, 2013, http://www.vicnews.com/opinion/letters/192524881.html; T. Knauss, "Niagara Mohawk Meters to Send Readings by Radio," *Post-Standard Syracuse*, September 17, 2002, A1.

22. S. Lubar, *Infoculture: The Smithsonian Book of Information Age Inventions* (Boston: Houghton, Mifflin, 1993).

23. J. MacDougall, "Why Radio Frequency Identification Makes Me Nervous," *National Post*, May 25, 2013, http://life.nationalpost.com/2013/05/25/jane-macdougall-rfids-make-me-nervous.

24. "What is RFID?" accessed April 19, 2016, at http://www.rfidjournal.com/site/faqs#Anchor-What-363.

25. R. Martin, "Diving Deep Into Loblaw's Loyalty Program: How Does Loblaw Bake Data Into Its PC Plus Program?" *Canadian Grocer*, March 13, 2016, http://www.canadiangrocer.com/top-stories/diving-deep-into-loblaws-loyalty-program-62823; J. Pachner, "This Little Yogurt Went to Market . . .," *Globe and Mail Report on Business*, October 31, 2008, htpp://www.theglobeandmail.com/report-on-business/rob-magazine/this-little-yogurt-went. . .

26. N. Rubenking, "Hidden Messages," *PC Magazine*, May 22, 2001, 86.

27. G. Stanley, "Diapers, Beer, and Data Science in Retail," *Contemporary Analysis: Predictive Analytics*, July 17, 2012, http://canworksmart.com/diapers-beer-retail-predictive-analytics/.

28. M. Overfelt, "A Better Way to Sell Tickets," *Fortune Small Business*, December 1, 2006, 76; R. Leth, "Sports Buzz in Toronto," April 3, 2013, http://globalnews.ca/video/458041/sports-buzz-in-toronto.

29. Teradata, "Hudson's Bay Company: Nailing Fraud and Raising ROI," 2013, http://www.teradata.com/customers/Retail-Hudsons-Bay.

30. "What Does Ford's Manufacturer Warranty Cover?", Bayfield Ford website, July 23, 2016, http://www.bayfieldford.com/what-does-ford-manufacturer-warranty-cover-.htm.

31. J.P. Mello, Jr, "Malware Poisons One-Third of World's Computers," *TechNewsWorld*, July 9, 2014, http://www.technewsworld.com/story/80707.html; D. Danchev, "Report: 48% of 22 Million Scanned Computers Infected With Malware," *ZDNet*, January 27, 2010, http://www.zdnet.com/blog/security/report-48-of-22-million-scanned-computers-infected-with-malware/5365; T. Samson,

"Malware Infects 30 Percent of Computers in U.S.," *InfoWorld*, 2010, http://www.infoworld.com/t/cyber-crime/malware-infects-30-percent-of-computers-in-us-199598; B. Gottesman and K. Karagiannis, "A False Sense of Security," *PC Magazine*, February 22, 2005, 72.

32. "Authentication," Webopedia.com, http://www.webopedia.com/TERM/a/authentication.html.

33. "Authorization," Webopedia.com, http://www.webopedia.com/TERM/a/authorization.html.

34. Morgan, "Announcing Our Worst Passwords of 2015," https://www.teamsid.com/worst-passwords-2015/; L. Seltzer, "Password Crackers," *PC Magazine*, February 12, 2002, 68.

35. W. Gordon, "Here's Everywhere You Should Enable Two-Factor Authentication Right Now," *LifeHacker*, December 10, 2013, http://lifehacker.com/5938565/heres-everywhere-you-should-enable-two-factor-authentication-right-now; L. Tung, "Google to Slap Two-Factor Across Apps via Suspicious Logins Trigger," *ZD Net*, May 15, 2014, http://www.zdnet.com/article/google-to-slap-two-factor-across-apps-via-suspicious-logins-trigger/.

36. Mercantile Mergers and Acquisitions Corporation, http://www.mercantilemergersacquisitions.com/aboutus/mark-borkowski.html; R. Carrick, "Storing Your Financial Data the Safe Way" *Globe and Mail*, September 6, 2012, http://www.theglobeandmail.com/globe-investor/personal-finance/storing-your-financial-data-the-safe-way/article4325109; C. Payette, "Mercantile Mergers Locks and Loads With Drive Crypt," April 22, 2009, http://www.theglobeandmail.com/technology/mercantile-mergers-locks-and-loads-with-drive-crypt/article1157409; C. Atchison, "Security: Stop, Thief?" *Profit Magazine*, October 2008, http://www.profitguide.com/manage-grow/strategy-operations/security-stop-thief-29453.

37. R. Gann, "How to Secure a Wireless Network: Top Tips for Securing Your Businesses Wireless Network," TechRadar, December 6, 2012, http://www.techradar.com/news/internet/how-to-secure-a-wireless-network-1075710.

38. J. DeAvila, "Wi-Fi Users, Beware: Hot Spots Are Weak Spots," *Wall Street Journal*, January 16, 2008, D1.

39. G. A. Fowler, "You Won't Believe How Adorable This Kitty Is! Click For More!" *Wall Street Journal*, March 26, 2013, http://www.wsj.com/articles/SB10001424127887324373204578373011392662962.

40. J. van den Hoven, "Executive Support Systems and Decision Making," *Journal of Systems Management* 47, no. 8 (March–April 1996): 48.

41. D. Hannon, "Colgate-Palmolive Empowers Senior Leaders With Executive Dashboards," InsiderProfiles, April 1, 2011, http://insiderprofiles.wispubs.com/article.aspx?Articled=5720.

42. "Intranet," Webopedia.com, http://www.webopedia.com/TERM/i/intranet.html.

43. Microsoft Office System Customer Solution Case Study, "Canadian Tire Rolls Out SharePoint® for Worker Collaboration," 2012, http://www.itreportcanada.ca/itpublic/Canadian_Tire_Rolls_Out_SharePoint.pdf; S. Holz, "Bring Your Intranet Into the 21st Century," Communication World, January–February 2008, 14–18.

44. "Accorda Therapeutics Announces Company Intranet Named One of Ten Best in the World," Yahoo! Finance, February 14, 2013, http://www.advfn.com/news/news_Acorda-Therapeutics-Announces-Company-Intranet-Nam_56292706.html; "Internal Communications—It's Not Rocket Science," Government of Nova Scotia, novascotia.ca/cns/pubs/ItsNotRocketScience.pdf; "Extranet," Webopedia, http://www.webopedia.com/TERM/E/extranet.html.

45. "Web Services," *PC Magazine*, http://www.pcmag.com/encyclopedia/term/54345/web-services.

46. K. C. Laudon, J. P. Laudon, and M. E. Brabston, *Management Information Systems: Managing the Digital Firm* (6th Canadian ed.) (Toronto: Pearson Canada, 2013).

47. J. Borzo, "Software for Symptoms," *Wall Street Journal*, May 23, 2005, R10.

48. Borzo, "Software for Symptoms."

49. R. Hernandez, "American Express Authorizer's Assistant," *Business Rules Journal*, http://bizrules.com/advice.htm.

17

1. WestJet, "1999 Initial Public Offering Prospectus," http://www.westjet.com/pdf/investorMedia/financialReports/062899prospectus.pdf.

2. WestJet, "InFlight Experience," http://www.westjet.com/guest/en/experience/inflightExperience/buyOnBoard.shtml.

3. J. Kirby, "West Jet's Plan to Crush Air Canada," *Maclean's*, October 6, 2013, http://www.thecanadianencyclopedia.ca/en/article/westjets-plan-to-crush-air-canada/#top.

4. C. Sorensen, "WestJet's Big Plans to Conquer Air Canada and Then the World," *Maclean's*, May 27, 2010, http://www2.macleans.ca/2010/05/27/ready-for-takeoff/2.

5. WestJet, "2015 Annual Report," http://www.westjet.com/pdf/investorMedia/financialReports/WestJet2015AR.pdf; "Top 10 Airlines, November 2015," Aviation Week Network, http://aviationweek.com/awin-only/us-airlines-employees-top-10-airlines-november-2015; "Management's Discussion and Analysis of Financial Results 2012," http://www.westjet.com/guest/en/media-investors/2012-annual-report/WestJet-MDA-2012.pdf.

6. K. Owram, "WestJet Airlines Taking the Fight to Air Canada With Plans to Debut Wide-Body Aircraft Next Year," *Financial Post*, July 7, 2014, http://business.financialpost.com/news/transportation/westjet-airlines-to-debut-wide-body-aircraft-next-year-as-it-broadens-offensive-against-air-canada.

7. Profile of the American Iron and Steel Institute 2014, https://www.steel.org/~/media/Files/AISI/Reports/AISI_Profile_14_FINAL.pdf.

8. G. Polek, "Automation Key to Boeing 777 Production Rate Increase," *AINonline*, June 17, 2013, http://www.ainonline.com/aviation-news/paris-air-show/2013-06-17/automation-key-boeing-777-production-rate-increase.

9. Web Desk, "Boeing Delivers First 777 Built With Faster Production Rate," *Q13Fox.com*, February 26, 2013, http://q13fox.com/2013/02/26/boeing-delivers-first-777-built-with-faster-production-rate/.

10. S. Gordon, "Intro to Productivity (That Thing Canadians Are Apparently So Bad At)," *Canadian Business*, June 4, 2013, http://www.canadianbusiness.com/economy/intro-to-productivity-that-thing-canadians-are-apparently-so-bad-at/.

11. TD Economics Topic Paper, "Canada's Productivity Challenge," October 5, 2005, https://www.td.com/document/PDF/economics/topic/td-economics-topic-el1005-prod.pdf.

12. "Solving (Almost) Canada's Productivity Puzzle," CBC News, August 11, 2009, http://www.cbc.ca/money/story/2009/08/10/f-productivity-statistics-canada-study.html.

13. D. Shaw, "Productivity: Its Increasing Influence Over Canadians' Standard of Living and Quality of Life Industry," Library of Parliament, Infrastructure and Resources Division, November 5, 2009, 4,

http://www2.parl.gc.ca/Content/LOP/Research Publications/prb0315-e.pdf.

14. "How Canada Performs, International Rankings, Economy, Labour Productivity Growth," The Conference Board of Canada, March 2013, http://www.conferenceboard.ca/hcp/details/economy/measuring-productivity-canada.aspx.

15. "How Canada Performs, Labour Productivity Growth," The Conference Board of Canada, March 2013, http://www.conferenceboard.ca/hcp/details/economy/measuring-productivity-canada.aspx.

16. Bureau of Labor Statistics, "Multifactor Productivity," http://stats.bls.gov/bls/productivity.htm.

17. A. Leonard, "Productivity in Canada: Concepts and Issues," Library of Parliament, Economics, Resources and International Affairs Division, September 16, 2014, http://www.lop.parl.gc.ca/content/lop/ResearchPublications/2014-84-e.pdf.

18. J. Baldwin and W. Gu, "The Canadian Productivity Review: Productivity Performance in Canada, 1961 to 2008: An Update on Long-Term Trends," August 2009, http://www.statcan.gc.ca/pub/15-206-x/15-206-x2009025-eng.pdf.

19. "Korean Brands Lead Industry in Initial Quality, While Japanese Brands Struggle to Keep Up With Pace of Improvement," J.D. Power U.S. Initial Quality Study, June 17, 2015, http://canada.jdpower.com/press-releases/2015-us-initial-quality-study-iqs#.

20. Toyota Company Info, Awards, J.D. Power, Quality Plant Awards, Toyota website, http://www.toyota.ca/cgi-bin/WebObjects.exe/WWW.woa/wa/vp?vp=Home.Vehicles.Quality.JDPower.

21. American Society for Quality, "Quality Glossary—Q," http://www.asq.org/glossary/q.html.

22. R. E. Markland, S. K. Vickery, and R. A. Davis, "Managing Quality" (Chapter 7), Operations Management: Concepts in Manufacturing and Services (Cincinnati: South-Western, 1998).

23. "WD Launches High-Performance, 7200 Rpm 2Tb Hard Drives for Desktop and Enterprise Systems," Western Digital, September 1, 2009, http://www.wdc.com.

24. J. Ewoldt, "A Brighter Day for LED Bulbs," StarTribune, April 3, 2013, http://www.startribune.com/business/201357281 .html?refer=y; M. White, "Light Switch: Why You'll Start Using LED Bulbs This Year," Time, April 25, 2013, http://business.time.com/2013/04/25/light-switch-why-youll-start-using-led-bulbs-this-year/.

25. L. L. Berry and A. Parasuraman, Marketing Services (New York: Free Press, 1991).

26. "Apple, Murphy USA, Tiffany & Co. Top New eMarketer Store Productivity Rankings," eMarketer Retail, May 26, 2014, http://retail.emarketer.com/apple-murphy-usa-tiffany-co -top-new-emarketer-store-productivity-rankings/; "10 Mind Blowing Facts About the Apple Store," Business Insider.com, http://www.businessinsider.com/apple-store-facts-2015-3#apple-stores-get-more-than-1-million-visitors-per-day-worldwide-thats-at-least-365-million-people-per-year-disney-theme-parks-only-get-about-130-million-visitors-per-year-3.

27. International Organization for Standardization, "FAQs—General Standards," http://www.iso.org/iso/home/standards.htm.

28. ISO in Brief, 2015, http://www.iso.org/iso/isoinbrief_2015.pdf.

29. International Organization for Standardization, "ISO 9000 Quality Management," http://www.iso.org/iso/home/standards/management-standards/iso_9000.htm.

30. International Organization for Standardization, "ISO 14000 Environmental Management," http://www.iso.org/iso/home/standards/management-standards/iso14000.htm.

31. J. Haimowitz and J. Warren, "Economic Value of Standardization" The Conference Board of Canada submitted to Standards Council of Canada, July 2000, http://www.scc.ca/sites/default/files/migrated_files/DLFE-342.pdf.

32. R. Henkoff, "The Not New Seal of Quality (ISO 9000 Standard of Quality Management)," Fortune, June 28, 1993, 116.

33. International Organization for Standardization, Home, Standards, Certification, http://www.iso.org/iso/home/standards/certification.htm.

34. J. W. Dean, Jr., and J. Evans, Total Quality: Management, Organization, and Strategy (St. Paul: West, 1994).

35. J. W. Dean, Jr., and D. E. Bowen, "Management Theory and Total Quality: Improving Research and Practice Through Theory Development," Academy of Management Review 19 (1994): 392–418.

36. B. Swallow, "Why Is a 20 Year Old Service Measure Still So Influential?" Mycustomer.com, May 1, 2014, http://www.mycustomer.com/service/management/esqi-why-is-a-20-year-old-service-measure-still-so-influential; R. Allen and R. Kilmann, "Aligning Reward Practices in Support of Total Quality Management," Business Horizons, May 1, 2001, 77.

37. iSixSigma, "What Is Six Sigma?", http://www.isixsigma.com/new-to-six-sigma/getting-started/what-six-sigma/; General Electric, "What Is Six Sigma?", http://www.ge.com/en/company/companyinfo/quality/whatis.htm.

38. "A Team Approach to Reducing Waiting Times," Globe and Mail, December 3, 2012, http://www.theglobeandmail.com/life/health-and-fitness/advsunnybrook/sunnybrookfeatures/a-team-approach-to-reducing-wait-times/article5913697.

39. J. Heskett, T. Jones, G. Loveman, W. Sasser, and L. Schlesinger, "Putting the Service–Profit Chain to Work," Harvard Business Review, July–August 2008 issue, https://hbr.org/2008/07/putting-the-service-profit-chain-to-work; R. Hallowell, L. A. Schlesinger, and J. Zornitsky, "Internal Service Quality, Customer and Job Satisfaction: Linkages and Implications for Management," Human Resource Planning 19 (1996): 20–31; J. L. Heskett, T. O. Jones, G. W. Loveman, W. E. Sasser, Jr., and L. A. Schlesinger, "Putting the Service–Profit Chain to Work," Harvard Business Review (March–April 1994): 164–74.

40. Harvard Business Review, "Putting the Service–Profit Chain to Work."

41. 2016 Winners Canada's Top 100 Employers, Vancity Vancouver City Savings Credit Union, http://content.eluta.ca/top-employer-vancity; A. Wahl, "Best Workplaces 2006: On the Money—Vancity," Canadian Business Online, April 10, 2006, http://www.canadianbusiness.com/business-strategy/the-best-workplaces-in-canada.

42. R. Eder, "Customer-Easy Doesn't Come Easy," Drug Store News, October 21, 2002, 52.

43. J. Heskett, T. Jones, G. Loveman, E. Sasser, and L. Schlesinger, "Putting the Service–Profit Chain to Work," Harvard Business Review 86 (July-August 2008): 118-129.

44. L. L. Berry and A. Parasuraman, "Listening to the Customer—The Concept of a Service-Quality Information System," Sloan Management Review 38, no. 3 (Spring 1997): 65; C. W. L. Hart, J. L. Heskett, and W. E. Sasser, Jr., "The Profitable Art of Service Recovery," Harvard Business Review (July–August 1990): 148–56.

45. Vancity Credit Union, "2002–2003 Accountability Report," https://www.vancity.com/lang/fr/AboutUs/OurBusiness/OurReports/AccountabilityReport/0203AccountabilityReport/CommitmentThree.

46. D. E. Bowen and E. E. Lawler III, "The Empowerment of Service Workers: What, Why,

How, and When," Sloan Management Review 33 (Spring 1992): 31–39; D. E. Bowen and E. E. Lawler III, "Empowering Service Employees," Sloan Management Review 36 (Summer 1995): 73–84.

47. Bowen and Lawler III, "The Empowerment of Service Workers."

48. Vancity Credit Union, "2002–2003 Accountability Report."

49. B. Gruel and S. Singh, "Deere's Big Green Profit Machine," Bloomberg Businessweek, July 5, 2012, http://www.businessweek.com/articles/2012-07-05/deeres-big -green-profit-machine.

50. G. V. Frazier and M. T. Spiggs, "Achieving Competitive Advantage Through Group Technology," Business Horizons 39 (1996): 83–88.

51. D. Lavrinc, "Peek Inside Tesla's Robotic Factory," Wired, July 16, 2013, http://www.wired.com/2013/07/tesla-plant-video/.

52. "What's Behind Canada's Drug Shortage? One Expert Says 'Money'" Global News, May 27, 2014, http://globalnews.ca/news/1355919/whats-behind-canadas-drug-shortage-one-expert-says-money/; M. Leung and A. Mulholland, "Drug Manufacturers Required to Report Drug Shortages Under New Rules," CTV News, February 10, 2015, http://www.ctvnews.ca/health/drug-manufacturers-required-to-report-shortages-under-new-rules-1.2229266; Health Canada, Drug & Health Products, Drug Products, Drug Shortages, http://www.hc-sc.gc.ca/dhp-mps/prodpharma/shortages-penuries/info-eng.php.

53. J. R. Henry, "Minimized Setup Will Make Your Packaging Line S.M.I.L.E.," Packaging Technology and Engineering, February 1, 1998, 24; J. Donoghue, "The Future Is Now," Air Transport World, April 1, 2001, 78; D. Evans, "Aftermarket Outlook," Aviation Maintenance Magazine, May 1, 2006, http://www.aviationtoday.com.

54. A. Madrigal, "Wow! Apple Turns Over Its Inventory Once Every 5 Days," The Atlantic, May 31, 2012, http://www.theatlantic.com/technology/archive/2012/05/wow-apple-turns-over-its-inventory-once-every-5-days/ 257915; "Gartner Announces Rankings of Its 2012 Supply Chain Top 25," Gartner.com, May 22, 2012, http://www.gartner.com/newsroom/id/2023116.

55. EFR-Central.com, "Welcome," http://www.efr-central.com/aboutefr.html.

56. J. R. Henry, "Minimized Setup Will Make Your Packaging Line S.M.I.L.E.," Packaging Technology and Engineering, February 1, 1998, 24.

57. J. Donoghue, "The Future Is Now," Air Transport World, April 1, 2001, 78; D. Evans, "Aftermarket Outlook," Aviation Maintenance Magazine, May 1, 2006, http://www.aviationtoday.com.

58. "The Way I Work: Marc Lore of Diapers.com," Inc., September 1, 2009, http://www.inc.com/magazine/20090901/the-way -i-work-marc-lore-of-diaperscom.html.

59. E. Powell, Jr., and F. Sahin, "Economic Production Lot Sizing With Periodic Costs and Overtime," Decision Sciences 32 (2001): 423–452

60. "Gartner Announces Rankings of Its 2012 Supply Chain Top 25," Gartner, May 22, 2012, http://www.gartner.com/newsroom /id/2023116; S. Sage, "Apple Boasts Strongest Manufacturing Supply Chain in the World, Turns Over Inventory in Five Days," iMore, June 1, 2012, http://www.imore.com/apple-boasts-strongest-supply-chain-world-turns-inventory-days.

61. N. Shirouzu, "Why Toyota Wins Such High Marks on Quality Surveys," Wall Street Journal, March 15, 2001, A1.

62. Shirouzu, "Why Toyota Wins."

63. G. Gruman, "Supply on Demand: Manufacturers Need to Know What's Selling Before They Can Produce and Deliver Their Wares in the Right Quantities," Info World, April 18, 2005.

Index

influences on ethical decision making, 46–52
practical steps to ethical decision making, 52–56
responses to demands for social responsibility, 61–62
social responsibility, 56–61
social responsibility and economic performance, 62–64
unethical workplace behaviours, 44–46
Ethics and Compliance Initiative (ECI), 44
Ethnicity, 233–234
European Union (EU), 136
Europe's Maastricht Treaty, 135–136
Evasive hiding, 309
Executive coaching, 18
Executive information system (EIS), 351, 353
Expatriate, 149, 150
Expectancy, 257
Expectancy theory, 257. *See also* Equity theory; Goal-setting theory; Reinforcement theory
components of, 257
to model, 258
motivating with, 257–259
Experienced employees, 282
Experiential approach to innovation, 117
Expert system, 353–354
Exporting, 140–141
External-employee factors, 94
External access and sharing of information, 352
External attribution, 296
External comparison, 254
External environments, 24
External recruiting, 205
Externals, 282
External value service, 367
Extinction, 261
Extranets, 352
Extrinsic rewards, 250–252
Extroversion, 237
Exxon/Imperial Oil, 271

F

Facebook, 14, 310, 320
Fadell, Tony, 112
"Fail Forward" message, 270
Fandray, Dayton, 55
Fast Company magazine, 283
Faulty action stage, 120
Fayol, Henri, 5
Fayol's management functions, 5
Federal Contractors Program (FCP), 227
Federal employment laws, 199–200
The Federal Government's Advisory Council, 272
FedEx, 89
Feedback, 307–308
Feedback control, 318
Feedback to sender, 298
Feedforward control, 318–319
Fiat, 288
Fiedler's contingency theory, 276–280
Field experience, 150
Figurehead role, 12

Financial perspectives, 324–325, 326–328
Financial Post, 316
Financial ratios, 326
Firewalls, 349
Firm-level strategies, 103. *See also* Corporate-level strategies; Industry-level strategies
basics of direct competition, 103–105
strategic moves of direct competition, 105–107
First-line managers, 9–10
First-mover advantage, 337–338
Five industry forces, 99–102
Fixed interval reinforcement schedule, 262
Fixed ratio reinforcement schedule, 262
Flexibility maintenance, 73
Flow, 115
FLYHTStream, 339–340
Focus strategy, 102
Followers as leaders, 276
Ford, Henry, 110
Foreign direct investment, 132–133
Formal authority system, 282
Formal communication channels, 298–300
Forming, 189
Forms of global business, 140
cooperative contracts, 141–142
exporting, 140–141
global new ventures, 144
phase model of globalization, 140
strategic alliances, 142–143
wholly owned affiliates, 144
Fortune 500 CEO, 9
Fortune 500 company, 98
Four generic strategies, 102
4G Light (4G LTE), 113
Franchise, 142
Franchisor, 142
Free trade agreements, 138
Friedman, Milton, 56
Frito-Lay, 261
Fry, Art, 116
Fuchs, Marcus, 131
Functional departmentalization, 156–157, 158
Functional turnover, 222
Fundamental attribution error, 296
Future Leaders of Manitoba award (FLM award), 153

G

Gainsharing, 194
Gallo, Carmine, 75
Gantt chart, 107
Gates, Bill, 37
Gates, Melinda, 185
Gender and leadership, 287
Gender discrimination, 230–233
General Agreement on Tariffs and Trade (GATT), 135
General Electric Co. (GE), 302
General Electric Workout, 127
General environment, 27. *See also* Task environment
economy, 28–29

political/legal component, 30–31
sociocultural component, 30
and specific environments, 28
technological component, 29–30
General Motors (GM), 61, 120
Generational change, 119
Generation gaps, 231
Geographic departmentalization, 158–160
Gillespie, Clay, 327
Glass ceiling, 231
Global business, 132
consumers, 138
forms of, 140–144
impact of, 132–133
trade agreements, 135–138
trade barriers, 133–135, 138
Global business units (GBUs), 155
Global consistency, 138–139
GlobalGap, 317
Globalization, phase model of, 140
Global joint ventures, 143
Global management, 132–151
aware of cultural differences, 149
finding best business climate, 144–145
forms of global business, 140–144
global business, 132–138
global consistency vs. local adaptation, 138–139
growing markets, 145–146
international assignment preparation, 149
language and cross-cultural training, 149–150
office/manufacturing location selection, 146
political risk minimization, 146–149
spouse, family, and dual-career issues, 151
Global new ventures, 144
Global positioning system (GPS), 24, 321
Globe and Mail, 13
Globe Investor, 137
Goal, 263
Goal acceptance, 264
Goal commitment, 71–72
Goal congruence rule, 285
Goal difficulty, 264
Goal-setting theory, 263. *See also* Equity theory; Expectancy theory; Reinforcement theory
components of, 264–265
motivating with, 265–266
Goal specificity, 264
Golden, Anne, 232
Gomez, Rosa, 315
Good, Ashley, 270
Google, 5, 88, 95, 191
Authenticator app, 349
Google Apps, 349
Google X, 191
Gossip, 300
Government import standards, 134
Government subsidies, 134
Graduate Management Admissions Test (GMAT), 208
Grand strategies, 98–99
Grant, Adam, 261

Judy Project, 234
Just-in-time inventory inventory system (JIT inventory system), 371, 373

K

Kanban system, 373
KFC, 59, 142
Kinesics, 303
King, Burger, 133
Knowledge, 353–354
Kohlberg's stages of moral development, 49
Kwik Kopy Printing Canada, 164

L

Labour Standards Tribunal, 201
Landale, Marjorie, 247
Language, 149–150
Lanzinger, Irene, 275
Large system interventions, 128
Lauzon, Armand, 127
Lawler, Edward, 191
Law School Admissions Test (LSAT), 208
Lawyers.com, 45
Leader information rule, 285
Leaderless group discussion, 209
Leader–member relations, 278
Leader role, 12
Leaders, 270
    Blake/Mouton leadership grid, 275
    derailment characteristics, 18
    female leader, 272
    followers as, 276
    leadership derailment, strategies to
        preventing, 18–19
Leadership
    behaviours, 273–275
    contingency theory, 276–280
    gender and leadership, 287
    leaders, 270–276
    leaders *vs.* managers, 270
    normative decision theory, 283–287
    path–goal theory, 280–283
    training, 18
    traits, 271–273
    visionary leadership, 287–291
Leadership style, 276, 277–278
    path–goal theory, 281–282
Leader's information, 285–286
Leading, 6–7
    and effectiveness paradigm, 239–241
    and growth perspectives, 325
Least Preferred Coworker Scale (LPC
    Scale), 277–278
Lee, Elizabeth, 335
Legal factors, 94
Legal responsibility, 59
Legislated Employment Equity Program
    (LEEP), 227
Leonard, Stew, 328
Lesbian, gay, bisexual, transgendered
    employees (LGBT employees), 243
Lewin's force field analysis, 123
Liaison role, 13
Licensing, 141–142

Lichtenberger, Shaun, 3
Line authority, 162
Line-flow production, 369
Line function, 162
LinkedIn, 310
Listening, 305–306
Live-streaming apps, 310
Loblaw, innovation at, 126
Local adaptation, 138–139
Locus of control, 282
London Times, 32
Lower order needs, 249

M

Maastricht Treaty of Europe, 136
Macdonald, Chelsea, 23
Mackey, John, 191
Magnitude of consequences, 47
Mahabadi, Hadi, 229
Mahler, Gustav, 270
Make-to-order operation, 368
Make-to-stock operation, 369
MakerBot, 144
Malaysia Airlines Flight 370, 339
Malware, 348
Management, 2
    companies in managers, 16–17
    issues, 4
    management functions, 5–7
    managerial roles, 11–16
    managers, 7–11
    mistakes made by managers, 17–19
    transition to, 19–20
Management by objectives, 74
Management functions, 3, 5
    controlling, 7
    leading, 6–7
    organizing, 6
    planning, 6
Management skills, 16
Managerial roles, 11
    decisional roles, 14–16
    informational roles, 13–14
    interpersonal roles, 12–13
Managers, 7, 262, 270
    characteristics of leaders derail, 18
    companies in, 16–17
    defining jobs, 20
    first-line managers, 9–10
    middle managers, 9, 10
    mistakes made, 17
    strategies to preventing leadership
        derailment, 18–19
    team leaders, 11
    top managers, 7–9
Manufacturing flexibility, 369
Manufacturing operations, 368
    amount of processing in, 368–369
    Electric Cars, 368–369
    flexibility of, 369–370
Maple syrup, 340
Marchionne, Sergio, 288
Market commonality, 104
Martin, Murray, 163
Maslow, hierarchy of needs, 249, 250

Master production schedule, 373–374
Material/product substitution, 333
Material Review Board (MRB), 76
Materials requirement planning (MRP),
    372, 373–374
Matrix departmentalization, 160–161
Matrix organizations, 162
Maximizing, 81
McCarthy Tétrault LLP, 166
McClelland's Learned Needs Theory, 248
McCubbin, Devon, 175
McDonald's, 104, 142, 164, 165, 227
Mechanistic organizations, 166
Media advocacy, 34
Meggy, Robert, 177
Meliones, Jon, 325
Melville, George, 4
Mentoring, 301–302
Mentorship, 301–302
Mentzer, Marc, 221
Mercantile Mergers & Acquisitions
    Corporation, 350
Metropolitan Life Insurance, 343
Meyer, Herbert, 217
Michigan studies, 274
Microsoft, 103
Middle-of-the-road style leadership, 275
Middle managers, 9, 10
Milestones, 117
Millennials, 230
Minhao, Huo, 253
Minjie, Huo, 253
Minority domination, 178, 186
Mintzberg, Henry, 11, 14, 270
Mintzberg's managerial roles, 12
Mission statement, 74
Modernizing Medicine, 340
Modular organizations, 169–170
Mohrman, Susan, 194
Mollick, Ethan, 10
Monitor role, 13
Moore, Gordon, 336–337
Moore's law, 336
moral development, 49
Morgan, Gwyn, 253
Morrissey, Helena, 239–240
Most favoured nation (MFN), 149
Motivation, 246
    basic model of motivation, 252
    effort and performance, 247–248
    eliminating pollution in China, 253
    equity theory, 253–257
    expectancy theory, 257–259
    extrinsic rewards, 250–252
    goal-setting theory, 263–266
    integrated model, 266
    intrinsic rewards, 250–252
    MARS model, 247
    need satisfaction, 248–250
    reinforcement theory, 259–263
    Sareena Sharma-Nickoli, 245
    set of forces, 246
    vacation, 251
Motivation, Ability, Role perceptions,
    Situational constraints model
    (MARS model), 247

S

CHAPTER REVIEW
Management

1

LEARNING OUTCOMES

1-1 (P. 4)

Describe what management is. Good management is working through others to accomplish tasks that help fulfill organizational objectives as efficiently as possible.

1-2 (P. 5)

Explain the four functions of management. Henri Fayol's classic management functions are known today as planning, organizing, leading, and controlling. Planning is determining organizational goals and a means for achieving them. Organizing is deciding where decisions will be made, who will do what jobs and tasks, and who will work for whom. Leading is inspiring and motivating workers to work hard to achieve organizational goals. Controlling is monitoring progress toward goal achievement and taking corrective action when needed. Studies show that performing the management functions well leads to better managerial performance.

1-3 (P. 7)

Describe different kinds of managers. There are four different kinds of managers. Top managers are responsible for creating a context for change, developing attitudes of commitment and ownership, creating a positive organizational culture through words and actions, and monitoring their company's business environments. Middle managers are responsible for planning and allocating resources, coordinating and linking groups and departments, monitoring and managing the performance of subunits and managers, and implementing the changes or strategies generated by top managers. First-line managers are responsible for managing the performance of nonmanagerial employees, teaching them how to do their jobs, and making detailed schedules and operating plans based on middle management's intermediate-range plans. Team leaders are responsible for facilitating team performance, fostering good relationships among team members, and managing external relationships.

1-4 (P. 11)

Explain the major roles and subroles that managers perform in their jobs. Managers perform interpersonal, informational, and decisional roles in their jobs. In fulfilling the interpersonal role, managers act as figureheads by performing ceremonial duties, as leaders by motivating and encouraging workers, and as liaisons by dealing with people outside their units. In performing their informational role, managers act as monitors by scanning their environment for information, as disseminators by sharing information with others in the company, and as spokespeople by sharing information with people outside their departments or companies. In fulfilling decisional roles, managers act as entrepreneurs by adapting their units to incremental change, as disturbance handlers by responding to larger problems that demand immediate action, as resource allocators by deciding on resource recipients and amounts, and as negotiators by bargaining with others about schedules, projects, goals, outcomes, and resources.

KEY TERMS

1-1

Management getting work done through others

Efficiency getting work done with a minimum of effort, expense, or waste

Effectiveness accomplishing tasks that help fulfill organizational objectives

1-2

Planning (management functions) determining organizational goals and a means for achieving them

Organizing deciding where decisions will be made, who will do what jobs and tasks, and who will work for whom

Leading inspiring and motivating workers to work hard to achieve organizational goals

Controlling monitoring progress toward goal achievement and taking corrective action when needed

1-3

Top managers executives responsible for the overall direction of the organization

Middle managers managers responsible for setting objectives consistent with top management's goals and for planning and implementing subunit strategies for achieving these objectives

First-line managers managers who train and supervise the performance of non-managerial employees who are directly responsible for producing the company's products or services

Team leaders managers responsible for facilitating team activities toward accomplishing a goal

1-4

Figurehead role the interpersonal role managers play when they perform ceremonial duties

Leader role the interpersonal role managers play when they motivate and encourage workers to accomplish organizational objectives

Liaison role the interpersonal role managers play when they deal with people outside their units

TO ACCESS MINDTAP: NELSON/STUDENT.COM

CHAPTER REVIEW 1

Monitor role the informational role managers play when they scan their environment for information

Disseminator role the informational role managers play when they share information with others in their departments or companies

Spokesperson role the informational role managers play when they share information with people outside their departments or companies

Entrepreneur role the decisional role managers play when they adapt themselves, their subordinates, and their units to change

Disturbance handler role the decisional role managers play when they respond to severe problems that demand immediate action

Resource allocator role the decisional role managers play when they decide who gets what resources

Negotiator role the decisional role managers play when they negotiate schedules, projects, goals, outcomes, resources, and employee raises

1-5

Technical skills the specialized procedures, techniques, and knowledge required to get the job done

Human skills the ability to work well with others

Conceptual skills the ability to see the organization as a whole, understand how the different parts affect one another, and recognize how the company fits into or is affected by its environment

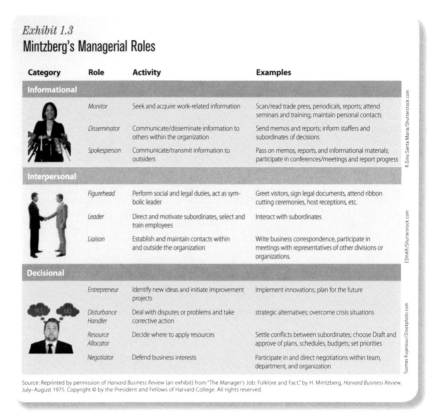

Exhibit 1.3
Mintzberg's Managerial Roles

Category	Role	Activity	Examples
Informational			
	Monitor	Seek and acquire work-related information	Scan/read trade press, periodicals, reports; attend seminars and training; maintain personal contacts
	Disseminator	Communicate/disseminate information to others within the organization	Send memos and reports; inform staffers and subordinates of decisions
	Spokesperson	Communicate/transmit information to outsiders	Pass on memos, reports, and informational materials; participate in conferences/meetings and report progress
Interpersonal			
	Figurehead	Perform social and legal duties, act as symbolic leader	Greet visitors, sign legal documents, attend ribbon cutting ceremonies, host receptions, etc.
	Leader	Direct and motivate subordinates, select and train employees	Interact with subordinates
	Liaison	Establish and maintain contacts within and outside the organization	Write business correspondence, participate in meetings with representatives of other divisions or organizations.
Decisional			
	Entrepreneur	Identify new ideas and initiate improvement projects	Implement innovations; plan for the future
	Disturbance Handler	Deal with disputes or problems and take corrective action	strategic alternatives; overcome crisis situations
	Resource Allocator	Decide where to apply resources	Settle conflicts between subordinates; choose Draft and approve of plans, schedules, budgets; set priorities
	Negotiator	Defend business interests	Participate in and direct negotiations within team, department, and organization

Source: Reprinted by permission of *Harvard Business Review* (an exhibit) from "The Manager's Job: Folklore and Fact," by H. Mintzberg, *Harvard Business Review*, July–August 1975. Copyright © by the President and Fellows of Harvard College. All rights reserved.

1-5 (P. 16)

Explain what companies look for in managers. Companies do not want one-dimensional managers. They want managers with a balance of skills. Managers need the knowledge and abilities to get the job done (technical skills), must be able to work effectively in groups and be good listeners and communicators (human skills), must be able to assess the relationships between the different parts of the company and the external environment and position their companies for success (conceptual skills), and should want to assume positions of leadership and power (motivation to manage). Technical skills are most important for lower-level managers, human skills are equally important at all levels of management, and conceptual skills and motivation to manage increase in importance as managers rise through the managerial ranks.

1-6 (P. 17)

Discuss the top mistakes that managers make in their jobs. Another way to understand what it takes to be a manager is to look at some common mistakes managers make. Management failure which often leads to career derailment is often associated with managers who experience difficulty adapting to change, have problems with interpersonal relationships, experience difficulty building a team, fail to meet business objectives, and have too narrow a functional orientation.

1-7 (P. 19)

Describe the transition that employees go through when they are promoted to management. Managers often begin their jobs by using more formal authority and less people management skill. However, most managers find that being a manager has little to do with "bossing" their subordinates. After six months on the job, the managers were surprised at the fast pace and heavy workload and that "helping" their subordinates was viewed as interference. After a year on the job, most of the managers had come to think of themselves not as doers but as managers who get things done through others. And, because they finally realized that people management was the most important part of their job, most of them had abandoned their authoritarian approach for one based on communication, listening, and positive reinforcement.

LEARNING OUTCOMES

2-1 (P. 24)
Discuss how changing environments affect organizations.
Environmental change, complexity, and resource scarcity are the basic components of external environments. Environmental change is the rate at which conditions or events cause change in a business. Environmental complexity is the number and intensity of external factors in an external environment. Resource scarcity is the scarcity or abundance of resources available in the external environment. As rates of environmental change increase, as the environment becomes more complex, and as resources become scarce, managers become less confident that they can understand, predict, and react effectively to the trends affecting their businesses. According to punctuated equilibrium theory, companies experience periods of stability followed by short periods of dynamic, fundamental change, followed by a return to periods of stability.

2-2 (P. 27)
Describe the four components of the general environment. The general environment consists of events and trends that affect all organizations. Because the economy influences basic business decisions, managers often use economic statistics and business confidence indices to predict future economic activity. Changes in technology, which transforms inputs into outputs, can be a benefit or a threat to a business. Sociocultural trends such as changing demographic characteristics affect how companies run their businesses, whether they are competing domestically or in international markets. Similarly, sociocultural changes in behaviour, attitudes, and beliefs affect the demand for a business's products and services. Court decisions and new federal and provincial laws have imposed much greater political/legal responsibility on companies. The best way to manage legal responsibilities is to educate managers and employees about laws and regulations as well as potential lawsuits in domestic or foreign markets that could affect a business.

2-3 (P. 31)
Explain the five components of the specific environment. The specific environment is made up of the customer, competitor, supplier, industry regulation, and advocacy group components. Companies can monitor customers' needs by identifying customer problems after they occur or by anticipating problems before they occur. Because they tend to focus on well-known competitors, managers often underestimate their competition or do a poor job of identifying future competitors. Suppliers and buyers are very dependent on each other, and that dependence sometimes leads to opportunistic behaviour, in which one benefits at the expense of the other. Regulatory agencies affect businesses by creating rules and then enforcing them. Advocacy groups cannot regulate organizations' practices, but through public communications, media advocacy, and product boycotts, they try to convince companies to change their practices.

KEY TERMS

2-1
External environments all events outside a company that have the potential to influence or affect it

Environmental change the rate at which a company's general and specific environments change

Stable environment an environment in which the rate of change is slow

Dynamic environment an environment in which the rate of change is fast

Punctuated equilibrium theory a theory according to which companies go through long, simple periods of stability (equilibrium), followed by short periods of dynamic, fundamental change (revolution), and ending with a return to stability (new equilibrium)

Environmental complexity the number of external factors in the environment that affect organizations

Simple environment an environment with few environmental factors

Complex environment an environment with many environmental factors

Resource scarcity the abundance or shortage of critical organizational resources in an organization's external environment

Uncertainty extent to which managers can understand or predict which environmental changes and trends will affect their businesses

2-2
General environment the economic, technological, sociocultural, and political trends that indirectly affect all organizations

Specific environment the customers, competitors, suppliers, industry regulations, and advocacy groups that are unique to an industry and directly affect how a company does business

Business confidence indices indices that show managers' level of confidence about future business growth

Technology the knowledge, tools, and techniques used to transform input into output

CHAPTER REVIEW 2

2-3

Competitors companies in the same industry that sell similar products or services to customers

Competitive analysis a process for monitoring the competition that involves identifying competition, anticipating their moves, and determining their strengths and weaknesses

Suppliers companies that provide material, human, financial, and informational resources to other companies

Supplier dependence the degree to which a company relies on a supplier because of the importance of the supplier's product to the company and the difficulty of finding other sources for that product

Buyer dependence the degree to which a supplier relies on a buyer because of the importance of that buyer to the supplier and the difficulty of finding other buyers for its products

Opportunistic behaviour a transaction in which one party in the relationship benefits at the expense of the other

Relationship behaviour mutually beneficial, long-term exchanges between buyers and suppliers

Industry regulation regulations and rules that govern the business practices and procedures of specific industries, businesses, and professions

Advocacy groups groups of concerned citizens who band together to try to influence the business practices of specific industries, businesses, and professions

Public communications an advocacy group tactic that relies on voluntary participation by the news media and the advertising industry to get the advocacy group's message out

Media advocacy an advocacy group tactic that involves framing issues as public issues; exposing questionable, exploitative, or unethical practices; and forcing media coverage by buying media time or creating controversy that is likely to receive extensive news coverage

Product boycott an advocacy group tactic that involves protesting a company's actions by convincing consumers not to purchase its product or service

2-4

Environmental scanning searching the environment for important events or issues that might affect an organization

2-4 (P. 35)

Describe the process that companies use to make sense of their changing environments. Managers use a three-step process to make sense of external environments: scanning the environment, interpreting information, and acting on the information. Managers scan their environments based on their organizational strategies, their need for up-to-date information, and their need to reduce uncertainty. When managers identify environmental events as threats, they take steps to protect the company from harm. When managers identify environmental events as opportunities, they formulate alternatives for taking advantage of them to improve company performance. Using cognitive maps can help managers visually summarize the relationships between environmental factors and the actions they might take to deal with them.

2-5 (P. 37)

Explain how organizational cultures are created and how they can help companies succeed. Organizational culture is the set of key values, beliefs, and attitudes shared by members of an organization. Organizational cultures are often created by company founders and then sustained by telling organizational stories and celebrating organizational heroes. Adaptable cultures that promote employee involvement, make clear the organization's strategic purpose and direction, and actively define and teach organizational values and beliefs can help companies achieve higher sales growth, return on assets, profits, quality, and employee satisfaction. Organizational cultures exist on three levels: the surface level, where cultural artifacts and behaviours can be observed; just below the surface, where values and beliefs are expressed; and deep below the surface, where unconsciously held assumptions and beliefs exist. Managers can begin to change company cultures by focusing on the top two levels.

2-5

Internal environment the events and trends inside an organization that affect management, employees, and organizational culture

Organizational culture the key values, beliefs, and attitudes shared by members of the organization

Organizational stories stories told by members to make sense of events and changes in an organization and to emphasize culturally consistent assumptions, decisions, and actions

Organizational heroes people celebrated for their qualities and achievements within an organization

Company vision a business's purpose or reason for existing

LEARNING OUTCOMES

3-1 (P. 44)

Identify unethical workplace behaviours. Ethics is the set of moral principles or values that define right and wrong. Workplace deviance is behaviour that violates important organizational norms about right and wrong and that harms the organization or its workers. There are four different types of workplace deviance. Production deviance and property deviance harm the company, whereas political deviance and personal aggression harm individuals within the company.

3-2 (P. 46)

Describe ethics guidelines and legislation in North America. In the United States, under the Sarbanes-Oxley Act, organizations found guilty of fraudulent practices and accounting errors may face fines and/or imprisonment. At the present time there is no national ethics legislation in Canada; however, an International Code of Ethics was released in 1997 to act as a guideline for Canadian businesses and a number of associations and regulatory bodies have adopted their own codes of ethics.

3-3 (P. 46)

Describe what influences ethical decision making. Three factors influence ethical decisions: the ethical intensity of the decision, the moral development of the manager, and the ethical principles used to solve the problem. Ethical intensity is strong when decisions have large, certain, immediate consequences and when we are physically or psychologically close to those affected by the decision. There are three phases of moral maturity. At the preconventional level, decisions are made for selfish reasons. At the conventional level, decisions conform to societal expectations. At the postconventional level, internalized principles are used to make ethical decisions. Each of these phases has two steps within it. Managers can use a number of different principles when making ethical decisions: long-term self-interest, personal virtue, religious injunctions, government requirements, utilitarian benefits, individual rights, and distributive justice.

3-4 (P. 52)

Explain what practical steps managers can take to improve ethical decision making. Employers can increase their chances of hiring ethical employees by testing all job applicants. Most large companies now have corporate codes of ethics. In addition to offering general rules, ethics codes must also provide specific, practical advice. Ethics training seeks to increase employees' awareness of ethical issues; to make ethics a serious, credible factor in organizational decisions; and to teach employees a practical model of ethical decision making. The most important factors in creating an ethical business climate are the personal examples set by company managers, the involvement of management in the company ethics program, a reporting system that encourages whistle blowers to report potential ethics violations, and fair but consistent punishment of violators.

KEY TERMS

3-1

Ethics the set of moral principles or values that defines right and wrong for a person or group

Ethical behaviour behaviour that conforms to a society's accepted principles of right and wrong

Workplace deviance unethical behaviour that violates organizational norms about right and wrong

Production deviance unethical behaviour that hurts the quality and quantity of work produced

Property deviance unethical behaviour aimed at the organization's property or products

Employee shrinkage employee theft of company merchandise

Political deviance using one's influence to harm others in the company

Personal aggression hostile or aggressive behaviour toward others

3-3

Ethical intensity the degree of concern people have about an ethical issue

Magnitude of consequences the total harm or benefit derived from an ethical decision

Social consensus agreement on whether behaviour is bad or good

Probability of effect the chance that something will happen and then harm others

Temporal immediacy the time between an act and the consequences the act produces

Proximity of effect the social, psychological, cultural, or physical distance between a decision maker and those affected by his or her decisions

Concentration of effect the total harm or benefit that an act produces on the average person

Preconventional level of moral development the first level of moral development, in which people make decisions based on selfish reasons

CHAPTER REVIEW 3

Conventional level of moral development the second level of moral development, in which people make decisions that conform to societal expectations

Postconventional level of moral development the third level of moral development, in which people make decisions based on internalized principles

Principle of long-term self-interest an ethical principle that holds that you should never take any action that is not in your or your organization's long-term self-interest

Principle of personal virtue an ethical principle that holds that you should never do anything that is not honest, open, and truthful and that you would not be glad to see reported in the newspapers, on TV or on the Internet

Principle of religious injunctions an ethical principle that holds that you should never take any action that is not kind and that does not build a sense of community

Principle of government requirements an ethical principle that holds that you should never take any action that violates the law, for the law represents the minimal moral standard

Principle of utilitarian benefits an ethical principle that holds that you should never take any action that does not result in greater good for society

Principle of individual rights an ethical principle that holds that you should never take any action that infringes on others' agreed-upon rights

Principle of distributive justice an ethical principle that holds that you should never take any action that harms the least fortunate among us: the poor, the uneducated, the unemployed

Self-dealing actions taken by a fiduciary that further his or her own best interest, rather than the benefit of the corporation

3-4

Overt integrity test a written test that estimates job applicants' honesty by directly asking them what they think or feel about theft or about punishment of unethical behaviours

Personality-based integrity test a written test that indirectly estimates job applicants' honesty by measuring psychological traits, such as dependability and conscientiousness

Whistle blowing reporting others' ethics violations to management or legal authorities

3-5

Social responsibility an individual's or a business's obligation to pursue policies, make decisions, and take actions that benefit society

3-5 (P. 56)

Explain to whom and for what organizations are socially responsible. Social responsibility is a business's obligation to benefit society. According to the shareholder model, a company's only social responsibility is to maximize shareholder wealth by maximizing company profits. According to the stakeholder model, companies must satisfy the needs and interests of multiple corporate stakeholders, not just shareholders. The needs of primary stakeholders, on which the organization relies for its existence, take precedence over those of secondary stakeholders.

3-6 (P. 61)

Explain how organizations can choose to respond to societal demands for social responsibility and how social responsibility impacts economic performance. Companies can best benefit their stakeholders by fulfilling their economic, legal, ethical, and discretionary responsibilities. Being profitable, or meeting one's economic responsibility, is a business's most basic social responsibility. Legal responsibility consists of following a society's laws and regulations. Ethical responsibility means not violating accepted principles of right and wrong when doing business. Discretionary responsibilities are social responsibilities beyond basic economic, legal, and ethical responsibilities.

Corporate social responsibility the voluntary activities undertaken by a company to operate in an economically, socially, and environmentally sustainable manner

Shareholder model a view of social responsibility that holds that an organization's overriding goal should be to maximize profit for the benefit of shareholders

Stakeholder model a theory of corporate responsibility that holds that management's most important responsibility, long-term survival, is achieved by satisfying the interests of multiple corporate stakeholders

Stakeholders persons or groups with a "stake" or legitimate interest in a company's actions

Primary stakeholder any group on which an organization relies for its long-term survival

Secondary stakeholder any group that can influence or be influenced by a company and can affect public perceptions about its socially responsible behaviour

Economic responsibility the expectation that a company will make a profit by producing a valued product or service

Legal responsibility a company's social responsibility to obey society's laws and regulations

Ethical responsibility a company's social responsibility not to violate accepted principles of right and wrong when conducting its business

Discretionary responsibility the expectation that a company will voluntarily serve a social role beyond its economic, legal, and ethical responsibilities

3-6

Social responsiveness a company's strategy for responding to stakeholders' economic, legal, ethical, or discretionary expectations concerning social responsibility

Reactive strategy a social responsiveness strategy in which a company does less than society expects

Defensive strategy a social responsiveness strategy in which a company admits responsibility for a problem but does the least required to meet societal expectations

Accommodative strategy a social responsiveness strategy in which a company accepts responsibility for a problem and does all that society expects to solve that problem

Proactive strategy a social responsiveness strategy in which a company anticipates responsibility for a problem before it occurs and does more than society expects to address the problem

LEARNING OUTCOMES

4-1 (P. 68)

Discuss the benefits and pitfalls of planning. Planning is choosing a goal and developing a method for achieving it. Planning offers four important benefits: provides direction, intensifies effort, reduces uncertainty, and facilitates decision making. However, planning also has three potential pitfalls. Companies that are overly committed to their plans may be slow to adapt to environmental changes. Planning is based on assumptions about the future, and when those assumptions are wrong, plans can fail. Finally, planning can fail when planners are detached from the implementation of plans.

4-2 (P. 69)

Describe how to make a plan that works. There are five steps to making a plan that works: (1) Set S.M.A.R.T. goals—goals that are **s**pecific, **m**easurable, **a**ttainable, **r**ealistic, and **t**imely. (2) Develop commitment to the goals. Managers can increase workers' goal commitment by encouraging worker participation in goal setting, making goals public, and getting top management to show support for workers' goals. (3) Develop action plans for goal accomplishment. (4) Track progress toward goal achievement by setting both proximal and distal goals and by providing workers with regular performance feedback. (5) Maintain flexibility by keeping options open.

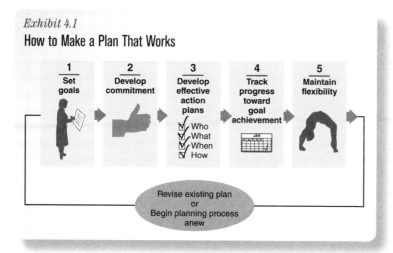

Exhibit 4.1
How to Make a Plan That Works

1 Set goals · 2 Develop commitment · 3 Develop effective action plans (☑ Who ☑ What ☑ When ☑ How) · 4 Track progress toward goal achievement · 5 Maintain flexibility

Revise existing plan or Begin planning process anew

4-3 (P. 73)

Discuss how companies can use plans at all management levels, from top to bottom. Proper planning requires that the goals at the bottom and middle of the organization support the objectives at the top of the organization. The goals at the top will be longer range than those at the bottom, as shown in Exhibit 4.1. Top management develops strategic plans, which start with the creation of an organizational vision and mission. Middle managers use techniques such as management by objectives (MBO) to develop tactical plans that direct behaviour, efforts, and priorities. Finally, lower level managers develop operational plans that guide daily activities in producing or delivering an organization's products and services. There are three kinds of operational plans: single-use plans, standing plans (policies, procedures, and rules and regulations), and budgets.

KEY TERMS

4-1

Planning choosing a goal and developing a strategy to achieve that goal

4-2

S.M.A.R.T. goals goals that are specific, measurable, attainable, realistic, and timely

Goal commitment the determination to achieve a goal

Action plan the specific steps (how), people (who), resources (what), and time period (when) for accomplishing a goal

Options-based planning maintaining flexibility by making small, simultaneous investments in many alternative plans

Slack resources a cushion of extra resources that can be used with options-based planning to adapt to unanticipated change, problems, or opportunities

4-3

Strategic plans overall company plans that clarify how the company will serve customers and position itself against competitors over the next two to five years

Vision statement a statement of a company's purpose and the ultimate destination it hopes to reach, acting as a guide to individuals in an organization

Mission statement a broad statement of an organization's purpose that distinguishes the organization from others of a similar type

Tactical plans plans created and implemented by middle managers that specify how the company will use resources, budgets, and people over the next six months to two years to accomplish specific goals within its mission

Operational plans day-to-day plans, developed and implemented by lower-level managers, for producing or delivering the organization's products and services over a 30-day to six-month period

Single-use plans plans that cover unique, one-time-only events

Standing plans plans used repeatedly to handle frequently recurring events

Policy a standing plan that indicates the general course of action that should be taken in response to a particular event or situation

CHAPTER REVIEW 4

Procedure a standing plan that indicates the specific steps that should be taken in response to a particular event

Rules and regulations standing plans that describe how a particular action should be performed or what must happen or not happen in response to a particular event

Budgeting quantitative planning through which managers decide how to allocate available money to best accomplish company goals

4-4

Decision making the process of choosing a solution from available alternatives

Rational decision making a systematic process of defining problems, evaluating alternatives, and choosing optimal solutions

Problem a gap between a desired state and an existing state

Decision criteria the standards used to guide judgments and decisions

Absolute comparisons a process in which each criterion is compared to a standard or ranked on its own merits

Relative comparisons a process in which each criterion is compared directly to every other

Maximizing choosing the best alternative

Satisficing choosing a "good enough" alternative

4-5

Groupthink a barrier to good decision making caused by pressure within a group for members to agree with one another

C-type conflict (cognitive conflict) disagreement that focuses on problem-and issue-related differences of opinion

A-type conflict (affective conflict) disagreement that focuses on individual or personal issues

Devil's advocacy a decision-making method in which an individual or a subgroup is assigned the role of a critic

Nominal group technique a decision-making method that begins and ends by having group members quietly write down and evaluate ideas to be shared with the group

Brainstorming a decision-making method in which group members build on one another's ideas to generate as many alternative solutions as possible

Electronic brainstorming a decision-making method in which group members use computers to build on one another's ideas and generate many alternative solutions

4-4 (P. 77)

Explain the steps and limits to rational decision making. Rational decision making is a six-step process in which managers define problems, evaluate alternatives, and compute optimal solutions. Step 1 is identifying and defining the problem. Problems are gaps between desired and existing states. Managers won't begin the decision-making process unless they are aware of the gap, are motivated to reduce it, and possess the necessary resources to fix it. Step 2 is defining the decision criteria used to judge alternatives. In Step 3, an absolute or relative comparison process is used to rate the importance of the decision criteria. Step 4 involves generating many alternative courses of action (i.e., solutions). Potential solutions are assessed in Step 5 by systematically gathering information and evaluating each alternative against each criterion. In Step 6, criterion ratings and weights are used to compute the optimal value for each alternative course of action. Rational managers then choose the alternative with the highest optimal value. Once the optimal alternative is chosen, Step 7 is to implement the decision and, following that, Step 8 entails evaluating the effectiveness of the decision. The rational decision-making model describes how decisions should be made in an ideal world without limits. However, bounded rationality recognizes that managers' limited resources, incomplete and imperfect information, and limited decision-making capabilities restrict their decision-making processes in the real world.

4-5 (P. 81)

Explain how group decisions and group decision-making techniques can improve decision making. When groups view problems from multiple perspectives, use more information, have a diversity of knowledge and experience, and become committed to solutions they help choose, they can produce better solutions than individual decision makers. However, group decisions can suffer from these disadvantages: groupthink, slowness, discussions dominated by just a few individuals, and unfelt responsibility for decisions. Group decisions work best when group members encourage c-type (cognitive) conflict. Group decisions don't work as well when groups become mired in a-type (affective) conflict. The devil's advocacy and dialectical inquiry approaches improve group decisions because they bring structured c-type conflict into the decision-making process. By contrast, the nominal group technique and the Delphi technique both improve decision making by reducing a-type conflict. Because it overcomes the problems of production blocking and evaluation apprehension, electronic brainstorming is more effective than face-to-face brainstorming.

LEARNING OUTCOMES

5-1 (P. 88)

Specify the components of sustainable competitive advantage and explain why it is important. Firms can use their resources to create and sustain a competitive advantage, that is, to provide greater value for customers than competitors can. A competitive advantage becomes sustainable when other companies cannot duplicate the benefits it provides and have, for now, stopped trying.

5-2 (P. 91)

Describe the steps involved in the strategy-making process. The first step in strategy making is determining whether a strategy needs to be changed to sustain a competitive advantage. The second step is to conduct a situational analysis that examines internal strengths and weaknesses as well as external threats and opportunities. The third step involves choosing a strategy. Strategic reference point theory suggests that when companies are performing better than their strategic reference points, top management will typically choose a risk-averse strategy. When performance is below strategic reference points, risk-seeking strategies are more likely to be chosen.

5-3 (P. 94)

Explain the different kinds of corporate-level strategies.
Corporate-level strategies, such as portfolio strategy and grand strategies, help managers determine what businesses they should be in. Portfolio strategy focuses on lowering business risk by being in multiple, unrelated businesses and by investing the cash flows from slow-growth businesses into faster growing businesses. One portfolio strategy is the BCG matrix. The most successful way to use the portfolio approach to corporate strategy is to reduce risk through related diversification.

The three kinds of grand strategies are growth, stability, and retrenchment/recovery. Companies can grow externally by merging with or acquiring other companies, or they can grow internally through direct expansion or by creating new businesses. Companies choose a stability strategy when their external environment changes very little or after they have dealt with periods of explosive growth. Retrenchment strategy—shrinking the size or scope of a business—is used to turn around poor performance. If retrenchment works, it is often followed by a recovery strategy that focuses on growing the business again.

5-4 (P. 99)

Describe the different kinds of industry-level strategies. Industry-level strategies focus on how companies choose to compete in their industry. The five industry forces determine an industry's overall attractiveness to corporate investors and its potential for long-term profitability. Together, a high level of these elements combine to increase competition and decrease profits. The three positioning strategies can help companies protect themselves from the negative effects of industry-wide competition.

KEY TERMS

5-1

Resources the assets, capabilities, processes, information, and knowledge that an organization uses to improve its effectiveness and efficiency, create and sustain competitive advantage, and fulfill a need or solve a problem

Competitive advantage providing greater value for customers than competitors can

Sustainable competitive advantage a competitive advantage that other companies have tried unsuccessfully to duplicate and have, for the moment, stopped trying to duplicate

Valuable resources resources that allow companies to improve efficiency and effectiveness

Rare resources resources that are not controlled or possessed by many competing firms

Imperfectly imitable resources resources that are impossible or extremely costly or difficult for other firms to duplicate

5-2

Competitive inertia a reluctance to change strategies or competitive practices that have been successful in the past

Strategic dissonance a discrepancy between a company's intended strategy and the strategic actions managers take when implementing that strategy

Situational analysis (SWOT analysis) an assessment of the strengths and weaknesses in an organization's internal envirnment and the opportunities and threats in its external environment

Distinctive competence what a company can make, do, or perform better than its competitors

Core capabilities the internal decision-making routines, problem-solving processes, and organizational cultures that determine how efficiently inputs can be turned into outputs

PESTEEL analysis analysis of the political, economic, social/demographic, technological, environmental, external-employee, and legal factors that affect a company and shape the company's strategy

CHAPTER REVIEW 5

5-3

Diversification a strategy for reducing risk by owning a variety of items (stocks or, in the case of a corporation, types of businesses) so that the failure of one stock or one business does not doom the entire portfolio

Portfolio strategy a corporate-level strategy that minimizes risk by diversifying investment among various businesses or product lines

Acquisition the purchase of a company by another company

Unrelated diversification creating or acquiring companies in completely unrelated businesses

BCG matrix a portfolio strategy, developed by the Boston Consulting Group, that categorizes a corporation's businesses by growth rate and relative market share and helps managers decide how to invest corporate funds

Star a company with a large share of a fast-growing market

Question mark a company with a small share of a fast-growing market

Cash cow a company with a large share of a slow-growing market

Dog a company with a small share of a slow-growing market

Related diversification creating or acquiring companies that share similar products, manufacturing, marketing, technology, or cultures

Grand strategy a broad corporate-level strategic plan used to achieve strategic goals and guide the strategic alternatives that managers of individual businesses or subunits may use

Growth strategy a strategy that concentrates on increasing profits, revenues, market share, or the number of places in which the company does business

Stability strategy a strategy that concentrates on improving the way in which the company sells the same products or services to the same customers

Retrenchment strategy a strategy that focuses on turning around very poor company performance by shrinking the size or scope of the business

Recovery the strategic actions taken after retrenchment to return to a growth strategy

5-4

Industry-level strategy a corporate strategy that addresses the question, "How should we compete in this industry?"

Competitive rivalry a measure of the intensity of competitive behaviour between companies in an industry

Threat of new entrants a measure of the degree to which barriers to entry make it easy or difficult for new companies to get started in an industry

Threat of substitute products or services a measure of the ease with which customers can find substitutes for an industry's products or services

Bargaining power of suppliers a measure of the influence that suppliers of parts, materials, and services to firms in an industry have on the prices of these inputs

Bargaining power of buyers a measure of the influence that customers have on a firm

Cost leadership the positioning strategy of producing a product or service of acceptable quality at consistently lower production costs than competitors can, so that the firm can offer the product or service at the lowest price in the industry

Differentiation the positioning strategy of providing a product or service that is sufficiently different from competitors' offerings that customers are willing to pay a premium price for it

Focus strategy the positioning strategy of using cost focus or differentiation focus to produce a specialized product or service for a limited, specially targeted group of customers in a particular geographic region or market segment

5-5

Firm-level strategy a corporate strategy that addresses the question, "How should we compete against a particular firm?"

Direct competition the rivalry between two companies that offer similar products and services, acknowledge each other as rivals, and react to each other's strategic actions

Market commonality the degree to which two companies have overlapping products, services, or customers in multiple markets

Resource similarity the extent to which a competitor has similar amounts and kinds of resources

Attack a competitive move designed to reduce a rival's market share or profits

Response a competitive countermove, prompted by a rival's attack, to defend or improve a company's market share or profit

5-5 (P. 103)

Explain the components and kinds of firm-level strategies. Firm-level strategies are concerned with direct competition between firms. Market commonality and resource similarity determine whether firms are in direct competition and thus likely to attack each other and respond to each other's attacks. In general, the more markets in which there is product, service, or customer overlap, and the greater the resource similarity between two firms, the more intense the direct competition between them. Market entries and exits are the most important kinds of attacks and responses.

LEARNING OUTCOMES

6-1 (P. 110)

Explain why innovation matters to companies. Technology cycles typically follow an S-curve pattern of innovation. Early in the cycle, technological progress is slow, and improvements in technological performance are small. As a technology matures, however, performance improves quickly. Finally, as the limits of a technology are reached, only small improvements occur. At this point, significant improvements in performance must come from new technologies. The best way to protect a competitive advantage is to create a stream of innovative ideas and products. Innovation streams begin with technological discontinuities that create significant breakthroughs in performance or function. Technological discontinuities are followed by discontinuous change, in which customers purchase new technologies and companies compete to establish the new dominant design. Dominant designs emerge because of critical mass, because they solve a practical problem, or because of the negotiations of independent standards bodies.

6-2 (P. 114)

Discuss the different methods that managers can use to effectively manage innovation in their organizations. To successfully manage innovation streams, companies must manage the sources of innovation and learn to manage innovation during both discontinuous and incremental change. Since innovation begins with creativity, companies can manage the sources of innovation by supporting a work environment in which creative thoughts and ideas are welcomed, valued, and encouraged. Creative work environments provide challenging work; offer organizational, supervisory, and work group encouragement; allow significant freedom; and remove organizational impediments to creativity.

Discontinuous and incremental change require different strategies. Companies that succeed in periods of discontinuous change typically follow an experiential approach to innovation. The experiential approach assumes that intuition, flexible options, and hands-on experience can reduce uncertainty and accelerate learning and understanding. A compression approach to innovation works best during periods of incremental change. This approach assumes that innovation can be planned using a series of steps and that compressing the time it takes to complete those steps can speed up innovation.

6-3 (P. 120)

Discuss why not changing can lead to organizational decline. The five-stage process of organizational decline begins when organizations don't recognize the need for change. In the blinded stage, managers fail to recognize the changes that threaten their organization's survival. In the inaction stage, management recognizes the need to change but doesn't act, hoping that the problems will correct themselves. In the faulty action stage, management focuses on cost cutting and efficiency rather than facing up to the fundamental changes needed to ensure survival. In the crisis stage, failure is likely unless fundamental reorganization occurs. Finally, in the dissolution stage, the company is dissolved through bankruptcy proceedings; by selling assets to pay creditors; or through the closing of stores, offices, and facilities. If companies recognize the need to change early enough, however, dissolution may be avoided.

KEY TERMS

6-1

Organizational innovation the successful implementation of creative ideas in organizations

Creativity the production of novel and useful ideas

Organizational change a difference in the form, quality, or condition of an organization over time

Technology cycle a cycle that begins with the birth of a new technology and ends when that technology reaches its limits and is replaced by a newer, substantially better technology

S-curve pattern of innovation a pattern of technological innovation characterized by slow initial progress, then rapid progress, and then slow progress again as a technology matures and reaches its limits

Innovation streams patterns of innovation over time that can create sustainable competitive advantage

Technological discontinuity a scientific advance or a unique combination of existing technologies creates a significant breakthrough in performance or function

Discontinuous change the phase of a technology cycle characterized by technological substitution and design competition

Technological substitution the purchase of new technologies to replace older ones

Design competition competition between old and new technologies to establish a new technological standard or dominant design

Dominant design a new technological design or process that becomes the accepted market standard

Technological lockout when a new dominant design (i.e., a significantly better technology) prevents a company from competitively selling its products or makes it difficult to do so

Incremental change the phase of a technology cycle in which companies innovate by lowering costs and improving the functioning and performance of the dominant technological design

CHAPTER REVIEW 6

6-2

Creative work environments workplace cultures in which workers perceive that new ideas are welcomed, valued, and encouraged

Flow a psychological state of effortlessness, in which you become completely absorbed in what you're doing and time seems to pass quickly

Experiential approach to innovation an approach to innovation that assumes a highly uncertain environment and uses intuition, flexible options, and hands-on experience to reduce uncertainty and accelerate learning and understanding

Design iteration a cycle of repetition in which a company tests a prototype of a new product or service, improves on that design, and then builds and tests the improved prototype

Product prototype a full-scale, working model that is being tested for design, function, and reliability

Testing the systematic comparison of different product designs or design iterations

Milestones formal project review points used to assess progress and performance

Multifunctional teams work teams composed of people from different departments

Compression approach to innovation an approach to innovation that assumes that incremental innovation can be planned using a series of steps and that compressing those steps can speed innovation

Generational change change based on incremental improvements to a dominant technological design such that the improved technology is fully backward compatible with the older technology

6-3

Organizational decline a large decrease in organizational performance that occurs when companies don't anticipate, recognize, neutralize, or adapt to the internal or external pressures that threaten their survival

6-4

Change forces forces that produce differences in the form, quality, or condition of an organization over time

Resistance forces forces that support the existing state of conditions in organizations

Resistance to change opposition to change resulting from self-interest, misunderstanding and distrust, a low tolerance for change, and time and cost factors

Unfreezing getting the people affected by change to believe that change is needed

6-4 (P. 122)

Discuss the different methods that managers can use to better manage change as it occurs. The basic change process involves unfreezing, change, and refreezing. Resistance to change stems from self-interest, misunderstanding, and distrust as well as a general intolerance for change. It can be managed through education and communication, participation, negotiation, top management support, and coercion. Knowing what not to do is as important as knowing what to do to achieve successful change. Managers should avoid these errors when leading change: not establishing urgency, not creating a guiding coalition, lacking a vision, undercommunicating the vision, not removing obstacles to the vision, not creating short-term wins, declaring victory too soon, and not anchoring changes in the corporation's culture. Finally, managers can use a number of change techniques. Results-driven change and the GE Workout reduce resistance to change by getting change efforts off to a fast start. Organizational development is a collection of planned change interventions (large system, small group, person-focused), guided by a change agent, that are designed to improve an organization's long-term health and performance.

Change intervention the process used to get workers and managers to change their behaviour and work practices

Refreezing supporting and reinforcing new changes so that they stick

Coercion using formal power and authority to force others to change

Results-driven change change created quickly by focusing on the measurement and improvement of results

General Electric Workout a three-day meeting in which managers and employees from different levels and parts of an organization quickly generate and act on solutions to specific business problems

Organizational development a philosophy and collection of planned change interventions designed to improve an organization's long-term health and performance

Change agent the person formally in charge of guiding a change effort

LEARNING OUTCOMES

7-1 (P. 132)

Discuss the impact of global business and the trade rules and agreements that govern it. Today, there are more than 77,000 multinational corporations worldwide. Historically, tariffs and nontariff trade barriers such as quotas, voluntary export restraints, government import standards, government subsidies, and customs classifications have made buying foreign goods much harder or more expensive than buying domestically produced products. In recent years, however, worldwide trade agreements such as GATT, along with regional trading agreements like the Maastricht Treaty of Europe, NAFTA, CAFTA-DR, UNASUR, ASEAN, and APEC have substantially reduced tariffs as well as nontariff barriers to international trade. Companies have responded by investing in growing markets in Asia, Eastern Europe, and Latin America. Consumers have responded by purchasing products based on value rather than geography.

7-2 (P. 138)

Explain why companies choose to standardize or adapt their business procedures. Global business requires a balance between global consistency and local adaptation. Global consistency means using the same rules, guidelines, policies, and procedures in each location. Managers at company headquarters like global consistency because it simplifies decisions. Local adaptation means adapting standard procedures to differences in markets. Local managers prefer a policy of local adaptation because it gives them more control. Not all businesses need the same combination of global consistency and local adaptation. Some thrive by emphasizing global consistency and ignoring local adaptation. Others succeed by ignoring global consistency and emphasizing local adaptation.

7-3 (P. 140)

Explain the different ways that companies can organize and act ethically to do business globally. The phase model of globalization says that, as companies move from a domestic to a global orientation, they use these organizational forms in sequence: exporting, cooperative contracts (licensing and franchising), strategic alliances, and wholly owned affiliates.
Yet not all companies follow the phase model. For example, global new ventures are global from their inception.

7-4 (P. 144)

Explain how to find a favourable business climate. The first step in deciding where to take your company global is finding an attractive business climate. Be sure to look for a growing market where consumers have strong purchasing power and foreign competitors are weak. When locating an office or manufacturing facility, consider both qualitative and quantitative factors. In assessing political risk, be sure to examine both political uncertainty and policy uncertainty. If the location you choose has considerable political risk, you can avoid it, try to control the risk, or use a cooperation strategy.

KEY TERMS

7-1

Global business the buying and selling of goods and services by people from different countries

Multinational corporations corporations that own businesses in two or more countries

Foreign direct investment a method of investment in which a company builds a new business or buys an existing business in a foreign country

Trade barriers government-imposed regulations that increase the cost and restrict the number of imported goods

Protectionism a government's use of trade barriers to shield domestic companies and their workers from foreign competition

Tariff a direct tax on imported goods

Nontariff barriers nontax methods of increasing the cost or reducing the volume of imported goods

Quotas limits on the number or volume of imported products

Voluntary export restraints voluntarily imposed limits on the number or volume of products exported to a particular country

Government import standards standards ostensibly established to protect the health and safety of citizens but, in reality, often used to restrict imports

Government subsidies government loans, grants, investments, and tax deferments given to domestic companies to protect them from foreign competition

Customs valuation/classification a classification assigned to imported products by government officials that affects the size of the tariff and imposition of import quotas

General Agreement on Tariffs and Trade (GATT) a worldwide trade agreement that reduced and eliminated tariffs, limited government subsidies, and established protections for intellectual property

World Trade Organization (WTO) the successor to GATT, the only international organization dealing with the global rules of trade between nations; its main function is to ensure that trade flows as smoothly, predictably, and freely as possible

CHAPTER REVIEW 7

Regional trading zones areas in which tariff and nontariff barriers on trade between countries are reduced or eliminated

Europe's Maastricht Treaty a regional trade agreement between most European countries

North American Free Trade Agreement (NAFTA) a regional trade agreement between the United States, Canada, and Mexico

Central America Free Trade Agreement (CAFTA-DR) a regional trade agreement between Costa Rica, the Dominican Republic, El Salvador, Guatemala, Honduras, Nicaragua, and the United States

Union of South American Nations (UNASUR) a regional trade agreement between Argentina, Brazil, Paraguay, Uruguay, Venezuela, Bolivia, Colombia, Ecuador, Peru, Guyana, Suriname, and Chile

Association of Southeast Asian Nations (ASEAN) a regional trade agreement between Brunei Darussalam, Cambodia, Indonesia, Lao PDR, Malaysia, Myanmar, the Philippines, Singapore, Thailand, and Vietnam

Asia-Pacific Economic Cooperation (APEC) a regional trade agreement between Australia, Canada, Chile, the People's Republic of China, Hong Kong, Japan, Mexico, New Zealand, Papua New Guinea, Peru, Russia, South Korea, Taiwan, the United States, and all members of ASEAN, except Cambodia, Lao PDR, and Myanmar

7-2

Global consistency when a multinational company has offices, manufacturing plants, and distribution facilities in different countries and runs them all using the same rules, guidelines, policies, and procedures

Local adaptation when a multinational company modifies its rules, guidelines, policies, and procedures to adapt to differences in foreign customers, governments, and regulatory agencies

7-3

Exporting selling domestically produced products to customers in foreign countries

Cooperative contract an agreement in which a foreign business owner pays a company a fee for the right to conduct that business in his or her country

Licensing an agreement in which a domestic company, the licensor, receives royalty payments for allowing another company, the licensee, to produce the licensor's product, sell its service, or use its brand name in a specified foreign market

Franchise a collection of networked firms in which the manufacturer or marketer of a product or service, the franchisor, licenses the entire business to another person or organization, the franchisee

Strategic alliance an agreement in which companies combine key resources, costs, risk, technology, and people

Joint venture a strategic alliance in which two existing companies collaborate to form a third, independent company

Wholly owned affiliates foreign offices, facilities, and manufacturing plants that are 100 percent owned by the parent company

Global new ventures new companies that are founded with an active global strategy and have sales, employees, and financing in different countries

7-4

Purchasing power a comparison of the relative cost of a standard set of goods and services in different countries

Political uncertainty the risk of major changes in political regimes that can result from war, revolution, the death of a political leader, social unrest, or other influential events

Policy uncertainty the risk associated with changes in laws and government policies that directly affect the way foreign companies conduct business

7-5 (P. 149)

Discuss the importance of identifying and adapting to cultural differences. When expatriates fail in overseas assignments, primarily it is because they find it difficult to adjust to linguistic, cultural, and social differences. Companies must identify these differences and help employees adapt to them, in order to maximize expatriate employees' effectiveness and the company's return on the sizable investment required to implement an overseas assignment.

7-6 (P. 149)

Explain how to successfully prepare workers for international assignments. Many expatriates return prematurely from international assignments because of poor performance. This is much less likely to happen if employees receive linguistic and cross-cultural training—such as documentary training, cultural simulations, or field experiences—before going on assignment. Adjustment of expatriates' spouses and families, which is the most important determinant of success in international assignments, can be improved through adaptability screening and intercultural training.

7-5

National culture the shared values and beliefs that affect the perceptions, decisions, and behaviour of the people of a particular country

7-6

Expatriate someone who lives and works outside his or her native country

LEARNING OUTCOMES

8-1 (P. 154)

Describe the departmentalization approach to organizational structure. There are five traditional departmental structures: functional, product, customer, geographic, and matrix. Functional departmentalization is based on the different business functions or types of expertise used to run a business. Product departmentalization is organized according to the different products or services a company sells. Customer departmentalization focuses its divisions on the different kinds of customers a company has. Geographic departmentalization is based on the different geographic areas or markets in which the company does business. Matrix departmentalization is a hybrid form that combines two or more forms of departmentalization, the most common being the product and functional forms. There is no single best departmental structure. Each structure has advantages and disadvantages.

8-2 (P. 162)

Explain organizational authority. Organizational authority is determined by the chain of command, line versus staff authority, delegation, and the degree of centralization in a company. The chain of command vertically connects every job in the company to higher levels of management and makes clear who reports to whom. Managers have line authority to command employees below them in the chain of command but have only staff, or advisory, authority over employees not below them in the chain of command. Managers delegate authority by transferring to subordinates the authority and responsibility needed to do a task; in exchange, subordinates become accountable for task completion. In centralized companies, most authority to make decisions lies with managers in the upper levels of the company. In decentralized companies, much of the authority is delegated to the workers closest to problems, who can then make the decisions necessary for solving the problems themselves.

8-3 (P. 164)

Discuss the different methods for job design. Companies use specialized jobs because they are economical and easy to learn and don't require highly paid workers. However, specialized jobs aren't motivating or particularly satisfying for employees. Companies have used job rotation, job enlargement, and job enrichment to make specialized jobs more interesting and motivating.

8-4 (P. 166)

Explain the methods that companies are using to redesign internal organizational processes (i.e., intra-organizational processes). Today, companies are using re-engineering and empowerment to change their intra-organizational processes. Re-engineering changes an organization's orientation from vertical to horizontal and changes its work processes by decreasing sequential and pooled interdependence and by increasing reciprocal interdependence. Re-engineering promises dramatic increases in productivity and customer satisfaction, but it has been criticized as simply an excuse to cut costs and lay off workers. Empowering workers means taking decision-making authority and

KEY TERMS

8-1

Organizational structure the vertical and horizontal configuration of departments, authority, and jobs within a company

Organizational process the collection of activities that transform inputs into outputs that customers value

Departmentalization subdividing work and workers into separate organizational units responsible for completing particular tasks

Functional departmentalization organizing work and workers into separate units responsible for particular business functions or areas of expertise

Product departmentalization organizing work and workers into separate units responsible for producing particular products or services

Customer departmentalization organizing work and workers into separate units responsible for particular kinds of customers

Geographic departmentalization organizing work and workers into separate units responsible for doing business in particular geographic areas

Matrix departmentalization a hybrid organizational structure in which two or more forms of departmentalization, most often product and functional, are used together

Simple matrix a form of matrix departmentalization in which managers in different parts of the matrix negotiate conflicts and resources

Complex matrix a form of matrix departmentalization in which managers in different parts of the matrix report to matrix managers, who help them sort out conflicts and problems

8-2

Authority the right to give commands, take action, and make decisions to achieve organizational objectives

Chain of command the vertical line of authority that clarifies who reports to whom throughout the organization

Span of control the number of individuals who report directly to a manager

CHAPTER REVIEW 8

Unity of command a management principle that workers should report to just one boss

Line authority the right to command immediate subordinates in the chain of command

Staff authority the right to advise, but not command, others who are not subordinates in the chain of command

Line function an activity that contributes directly to creating or selling the company's products

Staff function an activity that does not contribute directly to creating or selling the company's products, but instead supports line activities

Delegation of authority the assignment of direct authority and responsibility to a subordinate to complete tasks for which the manager is normally responsible

Centralization of authority the location of most authority at the upper levels of the organization

Decentralization the location of a significant amount of authority in the lower levels of the organization

Standardization solving problems by consistently applying the same rules, procedures, and processes

8-3

Job design the number, kind, and variety of tasks that individual workers perform in doing their jobs

Job specialization a job composed of a small part of a larger task or process

Job rotation periodically moving workers from one specialized job to another to give them more variety and the opportunity to use different skills

Job enlargement increasing the number of different tasks that a worker performs within one particular job

Job enrichment increasing the number of tasks in a particular job and giving workers the authority and control to make meaningful decisions about their work

8-4

Mechanistic organizations organizations characterized by specialized jobs and responsibilities; precisely defined, unchanging roles; and a rigid chain of command based on centralized authority and vertical communication

Organic organizations organizations characterized by broadly defined jobs and responsibility; loosely defined, frequently changing roles; and decentralized authority and horizontal communication based on task knowledge

responsibility from managers and giving it to workers. Empowered workers develop feelings of competence and self-determination and believe that their work has meaning and impact.

8-5 (P. 169)

Describe the methods that companies are using to redesign external organizational processes (i.e., inter-organizational processes). Organizations are using modular and virtual organizations to change inter-organizational processes. Because modular organizations outsource all noncore activities to other businesses, they are less expensive to run than traditional companies. However, modular organizations require extremely close relationships with suppliers, may result in a loss of control, and could create new competitors if the wrong business activities are outsourced. Virtual organizations participate in a network in which they share skills, costs, capabilities, markets, and customers. Virtual organizations can reduce costs, respond quickly, and, if they can successfully coordinate their efforts, produce outstanding products and services.

Intra-organizational process the collection of activities that take place within an organization to transform inputs into outputs that customers value

Re-engineering fundamental rethinking and radical redesign of business processes to achieve dramatic improvements in critical measures of performance, such as cost, quality, service, and speed

Task interdependence the extent to which collective action is required to complete an entire piece of work

Pooled interdependence work completed by having each job or department independently contribute to the whole

Sequential interdependence work completed in succession, with one group's or job's outputs becoming the inputs for the next group or job

Reciprocal interdependence work completed by different jobs or groups working together in a back-and-forth manner

Empowering workers permanently passing decision-making authority and responsibility from managers to workers by giving them the information and resources they need to make and carry out good decisions

Empowerment feelings of intrinsic motivation, in which workers perceive their work to have impact and meaning and perceive themselves to be competent and capable of self-determination

8-5

Inter-organizational process a collection of activities that take place among companies to transform inputs into outputs that customers value

Modular organizations organizations that outsource all other business activities to outside companies, suppliers, specialists, or consultants

Outsourcing obtaining goods and services from an outside supplier

Business process outsourcing (BPO) contracting operations of a specific business process to a third-party service provider

Virtual organization groups of geographically and/or organizationally distributed participants who collaborate toward a shared goal using a combination of information and communications technologies to accomplish a task

LEARNING OUTCOMES

9-1 (P. 176)

Explain the good and bad of using teams. In many industries, teams are growing in importance because they help organizations respond to specific problems and challenges. Teams have been shown to increase customer satisfaction, product and service quality, and employee job satisfaction. Although teams can produce significant improvements in these areas, using teams does not guarantee these positive outcomes. Teams and teamwork have the disadvantages of initially high turnover and social loafing (especially in large groups). Teams also share many of the advantages (multiple perspectives, generation of more alternatives, and more commitment) and disadvantages (groupthink, time, poorly run meetings, domination by a few team members, and weak accountability) of group decision making. Teams should be used for a clear purpose: when the work requires that people work together, when rewards can be provided for both teamwork and team performance, when ample resources can be provided, and when teams can be given clear authority over their work.

9-2 (P. 179)

Recognize and understand the different kinds of teams. Companies use different kinds of teams to make themselves more competitive. Autonomy is the key dimension that makes teams different. Traditional work groups (which execute tasks) and employee involvement groups (which make suggestions) have the lowest levels of autonomy. Semiautonomous work groups (which control major, direct tasks) have more autonomy, while self-managing teams (which control all direct tasks) and self-designing teams (which control membership and how tasks are done) have the highest levels of autonomy. Cross-functional, virtual, and project teams are common but are not easily categorized in terms of autonomy. Cross-functional teams combine employees from different functional areas to help teams attack problems from multiple perspectives and generate more ideas and solutions. Virtual teams use telecommunications and information technologies to bring coworkers together, regardless of physical location or time zone. Virtual teams reduce travel and work time, but communication may suffer since team members don't work face-to-face. Finally, project teams are used for specific, one-time projects or tasks that must be completed within a limited time. Project teams reduce communication barriers and promote flexibility; teams and team members are reassigned to their departments or new projects as old projects are completed.

9-3 (P. 184)

Understand the general characteristics of work teams. The most important characteristics of work teams are team norms, cohesiveness, size, conflict, and development. Norms let team members know what is expected of them and can influence team behaviour in positive and negative ways. Positive team norms are associated with organizational commitment, trust, and job satisfaction. Team cohesiveness helps teams retain members, promotes cooperative behaviour, increases motivation, and facilitates team performance. Attending team meetings

KEY TERMS

9-1

Work team a small number of people with complementary skills who hold themselves mutually accountable for pursuing a common purpose, achieving performance goals, and improving interdependent work processes

Cross-training training team members to do all or most of the jobs performed by the other team members

Social loafing behaviour in which team members withhold their efforts and fail to perform their share of the work

Groupthink when members of highly cohesive groups feel intense pressure not to disagree with one another so that the group can approve a proposed solution

9-2

Traditional work group a group composed of two or more people who work together to achieve a shared goal

Employee involvement team team that provides advice or makes suggestions to management concerning specific issues

Semiautonomous work group a group that has the authority to make decisions and solve problems related to the major tasks of producing a product or service

Self-managing team a team that manages and controls all of the major tasks of producing a product or service (also called a *self-directed work team*)

Self-designing team a team that has the characteristics of a self-managing team but also controls team design, work tasks, and team membership

Cross-functional team a team composed of employees from different functional areas of the organization

Virtual team a team composed of geographically and/or organizationally dispersed coworkers who use telecommunication and information technologies to accomplish an organizational task

Project team a team created to complete specific, one-time projects or tasks within a limited time

CHAPTER REVIEW 9

9-3

Norms informally agreed-on standards that regulate team behaviour

Cohesiveness the extent to which team members are attracted to a team and motivated to remain in it

Forming the first stage of team development, in which team members meet one another, form initial impressions, and begin to establish team norms

Storming the second stage of development, characterized by conflict and disagreement, in which team members disagree over what the team should do and how it should do it

Norming the third stage of team development, in which team members begin to settle into their roles, group cohesion grows, and positive team norms develop

Performing the fourth stage of team development, in which performance improves because the group has matured into an effective, fully functioning team

Adjourning the final stage of Bruce Tuckman's model of team development, in which a company wraps up the team and takes any lessons learned forward to other teams (with three important sub-stages: de-norming, de-storming, and de-forming)

9-4

Structural accommodation the ability to change organizational structures, policies, and practices in order to meet stretch goals

Bureaucratic immunity the ability to make changes without first getting approval from managers or other parts of an organization

Individualism–collectivism the degree to which a person believes that people should be self-sufficient and that loyalty to one's self is more important than loyalty to team or company

Team level the average level of ability, experience, personality, or any other factor on a team

Team diversity the variances or differences in ability, experience, personality, or any other factor on a team

Interpersonal skills skills, such as listening, communicating, questioning, and providing feedback, that enable people to have effective working relationships with others

Skill-based pay compensation system that pays employees for learning additional skills or knowledge

Gainsharing a compensation system in which companies share the financial value of performance gains such as productivity, cost savings, or quality with their workers

and activities, creating opportunities to work together, and engaging in nonwork activities can increase cohesiveness. Team size has a curvilinear relationship with team performance: teams that are very small or very large do not perform as well as moderate-sized teams of six to nine members. Teams of this size are cohesive and small enough for team members to get to know one another and contribute in a meaningful way but are large enough to take advantage of team members' diverse skills, knowledge, and perspectives. Conflict and disagreement are inevitable in most teams. The key to dealing with team conflict is to maximize cognitive conflict, which focuses on issue-related differences, and minimize affective conflict, the emotional reactions that occur when disagreements become personal rather than professional. As teams develop and grow, they pass through four stages of development: forming, storming, norming, and performing. If a team is not managed well, its performance may decline after a period of time as the team regresses through the stages of de-norming, de-storming, and de-forming.

9-4 (P. 190)

Explain how to enhance work team effectiveness. Companies can make teams more effective by setting team goals and managing how team members are selected, trained, and compensated. Team goals provide a clear focus and purpose, reduce the incidence of social loafing, and lead to higher team performance 93 percent of the time. Extremely difficult stretch goals can be used to motivate teams as long as teams have autonomy, control over resources, structural accommodation, and bureaucratic immunity. Not everyone is suited for teamwork. When selecting team members, companies should select people who have a preference for teamwork (individualism–collectivism) and should consider team level (average ability on a team) and team diversity (different abilities on a team). Organizations that successfully use teams provide thousands of hours of training to make sure that teams work. The most common types of team training are for interpersonal skills, decision-making and problem-solving skills, conflict resolution, technical training to help team members learn multiple jobs (i.e., cross training), and training for team leaders. Employees can be compensated for team participation and accomplishments in three ways: skill-based pay, gainsharing, and nonfinancial rewards.

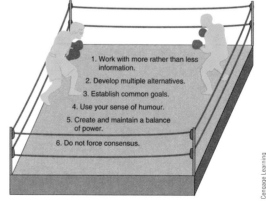

How Teams Can Have a Good Fight

1. Work with more rather than less information.
2. Develop multiple alternatives.
3. Establish common goals.
4. Use your sense of humour.
5. Create and maintain a balance of power.
6. Do not force consensus.

Cengage Learning

Source: K. M. Eisenhardt, J. L. Kahwajy, and L. J. Bourgeois III, "How Management Teams Can Have a Good Fight," *Harvard Business Review* 75, no. 4 (July–August 1997): 77–85.

TO ACCESS MINDTAP: NELSON/STUDENT.COM

CHAPTER REVIEW 10
Managing Human Resource Systems

LEARNING OUTCOMES

10-1 (P. 198)

Explain how different employment laws affect human resource practice. Human resource management is subject to major federal employment laws and subject to review by several federal agencies. In general, these laws indicate that sex, age, religion, colour, national origin, race, disability, and pregnancy may not be considered in employment decisions unless these factors can reasonably be seen as bona fide occupational qualifications.

10-2 (P. 202)

Explain how companies use HR planning and recruiting to find qualified job applicants. Recruiting is the process of finding qualified job applicants. The first step in recruiting is to conduct a job analysis, which is used to write a job description of basic tasks, duties, and responsibilities and to write job specifications indicating the knowledge, skills, and abilities needed to perform the job. Whereas internal recruiting involves finding qualified job applicants from inside the company, external recruiting involves finding qualified job applicants from outside the company.

10-3 (P. 205)

Describe the selection techniques and procedures that companies use when deciding which applicants should receive job offers. Selection is the process of gathering information about job applicants to decide who should be offered a job. Accurate selection procedures are valid, are legally defendable, and improve organizational performance. Application forms and résumés are the most common selection devices. Managers should check references and conduct background checks even though previous employers are often reluctant to provide such information for fear of being sued for defamation. Unfortunately, without this information, other employers are at risk of negligent hiring lawsuits. Selection tests generally do the best job of predicting applicants' future job performance. The three kinds of job interviews are unstructured, structured, and semistructured interviews.

10-4 (P. 211)

Describe how to determine training needs and select the appropriate training methods. Training is used to give employees the job-specific skills, experience, and knowledge they need to do their jobs or improve their job performance. To make sure training dollars are well spent, companies need to determine specific training needs, select appropriate training methods, and then evaluate the training.

10-5 (P. 214)

Discuss how to use performance appraisal to give meaningful performance feedback. The keys to successful performance appraisal are accurately measuring job performance and effectively sharing performance feedback with employees. Organizations should develop good performance appraisal scales; train raters how to accurately evaluate performance; and impress upon managers the value of providing feedback in a clear, consistent, and fair manner, as well as setting goals and monitoring progress toward those goals.

KEY TERMS

10-1

Human resource management (HRM) the process of finding, developing, and keeping the right people to form a qualified workforce

Bona fide occupational qualification (BFOQ) an exception in employment law that permits sex, age, religion, and the like to be used when making employment decisions, but only if they are "reasonably necessary to the normal operation of that particular business"

Sexual harassment a form of discrimination in which unwelcome sexual advances, requests for sexual favours, or other verbal or physical conduct of a sexual nature occur while performing one's job; another form of sexual harassment is when employment outcomes, such as hiring, promotion, or simply keeping one's job, depend on whether an individual submits to sexual harassment

Hostile work environment a form of harassment in which unwelcome and demeaning behaviour creates an intimidating and offensive work environment

10-2

Human resources planning an umbrella term that encompasses overarching philosophies, policies, and practices that are in line with the organization's strategy

Recruiting the process of developing a pool of qualified job applicants

Job analysis a purposeful, systematic process for collecting information on the important work-related aspects of a job in line with the organization's strategic direction

Job description a written description of the basic tasks, duties, and responsibilities required of an employee holding a particular job to help the organization realize its strategy

Job specifications a written summary of the qualifications needed to successfully perform a particular job to enable the organization to reach its organizational objectives

Internal recruiting the process of developing a pool of qualified job applicants from people who already work in the company

CHAPTER REVIEW 10

Succession planning deals with evaluating the needs that are required in future years in terms of staffing to replace people who retire, or who may leave, and to provide personnel for needed strategic growth requirements

External recruiting the process of developing a pool of qualified job applicants from outside the company

Realistic job previews a tool used to explain to potential new employees both the positive and negative aspects of a new job

10-3

Selection the process of gathering information about job applicants to decide who should be offered a job

Validation the process of determining how well a selection test or procedure predicts future job performance; the better or more accurate the prediction of future job performance, the more valid a test is said to be

Human resource information system (HRIS) a computerized system for gathering, analyzing, storing, and disseminating information related to the HRM process

Employment references sources such as previous employers or coworkers who can provide job-related information about job candidates

Background checks procedures used to verify the truthfulness and accuracy of information that applicants provide about themselves and to uncover negative, job-related background information not provided by applicants

Specific ability tests (aptitude tests) tests that measure the extent to which an applicant possesses the particular kind of ability needed to do a job well

Cognitive ability tests tests that measure the extent to which applicants have abilities in perceptual speed, verbal comprehension, numerical aptitude, general reasoning, and spatial aptitude

Biographical data (biodata) extensive surveys that ask applicants questions about their personal backgrounds and life experiences

Work sample tests tests that require applicants to perform tasks that are actually done on the job

Assessment centres a series of managerial simulations, graded by trained observers, that are used to determine applicants' capability for managerial work

Interviews a selection tool in which company representatives ask job applicants job-related questions to determine whether they are qualified for the job

Unstructured interviews interviews in which interviewers are free to ask the applicants anything they want

10-6 (P. 218)

Describe basic compensation strategies and discuss the four kinds of employee separations. Compensation includes both the financial and the nonfinancial rewards that organizations give employees in exchange for their work. There are three basic kinds of compensation decisions: pay level, pay variability, and pay structure. Employee separation is the loss of an employee, which can occur voluntarily or involuntarily. Companies use downsizing and early retirement incentive programs to reduce the number of employees in the organization and lower costs. However, companies generally try to keep the rate of employee turnover low to reduce costs associated with finding and developing new employees. Functional turnover, on the other hand, can be good for organizations.

Structured interviews interviews in which all applicants are asked the same set of standardized questions, usually including situational, behavioural, background, and job knowledge questions

10-4

Training developing the skills, experience, and knowledge employees need to perform their jobs or improve their performance

Needs assessment the process of identifying and prioritizing the learning needs of employees

10-5

Performance appraisal the process of assessing how well employees are doing their jobs

Objective performance measures measures of job performance that are easily and directly counted or quantified

Behavioural observation scale (BOS) a rating scale that indicates the frequency with which workers perform specific behaviours that are representative of the job dimensions critical to successful job performance

Rater training training performance appraisal raters in how to avoid rating errors and increase rating accuracy

360-degree feedback a performance appraisal process in which feedback is obtained from the boss, subordinates, peers and coworkers, and the employees themselves

10-6

Compensation the financial and nonfinancial rewards that organizations give employees in exchange for their work

Employee separation the voluntary or involuntary loss of an employee

Job evaluation a process that determines the worth of each job in a company by establishing the market value of the knowledge, skills, and requirements needed to perform it

Piecework a compensation system in which employees are paid a set rate for each item they produce

Commission a compensation system in which employees earn a percentage of each sale they make

Profit sharing a compensation system in which a company pays a percentage of its profits to employees in addition to their regular compensation

Employee stock ownership plan (ESOP) a compensation system that awards employees shares of company stock in addition to their regular compensation

Stock options a compensation system that gives employees the right to purchase shares of stock at a set price, even if the value of the stock increases above that price

Wrongful discharge a legal doctrine that requires employers to have a job-related reason to terminate employees

Downsizing the planned elimination of jobs in a company

Outplacement services employment-counselling services offered to employees who are losing their jobs because of downsizing

Early retirement incentive programs (ERIPs) programs that offer financial benefits to employees to encourage them to retire early

Phased retirement employees transition to retirement by working reduced hours over a period of time before completely retiring

Employee turnover loss of employees who voluntarily choose to leave the company

Functional turnover loss of poorly performing employees who voluntarily choose to leave a company

Dysfunctional turnover loss of high-performing employees who voluntarily choose to leave a company

CHAPTER REVIEW

Managing Individuals and a Diverse Workforce

LEARNING OUTCOMES

11-1 (P. 226)

Describe diversity and explain why it matters. Diversity exists in organizations when there are demographic, cultural, and personal differences among the people who work there and the customers who do business there. A common misconception is that workplace diversity and employment equity are the same. However, employment equity is more narrowly focused on demographics; diversity is broader in focus (going beyond demographics), voluntary, and more positive in that it encourages companies to value all kinds of differences. Employment equity and diversity thus differ in purpose, practice, and the reactions they produce. Diversity makes good business sense in terms of cost savings, attracting and retaining talent, and driving business growth (improving marketplace understanding and promoting higher-quality problem solving). The general purpose of diversity programs is to ensure that no one is advantaged or disadvantaged and that differences are respected and not ignored.

11-2 (P. 229)

Understand the special challenges that the dimensions of surface-level diversity pose for managers. Age, gender, race/ethnicity, and physical and mental disabilities are dimensions of surface-level diversity. Because those dimensions are (usually) easily observed, managers and workers tend to rely on them to form initial impressions and stereotypes. Sometimes this can lead to age, gender, racial/ethnic, or disability discrimination (i.e., treating people differently) in the workplace. In general, older workers, women, people of colour or different national origins, and people with disabilities are much less likely to be hired or promoted than are white males. This disparity is often due to incorrect beliefs or stereotypes such as "job performance declines with age," or "women aren't willing to travel on business," or "workers with disabilities aren't as competent as typical workers." To reduce discrimination, companies can determine the hiring and promotion rates for different groups, train managers to make hiring and promotion decisions on the basis of specific criteria, and make sure that everyone has equal access to training, mentors, reasonable work accommodations, and assistive technology. Finally, companies need to designate a go-to person whom employees can talk to if they believe they have suffered discrimination.

11-3 (P. 236)

Explain how the dimensions of deep-level diversity affect individual behaviour and interactions in the workplace. Deep-level diversity matters because it can reduce prejudice, discrimination, and conflict while increasing social integration. It consists of dispositional and personality differences that can be learned only through extended interaction with others. Research conducted in different cultures, settings, and languages indicates that there are five basic dimensions of personality: extroversion, emotional stability, agreeableness, conscientiousness, and openness to experience. Of these, conscientiousness is perhaps the most important because conscientious workers tend to be better performers on virtually any job. Extroversion is also related to performance in jobs that require significant interaction with others.

KEY TERMS

11-1

Diversity a variety of demographic, cultural, and personal differences among an organization's employees and customers

Employment equity an ongoing planning process used by an employer to eliminate barriers in an organization's employment procedures and to ensure appropriate representation of specific members of the workforce

Affirmative action purposeful steps taken by an organization to create employment opportunities for minorities and women

11-2

Surface-level diversity differences such as age, gender, race/ethnicity, and physical capabilities that are observable, typically unchangeable, and easy to measure

Deep-level diversity differences such as personality and attitudes that are communicated through verbal and nonverbal behaviours and are learned only through extended interaction with others

Social integration the degree to which group members are psychologically attracted to working with one another to accomplish a common objective

Age discrimination treating people differently (e.g., in hiring and firing, promotion, and compensation decisions) because of their age

Gender discrimination treating people differently because of their gender

Glass ceiling the invisible barrier that prevents women and minorities from advancing to the top jobs in organizations

Racial and ethnic discrimination treating people differently because of their race or ethnicity

Disability an activity limitation or participation restriction associated with a physical or mental condition or health problem

Disability discrimination treating people differently because of their disabilities

11-3

Disposition the tendency to respond to situations and events in a predetermined manner

Personality the relatively stable set of behaviours, attitudes, and emotions displayed over time that makes people different from one another

Extroversion the degree to which someone is active, assertive, gregarious, sociable, talkative, and energized by others

Emotional stability the degree to which someone is not angry, depressed, anxious, emotional, insecure, and excitable

Agreeableness the degree to which someone is cooperative, polite, flexible, forgiving, good-natured, tolerant, and trusting

Conscientiousness the degree to which someone is organized, hardworking, responsible, persevering, thorough, and achievement oriented

Openness to experience the degree to which someone is curious, broad-minded, and open to new ideas, things, and experiences; is spontaneous; and has a high tolerance for ambiguity

11-4

Organizational plurality a work environment where (1) all members are empowered to contribute in a way that maximizes the benefits to the organization, customers, and themselves, and (2) the individuality of each member is respected by not segmenting or polarizing people on the basis of their membership in a particular group

Awareness training training designed to raise employees' awareness of diversity issues and to challenge the underlying assumptions or stereotypes they may have about others

Skills-based diversity training training that teaches employees the practical skills they need for managing a diverse workforce, such as flexibility and adaptability, negotiation, problem solving, and conflict resolution

Diversity audits formal assessments that measure employee and management attitudes, investigate the extent to which people are advantaged or disadvantaged with respect to hiring and promotions, and review companies' diversity-related policies and procedures

Diversity pairing a mentoring program in which people of different cultural backgrounds, sexes, or races/ethnicities are paired together to get to know one another and change stereotypical beliefs and attitudes

11-4 (P. 238)

Explain the basic principles and practices that can be used to manage diversity. The three paradigms for managing diversity are the discrimination and fairness paradigm (equal opportunity, fair treatment, strict compliance with the law), the access and legitimacy paradigm (matching internal diversity to external diversity), and the learning and effectiveness paradigm (achieving organizational plurality by integrating deep-level diversity into the work of the organization). Unlike the other paradigms, which focus on surface-level differences, the learning and effectiveness paradigm values common ground, distinguishes between individual and group differences, minimizes conflict and divisiveness, and focuses on bringing different talents and perspectives together. What principles can companies use when managing diversity? Link diversity to strategic business goals. Include diversity in human resource planning. Recruit a diverse workforce. Select a diverse workforce. Train and develop a diverse staff. Monitor the effectiveness of staffing for diversity. Provide work–life flexibility. Create an inclusive working environment. Encourage senior executive support for diversity. The two types of diversity training are awareness training and skills-based diversity training. Companies also manage diversity through diversity audits and diversity pairing.

Paradigms for Managing Diversity

Diversity paradigm	Focus	Success measured by	Benefits	Limitations
Discrimination and fairness	Equal opportunity Fair treatment Recruitment of minorities Strict compliance with laws	Recruitment, promotion, and retention goals for underrepresented group	Results in fairer treatment Increases demographic diversity	Focuses on surface-level diversity
Access and legitimacy	Acceptance and celebration of differences	Diversity in company matches diversity of primary stakeholders	Establishes a clear business reason for diversity	Focuses on surface-level diversity
Learning and effectiveness	Integrating deep-level differences into organization	Valuing people on the basis of individual knowledge, skills, and abilities	Values common ground Distinguishes between individual and group differences Minimizes conflict, backlash, and divisiveness Brings different talents and perspectives together	Focuses on deep-level diversity, which is more difficult to measure and quantify

LEARNING OUTCOMES

12-1 (P. 246)

Explain the basics of motivation. Motivation is the set of forces that initiates, directs, and makes people persist in their efforts over time to accomplish a goal. Managers often confuse motivation and performance, but job performance is a multiplicative function of motivation times ability times situational constraints. Needs are the physical or psychological requirements that must be met to ensure survival and well-being. Different motivational theories (Maslow's Hierarchy of Needs, Alderfer's ERG Theory, and McClelland's Learned Needs Theory) specify a number of different needs. However, studies show that there are only two general kinds of needs: lower order needs and higher order needs. Both extrinsic and intrinsic rewards motivate people.

12-2 (P. 253)

Use equity theory to explain how employees' perceptions of fairness affect motivation. The basic components of equity theory are inputs, outcomes, and referents. After an internal comparison in which they compare their outcomes (O) to their inputs (I), employees make an external comparison in which they compare their O/I ratio with the O/I ratio of a referent, a person who works in a similar job or is otherwise similar. When their O/I ratio is equal to the referent's O/I ratio, employees perceive that they are being treated fairly. But, when their O/I ratio is different from their referent's O/I ratio, they perceive that they have been treated inequitably or unfairly.

12-3 (P. 257)

Use expectancy theory to describe how workers' expectations about rewards, effort, and the link between rewards and performance influence motivation. Expectancy theory holds that three factors affect the conscious choices people make about their motivation: valence, expectancy, and instrumentality. Expectancy theory holds that all three factors must be high for people to be highly motivated. If any one of these factors declines, overall motivation will decline too.

12-4 (P. 259)

Explain how reinforcement theory works and how it can be used to motivate. Reinforcement theory says that behaviour is a function of its consequences. Reinforcement has two parts: reinforcement contingencies and schedules of reinforcement. The four kinds of reinforcement contingencies are positive reinforcement and negative reinforcement, which strengthen behaviour, and punishment and extinction, which weaken behaviour. There are two kinds of reinforcement schedules, continuous and intermittent; intermittent schedules, in turn, can be divided into fixed and variable interval schedules and fixed and variable ratio schedules.

KEY TERMS

12-1

Motivation the set of forces that initiates, directs, and makes people persist in their efforts to accomplish a goal

Needs the physical or psychological requirements that must be met to ensure survival and well-being

Extrinsic rewards rewards that are tangible, visible to others, and given to employees contingent on the performance of specific tasks or behaviours

Intrinsic reward a natural reward associated with performing a task or activity for its own sake

12-2

Equity theory a theory that states that people will be motivated when they perceive that they are being treated fairly

Inputs in equity theory, the contributions employees make to the organization

Outcomes in equity theory, the rewards employees receive for their contributions to the organization

Referents in equity theory, others with whom people compare themselves to determine if they have been treated fairly

Outcome/input (O/I) ratio in equity theory, an employee's perception of how the rewards received from an organization compare with the employee's contributions to that organization

Under-reward a form of inequity in which you are getting fewer outcomes relative to inputs than your referent is getting

Over-reward a form of inequity in which you are getting more outcomes relative to inputs than your referent

Distributive justice the perceived degree to which outcomes and rewards are fairly distributed or allocated

Procedural justice the perceived fairness of the process used to make reward allocation decisions

CHAPTER REVIEW 12

12-3

Expectancy theory a theory that people will be motivated to the extent to which they believe that their efforts will lead to good performance, that good performance will be rewarded, and that they will be offered attractive rewards

Valence the attractiveness or desirability of a reward or outcome

Expectancy the perceived relationship between effort and performance

Instrumentality the perceived relationship between performance and rewards

12-4

Reinforcement theory a theory that behaviour is a function of its consequences, that behaviours followed by positive consequences will occur more frequently, and that behaviours followed by negative consequences, or not followed by positive consequences, will occur less frequently

Reinforcement the process of changing behaviour by changing the consequences that follow behaviour

Reinforcement contingencies cause-and-effect relationships between the performance of specific behaviours and specific consequences

Schedule of reinforcement rules that specify which behaviours will be reinforced, which consequences will follow those behaviours, and the schedule by which those consequences will be delivered

Positive reinforcement reinforcement that strengthens behaviour by following behaviours with desirable consequences

Negative reinforcement reinforcement that strengthens behaviour by withholding an unpleasant consequence when employees perform a specific behaviour

Punishment reinforcement that weakens behaviour by following behaviours with undesirable consequences

Extinction reinforcement in which a positive consequence is no longer allowed to follow a previously reinforced behaviour, thus weakening the behaviour

Continuous reinforcement schedule a schedule that requires a consequence to be administered following every instance of a behaviour

Intermittent reinforcement schedule a schedule in which consequences are delivered after a specified or average time has elapsed or after a specified or average number of behaviours has occurred

Fixed interval reinforcement schedule an intermittent schedule in which consequences follow a behaviour only after a fixed time has elapsed

Variable interval reinforcement schedule an intermittent schedule in which the time between a behaviour and the following consequences varies around a specified average

Fixed ratio reinforcement schedule an intermittent schedule in which consequences are delivered following a specific number of behaviours

Variable ratio reinforcement schedule an intermittent schedule in which consequences are delivered following a different number of behaviours, sometimes more and sometimes less, that vary around a specified average number of behaviours

12-5

Goal a target, objective, or result that someone tries to accomplish

12-5 (P. 263)

Describe the components of goal-setting theory and how managers can use them to motivate workers. A goal is a target, objective, or result that someone tries to accomplish. Goal-setting theory says that people will be motivated to the extent to which they accept specific, challenging goals and receive feedback that indicates their progress toward goal achievement. The basic components of goal-setting theory are goal specificity, goal difficulty, goal acceptance, and performance feedback. Goal specificity is the extent to which goals are detailed, exact, and unambiguous. Goal difficulty is the extent to which a goal is hard or challenging to accomplish. Goal acceptance is the extent to which people consciously understand and agree to goals. Performance feedback is information about the quality or quantity of past performance and indicates whether progress is being made toward the accomplishment of a goal.

12-6 (P. 266)

Discuss how the entire motivation model can be used to motivate workers. Each employee is likely to have personal motivators that differ from other employees'. See the other sections of this review for specifics.

Goal-setting theory a theory that people will be motivated to the extent to which they accept specific, challenging goals and receive feedback that indicates their progress toward goal achievement

Goal specificity the extent to which goals are detailed, exact, and unambiguous

Goal difficulty the extent to which a goal is hard or challenging to accomplish

Goal acceptance the extent to which people consciously understand and agree to goals

Performance feedback information about the quality or quantity of past performance that indicates whether progress is being made toward the accomplishment of a goal

LEARNING OUTCOMES

13-1 (P. 270)

Explain what leadership is. Management is getting work done through others; leadership is the process of influencing others to achieve group or organizational goals. Leaders are different from managers. The primary difference is that leaders are concerned about doing the right thing, while managers are concerned about doing things right. Organizations need both managers and leaders. But in general, companies are overmanaged and underled.

13-2 (P. 270)

Describe who leaders are and what effective leaders do. Trait theory says that effective leaders possess traits or characteristics that differentiate them from nonleaders. Those traits are drive, the desire to lead, honesty/integrity, self-confidence, emotional stability, cognitive ability, and knowledge of the business. These traits alone aren't enough for successful leadership; leaders who have many or all of them must also behave in ways that encourage people to achieve group or organizational goals. Two key leader behaviours are initiating structure, which improves subordinate performance, and consideration, which improves subordinate satisfaction. There is no ideal combination of these behaviours. The best leadership style depends on the situation.

13-3 (P. 276)

Explain Fiedler's contingency theory. Fiedler's theory assumes that leaders are effective when their work groups perform well, that leaders are unable to change their leadership styles, that leadership styles must be matched to the proper situation, and that favourable situations permit leaders to influence group members. According to the Least Preferred Coworker (LPC) scale, there are two basic leadership styles. People who describe their LPC in a positive way have relationship-oriented leadership styles. By contrast, people who describe their LPC in a negative way have task-oriented leadership styles. Situational favourableness, which occurs when leaders can influence followers, is determined by leader–member relations, task structure, and position power. In general, relationship-oriented leaders with high LPC scores are better leaders under moderately favourable situations, while task-oriented leaders with low LPC scores are better leaders in highly favourable and unfavourable situations. The key is to accurately measure and match leaders to situations or to teach leaders how to change situational factors.

13-4 (P. 280)

Describe how path–goal theory works. Path–goal theory states that leaders can increase subordinate satisfaction and performance by clarifying and clearing the paths to goals and by increasing the number and kinds of rewards available for goal attainment. For this to work, however, leader behaviour must be a source of immediate or future satisfaction for followers and must complement and not duplicate the characteristics of followers' work environments. In contrast to Fiedler's contingency theory, path–goal theory assumes that leaders can and do change their leadership styles (directive, supportive, participative, and achievement-oriented), depending on their subordinates (experience, perceived ability, internal or external locus of control) and the environment in which those subordinates work (task structure, formal authority system, primary work group).

KEY TERMS

13-1

Leadership the process of influencing others to achieve group or organizational goals

13-2

Trait theory a leadership theory that holds that effective leaders possess a similar set of traits or characteristics

Traits relatively stable characteristics, such as abilities, psychological motives, or consistent patterns of behaviour

Initiating structure the degree to which a leader structures the roles of followers by setting goals, giving directions, setting deadlines, and assigning tasks

Consideration the extent to which a leader is friendly, approachable, and supportive and shows concern for employees

13-3

Leadership style the way a leader generally behaves toward followers

Contingency theory a leadership theory that, in order to maximize work group performance, leaders must be matched to the situation that best fits their leadership style

Least Preferred Coworker (LPC) Scale consider (and scale or grade) all of the people with whom they have ever worked and then to choose the one person with whom they have worked least well

Situational favourableness the degree to which a particular situation either permits or denies a leader the chance to influence the behaviour of group members

Leader–member relations the degree to which followers respect, trust, and like their leaders

Task structure the degree to which the requirements of a subordinate's tasks are clearly specified

Position power the degree to which leaders are able to hire, fire, reward, and punish workers

CHAPTER REVIEW 13

13-4

Path–goal theory a leadership theory that leaders can increase subordinate satisfaction and performance by clarifying and clearing the paths to goals and by increasing the number and kinds of rewards available for goal attainment

Directive leadership a leadership style in which the leader lets employees know precisely what is expected of them, gives them specific guidelines for performing tasks, schedules work, sets standards of performance, and makes sure that people follow standard rules and regulations

Supportive leadership a leadership style in which the leader is friendly and approachable, shows concern for employees and their welfare, treats them as equals, and creates a friendly climate

Participative leadership a leadership style in which the leader consults employees for their suggestions and input before making decisions

Achievement-oriented leadership a leadership style in which the leader sets challenging goals, has high expectations of employees, and displays confidence that employees will assume responsibility and put forth extraordinary effort

13-5

Normative decision theory a theory that suggests how leaders can determine an appropriate amount of employee participation when making decisions

13-7

Strategic leadership the ability to anticipate, envision, maintain flexibility, think strategically, and work with others to initiate changes that will create a positive future for an organization

Visionary leadership leadership that creates a positive image of the future that motivates organizational members and provides direction for future planning and goal setting

Charismatic leadership the behavioural tendencies and personal characteristics of leaders that create an exceptionally strong relationship between them and their followers

Ethical charismatics charismatic leaders who provide developmental opportunities for followers, are open to positive and negative feedback, recognize others' contributions, share information, and have moral standards that emphasize the larger interests of the group, organization, or society

Unethical charismatics charismatic leaders who control and manipulate followers, do what is best for themselves instead of their organizations, want to hear only positive feedback, share only information that benefits themselves, and have moral standards that put their interests before everyone else's

Transformational leadership leadership that generates awareness and acceptance of a group's purpose and mission and gets employees to see beyond their own needs and self-interests for the good of the group

Transactional leadership leadership based on an exchange process, in which followers are rewarded for good performance and punished for poor performance

13-5 (P. 283)

Explain the normative decision theory. The normative decision theory helps leaders decide how much employee participation should be used when making decisions. Using the right degree of employee participation improves the quality of decisions and the extent to which employees accept and are committed to decisions. The theory specifies five different decision styles or ways of making decisions: autocratic (AI or AII), consultative (CI or CII), and group (GII). The theory improves decision quality via the decision rules of quality, leader information, subordinate information, goal congruence, and problem structure. Normative decision theory then operationalizes these decision rules in the form of yes/no questions, as shown in the decision tree displayed in Exhibit 13.8.

13-6 (P. 287)

Discuss gender and leadership. Stereotypes, prejudice, and discrimination contribute to women's under-representation in elite leadership roles by impacting perceptions of and responses to women as well as impacting the experiences of women themselves. The role of traits in understanding leadership emergence and effectiveness has been a controversial issue in the literature.

A study by Reuvers et al. showed that employees report more innovative behaviour when the transformational leadership is displayed by male in comparison with female managers, confirming our gender bias hypothesis. In a separate experimental study, Kulich et al. suggested that the romance of leadership does exist for both men and women but that the process of pay allocation differs as a function of gender. Generally, for a female leader, it is based on perceptions of her charisma and leadership ability rather than directly on company performance.

13-7 (P. 287)

Explain how visionary leadership (i.e., charismatic and transformational leadership) helps leaders achieve strategic leadership. Strategic leadership requires visionary, charismatic, and transformational leadership. Visionary leadership creates a positive image of the future that motivates organizational members and provides direction for future planning and goal setting. Charismatic leaders have strong, confident, dynamic personalities that attract followers, enable the leader to create strong bonds, and inspire followers to accomplish the leader's vision. Followers of ethical charismatic leaders work harder, are more committed and satisfied, are better performers, and are more likely to trust their leaders. The four components of transformational leadership are charisma or idealized influence, inspirational motivation, intellectual stimulation, and individualized consideration.

LEARNING OUTCOMES

14-1 (P. 294)

Explain the role that perception plays in communication and communication problems. Perception is the process by which people attend to, organize, interpret, and retain information from their environments. Perception is not a straightforward process. Because of perceptual filters such as selective perception and closure, people exposed to the same information stimuli often end up with very different perceptions and understandings. Perception-based differences can also lead to differences in the attributions (internal or external) that managers and workers make when explaining workplace behaviour. In general, workers are more likely to explain behaviour from a defensive bias, in which they attribute problems to external causes (i.e., the situation). Managers, on the other hand, tend to commit the fundamental attribution error, attributing problems to internal causes (i.e., the worker associated with a mistake or error). Consequently, when things go wrong, it's common for managers to blame workers and for workers to blame the situation or context in which they do their jobs. Finally, this problem is compounded by a self-serving bias that leads people to attribute successes to internal causes and failures to external causes. So, when workers receive negative feedback from managers, they may become defensive and emotional and not hear what their managers have to say. In short, perceptions and attributions represent a significant challenge to effective communication and understanding in organizations.

14-2 (P. 297)

Describe the communication process and the various kinds of communication in organizations. Organizational communication depends on the communication process, formal and informal communication channels, one-on-one communication, and nonverbal communication. The major components of the communication process are the sender, the receiver, noise, and feedback. Senders often mistakenly assume that they can pipe their intended messages directly into receivers' heads with perfect clarity. Formal communication channels such as downward, upward, and horizontal communication carry organizationally approved messages and information. By contrast, the informal communication channel, called the "grapevine," arises out of curiosity and is carried out through gossip or cluster chains. There are two kinds of one-on-one communication. Coaching is used to improve on-the-job performance, while counselling is used to communicate about non-job-related issues affecting job performance. Nonverbal communication, such as kinesics and paralanguage, accounts for as much as 93 percent of a message's content and understanding.

KEY TERMS

14-1

Communication the process of transmitting information from one person or place to another

Perception the process by which individuals attend to, organize, interpret, and retain information from their environments

Perceptual filters the personality-, psychology-, or experience-based differences that influence people to ignore or pay attention to particular stimuli

Selective perception the tendency to notice and accept objects and information consistent with our values, beliefs, and expectations while ignoring or screening out or not accepting inconsistent information

Closure the tendency to fill in gaps of missing information by assuming that what we don't know is consistent with what we already know

Attribution theory a theory that we all have a basic need to understand and explain the causes of other people's behaviour

Defensive bias the tendency for people to perceive themselves as personally and situationally similar to someone who is having difficulty or trouble

Fundamental attribution error the tendency to ignore external causes of behaviour and to attribute other people's actions to internal causes

Self-serving bias the tendency to overestimate our value by attributing successes to ourselves (internal causes) and attributing failures to others or the environment (external causes)

14-2

Encoding putting a message into a written, verbal, or symbolic form that can be recognized and understood by the receiver

Decoding the process by which the receiver translates the written, verbal, or symbolic form of a message into an understood message

Feedback to sender in the communication process, a return message to the sender that indicates the receiver's understanding of the message

Noise anything that interferes with the transmission of the intended message

CHAPTER REVIEW 14

Jargon vocabulary particular to a profession or group

Formal communication channel the system of official channels that carry organizationally approved messages and information

Downward communication communication that flows from higher to lower levels in an organization

Upward communication communication that flows from lower to higher levels in an organization

Horizontal communication communication that flows among managers and workers who are at the same organizational level

Informal communication channel the transmission of messages from employee to employee outside of formal communication channels; sometimes called "the grapevine" or "the rumour mill"

Coaching communicating with someone for the direct purpose of improving the person's on-the-job performance or behaviour

Mentorship communicating with someone with a focus on career development and knowledge transfer versus individual skill development or immediate performance improvement

Counselling communicating with someone about non-job-related issues that may be affecting or interfering with the person's performance

Nonverbal communication any communication that doesn't involve words

Kinesics movements of the body and face

Paralanguage the pitch, rate, tone, volume, and speaking pattern (use of silences, pauses, or hesitations) of one's voice.

14-3

Communication medium the method used to deliver an oral or written message

Hearing the act or process of perceiving sounds

Listening making a conscious effort to hear

Active listening assuming half the responsibility for successful communication by actively giving the speaker nonjudgmental feedback that shows you've accurately heard what he or she said

Empathetic listening understanding the speaker's perspective and personal frame of reference and giving feedback that conveys that understanding to the speaker

Destructive feedback feedback that disapproves without any intention of being helpful and almost always causes a negative or defensive reaction in the recipient

14-3 (P. 304)

Explain how managers can manage effective one-on-one communication. One-on-one communication can be managed by choosing the right communication medium, being a good listener, and giving effective feedback. Managers generally prefer oral communication because it provides the opportunity to ask questions and assess nonverbal communication. Oral communication is best suited to complex, ambiguous, or emotionally laden topics. Written communication is best suited for delivering straightforward messages and information. Listening is important for managerial success, but most people are terrible listeners. To improve your listening skills, choose to be an active listener (clarify responses, paraphrase, and summarize) and an empathetic listener (show your desire to understand, reflect feelings). Feedback can be constructive or destructive. To be constructive, feedback must be immediate, focused on specific behaviours, and problem-oriented.

14-4 (P. 308)

Describe how managers can manage effective organization-wide communication. Managers need methods for managing organization-wide communication and for making themselves accessible so that they can hear what employees throughout their organizations are feeling and thinking. Email, online collaboration tools, web or video conferencing, and cloud computing make it much easier for managers to improve message transmission and get the message out. By contrast, anonymous company hotlines, survey feedback, and frequent informal meetings help managers avoid organizational silence and improve reception by giving them the opportunity to hear what others in the organization feel and think. Monitoring social media sites is another way to find out what people are saying and thinking about your organization.

Constructive feedback feedback intended to be helpful, corrective, and/or encouraging

14-4

Organizational silence when employees withhold information about organizational problems or issues

LEARNING OUTCOMES

15-1 (P. 316)

Describe the basic control process. The control process begins by setting standards, measuring performance, and then comparing performance to the standards. The better a company's information and measurement systems, the easier it is to make these comparisons. The control process continues by identifying and analyzing performance deviations and then developing and implementing programs for corrective action. Control is a continuous, dynamic, cybernetic process, not a one-time achievement or result. Control requires frequent managerial attention. The three basic control methods are feedback control (after-the-fact performance information), concurrent control (simultaneous performance information), and feedforward control (preventive performance information). Control has regulation costs and unanticipated consequences and therefore isn't always worthwhile or possible.

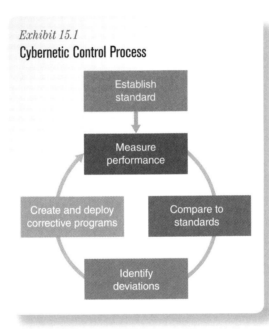

Exhibit 15.1
Cybernetic Control Process

- Establish standard
- Measure performance
- Compare to standards
- Identify deviations
- Create and deploy corrective programs

15-2 (P. 320)

Discuss the various methods that managers can use to maintain control. There are five methods of control: bureaucratic, objective, normative, concertive, and self-control (self-management). Bureaucratic and objective controls are top-down, management-based, and measurement-based. Normative and concertive controls represent shared forms of control because they evolve from company-wide or team-based beliefs and values. Self-control, or self-management, is a control system in which managers turn much, but not all, control over to the individuals themselves.

Bureaucratic control is based on organizational policies, rules, and procedures. Objective controls are based on reliable measures of behaviour or outputs. Normative control is based on strong corporate beliefs and careful hiring practices. Concertive control is based on the development of values, beliefs, and rules in autonomous work groups. Self-control is based on individuals' setting their own goals, monitoring themselves, and rewarding or punishing themselves with respect to goal achievement.

Each of these control methods may be more or less appropriate depending on the circumstances.

KEY TERMS

15-1

Control a regulatory process of establishing standards to achieve organizational goals, comparing actual performance to the standards, and taking corrective action when necessary

Standards a basis of comparison for measuring the extent to which various kinds of organizational performance are satisfactory or unsatisfactory

Benchmarking the process of identifying outstanding practices, processes, and standards in other companies and adapting them to your company

Cybernetic the process of steering or keeping on course

Feedback control a mechanism for gathering information about performance deficiencies after they occur

Concurrent control a mechanism for gathering information about performance deficiencies as they occur, thereby eliminating or shortening the delay between performance and feedback

Feedforward control a mechanism for monitoring performance inputs rather than outputs to prevent or minimize performance deficiencies before they occur

Control loss the situation in which behaviour and work procedures do not conform to standards

Regulation costs the costs associated with implementing or maintaining control

Cybernetic feasibility the extent to which it is possible to implement each step in the control process

15-2

Bureaucratic control the use of hierarchical authority to influence employee behaviour by rewarding or punishing employees for compliance or noncompliance with organizational policies, rules, and procedures

Objective control the use of observable measures of worker behaviour or outputs to assess performance and influence behaviour

Behaviour control the regulation of the behaviours and actions that employees perform on the job

CHAPTER REVIEW 15

Output control the regulation of employees' results or outputs through rewards and incentives

Normative control the regulation of employees' behaviour and decisions through widely shared organizational values and beliefs

Concertive control the regulation of employees' behaviour and decisions through work group values and beliefs

Self-control (or self-management) a control system in which managers and employees control their own behaviour by setting their own goals, monitoring their own progress, and rewarding themselves for goal achievement

15-3

Balanced Scorecard measurement of organizational performance from four equally important perspectives: customer, internal, and innovation and learning, and financial

Suboptimization performance improvement in one part of an organization at the expense of decreased performance in another part

Cash flow analysis a type of analysis that predicts how changes in a business will affect its ability to take in more cash than it pays out

Balance sheets (statements of financial position) accounting statements that provide a snapshot of a company's financial position at a particular point in time

Income statements (statements of comprehensive income) accounting statements that show what has happened to an organization's income, expenses, and net profit over a period of time (also historically called *profit and loss statements*)

Financial ratios calculations typically used to track a business's liquidity (cash), efficiency, and profitability over time compared to other businesses in its industry

Budgets quantitative plans through which managers decide how to allocate available money to best accomplish company goals

Economic value added (EVA) the amount by which company profits (revenues, minus expenses, minus taxes) exceed the cost of capital in a given year

Customer defections a performance assessment in which companies identify which customers are leaving and measure the rate at which they are leaving

Value customer perception that the product quality is excellent for the price offered

When to Use Different Methods of Control

BUREAUCRATIC CONTROL	▸ When it is necessary to standardize operating procedures ▸ When it is necessary to establish limits
BEHAVIOUR CONTROL	▸ When it is easier to measure what workers do on the job than what they accomplish on the job ▸ When cause–effect relationships are clear; that is, when companies know which behaviours will lead to success and which won't ▸ When good measures of worker behaviour can be created
OUTPUT CONTROL	▸ When it is easier to measure what workers accomplish on the job than what they do on the job ▸ When good measures of worker output can be created ▸ When it is possible to set clear goals and standards for worker output ▸ When cause–effect relationships are unclear
NORMATIVE CONTROL	▸ When organizational culture, values, and beliefs are strong ▸ When it is difficult to create good measures of worker behaviour ▸ When it is difficult to create good measures of worker output
CONCERTIVE CONTROL	▸ When responsibility for task accomplishment is given to autonomous work groups ▸ When management wants workers to take ownership of their behaviour and outputs ▸ When management desires a strong form of worker-based control
SELF-CONTROL	▸ When workers are intrinsically motivated to do their jobs well ▸ When it is difficult to create good measures of worker behaviour ▸ When it is difficult to create good measures of worker output ▸ When workers have or are taught self-control and self-leadership skills

Sources: L. J. Kirsch, "The Management of Complex Tasks in Organizations: Controlling the Systems Development Process," *Organization Science* 7 (1996): 1–21; S. A. Snell, "Control Theory in Strategic Human Resource Management: The Mediating Effect of Administrative Information," *Academy of Management Journal* 35 (1992): 292–327.

15-3 (P. 324)

Describe the behaviours, processes, and outcomes that today's managers are choosing to control in their organizations. Deciding what to control is just as important as deciding whether to control or how to control. In most companies, performance is evaluated using financial measures alone. However, the balanced scorecard encourages managers to measure and control company performance from four perspectives: financial, customer, internal operations, and innovation and learning. Traditionally, financial control has been achieved through cash flow analysis, balance sheets, income statements, financial ratios, and budgets. (For a refresher on these traditional financial control tools, see the next card, which is a Financial Review card.) Performance of internal operations is often measured in terms of quality, which is defined in three ways: excellence, value, and conformance to expectations. Minimizing waste has become an important part of innovation and learning in companies. The four levels of waste minimization are waste disposal, waste treatment, recycling and reuse, and waste prevention and reduction.

Basic Accounting Tools for Controlling Financial Performance

Steps for a Basic Cash Flow Analysis

1. Forecast sales (steady, up, or down).

2. Project changes in anticipated cash inflows (as a result of changes).

3. Project anticipated cash outflows (as a result of changes).

4. Project net cash flows by combining anticipated cash inflows and outflows.

Parts of a Basic Balance Sheet (Assets = Liabilities + Owner's Equity)

1. Assets
   a. Current Assets (cash, short-term investment, marketable securities, accounts receivable, etc.)
   b. Fixed Assets (land, buildings, machinery, equipment, etc.)

2. Liabilities
   a. Current Liabilities (accounts payable, notes payable, taxes payable, etc.)
   b. Long-Term Liabilities (long-term debt, deferred income taxes, etc.)

3. Owner's Equity
   a. Preferred stock and common stock
   b. Additional paid-in capital
   c. Retained earnings

Basic Income Statement

    SALES REVENUE
−   sales returns and allowances
+   other income
=   NET REVENUE
−   cost of goods sold (beginning inventory, costs of goods purchased, ending inventory)
=   GROSS PROFIT
−   total operating expenses (selling, general, and administrative expenses)
=   INCOME FROM OPERATIONS
−   interest expense
=   PRETAX INCOME
−   income taxes
=   NET INCOME

Common Kinds of Budgets

Revenue Budgets—used to project or forecast future sales.	▸ Accuracy of projection depends on economy, competitors, sales force estimates, etc. ▸ Determined by estimating future sales volume and sales prices for all products and services.
Expense Budgets—used within departments and divisions to determine how much will be spent on various supplies, projects, or activities.	▸ One of the first places that companies look for cuts when trying to lower expenses.
Profit Budgets—used by profit centres, which have "profit and loss" responsibility.	▸ Profit budgets combine revenue and expense budgets into one budget. ▸ Typically used in large businesses with multiple plants and divisions.

(Continued)

FINANCIAL REVIEW CARD

Cash Budgets—used to forecast how much cash a company will have on hand to meet expenses.

▸ Similar to cash flow analyses.
▸ Used to identify cash shortfalls, which must be covered to pay bills, or cash excesses, which should be invested for a higher return.

Capital Expenditure Budgets—used to forecast large, long-lasting investments in equipment, buildings, and property.

▸ Help managers identify funding that will be needed to pay for future expansion or strategic moves designed to increase competitive advantage.

Variable Budgets—used to project costs across varying levels of sales and revenues.

▸ Important because it is difficult to accurately predict sales revenue and volume.
▸ Lead to more accurate budgeting with respect to labour, materials, and administrative expenses, which vary with sales volume and revenues.
▸ Build flexibility into the budgeting process.

Common Financial Ratios

Ratios	Formula	What It Means	When to Use
Liquidity Ratios			
Current Ratio	$\dfrac{\text{Current Assets}}{\text{Current Liabilities}}$	▸ Whether you have enough assets on hand to pay for short-term bills and obligations. ▸ Higher is better. ▸ Recommended level is two times as many current assets as current liabilities	▸ Track monthly and quarterly. ▸ Basic measure of your company's health.
Quick (Acid Test) Ratio	$\dfrac{(\text{Current Assets} - \text{Inventories})}{\text{Current Liabilities}}$	▸ Stricter than current ratio. ▸ Whether you have enough (i.e., cash) to pay short-term bills and obligations. ▸ Higher is better. ▸ Recommended level is one or higher.	▸ Track monthly. ▸ Also calculate quick ratio with potential customers to evaluate whether they're likely to pay you in a timely manner.
Leverage Ratios			
Debt to Equity	$\dfrac{\text{Total Liabilities}}{\text{Total Equity}}$	▸ Indicates how much the company is leveraged (in debt) by comparing what is owed (liabilities) to what is owned (equity). ▸ Lower is better. A high debt-to-equity ratio could indicate that the company has too much debt. ▸ Recommended level depends on industry.	▸ Track monthly. ▸ Lenders often use this to determine the creditworthiness of a business (i.e., whether to approve additional loans).
Debt Coverage	$\dfrac{(\text{Net Profit} + \text{Noncash Expense})}{\text{Debt}}$	▸ Indicates how well cash flow covers debt payments. ▸ Higher is better.	▸ Track monthly. ▸ Lenders look at this ratio to determine if there is adequate cash to make loan payment.
Efficiency Ratios			
Inventory Turnover	$\dfrac{\text{Cost of Goods Sold}}{\text{Average Value of Inventory}}$	▸ Whether you're making efficient use of inventory. ▸ Higher is better, indicating that inventory (dollars) isn't purchased (spent) until needed. ▸ Recommended level depends on industry.	▸ Track monthly by using a 12-month rolling average.
Average Collections Period	$\dfrac{\text{Accounts Receivable}}{(\text{Annual Net Credit Sales Divided by 365})}$	▸ Shows on average how quickly your customers are paying their bills. ▸ Recommended level is no more than 15 days longer than credit terms. If credit is net 30 days, then average should not be longer than 45 days.	▸ Track monthly. ▸ Use to determine how long company's money is being tied up in customer credit.
Profitability Ratios			
Gross Profit Margin	$\dfrac{\text{Gross Profit}}{\text{Total Sales}}$	▸ Shows how efficiently a business is using its materials and labour in the production process. ▸ Higher is better, indicating that a profit can be made if fixed costs are controlled.	▸ Track monthly. ▸ Analyze when unsure about product or service pricing. ▸ Low margin compared to competitors means you're underpricing.
Return on Equity	$\dfrac{\text{Net Income}}{\text{Owner's Equity}}$	▸ Shows what was earned on your investment in the business during a particular period. Often called "return on investment." ▸ Higher is better.	▸ Track quarterly and annually. ▸ Use to compare to what you might have earned on the stock market, bonds, or government Treasury bills during the same period.

LEARNING OUTCOMES

16-1 (P. 336)

Explain the strategic importance of information. The first company to use new information technology to substantially lower costs or differentiate products or services often gains first-mover advantage, higher profits, and larger market share. Creating a first-mover advantage can be difficult, expensive, and risky, however. According to the resource-based view of IT, sustainable competitive advantage occurs when IT adds value, is different across firms, and is difficult to create or acquire.

16-2 (P. 339)

Describe the characteristics of useful information (i.e., its value and costs). Raw data are facts and figures. Raw data do not become information until they are in a form that can affect decisions and behaviour. For information to be useful, it has to be reliable and valid (accurate), of sufficient quantity (complete), pertinent to the problems you're facing (relevant), and available when you need it (timely). Useful information does not come cheap. The five costs of obtaining good information are the costs of acquiring, processing, storing, retrieving, and communicating information.

16-3 (P. 343)

Explain the basics of capturing, processing, and protecting information. Electronic data capture (bar codes, radio frequency identification [RFID] tags, scanners, and optical character recognition) is much faster, easier, and cheaper than manual data capture. Processing information means transforming raw data into meaningful information that can be applied to business decision making. Data mining helps managers with this transformation by discovering unknown patterns and relationships in data. Supervised data mining looks for patterns specified by managers, while unsupervised data mining looks for four general kinds of data patterns: association/affinity patterns, sequence patterns, predictive patterns, and data clusters. Protecting information ensures that data are reliably and consistently retrievable in a usable format by authorized users but no one else. Authentication and authorization, firewalls, antivirus software for PCs and corporate email and network servers, data encryption, virtual private networks (VPN), and web-based secure sockets layer (SSL) encryption are some of the best ways to protect information. Be careful with wireless networks, which are easily compromised even when security and encryption protocols are in place.

KEY TERMS

16-1

Moore's law the prediction that the cost of computing will drop by 50 percent every 18 months as computer-processing power doubles

Raw data facts and figures

Information useful data that can influence people's choices and behaviour

First-mover advantage the strategic advantage that companies earn by being the first to use new information technology to substantially lower costs or to make a product or service different from that of competitors

16-2

Acquisition cost the cost of obtaining data that you don't have

Processing cost the cost of turning raw data into usable information

Storage cost the cost of physically or electronically archiving information for later use and retrieval

Retrieval cost the cost of accessing already stored and processed information

Communication cost the cost of transmitting information from one place to another

16-3

Bar codes visual patterns that represent numerical data by varying the thickness and pattern of vertical bars

Radio frequency identification (RFID) tags tags containing minuscule microchips that transmit information via radio waves and can be used to track the number and location of the objects into which the tags have been inserted

Electronic scanner an electronic device that converts printed text and pictures into digital images

Optical character recognition the ability of software to convert digitized documents into ASCII (American Standard Code for Information Interchange) text or PDF documents that can be searched, read, and edited by word processing and other kinds of software

Processing information transforming raw data into meaningful information

CHAPTER REVIEW 16

Data mining the process of discovering patterns and relationships in large amounts of data

Data warehouse stores huge amounts of data that have been prepared for data mining analysis by being cleaned of errors and redundancy

Supervised data mining the process when the user tells the data mining software to look and test for specific patterns and relationships in a data set

Unsupervised data mining the process when the user simply tells the data mining software to uncover whatever patterns and relationships it can find in a data set

Association or affinity patterns when two or more database elements tend to occur together in a significant way

Sequence patterns when two or more database elements occur together in a significant pattern, but one of the elements precedes the other

Predictive patterns patterns that help identify database elements that are different

Data clusters when three or more database elements occur together (i.e., cluster) in a significant way

Protecting information the process of ensuring that data are reliably and consistently retrievable in a usable format for authorized users but no one else

Authentication making sure potential users are who they claim to be

Authorization granting authenticated users approved access to data, software, and systems

Biometrics identifying users by unique, measurable body features, such as fingerprint recognition or iris scanning

Two-factor authentication authentication based on what users know, such as a password, and what they have in their possession, such as a secure ID card or key

Firewalls protective hardware or software devices that sit between the computers in an internal organizational network and outside networks, such as the Internet

Virus a program or piece of code that, against your wishes, attaches itself to other programs on your computer and can trigger anything from a harmless flashing message to the reformatting of your hard drive to a system-wide network shutdown

Data encryption the transformation of data into complex, scrambled digital codes that can be unencrypted only by authorized users who possess unique decryption keys

16-4 (P. 351)

Describe how companies can access and share information and knowledge. Executive information systems, intranets, and corporate portals facilitate internal sharing and access to company information and transactions. Electronic data interchange and the Internet allow external groups such as suppliers and customers to easily access company information. Both decrease costs by reducing or eliminating data entry, data errors, and paperwork and by speeding up communication. Organizations use decision support systems and expert systems to capture and share specialized knowledge with nonexpert employees.

Virtual private network (VPN) software that securely encrypts data sent by employees outside the company network, decrypts the data when they arrive within the company computer network, and does the same when data are sent back to employees outside the network

Secure sockets layer (SSL) encryption Internet browser–based encryption that provides secure off-site Web access to some data and programs

16-4

Executive information system (EIS) a data processing system that uses internal and external data sources to provide the information needed to monitor and analyze organizational performance

Intranets private company networks that allow employees to easily access, share, and publish information using Internet software

Corporate portal a hybrid of executive information systems and intranets that allows managers and employees to use a web browser to gain access to customized company information and to complete specialized transactions

Extranets networks that allow companies to exchange information and conduct transactions with outsiders by providing them direct, web-based access to authorized parts of a company's intranet or information system

Electronic data interchange (EDI) when two companies convert their purchase and ordering information to a standardized format to enable the direct electronic transmission of that information from one company's computer system to the other company's computer system

Knowledge the understanding that one gains from information

Decision support system (DSS) an information system that helps managers understand specific kinds of problems and potential solutions and analyze the impact of different decision options using "what if" scenarios

Expert system an information system that contains the specialized knowledge and decision rules used by experts and experienced decision makers so that nonexperts can draw on this knowledge base to make decisions

LEARNING OUTCOMES

17-1 (P. 358)

Discuss the kinds of productivity and their importance in managing operations. Productivity is a measure of how many inputs it takes to produce or create an output. The greater the output from one input, or the fewer inputs it takes to create an output, the higher the productivity. Partial productivity measures how much of a single kind of input such as labour is needed to produce an output. Multifactor productivity is an overall measure of productivity that indicates how much labour, capital, materials, and energy are needed to produce an output.

$$\text{Partial productivity} = \frac{\text{Outputs}}{\text{Single kind of input}}$$

$$\text{Multifactor productivity} = \frac{\text{Outputs}}{(\text{Labour} + \text{Capital} + \text{Materials} + \text{Energy})}$$

17-2 (P. 360)

Explain the role that quality plays in managing operations. Quality can mean a product or service free of deficiencies or the characteristics of a product or service that satisfies customer needs. Quality products usually possess three characteristics: reliability, serviceability, and durability. Quality service means reliability, tangibles, responsiveness, assurance, and empathy. ISO 9000 is a series of five international standards for achieving consistency in quality management and quality assurance, while ISO 14000 is a set of standards for minimizing an organization's harmful effects on the environment. Total quality management (TQM) is an integrated organization-wide strategy for improving product and service quality. TQM is based on three mutually reinforcing principles: customer focus and satisfaction, continuous improvement, and teamwork.

17-3 (P. 365)

Explain the essentials of managing a service business. Services are different from goods. Goods are produced, tangible, and storable. Services are performed, intangible, and perishable. Likewise, managing service operations is different from managing production operations. The service–profit chain indicates that success begins with internal service quality, meaning how well management treats service employees. Internal service quality leads to employee satisfaction and service capability, which, in turn, lead to high-value service to customers, customer satisfaction, customer loyalty, and long-term profits and growth. Keeping existing customers is far more cost-effective than finding new ones. Consequently, to prevent disgruntled customers from leaving, some companies are empowering service employees to perform service recovery—restoring customer satisfaction to strongly dissatisfied customers—by giving them the authority and responsibility to immediately solve customer problems. The hope is that empowered service recovery will prevent customer defections.

KEY TERMS

17-1

Productivity a measure of performance that indicates how efficiently goods and services are produced

Partial productivity a measure of performance that indicates how much of a particular kind of input it takes to produce an output

Multifactor productivity an overall measure of performance that indicates how much labour, capital, materials, and energy it takes to produce an output

17-2

Quality a product or service free of deficiencies, or the characteristics of a product or service that satisfy customer needs

ISO 9000 a series of international standards for achieving consistency in quality management and quality assurance in companies throughout the world

ISO 14000 a series of international standards for managing, monitoring, and minimizing an organization's harmful effects on the environment

Total quality management (TQM) an integrated, principle-based, organization-wide strategy for improving product and service quality

Customer focus an organizational goal to concentrate on meeting customers' needs at all levels of the organization

Customer satisfaction an organizational goal to provide products or services that meet or exceed customers' expectations

Continuous improvement an organization's ongoing commitment to constantly assess and improve the processes and procedures used to create products and services

Variation a deviation in the form, condition, or appearance of a product from the quality standard for that product

Six Sigma a data-driven approach and methodology that strives to eliminate defects from products and services with a goal of having no more than 3.4 defects per million units or procedures

Teamwork collaboration between managers and non-managers, across business functions, and between companies, customers, and suppliers

CHAPTER REVIEW 17

17-3

Service recovery restoring customer satisfaction to strongly dissatisfied customers

17-4

Make-to-order operation a manufacturing operation that does not start processing or assembling products until a customer order is received

Assemble-to-order operation a manufacturing operation that divides manufacturing processes into separate parts or modules that are combined to create semi-customized products

Make-to-stock operation a manufacturing operation that orders parts and assembles standardized products before receiving customer orders

Manufacturing flexibility the degree to which manufacturing operations can easily and quickly change the number, kind, and characteristics of products they produce

Continuous-flow production a manufacturing operation that produces goods at a continuous rate, rather than a discrete rate

Line-flow production manufacturing processes that are pre-established, occur in a serial or linear manner, and are dedicated to making one type of product

Batch production a manufacturing operation that produces goods in large batches in standard lot sizes

Job shops manufacturing operations that handle custom orders or small batch jobs

17-5

Inventory the amount and number of raw materials, parts, and finished products that a company has in its possession

Average aggregate inventory average overall inventory during a particular time period

Weeks of supply the number of weeks it would take for a company to run out of its current supply of inventory

Stockout the situation when a company runs out of finished product

Inventory turnover the number of times per year that a company sells or "turns over" its average inventory

Ordering cost the costs associated with ordering inventory, including the cost of data entry, phone calls, obtaining bids, correcting mistakes, and determining when and how much inventory to order

17-4 (P. 368)

Describe the different kinds of manufacturing operations.
Manufacturing operations produce physical goods. Manufacturing operations can be classified according to the amount of processing or assembly that occurs after receiving an order from a customer.

Manufacturing operations can also be classified in terms of flexibility, and the degree to which the number, kind, and characteristics of products can easily and quickly be changed. Flexibility allows companies to respond quickly to competitors and customers and to reduce order lead times, but it can also lead to higher unit costs.

17-5 (P. 370)

Explain why and how companies should manage inventory levels. There are four kinds of inventory: raw materials, component parts, work-in-process, and finished goods. Because companies incur ordering, setup, holding, and stockout costs when handling inventory, inventory costs can be enormous. To control those costs, companies measure and track inventory in three ways: average aggregate inventory, weeks of supply, and turnover. Companies meet the basic goals of inventory management (avoiding stockouts and reducing inventory without hurting daily operations) through economic order quantity (EOQ) formulas, just-in-time (JIT) inventory systems, and materials requirement planning (MRP).

Use EOQ formulas when inventory levels are independent, and use JIT and MRP when inventory levels are dependent on the number of products to be produced.

Setup cost the costs of downtime and lost efficiency that occur when a machine is changed or adjusted to produce a different kind of inventory

Holding cost the cost of keeping inventory until it is used or sold, including storage, insurance, taxes, obsolescence, and opportunity costs

Stockout costs the costs incurred when a company runs out of a product, including transaction costs to replace inventory and the loss of customers' goodwill

Economic order quantity (EOQ) a system of formulas that minimizes ordering and holding costs and helps determine how much and how often inventory should be ordered

Just-in-time (JIT) inventory system an inventory system in which component parts arrive from suppliers just as they are needed at each stage of production

Kanban a ticket-based JIT system that indicates when to reorder inventory

Materials requirement planning (MRP) a production and inventory system that determines the production schedule, production batch sizes, and inventory needed to complete final products

Independent demand system an inventory system in which the level of one kind of inventory does not depend on another

Dependent demand system an inventory system in which the level of inventory depends on the number of finished units to be produced

Notes

Notes

Notes

Notes